CRAFTING FICTION
In Theory, In Practice

Marvin Diogenes
Stanford University

Clyde Moneyhun
The University of Delaware

Mayfield Publishing Company
Mountain View, California
London • Toronto

Library of Congress Cataloging-In-Publication Data

Diogenes Marvin.
    Crafting fiction : in theory, in practice / Marvin Diogenes, Clyde Moneyhun.
        p. cm.
    Includes index.
    ISBN: 0-7674-0207-3
    1. Fiction—Authorship. I. Moneyhun, Clyde. II. Title.
  PN3355 D56 2000
  808.3—dc21

                                             00-053289

Manufactured in the United States of America
10   9   8   7   6   5   4   3   2   1

Sponsoring editor, Renée Deljon; production editor, Melissa Williams; manuscript editor, Tom Briggs; design manager, Violeta Diaz; text and cover designer, Linda Robertson; permissions editor, Marty Granahan; manufacturing manager, Randy Hurst. The text was set in 10/12 Sabon by TBH Typecast, Inc. and printed on acid-free 45# Highland Plus by Malloy Lithographing, Inc.

Text credits appear on pages 637–639, which constitute an extension of the copyright page.

Preface

This book is an anthology of articles, interviews, memoirs, and critical and personal essays, mainly by fiction writers, focusing on the theory and practice of writing fiction. Initially, we wanted to write the book because we needed it. We had both been teaching fiction writing for about twenty years, and we had amassed an overstuffed file drawer of diverse readings that we liked to recommend to our students and that had become indispensable to our teaching over the years. Wouldn't it be nice, we thought, to have all of these readings together, in a single volume, for students to use? So here they are. We made the book we needed.

When we checked with friends and colleagues teaching fiction writing workshops from the beginning to the graduate level, we found that they, too, liked to use the kinds of readings we were anthologizing—often the very ones we were thinking of including. Early reviewers of the book likewise told us that we were on the right track and suggested ways they would use the book in their classes. We quickly saw that *Crafting Fiction* was a book that our colleagues also needed, or at least would have appreciated having for their students. As far as we know, there's still nothing else quite like it.

The book is organized into two parts, comprising 58 individual reading selections within four chapters. The selections are written mostly by fiction writers themselves, especially fiction writers who teach fiction writing, though a few are by important critics and theorists (and, of course, many fiction writers wear those hats, too). We tried to balance canonical and contemporary voices, and the pieces are by turns highly theoretical and thoroughly practical, illuminating a broad range of thought on how and why to write fiction and on what purposes fiction can serve. The book's organization, readings, and apparatus combine to further students' own development as fiction writers. Part One, "The Craft of Fiction," asks students to consider fiction and fictional craft. Specifically, Chapter One, "Realist, Romantic, and Avant-Garde Traditions," presents historical perspectives on fiction, showing how styles and philosophies have evolved and examining how traditions such as Realism, Romanticism, and Postmodernism have approached the issue of the relationship between fiction and real life. Here students encounter classic authors such as Nathaniel Hawthorne and Henry James and modern authors such as Flannery O'Connor, John Gardner, and William Gass. Chapter

Two, "Craft and the Elements of Fiction," gets into the nitty-gritty of fiction writing, such as character, plot, and point of view. Again, the chapter offers both germinal pieces by writers like E. M. Forster, Elizabeth Bowen, and Wayne Booth and newer pieces by R. V. Cassill, David Huddle, and David Michael Kaplan. Part Two, "Contexts for Fiction Writing," moves students to a consideration of their individual relationships with fiction as writers, students, and participants in contemporary life. Chapter Three, "The Writer's Life," includes autobiographical pieces, essays on the relation between fiction and life, and pieces on the relationship between fiction writing and the wider culture, by writers such as Ernest Hemingway, Virginia Woolf, James Baldwin, Bernard Malamud, Carol Bly, Annie Dillard, E. L. Doctorow, and Nadine Gordimer. Chapter Four, "The Teaching and Learning of Fiction Writing," explores how writing is taught and learned both in and out of the classroom, with pieces by writers like Raymond Carver, Richard Ford, Rita Mae Brown, Madison Bell, and D. G. Myers.

The text's apparatus is substantial, starting with a general introduction and chapter introductions, discussion questions following each selection, and writing activities concluding each chapter. The chapters are divided into titled subsections to make the progression of topics and ideas more apparent. The questions that follow each selection are aimed at facilitating in-class discussions of the reading's meaning, implications, and connections to other readings. The writing activities at the end of each chapter invite students to work with some of the ideas in the readings, especially in the form of scenes and stories of their own. For instance, some activities ask students to create a scene informed by some bit of advice in a reading; others ask them to imitate a piece of fiction explicated by a reading; and still others ask them to revisit and revise a passage they've already written in the light of what they've learned from a reading. Each writing activity, then, gives students the opportunity to put theory into practice.

Additionally, a compact and versatile craft "workshop" concludes Part One. The workshop's sequenced exercises, which focus on the elements of fictional craft, are activities that we have used ourselves both as writers and as teachers of writing. The activities center on both invention and an aspect of writing that we feel is too often neglected in fiction writing classes: revision. By "invention," we mean ways of exploring character, scene, and incident through brainstorming and drafting. These activities may generate background information that helps shape the story, or they may produce details and even scenes that are incorporated into the story. Our revision activities ask writers to revisit characters and plots from new perspectives and to explore other possibilities for motivation, emotion, incident, and scene.

THE BOOK'S FEATURES AT A GLANCE

- A substantial general introduction
- 58 reading selections, each introduced with a headnote
- A balanced and comprehensive introduction to the theory and practice of fiction writing

- A wide range of subjects, perspectives, time periods, and genres
- Consistent emphasis on students' own development as fiction writers
- Critical reading and creative writing apparatus
- A compact craft "workshop"
- A clear and effective overall structure
- A helpful appendix that provides guidelines for conducting effective workshops
- A detailed subject index as well as an index of authors and titles mentioned in the selections

We owe a lot to a lot of people for the existence of this book. We'd like to start by thanking our own fiction writing teachers at Columbia University, Stanford University, Arizona State University, and the University of Arizona, including Vance Bourjaily, Mary Carter, Elizabeth Hardwick, Robert Hemenway, Robert Houston, Bernard Kaplan, Sam Koperwas, Nancy Packer, Jonathan Penner, C. E. Poverman, Francine Prose, and Tobias Wolff. We also want to thank our fellow fiction writing students, who are too numerous to mention, for being so generous in helping us learn to write fiction. We remain friends with many of them and continue to depend on their generosity. Thanks as well to our many fiction writing students over the past twenty years for their good humor and hearts and open-mindedness as we experimented with many approaches to teaching fiction.

As we developed the book, many people also offered useful suggestions about potential selections, discussion questions, and writing activities. We thank our editors at Mayfield, especially Renée Deljon, who believed in the project from the beginning and who has been patient, persistent, and supportive. Thanks also to Tom Broadbent, who allowed Renée to talk him into signing the deal in the first place. We also owe special thanks to Donna Kimbler, who helped us research information for the headnotes; Melissa Williams, our production editor; and Tom Briggs, our manuscript editor. Thanks to the reviewers who made suggestions on several drafts of the manuscript, including Thomas Bracken, Northeastern Illinois University; Tom Bontly, University of Wisconsin at Milwaukee; Ron Carlson, Arizona State University; Robert Boswell, New Mexico State University; Kelly Cherry, University of Wisconsin at Madison; Alice LaPlante, San Francisco State University; Paul Lyons, University of Hawaii at Manoa; Renee Manfredi, University of Alaska-Fairbanks; Margaret McMullan, University of Evansville; Wendell Mayo, Bowling Green State University; Chris Mazza, University of Illinois at Chicago; Brian Morton, Sarah Lawrence College; William O'Rourke, University of Notre Dame; Susan Palwick, University of Nevada, Reno; Sharon Warner, University of New Mexico; Will Weaver, Bemidji State University; and Eugene Wildman, University of Illinois at Chicago.

Contents

CHAPTER TWO

Craft and the Elements of Fiction   131

Introduction   131

A WORKSHOP FOR WRITERS

Invention and Revision   281

PART TWO   Contexts for Fiction Writing   *295*

CHAPTER THREE
The Writer's Life   297

CHAPTER FOUR

The Teaching and Learning of Fiction Writing 457

You Making Art

Let's begin by proposing another title for the book, a rallying cry for fiction-writing classes, a credo underlying the contents of this collection of explorations, exhortations, and activities: *You Making Art.*

This book aims to inspire a particular action, the writing of fiction. Thus, *Crafting Narrative* is not primarily about you as a writer or about fiction as a literary art form, though both of these elements are ever present. The book's focus is on the *making,* the place where you and art come together to create new stories, new fiction.

You: The impulse, the desire, the need to express yourself, to announce your presence in the world, to voice and give narrative shape to your experience, are necessary but not sufficient to the writing of fiction. Creative writing, the wider discipline of which fiction writing is a part, is often considered a nonfield. Why? If creativity is personal and subjective, if creative genius is quicksilver and elusive, then how can you, the aspiring creative writer, be taught? Further, how can the fruits of the creative impulse, the children of your imagination, be evaluated? If the "You" in *You Making Art* is emphasized, what can be done to encourage your development of the "habits of art" fundamental to writing fiction?

In other words, what part of "you," aside from the ego-driven need for attention, for praise, for recognition of the value of your work, serves to provide substance for your fiction, fuel for the habits of art? Your experience and intuition and insight; your ability to discern patterns in behavior and events; your values and beliefs. Thus, the craft exercises in this book will draw on you in these ways—turning your sensory, intellectual, and moral experience of life into fiction. Another essential aspect of your experience that you bring to your writing is your vast experience with language. Everything you've heard or read, said or sung, serves as raw material for your making of art. From cliches to freshly made phrases, from jargon to stirring oratory, from small talk to soul talk—all the millions of words that make up your life you bring to your fiction.

Art: Knowledge and understanding of the history and traditions of fiction, study of the best that has been written about the principles and theoretical foundations of the art, are necessary but not sufficient to the writing of fiction.

Literary study preceded creative writing as an academic discipline, and literary critics and scholars specialize in the analysis and evaluation of finished works, generally those considered important enough to become part of the recognized canon. From these literary monuments they derive principles for what great art must do, what formal features and qualities such works manifest. Viewing fiction as art emphasizes the finished product, not the human process through which the art came to be. This approach is first descriptive, then evaluative, and ultimately prescriptive. This is the thing, its parts and qualities, and the would-be artist would do well to emulate what the critic/scholar has illuminated.

What aspect of literary study, then, can guide and support you as you make art? While English majors typically take a series of courses on major figures, periods, and genres, fiction writers apprentice themselves to the craft. For writers, then, major figures can best be studied as fellow artisans to imitate, to borrow and steal from, while genres can best be utilized as generative tools.

Making: The dynamic interaction of you and art, of your experiences of life and your reading of fiction, of your felt sense of what works and your reflections on literature are necessary to the writing of fiction. Inspiring and shaping this interaction is the aim of this book. Ultimately the book will succeed if it acts as a catalyst for "making," the central action of the credo "You Making Art."

A word about context: We should note that the elements of our triangle— you, the art of fiction, and the creative activity of making—do not exist in a vacuum. The writer does not live or write in isolation, though much creative work is solitary. Art does not exist on a Platonic plane removed from human experience and historical forces. Art is not separate from material conditions, the apparatus of schools and degree requirements and creative writing programs, the shifting conditions of the marketplace and the vagaries of literary taste, or the wider cultural context of values and ideologies related to work and art.

The book's chapters, while always circling among the key terms of *You Making Art* and the context of creative activity, do focus on its various elements separately:

Chapter One, on art, offers definitions of fiction as a whole, of the major traditions of fiction, and of important genres of fiction. The writers in this chapter speak from their own experiences and beliefs as makers of art, endorsing particular artistic values while laying out and describing categories and methods.

Chapter Two, on making surveys, the major elements of fiction, integrating description of these elements with specific advice to guide craft decisions. The Workshop for Writers at the end of the chapter moves beyond rules and exhortations to offer a sequence of specific writing activities designed to lead writers into a dynamic relationship with craft.

Chapter Three, on you in the context of personal and cultural experience, addresses the personal experience of writers from several perspectives: the texture of the individual writer's life, complete with challenges and anxieties;

and the life of the writer in the wider culture, wrestling with politics, the rigors of the marketplace, and advances in technology that call the nature of fiction into question.

Chapter Four, on you in the context of creative writing courses and programs, explores the particular context of writers teaching and learning, the long process of artistic education both inside and outside of classrooms and formal programs of study.

In this book we don't "talk up" to teachers or "talk down" to students. We're all fiction writers here, all makers of art, an attitude that we feel is vital to any good fiction workshop. Just as it is typical for fiction teachers to add rough drafts of their own stories to a workshop schedule rotation, so we offer these readings to teachers and students alike. So read, talk, think about it all—and go make some art.

PART ONE

The Craft of Fiction

CHAPTER 1

Realist, Romantic, and Avant-Garde Traditions

Aristotle insists that "imitation is natural to man from childhood" and that "it is natural for all to delight in works of imitation." This simple assertion provides the foundation for mimetic, or imitative, arts: We are delighted by representations of human experience, happily recognizing our own experience within the imitations. This may account for the most fundamental kind of pleasure afforded by stories; we are entertained by the familiar surfaces of human action and behavior. However, Aristotle makes another claim: "To be learning something is the greatest of pleasures not only to the philosopher but also the rest of mankind." The drama of Aristotle's day, and by extension the fiction of our own, cannot content itself with imitation; representations of experience must also teach, if the audience is to achieve the greatest pleasure, that of learning.

But what kind of teaching does fiction do? Not the academic kind—delivering lessons, transmitting facts, elucidating concepts. Novelist John Gardner defines fiction as "concrete philosophy," an inquiry into the nature of human experience, intent on discovering and illuminating the meanings of our thoughts and actions. Flannery O'Connor, along similar lines, emphasizes that fiction is dramatized meaning, not a form of preaching that explicitly states meaning. She even warns readers and critics against trying to isolate the theme of a piece of fiction, for this kind of analytical, didactic approach can kill what fiction has to offer, an experience of meaning.

The first section establishes some guiding principles for fiction that aims to represent, or imitate, human experience. Flannery O'Connor, in "Writing Short Stories," foregrounds the importance of persuading through the senses, claiming that this grounding in sensory experience serves as a springboard into the exploration of character, the mystery of why we act as we do. John Gardner, in "Basic Skills, Genre, and Fiction as Dream," echoes O'Connor in his discussion of fiction as "serious thought," the "concrete philosophy" referred to previously. The fiction writer, according to Gardner, must place the reader in a "vivid and continuous dream," constantly convincing the reader of the verisimilitude, or believability, of the imitation in order to engage in inquiry into the human condition. Both these writers argue for consistent, distinctive specification—of setting, dialogue, action, perception—as a keystone of effective mimesis. Rust Hills, in "Slick

Fiction and Quality Fiction," outlines a related standard for evaluating fiction: He criticizes "slick" fiction as soft, inchoate representation, a daydream that ignores the harder aspects of human experience. He praises "quality" fiction, linking it to the nightdream, a deeper form of engagement with character and motivation. His discussion of Chekhov and Maupassant as two poles in the short story tradition illuminates a debate about fiction that continues to this day, among writers and theorists alike.

The second section provides an overview of narrative, the root of all traditional fictional forms. Frank O'Connor's exploration of the short story genre was first delivered as a series of lectures and later collected in *The Lonely Voice*. He muses on the qualities that define the short story, highlighting the genre's focus on "submerged population groups," or, more colloquially, the "little man." In contrast to the novel, the short story focuses our attention on often-ignored nooks and crannies of human existence, representing the humble, the overlooked, the submerged. O'Connor offers Gogol's "The Overcoat" as the source of this emphasis in the short story. Francine Prose uses her experience teaching a fiction workshop to muse on the source of narrative in our lives and in our habits as writers, finding that reading Chekhov challenges every bit of advice she has ever given students about how to write fiction. Ursula Le Guin also emphasizes the central role that narrative plays in our lives, claiming (perhaps extravagantly) that making narratives is a mark of being fully human.

What we might call the "Realist tradition," as defined in the opening two sections of this chapter, is only one possible tradition, though it exerts a more powerful influence on most fiction writers today than do the other traditions. Only relatively recently—especially the later nineteenth century in both Europe and the United States—did fiction begin to obey the rules of Realism. American Realists like Mark Twain, Henry James, and Kate Chopin were reacting against what they considered the excesses of earlier writers. They wrote fiction about "real" people with "real" problems, set their stories in the present day, and used the kind of language "real" people used. The lesson of Realism was driven home by Modernists such as Steinbeck, Faulkner, and Hemingway (who counseled writers to "write what you know") and, more recently, by Minimalists such as Raymond Carver and Bobbie Ann Mason. However, the oldest narratives in our culture (for example, epics such as the *Iliad* and the Gilgamesh stories) are far from "realistic"; Greek tragedies usually involve mythic figures in struggles with gods; and even Shakespeare cared little for realistic "verisimilitude." Many writers today are recreating the older nonrealistic forms and also forging new experimental forms in reaction to the Realist tradition.

The "countertradition" we might label as Romance or Fabulation is sketched in the third section. American Romantics such as Nathaniel Hawthorne were well aware of the idea of "realistic" fiction and its requirement to be "true to life." In introductions to two of his most famous works, he explicitly valorizes the view by moonlight over the view by sunlight, a focus on "the clouds overhead" rather than "any portion of the actual soil of the County of Essex." He sees in Romance a fundamentally different approach to the fictional communication of a theme or moral about the human condition, one that sacrifices "realism" for a more oblique but ultimately deeper vision. In excerpts from appraisals of Hawthorne's Romanticism by Henry James, one of the most important American Realists, we see what James considered the strengths and weaknesses of such fiction. He clearly finds its "fabulistic" qualities rather superficial, almost naïve, but just as clearly he appreciates the possibilities for subtlety in its portrayal of life. Frank Norris, another writer often lumped with the Realists, writes in "A Plea for Romantic Fiction" that he has no use for "realism" and prefers "romance," if properly done. He ridicules "the drama of the broken teacup" but also rejects fiction that involves "cloaks and daggers or moonlight and golden hair." Real Romantic fiction, he says, goes "deep into the red, living heart of things." In the last selection, Robert Scholes asserts that the age of Realism is ending and that a lot of contemporary literature has much in common with the fables and allegories of an earlier time. He points to James Joyce and Iris Murdoch as two modern "fabulators" whose narratives echo the stuff of myth, legend, and fable.

The fourth section begins with "Philosophy and the Form of Fiction," by William Gass, a fiction writer and philosopher who establishes links between these genres while breaking fiction away from representation of the external world and imitation of human experience. Gass proposes instead that fiction is made up of language and that fiction writers offer propositions that create a "philosophically adequate world." He asserts forcefully that fiction writers should not aim to "render" the world, but rather should strive to create one out of language, the only medium available. Gass thus proposes a radically different purpose for fiction than writers like Flannery O'Connor and John Gardner. Annie Dillard, in "Fiction in Bits," distinguishes between the "traditional" excellences of mimetic fiction and the excellences pursued by writers she calls "contemporary modernists." She explores the nature of narrative collage, a technique that does not privilege linear plotting or other traditional unities of character, setting, and point of view. "Nothing temporal, spatial, perceptual, social, or moral is fixed" in narrative collage, according to Dillard, who then goes on to establish tentative guidelines for how such fragmented fiction can achieve "artistic integrity" and "coherence." Raymond Federman, in "Fiction Today or the Pursuit of Non-Knowledge," continues this discussion of fiction that leaves behind what he terms the "obsolete" traditions of Romanticism, devoted to individual expression, and Realism, devoted to the reproduction of the external world. Openly an advocate for this kind of "experimental" work, Federman endorses fiction that offers a "continual probing of its own medium," a central purpose of metafiction (or "surfiction," Federman's preferred term). Federman, like Gass, foregrounds the centrality of language in fiction. He also argues that "there is as much value in making nonsense as there is in making sense." His assertion that fiction should cancel out or erase its own formulations separates him from Gass and Dillard to some degree. To conclude the section, Philip Stevick provides additional historical context in "Form, Antiform, and Neoform: Verbal Collage." Stevick points out that writers have always challenged standard structures in fiction. In contrast to Dillard, Stevick admits the possibility of a writer achieving formal innovation while also representing the external world, pointing to James Joyce's *Ulysses* as an example. Further, he distinguishes between montage, a cinematic term concerned with editing techniques, and collage, a term associated with painting, citing writer Donald Barthelme's description and use of the technique. Stevick ends by proposing that "junctures" in the verbal collage help guide the reader, suggesting that every form ultimately generates technical guidelines.

Clearly, just as Realism was a reaction against the perceived excesses of Romanticism, recent developments in fiction are a reaction against the perceived artificiality and sterility of Realism. Some contemporary writers look to older traditions, spinning fables and allegories that remind us of ancient narratives. Others attempt to create entirely new narrative techniques that express what they see as the "realities" of modern life and forms of consciousness. While the conventions of Realism still prevail in most contemporary fiction, there are important and powerful countertraditions that preceded it and (in the opinion of some) are now succeeding it.

FOUNDATIONS OF FICTION

FLANNERY O'CONNOR

Writing Short Stories

Flannery O'Connor (1925–1964), in a brief life troubled by chronic illness, created some of the most important and influential fiction of the century, including her short story collections A Good Man Is Hard to Find *(1957) and* Everything That Rises Must Converge *(1965) and her novels* Wise Blood *(1952) and* The Violent Bear It Away *(1960). Her essays on the art of fiction writing, collected in* Mystery and Manners *(1969), are typical of her blend of earthy detail, biting wit, and high seriousness.*

I have heard people say that the short story was one of the most difficult literary forms, and I've always tried to decide why people feel this way about what seems to me to be one of the most natural and fundamental ways of human expression.* After all, you begin to hear and tell stories when you're a child, and there doesn't seem to be anything very complicated about it. I suspect that most of you have been telling stories all your lives, and yet here you sit—come to find out how to do it.

Then last week, after I had written down some of these serene thoughts to use here today, my calm was shattered when I was sent seven of your manuscripts to read.

After this experience, I found myself ready to admit, if not that the short story is one of the most difficult literary forms, at least that it is more difficult for some than for others.

---

*In another mood on another occasion Flannery O'Connor began as follows: "I have very little to say about short-story writing. It's one thing to write short stories and another thing to talk about writing them, and I hope you realize that your asking me to talk about story-writing is just like asking a fish to lecture on swimming. The more stories I write, the more mysterious I find the process and the less I find myself capable of analyzing it. Before I started writing stories, I suppose I could have given you a pretty good lecture on the subject, but nothing produces silence like experience, and at this point I have very little to say about how stories are written."

I still suspect that most people start out with some kind of ability to tell a story but that it gets lost along the way. Of course, the ability to create life with words is essentially a gift. If you have it in the first place, you can develop it; if you don't have it, you might as well forget it.

But I have found that the people who don't have it are frequently the ones hell-bent on writing stories. I'm sure anyway that they are the ones who write the books and the magazine articles on how-to-write-short-stories. I have a friend who is taking a correspondence course in this subject, and she has passed a few of the chapter headings on to me—such as, "The Story Formula for Writers," "How to Create Characters," "Let's Plot!" This form of corruption is costing her twenty-seven dollars.

I feel that discussing story-writing in terms of plot, character, and theme is like trying to describe the expression on a face by saying where the eyes, nose, and mouth are. I've heard students say, "I'm very good with plot, but I can't do a thing with character," or, "I have this theme but I don't have a plot for it," and once I heard one say, "I've got the story but I don't have any technique."

Technique is a word they all trot out. I talked to a writers' club once, and during the question time, one good soul said, "Will you give me the technique for the frame-within-a-frame short story?" I had to admit I was so ignorant I didn't even know what that was, but she assured me there was such a thing because she had entered a contest to write one and the prize was fifty dollars.

But setting aside the people who have no talent for it, there are others who do have the talent but who flounder around because they don't really know what a story is.

I suppose that obvious things are the hardest to define. Everybody thinks he knows what a story is. But if you ask a beginning student to write a story, you're liable to get almost anything—a reminiscence, an episode, an opinion, an anecdote, anything under the sun but a story. A story is a complete dramatic action— and in good stories, the characters are shown through the action and the action is controlled through the characters, and the result of this is meaning that derives from the whole presented experience. I myself prefer to say that a story is a dramatic event that involves a person because he is a person, and a particular person—that is, because he shares in the general human condition and in some specific human situation. A story always involves, in a dramatic way, the mystery of personality. I lent some stories to a country lady who lives down the road from me, and when she returned them, she said, "Well, them stories just gone and shown you how some folks *would* do," and I thought to myself that that was right; when you write stories, you have to be content to start exactly there— showing how some specific folks *will* do, *will* do in spite of everything.

Now this is a very humble level to have to begin on, and most people who think they want to write stories are not willing to start there. They want to write about problems, not people; or about abstract issues, not concrete situations. They have an idea, or a feeling, or an overflowing ego, or they want to Be A Writer, or they want to give their wisdom to the world in a simple-enough way for the world to be able to absorb it. In any case, they don't have a story and they wouldn't be willing to write it if they did; and in the absence of a story, they set out to find a theory or a formula or a technique.

Now none of this is to say that when you write a story, you are supposed to forget or give up any moral position that you hold. Your beliefs will be the light by which you see, but they will not be what you see and they will not be a substitute for seeing. For the writer of fiction, everything has its testing point in the eye, and the eye is an organ that eventually involves the whole personality, and as much of the world as can be got into it. It involves judgment. Judgment is something that begins in the act of vision, and when it does not, or when it becomes separated from vision, then a confusion exists in the mind which transfers itself to the story.

Fiction operates through the senses, and I think one reason that people find it so difficult to write stories is that they forget how much time and patience is required to convince through the senses. No reader who doesn't actually experience, who isn't made to feel, the story is going to believe anything the fiction writer merely tells him. The first and most obvious characteristic of fiction is that it deals with reality through what can be seen, heard, smelt, tasted, and touched.

Now this is something that can't be learned only in the head; it has to be learned in the habits. It has to become a way that you habitually look at things. The fiction writer has to realize that he can't create compassion with compassion, or emotion with emotion, or thought with thought. He has to provide all these things with a body; he has to create a world with weight and extension.

I have found that the stories of beginning writers usually bristle with emotion, but *whose* emotion is often very hard to determine. Dialogue frequently proceeds without the assistance of any characters that you can actually see, and uncontained thought leaks out of every corner of the story. The reason is usually that the student is wholly interested in his thoughts and his emotions and not in his dramatic action, and that he is too lazy or highfalutin to descend to the concrete where fiction operates. He thinks that judgment exists in one place and sense-impression in another. But for the fiction writer, judgment begins in the details he sees and how he sees them.

Fiction writers who are not concerned with these concrete details are guilty of what Henry James called "weak specification." The eye will glide over their words while the attention goes to sleep. Ford Madox Ford taught that you couldn't have a man appear long enough to sell a newspaper in a story unless you put him there with enough detail to make the reader see him.

I have a friend who is taking acting classes in New York from a Russian lady who is supposed to be very good at teaching actors. My friend wrote me that the first month they didn't speak a line, they only learned to see. Now learning to see is the basis for learning all the arts except music. I know a good many fiction writers who paint, not because they're any good at painting, but because it helps their writing. It forces them to look at things. Fiction writing is very seldom a matter of saying things; it is a matter of showing things.

However, to say that fiction proceeds by the use of detail does not mean the simple, mechanical piling-up of detail. Detail has to be controlled by some overall purpose, and every detail has to be put to work for you. Art is selective. What is there is essential and creates movement.

Now all this requires time. A good short story should not have less meaning than a novel, nor should its action be less complete. Nothing essential to the main experience can be left out of a short story. All the action has to be satisfactorily accounted for in terms of motivation, and there has to be a beginning, a middle, and an end, though not necessarily in that order. I think many people decide that they want to write short stories because they're short, and by short, they mean short in every way. They think that a short story is an incomplete action in which a very little is shown and a great deal suggested, and they think you suggest something by leaving it out. It's very hard to disabuse a student of this notion, because he thinks that when he leaves something out, he's being subtle; and when you tell him that he has to put something in before anything can be there, he thinks you're an insensitive idiot.

Perhaps the central question to be considered in any discussion of the short story is what do we mean by short. Being short does not mean being slight. A short story should be long in depth and should give us an experience of meaning. I have an aunt who thinks that nothing happens in a story unless somebody gets married or shot at the end of it. I wrote a story about a tramp who marries an old woman's idiot daughter in order to acquire the old woman's automobile. After the marriage, he takes the daughter off on a wedding trip in the automobile and abandons her in an eating place and drives on by himself. Now that is a complete story. There is nothing more relating to the mystery of that man's personality that could be shown through that particular dramatization. But I've never been able to convince my aunt that it's a complete story. She wants to know what happened to the idiot daughter after that.

Not long ago that story was adapted for a television play, and the adapter, knowing his business, had the tramp have a change of heart and go back and pick up the idiot daughter and the two of them ride away, grinning madly. My aunt believes that the story is complete at last, but I have other sentiments about it— which are not suitable for public utterance. When you write a story, you only have to write one story, but there will always be people who will refuse to read the story you have written.

And this naturally brings up the awful question of what kind of a reader you are writing for when you write fiction. Perhaps we each think we have a personal solution for this problem. For my own part, I have a very high opinion of the art of fiction and a very low opinion of what is called the "average" reader. I tell myself that I can't escape him, that this is the personality I am supposed to keep awake, but that at the same time, I am also supposed to provide the intelligent reader with the deeper experience that he looks for in fiction. Now actually, both of these readers are just aspects of the writer's own personality, and in the last analysis, the only reader he can know anything about is himself. We all write at our own level of understanding, but it is the peculiar characteristic of fiction that its literal surface can be made to yield entertainment on an obvious physical plane to one sort of reader while the selfsame surface can be made to yield meaning to the person equipped to experience it there.

Meaning is what keeps the short story from being short. I prefer to talk about the meaning in a story rather than the theme of a story. People talk about the theme of a story as if the theme were like the string that a sack of chicken feed is tied with. They think that if you can pick out the theme, the way you pick the right thread in the chicken-feed sack, you can rip the story open and feed the chickens. But this is not the way meaning works in fiction.

When you can state the theme of a story, when you can separate it from the story itself, then you can be sure the story is not a very good one. The meaning of a story has to be embodied in it, has to be made concrete in it. A story is a way to say something that can't be said any other way, and it takes every word in the story to say what the meaning is. You tell a story because a statement would be inadequate. When anybody asks what a story is about, the only proper thing is to tell him to read the story. The meaning of fiction is not abstract meaning but experienced meaning, and the purpose of making statements about the meaning of a story is only to help you to experience that meaning more fully.

Fiction is an art that calls for the strictest attention to the real—whether the writer is writing a naturalistic story or a fantasy. I mean that we always begin with what is or with what has an eminent possibility of truth about it. Even when one writes a fantasy, reality is the proper basis of it. A thing is fantastic because it is so real, so real that it is fantastic. Graham Greene has said that he can't write, "I stood over a bottomless pit," because that couldn't be true, or "Running down the stairs I jumped into a taxi," because that couldn't be true either. But Elizabeth Bowen can write about one of her characters that "she snatched at her hair as if she heard something in it," because that is eminently possible.

I would even go so far as to say that the person writing a fantasy has to be even more strictly attentive to the concrete detail than someone writing in a naturalistic vein—because the greater the story's strain on the credulity, the more convincing the properties in it have to be.

A good example of this is a story called "The Metamorphosis" by Franz Kafka. This is a story about a man who wakes up one morning to find that he has turned into a cockroach overnight, while not discarding his human nature. The rest of the story concerns his life and feelings and eventual death as an insect with human nature, and this situation is accepted by the reader because the concrete detail of the story is absolutely convincing. The fact is that this story describes the dual nature of man in such a realistic fashion that it is almost unbearable. The truth is not distorted here, but rather, a certain distortion is used to get at the truth. If we admit, as we must, that appearance is not the same thing as reality, then we must give the artist the liberty to make certain rearrangements of nature if these will lead to greater depths of vision. The artist himself always has to remember that what he is rearranging *is* nature, and that he has to know it and be able to describe it accurately in order to have the authority to rearrange it at all.

The peculiar problem of the short-story writer is how to make the action he describes reveal as much of the mystery of existence as possible. He has only a short space to do it in and he can't do it by statement. He has to do it by showing, not by saying, and by showing the concrete—so that his problem is really how to make the concrete work double time for him.

In good fiction, certain of the details will tend to accumulate meaning from the action of the story itself, and when this happens they become symbolic in the way they work. I once wrote a story called "Good Country People," in which a lady Ph.D. has her wooden leg stolen by a Bible salesman whom she has tried to seduce. Now I'll admit that, paraphrased in this way, the situation is simply a low joke. The average reader is pleased to observe anybody's wooden leg being stolen. But without ceasing to appeal to him and without making any statements of high intention, this story does manage to operate at another level of experience, by letting the wooden leg accumulate meaning. Early in the story, we're presented with the fact that the Ph.D. is spiritually as well as physically crippled. She believes in nothing but her own belief in nothing, and we perceive that there is a wooden part of her soul that corresponds to her wooden leg. Now of course this is never stated. The fiction writer states as little as possible. The reader makes this connection from things he is shown. He may not even know that he makes the connection, but the connection is there nevertheless and it has its effect on him. As the story goes on, the wooden leg continues to accumulate meaning. The reader learns how the girl feels about her leg, how her mother feels about it, and how the country woman on the place feels about it; and finally, by the time the Bible salesman comes along, the leg has accumulated so much meaning that it is, as the saying goes, loaded. And when the Bible salesman steals it, the reader realizes that he has taken away part of the girl's personality and has revealed her deeper affliction to her for the first time.

If you want to say that the wooden leg is a symbol, you can say that. But it is a wooden leg first, and as a wooden leg it is absolutely necessary to the story. It has its place on the literal level of the story, but it operates in depth as well as on the surface. It increases the story in every direction, and this is essentially the way a story escapes being short.

Now a little might be said about the way in which this happens. I wouldn't want you to think that in that story I sat down and said, "I am now going to write a story about a Ph.D. with a wooden leg, using the wooden leg as a symbol for another kind of affliction." I doubt myself if many writers know what they are going to do when they start out. When I started writing that story, I didn't know there was going to be a Ph.D. with a wooden leg in it. I merely found myself one morning writing a description of two women that I knew something about, and before I realized it, I had equipped one of them with a daughter with a wooden leg. As the story progressed, I brought in the Bible salesman, but I had no idea what I was going to do with him. I didn't know he was going to steal that wooden leg until ten or twelve lines before he did it, but when I found out that this was what was going to happen, I realized that it was inevitable. This is a story that produces a shock for the reader, and I think one reason for this is that it produced a shock for the writer.

Now despite the fact that this story came about in this seemingly mindless fashion, it is a story that almost no rewriting was done on. It is a story that was under control throughout the writing of it, and it might be asked how this kind of control comes about, since it is not entirely conscious.

I think the answer to this is what Maritain calls "the habit of art." It is a fact that fiction writing is something in which the whole personality takes part—the conscious as well as the unconscious mind. Art is the habit of the artist; and habits have to be rooted deep in the whole personality. They have to be cultivated like any other habit, over a long period of time, by experience; and teaching any kind of writing is largely a matter of helping the student develop the habit of art. I think this is more than just a discipline, although it is that; I think it is a way of looking at the created world and of using the senses so as to make them find as much meaning as possible in things.

Now I am not so naïve as to suppose that most people come to writers' conferences in order to hear what kind of vision is necessary to write stories that will become a permanent part of our literature. Even if you do wish to hear this, your greatest concerns are immediately practical. You want to know how you can actually write a good story, and further, how you can tell when you've done it; and so you want to know what the form of a short story is, as if the form were something that existed outside of each story and could be applied or imposed on the material. Of course, the more you write, the more you will realize that the form is organic, that it is something that grows out of the material, that the form of each story is unique. A story that is any good can't be reduced, it can only be expanded. A story is good when you continue to see more and more in it, and when it continues to escape you. In fiction two and two is always more than four.

The only way, I think, to learn to write short stories is to write them, and then to try to discover what you have done. The time to think of technique is when you've actually got the story in front of you. The teacher can help the student by looking at his individual work and trying to help him decide if he has written a complete story, one in which the action fully illuminates the meaning.

Perhaps the most profitable thing I can do is to tell you about some of the general observations I made about these seven stories I read of yours. All of these observations will not fit any one of the stories exactly, but they are points nevertheless that it won't hurt anyone interested in writing to think about.

The first thing that any professional writer is conscious of in reading anything is, naturally, the use of language. Now the use of language in these stories was such that, with one exception, it would be difficult to distinguish one story from another. While I can recall running into several clichés, I can't remember one image or one metaphor from the seven stories. I don't mean there weren't images in them; I just mean that there weren't any that were effective enough to take away with you.

In connection with this, I made another observation that startled me considerably. With the exception of one story, there was practically no use made of the local idiom. Now this is a Southern Writers' Conference. All the addresses on these stories were from Georgia or Tennessee, yet there was no distinctive sense of Southern life in them. A few place-names were dropped, Savannah or Atlanta or Jacksonville, but these could just as easily have been changed to Pittsburgh or Passaic without calling for any other alteration in the story. The characters spoke as if they had never heard any kind of language except what came out of a television set. This indicates that something is way out of focus.

There are two qualities that make fiction. One is the sense of mystery and the other is the sense of manners. You get the manners from the texture of existence that surrounds you. The great advantage of being a Southern writer is that we don't have to go anywhere to look for manners; bad or good, we've got them in abundance. We in the South live in a society that is rich in contradiction, rich in irony, rich in contrast, and particularly rich in its speech. And yet here are six stories by Southerners in which almost no use is made of the gifts of the region.

Of course the reason for this may be that you have seen these gifts abused so often that you have become self-conscious about using them. There is nothing worse than the writer who doesn't *use* the gifts of the region, but wallows in them. Everything becomes so Southern that it's sickening, so local that it is unintelligible, so literally reproduced that it conveys nothing. The general gets lost in the particular instead of being shown through it.

However, when the life that actually surrounds us is totally ignored, when our patterns of speech are absolutely overlooked, then something is out of kilter. The writer should then ask himself if he is not reaching out for a kind of life that is artificial to him.

An idiom characterizes a society, and when you ignore the idiom, you are very likely ignoring the whole social fabric that could make a meaningful character. You can't cut characters off from their society and say much about them as individuals. You can't say anything meaningful about the mystery of a personality unless you put that personality in a believable and significant social context. And the best way to do this is through the character's own language. When the old lady in one of Andrew Lytle's stories says contemptuously that she has a mule that is older than Birmingham, we get in that one sentence a sense of a society and its history. A great deal of the Southern writer's work is done for him before he begins, because our history lives in our talk. In one of Eudora Welty's stories a character says, "Where I come from, we use fox for yard dogs and owls for chickens, but we sing true." Now there is a whole book in that one sentence; and when the people of your section can talk like that, and you ignore it, you're just not taking advantage of what's yours. The sound of our talk is too definite to be discarded with impunity, and if the writer tries to get rid of it, he is liable to destroy the better part of his creative power.

Another thing I observed about these stories is that most of them don't go very far inside a character, don't reveal very much of the character. I don't mean that they don't enter the character's mind, but they simply don't show that he has a personality. Again this goes back partly to speech. These characters have no distinctive speech to reveal themselves with; and sometimes they have no really distinctive features. You feel in the end that no personality is revealed because no personality is there. In most good stories it is the character's personality that creates the action of the story. In most of these stories, I feel that the writer has thought of some action and then scrounged up a character to perform it. You will usually be more successful if you start the other way around. If you start with a real personality, a real character, then something is bound to happen; and you don't have to know what before you begin. In fact it may be better if you don't know what before you begin. You ought to be able to discover something from your stories. If you don't, probably nobody else will.

DISCUSSION QUESTIONS

1. O'Connor defines the short story as a "complete dramatic action" that explores the "mystery of human personality." What does O'Connor mean by each of these phrases? Why does she claim that the action of the story and the revelation of the characters must not only be present but also be interrelated?
2. O'Connor emphasizes the sensory dimension of fiction, asserting that short stories work first through the senses and then through the intellect. Do you agree that fiction must be an immersion into sensory experience before it can succeed emotionally and intellectually? Why or why not?
3. O'Connor criticizes some stories by young writers for not taking advantage of the writers' local idioms, the particulars of speech and behavior that are part of the writers' experiences. In the contemporary age of mass media, do you think that "manners," in O'Connor's sense, are still central to effective fiction? If the world has become a global village, as many argue, can fiction writers still be expected to work from the manners of a particular place?
4. O'Connor states that the writing of fiction is an activity in which "the whole personality takes part." What does she mean by this? How does her claim address the idea that fiction writing is primarily self-expression?

JOHN GARDNER

Basic Skills, Genre, and Fiction as Dream

John Gardner (1933–1982) was a medieval scholar by trade and a director of the writing program at SUNY Binghamton until his early death. He also wrote some of the most important fiction of the 1970s, including Grendel *(1971),* The Sunlight Dialogues *(1972),* Nickel Mountain *(1973), and* October Light *(1976). In addition, he wrote essays about the craft of fiction and the ethical dimension of fiction writing in collections such as* On Moral Fiction *(1978),* On Becoming a Novelist *(1983), and* The Art of Fiction: Notes on Craft for Young Writers *(1984). It is possible that his most enduring influence was as a teacher of fiction writing; among the writers inspired by him to devote their lives to fiction was Raymond Carver, who writes lovingly of his teaching and his spirit.*

. . . Let us suppose the writer has mastered the rudiments. How should he begin on fiction? What should he write about, and how can he know when he's done it well?

A common and usually unfortunate answer is "Write about what you know." Nothing can be more limiting to the imagination, nothing is quicker to turn on the psyche's censoring devices and distortion systems, than trying to write truthfully and interestingly about one's own home town, one's Episcopalian mother, one's crippled younger sister. For some writers, the advice may work, but when it does, it usually works by a curious accident: The writer writes well about what he knows because he has read primarily fiction of just this kind—realistic fiction of the sort we associate with *The New Yorker,* the *Atlantic Monthly,* or *Harper's.* The writer, in other words, is presenting not so much what he knows about life as what he knows about a particular literary genre. A better answer, though still not an ideal one, might have been "Write the kind of story you know and like best— a ghost story, a science-fiction piece, a realistic story about your childhood, or whatever."

Though the fact is not always obvious at a glance when we look at works of art very close to us in time, the artist's primary unit of thought—his primary conscious or unconscious basis for selecting and organizing the details of his work— is *genre.* This is perhaps most obvious in the case of music. A composer writes an opera, a symphony, a concerto, a tone poem, a suite of country dances, a song cycle, a set of variations, or a stream-of-consciousness piece (a modern psychological adaptation of the tone poem). Whatever genre he chooses, and to some extent depending on which genre he chooses, he writes within, or slightly varies, traditional structures—sonata form, fugal structure, ABCBA melodic structure, and so forth; or he may create, on what he believes to be some firm basis, a new structure. He may cross genres, introducing country dances into a symphony or, say, constructing a string quartet on the principle of theme and variations. If he's looking for novelty (seldom for any more noble reason), he may try to borrow structure from some other art, using film, theatrical movement, or something else. When new forms arise, as they do from time to time, they rise out of one of two processes, genre-crossing or the elevation of popular culture. Thus Ravel, Gershwin, Stravinsky, and many others blend classical tradition and American jazz—in this case simultaneously crossing genres and elevating the popular. Occasionally in music as in the other arts, elevating popular culture must be extended to mean recycling trash. Electronic music began in the observation that the beeps and boings that come out of radios, computers, and the like might sound a little like music if structure were imposed—rhythm and something like melody. Anything, in fact—as the Dadaists, Spike Jones, and John Cage pointed out—might be turned into something like music: the scream of a truck-tire, the noise of a windowshade, the bleating of a sheep.

We see much the same in the visual arts. In any culture certain subjects become classical, repeated by artist after artist—for instance, in the Christian Middle Ages, the theme of the dead Christ's descent from the cross, the martyrdom of St. Stephen, the mother and child. As the surrounding culture changes, the treatment of classical subjects changes, popular culture increasingly impinges, new forms arise—literary illustration replacing Biblical illustration, secular figures parodying religious figures, "real life" edging out illustrative painting, new ventures of thought (psychology, mathematics) transforming traditional still lifes, rooms, and landscapes to dream images or spatial puzzles. The process of change in the visual arts, in other words, is identical to that in music. Sometimes it rises out of genre-crossing, as when Protestant Flemish painters present a secular family portrait in the triangular organization of Catholic holy-family painters; sometimes it rises out of an elevation of the popular, or of trash, as on Giotto's campanile, in Matisse's cut-outs, or in the trash collages of Robert Rauschenberg; and sometimes change comes—the usual case—out of both at once.

The same holds true for literature. Novelty comes chiefly from ingenious genre-crossing or elevation of familiar materials. As an example of genre-crossing, think of the best of the three versions of Faulkner's "Spotted Horses" (the one that begins with the words "That Flem"), where techniques of the yarn—mainly diction, comic exaggeration, and cruel humor—are combined with techniques of the realistic-symbolic short story. Genre-crossing of one sort or another is behind most of the great literary art in the English tradition. Chaucer again and again plays one form off against another, as in the *Knight's Tale,* where, along with other, less-well-known forms, he blends epic and romance. The greatest of all medieval alliterative poems, *Sir Gawain and the Green Knight,* blends elements of the earthy *fabliau* (in the temptation scenes) with romance elements. Shakespeare's most powerful techniques are all results of genre-crossing: his combination of prose and verse to expand the emotional range of drama; his combination of Roman high-style convention with conventions drawn from the English folk plays, rowdy medieval mystery plays (or guild plays), and so on; and his crossing of tragic convention and comic convention for the "dark comedies." Milton's fondness for genre-crossing is one of the commonplaces of scholarship. As for the elevation of popular materials or trash—alone or in combination with nobler forms—think of John Hawkes' blend of the psychological-symbolic novel and the American hard-boiled mystery, Italo Calvino's blend (in *t-zero* and *Cosmicomics*) of sci-fi, fantasy, comic-book language and imagery, movie melodrama, and nearly everything else, or Donald Barthelme's transformation of such cultural trash as the research questionnaire, the horror-show and animated cartoon, the travelogue and psychiatrist's transcript. Like genre-crossing, the elevation of popular or trash materials is an old and familiar form of innovation. It was a favorite method of late Greek poets like Apollonios Rhodios (in the *Argonautica*), Roman comic poets, many of the great medieval poets (think of Chaucer's *Rime of Sir Thopas*), and poets of the Renaissance. The noblest of modern literary forms, equivalent in range and cultural importance to the noblest of musical forms, the symphony, began in the elevation and transformation of trash when Defoe, Richardson, and Fielding began transmuting junk into art. *Robinson Crusoe* and *Moll Flanders* spring, respectively, from the naive shipwreck narrative and the rogue's confession; *Pamela* and *Clarissa* add character and plot to the popular collection of epistolary models for the guidance of young ladies; *Jonathan Wilde* comes from the gallows broadside, or story of the character and horrible crimes of the felon about to be hanged.

None of these writers, ancient or modern, sat down to write "to express himself." They sat down to write this kind of story or that, or to mix this form with that form, producing some new effect. Self-expression, whatever its pleasures, comes about incidentally. It also comes about inevitably. The realistic writer may set out to conjure up the personality of his aunt, creating for her, or copying from life, some story through which her character is revealed, and thus he reveals his strong feelings about his aunt; that is, he expresses himself. The fabulist—the writer of nonrealistic yarns, tales, or fables—may seem at first glance to be doing something quite different; but he is not. Dragons, like bankers and candy-store owners, must have firm and predictable characters. A talking tree, a talking refrigerator, a talking clock must speak in a way we learn to recognize, must influence events in ways we can identify as flowing from some definite motivation; and since character can come only from one of two places, books or life, the writer's aunt is as likely to show up in a fable as in a realistic story. Thus the process by which one writes a fable, on one hand, or a realistic story, on the other, is not much different. Let us look more closely at the similarities and differences.

In any piece of fiction, the writer's first job is to convince the reader that the events he recounts really happened, or to persuade the reader that they might have happened (given small changes in the laws of the universe), or else to engage the reader's interest in the patent absurdity of the lie. The realistic writer's way of making events convincing is verisimilitude. The tale writer, telling stories of ghosts, or shape-shifters, or some character who never sleeps, uses a different approach: By the quality of his voice, and by means of various devices that distract the critical intelligence, he gets what Coleridge called—in one of the most clumsy famous sentences in all literature—"the willing suspension of disbelief for the moment, which constitutes poetic faith." The yarn writer—like Mark Twain in "The Celebrated Jumping Frog of Calaveras County" or "Baker's Bluejay Yarn"—uses yet another method: He tells outrageous lies, or has some character tell the poor narrator some outrageous lie, and he simultaneously emphasizes both the brilliance and the falsehood of the lie; that is, he tells the lie as convincingly as he can but also raises objections to the lie, either those objections the reader might raise or, for comic effect, literal-minded country-bumpkin objections that, though bumpkinish, call attention to the yarn's improbabilities.

All three kinds of writing, it should be obvious at a glance, depend heavily on precision of detail. In writing that depends on verisimilitude, the writer in effect argues the reader into acceptance. He places his story in some actual setting— Cleveland, San Francisco, Joplin, Missouri—and he uses characters we would be likely to meet in the setting he has chosen. He gives us such detail about the streets, stores, weather, politics, and concerns of Cleveland (or whatever the setting is) and such detail about the looks, gestures, and experience of his characters that we cannot help believing that the story he tells us must be true. In fact it may be true, as is Truman Capote's novel *In Cold Blood* or Norman Mailer's *The Executioner's Song*. The fact that the story is true of course does not relieve the novelist of the responsibility of making the characters and events convincing. Second by second we ask, "Would a mother really say that?" "Would a child really think that?" and if the novelist has done his work well we cannot help answering, "Yes." If he has done his work badly, on the other hand, the reader feels unconvinced even when the writer presents events he actually witnessed in life. What has gone wrong, in this case, is that the writer missed or forgot to mention something important to the development of the scene. For instance, if a fictional husband and wife are arguing bitterly and the wife suddenly changes her tactics, speaking gently, even lovingly, the reader cannot understand or believe the change unless some clue is provided as to the reason for it. The clue may be an event, perhaps a noise in another part of the house, that reminds her that the children are nearby; or it may be a thought, perhaps the wife's reflection that this is how her mother used to argue with her father; or the clue may be a gesture, as when the wife, after something the husband says, turns and looks out the window, providing a pause that allows her to collect herself. When the realist's work convinces us, all effects, even the most subtle, have explicit or implicit causes. This kind of documentation, moment by moment authenticating detail, is the mainstay not only of realistic fiction but of all fiction.

In other words, while verisimilar fiction may be described generally as fiction that persuades us of its authenticity through real-world documentation, using real or thoroughly lifelike locations and characters—real cities or cities we believe to be real although their names have been changed, real-life characters with actual or substituted names, and so forth—the line-by-line bulk of a realist's work goes far beyond the accurate naming of streets and stores or accurate description of people and neighborhoods. He must present, moment by moment, concrete images drawn from a careful observation of how people behave, and he must render the connections between moments, the exact gestures, facial expressions, or turns of speech that, within any given scene, move human beings from emotion to emotion, from one instant in time to the next.

Compare the technique of the writer of tales. Whereas the realist argues the reader into acceptance, the tale writer charms or lulls him into dropping objections; that is, persuades him to suspend disbelief. Isak Dinesen begins one of her tales: "After the death of his master Leonidas, Angelino Santasillia resolved that he would never again sleep. Will the narrator be believed when he tells the reader that Angelino kept this resolve? Nevertheless, it is the case." No realist, of course, could tell this story, since no amount of argument will convince us that a character really might stay awake for weeks, months, years. The tale writer simply walks past our objections, granting that the events he is about to recount are incredible but winning our suspension of disbelief by the confidence and authority of the narrator's voice. Yet after establishing the impossible premise, one that opens the door to further improbabilities—in the case of Isak Dinesen's tale, as it happens, the appearance of Judas, at the end of the narrative, counting his silver in a small, dimly lit room—the tale writer documents his story moment by moment by details of exactly the kind realists use. The opening lines slightly alter natural law, but granting the alteration, what follows is made to seem thoroughly probable and at least poetically true by the writer's close attention to the natural flow of moral cause and effect, a flow minutely documented with details drawn from life. As the story progresses, the sleepless Angelino walks, talks, and thinks more and more slowly. Sometimes whole days pass between the beginnings and ends of his sentences. We "believe" the narrative not just because the tale voice has charmed us but also, and more basically, because the character's gestures, his precisely described expression, and the reaction of others to his oddity all seem to us exactly what they would be in this strange situation. The images are as sharp and accurately rendered as any in Tolstoy's *Childhood* or *Anna Karenina*. The streets he walks, the weather, the city's sounds and smells all authenticate the sleepless man's existence. There is, admittedly, one great difference between the use of authenticating detail by a realist and the use of the same by a tale writer. The realist must authenticate continually, bombarding the reader with proofs; the writer of tales can simplify, persuading us partly by the beauty or interest of his language, using authenticating detail more sparingly, to give vividness to the tale's key moments. Thus, for example, once the writer of a tale has convinced us, partly by charm, partly by detail, that a certain king has a foul temper, he can make such bald statements as: "The king was furious. He sent everyone home, locked all the doors, and had chains wrapped tight around his castle." Nevertheless the difference is one of degree. Neither the realist nor the writer of tales can get by without documentation through specific detail.

It's the same in the yarn. Consider the following, from Mark Twain's "Baker's Bluejay Yarn."

> "When I first begun to understand jay language correctly, there was a little incident happened here. Seven years ago, the last man in this region but me moved away. There stands his house—been empty ever since; a log house, with a plank roof—just one big room, and no more; no ceiling—nothing between the rafters and the floor. Well, one Sunday morning I was sitting out here in front of my cabin, with my cat, taking the sun, and looking at the blue hills, and listening to the leaves rustling so lonely in the trees, and thinking of the home away yonder in the states, that I hadn't heard from in thirteen years, when a bluejay lit on that house, with an acorn in his mouth, and says, 'Hello, I reckon I've struck something.' When he spoke, the acorn dropped out of his mouth and rolled down the roof, of course, but he didn't care; his mind was all on the thing he had struck. It was a knot-hole in the roof. He cocked his head to one side, shut one eye and put the other one to the hole, like a 'possum looking down a jug; then he glanced up with his bright eyes, gave a wink or two with his wings—which signifies gratification, you understand—and says, 'It looks like a hole, it's located like a hole—blamed if I don't believe it *is* a hole!'"

Baker, we understand, has been out in the wilderness too long and has gone a little dotty—or else (more likely) he's pulling the leg of the credulous narrator who reports his story as gospel. Either way, no one but the narrator imagines for a moment that what Baker is saying is true. What makes the lie delightful is the pains Baker takes to make it credible. The cabin with the knothole in the roof exists: It has a history and physical features—in fact Baker can point to it. Details convince us that Baker really did sit looking at it: It was a Sunday morning; his cat was with him; he was looking at and listening to specific things, thinking specific thoughts. The bluejay really did speak—the acorn is the proof—and further details labor valiantly to persuade us that bluejays think: the cocked head, the one closed eye, the vivid image of the open eye pressed to the knot-hole "like a 'possum looking down a jug."

In all the major genres, vivid detail is the life blood of fiction. Verisimilitude, suspension of disbelief through narrative voice, or the wink that calls attention to the yarn-teller's lie may be the *outer* strategy of a given work; but in all major genres, the inner strategy is the same: The reader is regularly presented with proofs—in the form of closely observed details—that what is said to be happening is really happening. Before we turn to the technical implications of this fact, let us look, briefly, at a few more examples, since the point is one of great importance. Take a short scene from Peter Taylor's "The Fancy Woman." George has brought Josephine, the "fancy woman" or prostitute he loves, home to meet the family. Josephine has been drinking, and George is determined to sober her up.

> As he pushed Josephine onto the white, jumpy beast he must have caught a whiff of her breath. She knew that he must have! He was holding the reins close to the bit while she tried to arrange herself in the flat saddle. Then he grasped her ankle and asked her, "Did you take a drink upstairs?" She laughed, leaned forward in her saddle, and whispered:
>
> "Two. Two jiggers."
>
> She wasn't afraid of the horse now, but she was dizzy. "George, let me down," she said faintly. She felt the horse's flesh quiver under her leg and looked over her shoulder when it stomped one rear hoof.
>
> George said, "Confound it, I'll sober you." He handed her the reins, stepped back, and slapped the horse on the flank. "Hold on!" he called, and her horse cantered across the lawn.
>
> Josie was clutching the leather straps tightly, and her face was almost in the horse's mane. "I could kill him for this," she said, slicing out the words with a sharp breath. God damn it! The horse was galloping along a dirt road. She saw nothing but the yellow dirt. The hoofs crumbled over a three-plank wooden bridge, and she heard George's horse on the other side of her. She turned her face that way and saw George through the hair that hung over her eyes. He was smiling. "You dirty bastard," she said.

Who can doubt the scene? Taylor tells us that the horse is "jumpy" and proves it by a closely observed detail: George holds the reins—as one must to control a jumpy horse when one is standing on the ground—"close to the bit." That Josie is sitting on a real horse, and a jumpy one, is proved by further authenticating details: The horse's flesh quivers "under her leg," and when the writer tells us that Josephine "looked over her shoulder when it stomped one rear hoof," we are at once convinced by both the horse's action and the woman's response. Since Josie is dizzy and presumably not a good rider, we are fully persuaded by the detail telling us "her face was almost in the horse's mane," by the panicky way in which she talks to herself, "slicing out the words with a sharp breath," by the fact that, riding down the dirt road, she "saw nothing but the yellow dirt," by the "three-plank wooden bridge" (in her alarm she looks closely), by the fact that she hears George's horse before she sees it, and by the fact that, turning to look at him, she sees George "through the hair that hung over her eyes." Examining the scene carefully, we discover that something like half of it is devoted to details that prove its actuality.

Compare a short passage from a comic tale in Italo Calvino's *Cosmicomics* (translated from the Italian by William Weaver). The narrator, old Qfwfq, is recalling the days, in the Carboniferous period of the planet, when osseous, pulmonate fish, including Qfwfq, moved up from the sea onto land.

> Our family, I must say, including grandparents, was all up on the shore, padding about as if we had never known how to do anything else. If it hadn't been for the obstinacy of our great-uncle N'ba N'ga, we would have long since lost all contact with the aquatic world.
>
> Yes, we had a great-uncle who was a fish, on my paternal grandmother's side, to be precise, of the Coelacanthus family of the Devonian period (the fresh-water branch: who are, for that matter, cousins of the others—but I don't want to go into all these questions of kinship, nobody can ever follow them anyhow). So as I was saying, this great-uncle lived in certain muddy shallows, among the roots of some protoconifers, in that inlet of the lagoon where all our ancestors had been born. He never stirred from there: at any season of the year all we had to do was push ourselves over the softer layers of vegetation until we could feel ourselves sinking into the dampness, and there below, a few palms' lengths from the edge, we could see the column of little bubbles he sent up, breathing heavily the way old folks do, or the little cloud of mud scraped up by his sharp snout, always rummaging around, more out of habit than out of the need to hunt for anything.

Partly we believe, or forget to disbelieve, what Calvino tells us because of the charm of old Qfwfq's voice; and partly we're convinced by vivid detail. I will not labor the point—the fish-animals "padding about" on shore, the vivid picturing of great-uncle N'ba N'ga's home (the muddy shallows among the roots of protoconifers), the vivid image of the fish-animals pushing themselves "over the softer layers of vegetation until we could feel ourselves sinking into the dampness," the specificity and appropriateness of the measure "a few palms' lengths," the column of little bubbles, the great-uncle's habit of "breathing heavily the way old folks do," the "little cloud of mud scraped up by his sharp snout, always rummaging around, more out of habit than out of the need to hunt for anything."

Consider, finally, the piling up of authenticating details in Ivan Bunin's "The Gentleman from San Francisco," a more conventionally narrated, serious tale. The passage presents an ocean liner crossing the Atlantic.

> On the second and third night there was again a ball—this time in mid-ocean, during the furious storm sweeping over the ocean, which roared like a funeral mass and rolled up mountainous seas fringed with mourning silvery foam. The Devil, who from the rocks of Gibraltar, the stony gateway of two worlds, watched the ship vanish into night and storm, could hardly distinguish from behind the snow the innumerable fiery eyes of the ship. The Devil was as huge as a cliff, but the ship was even bigger, a many-storied, many-stacked giant. . . . The blizzard

battered the ship's rigging and its broad-necked stacks, whitened with snow, but it remained firm, majestic—and terrible. On its uppermost deck, amidst a snowy whirlwind there loomed up in loneliness the cozy, dimly lighted cabin, where, only half awake, the vessel's ponderous pilot reigned over its entire mass, bearing the semblance of a pagan idol. He heard the wailing moans and the furious screeching of the siren, choked by the storm, but the nearness of that which was behind the wall and which in the last account was incomprehensible to him, removed his fears. He was reassured by the thought of the large, armored cabin, which now and then was filled with mysterious rumbling sounds and with the dry creaking of blue fires, flaring up and exploding around a man with a metallic headpiece, who was eagerly catching the indistinct voices of the vessels that hailed him, hundreds of miles away. . . .

One can see at a glance that the details are symbolic, identifying the ship as a kind of hell constructed by the pride of modern man and more terrible than the power of the Devil. But my point at the moment is only this: that here too, as everywhere in good fiction, it's physical detail that pulls us into the story, makes us believe or forget not to believe or (in the yarn) accept the lie even as we laugh at it.

If we carefully inspect our experience as we read, we discover that the importance of physical detail is that it creates for us a kind of dream, a rich and vivid play in the mind. We read a few words at the beginning of the book or the particular story, and suddenly we find ourselves seeing not words on a page but a train moving through Russia, an old Italian crying, or a farmhouse battered by rain. We read on—dream on—not passively but actively, worrying about the choices the characters have to make, listening in panic for some sound behind the fictional door, exulting in characters' successes, bemoaning their failures. In great fiction, the dream engages us heart and soul; we not only respond to imaginary things—sights, sounds, smells—as though they were real, we respond to fictional problems as though they were real: We sympathize, think, and judge. We act out, vicariously, the trials of the characters and learn from the failures and successes of particular modes of action, particular attitudes, opinions, assertions, and beliefs exactly as we learn from life. Thus the value of great fiction, we begin to suspect, is not just that it entertains us or distracts us from our troubles, not just that it broadens our knowledge of people and places, but also that it helps us to know what we believe, reinforces those qualities that are noblest in us, leads us to feel uneasy about our faults and limitations.

This is not the place to pursue that suspicion—that is, the place to work out in detail the argument that the ultimate value of fiction is its morality, though the subject is one we must return to—but it is a good place to note a few technical implications of the fact that, whatever the genre may be, fiction does its work by creating a dream in the reader's mind. We may observe, first, that if the effect of the dream is to be powerful, the dream must probably be vivid and continuous—*vivid* because if we are not quite clear about what it is that we're dreaming, who and where the characters are, what it is that they're doing or trying to do and why, our emotions and judgments must be confused, dissipated, or blocked; and *continuous* because a repeatedly interrupted flow of action must necessarily have less force than an action directly carried through from its beginning to its conclusion. There may be exceptions to this general rule—we will consider that possibility later—but insofar as the general rule is persuasive it suggests that one of the chief mistakes a writer can make is to allow or force the reader's mind to be distracted, even momentarily, from the fictional dream.

Let us be sure we have the principle clear. The writer presents a scene—let us say a scene in which two rattlesnakes are locked in mortal combat. He makes the scene vivid in the reader's mind; that is, he encourages the reader to "dream" the event with enormous clarity, by presenting as many concrete details as possible. He shows, with as much poetic force as he can muster, how the heads hover, jaws wide, slowly swaying, and then strike; how the teeth sink in; how the tails switch and lash, grope for a hold, pound up dust clouds; how the two snakes hiss, occasionally strike and miss, the two rattles roaring like motors. By detail the writer achieves vividness; to make the scene continuous, he takes pains to avoid anything that might distract the reader from the image of fighting snakes to, say, the manner in which the image is presented or the character of the writer. This is of course not to say that the writer cannot break from the scene to some other—for instance, the conservationist rushing toward the snakes in his jeep. Though characters and locale change, the dream is still running like a movie in the reader's mind. The writer distracts the reader—breaks the film, if you will—when by some slip of technique or egoistic intrusion he allows or forces the reader to stop thinking about the story (stop "seeing" the story) and think about something else.

Some writers—John Barth, for instance—make a point of interrupting the fictional dream from time to time, or even denying the reader the chance to enter the fictional dream that his experience of fiction has led him to expect. We will briefly examine the purpose and value of such fiction later. For now, it is enough to say that such writers are not writing fiction at all, but something else, *metafiction*. They give the reader an experience that assumes the usual experience of fiction as its point of departure, and whatever effect their work may have depends on their conscious violation of the usual fictional effect. What interests us in their novels is that they are *not* novels but, instead, artistic comments on art.

We've come a long way from our opening question, "If there are no rules, or none worth his attention, where is the beginning writer to begin?" Among other things, you may impatiently object, we've raised the specter of a great morass of rules: Don't try to write without the basic skills of composition; don't try to write "what you know," choose a genre; create a kind of dream in the reader's mind, and avoid like the plague all that might briefly distract from that dream—a notion wherein a multitude of rules are implied.

But nothing in all this, I patiently answer, has anything to do with aesthetic law or gives rules on how to write. That literature falls into genres is simply an observation from nature, comparable to Adam's observation that the animals need names. If one is to write, it helps to know what writing is. And the fact that all three of the major genres have one common element, the fictional dream, is another observation, nothing more. We are speaking, remember, only of realistic narratives, tales, and yarns—that is, fiction's primary forms—so that in listing ways in which the reader can be distracted from the fictional dream, as I will in

Part Two, I am in fact dealing only with things to watch out for when striving for the effects of traditional fiction. My premise of course is that before one can work well with metafiction, one needs some understanding of how the primary forms work.

Let us turn again, then, to [the] opening question: Where should one begin?

I have said that a good answer, but not an ideal one, is "Write the kind of story you know and like best"; in other words, choose a genre and try to write in it. Since we're living in an age very rich in genres—since a given student may have encountered almost anything, from tales like Isak Dinesen's to *New Yorker* realistic fiction, from surreal, plotless fictions-in-question-and-answer-form to philosophically enriched and dramatically intensified prose renderings of something like the vision in *Captain Marvel* comics—such instructions to the writer may produce almost anything. Set off in this way, the writer is sure to enjoy himself, first riffling through genres, discovering how many and how complex they are, then—tongue between his teeth—knocking off his brilliant example. The approach has the advantage of reminding the student of what freedom he has, how vast the possibilities are, and the advantage of encouraging him to find his own unique path.

The reason the approach seems to me not ideal is that, except in the extraordinary case, it wastes the writer's time. It instructs him to do something he cannot realistically be expected to do well—and here I mean "well" in the always urgent artist's sense, not the more casual, more gentlemanly way in which we do things badly or well in other university programs. Let me explain. True artists, whatever smiling faces they may show you, are obsessive, driven people—whether driven by some mania or driven by some high, noble vision need not presently concern us. Anyone who has worked both as artist and as professor can tell you, I think, that he works very differently in his two styles. No one is more careful, more scrupulously honest, more devoted to his personal vision of the ideal, than a good professor trying to write a book about the *Gilgamesh*. He may write far into the night, he may avoid parties, he may feel pangs of guilt about having spent too little time with his family. Nevertheless, his work is no more like an artist's work than the work of a first-class accountant is like that of an athlete contending for a championship. He uses faculties of the mind more easily available to us; he has, on all sides of him, stays, checks, safeties, rules of procedure that guide and secure him. He's a man sure of where he stands in the world. He belongs on sunlit walkways, in ivied halls. With the artist, not so. No critical study, however brilliant, is the fierce psychological battle a novel is. The qualities that make a true artist— nearly the same qualities that make a true athlete—make it important that the student writer never be prevented from working as seriously as he knows how to. In university courses we do exercises. Term papers, quizzes, final examinations are not meant for publication. We move through a course on Dostoevsky or Poe as we move through a mildly good cocktail party, picking up the good bits of food or conversation, bearing with the rest, going home when it comes to seem the reasonable thing to do. Art, at those moments when it feels most like art—when we feel most alive, most alert, most triumphant—is less like a cocktail party than a tank full of sharks. Everything's for keeps, nothing's just for exercise. (Robert

Frost said, "I never write exercises, but sometimes I write poems which fail and then I call them exercises.") A course in creative writing should be like writing itself; everything required should be, at least potentially, usable, publishable: for keeps. "A *mighty will*," Henry James said, "that's all there is!" Let no one discourage or undermine that mighty will.

I would begin, then, with something real—smaller than a short story, tale, yarn, sketch—and something primary, not secondary (not parody, for example, but the thing itself). I would begin with some one of those necessary parts of larger forms, some single element that, if brilliantly done, might naturally become the trigger of a larger work—some small exercise in technique, if you like, as long as it's remembered that we do not really mean it as an exercise but mean it as a possible beginning of some magnificent work of art. A one-page passage of description, for example; description keyed to some particular genre—since description in a short story does not work in the same way description works in the traditional tale. And I would make the chief concern of this small exercise the writer's discovery of the *full meaning* of fiction's elements. Having written one superb descriptive passage, the writer should know things about description that he'll never need to think about again. Working element by element through the necessary parts of fiction, he should make the essential techniques second nature, so that he can use them with increasing dexterity and subtlety, until at last, as if effortlessly, he can construct imaginary worlds—huge thoughts made up of concrete details—so rich and complex, and so awesomely simple, that we are astounded, as we're always astounded by great art.

This means, of course, that he must learn to see fiction's elements as only a writer does, or an occasional great critic: as the fundamental units of an ancient but still valid kind of thought. Homer's kind of thought; what I have sometimes called "concrete philosophy." We're not ready just yet to talk about what that kind of thought entails, but we can make a beginning by describing how an exercise in description might work.

To the layman it may seem that description serves simply to tell us where things are happening, giving us perhaps some idea of what the characters are like by identifying them with their surroundings, or providing us with props that may later tip over or burn down or explode. Good description does far more: It is one of the writer's means of reaching down into his unconscious mind, finding clues to what questions his fiction must ask, and, with luck, hints about the answers. Good description is symbolic not because the writer plants symbols in it but because, by working in the proper way, he forces symbols still largely mysterious to him up into his conscious mind where, little by little as his fiction progresses, he can work with them and finally understand them. To put this another way, the organized and intelligent fictional dream that will eventually fill the reader's mind *begins as a largely mysterious dream in the writer's mind*. Through the process of writing and endless revising, the writer makes available the order the reader sees. Discovering the meaning and communicating the meaning are for the writer one single act. One does not simply describe a barn, then. One describes a barn as seen by someone in some particular mood, because only in that way can the barn—or the writer's experience of barns combined with whatever lies deepest in his feelings—be tricked into mumbling its secrets. . . .

1. Gardner advises young writers not to write from personal experience, but rather to write the kind of story the writer likes best. Why does he give this advice?
2. Gardner asserts that originality in art often comes from combining existing genres in new ways. What examples are you familiar with that illustrate this process? Do you agree with Gardner's belief that originality derives from working with familiar forms?
3. Gardner claims that fiction is a form of "concrete philosophy" and "serious thought." In what ways do these definitions conflict with other definitions of fiction as primarily a matter of storytelling or self-expression?
4. Gardner offers a partial taxonomy of fiction, describing the realistic short story, the tale, and the yarn. What are the important characteristics of each type of story? What other types of fiction would you add to Gardner's list?

RUST HILLS

Slick Fiction and Quality Fiction

Rust Hills (b. 1924) was an influential fiction editor for Esquire *magazine during its heyday of discovering new voices in American fiction. He co-edited* Lust, Violence, Sin, Magic: Sixty Years of Esquire Fiction *(1993) with Will Blythe and Erika Mansourian. He also wrote the textbooks* How We Live: Contemporary Life in Contemporary American Fiction *(1968) and* Writing in General and the Short Story in Particular *(1977). As a reader of thousands of unpublished short stories and novels, he has a sharp eye for fiction that works.*

We had submitted to us at *Esquire* recently a short story by a very distinguished author. One of his stories, at least, has become a semiclassic; I remember teaching it in freshman English classes. But, like many celebrated authors who may not have *it* anymore, the author has turned to slick fiction, thinking, perhaps, that his skill and his name would carry the fake plot.

It started off well enough, with a neatly characterized sketch: a doting mother trying to console her businessman husband, both worried about the laziness of their college-boy son, who, the father storms, is learning nothing practical and useful in school. In the basement playroom, the scampish young man meanwhile vows to his fiancee he'll make her a million dollars.

Charming to this point, the story turns slick. The boy returns to college, listens listlessly as his English instructor tells of the fortune one could make if he discovered a lost play of Shakespeare's. Suddenly he remembers an old book his mother brought from Italy, rushes back home, steals the book (nothing is made of the ethics of this), annotates it (while lying in the sun on the Riviera), and gets ready to make his million publishing it.

We next see him in a magnificent suite in a magnificent London hotel preparing for tea with the Queen. The father reappears, still suspicious, for he has never heard of Shakespeare; but as his son drives off in his chauffeur-driven Daimler, he looks at him "with a curious awe."

Needless to say, the distinguished author of this undistinguished story is a college professor. In an academic, this story represents the most undisguised sort of daydreaming. Not by any commercial means, but solely by his own academic skills and his scholarship, the hero (and the author with him in his fantasying) is able to make so much money and become so successful that even his old man looks at him "with a curious awe." That last phrase is interesting, because when slick takes over, even the words and phrases turn to cliché.

The story is a harmlessly genial and gentle kind of daydreaming, and one wishes some magazine would publish it, and pay the author a million dollars, and make all his dreams come true.

Leonard Wallace Robinson, who was Managing Editor of *Esquire* when I came here, had a good eye for both slick and quality fiction. More interesting, he was invariably able to tell the difference between them. As I recall his distinction, it was that quality fiction partakes of the nightdream—while slick fiction partakes of the daydream.

In terms of literary history, it seems to me, the distinction between slick and quality goes back to the two writers that Paul Roche calls the twin pillars of the short story: Maupassant and Chekhov. I argue with people a lot about short stories and I argued with Paul Roche about this. For he claimed that we were too much under the influence of Chekhov and needed more Maupassant. My disagreement is: that the Maupassant method is at the very heart of the more pretentious sort of slick; that his stories are full of beautiful, oversexed women and trick, twisty plot devices; that the stories may occasionally be seamy, but that their plots are such that they are without a truly accurate view of life; but that Chekhov sees life as it is and renders it so; and that his accurate vision and uncompromising plotting stand at the head of a literary tradition recently come to a fine flowering in the works of contemporary writers like Bernard Malamud and Saul Bellow; but that this Chekhov influence is still not in actual ascendancy, as the majority of magazine fiction is committed to the slick, trick, glamourized methods of Maupassant's fake daydreaming writing.

Too much of the daydream is what's the trouble with most of the fiction we see. Daytime fantasying is at the heart of all the slick, trick, sexy, sadistic, self-pitying, snappy-dialogued, romanticized, glamourized, hard-boiled, or sentimentalized stories that come our way, that we occasionally publish (more or less by accident), and that I read too often in other magazines. The concept of writing as some sort of catharsis, some sort of working out of symbolic terms of a writer's fantasies known or unknown, is a perfectly acceptable concept as long as the writing is successful. But you'll find that the successful writing of this sort stems from the nightdream, not the daydream. When cathartic writing is unsuccessful, it is so unsuccessful that almost anything is better: six years of psychoanalysis for the writer; finger painting; or the cold shower and walk around the block that the YMCA is supposed to advise.

This sort of daydreaming, which is at the heart of all slick fiction (both hard-boiled and romantic), is much more forgivable in the young than in the old: In the young writer it may represent a persistence of illusion; in the old it represents an escape from reality. We are much more tolerant of the fantasying slick attitudes in a new, inexperienced writer than in someone who has the craft to draw a story about how things really are, but hasn't the vision or integrity to do it.

A lot of the undergraduate writing that we see, for instance, will have an overly romantic or false-cynical slickness that we will try to overlook for the promise of a talent and an eye and an ear not yet realized. There was recently, as an example, some very promising work from a very young writer studying at Columbia. *Three Sketches* he called his submission, and one of them, titled "A Momentary Thing," told of a young American sitting at a cafe in Paris approached by an attractive prostitute. The boy has a warm and friendly discussion with her, and the two are obviously very *simpatico*; but at the end he tells her to go on her way, and speaks of her to his friends as "just another whore."

It was a romantic little sketch, and it seemed slick in its youngishness and in its melancholy irony—sentimentalized prostitutes are, I suppose, the cliche of cliches. But somehow the story managed not to be slick romantic, but just young romantic, which, as I say, is a very forgivable thing—at least in the young. Forgivable—but not publishable.

As in many of the stories that we get from universities, there was in this sketch a lack of body—a nonattention to standard story values: plot, suspense, characterization in depth, and so forth. Students generally shy away from telling a full-bodied story under the excuse that it is old-fashioned writing. And shying away is actually very sensible of them, because they haven't yet the equipment to handle a full-fledged plot with full-fledged characters—they find their story is likely to bog down into a melodrama, with unconvincing dialogue, unconvincing character shifts, and unsustained tone and mood.

Often they will turn then to some sort of experimental story—full of stream-of-consciousness mixed with newspaper headlines and dirty words. This is useful as an exercise, but the results are seldom worth much. *Esquire* has never, for instance, published an experimental story, even by a celebrated author. It would seem that if a writer has written stories with the control of technique that James Joyce showed in *Dubliners,* he would then be ready to go on to publish experimental work like *Finnegans Wake*—not before. Experimentalism in new writers is too often a cover for lack of craft.

Undergraduate writers and beginning writers are much more likely to be successful when they write fragments like these three sketches sent to us from Columbia—because these are, in effect, exercises—and as exercises they are, of course, very useful to a new writer.

Sketches such as these are the first workings out of the amateur writer's "wonderful idea for a short story"—which usually means plot, not idea at all. More is needed: a true something to say. In a mature writer who has found what he has to say, and has said it in many ways and in many stories, this becomes a body of work—with a world of its own: Fitzgerald's world; Hemingway's world; Dickens' world. But it must be found first, with experiments and exercises.

The trouble is that new young writers always want to publish their more or less successful exercises, and they are not savvy enough to know that these are traditionally published in little magazines, not in the big national commercial ones. It is too bad, because publication in the small literary quarterlies, no matter how small, can be a great help. A new writer cannot usually expect to publish first in the large national commercial magazines, and he can't even expect, perhaps, to first publish in some of the more renowned quarterlies like *Kenyon Review, Partisan Review, Sewanee Review,* etc. But publication in the littler of the little—magazines like *Accent* and *Epoch* and *Audience*—and even in any little magazine the writer and his friends might start for themselves is the natural and traditional road to publishing for pay. Charles Allen published (in *Sewanee Review,* July, 1943) a study showing that of 100 writers important since 1914, eighty-five of them had first appeared in little magazines. And if anyone would take the trouble to read these early contributions, he would see how impossible (and, indeed, how unwarranted) publication of most of these pieces in a large national commercial magazine would have been.

To be worth considering at all, it seems to me, a story must have a point—some point, any point; some intention. But for the story to be good, the point must be inextricably bedded in all the other aspects of the story—in the plot, the characterizations, the mood, the style, the setting, the structure, and so on. If a story has no point, then it is pointless. And if the story does have a point or purpose, but it is not inextricably bedded in all the other aspects, then what one has is at worst a tract, at best some sort of allegory or parable—a "message" story. The point need not then, indeed, *must* not, be demonstrable, capable of being removed, paraphrased.

But if the point of the story *is* inextricably bedded in all the other aspects of a story, then that story says something, tells you something, without being a tract. You get the absolute fusion of form and content that is Art. And further, whatever the theme or point or purpose or intention of the story is, will become a *controlling* intention. The controlling intention will control the selection and presentation of all the other aspects of a short story: the mood the author creates; the style he selects; the structure of the story; the workings-out of the narrative or plot line through the various crises (also determined by the controlling intention); it will control the original delineation and the subsequent development of the characters. In sum: the intention or purpose of a story must be inseparable from all the other aspects, and will at the same time control them.

I always seem to be misunderstood here, and I don't want to be. A key to the quality story is characterization, and let me use the interaction between characterization and theme as an example to qualify what I say about controlling intent. The distinction made between tragedy and melodrama (or between comedy and farce) is that in tragedy plot yields to character, while in melodrama the characterizations will shift according to the devisings of the plot. What is true of drama seems to me equally true of the difference between quality and slick in prose fiction; and what is true of the interaction between characterization and plot seems equally true of the relation of characterization to theme. Characters will not be just chosen to demonstrate the point of the story, they must "somehow live themselves"—and I find I've found a cliche here, myself. The cliche is at the very heart of the slick. In a slick story the conception of the characters will be stereotype—every delineation of them will stem from a stock figure: "a guy who works in a bank"; even simply "a waitress." The situation (and eventually the plot) will partake of the same sort of cliche: "this woman is seated at a bar"; "a young American student is sitting in a Paris cafe"; "this college kid who worries his parents." In quality writing stereotyping can never be a substitute for characterization; in slick, it always is. In good writing the characterization somehow *becomes* the point of the story. The point of the story must be concealed, must in some way be added *into* it, not just worked out. The story's controlling intention must never be thought of as wholly interchangeable with its theme.

How will this work in actual practice? Which will come first? The intention?—the point the author wants to make, and for which he will subsequently find a story to illustrate? Or will the story come first?—the "some incident observed in the subway" which naggles away at the author, until he begins to write about it, seeing only then (but perhaps not really clearly, himself, ever at all) the point of what he is saying, and through the discovered (or, at least, sensed) controlling intention carving and creating all the other aspects further to fit?

It could, of course, be either of these two methods—but it seems to me more likely that the process of creating a successful story is some combination of the two. It seems usual, for instance, that a writer keeps a notebook and in this notebook puts down thoughts and ideas which occur to him and also makes a note of any incident which he has observed or been told of or read of in the newspaper, and which has captured his fancy. It is the marriage of these two elements—the thought and the incident, whether in a notebook or in his own mind alone—that produces the seed that grows (or, more accurately, is *made* to grow through the author's bringing to bear imagination or hard work—depending on which is most necessary) into the final story—which, if it is truly successful, will (as I emphasized at the beginning) appear as if its elements had never been unfused.

And perhaps they never were. I am not a writer, and I have no way of knowing. I used to try, about once every year or so, but I never wrote a story that was even remotely successful. I finally gave it up, under the theory that to try to be a good editor is not much less a thing than being a bad writer, and while it probably isn't much better paid, it is an awful lot happier. A great weight was lifted from me, and I found I could look at life around me with some other interest than just as potential material. No one should ever be encouraged to write. There are too many writers already, and the world is especially full of people who don't want to write, but do want to be writers. What begins as a harmless catharsis will, with encouragement, become a compulsion to publish. We feel it is wrong to encourage bad writers with a soft rejection, no matter how the letter of submission may beg for "just some comment." Writing is hard—almost anything else is easy (again, something Len Robinson used to say). You can do almost anything else if you have a cold or a hangover or a lot of worries—but it is just about impossible to write.

Even if never having written anything successful himself makes it unlikely that a person will be very accurate or positive about how it's done, it shouldn't rule out his chances of recognizing a good piece of writing. I won't develop this, but just state: I think it may improve his chances. And, so far as helping an author to rewrite is concerned, then—if, as I believe, good editing is the ability first to comprehend the work's intentions; and second, to demonstrate to the author ways in which he can more successfully realize them—the value of the editor's ability to write is in inverse ratio to the author's ability to edit.

Judging stories, I work on a basis of a mixture of the too academic and the too emotional—and they tend to balance out. The too academic approach is a method (much modified from the lectures of Fred B. Millett, who taught me Freshman English one hundred and eighty years ago at Wesleyan) of asking a series of four questions about the story:

1. What is the author trying to say?
2. How does he say it?
3. How well does he say it?
4. Was it worth saying?

The first two questions are, of course, of interpretation, which must always precede evaluation (the last two). Questions two and three concern form; and, questions one and four, content. As I say, this four-point approach to the criticism (interpretation and evaluation) of writing is perhaps too neat and pedantic (question four, for instance, is to all intents and purposes useless, and has as its primary value neatness—although there is this to say: A short story may be defeated right from the start by too limited a conception), but following the method does seem to me to have two advantages: first, by focusing your attention early on the author's purpose (and I'm ignoring what is known in aesthetic theory as The Intentional Fallacy, and I know it and don't think it makes much difference in magazine editing), these questions get you to thinking of the work in its own terms and cut down on snap judgments; and second, by encouraging you to give a run-down to a story you may have been initially enthusiastic about, it gives you a chance to pause, and to see how the effects that made you enthusiastic were created, and why, and if it's a serious story, or merely just a fake one, whose emotion was based in sentimentality, and deliberately evoked.

So much for the too academic approach. The second, the too emotional approach, is responding to what Edmund Wilson may not have had in mind at all with the term "the shock of recognition"—but it's a marvelous term for the experience anyway. The quality of the unsolicited manuscripts we see is so dreadfully low, that when we read a story of any promise at all, we certainly experience some recognition. But when a *really* good story comes in—solicited or unsolicited— when one reads that really good story, it is really a shock!

These are the full-bodied stories that are totally unlike one another and totally unlike any other story. And they are also characterized by a view of life which is neither wishful nor stereotyped.

DISCUSSION QUESTIONS

1. Hills contrasts Chekhov and Maupassant, the twin pillars of the short story tradition, preferring Chekhov's emphasis on character to Maupassant's high-quality "slick" fiction. Especially if you're familiar with these writers, do you agree with Hills' judgment? Can you apply Hills' judgment to other writers you've read?

2. Hills claims that slick fiction is like a daydream, while quality fiction has the feel of a "nightdream." What does he mean? Why does he use the term "night-dream" rather than "nightmare"? How does this distinction relate to his central distinction between slick and quality fiction?

3. Hills pronounces that "experimentalism in new writers is too often a cover for lack of craft." To what extent do you agree with this judgment? What reasons might you or other new writers have for experimenting with fiction?

FRANK O'CONNOR

Introduction to *The Lonely Voice*

Frank O'Connor (1903–1966), born as Michael Francis O'Donovan, was an Irish short story writer, novelist, playwright, essayist, biographer, autobiographer, editor, and translator. His short story collections include Guests of the Nation *(1931),* Bones of Contention *(1936),* Domestic Relations *(1957), and* My Oedipus Complex and Other Stories *(1963); his novels are* The Saint and Mary Kate *(1932) and* Dutch Interior *(1940). In* The Lonely Voice: A Study of the Short Story *(1963), he lays out his basic aesthetic for fiction.*

"By the hokies, there was a man in this place one time by the name of Ned Sullivan, and a queer thing happened him late one night and he coming up the Valley Road from Durlas."

That is how, even in my own lifetime, stories began. In its earlier phases storytelling, like poetry and drama, was a public art, though unimportant beside them because of its lack of a rigorous technique. But the short story, like the novel, is a modern art form; that is to say, it represents, better than poetry or drama, our own attitude to life.

No more than the novel does it begin with "By the hokies." The technique which both have acquired was the product of a critical, scientific age, and we recognize the merits of a short story much as we recognize the merits of a novel—in terms of plausibility. By this I do not mean mere verisimilitude—that we can get from a newspaper report—but an ideal action worked out in terms of verisimilitude. As we shall see, there are dozens of ways of expressing verisimilitude—as many perhaps as there are great writers—but no way of explaining its absence, no way of saying, "At this point the character's behavior becomes completely inexplicable." Almost from its beginnings the short story, like the novel, abandoned the devices of a public art in which the storyteller assumed the mass assent of an audience to his wildest improvisations—"and a queer thing happened him late one night." It began, and continues to function, as a private art intended to satisfy the standards of the individual, solitary, critical reader.

Yet, even from its beginnings, the short story has functioned in a quite different way from the novel, and, however difficult it may be to describe the difference, describing it is the critic's principal business.

"We all came out from under Gogol's 'Overcoat'" is a familiar saying of Turgenev, and though it applies to Russian rather than European fiction, it has also a general truth.

Read now, and by itself, "The Overcoat" does not appear so very impressive. All the things Gogol has done in it have been done frequently since his day, and sometimes done better. But if we read it again in its historical context, closing our minds so far as we can to all the short stories it gave rise to, we can see that Turgenev was not exaggerating. We have all come out from under Gogol's "Overcoat."

It is the story of a poor copying clerk, a nonentity mocked by his colleagues. His old overcoat has become so threadbare that even his drunken tailor refuses to patch it further since there is no longer any place in it where a patch would hold. Akakey Akakeivitch, the copying clerk, is terrified at the prospect of such unprecedented expenditure. As a result of a few minor fortunate circumstances, he finds himself able to buy a new coat, and for a day or two this makes a new man of him, for after all, in real life he is not much more than an overcoat.

Then he is robbed of it. He goes to the Chief of Police, a bribe-taker who gives him no satisfaction, and to an Important Personage who merely abuses and threatens him. Insult piled on injury is too much for him and he goes home and dies. The story ends with a whimsical description of his ghost's search for justice, which, once more, to a poor copying clerk has never meant much more than a warm overcoat.

There the story ends, and when one forgets all that came after it, like Chekhov's "Death of a Civil Servant," one realizes that it is like nothing in the world of literature before it. It uses the old rhetorical device of the mock-heroic, but uses it to create a new form that is neither satiric nor heroic, but something in between—something that perhaps finally transcends both. So far as I know, it is the first appearance in fiction of the Little Man, which may define what I mean by the short story better than any terms I may later use about it. Everything about Akakey Akakeivitch, from his absurd name to his absurd job, is on the same level of mediocrity, and yet his absurdity is somehow transfigured by Gogol.

> Only when the jokes were too unbearable, when they jolted his arm and prevented him from going on with his work, he would bring out: "Leave me alone! Why do you insult me?" and there was something strange in the words and in the voice in which they were uttered. There was a note in it of something that roused compassion, so that one young man, new to the office, who, following the example of the rest, had allowed himself to mock at him, suddenly stopped as though cut to the heart, and from that day forth, everything was as it were changed and appeared in a different light to him. Some unnatural force seemed to thrust him away from the companions with whom he had become acquainted, accepting them as well-bred, polished people. And long afterwards, at moments of the greatest gaiety, the figure of the humble little clerk with a bald patch on his head rose

before him with his heart-rending words "Leave me alone! Why do you insult me?" and in those heart-rending words he heard others: "I am your brother." And the poor young man hid his face in his hands, and many times afterwards in his life he shuddered, seeing how much inhumanity there is in man, how much savage brutality lies hidden under refined, cultured politeness, and my God! even in a man whom the world accepts as a gentleman and a man of honour.

One has only to read that passage carefully to see that without it scores of stories by Turgenev, by Maupassant, by Chekhov, by Sherwood Anderson and James Joyce could never have been written. If one wanted an alternative description of what the short story means, one could hardly find better than that single half-sentence, "and from that day forth, everything was as it were changed and appeared in a different light to him." If one wanted an alternative title for this work, one might choose "I Am Your Brother." What Gogol has done so boldly and brilliantly is to take the mock-heroic character, the absurd little copying clerk, and impose his image over that of the crucified Jesus, so that even while we laugh we are filled with horror at the resemblance.

Now, this is something that the novel cannot do. For some reason that I can only guess at, the novel is bound to be a process of identification between the reader and the character. One could not make a novel out of a copying clerk with a name like Akakey Akakeivitch who merely needed a new overcoat any more than one could make one out of a child called Tommy Tompkins whose penny had gone down a drain. One character at least in any novel must represent the reader in some aspect of his own conception of himself—as the Wild Boy, the Rebel, the Dreamer, the Misunderstood Idealist—and this process of identification invariably leads to some concept of normality and to some relationship—hostile or friendly—with society as a whole. People are abnormal insofar as they frustrate the efforts of such a character to exist in what he regards as a normal universe, normal insofar as they support him. There is not only the Hero, there is also the Semi-Hero and the Demi-Semi-Hero. I should almost go so far as to say that without the concept of a normal society the novel is impossible. I know there are examples of the novel that seem to contradict this, but in general I should say that it is perfectly true. The President of the Immortals is called in only when society has made a thorough mess of the job.

But in "The Overcoat" this is not true, nor is it true of most of the stories I shall have to consider. There is no character here with whom the reader can identify himself, unless it is that nameless horrified figure who represents the author. There is no form of society to which any character in it could possibly attach himself and regard as normal. In discussions of the modern novel we have come to talk of it as the novel without a hero. In fact, the short story has never had a hero.

What it has instead is a submerged population group—a bad phrase which I have had to use for want of a better. That submerged population changes its character from writer to writer, from generation to generation. It may be Gogol's officials, Turgenev's serfs, Maupassant's prostitutes, Chekhov's doctors and teachers, Sherwood Anderson's provincials, always dreaming of escape.

"Even though I die, I will in some way keep defeat from you," she cried, and so deep was her determination that her whole body shook. Her eyes glowed and she clenched her fists. "If I am dead and see him becoming a meaningless drab figure like myself, I will come back," she declared. "I ask God now to give me that privilege. I will take any blow that may fall if but this my boy be allowed to express something for us both." Pausing uncertainly, the woman stared about the boy's room. "And do not let him become smart and successful either," she added vaguely.

This is Sherwood Anderson, and Anderson writing badly for him, but it could be almost any short-story writer. What has the heroine tried to escape from? What does she want her son to escape from? "Defeat"—what does that mean? Here it does not mean mere material squalor, though this is often characteristic of the submerged population groups. Ultimately it seems to mean defeat inflicted by a society that has no sign posts, a society that offers no goals and no answers. The submerged population is not submerged entirely by material considerations; it can also be submerged by the absence of spiritual ones, as in the priests and spoiled priests of J. F. Powers' American stories.

Always in the short story there is this sense of outlawed figures wandering about the fringes of society, superimposed sometimes on symbolic figures whom they caricature and echo—Christ, Socrates, Moses. It is not for nothing that there are famous short stories called "Lady Macbeth of the Mtsensk District" and "A Lear of the Steppes" and—in reverse—one called "An Akoulina of the Irish Midlands." As a result there is in the short story at its most characteristic something we do not often find in the novel—an intense awareness of human loneliness. Indeed, it might be truer to say that while we often read a familiar novel again for companionship, we approach the short story in a very different mood. It is more akin to the mood of Pascal's saying: *Le silence éternel de ces espaces infinis m'effraie.*

I have admitted that I do not profess to understand the idea fully: it is too vast for a writer with no critical or historical training to explore by his own inner light, but there are too many indications of its general truth for me to ignore it altogether. When I first dealt with it I had merely noticed the peculiar geographical distribution of the novel and the short story. For some reason Czarist Russia and modern America seemed to be able to produce both great novels and great short stories, while England, which might be called without exaggeration the homeland of the novel, showed up badly when it came to the short story. On the other hand my own country, which had failed to produce a single novelist, had produced four or five storytellers who seemed to me to be first-rate.

I traced these differences very tentatively, but—on the whole, as I now think, correctly—to a difference in the national attitude toward society. In America as in Czarist Russia one might describe the intellectual's attitude to society as "It may work," in England as "It must work," and in Ireland as "It can't work." A young American of our own time or a young Russian of Turgenev's might look forward with a certain amount of cynicism to a measure of success and influence; nothing but bad luck could prevent a young Englishman's achieving it, even today; while a young Irishman can still expect nothing but incomprehension, ridicule, and injustice. Which is exactly what the author of *Dubliners* got.

The reader will have noticed that I left out France, of which I know little, and Germany, which does not seem to have distinguished itself in fiction. But since those days I have seen fresh evidence accumulating that there was some truth in the distinctions I made. I have seen the Irish crowded out by Indian storytellers, and there are plenty of indications that they in their turn, having become respectable, are being outwritten by West Indians like Samuel Selvon.

Clearly, the novel and the short story, though they derive from the same sources, derive in a quite different way, and are distinct literary forms; and the difference is not so much formal (though, as we shall see, there are plenty of formal differences) as ideological. I am not, of course, suggesting that for the future the short story can be written only by Eskimos and American Indians: without going so far afield, we have plenty of submerged population groups. I am suggesting strongly that we can see in it an attitude of mind that is attracted by submerged population groups, whatever these may be at any given time—tramps, artists, lonely idealists, dreamers, and spoiled priests. The novel can still adhere to the classical concept of civilized society, of man as an animal who lives in a community, as in Jane Austen and Trollope it obviously does; but the short story remains by its very nature remote from the community—romantic, individualistic, and intransigent.

But formally as well the short story differs from the novel. At its crudest you can express the difference merely by saying that the short story is short. It is not necessarily true, but as a generalization it will do well enough. If the novelist takes a character of any interest and sets him up in opposition to society, and then, as a result of the conflict between them, allows his character either to master society or to be mastered by it, he has done all that can reasonably be expected of him. In this the element of Time is his greatest asset; the chronological development of character or incident is essential form as we see it in life, and the novelist flouts it at his own peril.

For the short-story writer there is no such thing as essential form. Because his frame of reference can never be the totality of a human life, he must be forever selecting the point at which he can approach it, and each selection he makes contains the possibility of a new form as well as the possibility of a complete fiasco. I have illustrated this element of choice by reference to a poem of Browning's. Almost any one of his great dramatic lyrics is a novel in itself but caught in a single moment of peculiar significance—Lippo Lippi arrested as he slinks back to his monastery in the early morning, Andrea Del Sarto as he resigns himself to the part of a complaisant lover, the Bishop dying in St. Praxed's. But since a whole lifetime must be crowded into a few minutes, those minutes must be carefully chosen indeed and lit by an unearthly glow, one that enables us to distinguish present, past, and future as though they were all contemporaneous. Instead of a novel of five hundred pages about the Duke of Ferrara, his first and second wives and the peculiar death of the first, we get fifty-odd lines in which the Duke, negotiating a second marriage, describes his first, and the very opening lines make our blood run cold:

> That's my last Duchess painted on the wall,
> Looking as if she were alive.

This is not the essential form that life gives us; it is organic form, something that springs from a single detail and embraces past, present, and future. In some book on Parnell there is a horrible story about the death of Parnell's child by Kitty O'Shea, his mistress, when he wandered frantically about the house like a ghost, while Willie O'Shea, the complaisant husband, gracefully received the condolences of visitors. When you read that, it should be unnecessary to read the whole sordid story of Parnell's romance and its tragic ending. The tragedy is there, if only one had a Browning or a Turgenev to write it. In the standard composition that the individual life presents, the storyteller must always be looking for new compositions that enable him to suggest the totality of the old one.

Accordingly, the storyteller differs from the novelist in this: he must be much more of a writer, much more of an artist—perhaps I should add, considering the examples I have chosen, more of a dramatist. For that, too, I suspect, has something to do with it. One savage story of J. D. Salinger's, "Pretty Mouth and Green My Eyes," echoes that scene in Parnell's life in a startling way. A deceived husband, whose wife is out late, rings up his best friend, without suspecting that the wife is in the best friend's bed. The best friend consoles him in a rough-and-ready way, and finally the deceived husband, a decent man who is ashamed of his own outburst, rings again to say that the wife has come home, though she is still in bed with her lover.

Now, a man can be a very great novelist as I believe Trollope was, and yet be a very inferior writer. I am not sure but that I prefer the novelist to be an inferior dramatist; I am not sure that a novel could stand the impact of a scene such as that I have quoted from Parnell's life, or J. D. Salinger's story. But I cannot think of a great storyteller who was also an inferior writer, unless perhaps Sherwood Anderson, nor of any at all who did not have the sense of theater.

This is anything but the recommendation that it may seem, because it is only too easy for a short-story writer to become a little too much of an artist. Hemingway, for instance, has so studied the artful approach to the significant moment that we sometimes end up with too much significance and too little information. I have tried to illustrate this from "Hills like White Elephants." If one thinks of this as a novel one sees it as the love story of a man and a woman which begins to break down when the man, afraid of responsibility, persuades the woman to agree to an abortion which she believes to be wrong. The development is easy enough to work out in terms of the novel. He is an American, she perhaps an Englishwoman. Possibly he has responsibilities already—a wife and children elsewhere, for instance. She may have had some sort of moral upbringing, and perhaps in contemplating the birth of the child she is influenced by the expectation that her family and friends will stand by her in her ordeal.

Hemingway, like Browning in "My Last Duchess," chooses one brief episode from this long and involved story, and shows us the lovers at a wayside station on the Continent, between one train and the next, as it were, symbolically divorced from their normal surroundings and friends. In this setting they make a decision which has already begun to affect their past life and will certainly affect their future. We know that the man is American, but that is all we are told about him. We can guess the woman is not American, and that is all we are told about her. The light is focused fiercely on that one single decision about the abortion. It is the abortion, the whole abortion, and nothing but the abortion. We, too, are compelled to make ourselves judges of the decision, but on an abstract level. Clearly, if we knew that the man had responsibilities elsewhere, we should be a little more sympathetic to him. If, on the other hand, we knew that he had no other responsibilities, we should be even less sympathetic to him than we are. On the other hand, we should understand the woman better if we knew whether she didn't want the abortion because she thought it wrong or because she thought it might loosen her control of the man. The light is admirably focused but it is too blinding; we cannot see into the shadows as we do in "My Last Duchess."

> She had
> A heart—how shall I say?—too soon made glad,
> Too easily impressed; she liked whate'er
> She looked on, and her looks went everywhere.

And so I should say Hemingway's story is brilliant but thin. Our moral judgment has been stimulated, but our moral imagination has not been stirred, as it is stirred in "The Lady with the Toy Dog" in which we are given all the information at the disposal of the author which would enable us to make up our minds about the behavior of his pair of lovers. The comparative artlessness of the novel does permit the author to give unrestricted range to his feelings occasionally—to *sing*; and even minor novelists often sing loud and clear for several chapters at a time, but in the short story, for all its lyrical resources, the singing note is frequently absent.

That is the significance of the difference between the *conte* and the *nouvelle* which one sees even in Turgenev, the first of the great storytellers I have studied. Essentially the difference depends upon precisely how much information the writer feels he must give the reader to enable the moral imagination to function. Hemingway does not give the reader enough. When that wise mother Mme. Maupassant complained that her son, Guy, started his stories too soon and without sufficient preparation, she was making the same sort of complaint.

But the *conte* as Maupassant and even the early Chekhov sometimes wrote it is too rudimentary a form for a writer to go very far wrong in; it is rarely more than an anecdote, a *nouvelle* stripped of most of its detail. On the other hand the form of the *conte* illustrated in "My Last Duchess" and "Hills like White Elephants" is exceedingly complicated, and dozens of storytellers have gone astray in its mazes. There are three necessary elements in a story—exposition, development, and drama. Exposition we may illustrate as "John Fortescue was a solicitor in the little town of X"; development as "One day Mrs. Fortescue told him she was about to leave him for another man"; and drama as "You will do nothing of the kind," he said.

In the dramatized *conte* the storyteller has to combine exposition and development, and sometimes the drama shows a pronounced tendency to collapse under the mere weight of the intruded exposition—"As a solicitor I can tell you you will do nothing of the kind," John Fortescue said. The extraordinary brilliance of "Hills like White Elephants" comes from the skill with which Hemingway has excluded unnecessary exposition; its weakness, as I have suggested, from the fact that much of the exposition is not unnecessary at all. Turgenev probably invented the dramatized *conte,* but if he did, he soon realized its dangers because in his later stories, even brief ones like "Old Portraits," he fell back on the *nouvelle.*

The ideal, of course, is to give the reader precisely enough information, and in this again the short story differs from the novel, because no convention of length ever seems to affect the novelist's power to tell us all we need to know. No such convention of length seems to apply to the short story at all. Maupassant often began too soon because he had to finish within two thousand words, and O'Flaherty sometimes leaves us with the impression that his stories have either gone on too long or not long enough. Neither Babel's stories nor Chekhov's leave us with that impression. Babel can sometimes finish a story in less than a thousand words; Chekhov can draw one out to eighty times the length.

One can put this crudely by saying that the form of the novel is given by the length; in the short story the length is given by the form. There is simply no criterion of the length of a short story other than that provided by the material itself, and either padding to bring it up to a conventional length or cutting to bring it down to a conventional length is liable to injure it. I am afraid that the modern short story is being seriously affected by editorial ideas of what its length should be. (Like most storytellers, I have been told that "nobody reads anything longer than three thousand words.") All I can say from reading Turgenev, Chekhov, Katherine Anne Porter, and others is that the very term "short story" is a misnomer. A great story is not necessarily short at all, and the conception of the short story as a miniature art is inherently false. Basically, the difference between the short story and the novel is not one of length. It is a difference between pure and applied storytelling, and in case someone has still failed to get the point, I am not trying to decry applied storytelling. Pure storytelling is more artistic, that is all, and in storytelling I am not sure how much art is preferable to nature.

Nor am I certain how one can apply this distinction if one can apply it at all. In trying to distinguish between Turgenev's novels and *nouvelles,* Dmitry Mirsky has suggested that the *nouvelles* omit conversations about general ideas which were popular in the nineteenth-century Russian novel. I have tried to assimilate this to my own vague feelings on the subject by suggesting that this is merely another way of saying that the characters in the *nouvelles* were not intended to have general significance. In a marvelous story like "Punin and Baburin," the two principal characters seem to have no general significance at all as they would have been bound to have had they been characters in a novel. In fact when they do appear in a novel like "On the Eve" they have considerable general significance, and the reader is bound to take sides between them. The illegitimate defender of human liberty and the gas-bag poet are not people we take sides with. We sympathize and understand, all right, but they both remain members of a submerged population, unable to speak for themselves.

Even in Chekhov's "Duel," that fantastic short story which is longer than several of Turgenev's novels, the characters are too specific, too eccentric for any real generalization, though generalized conversations are strewn all over the place. We look at Laevsky and Nadyezhda Fyodorovna as we look at Punin and Baburin, from outside, with sympathy and understanding but still feeling, however wrongly, that their problems are their own, not ours. What Turgenev and Chekhov give us is not so much the brevity of the short story compared with the expansiveness of the novel as the purity of an art form that is motivated by its own necessities rather than by our convenience.

As I have said, this is not all gain. Like the Elizabethan drama the novel is a great popular art, and full of the impurities of a popular art, but, like the Elizabethan drama, it has a physical body which a purer art like the short story is constantly in danger of losing. I once tried to describe my own struggle with the form by saying that "Generations of skilful stylists from Chekhov to Katherine Mansfield and James Joyce had so fashioned the short story that it no longer rang with the tone of a man's voice speaking." Even in the nineteenth century there were writers who seem to have had the same uncomfortable feeling. One is Leskov, the only great Russian writer whose work has not been adequately translated.

Even from the miserable number of his stories that have been translated it is clear that he wanted literature to have a physical body. He has tried to revive the art of the folk storyteller so that we can hear the tone of a man's voice speaking. The folk storyteller, because his audience (like a child listening to a bedtime story) can only apprehend a few sentences at a time, unlike a reader who can hold a score of details before his mind simultaneously, has only one method of holding its attention, and that is by piling incident on incident, surprise on surprise. One old folk storyteller, who got someone to read him a couple of my stories, said sadly, "There aren't enough marvels in them." In Leskov's "Enchanted Wanderer" he would have found enough marvels to satisfy even him.

Leskov had also the popular taste for excess. He liked people to be full-blooded. When they were drunk he liked them very drunk, and when they fell in love he did not care for them to be too prudent. "Lady Macbeth of the Mtsensk District" is no understatement as a title. The heroine, consumed by passion, first murders her father-in-law, then her husband, then her co-heir, and finally in destroying herself murders her lover's mistress as well. I think my old friend the folk storyteller would have smacked his lips over that, but I cannot bear to imagine his disappointment over "The Lady with the Toy Dog." "And no one got killed at all?" I can almost hear him cry. He could not have told it to an audience in his little cottage without adding two farcical incidents, two murders, and at least one ghost.

But if this were all, Leskov would be merely a Russian Kipling, and so far as my understanding of his work goes, beyond the superficial resemblances—the episodic treatment and the taste for excess—he had very little in common with

Kipling. Kipling, I should say, took the superficial things that belong to oral storytelling without that peculiar sense of the past that illuminates its wildest extravagances. In one very amusing story Kipling describes the native descendants of an Irish rebel in the British forces in India singing "The Wearing of the Green" before a Crucifix and a cap badge at the time of the Angelus, but in his usual way he vulgarizes it, throwing the Crucifix, the Angelus, the cap badge, and the Irish rebel song in with the mutilation of cattle as the essential Irish things—a mistake that Leskov would not have made. Superficially, there is little to distinguish Leskov's "Lady Macbeth" from "Love-O'-Women," but you could put the former into an Icelandic family saga without anyone's noticing anything peculiar about it. Try to think of someone putting the latter in without someone's noticing that "I'm dyin', Aigypt, dyin'" is not the language of saga! It is irremediably the language of the gin palace.

No, Leskov is important because he is really defining a difference of outlook not between an English Conservative and an English Labour man but between two types of human being. Kipling loves the physical only if the physical happens to be his side and to be well equipped with repeating rifles. Leskov loves it for his own sweet sake. Both to Turgenev and to Chekhov flogging was a horror—to Turgenev because he felt that history had cast him for the part of the flogger, to Chekhov, the slave's grandson, because he felt that every blow of the whip was directed at his own back. Leskov, without prejudice—we might as well face it— found the whole vile business vastly entertaining. To him flogging was an endurance test like any other, and the essence of masculinity was the capacity to endure. He would probably have defended torture on the same grounds.

> They gave me a terrible flogging, so that I could not even stand on my feet afterwards, and they carried me to my father on a piece of straw matting, but I didn't mind that very much; what I did mind was the last part of my sentence, which condemned me to go down on my knees and knock stones into a garden path. . . . I felt so bad about it that after vainly casting about in my mind how to find a way out of my trouble I decided to do away with myself.

That is an extraordinary attitude which you can find in at least one other story of Leskov's, and quite characteristic of him. For instance when the hero of "The Enchanted Wanderer" has gambled away his boss's money he realizes that the only punishment that fits his case is a flogging, so he goes to his boss with bowed head.

> "What are you up to now?" he asked.
> "Give me a good beating at any rate, sir," I said.

Now, this is not mock-heroics; it is not the maunderings of a sexual pervert; it is identical with the extraordinary scene in Gauguin's *Journal* when his mistress, who has been unfaithful to him, asks to be beaten, not so much because she feels any particular guilt about her own behavior as that she knows instinctively that Gauguin will feel better afterward. It is part of the primitive childish psychology of Lawrence's "Tickets, Please!" and between grown-up, civilized people there is literally nothing to be said about it. It is a fact of childish and primitive psychology, but it means that Leskov is often right about that when liberals and humanitarians like Turgenev and Chekhov are wrong.

It must be twenty years since I read a story of Leskov's called "The Stinger" that reminded me at once of Chekhov's "At the Villa." Chekhov's is a tragic story of a civilized engineer who, with his wife and family, is trying to do everything for the unenlightened peasants about him but incurs their scorn, and is driven out of his home by their malice. Leskov's, as best I can remember it, is about a civilized English factory manager in Russia who replaces the barbaric floggings with mild and meaningless punishments. The peasants, who had hoped that the Englishman would treat them like a father and beat them when they did wrong, are absolutely horrified when they are bidden to stand in a corner, and finally, in despair, burn the Englishman's home about him. The same story, but this time told from inside.

Once again, we could argue till the cows come home and get no nearer a solution. The principal difference is that Leskov, by his very extravagance, convinces us that he knows the peasants, while Chekhov, the saintly doctor, trying to help them from without, simply has no clue to the workings of their minds. Russian and all as he is, he is simply an alien in the world of Leskov and Gauguin.

I do not like that world, but about certain things Leskov is the truer artist. . . .

We have been told that the novel is dead, and I am sure that someone has said as much for the short story. I suspect that the announcement may prove a little premature, and I should be much readier to listen to an argument that poetry and the theater were dead. I should not be too enthusiastic about that either, but I should be prepared to admit that since they are both primitive arts there would be some sort of case to answer. But the novel and the short story are drastic adaptations of a primitive art form to modern conditions—to printing, science, and individual religion—and I see no possibility of or reason for their supersession except in a general supersession of all culture by mass civilization. I suppose if this takes place, we shall all have to go into monasteries, or—if mass civilization forbids—into catacombs and caves, but even there, I suspect, more than one worshiper will be found clutching a tattered copy of *Pride and Prejudice* or *The Short Stories of Anton Chekhov.*

DISCUSSION QUESTIONS

1. O'Connor points to Gogol's "Overcoat" as essential to an understanding of the development of the short story, emphasizing the importance of "the Little Man" in the genre. What are the features of "the Little Man," and what separates this type from the protagonist of the novel?

2. Extending his idea of "the Little Man," O'Connor offers the "submerged population group" as the subject of the short story writer's attention. What does he mean by this term? How do the ideas of "the Little Man" and the "submerged population group" relate to O'Connor's sense of "intense awareness of human loneliness" in the short story?

3. O'Connor writes that "for the short-story writer there is no such thing as essential form." What does he mean by this? If there is not essential form, how may a short story writer structure and shape a story?

FRANCINE PROSE

Learning from Chekhov

Francine Prose (b. 1947) has published short stories, novellas, children's books, and novels, including Marie Laveau *(1977),* Animal Magnetism *(1978),* Household Saints *(1981),* Hungry Hearts *(1983),* Hunters and Gatherers *(1995),* Guided Tours of Hell *(1997), and* Blue Angel *(2000). She has taught fiction writing at the University of Arizona, Harvard, and Sarah Lawrence. This selection testifies to her intensely personal approach to fiction writing.*

This past year I taught at a college two and a half hours from my home. I commuted down once a week, stayed overnight, came back. Through most of the winter I took the bus. The worst part was waiting to go home in the New Rochelle Greyhound station. The bus was unreliable, as was the twenty-minute taxi ride I took to get there, so I wound up being in the station, on the average, forty minutes a week.

One thing you notice if you spend any time there is that although the bus station is a glassed-in corner storefront, none of the windows open, so the only time air moves is when someone opens the door. There is a ticket counter, a wall of dirty magazines, a phone, a rack of dusty candy. It's never very crowded, which is hardly a comfort when half the people who *are* there look like they'd happily blow your brains out on the chance of finding a couple of Valiums in your purse.

Usually I bought a soda and a greasy sugar cookie to cheer myself up and read *People* magazine because I was scared to lose touch with reality for any longer than it took to read a *People* magazine article. Behind the counter worked a man about sixty and a woman about fifty, and in all the time I was there I never heard them exchange one personal word. Behind them was a TV, on constantly, and it will give you an idea of what kind of winter I had when I say that the first ten times I saw the *Challenger* blow up were on the bus station TV. I was having a difficult time in my life, and every minute that kept me from getting home to my husband and kids was painful. Many of you who have commuted will probably know what I mean.

Finally the bus came; the two drivers who alternated—the nasty younger one who seemed to slip into some kind of trance between Newburgh and New Paltz and went slower and slower up the thruway, and the older one who looked like a Victorian masher and had a fondness for some aerosol spray which smelled like a cross between cherry Lifesavers and Raid. The bus made Westchester stops for half an hour before it even got to the highway.

As soon as I was settled and had finished the soda and cookie and magazine from the bus station, I began reading the short stories of Anton Chekhov. It was my ritual and my reward. I began where I'd left off the week before, through volume after volume of the Garnett translations. And I never had to read more than a page or two before I began to think that maybe things weren't so bad. The stories were not only—it seemed to me—profound and beautiful, but also involving, so that I would finish one and find myself, miraculously, a half hour closer to home. And yet there was more than the distraction, the time so painlessly and pleasantly spent. A great sense of comfort came over me, as if in those thirty minutes I myself had been taken up in a spaceship and shown the whole world, a world full of sorrows, both different and very much like my own, and also a world full of promise, an intelligence large enough to embrace bus drivers and bus station junkies, a vision so piercing it would have kept seeing those astronauts long after that fiery plume disappeared from the screen. I began to think that maybe nothing was wasted, that someday I could do something with what was happening to me, to use even the New Rochelle bus station in some way, in my work.

Reading Chekhov, I felt not happy, exactly, but as close to happiness as I knew I was likely to come. And it occurred to me that this was the pleasure and mystery of reading, as well as the answer to those who say that books will disappear. For now, books are still the best way of taking great art and its consolations along with us on the bus.

In the spring, at the final meeting of the course I was commuting to teach, my students asked me this: if I had one last thing to tell them about writing, what would it be? They were half joking, partly because by then they knew me well enough to know that whenever I said anything about writing, I could usually be counted on to come up—often when we'd gone on to some other subject completely—with qualifications and even counterexamples proving that the opposite could just as well be true. And yet they were also half serious. We had come far in that class. From time to time, it had felt as if, at nine each Wednesday morning, we were shipwrecked together on an island. Now they wanted a souvenir, a fragment of seashell to take home.

Still it seemed nearly impossible to come up with that one last bit of advice. Often, I have wanted to somehow get in touch with former students and say: remember such and such a thing I told you? Well, I take it back, I was wrong! Given the difficulty of making any single true statement, I decided that I might just as well say the first thing that came to mind—which, as it happened, was this: the most important things, I told them, were observation and consciousness. Keep your eyes open, see clearly, think about what you see, ask yourself what it means.

After that came the qualifications and counterexamples: I wasn't suggesting that art necessarily be descriptive, literal, autobiographical or confessional. Nor should the imagination be overlooked as an investigational tool. Italo Calvino's story, "The Distance of the Moon," about a mythical time when the moon could be reached by climbing a ladder from the earth, has always seemed to me to be a work of profound observation and accuracy. If clearsightedness—meant literally—were the criterion for genius, what should we do about Milton? But still, in most cases the fact remains: The wider and deeper your observational range, the better, the more interestingly and truthfully you will write.

My students looked at me and yawned. It was nine in the morning, and they'd heard it before. And perhaps I would not have repeated it, or repeated it with such conviction, had I not spent the year reading and rereading all that Chekhov, all those stories filled and illuminated with the deepest and broadest— at once compassionate and dispassionate—observation of life that I know.

I have already told you what reading the Chekhov stories did for me, something of what they rescued me from and what they brought me to. But what I have to add now is that after a while I started noticing a funny thing. Let's say, for example, that I had just come from telling a student that one reason the class may have had trouble telling his two main characters apart is that they were named Mikey and Macky. I wasn't saying that the two best friends in his story couldn't have similar names. But, given the absence of other distinguishing characteristics, it might be better—in the interests of clarity—to call one Frank, or Bill. The student seemed pleased with this simple solution to a difficult problem; I was happy to have helped. And then, as my bus pulled out of New Rochelle, I began Chekhov's "The Two Volodyas."

In that story, a young woman named Sofya deceives herself into thinking she is in love with her elderly husband Volodya, then deceives herself into thinking she is in love with a childhood friend, also named Volodya; in the end, we see her being comforted by an adoptive sister who has become a nun, and who tells her "that all this is of no consequence, that it would all pass and God would forgive her." What I want to make clear is that the two men's having the same name is not the point of the story; here, as in all of Chekhov's work, there is never exactly "a point." Rather, we feel that we are seeing into this woman's heart, into what she perceives as her "unbearable misery." That she should be in love or not in love—with two men named Volodya—is simply a fact of her life.

The next week, I suggested to another student that what made her story confusing was the multiple shifts in point of view. It's only a five-page story, I said. Not *Rashomon*. And that afternoon I read "Gusev," one of the most beautiful of Chekhov's stories about a sailor who dies at sea. The story begins with the sailor's point-of-view, shifts into long stretches of dialogue between him and another dying man. When Gusev dies—another "rule" I was glad I hadn't told my students was that, for "obvious" reasons, you can't write a story in which the narrator point-of-view character dies—the point of view shifts to that of the sailors burying him at sea and then on to that of the pilot fish who see his body fall, to the shark who comes to investigate, until finally—as a student of mine once wrote—we feel we are seeing through the eyes of God. What I have found—what I've just proved—is that it's nearly impossible to *describe* the end of this story with any accuracy at all. So I will quote the last few marvelous paragraphs. What I want to point out—what needs no pointing out—is how much would have been lost had Chekhov followed the rules.

> He went rapidly towards the bottom. Did he reach it? It was said to be three miles to the bottom. After sinking sixty or seventy feet, he began moving more and more slowly, swaying rhythmically, as though he were hesitating, and, carried along by the current, moved more rapidly sideways than downwards.

Then he was met by a shoal of fish called harbor pilots. Seeing the dark body the fish stopped as though petrified, and suddenly turned round and disappeared. In less than a minute they flew back swift as an arrow to Gusev, and began zigzag-ging round him in the water.

After that another dark body appeared. It was a shark. It swarmed under Gusev with dignity and no show of interest, as though it did not notice him, and sank down upon its back, then it turned belly upwards, basking in the warm transparent water, and languidly opened its jaws with two rows of teeth. The har-bor pilots are delighted, they stop to see what will come next. After playing a little with the body the shark nonchalantly puts its jaws under it, cautiously touches it with its teeth, and the sailcloth is rent its full length from head to foot; one of the weights falls out and frightens the harbor pilots, and, striking the shark on the ribs, goes rapidly to the bottom.

Overhead at this time the clouds are massed together on the side where the sun is setting; one cloud like a triumphal arch, another like a lion, a third like a pair of scissors. . . . From behind the clouds a broad green shaft of light pierces through and stretches to the middle of the sky; a little later another, violet-colored, lies beside it; next to that, one of gold, then one rose-colored. . . . The sky turns a soft lilac. Looking at this gorgeous enchanted sky, at first the ocean scowls, but soon it too takes tender, joyous, passionate colors for which it is hard to find a name in human speech.

Around this same time, I seem to remember myself telling my class that we should, ideally, have some notion of whom or what a story is about—in other words, whose story is it? To offer the reader that simple knowledge, I said—I must have been in one of my ironic moods—wasn't really giving much. A little clarity of focus cost the writer almost nothing and paid off, for the reader, a hun-dredfold. And it was about this same time that I first read "In the Ravine," per-haps the most heartbreaking and most powerful Chekhov story I know, in which we don't realize that the peasant girl Lipa is our heroine until almost halfway through. Moreover, the story turns on the death of a baby—just the sort of inci-dent I advise students to stay away from because it is so difficult to write well and without sentimentality. Here—I have no pedagogical excuse to quote this, but am only including it because I so admire it—is the extraordinarily lovely scene in which Lipa plays with her baby.

Lipa spent her time playing with the baby which had been born to her before Lent. It was a tiny, thin, pitiful little baby, and it was strange that it should cry and gaze about and be considered a human being, and even be called Nikifor. He lay in his cradle, and Lipa would walk away towards the door and say, bowing to him: "Good day, Nikifor Anisimitch!"

And she would rush at him and kiss him. Then she would walk away to the door, bow again, and say: "Good day, Nikifor Anisimitch!" And he kicked up his little red legs and his crying was mixed with laughter like the carpenter Elizarov's.

By now I had learned my lesson. I began telling my class to read Chekhov instead of listening to me. I invoked Chekhov's name so often that a disgruntled student accused me of trying to make her write like Chekhov. She went on to tell me that she was sick of Chekhov, that plenty of writers were better than Chekhov, and when I asked her who, she said: Thomas Pynchon. I said I thought both writers were very good, suppressing a wild desire to run out in the hall and poll the entire faculty on who was better—Chekhov or Pynchon—only stopping myself because—or so I'd like to think—the experience of reading Chekhov was proving not merely enlightening, but also humbling.

Still there were some things I thought I knew. A short time later I suggested to yet another student that he might want to think twice about having his character—in the very last paragraph of his story—pick up a gun and blow his head off for no reason. I wasn't saying that this couldn't happen, it was just that it seemed so unexpected, so melodramatic. Perhaps if he prepared the reader, ever so slightly, hinted that his character was, if not considering, then at least capable of this. A few hours later I got on the bus and read the ending of "Volodya":

> Volodya put the muzzle of the revolver to his mouth, felt something like a trigger or a spring, and pressed it with his finger. Then he felt something else projecting, and once more pressed it. Taking the muzzle out of his mouth, he wiped it with the lapel of his coat, looked at the lock. He had never in his life taken a weapon in his hand.
>
> "I believe one ought to raise this," he reflected. "Yes, it seems so."
>
> Volodya put the muzzle in his mouth again, pressed it with his teeth, and pressed something with his fingers. There was the sound of a shot. Something hit Volodya in the back of his head with terrible violence and he fell on the table with his face downwards among the bottles and glasses. Then he saw his father as in Mentone, in a top hat with a wide black band on it, wearing mourning for some lady, suddenly seize him by both hands, and they fell headlong into a very deep dark pit. Then everything was blurred and vanished.

Until that moment we'd had no indication that Volodya was troubled by anything more than the prospect of school exams and an ordinary teenage crush on a flirtatious older woman. Nor had we heard much about his father, except that Volodya blames his frivolous mother for having wasted his money.

What seemed at issue here was far more serious than a question of similar names and divergent points of view. For as anyone who has ever attended a writing class knows: the bottom line of the fiction workshop is motivation. We complain, we criticize, we say that we don't understand why this or that character says or does something. Like parody method actors, we ask: what is the motivation? Of course, all this is based on the comforting supposition that things, in fiction as in life, are done for a reason. But here was Chekhov telling us that—hadn't we ever noticed?—quite often people do things—terrible, irrevocable things—for no good reason at all. No sooner had I assimilated this critical bit of information than I happened to read "A Dull Story," which convinced me that I had not only been overestimating, but also oversimplifying the depths and complexities of motivation. How could I have demanded to know clearly how a certain character felt about another character when—as the narrator of "A Dull Story" reveals on every page—our feelings for each other are so often elusive, changing, contradictory, hidden in the most clever disguises even from ourselves?

Clearly Chekhov was teaching me how to teach, and yet I remained a slow learner. The mistakes—and the revelations—continued. I had always assumed and probably even said that being insane was not an especially happy state, that the phrase "happy idiot" was generally an inaccurate one and that, given the choice, most hallucinating schizophrenics would opt for sanity. And maybe this is mostly true, but as Chekhov is always reminding us, "most" is not "all." For Kovrin, the hero of "The Black Monk," the visits from an imaginary monk are the sweetest and most welcome moments in his otherwise unsatisfactory life. And what of the assumption that, in life and in fiction, a crazy character should "act" crazy, should early on clue us into his craziness? Not Kovrin, who, aside from these hallucinatory attacks and a youthful case of "upset nerves," is a university professor, a husband, a functioning member, as they say, of society, a man whose consciousness of his own "mediocrity" is relieved only by his conversations with the phantasmagorical monk, who assures him that he is a genius.

Reading another story, "The Husband," I remembered asking: What is the point of writing a story in which everything's rotten and all the characters are terrible and nothing much happens and nothing changes? In "The Husband," Shalikov, the tax collector, watches his wife enjoying a brief moment of pleasure as she dances at a party, has a jealous fit and blackmails her into leaving the dance and returning to the prison of their shared lives. The story ends:

> Anna Pavlovna would scarcely walk. She was still under the influence of the dancing, the music, the talk, the lights, and the noise; she asked herself as she walked along why God had thus afflicted her. She felt miserable, insulted, and choking with hate as she listened to her husband's heavy footsteps. She was silent, trying to think of the most offensive, biting and venomous word she could hurl at her husband, and at the same time she was fully aware that no word could penetrate his tax collector's hide. What did he care for words? Her bitterest enemy could not have contrived for her a more helpless position. And meanwhile the band was playing, and the darkness was full of the most rousing, intoxicating dance tunes.

The "point"—and, again, there is no conventional "point"—is that in just a few pages, the curtain concealing these lives has been drawn back, revealing them in all their helplessness and rage and rancor. The point is that lives go on without change, so why should fiction insist that major reverses should always—conveniently—occur?

And finally, this revelation. In some kind of fit of irritation, I told my class that it was just a fact that the sufferings of the poor are more compelling, more worthy of our attention than the vague discontents of the rich. So it was with some chagrin that I read "A Woman's Kingdom," a delicate and astonishingly moving story about a rich, lonely woman—a factory owner, no less—who finds herself attracted to her foreman . . . until a casual remark by a member of her own class awakens her to the impossibility of her situation. By the time I had finished the story, I felt that I had been challenged, not only in my more flippant statements about fiction but in my most basic assumptions about life. In this case, truth had nothing to do with social justice, or with morality, with right and wrong. The truth was what Chekhov had seen and I—with all my fancy talk of observation—had somehow overlooked: cut a rich woman and she will bleed just like a poor one. Which isn't to say that Chekhov didn't know and know well: the world being what it is, the poor do get cut somewhat more often and more deeply.

And now, since we are speaking of life, a brief digression, about Chekhov's. By the time Chekhov died of tuberculosis at the age of forty-four, he had written—in addition to his plays—588 short stories. He was also a medical doctor. He supervised the construction of clinics and schools, he was active in the Moscow Art Theater, he married the famous actress, Olga Knipper, he visited the infamous prison on Sakhalin Island and wrote a book about that. Once when someone asked him about his method of composition, Chekhov picked up an ashtray. "This is my method of composition," he said. "Tomorrow I will write a story called 'The Ashtray.'" Along the way, he was generous with advice to young writers. And now, to paraphrase what I said to my class, listen to Chekhov instead of me. Here are two quotations from Chekhov's letters, both on the subject of literary style:

> In my opinion a true description of Nature should be very brief and have the character of relevance. Commonplaces such as "the setting sun bathing in the waves of the darkening sea, poured its purple gold, etc."—"the swallows flying over the surface of the water twittered merrily"—such commonplaces one ought to abandon. In descriptions of Nature one ought to seize upon the little particulars, grouping them in such a way that, in reading when you shut your eyes, you get the picture.
>
> For instance you will get the full effect of a moonlit night if you write that on the milldam, a little glowing star point flashed from the neck of a broken bottle, and the round black shadow of a dog or a wolf emerged and ran, etc. . . .
>
> In the sphere of psychology, details are also the thing. God preserve us from commonplaces. Best of all is it to avoid depicting the hero's state of mind; you ought to try to make it clear from the hero's actions. It is not necessary to portray many characters. The center of gravity should be in two people: he and she.

> You understand it at once when I say "The man sat on the grass." You understand it because it is clear and makes no demands on the attention. On the other hand it is not easily understood if I write, "A tall, narrow-chested, middle-sized man, with a red beard, sat on the green grass, already trampled by pedestrians, sat silently, shyly, and timidly looked about him." That is not immediately grasped by the mind, whereas good writing should be grasped at once—in a second.

Another quotation, on the subject of closure:

> My instinct tells me that at the end of a story or a novel I must artfully concentrate for the reader an impression of the entire work, and therefore must casually mention something about those whom I have already presented. Perhaps I am in error.

And here are a number of quotations on a theme which comes up again and again in his letters—the writer's need for objectivity, the importance of seeing clearly, without judgment, certainly without prejudgment, the need for the writer to be, in Chekhov's words, "an unbiased observer."

> That the world "swarms with male and female scum" is perfectly true. Human nature is imperfect. . . . But to think that the task of literature is to gather the pure grain from the muck heap is to reject literature itself. Artistic literature is called so because it depicts life as it really is. Its aim is truth—unconditional and honest. . . . A writer is not a confectioner, not a dealer in cosmetics, not an entertainer; he is a man bound under compulsion, by the realization of his duty and by his conscience. . . . To a chemist, nothing on earth is unclean. A writer must be as objective as a chemist.

> It seems to me that the writer should not try to solve such questions as those of God, pessimism, etc. His business is but to describe those who have been speaking or thinking about God and pessimism, how and under what circumstances. The artist should be not the judge of his characters and their conversations, but only an unbiased observer.

> You are right in demanding that an artist should take an intelligent attitude to his work, but you confuse two things: solving a problem and stating a problem correctly. It is only the second that is obligatory for the artist.

> You abuse me for objectivity, calling it indifference to good and evil, lack of ideas and ideals, and so on. You would have me, when I describe horse thieves, say: "Stealing horses is an evil." But that has been known for ages without my saying so. Let the jury judge them; it's my job simply to show what sort of people they are. I write: you are dealing with horse thieves, so let me tell you that they are not beggars but well fed people, that they are people of a special cult, and that horse stealing is not simply theft but a passion. Of course it would be pleasant to combine art with a sermon, but for me personally it is impossible owing to the conditions of technique. You see, to depict horse thieves in 700 lines I must all the time speak and think in their tone and feel in their spirit, otherwise . . . the story will not be as compact as all short stories ought to be. When I write, I reckon entirely upon the reader to add for himself the subjective elements that are lacking in the story.

And now, one final quotation, which given my track record for making statements and having to retract them a week later, struck me with particular force:

> It is time for writers to admit that nothing in this world makes sense. Only fools and charlatans think they know and understand everything. The stupider they are, the wider they conceive their horizons to be. And if an artist decides to declare that he understands nothing of what he sees—this in itself constitutes a considerable clarity in the realm of thought, and a great step forward.

Every great writer is a mystery, if only in that some aspect of his or her talent remains forever ineffable, inexplicable and astonishing. The sheer population of

Dickens' imagination, the fantastic architecture Proust constructs out of minutely examined moments, etc., etc. We ask ourselves: How could anyone do that? And of course, different qualities of the work will mystify different people. For me, Chekhov's mystery is first of all one of knowledge: how does he know so much? He knows everything we pride ourselves on having learned, and of course much more. "The Name Day Party," a story about a pregnant woman, is full of observations about pregnancy which I had thought were secrets.

The second mystery is how, without ever being direct, he communicates the fact that he is not describing The World or how people should see The World or how he, Anton Chekhov, sees The World, but only one or another character's world for a certain span of time. When the characters are less than attractive, we never feel the author hiding behind them, peeking out from around their edges to say: "This isn't me, this isn't me!" We never feel that Gurov, the "hero" of "The Lady with the Pet Dog" is Chekhov, though, for all we know, he could be. Rather we feel we are seeing his life—and his life transformed. Chekhov is always, as he says in his letters, working from the particular to the general.

The greatest mystery for me—and it's what, I think, makes Chekhov so different from any other writer I know—is this matter he keeps alluding to in his letters: the necessity of writing without judgment. Not saying, Stealing horses is an evil. To be not the judge of one's characters and their conversations but rather the unbiased observer. What should, I imagine, be clear, is that Chekhov didn't live without judgment. I don't know if anyone does, or if it is even possible except for psychotics and Zen monks who've trained themselves to suspend all reflection, moral and otherwise. My sense is that living without judgment is probably a terrible idea. Nor, again, is any of this prescriptive. Balzac judged everyone and found nearly all of them wanting; their smallness and the ferocity of his outrage is part of the greatness of his work. But what Chekhov believed and acted on more than any writer I can think of is that judgment and especially prejudgment was incommensurate with a certain kind of literary art. It is, I believe, what—together with his range of vision—makes him wholly unique among writers. And why, for reasons I still can't quite explain, his work comforted me in ways Balzac just simply could not.

Before I finish, I'd like to quote Vladimir Nabokov's summation of his lecture on Chekhov's story, "The Lady with the Pet Dog":

> All the traditional rules of storytelling have been broken in this wonderful story of twenty pages or so. There is no problem, no regular climax, no point at the end. And it is one of the greatest stories ever written.
>
> We will now repeat the different features that are typical for this and other Chekhov tales.
>
> First: The story is told in the most natural way possible, not beside the after-dinner fireplace as with Turgenev or Maupassant, but in the way one person relates to another the most important things in his life, slowly and yet without a break, in a slightly subdued voice.
>
> Second: Exact and rich characterization is attained by a careful selection and careful distribution of minute but striking features, with perfect contempt for the

sustained description, repetition, and strong emphasis of ordinary authors. In this or that description one detail is chosen to illume the whole setting.

Third: There is no special moral to be drawn and no special message to be received.

Fourth: The story is based on a system of waves, on the shades of this or that mood. . . . In Chekhov, we get a world of waves instead of particles of matter. . . .

Sixth: The story does not really end, for as long as people are alive, there is no possible and definite conclusion to their troubles or hopes or dreams.

Seventh: The storyteller seems to keep going out of his way to allude to trifles, every one of which in another type of story would mean a signpost denoting a turn of the action . . . but just because these trifles are meaningless, they are all-important in giving the real atmosphere of this particular story.

Let me repeat one sentence which seems to me particularly significant. "We feel that for Chekhov the lofty and the base are not different, that the slice of watermelon and the violet sea and the hands of the town governor are essential points of the beauty plus pity of the world." And what I might add to this is: the more Chekhov we read, the more strongly we feel this. I have often thought that Chekhov's stories should not be read singly but as separate parts of a whole. For like life, they present contradictory views, opposing visions. Reading them, we think: How broad life is! How many ways there are to live! In this world, where anything can happen, how much is possible! Our whole lives can change in a moment. Or: Nothing will ever change—especially the fact that the world and the human heart will always be wider and deeper than anything we can fathom.

And this is what I've come to think about what I learned and what I taught and what I should have taught. Wait! I should have said to that class: Come back! I've made a mistake. Forget about observation, consciousness, clearsightedness. Forget about life. Read Chekhov, read the stories straight through. Admit that you understand nothing of life, nothing of what you see. Then go out and look at the world.

DISCUSSION QUESTIONS

1. Prose begins with a narrative describing her situation in life and her immediate surroundings at the time she was reading Chekhov's stories. Why does she begin this way? How do the descriptions of the bus station and the people frame her exploration of Chekhov?
2. Prose states that reading Chekhov brings her "as close to happiness as I knew I was likely to come." What does this mean? What is the relationship in your life between the experience of reading your favorite writers and the experience of happiness?
3. In Chekhov's work "there is never exactly a 'point,'" according to Prose. How does this assertion fit or clash with your understanding of meaning in fiction? What does this suggest about the manner in which fiction can communicate meaning?

4. Prose credits Chekhov with "teaching me how to teach." What are the lessons Chekhov teaches? How do these lessons illuminate the relationship between life and fiction?

5. Prose offers a brief sketch of Chekhov's life, mentioning his work as a medical doctor and a journalist (in his book on Sakhalin Island). Why are these details important? How does this biographical information relate to Chekhov's artistic method and views about how stories should work?

6. Though Chekhov writes in a letter that it is a "great step forward" for an artist to "declare that he understands nothing of what he sees," Prose asks in admiration, "how does he know so much?" What do you make of this apparent paradox?

URSULA K. LE GUIN

Some Thoughts on Narrative

Ursula Le Guin (b. 1929) has published over thirty volumes of short stories and novels, including The Dispossessed *(1974),* The Ones Who Walk Away from Omelas *(1993),* Worlds of Exile and Illusion *(1996), and the Earthsea series, as well as poetry, nonfiction, and theory on the writing of fiction. Her writing about fiction includes the textbook* Steering the Craft: Exercises and Discussions on Story Writing for the Lone Navigator or the Mutinous Crew *(1998). Her fiction, sometimes classified as science fiction, fantasy, or magical realism, has won Nebula and Hugo awards, a National Book Award, and a Pushcart Prize.*

This paper incorporates parts of the Nina Mae Kellogg Lecture given at Portland State University in the spring of 1980.

Recently, at a three-day-long symposium on narrative, I learned that it's unsafe to say anything much about narrative, because if a poststructuralist doesn't get you a deconstructionist will. This is a pity, because the subject is an interesting one to those outside the armed camps of literary theory. As one who spends a good deal of her time telling stories, I should like to know, in the first place, why I tell stories, and in the second place, why you listen to them; and vice versa.

Through long practice I know how to tell a story, but I'm not sure I know what a story is; and I have not found much patience with the question among those better qualified to answer it. To literary theorists it is evidently too primitive, to linguists it is not primitive enough; and among psychologists I know of only one, Simon Lesser, who has tried seriously to explain narration as a psychic process. There is, however, always Aristotle.

Aristotle says that the essential element of drama and epic is "the arrange-ment of the incidents." And he goes on to make the famous and endearing remark that this narrative or plotly element consists of a beginning, a middle, and an end:

> A beginning is that which is not itself necessarily after anything else, and which has naturally something else after it; an end, that which is naturally after some-thing else, either as its necessary or usual consequent, and with nothing else after it; and a middle, that which is by nature after one thing and has also another after it.

According to Aristotle, then, narrative connects events, "arranges incidents," in a directional temporal order analogous to a directional spatial order. Causality is implied but not exactly stated (in the word "consequent," which could mean "result" or merely "what follows"); the principal linkage as I understand it is temporal (E. M. Forster's story sequence, "and then . . . and then . . . and then . . ."). So narrative is language used to connect events in time. The connec-tion, whether conceived as a closed pattern, beginning-middle-end, or an open one, past-present-future, whether seen as lineal or spiral or recursive, involves a movement "through" time for which spatial metaphor is adequate. Narrative makes a journey. It goes from A to Z, from then to then-prime.

This might be why narrative does not normally use the present tense except for special effect or out of affectation. It locates itself in the past (whether the real or an imagined, fictional past) in order to allow itself forward movement. The present not only competes against the story with a vastly superior weight of real-ity, but limits it to the pace of watch hand or heartbeat. Only by locating itself in the "other country" of the past is the narrative free to move towards its future, the present.

The present tense, which some writers of narrative fiction currently employ because it is supposed to make the telling "more actual," actually distances the story (and some very sophisticated writers of narrative fiction use it for that pur-pose). The present tense takes the story out of time. Anthropological reports con-cerning people who died decades ago, whose societies no longer exist, are written in the present tense; this paper is written in the present tense. Physics is normally written in the present tense, in part because it *generalizes,* as I am doing now, but also because it deals so much with nondirectional time.

Time for a physicist is quite likely to be reversible. It doesn't matter whether you read an equation forwards or backwards—unlike a sentence. On the sub-atomic level directionality is altogether lost. You cannot write the history of a photon; narration is irrelevant; all you can say of it is that it might be, or, other-wise stated, if you can say where it is you can't say when and if you can say when it is you can't say where.

Even of an entity relatively so immense and biologically so complex as a gene, the little packet of instructions that tells us what to be, there is no story to be told; because the gene, barring accident, is immortal. All you can say of it is that it is, and it is, and it is. No beginning, no end. All middle.

The past and future tenses become useful to science when it gets involved in irreversible events, when beginning, middle, and end will run only in that order.

What happened two seconds after the Big Bang? What happened when Male Beta took Male Alpha's banana? What will happen if I add this hydrochloric acid? These are events that made, or will make, a difference. The existence of a future—a time different from now, a then-prime—depends on the irreversibility of time; in human terms, upon mortality. In Eternity there is nothing novel, and there are no novels.

So when the storyteller by the hearth starts out, "Once upon a time, a long way from here, lived a king who had three sons," that story will be telling us that things change; that events have consequences; that choices are to be made; that the king does not live forever.

Narrative is a stratagem of mortality. It is a means, a way of living. It does not seek immortality; it does not seek to triumph over or escape from time (as lyric poetry does). It asserts, affirms, participates in directional time, time experienced, time as meaningful. If the human mind had a temporal spectrum, the nirvana of the physicist or the mystic would be way over in the ultraviolet, and at the opposite end, in the infrared, would be *Wuthering Heights*.

To put it another way: Narrative is a central function of language. Not, in origin, an artifact of culture, an art, but a fundamental operation of the normal mind functioning in society. To learn to speak is to learn to tell a story.

I would guess that preverbal narration takes place almost continuously on the unconscious level, but pre- or nonverbal mental operations are very hard to talk about. Dreams might help.

It has been found that during REM (rapid eye movement) sleep, the recurrent phase of sleep during which we dream abundantly, the movement of the eyes is intermittent. If you wake the dreamer while the eyes are flickering, the dreams reported are disconnected, jumbled, snatches and flashes of imagery; but, awakened during a quiet-eye period, the dreamer reports a "proper dream," a *story*. Researchers call the image-jumble "primary visual experience" and the other "secondary cognitive elaboration."

Concerning this, Liam Hudson wrote (in the *Times Literary Supplement* of January 25, 1980):

> While asleep, then, we experience arbitrary images, and we also tell ourselves stories. The likelihood is that we weave the second around the first, embedding images that we perceive as bizarre in a fabric that seems to us more reasonable. If I confront myself, while asleep, with the image of a crocodile on the roof of a German *Schloss,* and then, while still fast asleep, create for myself some plausible account of how this implausible event has occurred, I am engaged in the manoeuvre of rationalisation—of rendering sensible-seeming something that is not sensible in the least. In the course of this manoeuvre, the character of the original image is falsified. . . .
>
> The thinking we do without thinking about it consists in the translation of our experience to narrative, irrespective of whether our experience fits the narrative form or not. . . . Asleep and awake it is just the same: we are telling ourselves stories all the time, . . . tidier stories than the evidence warrants.

Mr. Hudson's summary of the material is elegant, and his interpretation of it is, I take it, Freudian. Dreamwork is *rationalization,* therefore it is *falsification:* a cover-up. The mind is an endless Watergate. Some primitive "reality" or "truth" is forever being distorted, lied about, tidied up.

But what if we have no means of access to this truth or reality except through the process of "lying," except through the narrative? Where are we supposed to be standing in order to judge what "the evidence warrants"?

Take Mr. Hudson's crocodile on the roof of a German castle (it is certainly more interesting than what I dreamed last night). We can all make that image into a story. Some of us will protest, No no I can't, I can't tell stories, etc., having been terrorized by our civilization into believing that we are, or have to be, "rational." But all of us can make that image into some kind of story, and if it came into our head while we were asleep, no doubt we would do so without a qualm, without giving it a second thought. As I have methodically practiced irrational behavior for many years, I can turn it into a story almost as easily waking as asleep. What has happened is that Prince Metternich was keeping a crocodile to frighten his aunt with, and the crocodile has escaped through a skylight onto the curious, steep, leaden roofs of the castle, and is clambering, in the present tense because it is a dream and outside time, towards a machicolated nook in which lies, in a stork's nest, but the stork is in Africa, an egg, a wonderful, magical Easter egg of sugar containing a tiny window through which you look and you see—But the dreamer is awakened here. And if there is any "message" to the dream, the dreamer is not aware of it; the dream with its "message" has gone from the unconscious to the unconscious, like most dreams, without any processing describable as "rationalization," and without ever being verbalized (unless and until the dreamer, in some kind of therapy, has learned laboriously to retrieve and hold and verbalize dreams). In this case all the dreamer—we need a name for this character, let us call her Edith Driemer—all Edith remembers, fleetingly, is something about a roof, a crocodile, Germany, Easter, and while thinking dimly about her great-aunt Esther in Munich, she is presented with further "primary visual (or sensory) experiences" running in this temporal sequence: A loud ringing in the left ear. Blinding light. The smell of an exotic herb. A toilet. A pair of used shoes. A disembodied voice screaming in Parsee. A kiss. A sea of shining clouds. Terror. Twilight in the branches of a tree outside the window of a strange room in an unknown city . . .

Are these the "primary experiences" experienced while her eyes move rapidly, furnishing material for the next dream? They could well be; but by following Aristotle's directions and making purely temporal connections between them, we can make of them a quite realistic narration of the day Edith woke up and turned off the alarm clock, got up and got dressed, had breakfast listening to the radio news, kissed Mr. Driemer goodbye, and took a plane to Cincinnati in order to attend a meeting of market analysts.

I submit that though this network of "secondary elaboration" may be more rationally controlled than that of the pretended dream, the primary material on which it must work can be considered inherently as bizarre, as absurd, as the crocodile on the roof, and that the factual account of Edith Driemer's day is no more and no less than the dream-story a "manoeuvre," "rendering sensible-seeming something that is not sensible in the least."

Dream narrative differs from conscious narrative in using sensory symbol more than language. In dream the sense of the directionality of time is often replaced by spatial metaphor, or may be lowered, or reversed, or vanish. The connections dream makes between events are most often unsatisfactory to the rational intellect and the aesthetic mind. Dreams tend to flout Aristotle's rules of plausibility and muddle up his instructions concerning plot. Yet they are undeniably narrative: they connect events, fit things together in an order or a pattern that makes, to some portion of our mind, sense.

Looked at as a "primary visual (sensory) experience," in isolation, without connection to any context or event, each of our experiences is equally plausible or implausible, authentic or inauthentic, meaningful or absurd. But living creatures go to considerable pains to escape equality, to evade entropy, chaos, and old night. They arrange things. They make sense, literally. Molecule by molecule. In the cell. The cells arrange themselves. The body is an arrangement in spacetime, a patterning, a process; the mind is a process of the body, an organ, doing what organs do: organize. Order, pattern, connect. Do we have any better way to organize such wildly disparate experiences as a half-remembered crocodile, a dead great-aunt, the smell of coffee, a scream from Iran, a bumpy landing, and a hotel room in Cincinnati, than the narrative?—an immensely flexible technology, or life strategy, which if used with skill and resourcefulness presents each of us with that most fascinating of all serials, The Story of My Life.

I have read of a kind of dream that is symptomatic of one form of schizophrenia. The dream presents an object, a chair perhaps, or a coat, or a stump. Nothing happens, and there is nothing else in the dream.

Seen thus in spatial and temporal isolation, the primary experience or image can be the image of despair itself (like Sartre's tree root). Beckett's work yearns toward this condition. In the other direction, Rilke's celebration of "Things"—a chair, a coat, a stump—offers connection: a piece of furniture is part of the pattern of the room, of the life, a bed is a table in a swoon (in one of his French poems), forests are in the stump, the pitcher is also the river, and the hand, and the cup, and the thirst.

Whether the technique is narrative or not, the primary experience has to be connected with and fitted into the rest of experience to be useful, probably even to be available, to the mind. This may hold even for mystical perception. All mystics say that what they have experienced in vision cannot be fitted into ordinary time and space, but they try—they have to try. The vision is ineffable, but the story begins, "In the middle of the road of our life . . ."

It may be that an inability to fit events together in an order that at least seems to make sense, to make the narrative connection, is a radical incompetence at being human. So seen, stupidity could be defined as a failure to make enough connections, and insanity as severe repeated error in making connections—in telling The Story of My Life.

But nobody does it right all the time, or even most of the time. Even without identifying narration with falsification, one must admit that a vast amount of our life narration is fictional—how much, we cannot tell.

But if narration is a life stratagem, a survival skill, how can I get away, asleep and awake, with mistaking and distorting and omitting data, through wishful thinking, ignorance, laziness, and haste? If the ghostwriter in my head writing The Story of My Life is forgetful, careless, mendacious, a hack who doesn't care what happens so long as it makes some kind of story, why don't I get punished? Radical errors in interpreting and reacting to the environment aren't let off lightly, in either the species or the individual.

Is the truthfulness of the story, then, the all-important value; or is the quality of the fiction important too? Is it possible that we all keep going in very much the same way as Queen Dido or Don Quixote keeps going—by virtue of being almost entirely fictional characters?

Anyone who knows J. T. Fraser's work, such as his book *Of Time, Passion, and Knowledge,* and that of George Steiner, will have perceived my debt to them in trying to think about the uses of narrative. I am not always able to follow Mr. Steiner; but when he discusses the importance of the future tense, suggesting that statements about what does not exist and may never exist are central to the use of language, I follow him cheering and waving pompoms. When he makes his well-known statement "Language is the main instrument of man's refusal to accept the world as it is," I continue to follow, though with lowered pompoms. The proposition as stated worries me. Man's refusal to accept the world as it is? Do women also refuse? What about science, which tries so hard to see the world as it is? What about art, which not only accepts the dreadful world as it is but praises it for being so? "Isn't life a terrible thing, thank God!" says the lady with the backyard full of washing and babies in *Under Milk Wood,* and the sweet song says, "Nobody knows the trouble I seen, Glory, Hallelujah!" I agree with them. All grand refusals, especially when made by Man, are deeply suspect.

So, caviling all the way, I follow Mr. Steiner. If the use of language were to describe accurately what exists, what, in fact, would we want it for?

Surely the primary, survival-effective uses of language involve stating alternatives and hypotheses. We don't, we never did, go about making statements of fact to other people, or in our internal discourse with ourselves. We talk about what may be, or what we'd like to do, or what you ought to do, or what might have happened: warnings, suppositions, propositions, invitations, ambiguities, analogies, hints, lists, anxieties, hearsay, old wives' tales, leaps and cross-links and spiderwebs between here and there, between then and now, between now and sometime, a continual weaving and restructuring of the remembered and the perceived and the imagined, including a great deal of wishful thinking and a variable quantity of deliberate or non-deliberate fictionalizing, to reassure ourselves or for the pleasure of it, and also some deliberate or semi-deliberate falsification in order to mislead a rival or persuade a friend or escape despair; and no sooner have we made one of these patterns of words than we may, like Shelley's cloud, laugh, and arise, and unbuild it again.

In recent centuries we speakers of this lovely language have reduced the English verb almost entirely to the indicative mood. But beneath that specious and arrogant assumption of certainty all the ancient, cloudy, moody powers and options of the subjunctive remain in force. The indicative points its bony finger at primary experiences, at the Things; but it is the subjunctive that joins them, with the bonds of analogy, possibility, probability, contingency, contiguity, memory, desire, fear, and hope: the narrative connection. As J. T Fraser puts it, moral choice, which is to say human freedom, is made possible "by language, which permits us to give accounts of possible and impossible worlds in the past, in the future, or in a faraway land."

Fiction in particular, narration in general, may be seen not as a disguise or falsification of what is given but as an active encounter with the environment by means of posing options and alternatives, and an enlargement of present reality by connecting it to the unverifiable past and the unpredictable future. A totally factual narrative, were there such a thing, would be passive: a mirror reflecting all without distortion. Stendhal sentimentalized about the novel as such a mirror, but fiction does not reflect, nor is the narrator's eye that of a camera. The historian manipulates, arranges, and connects, and the storyteller does all that as well as intervening and inventing. Fiction connects possibilities, using the aesthetic sense of time's directionality defined by Aristotle as plot; and by doing so it is useful to us. If we cannot see our acts and being under the aspect of fiction, as "making sense," we cannot act as if we were free.

To describe narrative as "rationalization" of the given or of events is a blind alley. In the telling of a story, reason is only a support system. It can provide causal connections; it can extrapolate; it can judge what is likely, plausible, possible. All this is crucial to the invention of a good story, a sane fantasy, a sound piece of fiction. But reason by itself cannot get from the crocodile to Cincinnati. It cannot see that Elizabeth is, in fact, going to marry Darcy, and why. It may not even ever quite understand who it was, exactly, that Oedipus did marry. We cannot ask reason to take us across the gulfs of the absurd. Only the imagination can get us out of the bind of the eternal present, inventing or hypothesizing or pretending or discovering a way that reason can then follow into the infinity of options, a clue through the labyrinths of choice, a golden string, the story, leading us to the freedom that is properly human, the freedom open to those whose minds can accept unreality.

DISCUSSION QUESTIONS

1. Le Guin claims that "narrative is a stratagem of mortality. It is a means, a way of living." What does she mean by this? How does narrative provide humans with a way of being in the world?

2. Le Guin goes further in her advocacy of narrative to claim that an inability to narrate qualifies as "a radical incompetence at being human." How does her definition of "being human" lead her to place narrative in such a central role?

3. Le Guin writes of lying to tell the truth. What does she mean by this? Does this credo apply equally well to all narratives—those told orally in everyday interactions along with literary fictions?

NATHANIEL HAWTHORNE

Hawthorne on Romance
Excerpt from "The Custom-House" / *The Scarlet Letter*
and
Preface to *The House of the Seven Gables*

Nathaniel Hawthorne (1804–1864) is most famous as the author of The Scarlet Letter
*(1850). He also published dozens of short stories that helped define the genre in America, as well
as eight other novels, including* The House of the Seven Gables *(1851),* The Blithedale Romance *(1852), and* The Marble Faun *(1860). In addition, he wrote travel pieces,
sketches, children's books, and biographies. In his nonfiction, especially in his own introductions
to his novels, he gives insight into his aims as a fiction writer and the means he used to achieve
those aims.*

Excerpt from "The Custom-House"

. . . Moonlight, in a familiar room, falling so white upon the carpet, and showing
all its figures so distinctly,—making every object so minutely visible, yet so unlike
a morning or noontide visibility,—is a medium the most suitable for a romance-
writer to get acquainted with his illusive guests. There is the little domestic
scenery of the well-known apartment; the chairs, with each its separate individuality; the centre-table, sustaining a work-basket, a volume or two, and an extin-
guished lamp; the sofa; the book-case; the picture on the wall; all these details, so
completely seen, are so spiritualized by the unusual light, that they seem to lose
their actual substance, and become things of intellect. Nothing is too small or too
trifling to undergo this change, and acquire dignity thereby. A child's shoe; the
doll, seated in her little wicker carriage; the hobby-horse;—whatever, in a word,
has been used or played with, during the day, is now invested with a quality of
strangeness and remoteness, though still almost as vividly present as by daylight.
Thus, therefore, the floor of our familiar room has become a neutral territory,

somewhere between the real world and fairy-land, where the Actual and the Imaginary may meet, and each imbue itself with the nature of the other. Ghosts might enter here, without affrighting us. It would be too much in keeping with the scene to excite surprise, were we to look about us and discover a form, beloved, but gone hence, now sitting quietly in a streak of this magic moonshine, with an aspect that would make us doubt whether it had returned from afar, or had never once stirred from our fireside.

The somewhat dim coal-fire has an essential influence in producing the effect which I would describe. It throws its unobtrusive tinge throughout the room, with a faint ruddiness upon the walls and ceiling, and a reflected gleam from the polish of the furniture. This warmer light mingles itself with the cold spirituality of the moonbeams, and communicates, as it were, a heart and sensibilities of human tenderness to the forms which fancy summons up. It converts them from snow-images into men and women. Glancing at the looking-glass, we behold—deep within its haunted verge—the smouldering glow of the half-extinguished anthracite, the white moonbeams on the floor, and a repetition of all the gleam and shadow of the picture, with one remove farther from the actual, and nearer to the imaginative. Then, at such an hour, and with this scene before him, if a man, sitting all alone, cannot dream strange things, and make them look like truth, he need never try to write romances. . . .

Preface by the Author

When a writer calls his work a Romance, it need hardly be observed that he wishes to claim a certain latitude, both as to its fashion and material, which he would not have felt himself entitled to assume had he professed to be writing a Novel. The latter form of composition is presumed to aim at a very minute fidelity, not merely to the possible, but to the probable and ordinary course of man's experience. The former—while, as a work of art, it must rigidly subject itself to laws, and while it sins unpardonably so far as it may swerve aside from the truth of the human heart—has fairly a right to present that truth under circumstances, to a great extent, of the writer's own choosing or creation. If he think fit, also, he may so manage his atmospherical medium as to bring out or mellow the lights and deepen and enrich the shadows of the picture. He will be wise, no doubt, to make a very moderate use of the privileges here stated, and, especially, to mingle the Marvelous rather as a slight, delicate, and evanescent flavor than as any portion of the actual substance of the dish offered to the public. He can hardly be said, however, to commit a literal crime even if he disregard this caution.

In the present work, the author has proposed to himself—but with what success, fortunately, it is not for him to judge—to keep undeviatingly within his immunities. The point of view in which this tale comes under the Romantic definition lies in the attempt to connect a bygone time with the very present that is flitting away from us. It is a legend prolonging itself, from an epoch now gray in the distance, down into our own broad daylight, and bringing along with it some of its legendary mist, which the reader, according to his pleasure, may either disregard, or allow it to float almost imperceptibly about the characters and events for the sake of a picturesque effect. The narrative, it may be, is woven of so humble a texture as to require this advantage, and, at the same time, to render it the more difficult of attainment.

Many writers lay very great stress upon some definite moral purpose, at which they profess to aim their works. Not to be deficient in this particular, the author has provided himself with a moral—the truth, namely, that the wrongdoing of one generation lives into the successive ones, and, divesting itself of every temporary advantage, becomes a pure and uncontrollable mischief, and he would feel it a singular gratification if this romance might effectually convince mankind—or, indeed, any one man—of the folly of tumbling down an avalanche of ill-gotten gold, or "real" estate, on the heads of an unfortunate posterity, thereby to maim and crush them, until the accumulated mass shall be scattered abroad in its original atoms. In good faith, however, he is not sufficiently imaginative to flatter himself with the slightest hope of this kind. When romances do really teach anything, or produce any effective operation, it is usually through a far more subtile process than the ostensible one. The author has considered it hardly worth his while, therefore, relentlessly to impale the story with its moral as with an iron rod—or, rather, as by sticking a pin through a butterfly—thus at once deprived it of life, and causing it to stiffen in an ungainly and unnatural attitude. A high truth, indeed, fairly, finely, and skillfully wrought out, brightening at every stop, and crowning the final development of a work of fiction, may add an artistic glory, but is never any truer, and seldom any more evident, at the last page than at the first.

The reader may perhaps choose to assign an actual locality to the imaginary events of this narrative. If permitted by the historical connection—which, though slight, was essential to his plan—the author would very willingly have avoided anything of this nature. Not to speak of other objections, it exposes the romance to an inflexible and exceedingly dangerous species of criticism, by bringing his family pictures almost into positive contact with the realities of the moment. It has been no part of his object, however, to describe local manners, nor in any way to meddle with the characteristics of a community for whom he cherishes a proper respect and a natural regard. He trusts not to be considered as unpardonably offending by laying out a street that infringes upon nobody's private rights, and appropriating a lot of land which had no visible owner, and building a house of materials long in use for constructing castles in the air. The personages of the tale—though they give themselves out to be of ancient stability and considerable prominence—are really of the author's own making, or, at all events, of his own mixing; their virtues can shed no luster, nor their defects redound, in the remotest degree, to the discredit of the venerable town of which they profess to be inhabitants. He would be glad, therefore, if—especially in the quarter to which he alludes—the book may be read strictly as a Romance, having a great deal more to do with the clouds overhead than with any portion of the actual soil of the County of Essex.

DISCUSSION QUESTIONS

1. What is the difference, according to Hawthorne, between a "Romance" and a "Novel"? What contrasting sets of "rules" does he propose?
2. What, more generally, are differences between "romantic" and "realistic" points of view, approaches to life, and approaches to the fictional depiction of life's truths?
3. Why do you think Hawthorne appears to be defending Romanticism against criticism? Examining his defenses, what objections do you see him both acknowledge and attempt to answer?
4. Hawthorne mentions the idea of communicating "truth" through his Romances in several places in these passages. Putting together everything he says about it, how can he claim to embody "truth" in his fanciful and "unrealistic" fiction?

HENRY JAMES

James on Hawthorne's Romances
Hawthorne Was a Man of Fancy, excerpt from *Hawthorne,* 1879
That Feeling of Latent Romance,
excerpt from "Hawthorne," 1896
Why Hawthorne Has Borne the Test of Time,
excerpt from "Letter to the Hon. Robert S. Rantoul," 1905

Henry James (1843–1916), a pivotal figure in American fiction, published over twenty collections of short stories, two dozen novels, and countless volumes of essays, travel sketches, biographies, and criticism. Some of his more famous fiction includes Washington Square *(1881),* The Portrait of a Lady *(1881),* The Turn of the Screw *(1898), and* The Wings of the Dove *(1902). When his collected stories and novels were to be republished in thirty-five volumes, he took the opportunity to revise every one of them, some extensively, and to write critical prefaces to each one, which are brought together in the widely read collection* The Art of the Novel *(1934). He was acutely aware of his literary lineage and wrote extensively on Nathaniel Hawthorne, whom he considered a kind of literary ancestor.*

Hawthorne Was a Man of Fancy

. . . Hawthorne was a man of fancy, and I suppose that in speaking of him it is inevitable that we should feel ourselves confronted with the familiar problem of the difference between the fancy and the imagination. Of the larger and more potent faculty he certainly possessed a liberal share; no one can read *The House of the Seven Gables* without feeling it to be a deeply imaginative work. But I am often struck, especially in the shorter tales, of which I am now chiefly speaking, with a kind of small ingenuity, a taste for conceits and analogies, which bears more particularly what is called the fanciful stamp. The finer of the shorter tales are redolent of a rich imagination . . . ; but as a general thing I should characterise the more metaphysical of our author's short stories as graceful and felicitous conceits. They seem to me to be qualified in this manner by the very fact that they belong to the province of allegory. Hawthorne, in his metaphysical moods, is nothing if not allegorical, and allegory, to my sense, is quite one of the lighter exercises of the imagination. Many excellent judges, I know, have a great stomach for it; they delight in symbols and correspondences, in seeing a story told as if it were another and a very different story. I frankly confess that I have as a general thing but little enjoyment of it and that it has never seemed to me to be, as it were, a first-rate literary form. It has produced assuredly some first-rate works; and Hawthorne in his younger years had been a great reader and devotee of Bunyan and Spenser, the great masters of allegory. But it is apt to spoil two good things— a story and a moral, a meaning and a form; and the taste for it is responsible for a large part of the forcible feeble writing that has been inflicted upon the world. The only cases in which it is endurable is when it is extremely spontaneous, when the analogy presents itself with eager promptitude. When it shows signs of having been groped and fumbled for, the needful illusion is of course absent and the failure complete. Then the machinery alone is visible, and the end to which it operates becomes a matter of indifference. There was but little literary criticism in the United States at the time Hawthorne's earlier works were published; but among the reviewers Edgar Poe perhaps held the scales the highest. . . . He wrote a chapter upon Hawthorne, and spoke of him on the whole very kindly; and his estimate is of sufficient value to make it noticeable that he should express lively disapproval of the large part allotted to allegory in his tales—in defence of which, he says, "however, or for whatever object employed, there is scarcely one respectable word to be said. . . . The deepest emotion," he goes on, "aroused within us by the happiest allegory *as* allegory, is a very, *very* imperfectly satisfied sense of the writer's ingenuity in overcoming a difficulty we should have preferred his not having attempted to overcome. . . . One thing is clear, that if allegory ever establishes a fact, it is by dint of overturning a fiction"; and Poe has furthermore the courage to remark that the *Pilgrim's Progress* is a "ludicrously overrated book." Certainly, as a general thing, we are struck with the ingenuity and felicity of Hawthorne's analogies and correspondences; the idea appears to have made itself at home in them easily. Nothing could be better in this respect than *The Snow-Image* (a little masterpiece), or *The Great Carbuncle*, or *Doctor Heidegger's Experiment*, or *Rappaccini's Daughter*. But in such things as *The Birth-Mark* and *The Bosom-Serpent*, we are struck with something stiff and mechanical, slightly incongruous, as if the kernel had not assimilated its envelope. But these are matters of light impression, and there would be a want of tact in pretending to discriminate too closely among things which all, in one way or another, have a charm. The charm—the great charm—is that they are glimpses of a great field, of the whole deep mystery of man's soul and conscience. They are moral, and their interest is moral; they deal with something more than the mere accidents and conventionalities, the surface occurrences of life. The fine thing in Hawthorne is that he cared for the deeper psychology, and that, in his way, he tried to become familiar with it. This natural, yet fanciful familiarity with it, this air, on the author's part, of being a confirmed *habitué* of a region of mysteries and subtleties, constitutes the originality of his tales. And then they have the further merit of seeming, for what they are, to spring up so freely and lightly. The author has all the ease, indeed, of a regular dweller in the moral, psychological realm; he goes to and fro in it, as a man who knows his way. His tread is a light and modest one, but he keeps the key in his pocket. . . .

That Feeling of Latent Romance

[Hawthorne's fictions] . . . sounded, with their rare felicity, from the very first the note that was to be Hawthorne's distinguished mark,—that feeling for the latent romance of New England, which in summary form is the most final name to be given, I think, to his inspiration. This element, which is what at its best his genius most expresses, was far from obvious,—it had to be looked for; and Hawthorne found it, as he wandered and mused, in the secret play of the Puritan faith: the secret, I say particularly, because the direct and ostensible, face to face with common tasks and small conditions (as I may call them without prejudice to their general grimness), arrived at forms of which the tender imagination could make little. It could make a great deal, on the other hand, of the spiritual contortions, the darkened outlook, of the ingrained sense of sin, of evil, and of responsibility. There had been other complications in the history of the community surrounding him,—savages from behind, soldiers from before, a cruel climate from every quarter and a pecuniary remittance from none. But the great complication was the pressing moral anxiety, the restless individual conscience. These things were developed at the cost of so many others, that there were almost no others left to help them to make a picture for the artist. The artist's imagination had to deck out the subject, to work it up, as we nowadays say; and Hawthorne's was,—on intensely chastened lines, indeed,—equal to the task. In that manner it came into exercise from the first, through the necessity of taking for granted, on the part of the society about him, a life of the spirit more complex than anything that met the mere eye of sense. It was a question of looking behind and beneath for the suggestive idea, the artistic motive; the effect of all of which was an invaluable training for the faculty that evokes and enhances. This ingenuity grew alert and irrepressible as it manœuvred for the back view and turned up the under side of common aspects,—the laws secretly broken, the impulses secretly felt, the hidden passions, the double lives, the dark corners, the closed rooms, the skeletons in the cupboard and at the feast. It made, in short, and cherished, for fancy's sake, a mystery and a glamour where there were otherwise none very ready to its hand; so that it ended by living in a world of things symbolic and allegoric, a presentation of objects casting, in every case, far behind them a shadow more curious and more amusing than the apparent figure. Any figure therefore easily became with him an emblem, any story a parable, any appearance a cover: things with which his concern is—gently, indulgently, skillfully, with the lightest hand in the world—to pivot them round and show the odd little stamp or sign that gives them their value for the collector. . . .

. . . In truth, for many persons his great, his most touching sign will have been his aloofness wherever he is. He is outside of everything, and an alien everywhere. He is an æsthetic solitary. His beautiful, light imagination is the wing that on the autumn evening just brushes the dusky window. It was a faculty that gave him much more a terrible sense of human abysses than a desire rashly to sound them and rise to the surface with his report. On the surface—the surface of the soul and the edge of the tragedy—he preferred to remain. He lingered, to weave his web, in the thin exterior air. This is a partial expression of his characteristic habit of dipping, of diving just for sport, into the moral world without being in the least a moralist. He had none of the heat nor of the dogmatism of that character; none of the impertinence, as we feel he would almost have held it, of any intermeddling. He never intermeddled; he was divertedly and discreetly contemplative, pausing oftenest where, amid prosaic aspects, there seemed most of an appeal to a sense for subtleties. But of all cynics he was the brightest and kindest, and the subtleties he spun are mere silken threads for stringing polished beads. His collection of moral mysteries is the cabinet of a dilettante.

Why Hawthorne Has Borne the Test of Time

. . . [T]here is a reason, in particular, why he has borne it so well, and I think you will recognize with me, in the light of what I have tried to say, that he has done so by very simply, quietly, slowly and steadily, becoming for us a Classic. If we look at the real meaning of our celebration to-day, ask ourselves what is at the back of our heads or in the bottom of our hearts about it, we become conscious of that interesting process and eloquent plea of the years on Hawthorne's behalf—of that great benefit, that effect of benevolence, for him, from so many of the things the years have brought. We are in the presence thus of one of the happiest opportunities to see how a Classic comes into being, how three such things as the Scarlet Letter, the Gables, and Blithedale—to choose only a few names where I might choose many—acquire their final value. They acquire it, in a large measure, by the manner in which later developments have worked in respect to them—and, it is scarce too much to say, acquire it in spite of themselves and by the action of better machinery than their authors could have set in motion, stronger (as well as longer!) wires than their authors could have pulled. Later developments, I think, have worked in respect to them by *contrast*—that is the point—so much more either than by a generous emulation or by a still more generous originality. They have operated to make the beauty—the other beauty—delicate and noble, to throw the distinction into relief. The scene has changed and everything with it—the pitch, and the tone, and the quantity, and the quality, above all; reverberations are gained, but proportions are lost; the distracted Muse herself stops her ears and shuts her eyes: the brazen trumpet has so done its best to deafen us to the fiddle-string. But to the fiddle-string we nevertheless return; it sounds, for our sense, with the slightest lull of the general noise—such a lull as, for reflection, for taste, a little even for criticism, and much, certainly, for a legitimate complacency, our present occasion beneficently makes. Then it is that such a mystery as that of the genius we commemorate may appear a perfect example of the truth that the state of being a classic is a *comparative* state—considerably, generously, even when blindly, brought about, for the author on whom the crown alights, by the generations, the multitudes worshipping other gods, that have followed him. He must obviously have been in himself exquisite and right, but it is not to that only, to being in himself exquisite and right, that any man ever was so fortunate as to owe the supreme distinction. He owes it more or less, at the best, to the *relief* in which some happy, some charming combination of accidents has placed his intrinsic value. This combination, in our own time, has been the contagion of the form that we may, for convenience, and perhaps, as regards much of it, even for compliment, call the journalistic—so pervasive, so ubiquitous, so unprecedentedly prosperous, so wonderful for outward agility, by so unfavorable, even so fatal, to development from within. Hawthorne saw it—and it saw him—but in its infancy, before these days of huge and easy and immediate success, before the universal, the overwhelming triumph of the master. He *had* developed from within—as to feeling, as to form, as to sincerity and character. So it is, as I say, that he enjoys his relief, and that we are thrown back, by the sense of difference, on his free possession of himself. He lent himself, of course, to his dignity—by the way the serious, in him, flowered into the grace of art; but our need of him, almost quite alone as he stands, in one tray of the scales of Justice, would add, if this were necessary, to the earnestness of our wish to see that he be undisturbed there. Vigilance, in the matter, however, assuredly, is happily not necessary! The grand sign of being classic is that when you have "passed," as they sat at examinations, you have passed; you have become one once for all, you have taken your degree and may be left to the light and the ages.

DISCUSSION QUESTIONS

1. James mentions Hawthorne's tendency toward allegory. What is allegory? Why is it acceptable for Romance but antithetical to Realism?
2. What is James' criticism of Hawthorne's more "allegorical" tales? Why does he consider them "one of the lighter exercises of the imagination"?
3. In spite of his criticism of Hawthorne, what strengths does James see in romances such as Hawthorne's if they are written as well as Hawthorne at his best?
4. Why, in James' opinion, was Hawthorne so popular in James' own time, half a century after the time of his first popularity, during an era of the new "realism" in fiction?

FRANK NORRIS

A Plea for Romantic Fiction

Frank Norris (1870–1902) was the most famous proponent of American Naturalism, writing of the seamier side of life—of lust, greed, and violence among the poor and desperate. His novels McTeague *(1899),* The Octopus *(1901), and* The Pit *(1902) are classics of the form. He had strong opinions about what fiction should and should not do, which he expressed in the collection* The Responsibilities of the Novelist *(1903), from which this selection comes.*

Let us at the start make a distinction. Observe that one speaks of romanticism and not sentimentalism. One claims that the latter is as distinct from the former as is that other form of art which is called Realism. Romance has been often put upon and overburdened by being forced to bear the onus of abuse that by right should fall to sentiment; but the two should be kept very distinct, for a very high and illustrious place will be claimed for romance, while sentiment will be handed down the scullery stairs.

Many people to-day are composing mere sentimentalism, and calling it and causing it to be called romance; so with those who are too busy to think much upon these subjects, but who none the less love honest literature, Romance, too, has fallen into disrepute. Consider now the cut-and-thrust stories. They are all labeled Romances, and it is very easy to get the impression that Romance must be an affair of cloaks and daggers, or moonlight and golden hair. But this is not so at all. The true Romance is a more serious business than this. It is not merely a conjurer's trick-box, full of flimsy quackeries, tinsel and claptraps, meant only to amuse, and relying upon deception to do even that. Is it not something better than this? Can we not see in it an instrument, keen, finely tempered, flawless—an instrument with which we may go straight through the clothes and tissues and wrappings of flesh down deep into the red, living heart of things?

Is all this too subtle, too merely speculative and intrinsic, too *precieuse* and nice and "literary"? Devoutly one hopes the contrary. So much is made of so-called Romanticism in present-day fiction that the subject seems worthy of discussion, and a protest against the misuse of a really noble and honest formula of literature appears to be timely—misuse, that is, in the sense of limited use. Let us suppose for the moment that a romance can be made out of a cut-and-thrust business. Good Heavens, are there no other things that are romantic, even in this—falsely, falsely called—humdrum world of to-day? Why should it be that so soon as the novelist addresses himself—seriously—to the consideration of contemporary life he must abandon Romance and take up that harsh, loveless, colourless, blunt tool called Realism?

Now, let us understand at once what is meant by Romance and what by Realism. Romance, I take it, is the kind of fiction that takes cognizance of variations from the type of normal life. Realism is the kind of fiction that confines itself to the type of normal life. According to this definition, then, Romance may even treat of the sordid, the unlovely—as for instance, the novels of M. Zola. (Zola has been dubbed a Realist, but he is, on the contrary, the very head of the Romanticists.) Also, Realism, used as it sometimes is as a term of reproach, need not be in the remotest sense or degree offensive, but on the other hand respectable as a church and proper as a deacon—as, for instance, the novels of Mr. Howells.

The reason why one claims so much for Romance, and quarrels so pointedly with Realism, is that Realism stultifies itself. It notes only the surface of things. For it, Beauty is not even skin deep, but only a geometrical plane, without dimensions and depth, a mere outside. Realism is very excellent so far as it goes, but it goes no further than the Realist himself can actually see, or actually hear. Realism is minute; it is the drama of a broken teacup, the tragedy of a walk down the block, the excitement of an afternoon call, the adventure of an invitation to dinner. It is the visit to my neighbour's house, a formal visit, from which I may draw no conclusions. I see my neighbour and his friends—very, oh, such very! probable people—and that is all. Realism bows upon the doormat and goes away and says to me, as we link arms on the sidewalk: "That is life." And I say it is not. It is not, as you would very well see if you took Romance with you to call upon your neighbour.

Lately you have been taking Romance a weary journey across the water—ages and the flood of years—and haling her into the fusty, musty, worm-eaten, moth-riddled, rust-corroded "Grandes Salles" of the Middle Ages and the Renaissance, and she has found the drama of a bygone age for you there. But would you take her across the street to your neighbour's front parlour (with the bisque fisherboy on the mantel and the photograph of Niagara Falls on glass hanging in the front window); would you introduce her there? Not you. Would you take a walk with her on Fifth Avenue, or Beacon Street, or Michigan Avenue? No, indeed. Would you choose her for a companion of a morning spent in Wall Street, or an afternoon in the Waldorf-Astoria? You just guess you would not.

She would be out of place, you say—inappropriate. She might be awkward in my neighbour's front parlour, and knock over the little bisque fisher-boy. Well, she might. If she did, you might find underneath the base of the statuette, hidden away, tucked away—what? God knows. But something that would be a complete revelation of my neighbour's secretest life.

So you think Romance would stop in the front parlour and discuss medicated flannels and mineral waters with the ladies? Not for more than five minutes. She would be off upstairs with you, prying, peeping, peering into the closets of the bedroom, into the nursery, into the sitting-room; yes, and into that little iron box screwed to the lower shelf of the closet in the library; and into those compartments and pigeon-holes of the *secretaire* in the study. She would find a heartache (maybe) between the pillows of the mistress's bed, and a memory carefully secreted in the master's deed-box. She would come upon a great hope amid the books and papers of the study-table of the young man's room, and—perhaps—who knows—an affair, or, great Heavens, an intrigue, in the scented ribbons and gloves and hairpins of the young lady's bureau. And she would pick here a little and there a little, making up a bag of hopes and fears and a package of joys and sorrows—great ones, mind you—and then come down to the front door, and, stepping out into the street, hand you the bags and package and say to you—"That is Life!"

Romance does very well in the castles of the Middle Ages and the Renaissance chateaux, and she has the *entree* there and is very well received. That is all well and good. But let us protest against limiting her to such places and such times. You will find her, I grant you, in the chatelaine's chamber and the dungeon of the man-at-arms; but, if you choose to look for her, you will find her equally at home in the brownstone house on the corner and in the office-building downtown. And this very day, in this very hour, she is sitting among the rags and wretchedness, the dirt and despair of the tenements of the East Side of New York.

"What?" I hear you say, "look for Romance—the lady of the silken robes and golden crown, our beautiful, chaste maiden of soft voice and gentle eyes—look for her among the vicious ruffians, male and female, of Allen Street and Mulberry Bend?" I tell you she is there, and to your shame be it said you will not know her in those surroundings. You, the aristocrats, who demand the fine linen and the purple in your fiction; you, the sensitive, the delicate, who will associate with your Romance only so long as she wears a silken gown. You will not follow her to the slums, for you believe that Romance should only amuse and entertain you, singing you sweet songs and touching the harp of silver strings with rosy-tipped fingers. If haply she should call to you from the squalour of a dive, or the awful degradation of a disorderly house, crying: "Look! listen! This, too, is life. These, too, are my children! Look at them, know them and, knowing, help!" Should she call thus you would stop your ears; you would avert your eyes and you would answer, "Come from there, Romance. Your place is not there!" And you would make of her a harlequin, a tumbler, a sword-dancer, when, as a matter of fact, she should be by right divine a teacher sent from God.

She will not often wear the robe of silk, the gold crown, the jeweled shoon; will not always sweep the silver harp. An iron note is hers if so she choose, and coarse garments, and stained hands; and, meeting her thus, it is for you to know her as she passes—know her for the same young queen of the blue mantle and lilies. She can teach you if you will be humble to learn—teach you by showing. God help you if at last you take from Romance her mission of teaching; if you do not believe that she has a purpose—a nobler purpose and a mightier than mere amusement, mere entertainment. Let Realism do the entertaining with its meticulous presentation of teacups, rag carpets, wall-paper and haircloth sofas, stopping with these, going no deeper than it sees, choosing the ordinary, the untroubled, the commonplace.

But to Romance belongs the wide world for range, and the unplumbed depths of the human heart, and the mystery of sex, and the problems of life, and the black, unsearched penetralia of the soul of man. You, the indolent, must not always be amused. What matter the silken clothes, what matter the prince's houses? Romance, too, is a teacher, and if—throwing aside the purple—she wears the camel's-hair and feeds upon the locusts, it is to cry aloud unto the people, "Prepare ye the way of the Lord; make straight his path."

DISCUSSION QUESTIONS

1. How does Norris define (by contrasting them) "Romance" and "Realism"? What is the difference in the way each says, "That is life"?
2. How does Norris criticize Realism? What are its limits as a fictional technique?
3. What two ideas of Romance does Norris contrast, and how does he criticize the one and recommend the other?
4. In what ways is Romance, at least as Norris says it should be done, preferable to Realism, at least as Norris criticizes it?

ROBERT SCHOLES

Fabulation and Romance

Robert Scholes (b. 1929) has taught at Brown University since 1970. He is the author of over thirty works of literary criticism, anthologies of literature, and literature textbooks, including The Nature of Narrative *(1966),* Elements of Fiction *(1968),* Structural Fabulation *(1975), and* Fabulation and Metafiction *(1979), from which we have taken our selection. He is an astute reader and theorist of contemporary fiction, tracing its roots in tradition and mapping its explorations.*

FACT, FICTION, AND FALLIBILISM

It will be useful to begin by considering the definition of reality offered to us a century ago by the brilliant pragmatist philosopher Charles Saunders Peirce. In an essay called "How to Make Our Ideas Clear" Peirce suggested that we could arrive at a clear notion of the real "by considering the points of difference between reality and its opposite, fiction" (Justus Buchler, ed., *Philosophical Writings of Peirce*, p. 36). The products of imagination are real, said Peirce, in the sense that we really imagine them. If we have a thought or a dream, the thinking and dreaming are themselves real:

> Thus a dream has real existence as a mental phenomenon, if somebody really dreamt it; that he dreamt so and so, does not depend on what anybody thinks was dreamt, but is completely independent of all opinion on the subject. On the other

hand, considering not the fact of dreaming, but the thing dreamt, it retains its peculiarities by virtue of no other fact than that it was dreamt to possess them. Thus we may define the real as that whose characters are independent of what anybody may think them to be. (p. 36)

Our fictions are real enough in themselves, but, as signs pointing to any world outside the fiction or the dream, they have no factual status. All thought, being fiction, tends toward this situation. We may think about reality all we please, but we shall never reach it in thought. Reality is absolute for Peirce, but human attempts to signify the truth are relative: "The opinion which is fated to be ultimately agreed to by all who investigate, is what we mean by truth, and the object represented in this opinion is the real" (p. 38).

In life, we do not attain the real. What we reach is a notion of the real which contents us enough so that we can found our behavior upon it. In a word, we arrive at belief. "And what is belief? It is the demi-cadence which closes a musical phrase in the symphony of our intellectual life" (p. 28). To acquiesce in belief would be to end the symphony of life prematurely. Belief is comfortable, but it is in a sense the enemy of truth, because it stifles inquiry. And, since "people cannot attain absolute certainty concerning questions of fact" (p. 50), the appropriate intellectual position for a human being must be what Peirce called "fallibilism," which he expressed in this fashion: "On the whole, then, we cannot in any way reach perfect certitude nor exactitude. We never can be absolutely sure of anything, nor can we with any probability ascertain the exact value of any measure or general ratio" (p. 58).

It is my contention that modern fabulation grows out of an attitude which may be called "fallibilism," just as nineteenth-century realism grew out of an earlier attitude called positivism. Fabulation, then, means not a turning away from reality, but an attempt to find more subtle correspondences between the reality which is fiction and the fiction which is reality. Modern fabulation accepts, even emphasizes, its fallibilism, its inability to reach all the way to the real, but it continues to look toward reality. It aims at telling such truths as fiction may legitimately tell in ways which are appropriately fictional. It will be useful to test that thesis provisionally on a writer who has been one of the major influences on the contemporary fabulative movement, and who is often described as one who has turned his back on reality to play in a purely verbal universe.

WHAT GOOD IS PURE ROMANCE?

A fair question, apparently. Plato asked it and nobody has answered it. Maybe it isn't as fair as it looks. What the question actually meant to him requires a bit of explanation. As I understand it, however, we can approximate Plato's intention by breaking the question into two parts: a) What good effect will listening to stories have on our understanding of the world?, and b) What good effect will listening to stories have on our behavior in the world? Like the good philosopher he was, Plato discovered that philosophy could do both a) and b) better than fiction could. That is, philosophy could tell us more truly both the nature of the cosmos and the attributes of right action. All those apologists for poetry who have accepted Plato's gambit have been reduced to presenting fiction either as sugar coating for the pill of philosophy, or as a handy and accurate shorthand notation of reality—that is, as allegory or as realism.

What Plato was really asking was "What good is poetry *as philosophy?*"— since for him philosophy already had a monopoly on both truth and goodness. Now that science owns truth, and goodness knows where goodness went (religion had it last but seems to have mislaid it), Plato's question has shifted its meaning so far as to expose its underpinnings. Zola tried to answer the question, "What good is fiction *as science?*" and worked himself into the absurd corner of the "experimental" novel, a notion he seems to have had the good sense not to believe but merely to use as journalistic puffery for his own productions, much as his heirs are now crying "phenomenological" novel for similar reasons. Matthew Arnold tried to answer the question, "What good is fiction *as religion?*" and twisted himself around to the point where he could see literature replacing dogma. Now the Marxist asks, "What good is fiction *as politics?*," and the Freudian asks, "What good is fiction *as psychology?*," and so on. But the real question, the one that Plato pretended to be asking, has gotten lost. Probably Plato could not see it himself. Since literary criticism started as a branch of philosophy, it was doubtless necessary to see Plato's question in terms of metaphysics and ethics. Even Aristotle succeeded only in adding a psychological concept, *katharsis,* to his notion of literature, and then returned quickly to its philosophical value as "imitation." But now that we can see criticism as a branch of literature itself, we should be able to set Plato's question in its proper context and make it mean what it should mean: What are the special qualities of fiction for which we value it? In other words, "What good is fiction *as fiction?*"

Not as the "representation of an action," but as an imaginative construct. Not in terms of what it tells us about, even including the imagination itself, but in terms of what makes our experience of fiction a good experience. The Aristotle of *katharsis* is much closer to the mark than the Aristotle of *mimesis.* The students of sleep have discovered that dreaming is necessary to the well-being of the human organism, and perhaps to the higher animals as well. It is not that our dreams teach us anything; they are simply a means of expression for us, a nightly cinema in which we are producer, director, all the actors, and all the audience. And if we are cheated of this imaginative performance in our sleep, we suffer for it during our waking existence in ways still not entirely understood.

I do not think fiction is a substitute for dream, but I think it must work for us in a similar way. It must provide us with an imaginative experience which is necessary to our imaginative well-being. And that is quite enough justification for it. We need all the imagination we have, and we need it exercised and in good condition. The simplest kind of fabling will do this for us to some extent, as long as we can respond to it fully, as long as it can engage our imagination totally. But as our imagination stretches and as we grow more serious (this combination of processes being what we mean, ideally, by the verb "to mature"), we require not fabling but fabulation. Pure romance must be enriched, like skim milk, if it is to sustain a full imaginative life. Allegory is one way of enriching pure romance. . . .

A FABLE AND ITS GLOSS

Once there was a country called Fiction, bordered on one side by the mountains of Philosophy and on the other by a great bog called History. The people of Fiction had a great gift, the gift of telling stories which could amuse men. As long as they had no contact with the peoples of the neighboring territories, they were perfectly satisfied with their gift and wanted nothing. But progress, and improved communications, brought them into contact with the strange peoples who lived on their borders and beyond. These peoples were not storytellers like the Fiction people, but they had something called Ideas. And when the Fiction people learned about Ideas they yearned for them terribly and wanted to use them to give their stories more dignity. A story without Ideas, they came to think, was fit only for children. So the Fiction people agreed that they would begin trading with their neighbors to get some Ideas.

This only made things worse. For the people on the Philosophy side of the land of Fiction insisted that Fictional Ideas should come from Philosophy, or from Theology just back in the hills, while the people on the other side said the only Ideas any good for fiction were those of the Historians. For a while those who favored Philosophy and Theology won. They called their part of Fiction "Allegory" and they flourished under leaders like Dante and Spenser. But after a while the Ideas from Philosophy and Theology began to lose their zip, and even the Philosophers started saying that the Historians had a lot of good Ideas. Then the Allegorists grew weak and the other party, who called themselves "Realists," began to grow in size and power. They took Ideas from the Historians and discovered other territories, way back in the bog, peopled by an aggressive breed known as Social Scientists. These fellows had Ideas too, and the Realists took as many as they could get.

Then a strange thing happened. The Historians and Social Scientists got tired of having other folks put their Ideas into stories. They decided to muscle in on the story racket themselves. So they climbed out of the bog and invaded the fertile fields of Fiction, and everybody who stayed on in the territory they occupied had to agree to write non-Fiction novels. At the same time the Philosophers and Theologians got a whole new batch of Ideas called Existentialism and Wittgenstein which frightened them so much that they lit out for the highest peaks leaving Ideas strewn all over the foothills. But some Philosophers had got to like that territory so much that they wouldn't leave. They were still there when the refugees from Realism started to pour in and take over. Finally, in order to stay, they had to agree to show these refugees a new way to do Allegory with all these new Ideas. A few of the refugees had smuggled some Ideas called Jung and Freud with them, and when the leftover Philosophers saw them they said they weren't Social Science Ideas anyway, but things those rascals had stolen from Theology and Philosophy to begin with. So they took all the old and new Ideas they could find and began trying to work out a kind of Allegory. One of the leftover Philosophers who showed the refugees from Fiction the most was a nice lady named Iris Murdoch.

Well. This little exemplum is a pretty feeble fable, just a discursive convenience, really, and not a proper allegory. Its characters and events are too shadowy, of too little interest in themselves, to be thought of as truly allegorical. In the great allegories, tension between the ideas illustrated by the characters and the human qualities in their characterization makes for a much richer and more powerful kind of meaning. The great allegories are never entirely allegorical, just as the great realistic novels are never entirely real. And, in allegory, it is often the tension between the ideational side of a situation and the human side which makes for the power and the meaning—and the power *of* the meaning. Take, for example, the concept of damnation, which is derived from analogies with actual punishment by torture but is referred to an "ideal" eternal world outside the visible universe. And take also a little human situation, a pair of young lovers such as might people a harmless novella of cuckoldry. Put these two things together and you have Francesca da Rimini and her lover Paolo, burning forever in Dante's hell. This is allegory. My fable, on the other hand, was only a nod from criticism in the direction of allegory.

That fable, however, was the shortest and clearest way that I could sketch out my view of the relations of allegory and realism to fiction—both the conceptual relations and the historical ones. Now I must gloss that brief paradigm a bit. Allegory amounts to seeing life through ideational filters provided by philosophy or theology. When realism supplanted allegory as the great form of serious narrative, it claimed to be superior because it looked directly at life—without filters of any kind. The manifestoes of realism are full of terms like "objectivity," "detachment," "experiment," and so on, which suggest a clear and scientific view of life. But we can see now that it is impossible to look directly at life. It is like gazing right into the sun; we see so much that we are blinded.

For a writer, language itself is a great filter which colors his view of life. For the realistic novelist, other filters in the form of concepts of time, space, causality, society, and a whole collection of psychological types and tropes enable him to capture what he calls "life" on paper. He may be unaware of these, simply imitating his predecessors or seeing in the same way his contemporaries see, but the filters are there—and indispensable—whether the novelist knows it or not. As one of realism's great apologists, Georg Lukács, has put it, realism depends on types:

> The central category and criterion of realist literature is the type, a peculiar synthesis which organically binds together the general and the particular both in characters and situations. What makes a type a type is not its average quality, not its mere individual being, however profoundly conceived: what makes it a type is that in it all the humanly and socially essential determinants are present on their highest level of development, in the ultimate unfolding of the possibilities latent in them, in extreme presentation of their extremes, rendering concrete the peaks and limits of men and epochs.

Allegory also depends on types, but the types of allegory are referable to a philosophy and theology concerned with ideals and essences; while the types of realism are referable to social sciences concerned with recording and understanding the processes that govern existence. The types of realism are committed to the visible world, while the types of allegory are committed to the invisible. This is why allegory was the great narrative form of the later Middle Ages and early Renaissance. When the Christian cosmos, based on the invisible world of eternity, was challenged by a humanism that put man and his visible world at the cosmic center of things, allegory became the best literary mode for controlling and reconciling these two visions. Francesca da Rimini in Dante's hell is a perfect example of the invisible world controlling the visible, of Christianity acknowledging humanism but mastering it—with difficulty, of course. That is why Dante faints after hearing Francesca. And the faint of the character Dante reflects the effort expended by the author Dante in giving humanism such a fair display and still keeping it subordinate. In a way, the rise of the novel simply reflects the triumph of humanism and the empirical attitudes which came in its train. As the invisible world lost its reality, the visible world became realer. And as dogmatic theology and systematic philosophy lost their control over men's minds, they were supplanted by positivistic or pragmatic and relativistic views of life and conduct. The realistic novel, which presents views of life and conduct in terms of manners and mores, was the appropriate form for serious fiction in the age of Comte.

But that age is ending. Now positivism and realism itself are fading and losing their hold on the minds of men. Instead of being The Way, they now just seem a way. They seem like dogma, and tired old dogma at that. Furthermore, psychology, when it moves away from statistics and experiments with animals and probes into depths of the human psyche, is moving from social science toward philosophy; for the deeps of the psyche are an invisible world also, one which modern men accept with the same unquestioning faith once reserved for the invisible world of Christianity. Freud and Jung together have presented the modern writer with a new scheme of the invisible world which cries out for allegorization. The depths, of course, are murkier than the heavens, and any allegory based on depth psychology will have to be more tentative than an allegory based on the Christian cosmos needed to be. But the archetypal system of Joyce's *Finnegans Wake* is as allegorical as anything in Dante. . . .

DISCUSSION QUESTIONS

1. In what ways, according to Scholes, does "fabulation" still aim at "the real"? How does fabulation—the creation of patently "unreal" characters and narratives—"aim at telling truths"?
2. What might Scholes mean by "pure romance"? What is "romance" (or "fiction *as fiction*") not good for and why? What is it good for and why?
3. What sense do you make of Scholes' little "allegory"? As a way of understanding it, can you attach some more real writers' names to his story, as he does with Dante, Spenser, and Iris Murdoch?

4. What might Scholes mean when he says, "The great allegories are never entirely allegorical, just as the great realistic novels are never entirely real"?
5. Scholes asserts that "realism" is no more "real" or "objective" or "detached" than any other fictional technique, including allegory. What is his reasoning? How might his idea be true?
6. Do you agree with Scholes that the age of realism is ending? What evidence can you present either (or both) supporting or criticizing his view?

MODERNIST AND POSTMODERNIST FICTION

WILLIAM GASS

Philosophy and the Form of Fiction

William Gass (b. 1924) has taught at Washington University since 1969, where he is now David May Distinguished University Professor. Since his ground-breaking Omensetter's Luck *(1966) and* In the Heart of the Heart of the Country *(1968), he has been a unique voice in American fiction, winning the National Book Critics Circle Award (1986 and 1997) and the PEN/Faulkner Award and the American Book Award (1996). He is an equally important critic and theorist of fiction in collections such as* Fiction and the Figures of Life *(1970),* Writing in Politics *(1996), and* Reading Rilke: Reflections on the Problems of Translation *(1999).*

So much of philosophy is fiction. Dreams, doubts, fears, ambitions, ecstasies . . . if philosophy were a stream, they would stock it like fishes. Although fiction, in the manner of its making, is pure philosophy, no novelist has created a more dashing hero than the handsome Absolute, or conceived more dramatic extrications—the soul's escape from the body, for instance, or the will's from cause. And how thin and unlaced the forms of *Finnegans Wake* are beside any of the *Critiques;* how sunlit Joyce's darkness, how few his parallels, how loose his correspondences. With what emotion do we watch the flight of the Alone to the Alone, or discover that *"der Welt ist alles, was der Fall ist,"* or read that in a state of nature the life of man is "solitary, poor, nasty, brutish, and short." Which has written the greater *Of Human Bondage,* or brooded more musically upon life's miseries, or dwelled more lovingly upon the outlines of its own reflection? Is it not exhilarating to be told that the "desire and pursuit of the whole is called love"? And if we wish to become critical we can observe that Descartes' recourse to a gland in the skull to account for our intercourse with ourselves is a simple failure of the imagination, and that for the philosophers, God is always in His machine, flying about on wires like Peter Pan.

Novelist and philosopher are both obsessed with language, and make themselves up out of concepts. Both, in a way, create worlds. Worlds? But the worlds of the novelist, I hear you say, do not exist. Indeed. As for that—they exist more often than the philosophers'. Then, too—how seldom does it seem to matter. Who honestly cares? They are divine games. Both play at gods as others play at bowls; for there is frequently more reality in fairy tales than in these magical constructions of the mind, works equally of thought and energy and will, which raise up into sense and feeling, as to life, acts of pure abstraction, passes logical, and intuitions both securely empty and as fitted for passage as time.

Games—yet different games. Fiction and philosophy often make most acrimonious companions. To be so close in blood, so brotherly and like in body, can inspire a subtle hate; for their rivalry is sometimes less than open in its damage. They wound with advice. They smother with love. And they impersonate one another. Then, while in the other's guise and gait and oratory, while their brother's smiling ape and double, they do his suicide. Each expires in a welter of its own surprise.

Philosophers multiply our general nouns and verbs; they give fresh sense to stale terms; "man" and "nature" are their characters; while novelists toil at filling in the blanks in proper names and at creating other singular affairs. A novelist may pin a rose to its stem as you might paper a tail to its donkey, the rose may blush at his command, but the philosopher can elevate that reddening from an act of simple verbal predication to an angel-like ingression, ennobling it among Beings. The soul, we must remember, is the philosopher's invention, as thrilling a creation as, for instance, Madame Bovary. So I really should point out, though I shall say little more about it, that fiction is far more important to philosophy than the other way round. However, the novelist can learn more from the philosopher, who has been lying longer; for novelizing is a comparatively new, unpolished thing. Though philosophers have written the deeper poetry, traditionally philosophy has drawn to it the inartistic and the inarticulate, those of too mechanical a mind to move theirs smoothly, those too serious to see, and too fanatical to feel. All about us, now, the dull and dunce-eyed stool themselves to study corners.

Souls, essences, the bickering legions of immortals, the countless points of view which religion and philosophy have shaped, are seldom understood as metaphorical, as expressions of our wishes and our fears, as desperate political maneuvers, strategies of love or greed, as myths which make a sense which some men may, at moments, need; for the celebrated facts of life, whatever they are, are not very forceful, and even the most stubborn and most brutish ones (that man must eat to live, for instance) allow an indefinite number of attitudes and interpretations, including vegetarianism or solemn pronouncements in favor of fish or stern edicts against pork and beans.

If games, then sometimes dangerous ones. Let us suppose for a moment that both our Russells and our Becketts are engaged in telling us *how it is,* that the novelist and the philosopher are companions in a common enterprise, though they go about it in different ways. The objects I see and sometimes label—pencil, paper, table, penny, chair—each seems solid yet is pocked with spaces, each seems steady yet is made of moving pieces: shape, steadiness, solidity, and color . . . are these illusions? I call the penny round, but I'm reminded I see an ellipse. I say the pencil's yellow, yet perhaps the yellow's painted in by eye, the yellow is the reading of a signal maybe, although the reading does not reside within the receiver, and possibly its actual home is in the mind. The what? The mind. Who, or what, is that? A character. Like Micawber. Going on in the firm belief that something will turn up. Hasn't he made my world strange, this philosopher? I find I have a body, then a mind. I find that the world I live in, the objects I manipulate, are in great part my constructions. I shortly come to believe in many invisible beings, gods and angels, wills and powers, atoms, voids. Once where I thought an anger "out there" like a demon, a color "out there" in an object, connections "out there" holding hands with things, I now think otherwise. Loose bundles of affections and sensations pass me like so many clouds of dust in space (and, dear heaven, who am I?).

Beckett tells us that we live in garbage cans; sit at the side of empty roads, in emptiness awaiting emptiness; crawl blindly through mud. My skin is the tattered dirty clothing of a tramp, my body a broken bicycle, my living space is earth to just beneath my shoulders, my speech the twittering of an unoiled pump. Hasn't he made my world strange, this novelist? No, of course our lives are not a muddy crawl—*apparently.* But that is mere appearance. We're fooled constantly. We think our emotions fine when they are coarse; we think our ideas profound when they are empty, original when commonplace; we think at first we are living richly, deeply, when all we possess is a burlap bag, unopened tins, dirty thoughts, and webby privates.

I cannot help my home still looks well furnished, or my body trim; I cannot help the colors which I seem to come upon, or the unflinching firmness of my chair; I cannot help I glory in my sex or feel and think and act as one and not as a divided community; for I'm incurably naïve, incurably in love with deception; still, I can be taught, I can learn suspicion, learn that things aren't really what they seem; I can learn to hate my pleasures, condemn my desires, doubt my motives, deny my eyes, put unseen creatures in the world and then treat them with greater reverence, give them greater powers than those I innocently know—to bow and bow and bow in their direction; I can replace my love for people with a love for principle, and even pursue a life beyond the grave as a program for the proper pursuit of this one. Bravo, novelists and philosophers; good show.

Save the appearances, Plato said. Then make them all realities. No better way. Yet without that splendid distinction, the novelist as philosopher and the philosopher as novelist would both be out of business.

2

The esthetic aim of any fiction is the creation of a verbal world, or a significant part of such a world, alive through every order of its Being. Its author may not purpose this—authors purpose many things—but the construction of some sort of object, whether too disorderly to be a world or too mechanical to be alive, cannot be avoided. The story must be told and its telling is a record of the choices, inadvertent or deliberate, the author has made from all the possibilities of language. Whether or not it was correct of Aristotle to reason, as he apparently sometimes did, from the syntax of the Greek language to the syntax of reality, the art of fiction consists of such reasoning, since its people and their destinies, the things they prize, the way they feel, the landscapes they inhabit, are indistinct from words and all their orderings.

The artist's task is therefore twofold. He must show or exhibit his world, and to do this he must actually make something, not merely describe something that might be made. This takes tremendous technical skill, and except in rare and highly favored persons, great labor. Furthermore, he must present us with a world that is philosophically adequate, and this requires of him the utmost exercise of thought and sensibility. No one should mistake the demand. It is not for a comprehensive and correct philosophy. Truth, I am convinced, has antipathy for art. It is best when a writer has a deep and abiding indifference to it, although as a private person it may be vital to him. If the idea of truth is firmly defined and firmly held in line; if it is not, like Proteus, permitted to change its shape at every questioning, the very great difference between the theoretical formulations of the philosopher and the concrete creations of the novelist must make itself felt. The concepts of the philosopher speak, the words of the novelist are mute; the philosopher invites us to pass through his words to his subject: man, God, nature, moral law; while the novelist, if he is any good, will keep us kindly imprisoned in his language—there is literally nothing beyond. Of course, if the philosopher has made up his subject, as I suspect he has made up God, sin, and sense data, then he is performing for us, at least in part, as the novelist performs. Theology, it appears, is one-half fiction, one-half literary criticism.

A philosophy may be "adequate" without being true. If it answers, or shows how to answer, the questions its assumptions and its inferential laws allow, it is complete; if its conclusions follow from these assumptions as its rules dictate, it is consistent; and if the questions it permits are, in any degree, the same that everyday life puts to the ordinary man, it and its answers are to that degree significant; for the everyday questions of ordinary life are always addressed to those ultimate appearances which we remember must be saved. Any philosophy complete, consistent, and significant is, in the sense here used, adequate. It is adequate within its range, although its range may not be vast. A long and complex novel, or series of novels, however, may present us with a world complete through every principle and consequence, rivaling in its comprehensiveness the most grandiose philosophical systems; while a brief story may exhibit only an essential part from which we may infer, at our desire and leisure, much of the remainder. Finally, the artist is not asked to construct an adequate philosophy, but a philosophically adequate world, a different matter altogether. He creates an object, often as intricate and rigorous as any mathematic, often as simple and undemanding as a baby's toy, from whose nature, as from our own world, a philosophical system may be inferred; but he does not, except by inadvertence or mistaken esthetic principle, deem it his task to philosophize. A man who makes a thing that moves utilizes the laws of motion, although he may be unaware of their existence. All he cares about is the accomplishment of his particular design. The worlds which, in like manner, the writer creates, are only imaginatively possible ones; they need not be at all like any real one, and the metaphysics which any fiction implies is likely to be meaningless or false if taken as nature's own. The man who makes machines intuitively, the laws of heat and light and motion in his fingers, is inventive. Indeed, he may invent, in the principles of its running, what science knows nothing of. The writer, similarly, thinks through the medium of which he is the master, and when his world arises, novel and complete—sometimes as arbitrary and remote from real things as the best formal game, sometimes as searchingly advanced and sharp to the fact as the gadget of the most inspired tinker—his world displays that form of embodied thought which is imagination.

Nature is more than its regulations. Galileo follows the swinging Pisa Cathedral lamps with his dreadful eyes, but it is not the spill of light and shadow, the halo or the burning, that attracts him. It is the quantity in the action, the principle in the thing. So any maker, bent on rendering concrete the dominion of number, must find the qualities of sensation which will embody them. Nor can he merely name the qualities over, for what he makes is a world, not a diagram, and what he makes must live. Swinging has a law, but before the law of swinging come the swings.

Writers whose grasp of esthetic principles is feeble, or whose technique is poor and unpracticed, or whose minds are shallow and perceptions dim, give us stories which are never objects for contemplation, but arguments; they give us, at best, dramatized philosophy, not philosophically significant drama; or, if they know they must exhibit or present, show us Bradleyan selves in Berkeleyan suits sitting down to Boolean tea.

The philosophy that most writers embody in their work, with those amendments and additions which any strong personality will invariably insist upon, since it can only identify itself with what it calls its own begetting, is usually taken unconsciously from the tradition with which the writer is allied. As a result, a writer whose work has little esthetic merit may retain an historical or a philosophical interest. He may have represented, in just the confused way it existed, the world his generation saw and believed they lived in; or he may have produced a model of some philosopher's theoretical vision; and since the philosopher's vision is as often as not blind at the last to the signals of reality, it may be as near to the sight of fact his theory will ever come. On such occasions the work is commentary. Some novels are of very great philosophical importance, as it is doubtless one test of a philosophy to imagine, more simply than the cosmos itself does, what it would be like to live under its laws—whether, in other words, with its principles it is possible to build something that will run. Such imaginative construction is particularly useful for the evaluation of moral and political systems. One wants to know what people, good according to Kant or Nietzsche or William James, are like, and how it feels to house the conscience of Saint Paul or guard with the eyes of Augustine the affairs of the city of God. An artist may precede the sciences in discovery, just as the inventor may, by incorporating in his work ideas which turn out true, but his success in this is not esthetic, and depends entirely on what science decides.

An idea must first be thought before it can be tested, but a principle encased in fiction has, most likely, not been thought of at all. It has been used. This may have been what Plato had in mind when he classified his citizens according to their nearness to the Forms. Certainly it is one thing to employ an idea, another to state it in a manner suitable to thought, while yet another to carry out the tests which make it true or false. It is a sadly limited view of the power of mind in man to suppose that only truth employs or pleasures it. It appears that any expression suitable to science must be quantitatively abstract, and that thought itself proceeds by quantities and extensions, yet one may contemplate the most purely abstract and most purely quantitative system for the values of the system's sake, and so far as this is done, and is the end of such pure systems, they, and the opposite pole of art, have the same appreciative aim, and are in value much akin; for creative thought and creative imagination are not so much stirred on by truth in any synthetic sense as by sublimity—a vision of absolute organization. It is really a moral insistence, this insistence that truth be first, whether it is the Platonist, who requires that Ideas do the work of things, or the Pragmatist, who demands that things perform the functions of ideas.

3

For the purposes of analysis we can regard the sentences of fiction as separate acts of creation. They are the most elementary instances of what the author has constructed. Wittgenstein believed for a time that a proposition, in the disposition of its names, pictured a possibly equivalent arrangement of objects. This is a pleasant fancy, and plainly must be true . . . of fictions; though sentences in stories should do more than simply configure things. Each should contrive (through order, meaning, sound, and rhythm) a moving unity of fact and feeling.

Before us is the empty page, the deep o'er which, like God, though modestly, we brood. But that white page, what is it? Perhaps it is the ideally empty consciousness of the reader—a dry wineskin or a *tabula rasa*. And if, as authors, we think this way, then what we want is a passive mind and, as in love, an utterly receptive woman. Thus our attitudes, before the first act of creation, make a philosophical difference. What shall we sail upon it first?

> All known all white bare white body fixed one yard legs joined like sewn.

Beckett's "Ping" begins. An audacious first term: all. The sentence isolates its words; they slowly fall, slowly revolve, slowly begin to group themselves. We are in the hands of an ancient atomist.

> All known all white bare white body fixed one yard legs joined like sewn.
> Light heat white floor one square yard never seen. White walls one yard by two white ceiling one square yard never seen.

Stately monotonous strokes, like measured beats of a gong, occur within, but do not fill, this void. Though here the gong sometimes emits a ping. Truly, nothing is previous. Groups first formed form the first connections, and are repeated.

> Bare white body fixed only the eyes only just. Traces blurs light grey almost white on white. Hands hanging palms front white feet heels together right angle. Light heat white planes shining white bare white body fixed ping fixed elsewhere.

With what remarkable confidence, on the other hand, does Jane Austen reach for our responses. She does not form a chaos or create from nothing. Her pen moves through us; we part a bit and yield the paths of her design. How much we are expected to know already: manners, values, social structure. She thinks in far, far longer lengths; her silences are like the silences which occur in happy conversations; her spaces are interiors, tamed and quiet; she does not begin, she ends, in terror, and the metaphysical.

Let's descend into the sentence briefly, on a rope for our return. How amazing they can be, how strange. The shortest one can spell us back to infancy. ("A cow broke in tomorrow morning to my Uncle Toby's fortifications," for instance.) The meaning of a sentence may make a unity, comprise some whole, but inevitably its concepts are loosed one by one like the release of pigeons. We must apprehend them, then, like backward readers: here's a this, now a that, now a this. The sentence must be sounded, too; it has a rhythm, speed, a tone, a flow, a pattern, shape, length, pitch, conceptual direction. The sentence confers reality upon certain relations, but it also controls our estimation, apprehension, and response to them. Every sentence, in short, takes metaphysical dictation, and it is the sum of these dictations, involving the whole range of the work in which the sentences appear, which accounts for its philosophical quality, and the form of life in the thing that has been made.

In Beckett's sentences, quoted above, there is no subordination, but a community of equals—well, hardly a community either, though the primordial relationship of adjective to noun is not entirely suppressed. This is not the place to get lost in details, but we are all aware of the kind of influence Aristotle's subject-predicate logic had on his philosophy, and on all those which followed for quite a long time. The novelist's characteristic grammatical forms affect the building of his book at least as much, though we must be careful to notice not only his words' syntactical pasts, but their present syntactical functions. So some sentences are crowded with nouns; some contain largely connectives. Some sentences are long and tightly wound; others are as hard and blunt as a hammer. Some combine events of contrasting sizes, like a sneeze and the fall of Rome; others set dogs at bears, link the abstract and the concrete, quality and number, relation and property, act and thing. In some worlds the banjo and its music are two banjos, in others all the instruments dissolve into their music, that into a landscape or a climate, thus finally, through the weather, to an ear.

The Humean sentence will reduce objects to their qualities, maintain an equality between them by using nonsubordinating conjunctions, be careful not to confuse emotion and reflection with perception, but at the same time will allow their presence in the same onward flow. Everywhere, Hume makes his world out of lists and collections. Some novelists, like I. B. Singer, for example, drain the mental from their books as if it were pus in a wound. Thoughts are rendered as public speech; there is recourse to journals; incidents and objects are presented always as the public might see them; and even inner temptations—lusts, hates, fears—receive embodiment as visibly material demons. Henry James's sentences are continuous qualifications, nuance is the core and not the skin; and the average idealist, proceeding with a similar scrupulosity, treats his entire work as the progressive exploration and exposure of a single subject. It would suit him if there were no ordinary periods, no real beginning or real end, if every word were an analytic predicate of one ultimate Idea.

Imagine for a moment we are making up a man, breathing life into a clay lung.

> He stood in the mud: long, thin, brown in his doctor's gown of fur, with his black flapped cap that buttoned well under his chin and let out his brown, lean, shaven and humorous face like a woodpecker's peering out of a hole in a tree.

What is the shape of Achilles' nose? what color were his eyes? Achilles is what Achilles does; he has no secret wishes, secret dreams; he has no cautiously hidden insides. Shall we make our man on that model, out of deeds? or shall we see him through his station: prince or clown, clerk or plumber, servant or secretary, general or priest? Shall we dress him in his features as Ford here puts Magister Nicholas Udal in his clothes? Whether a man has thick lips or thin, crafty ones or cruel, we can always count on Ford to tell us, though in other men's fictions many are lipless. The colon contrives to give the qualities which follow it to Udal's whole muddy standing, not to Udal and his form alone. Observe what happens if we remove it, and at the same time alter the order of our apprehension of these details:

> *He was long, thin, and brown in his doctor's gown of fur, with his black flapped cap that buttoned well under his chin and let out his brown, lean, shaven and humorous face like a woodpecker's peering out of a hole in a tree. He stood in the mud.*

The original passage is packed with possessives, the dominant relation is that of ownership, but the Magister need not own everything. Can we feel the effect of progressively loosening these ties, the clothing first, and then the features?

> *He stood in the mud: long, thin, brown in a doctor's gown of fur, with a black flapped cap that buttoned well under his chin and let out his brown, lean, shaven and humorous face like a woodpecker's peering out of a hole in a tree.*

> *He stood in the mud: long, thin, brown in a doctor's gown of fur, with a black flapped cap that buttoned well under a chin and let out a brown, lean, shaven and humorous face like a woodpecker's peering out of a hole in a tree.*

Perversely, let us let him own his clothes but not his face.

> *He stood in the mud: long, thin, brown in his doctor's gown of fur, with his black flapped cap that buttoned well under a chin and let out a brown, lean, shaven and humorous face like a woodpecker's peering out of a hole in a tree.*

It is not simply that our understanding of Udal changes; our understanding changes because Udal has become a figure in a changed world.

We might at first be inclined to think that style is a form of perception; that each sentence reveals the way the writer looks at the world—

for example, observe the differences between (1) We walked through the woods. The trees had leaves. The leaves were newly green. (2) We walked through the woods. New leaves greened the trees. (3) We walked the greening woods. (4) It seemed the greening woods walked while we stood.

—but strictly speaking style cannot be, itself, a kind of vision, the notion is very misleading, for we do not have before us some real forest which we might feel ourselves free to render in any number of different ways; we have only the words which make up this one. There are no descriptions in fiction, there are only constructions, and the principles which govern these constructions are persistently philosophical. The same, for that matter, is true of narration, dialogue, character, and the rest. Just as the painter's designs help make his object, the lines of the novelist offer no alternatives, they are not likely interpretations of anything, but are the thing itself.

4

Thus so many of the things which are false or foolish when taken to the world— in religion or philosophy—become the plainest statements of what's true when taken to fiction, for in its beginning *is* the word, and if the esthetic aim of any fiction is the creation of a world, then the writer is creator—he is god—and the relation of the writer to his work represents in ideal form the relation of the fabled Creator to His creation.

Once God was regarded as the cause of all, as the Great Historian with a plan for His people, the Architect, the Lawgiver, the principle of Good; so that if Mary sickened, the cause was God, and if Mary died, it was God who called her Home, and if anything happened whatever, it was ordained by Him, indeed it was counted on, by Him, from the beginning. He saw things, all things, plain—plainer surely than any novelist ever saw his story before a word of it went down. So that really, in this created world, there are no necessary beings, there are no categorical creatures, and events do not follow one another out of the past, because of the past, but everlastingly out of God, because of God. In a movie, too, where everything is predestined, the illusion of internal structure is maintained, as though one part of the film explained the occurrence of another. However, the director had the scenes shot; had them spliced as he desired; and the sensation that the villain's insult has provoked the hero's glove is an appearance often not even carefully contrived. In the story of Mary, if Mary dies, the novelist killed her, her broken heart did not. The author of any popular serial knows, as Dickens did, that to the degree he makes his world real to his readers, to that degree they will acknowledge his authorship; hold him responsible; and beg him to make the world good, although evil seems present in it; beg him to bring all to a moral and materially glorious close, in clouds and hallelujahs. Though such appeals may cause smiles in the sophisticated, they are appeals more rationally directed to the actual power than those, exactly parallel, delivered by the faithful in their prayers to God. The novelist is uncomfortable. He may enjoy his alleged omnipotence, his omniscience and omnipresence, but with it, spoiling it, is responsibility. What about all that perfection? Can he take upon himself this burden? Can he assure his readers that his world is good, whatever happens? He can explain evil no better than the theologian; therefore shortly the novelist who assumes the point of view of the omnipotent, omniscient, and omnipresent narrator begins to insist upon his imperfection; apologize, in a gentle way perhaps, for his cutpurses, whores, his murderers, and in general surrender his position. "I'm sorry Becky doesn't seem as sweet as she should, but what can I do about it? That's just how she is." "Well, I'm terribly sorry about all this sordidness, as sorry as you are," he may say, "but that's how the world is, and what am I, poor fellow, but a dime-store mirror held to it?" This is a sly device. And the worlds which the novelist creates are shortly deprived of their deities. At last the convention seems acceptable only if it's all in fun. God snickers and pushes parsons into ditches. And when the novelist begins to explain that, of course, omnipotence is artistically vulgar; that one must limit oneself to a point of view, he is insisting, for *his* world, upon the restriction of knowledge to the human, and often only to a few of these, and finally only to rare moments occurring in the best minds. He gives up his powers to a set of principles. He allows himself to be governed by them, not to govern, as if God stepped down in favor of moving mass and efficient causes, so to say: "This is not mine; I do not this; I am not here." Novels in which the novelist has effaced himself create worlds without gods.

Even outside books time passes. These days, often, the novelist resumes the guise of God; but he is merely one of us now, full of confusion and error, sin and cleverness. He creates as he is able; insists upon his presence and upon his wickedness and fallibility too. He is not sure about what he knows; his powers have no great extension; he's more imperfect than otherwise; he will appeal to us, even, for sympathy. Why not? He's of his time. Are there any deities who still have size?

An author may make up his own rules, like the god of the Deists, or take them from experience where he thinks he finds them ready-made; but the control which these rules exercise is little like that exercised by the laws of nature, whatever they are. The star-crossed lovers in books and plays are doomed, not because in the real world they would be, but because, far more simply, they are star-crossed. Simple slum conditions, as we know, do not so surely produce a certain sort as in novels they are bound to, and no amassing of detail is sufficient to ensure a perfectly determinate Newtonian conclusion. Authors who believe they must, to move their fictions, hunt endlessly through circumstances for plausible causes as they might hunt for them in life, have badly misunderstood the nature of their art—an enterprise where one word and one inferring principle may be enough.

As in a dice race, when we move over the squares with our colored disks, the dice impel us and the ruled lines guide. There are no choices. The position of each disk is strictly determined. We see the track, we know the throw, we can predict the new arrangement. Such a game is the simplest kind, and forms the simplest system. There is one rule of inference. Any principle that permits the rational expectation of some situation upon the occurrence of another is a principle of inference, and such a principle is called a rule when the conclusion to be inferred awaits an inferring power—a power that must be, therefore, ordered to its task—and is called a law when the inferring power acts, as it were, from within its premises. The form of the game, however, lies in number, the winner he who rolls the highest score; but this form is imaged out upon a table; disks describe the level of addition; and these are transmogrified by fancy into thoroughbreds, while the player, through this really peculiar evidence of the superiority of man, becomes the owner of a stable. The adding of the dice can be expressed in many ways. This simple system is the foundation of many more complicated ones. There are principles, one might call them, of embodiment, wherein the players are enjoined to treat the disks and the squared path as representing the units and the total of addition. There are yet other principles, here assumed, that call the squared-up path a track, the flat disks horses. The game may make these assumptions explicit, but if it does not, the player may imagine for himself any other suitable kind of linear contest.

When God abdicates, or at least sanctions a belief in the end of miracle, he gives over his rule to inference. For fiction, the rules can be as many as the writer wishes, and they can be of any kind he wishes. They establish the logic, the order, of his world. They permit us to expect one event will follow another, or one sentence another, or one word another. To the degree words, sentences, and, materially, things and happenings follow without rule, the world is a world of chance. Since no work can exhibit a conformity to principle so complete each word is, in its place and time, inevitable and predictable, all fictional worlds contain at least an element of chance, and some, of course, a very high degree of it. It is merely a critical prejudice that requires from fiction a rigidly determined order. Chance, too, is a kind of principle, and can be brought to the understanding of reason. In the natural realm, the principle of causality is often regarded as the inferring instrument. Causality, in general, makes out the possibility of predicting events from the evidence of others. Since the inferring power is thought to reside otherwise than in the observer, any particular expression of it is a law. When, as in the game above, it is impossible to predict the future organization of a system on the basis simply of its present state and its governing rules or laws, and when the prediction must await the unpredictable disclosure of further facts, for instance what the dice will read, then the system is a system based on chance. It must be borne in mind that the results of the game proceed inevitably from its nature, and that a system based on chance remains as beautifully systematic as any other. If what the fates decree must come to pass, chance can lie only in the way to it. Or each affair may be seen necessarily to unfold out of its past without anyone's being able to guess the ultimate consequences. Again, certainty and doubt about both end and means may be so shrewdly mixed, the reader is delightfully tossed between cruel suspense and calm inevitability. In the dice game, the players finger disks, but if the game, by its conventions, calls them horses, they are horses. However, to a fellow who, his disk dead even with the others, resolutely calls all disks, and only waits the adding up of his account, art must ever be a failure; for it can succeed only through the cooperating imagination and intelligence of its consumers, who fill out, for themselves, the artist's world and make it round, and whose own special genius partly determines the ultimate glory of it.

The causal relation itself may be logically necessary or psychologically customary, formal or final, mechanical or purposive. It may be divinely empowered or materially blind. Causality in fiction is usually restricted to the principle that controls the order of constructed events, considered separately from whatever rule may govern the placement of symbols, the dress of the heroine, the names of the characters, and so on, if any rule does govern them. An event, however, may be anything from the twitch of an eyebrow to the commission of adultery, and a cause, any event which leads beyond itself to another. The plot (to risk that rightly abused word) is composed of those events the novelist has troubled to freshly arrange as causes, as opposed to those he has thrown in for vividness, but which cause nothing, or those concerning which he has let nonfictitious nature have its way. Nonfictitious nature has its way about a good deal. If in a story it rains, the streets usually get wet; if a man is stabbed, he bleeds; smoke can still be a sign of fire, and screams can be sounds of damsels in distress. No novel is without its assumptions. It is important to find them out, for they are not always the same assumptions the reader is ready, unconsciously, to make. Hawthorne could count on more than Henry James, as James complained. Do we any longer dare to infer goodness from piety, for example, evil from promiscuity, culture from rank?

And has not the world become, for many novelists, a place not only vacant of gods, but also empty of a generously regular and peacefully abiding nature on which the novelist might, in large, rely, so to concentrate on cutting a fine and sculptured line through a large mass taken for granted, and has it now also seemed to him absent of that perceptive and sympathetic reader who had his own genius and would undertake the labor, rather easy, of following the gracious turns that line might take; so that, with all these forms of vacantness about him, he has felt the need to reconstitute, entire, his world; to take nothing, if he felt the spur of that conceit, for granted, and make all new, distinct, apart, and finally, even, to provide, within the framework of his vision, the ideal reader, the writer's words his mind and eyes?

5

The use of philosophical ideas in the construction of fictional works—in a very self-conscious and critical way, I mean—has been hastened by the growing conviction that not only do these ideas often represent conceptual systems of considerable complexity, they have the further advantage of being almost wholly irrelevant as accounts of the real world. They are, that is, to a great degree *fictional* already, and ripe for fun and games. Then, too, the novelist now better understands his medium; he is ceasing to pretend that his business is to render the world; he knows, more often now, that his business is to *make* one, and to make one from the only medium of which he is a master—language. And there are even more radical developments.

There are metatheorems in mathematics and logic, ethics has its linguistic oversoul, everywhere lingos to converse about lingos are being contrived, and the case is no different in the novel. I don't mean merely those drearily predictable pieces about writers who are writing about what they are writing, but those, like some of the work of Borges, Barth, and Flann O'Brien, for example, in which the forms of fiction serve as the material upon which further forms can be imposed. Indeed, many of the so-called antinovels are really metafictions.

Still, the philosophical analysis of fiction has scarcely taken its first steps. Philosophers continue to interpret novels as if they were philosophies themselves, platforms to speak from, middens from which may be scratched important messages for mankind; they have predictably looked for content, not form; they have regarded fictions as ways of viewing reality and not as additions to it. There are many ways of refusing experience. This is one of them.

So little is known of the power of the gods in the worlds of fiction, or of the form of cause, or of the nature of soul, or of the influence of evil, or of the essence of good. No distinction is presently made between laws and rules of inference and conventions of embodiment, or their kinds. The role of chance or of assumption, the recreative power of the skillful reader, the mastery of the sense of internal life, the forms of space and time: how much is known of these? The ontological significance of the subordinate clause, or the short stiff sentence regularly conjoined to more, or new words, or inversion—all passed over. Writers are seldom recognized as empiricists, idealists, skeptics, or stoics, though they ought—I mean, now, in terms of the principles of their constructions, for Sartre is everywhere recognized as an existentialist leaning left, but few have noticed that the construction of his novels is utterly bourgeois. No search is made for first principles, none for rules, and in fact all capacity for thought in the face of fiction is so regularly abandoned as to reduce it to another form of passive and mechanical amusement. The novelist has, by this ineptitude, been driven out of healthy contact with his audience, and the supreme values of fiction sentimentalized. The art of the novel is now a mature art, as constantly the source of that gratification found in the purest and profoundest contemplation as any art has ever been, and the prospect of a comprehensive esthetic that will provide for its understanding and its judgment is promising and grand. The novel is owed this. It has come, in darkness, far. But it will not stir farther until the appreciation of it has become *properly* philosophical.

DISCUSSION QUESTIONS

1. Gass begins by equating philosophy and fiction. What is your initial response to this affiliation? In your experience, are these kindred terms, or are they ways of thinking and writing that should be kept separate?
2. Gass's opening paragraph refers to several important philosophical ideas about the nature of existence. Are these philosophical terms and positions familiar to you? Where did you learn about them? In what ways can you think about these ideas as fictions, in the sense Gass describes?
3. In developing his argument, Gass asserts that "man" and "nature" are the characters used by philosophers in their exploration of existence and consciousness, and that the "soul" itself is "the philosopher's invention." What does he mean by this? Are you comfortable thinking about "man" and "nature" as characters and the soul as an invention? Why?
4. Gass claims that "the artist is not asked to construct an adequate philosophy, but a philosophically adequate world." What is the distinction he is trying to

make here? How does this relate to his earlier assertion that "truth . . . has antipathy for art"?

5. Gardner, earlier in this chapter, writes of fiction as "concrete philosophy." How does Gardner's definition differ in substance from Gass's reflections on fiction and philosophy? How would Gardner respond to Gass's idea that "a principle, encased in fiction has, most likely, not been thought of at all. It has been used"?

6. What is Gass's purpose in rewriting and analyzing multiple versions of the passage about Magister Nicholas Udal? How does this analysis lead to his assertion that "there are no descriptions in fiction, only constructions"?

7. Gass positions the fiction writer as a god, creating a world out of words, and then states that many fiction writers wish to avoid this power and responsibility. The result: "Novels in which the novelist has effaced himself create worlds without gods." What does this mean? Why is it important?

8. Toward the end of the essay Gass asserts that the novelist is "ceasing to pretend that his business is to render the world; he knows, more often now, that his business is to make one, and to make one from the only medium of which he is a master—language." Do you count yourself among the writers Gass describes? How did you come to this sense of your purpose?

ANNIE DILLARD

Fiction in Bits

Annie Dillard (b. 1943) has been Writer in Residence at Wesleyan University since 1987. She won the Pulitzer Prize for Pilgrim at Tinker Creek *(1974), was nominated for an LA Times Book Prize for* Living by Fiction *(1982), and was nominated for a National Book Critics Circle Award for* An American Childhood *(1987). In addition to her nonfiction, she has published poetry (most recently,* Mornings like This, *1995) and a novel (*The Living, *1992). Many of her essays reflect on the meaning of viewing life through a writer's eye.*

Many contemporaries write a fiction intended to achieve traditional kinds of excellence. Many others write a fiction which is more abstracted—the kind of fiction Borges wrote in *Ficciones,* or Nabokov wrote in *Pale Fire.* This latter kind of fiction has no name, and I do not intend to coin one. Some people call it "metafiction," "fabulation," "experimental," "neo-Modernist," and, especially, "Post-Modernist"; but I find all these terms misleading. "Post-Modernist" is the best, but it suffers from the same ambiguity which everyone deplores in its sibling term, "Post-Impressionist."

Recently a stranger from New York City sent me a green button, a big green button, which read: POST-MODERNIST. From his letter I inferred that he disliked Modernism, found it baffling and infuriating, and for reasons I could not fathom, included me on his team.

But Modernism is not over. The historical Modernists are dead: Kafka, Joyce, Faulkner, and also Biely, Gide, Malraux, Musil, Woolf. But one could argue—and I do—that diverse contemporary writers are carrying on, with new emphases and further developments, the Modernists' techniques.

I am going to use the dreadful mouthful "contemporary modernist" to refer to these contemporary writers and their fiction. I trust that the clumsiness of the term will prevent its catching on. I will also use the lowercase, nonhistorical term "modernist" loosely, to refer to the art of surfaces in general. The historical Modernists explored this art and bent it, in most cases, to surprisingly traditional ends. Transitional writers like Knut Hamsun, Witold Gombrowicz, and Bruno Schulz expanded its capacity for irony. Now various contemporaries are pushing it to various interesting extremes: Jorge Borges, Vladimir Nabokov, Samuel Beckett, and Robert Coover, John Barth, John Hawkes, William Burroughs, Donald Barthelme, Thomas Pynchon, Rudolph Wurlitzer, Thomas M. Disch, Alain Robbe-Grillet, Jonathan Baumbach, William Hjorstberg, and Flann O'Brien, Italo Calvino, Tommaso Landolfi, Julio Cortázar, Manuel Puig, Elias Canetti, and Carlos Fuentes.

TIME IN SMITHEREENS

Nothing is more typical of modernist fiction than its shattering of narrative line. Just as Cubism can take a roomful of furniture and iron it onto nine square feet of canvas, so fiction can take fifty years of human life, chop it to bits, and piece those bits together so that, within the limits of the temporal form, we can consider them all at once. This is narrative collage. The world is a warehouse of forms which the writer raids: this is a stickup. Here are the narrative leaps and fast cuttings to which we have become accustomed, the clenched juxtapositions, interpenetrations, and temporal enjambments. These techniques are standard practice now; we scarcely remark them. No degree of rapid splicing could startle an audience raised on sixty-second television commercials; we tend to be bored without it. But to early readers of Faulkner, say, or of Joyce, the surface bits of their work must have seemed like shrapnel from some unimaginable offstage havoc.

The use of narrative collage is particularly adapted to various twentieth-century treatments of time and space. Time no longer courses in a great and widening stream, a stream upon which the narrative consciousness floats, passing fixed landmarks in orderly progression, and growing in wisdom. Instead, time is a flattened landscape, a land of unlinked lakes seen from the air. There is no requirement that a novel's narrative bits follow any progression in narrative time; there is no requirement that the intervals between bits represent equal intervals of elapsed time. Narrative collage enables Carlos Fuentes in *Terra Nostra* to approximate the eternal present which is his subject. We read about quasars one minute; we enter an elaborated scene with Pontius Pilate the next. Narrative collage enables Grass in *The Flounder* to bite off even greater hunks of time and to include such disparate elements as Watergate, the history of millet, Vasco da Gama, a neolithic six-breasted woman, and recipes for cooking eel. Narrative collage enables Charles Simmons, in *Wrinkles,* artistically to fracture a human life and arrange the broken time bits on the page. And it enables Michael Ondaatje, a Canadian novelist, to include in his novel *The Collected Works of Billy the Kid* not only prose narration in many voices and tenses, but also photographs ironic and sincere, and blank spaces, interviews, and poems.

Joyce, 163 years after Sterne, started breaking the narrative in *Ulysses.* The point of view shifts, the style shifts; the novel breaks into various parodies, a question-and-answer period, and so forth. Later writers have simply pushed farther this notion of disparate sections. They break the narrative into ever finer particles and shatter time itself to smithereens. Often writers call attention to the particles by giving them each a separate chapter, or number, or simply a separate title, as Gass does in "In the Heart of the Heart of the Country." Donald Barthelme has a story ("The Glass Mountain") in which each sentence constitutes a separate, numbered section. All these cosmetics point to a narration as shattered, and as formally ordered, as a Duchamp nude.

If and when the arrow of time shatters, cause and effect may vanish, and reason crumble. This may be the point. I am thinking here of Robert Coover's wonderful story "The Babysitter," in which the action appears as a series of bits told from the point of view of several main characters. Each version of events is different and each is partially imaginary; nevertheless, each event triggers other events, and they all converge in a final scene upon whose disastrous particulars the characters all of a sudden agree. No one can say which causal sequence of events was more probable. Time itself is, as in the Borges story, a "garden of forking paths." In other works of this kind, events do not trigger other events at all; instead, any event is possible. There is no cause and effect in Julio Cortázar's *Hopscotch,* an unbound novel whose pages may be shuffled. There is no law of noncontradiction in Barthelme's story "Views of My Father Weeping." Barthelme writes the story in pieces, half of which examine a father's death and half of which depict the father, in the same time frame, alive and weeping.

Narrative collage, and the shifting points of view which accompany it, enable fiction to make a rough literature of physics, a better "science fiction" which acknowledges the equality of all relative positions by assigning them equal value. One extreme of this kind of fiction is an art without center. The world is an undirected energy; it is an infinite series of random possibilities. (Barthelme ends "Views of My Father Weeping" with a section which reads only "Etc.") The world's coherence derives not from a universal order but from any individual stance. God knows this is a common enough position. It is not really physics but ordinary relativism. (In literature, relativism need not be cynical; in "The Babysitter" and *Hopscotch* it is downright gleeful. Relativism is particularly suited to artists and writers, who, as a class, have often been dedicated to private vision anyway, and especially to the private vision of the world as a storehouse of manipulable ideas and things.)

Not only does time shift rapidly in contemporary modernist narrative; so does everything else. Space, for instance, is no longer a three-dimensional "setting"—the great house into which generations of little lords are born, the setting into which readers sitting in their own great houses can settle. Instead, space is, or may be, a public, random, or temporary place. Instead of being exotic, places may be merely alien—rucks in the global fabric where no one is at home. The action may occur all over the globe, with everywhere the same narrative distance, so that works of this sort (*V., Terra Nostra*) may have geographical breadth without emotional depth. (I am not speaking pejoratively here in the least; I mean merely to distinguish between sets of excellences.) The traditional novelist labors to render an exotic setting familiar, to put us at our ease in the Alps or at home in burning Moscow. But contemporary writers may flaunt their multiple, alien settings, as Pynchon does, or make of the familiar world someplace alien and strange, as Thomas M. Disch does with Manhattan. Narrative collage touches every aspect of the fiction in which it appears. The point of view shifts; the prose style shifts and its tone; characters turn into things; sequences of events abruptly vanish. Images clash; realms of discourse bang together. Zeus may order a margarita; Zsa Zsa Gabor may raise the siege of Orléans. In a recent *TriQuarterly* story, Heathcliff meets Chateaubriand on a golf course. These things have almost become predictable.

The use of narrative collage, then, enables a writer to recreate, if he wishes, a world shattered, and perhaps senseless, and certainly strange. It may emphasize the particulate nature of everything. We experience a world unhinged. Nothing temporal, spatial, perceptual, social, or moral is fixed.

This is the fiction of quantum mechanics; a particle's velocity and position cannot both be known. Similarly, it may happen that in the works of some few writers, the narrative itself cannot be located. Events occur without discernible meaning; "mere anarchy is loosed upon the world." What if the world's history itself, and the events of our own lives in it, were as jerked, arbitrary, and fundamentally incoherent as is the sequence of episodes in some contemporary fictions? It is, these writers may say; they are.

THE EGG IN THE CAGE

I would like to pause here to talk about artistic integrity. Distinctions of value need to be made among contemporary modernist works, as among all works, and I think they can be made most pointedly here, where technique fades into meaning and raises the issue of integrity.

Interestingly enough, contemporary modernist fiction, unlike traditional fiction, has no junk genres. Like poetry so long as it is serious, fiction, so long as it is witty, is almost always assumed to be literature. Well, then, it has already passed the qualifying rounds and must go on to the finals: Does it have meaning? For any art, including an art of surface, must do more than dazzle. Is this art in the service of idea? And it is right here that *some* contemporary modernist fiction can claim, Yes, it does mean; it recreates in all its detail the meaninglessness of the modern world. And I cry foul. When is a work "about" meaninglessness and when is it simply meaningless?

Clearly the shattering of what we feel as the rondure of experience (or of what, according to this theory, we who were born after 1911 have never felt as the rondure of experience), and the distant and ironic examination of the resultant fragments, serve, in Robbe-Grillet's terms, "to exile the world to the life of its own surface"—and, by extension, to express our sense of exile on that surface. If meaning is contextual, and it is, then the collapse of ordered Western society and its inherited values following World War I cannot be overstressed; when we lost our context, we lost our meaning. We became, all of us in the West, more impoverished and in one sense more ignorant than pygmies, who, like the hedgehog, know one great thing: in this case, why they are here. We no longer know why we are here—if, indeed, we are to believe that large segments of European society ever did. At any rate, our contemporary questioning of why we are here finds a fitting objective correlative in the worst of the new fictions, whose artistic recreation of our anomie, confusion, and meaninglessness elicits from us the new question, Why am I reading this?

We judge a work on its integrity. Often we examine a work's integrity (or at least I do) by asking what it makes for itself and what it attempts to borrow from the world. Sentimental art, for instance, attempts to force preexistent emotions upon us. Instead of creating characters and events which will elicit special feelings unique to the text, sentimental art merely gestures toward stock characters and events whose accompanying emotions come on tap. Bad poetry is almost always bad because it attempts to claim for itself the real power of whatever it describes in ten lines: a sky full of stars, first love, or Niagara Falls. An honest work generates its own power; a dishonest work tries to rob power from the cataracts of the given. That is why scenes of high drama—suicide, rape, murder, incest—or scenes of great beauty are so difficult to do well in genuine literature. We already have strong feelings about these things, and literature does not operate on borrowed feelings.

As in the realm of feeling, so in the realm of intellect. Naming your characters Aristotle and Plato is not going to make their relationship interesting unless you make it so on the page; having your character shoot himself in the end does not mean that anyone has learned anything; and setting your novel in Buchenwald does not give it moral significance. Now: may a work of art borrow meaning by being itself meaningless? May it claim thereby to have criticized society? Or to have recreated our experience? May a work claim for itself whole hunks of other people's thoughts on the flimsy grounds that the work itself, being so fragmented, typifies our experience of this century? Can a writer get away with this? I don't think so.

But let me state the question more sympathetically, from the writer's point of view. The writer's question is slightly different. If the writer's honest intention is to recreate a world he finds meaningless, must his work then be meaningless? If he writes a broken book, is he not then a bad artist? On the other hand, if he unifies a world he sees as shattered, is he not dishonest? All this is an old problem for any writer, for a traditional one as well as a contemporary one. Stated broadly, the question is, What is negative art? What can it be? What can a writer do when his intention is to depict seriously a boring conversation? Must he bore everybody? How should he handle a dull character, a hateful scene? (Everyone knows how the hated voice of a hated character can ruin a book.) Or, in the big time, how can a writer show, as a harmonious, artistic whole, times out of joint, materials clashing, effects without cause, life without depth, and all history without meaning?

There are several strategies which may ameliorate these difficulties. A writer may make his aesthetic surfaces very, very good and even appealing, in the hope that those surface excellences will impart to the work enough positive value, as it were, to overwhelm its negativity. Better, he may widen his final intention to include possibilities for meaning which illuminate, without relieving, suffering: but this solution, the writing of tragedy or of contemporary art whose intentions are wider than those posited, does not address the problem. The only real solution is this, which obtains in all art: the writer makes real artistic meaning of meaninglessness the usual way, the old way, by creating a self-relevant artistic whole. He produces a work whose parts cohere. He imposes a strict order upon chaos. And this is what most contemporary modernist fiction does. Art may imitate anything but disorder. The work of art may, like a magician's act, pretend to any degree of spontaneity, randomality, or whimsy, so long as the effect of the whole is calculated and unified. No subject matter whatever prohibits a positive and unified handling. After all, who would say of "The Waste Land" that it is meaningless, or of *Molloy,* or *Mrs. Bridge?* We see in these works, and in traditional black works like Greene's *Brighton Rock* and Lowry's *Under the Volcano,* the unity which characterizes all art. In this structural unity lies integrity, and it is integrity which separates art from nonart.

Let me tread shaky ground in order to insert a note from René Magritte on this business of integrity. Any juxtaposition may be startling. Narrative collage is a cheap source of power. An onion ring in a coffin! Paul of Tarsus and Shelly Hack! We can all do this all day. But in the juxtaposition of images, as in other juxtapositions, there is true and false, says Magritte. Magritte says we know birds in a cage. The image gets more interesting if we have, instead of a bird, a fish in the cage, or a shoe in the cage; "but though these images are strange they are unhappily accidental, arbitrary. It is possible to obtain a new image which will stand up to examination through having something final, something right about it: it's the image showing an egg in the cage."

Now, what do we make of this curious assertion of Magritte's, that surrealist images may be right or wrong? What can be right about a surrealist image? I am certainly not going to endorse as an artistic criterion Magritte's vague, emotional phrase "something right about it." But I do endorse his notion that the right image will "stand up to examination." After all, there is nothing too mysterious about the rightness of an egg's replacing a bird. The two have met. In other words, the "something right" which "will stand up to examination" is ordinary unity. Notice that Magritte's surrealism by no means intends to traffic in "accidental" or "arbitrary" images. He uses these words to damn. Must arbitrariness always be damning? Must it forever be out of bounds not as a subject but as a technique? I think so.

Let me insert here a regret that criticism has no other terms than "device" and "technique" for these deliberate artistic causes which yield deliberate artistic effects. In painting and in music, the word "technique," at least, has a respectable sound; but in fiction, and especially to laymen, both "device" and "technique" sound sinister, as though writers were cold-blooded manipulators and gadgeteers who for genius substitute a bag of tricks. They are; of course they are. But the trick is the work itself. The trick is intrinsic. One does not produce a work and then give it a twist by inserting devices and techniques here and there like acupuncture needles. The work itself is the device. In traditional fiction the work is device made flesh; in contemporary modernist fiction the work may be technique itself or device laid bare.

All this is not to say that the fragmentation of the great world is the only theme of narrative collage: far from it. These techniques—abrupt shifts, disjunctive splicings and enjambments of time, space, and voice—are common coin. Almost all contemporary writers, including writers of traditional fiction, use them toward any number of different ends. For that matter, the historical Modernists themselves used them for various, often traditional ends. In Joyce's *Ulysses,* in Faulkner's *The Sound and the Fury,* the use of segmented narrative deepens the reader's sense of the fictional world and its complex characters and scenes. The technique serves the works' other themes, as it does in Garrett's *Death of the Fox,* Ellison's *Invisible Man,* Lessing's *The Golden Notebook,* and Durrell's *Alexandria Quartet.* And even when a work's theme is fragmentation, the work may itself be unified, and the fragmentation may not be bad news; James and many other writers have celebrated the world's "blooming, buzzing confusion."

Note, then, that the fragmentation of narrative line may be, and usually is, as formally controlled as any other aspect of fiction. There is nothing arbitrary whatsoever about fragmentation itself. In fact, as a technique it may elicit *more* formal control than a leisured narrative technique which imitates the thickened flow of time in orderly progression, if only because it requires the writer clearly to identify the important segments of his work and skip the rest. No charming narrative dalliances prevent our seeing his scenes as parts of a whole; no emotional coziness lulls our minds to sleep.

The virtues of contemporary modernist fiction are literary, are intellectual and aesthetic. They are the solid excellences of complex, formally ordered pattern. Most contemporary modernist fiction, and the best of it, does not claim these virtues *and* the incidental virtues of realistic fiction as well. You do not find Calvino promoting "verisimilitude"; you do not read Nabokov as a document of the times. This is as it should be. I bring up the question of integrity here only because it is here that a writer may most readily fool himself—always an attractive possibility. On one hand, sophisticated, hurried readers continue to judge works on the sophistication of their surfaces. On the other hand, our culture continues to pay lip service to the incidental and dull virtues of realism. So a writer may combine the two sets of excellence inappropriately. He may fool himself into reproducing the broken, sophisticated-looking forms of good contemporary modernist fiction without its unified content, in the hope that the narrative technique, *as an end in itself,* has an intrinsic significance. It not only looks good, it is "realistic." It is "social criticism." He may fool himself into shirking the difficult, heartbreaking task of structuring a work of art on the grounds that art is imitation (all of a sudden) and a slapdash fiction imitates a seriously troubled world.

But I am exaggerating, and speaking here more in theory than in fact. I am pummeling an unnamed straw man, a straw author, who composes, like Dadaist Tristan Tzara, by stirring a hatful of scraps. I am certainly not thinking here of a great writer like Cortázar, or Coover. In fact, I know for certain of no such writer of fiction, and I'm afraid I would not name one if I did. Serious writers are not consciously dishonest. I mean only to mutter darkly that in the present confusion of technical sophistication and significance, an emperor or two might slip by with no clothes.

Anyone with wit and training can search a work for sense. And sense is by no means an obsolete virtue: sense, and not the skill to dazzle, is the basal criterion for art. Surface obscurity is, of course, by no means a sign of its absence. On the contrary, such obscurity usually proves to be smoke from some wonderfully interesting fire. We simply must not mistake the smoke for the fire. I am certain that much, if not most, of today's lasting fiction derives from contemporary modernist writers of integrity (writers like Nabokov, Borges, Beckett, Barth, Calvino). That other writers may produce fictional surfaces similar to theirs, but without their internal integrity, does not in any way dim their achievement. But someone must distinguish between art and mere glibness.

All we need are responsible readers who demand real artistic coherence from a work. And we need book reviewers who understand how literature works and do not forget their training when they read a dust jacket. After all, new, subtle, and intellectualized forms of sense demand, and must continue to produce, detailed critical effort. We need much more serious textual criticism of contemporary work—work to whose formal intentions publishers and reviewers are usually indifferent—and we need a wide forum for such criticism. It's a pity it's so dull. Nevertheless, such effort gave us Wallace Stevens and Nabokov; it must continue, undaunted by fluff, to locate the great work being produced today. (Or the philistines will get us, or the paperbacks won't.)

Let me conclude this excursus with a few bald assertions. Meaninglessness in art is a contradiction in terms. Meaning in art is contextual. What does a whale mean? A whale means whatever an artist can make it mean in a given work. Art is the creation of coherent contexts. Since words necessarily refer to the world, as paint does not, literary contexts must be more responsible to the actual world than painting contexts must be. That is, it is easily conceivable that a painted blue streak should represent a ship's hull in one painting and a curved arm in another.

But that fictional element in *Moby-Dick* had better be a whale or something mighty like one. The blue streak can hold up its end of the artistic structure in virtually any context, but whales belong at sea. Writers do not create whales; whales are known and given; you can only do so much with them. You would be hard put in your serious novel to make a whale stand for a repressive Middle Eastern regime, or baseball, or agriculture. You would violate the bonds of unity if you tried to force a serious narrative connection between a vicious whale and, say, Isabel Archer. It would be precious to yoke them together without just cause. It would be mere comedy. It would be painting a shoe in the cage.

In all the arts, coherence in a work means that the relationship among parts—the jointed framework of the whole—is actual, solid, nailed down. (Of course, a proper demonstration of valid connection among parts would require a full-scale exegesis of a text, an interruption which I am unwilling to suffer. There are solid readings of standard works. Reliable readings of intelligent lyric poetry usually demonstrate the relationship of parts very clearly, if only because the texts at hand are so small. I could refer the reader to, say, Bloom or Ellman on Yeats, Frye on Blake, Vendler or Sukenick on Stevens. In contemporary fiction, the *Hollins Critic* essays such as those collected in *The Sounder Few* give intelligent exegeses of contemporary texts.) In all the arts, coherence and integrity go hand in hand. One cannot toss onto one's canvas a patch of blue paint and hope one's friends like it or some clever critic finds a reason for it. Similarly, one cannot add the weight of idea to a piece of fiction by setting a whale swimming through it, or by inserting Adolf Hitler with a larding needle, or by scrambling the world's contents with a pen.

Contemporary modernist fiction, in fact, requires *more* coherence than traditional fiction does. For one of the things this new fiction does is bare its own structure. (How long a novel would *Pale Fire* be in the hands of Thomas Mann?) This fiction sees that the formal relationship among parts is the essential value of all works of art. So it strips the narration of inessentials: like Hugo's excursions into the history of all aspects of human culture, like the unities of time, space, and action, like emotion. It bares instead its structural bones, as *Pale Fire* does, and *Invisible Cities,* and *Ficciones;* it bares its structural bones, brings them to the surface, and retires. Those bones had better be good. If a writer is going to use forms developed by intelligent people, he should use them intelligently. It does not do to mimic results without due process. Traditional fiction has the advantage here, I think. In a conservative work well fleshed, we may not notice at once that the joints do not articulate, nor the limbs even meet the torso. There may in fact be so much flesh that the parts cohere as it were bonelessly. But it is easy to see, if we look, taped joints on a skeleton.

It is interesting that John Fowles rewrote *The Magus. The Magus* is in many ways a contemporary modernist piece of fiction—in its fantastic transfigurations, its object-like and grotesque characters, and its emphasis on the irrational. But the first edition of *The Magus*—now it can be told—was dishonest work, the relationship of whose parts was pleaded. Its structure collapsed at a touch. It is interesting that Fowles rewrote it because, I fancy, Fowles understood that in order to make his bid as an important writer he needed to set his house in order and redress his crimes against integrity.

At best, integrity and intelligence go hand in hand to ensure against laziness, false analogies, pleaded connections, and sleight of word. Integrity demands of intelligence that it forge true connections on the page. Intelligence calls for integrity for the challenge of it, and from intelligent respect for the audience of literature, and respect for the art of literature itself, and for its capacity to mean.

DISCUSSION QUESTIONS

1. Dillard begins by distinguishing the fiction she will discuss from fiction that aims for "traditional kinds of excellence." These are the excellences of the representational, or mimetic, fiction described by several writers in this chapter. What do you know about the writers Dillard lists as "contemporary modernists"? What are the features of their work in contrast to the features of traditional mimetic fiction?

2. What does Dillard mean by "narrative collage"? How does this technique relate to "various twentieth-century treatments of time and space" in the arts and sciences? What concepts or worldviews have you studied in the sciences and social sciences that seem to connect to the fiction writer's use of narrative collage?

3. How does Dillard's point about the "relativism" of narrative collage and shifting points of view relate to Gass's point about the contemporary novelist's refusal to act as god in the construction of fictional worlds?

4. Dillard asserts that "nothing temporal, spatial, perceptual, social, or moral is fixed" in narrative collage. Are you attracted, in your reading and your writing, to this absence of what might be considered the unities of more traditional fiction? Why? What in your personal experience and knowledge of history leads you toward or away from the technique of narrative collage?

5. What does Dillard mean by "artistic integrity"? By a "self-relevant artistic whole"? Do you agree with her that "no subject matter whatsoever prohibits a positive and unified handling"? Why?

6. Dillard to some degree attempts to reclaim the word "trick" from its negative connotations when she writes that "the work itself is a device." What does she mean by this, and how does she see a work of art transcending its nature as a trick, or device, to achieve meaning and integrity?

7. Dillard claims that "contemporary modernist fiction" aims for the "solid excellences of complex, formally ordered pattern" and not the virtues of "realistic fiction." Are these virtues and excellences necessarily antithetical? Why?

8. Dillard defines "coherence" in art in the following way: "the relationship among parts—the jointed framework of the whole—is actual, solid, nailed down." What does she mean by this? Is this too rigorous a demand for work that defies representation?

RAYMOND FEDERMAN

Fiction Today or the Pursuit of Non-Knowledge

Raymond Federman (b. 1928) is Distinguished Professor Emeritus at SUNY-Buffalo. Among his novels are Double or Nothing *(1971),* Take It or Leave It *(1976),* The Twofold Vibration *(1982), and* To Whom It May Concern *(1990). He has written two novels in French (*Amer Eldorado, *1974; and* La Fourrure de ma tante Rachel, *1996) and a memoir in German (*Eine Version Meines Lebens, *1993). He has also published poetry and important literary criticism, including* Surfiction: Fiction Now and Tomorrow *(1981) and* Critifiction: Postmodern Essays *(1993). In his own fiction and in his theoretical works on fiction, notably on Samuel Beckett, he emphasizes the central role of language, which in his view precedes meaning.*

Reality, whether approached imaginatively, or empirically remains a surface, hermetic. Imagination, applied to what is absent, is exercised in a vacuum and cannot tolerate the limits of the real

—SAMUEL BECKETT

TO BEGIN: some thoughts, pieces of thoughts—for one never knows where one's thoughts originate, and when these thoughts merge with those of others, where one's language begins and where it converges with that of others within the dialogue all of us entertain with ourselves and with others.

1. In the beginning was not MIMESIS (the art of imitation), but the necessity to achieve MIMESIS.

2. Artistic activity begins when man finds himself face to face with the visible world as with something immensely enigmatical. In the creation of a work of art, man engages in a struggle with Nature not for his physical but for his mental existence.

3. The reality of imagination is more real than reality without imagination, and besides reality as such has never really interested anyone, it is and has always been a form of disenchantment. What makes reality fascinating is the imaginary catastrophe that hides behind it.

4. Contemporary works of fiction are often experienced with a certain anxiety, not because they threaten to extinguish the novel or the short story as recognizable genres, but because they challenge the traditional bases of both cultural and aesthetic judgment. Literature has most often been accepted as culturally significant to the extent that it represents the exter-

nal world, either through the depiction of a socio/historical situation, or through the verbalization of psychological states. Much of contemporary fiction does not relate the reader directly to the external world (*reality*), nor does it provide the reader with a sense of lived experience (*truth*), instead contemporary fiction dwells on the circumstances of its own possibilities, on the conventions of narrative, and on the openness of language to multiple meanings, contradictions, paradoxes, and irony.

In other words, at the center of the discussion (or perhaps one should say, the controversy) which has been going on now for more than four decades about NEW (innovative/experimental) FICTION versus OLD (traditional/realistic) FICTION is the problem of REPRESENTATION, that is to say the relationship of fiction to reality and life: MIMESIS.

As soon as a work of fiction refuses deliberately TO REPRESENT the world (*to mirror reality*), or refuses TO EXPRESS the innerself of man (*to mirror the soul*), it is immediately considered a failure, quickly labeled experimental, and therefore declared irrelevant, useless, boring, unreadable, and of course unmarketable.

According to the traditional view of fiction, there lies at the base of a text (a novel, a story), like an irreducible foundation, an established meaning (A SOMETHING-TO-BE-SAID) constituted even before the work is completed. This preexisting meaning affects two domains: the SELF and the WORLD.

The manifestation of this established meaning is thus divided into two parallel ideas: the aspects of the self are expressed, the aspects of the world are represented. Although still dominant today in much of literature, this concept of a text, with its two key notions of expression and representation, is highly inconsistent.

It rose to its height in a precise historical period: the nineteenth century—an era too recent for the still-innumerable believers of the EXPRESSION/REPRESENTATION DOCTRINE to see how they fit into a long and obsolete tradition, but already an era too distant for its believers to have maintained any freshness of vision.

As we learned in our schoolbooks, two literary movements dominated the nineteenth century: ROMANTICISM dealt with expression, REALISM with representation. To oppose these two movements, as it is too often done in literature courses, in term-papers, dissertations, and manuals of literary history, is to hide the fact that Romanticism and Realism are really two faces of the same coin. Both subordinate the literary text to an already established meaning present in the world even before the poem or the novel is written. It is not by chance that Victor Hugo's poems which were called *"mirrors of the soul"* find a parallel in Balzac's novels which he himself called *"mirrors that one drags along the road of reality."* [The sarcasm here is not meant to demean the greatness and the relevance of Balzac's novels or Victor Hugo's poems—these writers lived and wrote in the nineteenth century; we live and write in the twentieth century, in fact almost in the twenty-first century. Our relation to the world (however real or unreal it may be) has undergone radical changes.]

This expression/representation doctrine is, of course, still with us, or at least it was the dominant and valid view of the literary act until the end of the EXISTENTIALIST ERA (sometime at the beginning of the 1950s). It is only with the advent of what has been called New Fiction, Antifiction, Metafiction, Postmodern Fiction, or what I prefer to call Surfiction, that this view began to be questioned, challenged, undermined, and even rejected.

In fact, one can consider the New Fiction that begins to take shape in the middle of the 1950s and which is still being written today in many parts of the world, as fitting into the POST-EXISTENTIALIST ERA, suggesting thereby that this New Fiction (*Nouveau Roman,* it was called in France in the 50s) turned its back on Reality, Life, and Man, or at least on the notion that fiction should only express or represent Reality, Life, and Man.

In order to understand how the New Fiction functions, and why it turned away from its own tradition, it is necessary to return for a moment to that EXISTENTIALIST ERA—that period which immediately preceded, traversed, and followed World War II—and examine its literary vision.

In 1947, Jean-Paul Sartre raised a crucial question for anyone seriously involved in literature as a creator, a critic, or simply as a student. He asked: What is Literature? (*Qu'est-ce que la littérature?*) Not only a question, but a lengthy essay which served first as an introduction to *Les Temps Modernes* (the literary journal Jean-Paul Sartre launched in 1947), and which subsequently became the volume entitled *Situations* II. At the center of this essay Sartre argued the question of literary commitment—engagement.

The whole problematic of the *Nouveau Roman* in France during the 1950s, but also of all literary activities since World War II anywhere in the world, can only be postulated in function of Sartre's fundamental concept of literary commitment—what he called *la littérature engagée.*

What did Sartre propose?

1. An optimistic and rationalistic conception of literary activities.
2. The book as a means of communication.
3. Literature as *une prise de position*—a stance on all moral, social, and political questions.
4. The writer as participating in the shaping of history.
5. Writing as a form of liberation, a force that liberates others from moral, social, and political oppression.

This is certainly a most noble set of propositions. It means that the writer can function within this set of rules only if he participates in history in the sense of a universal event relating to individual freedom. Therefore, the act of writing is accomplished within the narrow space of a relative possibility. The writers fulfills the essential demands of his function and of his art only when he unmasks our world—that world which is but an immense mechanism of injustices.

Since the writer cannot escape his time, he must embrace it. Literature, here and now, prepares the social and socialistic revolution [*one must remember that Sartre was writing at the time from a Marxist point of view*]. Literature, he went on to argue, becomes a conquest of total freedom for everyone. It prepares the freedom of the future.

These are indeed beautiful thoughts, and yet, in spite of their impact at the time, in spite of all the debates around them, the literature (and especially fiction) that followed these pronouncements, in France particularly, but everywhere else as well, did not respect Jean-Paul Sartre's ideas.

Instead of getting involved with the CRISIS OF CONSCIENCE and the CRISIS OF CONSCIOUSNESS which underline Sartre's proposal, the literature of the last forty-five years concerned itself with itself, with literature, with the crisis of literature, with the crisis of language and of communication, with the crisis of knowledge, and not with social and political problems—except for a few rare cases in specific places and situations (in Germany, for instance, at least for a decade or so following World War II, in South Africa, or in certain Latin American countries). Everywhere else, the novel per se—that is to say the New Fiction—turned its back on Jean-Paul Sartre and the Existentialist vision.

In fact, that New Fiction [*poetry, of course, had already done so more than a century ago when it was declared useless by the Bourgeoisie*] moved from a moral and ethical purpose to an aesthetic and formalistic level to tell us, to show us, to repeat endlessly, that writers write simply to reveal the impossibility of writing in a postmodern era.

Alain Robbe-Grillet, Michel Butor, Robert Pinget, Georges Perec, Claude Simon, Nathalie Sarraute, and many others (including the great Samuel Beckett) in France; John Barth, John Hawkes, William Gass, Donald Barthelme, Robert Coover, Ronald Sukenick, Walter Abish, and many others (including myself, I suppose), in the United States; but also Italo Calvino, Julio Cortázar, Jorge Luis Borges, Severo Sarduy, Jürgen Becker, Peter Handke, B. S. Johnson, Christine Brooke-Rose, and many others all over the world (the Western world), seemed to be more concerned with the problems of writing their books, of letting the difficulties of writing fiction transpire in the fiction itself, rather than commit themselves to the problems of Man and of the injustices of society.

But this is not new. This deliberate refusal to confront social consciousness in favor of the crisis of literature goes way back to the beginning of the century: to Marcel Proust, certainly, in fiction, and to Mallarmé, in poetry. Proust who wrote a fifteen volume novel (over three thousand pages) to ask himself what it meant to write a novel; Mallarmé who, in questioning the act of writing poetry, dismantled conventional prosody and brought poetry to an impasse of self-negation from which it has not been able to extricate itself. However, Proust and his contemporaries managed to escape the failure implicit in their undertaking, whereas the new novelists seem to make of failure an occasion, or, as Samuel Beckett so well exemplified in his work, to reveal that to be a writer is to be willing to admit the inevitability of failure.

But the fact that failure is an indeniable aspect of contemporary art had already been stated, quite forcefully and movingly, in 1923, by a young, unknown French poet in a series of letters he wrote to Jacques Rivière, the editor of a French magazine (*La Nouvelle Revue Française*) who had rejected some of his poems. I mean, of course, Antonin Artaud whose poems had been refused by Jacques Rivière. The correspondence between Artaud and Rivière remains an important set of documents concerning the crisis of literature in the twentieth century.

Artaud had written in one of his poems:

> All communications are cut
> in front
> behind
> all around
> and the last ties which still cling to man must be cut
> we are without roots

And in one of the letters to Jacques Rivière he states: "I suffer from a frightening sickness of the mind. My thoughts abandon me—from the simple fact of thinking to the exterior fact of materializing thoughts into words, there is something that destroys my thoughts, something that prevents me from being what I could be, and which leaves me . . . in suspense."

Suddenly literature becomes the explanation of why the writer cannot write, why he constantly confronts the failure of expression and communication, why he can no longer represent the world faithfully and truthfully.

This is indeed the dilemma which many writers encountered throughout the first half of the twentieth century, especially those who were considered avant-garde: James Joyce, Franz Kafka, Louis-Ferdinand Céline, André Gide, Thomas Mann, John Dos Passos, William Faulkner, and Jean-Paul Sartre himself. Even though these writers wanted to affirm human dignity, they were forced to do so at times in a somewhat fragmented and seemingly incoherent style. However, these writers, and many others too, starting with Proust, managed to transfer their dilemma to their characters, and not to the writing itself, as is the case in much of the New Fiction.

It is Edouard, the fictitious novelist of André Gide's *Les Faux-monnayeurs (The Counterfeiters)* who confronts the crisis of writing and as such becomes a pathetic, almost tragic figure, while Gide, the real novelist, pretends playfully to have relinquished his responsibility toward the novel and its characters. It is Philip Quarles, in Aldous Huxley's *Point Counter Point,* who struggles with the creation and failure of fiction while the real author laughs at him. And there are similar writers-protagonists in novels by Thomas Mann, James Joyce, Louis-Ferdinand Céline who confront the failure of their own fictitious world. Even Roquentin, in Sartre's *La Nausée,* eventually abandons out of despair the book he is writing.

But if Antonin Artaud expressed, in a kind of lucid madness, the writer's dilemma, if his own works, which he called "these incredible rags," reveal the obstacles, denounce the limits, pinpoint the lacks, expose the inadequacies of language, they do so with such lucidity, that ultimately Artaud found in failure a reason to go on writing. In other words, like many of his contemporaries, he pursued his work with clairvoyance in the most opaque region of imagination.

Nevertheless, from Proust to Beckett, there is a feeling that something is wrong with literature, something is wrong with the act of expressing. "There is no communication," writes Beckett in 1930 in his monograph on Proust, "because there are no vehicles of communication." And even Sartre points to this crisis of communication when he writes at the beginning of his 1947 essay:

> There has been a crisis of rhetoric, then a crisis of language. Most writers have now resigned themselves to being mere nightingales. Most writers now insist that the secret goal of all literature is the destruction of language, and to reach this goal one merely needs to speak to say nothing.

Sartre, of course, is being sarcastic here, but this statement almost reads like a manifesto for the New Fiction. However, in spite of all the anguish, of all the anxiety of literature in the first half of the twentieth century in facing up to its crisis, it is the New Fiction (and to some extent the New Theater which received the unfortunate name of THEATER OF THE ABSURD) which made the most homogeneous effort to demystify and expose the problem, and destroy those social and cultural reflexes which kept literature blind to its own crisis.

How can the writer, then, in the light of what I have just stated, confront the human condition? How can the writer today cope with his subject? That is to say reality, Man, and social injustices. He can either follow Sartre's suggestion and become a social worker of literature, and simply write political pamphlets [or make speeches standing on top of a garbage can, as Sartre himself did in 1968, during the failed student uprising]; or else he can stop writing and become a politician [mayor of New York City, as Norman Mailer once tried], or Minister of Cultural Affairs [as André Malraux did in order to give Paris a face-lift], or flirt with the possibility of becoming a member of the government [as Günter Grass repeatedly attempted for the past forty years or so]. Or else, the writer confronts the real problem, the crisis of literature today, at the risk of losing his audience, and of locking himself into pure formalism.

Baffled by the world in which he lives, the writer is plunged into a state of anguish—intellectual anguish—because he does not comprehend that world any more, or rather because the more he knows about the world the less it makes sense. The writer knows nothing or comprehends nothing because there is nothing more to know or comprehend, or rather because there is too much to know and comprehend. In any event, absolute knowledge, like absolute truth, no longer exists. This does not mean, however, that the contemporary writer has become a nihilist, as many antagonistic critics of the New Fiction have claimed. Nihilism implies that there is nothing, and that's it. Whereas in our present state of intellectual anguish we realize that there is either too much to know, hence the confusion, or nothing more to know, hence the impossibility and futility of writing in the same old forms, but this is no cause for despair. In the impossibility of literature today, the writer also discovers the necessity of going on with literature, not simply to affirm a knowledge which is constantly slipping away, but to make of literature an act of survival.

Since the Greeks, literature has constituted itself as the vehicle of knowledge in the form of apologies, commentaries, amplifications on other texts, decorations or explanations of knowledge. In other words, literature was an affirmation of faith, of certitude in knowledge. Literature was in fact knowledge, and therefore:

> Most works of fiction achieved coherence and meaningfulness through a logical accumulation of facts about specific situations and, more or less, credible characters. In the process of recording, or gradually revealing mental and physical experiences, organized in an aesthetic and ethical form, these works progressed toward a definite goal—the revelation of knowledge. To read a novel was to learn something about the world and about man.

This statement is quoted from *Journey to Chaos* [a book I published in 1965, devoted to the fiction of Samuel Beckett], in which I go on saying that "Beckett's novels seem to progress in exactly the opposite direction, retracting knowledge, canceling knowledge, dragging us slowly and painfully toward chaos and meaninglessness."

This is also the case with most works of contemporary fiction known as avant-garde or experimental. The more pages we accumulate to the left as we read a novel, let's say by Alain Robbe-Grillet [*Jealousy,* for instance] or Walter Abish [*Alphabetical Africa*], the less we seem to know. As we read we encounter repetition after repetition, the text circles upon itself, cancels itself, and instead of moving toward a resolution or a conclusion, it seems to stumble relentlessly toward a gap at the center of the book, toward a GREAT HOLE. Thomas Pynchon's *Gravity's Rainbow* also leads us toward deliberate confusion and chaos. There are many such contemporary novels that make a shamble of traditional epistemology, and do so with effrontery and even playfulness, as for instance my own novel *Take It or Leave It*.

Therefore, the question can be asked: can there be a literature that refuses to represent the world or to express the inner-self of man? The entire oeuvre of Samuel Beckett is but that. Molloy (that grandiose figure of postmodern fiction, in Beckett's novel by that title) seems to be speaking for contemporary writers when he says:

> For to know nothing is nothing, not to want to know anything likewise, but to be beyond knowing anything, to know you are beyond knowing anything, that is when peace enters into the soul of the incurious seeker.

Today's New Fiction seeks to avoid knowledge deliberately, particularly the kind of knowledge that is received, approved, determined by conventions. In order to succeed (paradoxically one might say) in this pursuit of non-knowledge, the New Fiction invents its own reality, cuts itself off from referential points with the external world. The New Fiction affirms its own autonomy by exposing its own lies: it tells stories that openly claim to be invented, to be false, inauthentic; it dismisses absolute knowledge and what passes for reality; it even states, defiantly, that reality as such does not exist, that the idea of reality is an imposture.

Ronald Sukenick, one of the leading experimental fictioneers in the United States, has one of his characters (himself a novelist) state in a collection of stories appropriately entitled *The Death of the Novel and Other Stories:*

> Fiction constitutes a way of looking at the world. Therefore I will begin by considering how the world looks in what I think we may now begin to call the contemporary post-realistic novel. Realistic fiction presupposes chronological time as the medium of a plotted narrative, an irreducible individual psyche as the subject of its characterization, and, above all, the ultimate concrete reality of things as the object and rationale of its description. In the world of post-realism, however, all of these absolutes have become absolutely problematic.

> The contemporary writer—the writer who is acutely in touch with the life of which he is part—is forced to start from scratch: reality does not exist, time does not exist, personality does not exist.

What replaces knowledge of the world and of man is the act of searching (researching even) within the fiction itself for the implications of what it means to write fiction. This becomes an act of self-reflection, and therefore fiction becomes the metaphor of its own narrative progress. It establishes itself as it writes itself. In other words, fiction now becomes a continual probing of its own medium, but a probing that cancels, erases, abolishes whatever it discovers, whatever it formulates as it is performed.

In his novel entitled *Out*, Ronald Sukenick [not the real author, but the mythical author-protagonist by that name] states: "I want to write a novel that changes like a cloud as it goes along." In my own novel *Take It or Leave It*, the narrator whose name is Federman replies to Sukenick: "I want to write a novel that cancels itself as it goes along."

These two statements suggest a kind of writing which negates whatever transitory conclusions it makes, and in fact both novels illustrate their own system of self-cancellation, and playfully acknowledge their denial of absolute knowledge—*Out* by a process of diminution and disappearance, that of the count-down; *Take It or Leave It* by a process of digression and erasure, described in the novel as the leapfrog technique.

To some extent these novels function like scientific research whereby one experiment after another abolishes the truths of yesterday. And it is true that more and more we have come to recognize that modern art cancels itself as it is created. The Tinguely machine is set in motion in order to destroy itself in front of the viewers. The white canvas of Abstract Expressionism pretends to deny its own existence. Avant-garde music abolishes itself into discordance or silence. Concrete poetry empties itself of meaning, while New Fiction writes itself into nonsense and non-knowledge, or to play on the title of a Beckett text: fiction seeks LESSNESSness.

Modern Art and New Fiction reveal that we exist in a temporary situation, surrounded by temporary landscapes. Faced with this transitory aspect of life and of the world, literature confronts its own impossibility. But since writers go on writing (fiction or poetry) in spite of this impossibility, it can also be said that literature, nonetheless, continues to search for new possibilities. It searches, within itself, for its subject, because the subject is no longer outside the work of art, it is no longer simply Nature or Man.

As a result we now have poems of poetry, theater of theater, novels of novel. For instance, the poem/explication of John Ashbery and Francis Ponge; the play-within-the-play of Jean Genet; the novel in spiral [*en abîme*] that circles around its own interrogations of John Barth, Walter Abish, Michel Butor, Julio Cortázar. But going even further, novels are written without characters (George Chambers, Maurice Roche, Georges Perec), and even without pronominal persons (Philippe Sollers, Samuel Beckett, Raymond Federman). There now exists a literature that appropriates objects rather than inscribe subjects; a literature that plays tricks on its readers (Harry Matthews, Vladimir Nabokov, Italo Calvino); a literature that empties itself of all the old pretensions, postures and impostures; a literature that seems exhausted and yet refuses to die—a LITERATURE OF EXHAUSTION, as John Barth called it in his 1968 seminal essay.

This crisis, however, did not reveal itself in our time with the advent of the New Fiction. It began to be felt in the middle of the nineteenth century—first as an existential crisis and then as an epistemological crisis. All the great thinkers and philosophers since the middle of the last century tried to offer means of solving the crisis—means of giving a sense of stability and continuity, and even a sense of permanence to a world that was falling apart: Darwin with the theory of evolution; the Positivists such as Ernest Renan and Auguste Comte with their affirmation of facts; Henri Bergson with the notion of intuitive thought based on movement and duration; Albert Einstein with his theory of relativity; Bertrand Russell with logical anatomism; the Phenomenologists with their insistence on beingness; and closer to us the Existentialists with their idea that existence precedes essence. Nietzsche was perhaps the only thinker to admit a rupture, and to proclaim a fragmentation of the world and of man's vision of the world.

Many artists and writers too attempted to preserve that vision of the world as a continuous, stable, and fixed succession of events. Realism affirmed logical and sequential continuity of experience, and Naturalism went even as far as demonstrating how man is predetermined by heredity, environment, and climate. However, in some cases, the great artists and writers of the end of the last century and of the twentieth century used this crisis as a source of inspiration. Consequently, fragmentation, incoherence, discontinuity, montage, collage, nonsense, chance happening, automatism, abstraction, stream of consciousness, and so on, became the governing elements of great art in the twentieth century.

Painting, through Impressionism, Cubism, and Constructivism blurred the lines of the real, and eventually reached total abstraction, that is to say the total erasing of reality. In poetry, symbolist poets such as Rimbaud, Lautréamont, Mallarmé (at least in France) dismantled conventional forms and poetic language, and after them the Dadaists, the Futurists, the Surrealists, and the Imagists, forced the entire logic of discursive language to fall apart. In fiction the progress (or perhaps one should say the process) was slower, because realism (the great imposture of illusionism) held fiction captive, except in a novel such as James Joyce's *Finnegans Wake* which outrageously blurred meaning by dislocating words and syntax to become a gigantic verbal edifice of unreadability.

In other words, at the same time as the world becomes more and more unintelligible, artists, poets, novelists realize that the real world is perhaps somewhere else—AILLEURS says the French poet Henri Michaux in a book by that title. And even if the world is not ELSEWHERE, it is a world no longer to be known, no longer to be expressed or represented, but to be imagined, to be invented anew.

The real world is now to be found in language, but not in the conventional, syntactical discourse that connected fiction to reality—the known world, the coherent, continuous, expressible world where, supposedly, words and things stuck to each other. On the contrary, the real world is now inside language, and can only be recreated by language, or what Rimbaud called *l'alchimie du verbe*. In our present world, words and things—*LES MOTS ET LES CHOSES,* as Michel Foucault so well demonstrated—no longer stick to each other, because language too is an autonomous reality.

Of course, not everyone is willing to accept this new conception of THE WORLD WITHIN THE WORD (as William Gass proposes in his collection of essays by that title), not all writers are willing to recognize a world without a preexisting meaning—a world of non-knowledge. The Positivists (and they are still very much present among us) want to stabilize knowledge, and consequently stabilize language at the same time. But this is a false premise. Logical Positivism wants to make sense out of the world, but faced with the limits of reality, it sets limits to language. "The limits of my world," wrote Wittgenstein, "are the limits of my language. What cannot be said cannot have meaning." Wittgenstein's statement is obviously meant as an anti-metaphysical proposition, but nonetheless it rationalizes language.

The New Fiction, on the contrary, rather than accepting the limitations of the possible, proposes no limits for language into the impossible, even if that language becomes contradictory or irrational. Indeed, the language of the New Fiction reaches beyond the rational, where the real and the imaginary, past and future, conscious and subconscious, and even life and death are no longer dichotomous. The New Fiction no longer opposes what is communicable to what is not communicable, what makes sense to what does not make sense, for there is as much value in making nonsense as there is in making sense. It is only a matter of direction.

Many characters in the New Fiction—or what I prefer to call the WORD-BEINGS of fiction—exist beyond reality as we know it, beyond life even, in a kind of absurd post-life condition, and in a totally illogical temporality and spatiality, free of all contradictions. As they wander in this liberated time and space (in novels such as *Cosmicomics* and *T/Zero,* by Calvino, or *How It Is* and *The Lost Ones,* by Beckett), these characters no longer need to rely on reason or memory to govern their activities since they exist only as beings made of words—the words of their fiction.

The impossible becomes possible in the New Fiction because language escapes analytical logic. It is a language which accepts and even indulges in contradictions; a language that plays with repetitions, permutations, neologisms, puns; a language that dislocates conventional syntax while designing a new typography, and in so doing renders the world even more unintelligible.

How, then, can the contemporary writer be *engagé*—socially and politically committed—since to be *engagé,* in the old Sartrean sense, there must be an intelligible and recognizable world, a world of stable and accepted values? To a great extent, the reason why Sartre's idea of a literary commitment failed is because he wanted all writers to agree on a system of moral, social, and political values, therefore denying the possibility of exploration and innovation into other systems. However, the one aspect of Sartre's thought that remains valid today is that of freedom, but a freedom which is not strictly and necessarily inclined socially, politically, or morally. It is above all, for today's writers, a linguistic freedom—a freedom of speech, one might say—a freedom to be able to say or write anything and everything, in any possible way. In this sense, this linguistic freedom to explore the impossible becomes as essential and as subversive as what Sartre proposed some forty-five years ago.

Of course, one can always argue that since there is nothing to know, then there is nothing to say. Or, as Robert Pinget once put it: "What is said is never said since one can always say it differently." And it is true that much of the New Fiction builds itself out of its own linguistic incapacity to express what cannot be expressed, and as such seems to make itself while unmaking itself. But since nothing is said, since nothing can be said, or since it can always be said differently, writers are now freed from what was denying them, what was negating them, and what was determining how they should write.

As far back as 1956, in a controversial essay entitled "A Future for the Novel," Alain Robbe-Grillet emphasized the absurdity and the impossibility of saying the world:

> The world is neither significant nor absurd. It IS, quite simply. That, in any case, is the more remarkable thing about it. And suddenly, the obviousness of this strikes us with irresistible force. All at once the whole splendid construction collapses; opening our eyes unexpectedly, we have experienced, once too often, the shock of this stubborn reality we were pretending to have mastered. Around us, defying the noisy pack of our animistic or protective adjectives, things ARE THERE. Their surfaces are distinct and smooth, intact, neither suspiciously brilliant nor transparent. All our literature has not yet succeeded in eroding their smallest corner, in flattening their slightest curve.

Suddenly in this impossibility of saying the world appears the incredible possibility that everything can be said now, everything is on the verge of being said anew. This explains why in much of New Fiction one finds long meandering sentences, delirious verbal articulations, repetitions, lists, questions without answers, fractured parcels of words, blank spaces where words should have been inscribed—an entire mechanism of linguistic montage and collage. It is as though the language of fiction was taking an inventory of itself in an effort to grab things as they are, to reassess the world, but without imposing a pre-established signification upon it.

That is why much of the New Fiction often appears like a catalogue of WHAT IS in the world, or HOW IT IS (as Beckett entitled one of his novels), and no longer what we thought we KNEW of the world. There is, therefore, behind this project an effort of sincerity—a search for a new truth; a genuine effort to reinstate things, the world, and people in their proper place—in a purified state. That, in my opinion, is also a form of literary commitment. This extreme exigency of truth constitutes the honor and the purpose of the New Fiction at a time when literature (or what passes for literature on the best-sellers lists) remains all too often an inconsequential network of illusions that perpetuates an obsolete vision of the world.

This lucidity, this search for a new truth was already present in the work of Artaud in the form of self-consciousness which forced him to reply to those who reproached him for attaching too much importance to language:

> You don't see my thought . . . I know myself because I am my own spectator, I am Antonin Artaud's spectator . . . I am the one who has most clearly felt the

bewildering confusion of his language to its relation with the world. I am the one who has best marked the moment of its most intimate, imperceptible shifts.

This questioning of one's existence and one's language becomes in the New Fiction its highest justification—if a justification is needed.

Reduced to non-sense, non-signification, non-knowledge, the world is no longer to be known or to be explained, it is to be EXPERIENCED as it is now recreated in the New Fiction, but no longer as an image (a realistic representation) or as an expression (vague feelings) of what we thought it was, but as a newly invented, newly discovered reality—a real fictitious reality.

DISCUSSION QUESTIONS

1. Federman, like Dillard, addresses fiction that doesn't aim to represent the material world or reproduce lived experience. What does he put in place of mimesis as fiction's aim?
2. What does Federman highlight as the flaw in the hybrid tradition of Romanticism (devoted to expression) and Realism (devoted to representation)? How does he see these two traditions working together to establish the goals of mimetic fiction? Do you agree that this tradition is "obsolete"? Why?
3. What are the important elements of Sartre's literature of engagement, as described by Federman? What historical circumstances do you think contributed to Sartre's insistence on the writer's engagement with history, politics, and social activism?
4. Federman claims that writers of "New Fiction" rejected Sartre's literature of engagement and instead concerned themselves with aesthetic and formalistic issues. Why did these writers do this? What historical events account for Federman's claim that these writers acknowledged the "inevitability of failure" of their literary work? What kind of failure is he referring to?
5. To what does Federman attribute "the impossibility of literature today"? How does this impossibility paradoxically affirm "the necessity of going on with literature" in order to survive?
6. Federman writes about experimental work: "Fiction now becomes a continual probing of its own medium, but a probing that cancels, erases, abolishes whatever it discovers, whatever it formulates as it is performed." Why would writers choose to pursue this "non-knowledge"?
7. Like Gass, Federman places much emphasis on language, not reality, as the substance of the world of fiction. He further claims that "there is as much value in making nonsense as there is in making sense." How does this bring him into conflict with Dillard's insistence on artistic integrity and coherence? What are the excellences Federman would substitute for Dillard's?
8. How does Federman's sense that "New Fiction" catalogues "WHAT IS" and "HOW IT IS" shift our experience of fiction? How would Flannery O'Connor and Gardner, among others, respond to this description of fiction's relationship to the world?

PHILIP STEVICK

Form, Antiform, and Neoform:
Verbal Collage

Philip Stevick (b. 1930) taught at Temple University from 1965 until his recent retirement. He is the author of several important studies of traditional and contemporary fiction, including The Theory of the Novel *(1967),* The Chapter in Fiction: Theories of Narrative Division *(1970), and* Alternative Pleasures: Postrealist Fiction and the Tradition *(1981).*

Implicit in the ideas of fictional form current in every period is a set of counter ideas, or, if not ideas, impulses, that complicate ideas of form by asserting ideas of antiform. Fielding, for example, defined fictional form by analogy with historical form; he obviously believed in his analogy and to some extent fulfilled it; yet he consistently mocked the formula, writing novels, finally, that are not very much like the models of historical writing he and his readers knew. Fielding also made large claims for ideas of organic form long before the phrase became widely used, defining fictional form by reference to transcendent aesthetic categories such as unity, contrast, proportion, coherence, and consistent relevance to the general design. Yet he permitted himself to write such chapter titles as "A discourse between the poet and player; of no other use in this history, but to divert the reader" or "Containing little more than a few odd Observations." Fielding was more aware than most novelists since his time of the relation of concept to counterconcept. And part of the pleasure of reading him derives from watching the splendid self-irony with which he plays off the conviction that he has discovered the nature of the thing he is doing against the equal but antithetical conviction that the thing he is doing is forever escaping his description of it.

Every novel, merely by virtue of its constant contact with the amplitude and multifariousness of daily experience, contains material tangential or even antithetical to its apparent formal principles, whether those formal principles are stated by the author, assumed by the readers, or formulated after the fact by critics. Yet it is customary for writers and critics to suppress a sense of the contradictoriness of prose fiction, assuming, for purposes of description, that it is a much more constricted art than it is. Neither Dickens nor his readers or critics have ever quite come to terms with the vast number of different things that happen in *Bleak House,* some of which surely escape even the most comprehensive statement of that novel's formal principles. And even works that strike us as pursuing aesthetic unity much more relentlessly than Dickens ever did—*Madame Bovary,* for example—contain material not altogether relevant to any formulable statement of their form. No one would wish away Charles Bovary's cap, in the first chapter of

Madame Bovary. But the mimetic premises of Flaubert's novel leave the reader quite unprepared for that grotesque effusion, as if Flaubert had permitted the imagination of Gogol to intrude into his second page. And the rhythms of that novel, its allocation of interest and its solicitation of our sympathy, insofar as these can be abstracted from the novel, intellectualized, and put into words, provide us with no justification for that strange but wonderful paragraph.

Certain works of the modernist period do display within themselves a recognition of the contrasting claims of form and the simultaneous wish to violate form. *The Counterfeiters* is an example of one kind. Again and again in the *Notebooks,* Gide writes that the intention of his novel, indeed the very imperatives of fictional form at the time of his writing, compel him to do one thing; yet almost against his will the very passage he has just written and upon which he comments in his *Notebooks* does something else. "It can be said of almost all 'rules of life' that it would be wiser to take the opposite course than to follow them."[1] Joyce's *Ulysses* is the clearest example in English, though an example of a much different kind from Gide's, of the contrast between the two claims—to define form, to contemplate form, to pursue formal control, to take formal imperatives with such seriousness that the design of the novel becomes a veritable synthesis of narrative history, and to permit clutter, mess, muddle, trivia, the false lead, the unexplainable event, the irrelevant detail. It has been a commonplace of Joyce criticism almost since the appearance of *Ulysses* that countless local details appear in the book not because of formal demands but because they existed in *Thom's Official Directory* of 1905. And it has been a commonplace of Joyce criticism that the Man in the MacIntosh is a figure full of portent, a motif promising incremental meaning, a structural device promising symbolic reference, but that the Man in the MacIntosh is finally devoid of significance, a nullity, meaning anything or nothing, a device, as I would put it, of antiform. True to his idea of the nature of fiction, true to the particular architectonics of his novel, Joyce was also true to Dublin, and Dublin, not being organized according to aesthetic principles, compelled the inclusion of details that, even now, after half a century of obsessive Joyce scholarship, confound the expositors.

Recent fiction, in a remarkable number of cases, rather than suppressing the principle of antiform, extends the implicit examples of Gide and Joyce and the earlier examples of Fielding and Sterne by embracing it. The best-known passage of Barthelme's *Snow White,* for example, is the questionnaire that Barthelme inserts into the middle of his book. "1. Do you like the story so far? Yes ( ) No ( ) 2. Does Snow White resemble the Snow White you remember? Yes ( ) No ( ) . . . 5. In the further development of the story, would you like to see more emotion ( ) or less emotion ( )?"[2] *Snow White* is a strange and unpredictable book. Yet, however one apprehends its form, a questionnaire is not intrinsic to it. Other novels *assimilate* diverse materials. Perhaps it would be possible to say that even *Ulysses* finally assimilates all of its clutter and trash to its highly formulaic whole. But the questionnaire is not assimilated into *Snow White.* It is simply, perversely, there.

In lesser known books, versions of the same impulse appear. The snips and scraps of Charles Newman's *The Promisekeeper* or Constance Urdang's *Natural History,* for example—newspaper articles in narrow-column format, graffiti, handbills, signs, and diagrams—are not exactly assimilated, like realistic detail in Balzac, or like Joyce's clutter. Their appearance is perverse and discontinuous. In a different way, Stanley Elkin's *The Making of Ashenden* and Don DeLillo's *End Zone* change their formal premises as they go, not merely evolving as many traditional novels do, but transforming themselves into something not implicit in their beginnings. The first begins with the self-congratulatory reflections of an affluent, overrefined, almost Jamesean character and ends with his copulation with a bear. The second begins with an account of a football team in an East Texas college and ends as a meditation on global politics and eschatology. The most stunning examples of the embracing of formal contrariety are in the short fiction of John Barth in *Lost in the Funhouse.* Variously, within the same fictions—stories "about" Ambrose and his family; love and death; the life and times of the Eastern shore in the 40s; the technique of writing codified by a naïf; the technique of writing agonizingly faced by Barth; the relationship between print and reader; the relationship between pleasure and pain; the possibilities of continuity, coherence, and form; the vitality of narration; and the exhaustion of narration—they embrace, like nothing in prose fiction since Sterne and nothing except Sterne, the principle of formal perversity.

What I am beginning to describe is a narrative art far more audacious than the kind for which Dos Passos and others have borrowed the term *montage* from the art of the film. A French word meaning, roughly, *editing,* it has taken on an uncommon power, partly because of the associations the word has come to have with Eisenstein's great *Potemkin,* partly because of the theoretical debates between Eisenstein and Pudovkin concerning the nature and effect of sequence in film, partly because, whatever Eisenstein said or did, there *is* something uncanny and mysterious about the way in which the mind perceives the relationship between shots in a film.

Clearly Flaubert, in the scene at the agricultural fair in *Madame Bovary,* cuts, edits, or makes a montage with his unmodulated movement from the auctioneer selling swine, to Emma and Rodolphe professing love, even though there were no motion pictures to teach him how to arrange that scene. Anachronistically describing Flaubert's technique as a montage tells us something important about his art because it reminds us—all of us being initiates in the experience of film—of the way in which Flaubert structures and implicitly comments by the sequence of his "shots." Yet Flaubert's scene or, to choose the most obvious example from the period of film, the newsreel section of Dos Passos's *U.S.A.* uses discontinuities in the service of continuities. Both passages carry forward an unmistakable sense of thematic selectivity; and what they begin to be, they become. For all of the audacity in its movement from shot to shot, one cannot imagine *Potemkin* containing, apropos of nothing in particular, a brief sequence showing a camel, a moving van, a rising soufflé. For all of the audacity in its movement from auction to Emma, one cannot imagine Flaubert's extended scene including, apropos of nothing in particular, a brief account of the climate of Tierra del Fuego. And, for all of the audacity in its movement from one news event to another, one cannot imagine Dos Passos including, apropos of nothing in particular, a description of a man sleeping.

Going beyond the fictional techniques that can be named by analogy with montage, the fiction I describe goes to exactly that point at which the violation of the implicit formal premises of a work by apparently antithetical elements becomes, in fact, normative. If what seem antiformal elements do become normative and take over the work, what we have is a new kind of form, one for which Aristotelean descriptions will not apply. Such fiction is not likely to have a beginning, a middle, and an end. It is not likely to fulfill long-term expectations. And it is not likely to structure itself, in any valid sense, upon a plot. As so often happens when the descriptive terminology of one art suddenly seems deficient, it is natural and useful to begin to reconstruct a terminology by borrowing from the description of another art—not film this time, useful as montage was for a time, but from the graphic arts. It is a move which, in this case, carries the authority of Barthelme.

In an interview the interviewer quotes an earlier sentence of Barthelme's, in which he says that "The principle of collage is the central principle of all art in the twentieth century in all media." Would he expand on that sentence? asks the interviewer. "I was probably wrong," replies Barthelme, "or too general. I point out however that New York City is or can be regarded as a collage, as opposed to, say, a tribal village in which all of the huts are the same hut duplicated. The point of collage is that unlike things are stuck together to make, in the best case, a new reality. This new reality, in the best case, may be or imply a comment on the other reality from which it came, and may be also much else. It's an *itself,* if it's successful: Harold Rosenberg's 'anxious object,' which does not know whether it's a work of art or a pile of junk."[3] It is one of the perils of the use of collage as an analogy, as Barthelme illustrates, that it expands so as to seem to include almost everything. New York is a collage. Fiction is a collage. The top of one's desk is a collage. The contents of one's pockets is a collage. Still, the analogy persists in the criticism of recent fiction, not merely because Barthelme used it but because it is a usable start in the restructuring of formal description.

Techniques that might, with some justification, be called collage have, of course, been around for a long time. *Anatomy of Melancholy* is an assemblage of one kind, and in our century, portions of *The Waste Land* and the *Cantos* are assemblages of another kind. American literature of the twentieth century sometimes shows the impulse to assemble. Evan Connell's *Points for a Compass Rose* is a splendid gathering of bits and pieces; Paul Metcalf's *Genoa* splices together fictive-autobiographical material from contemporary experience, materials from Melville's life, the words of his fiction, the words of his critics, the words of Columbus, bits of geographical and navigational information. And Agee, in *Let Us Now Praise Famous Men,* wishes that instead of describing the clothing of a sharecropper's family, he could paste a shoe itself into the text, an impulse to collage that, at that point, transcends words altogether. But all of these earlier acts of assemblage either declare themselves marginal and eccentric, as Connell's certainly does, or their acts of assemblage exist to serve larger purposes. Clearly the analogy *verbal collage* seems most appropriate when it names a fictional technique that is central to the aesthetic motives of its period and when the principle of assemblage is, radically and irreducibly, the principle of the whole work.

Just as clearly, the analogy verbal collage means something rather different from those modernist techniques so brilliantly discussed by Joseph Frank as "spatial form."[4] The intersecting simultaneities of *Ulysses* and the transcendence of time in Proust do result, no doubt, as Frank argues they do, in the kind of spatialization of literature that he names, a replacement of the sequentiality that has always been assumed to be of the nature of literature by the nonsequential sense of design that has always been assumed to be of the nature of the visual arts. Still, nobody would call *Swann's Way* a verbal collage. For, despite the transmutation of narrative into something that begins to resemble painting in its spatial effect, the images and events of Proust's novel are still apprehensible as elements of a linear design, continuous and coherent.

The principle of collage does seem to be clearly the case in Barthelme's story "The Party." "I went to a party and corrected a pronunciation," the story begins.

> The man whose voice I had adjusted fell back into the kitchen. I praised a Bonnard. It was not a Bonnard. My new glasses, I explained, and I'm terribly sorry, but significant variations elude me, vodka exhausts me, I was young once, essential services are being maintained. Drums, drums, drums, outside the windows. I thought that if I could persuade you to say "no," then my own responsibility would be limited, or changed, another sort of life would be possible, different from the life we had previously, somewhat skeptically, enjoyed together. But you had wandered off into another room, testing the effect on members of the audience of your ruffled blouse, your long magenta skirt. Giant hands, black, thick with fur, reaching in through the windows. Yes, it was King Kong, back in action, and all of the guests uttered loud exclamations of fatigue and disgust, examining the situation in the light of their own needs and emotions, hoping that the ape was real or papier-mache according to their temperaments, or wondering whether other excitements were possible out in the crisp, white night.
>
> "Did you see him?"
>
> "Let us pray."
>
> The important tasks of a society are often entrusted to people who have fatal flaws. Of course we tried hard, it was intelligent to do so, extraordinary efforts were routine. . . . Zest is not fun for everybody. I am aware that roles change. Kong himself is now adjunct professor of art history at Rutgers, co-author of a text on tomb sculpture; if he chooses to come to a party through the window he is simply trying to make himself interesting.[5]

I have argued for a progression in which fiction has moved from a willing acceptance of a certain antiformal perversity to a new arrangement in which the undermining of the ostensible formal premises of a work become no longer perverse intrusions but norms. Still, judging from Barthelme's story, the collage that results is far from either a willed randomness or a kind of arty detachment from experience, mere word games, design for its own sake. However startling its movements from sentence to sentence and image to image, Barthelme's story begins to lay out a series of motifs and antitheses rather more controlled and less random than the continuity of a realistic art story—for example its alternation between references to energy and zest on the one hand and to fatigue and boredom on the other; or its modulations between the domestic interior within which the party takes place and the "outside"; or in its modulation among at least three levels of cultural experience, the level of impersonal officialese, the level of personal encounter, and the level of the intersection of person and mass culture. Far from being random, Barthelme's collage is also far from being pure design. What it seeks to be, I think, and what it seems to be for most readers is a stylized and intensified version of parties, those parties being, in experience, of the nature of collage—disjointed, fragmentary, full of social formulas, chic tastes, and ritual phrases. In that sense, the principle of collage curiously serves the classic function of mimetic art by devising a structural vehicle that indicates the rhythms, the feeling tone, and the perceived content of the experience itself.

Visual collage can be made of anything, chair caning, egg shells, rusty nails, paint, ticket stubs; and the finished composition need not suggest anything about the areas of experience from which those assembled objects came. *Verbal collage,* on the other hand, can only be made successfully of those scraps that belong to areas of experience which seem to be collages already—a commercial strip of urban roadway, an evening of television, a recollection of a political campaign, a large party. Visual objects do not carry with them the same organizational imperatives that words do. A piece of chair caning and a ticket stub, placed beside each other, "mean" nothing because no prior value determines that they should be perceived in any relation to each other. Syntax, rhetorical order, and linear narration, however, *are* prior imperatives; and, thus, if they are violated, their violation will seem purposefully expressive of disorder.

Structurally, a visual collage implies these principles. First, implicit in the enterprise is the wish to make textural shifts, moving from paint, to cloth, to pasted paper, to wicker, to cemented, three-dimensional objects. Second, implicit in the enterprise is a wish to make the most of a certain interplay between the hidden and the manifest. In realist painting, to be sure, as in experience, objects are concealed behind other objects. In a picture containing a sunset, however, the sun, although receding behind a hill, would not be spoken of as being *hidden* by the hill. In a Rauschenberg collage, on the other hand, one recognizes a replica of a newsprint photograph of John Kennedy, hidden in part by the willful superimposition of other elements of the composition. So it is with visual collage in general. We do not see scraps and fragments but whole artistic gestures such as parallel paint marks, overlapping as it were, so that each element appears as a recognizable whole, partly obscured by the overlapping effect of one or more adjacent elements. Third, implicit in the enterprise is a wish to move tonally between elements that are serious and elements that are frivolous, elements that seem to belong to the realm of pure aesthetic—nonsignificant shapes and paint marks—and elements that are chosen to seem especially quotidian, scraps from a newspaper, theater tickets, found objects. Fourth, implicit in the enterprise is a wish to make a gestalt out of objects that, by their nature, would seem to be irreconcilable, disparate, and totally heterogeneous, making them, by a sheer force of the aesthetic imagination, into a whole.

Barthelme's "The Party" does present structural rhythms for which existing literary description is plainly inapplicable and for which the analogy of collage is both an apt descriptive tool and an enabling fact of aesthetic history, since without the rich possibilities exploited by the visual media "The Party" would not have come to exist. Nothing in fictional theory prepares us for that movement in the story toward the sentence "Drums, drums, drums, outside the windows," a sentence suggestive both of one of the forgettable clichés of B movies of the forties and of the not altogether fanciful imagination of an apocalyptic tribal life beyond the apartment in which the party takes place. The rhythms of collage plainly do describe that narrative movement, not simply in the abruptness of the shift but also in the textural difference in moving from the bureaucratese of the sentence before it to the overcivilized, personal analysis of the sentence following.

For those characteristic shifts between the elements of collage, shifts at once of subject matter, tone, style, and relation to experience, I suggest the word *juncture*. In a visual collage, one is always aware of its junctures because one takes in the composition as a whole and every part insists upon its willed, pasted, juxtaposed quality. In a verbal collage, on the other hand, the junctures must be frequent enough to keep us aware of its mode of composition, since a verbal collage is experienced sequentially. The early sections of Waugh's *A Handful of Dust* are remarkably discontinuous. But each section is some pages long. And thus the remarkable absence of transition that marks the movement from section to section in Waugh's novel occurs at wide intervals, spaced between continuous passages of conventional narration; and, although the effect is disconcerting, it is not of the nature of collage. This suggests a principle: the most audacious and startling junctures can occur in a fiction without that fiction seeming unconventional; the degree to which a fiction seems of the nature of collage will seem, more than the result of any other force, directly proportional to the frequency of the juncture. Among contemporary novels, for example, Evan Connell's *Mrs. Bridge* makes a stark juncture between each section, those sections being generally between one and three pages. The effect is of a scrapbook, perhaps, but not a collage. It is a wonderful novel, rich, wise, witty, and intricately observed. But it does not seem to occupy the same ground with clearly postmodernist novels. Renata Adler's *Speedboat* makes a juncture at the end of nearly every paragraph, which is to say that almost no two consecutive paragraphs are "about" the same events or even tap the same cultural level with the same stylistic and tonal resources. If for no other reason than the rhythms of its junctures, it seems technically postmodernist, although less relentlessly and audaciously so than Barthelme's "The Party." Different purposes are being served and different sensibilities are on display in the fiction of Jerzy Kosinski, Leonard Michaels, Walter Abish, and Ronald Sukenick. But all of these, and many more, find a common usefulness in the manipulation of comparably unmodulated movements.

To make a fiction, we have always thought, is to tell a story, although we have learned that one can tell it from the inside or the outside, backward or forward, implicitly or directly, with a set of stylistic resources that is self-consistent or mixed and various. What is now obvious is that one can make a fiction not by telling a story at all but by a verbal activity that is analogous to cutting and pasting. What the eighteenth-century novelists knew and acknowledged, and what the nineteenth-century novelists knew and suppressed, is that, having begun to tell a story, one allows, necessarily, a certain latitude of effect and a certain range of inclusiveness that sooner or later violates the implicit principles of the story one began to tell. What certain fiction of our own time proposes is a form in which the violations of principle are perpetual, the form continually redefined, so that discontinuity is the norm and linearity is superseded by the arrangement of fragments: What is important, however, is less the discovery of the formal possibility than the discovery of its power. For, as Pynchon's monumental collages surely demonstrate, the result of cutting and pasting, far from being a mere exercise in arrangement, becomes, as does fiction in all times and places that finds its own formal ways to its own vision, a way of knowing.

NOTES

1. André Gide, *The Counterfeiters* (New York: Modern Library, 1951), p. 450.
2. Donald Barthelme, *Snow White* (New York: Bantam, 1968), p. 82.
3. Joe David Bellamy, *The New Fiction: Interviews with Innovative American Writers* (Urbana: University of Illinois Press, 1974), pp. 51–52.
4. "Spatial Form in Modern Literature," *Sewanee Review* 53 (1945):221–40, 433–56, 643–53.
5. *Sadness* (New York: Bantam, 1974), pp. 57–58.

DISCUSSION QUESTIONS

1. Stevick further contextualizes Dillard and Federman's explorations of twentieth-century fiction by stating that in every historical period writers have challenged "ideas of form by asserting ideas of antiform." In your study of literature, have you been drawn to these challenges to form? Which of your favorite writers or other artists have worked with antiforms?
2. Dillard suggests in "Fiction in Bits" that contemporary modernists cannot pursue contrasting sets of excellences, Formalist and Realist. Stevick's analysis of Joyce's *Ulysses* asserts that Joyce was true both to artistic form and to the actual setting of Dublin. Do you think that this dual allegiance is possible? How can a writer accomplish this?
3. What does Stevick mean by "formal perversity" in his description of Barth's "Lost in the Funhouse"? What other works strike you as examples of this strategy of assimilating varied materials into a piece of fiction?
4. Stevick discusses "montage" as a film technique that still serves a kind of narrative continuity. Like Dillard, he foregrounds the term "collage," quoting Barthelme about the nature of the term. What is the essence of "collage," according to Barthelme?
5. Stevick offers the term "juncture" to describe the "characteristic shifts" between elements of verbal collage. How do these junctures help guide the reader through this kind of fiction? In what ways can a story using collage teach the reader to read the story? What "way of knowing" does this kind of structure lead to?

WRITING ACTIVITIES

1. Sketch several ideas for short stories, keeping in mind Flannery O'Connor's advice that it's better to start with a character who interests you than with a preconceived action you need a character to perform. Begin by thinking of a particular character; then outline a sequence of events that you feel would explore and reveal the character.

2. Write a scene involving a character (possibly one from the activity above) that foregrounds the sensory dimension of the character's world. In other words, emphasize what can be seen, heard, smelled, and touched in a particular setting that the character spends time in.

3. Hawthorne speaks (fancifully, as we might expect) about the frame of mind a writer must be in to produce a certain style of fiction—specifically the dreamy, shadowy, eerie frame of mind that produces Romantic fiction. Try his exercise: seek out a specific setting to put yourself in a specific frame of mind, and then see whether the scene you write flows from that frame of mind.

4. Try your hand at writing a brief allegory, preferably one better than the one that Scholes admits is "pretty feeble." Based on the experience, be prepared to say what advantages the allegory as a form has over the more "realistic" story.

5. Take a short passage from one of your stories and play with its language in the way Gass plays with the passage from Ford Madox Ford. What happens when you move things around? Does your sense of the meaning of your work—the way it communicates with the reader—change as you do this. How does this kind of work make the language more visible as a form of philosophy? Put together some juxtapositions of people, places, and things in a narrative collage that you feel creates "true" meaning, in the way Dillard describes it in "Fiction in Bits."

6. Take one of your "traditional" stories and break it into parts; then put the story back together into some kind of coherent form that has "artistic integrity." As you work with the narrative collage, what kinds of choices do you have to make?

7. Write an imitation of the section of Barthelme's "The Party" printed in Stevick's essay on verbal collage. Begin with a recognizable setting, perhaps, but then let go of linearity and other kinds of unity you're used to pursuing. What happens? Do you notice "motifs and antitheses" in your collage? How can you revise to create a pattern out of these motifs and antitheses? Does your imitation ultimately seem to represent experience? How?

8. Write a short story in three forms: the realistic short story, the fabulistic tale, and the fragmented experimental nonstory. How do the elements of the story change as you work with the conventions of the genre?

CHAPTER 2

Craft and the Elements of Fiction

Fiction writers work with certain elements the way painters work with oil paint and canvas, color and light, proportion and perspective, or (as the title of this chapter's first section implies) the way scientists work with the literal "elements" of the periodic table and their properties. On the face of it, the elements of fiction are simple: little imitation people move through little imitation lives, or "characters" move through "plots." At the same time, the ways in which these elements are endlessly recombined are the stuff of magic. Look at the way daVinci can create the illusion of vast three-dimensional space on a small two-dimensional rectangle of shape and color. Look at the way nature can put together carbon and nitrogen to create human beings. To say that the elements of fiction are simple is to speak the truth, but only part of the truth.

The first section's selections lay out with great simplicity the elements of fiction, and then proceed to complicate them in ways that may be new to some readers. The writers in this section give us a vocabulary that is still the most common one we have for talking about this "craft" aspect of fiction. For example, in excerpts from his classic *Aspects of the Novel,* E. M. Forster tells us the difference between "flat" and "round" characters (a distinction that will be echoed by R. V. Cassill in the second section), and between "story" and "plot." Elizabeth Bowen spells out what now seems obvious: fiction is made of characters, action, dialogue, movement toward a conclusion, a meaning. Wayne Booth begins with the usual categorizations of "point of view" into first and third person, but he goes on to show how many more points of view there actually are and how their various natures are determined by a balance of "distances" among character, author, and reader. Leon Surmelian goes into detail about the difference between "scene" and "summary," the characteristics and uses of each. The writers in this section tend to present the tools in the toolbox and talk about what they're good for, without much commentary about how they are used well or poorly. Forster defends the need for "flat" characters, for example, and Surmelian talks about the usefulness of "summary," two elements fiction writers are often told to avoid. Eudora Welty rounds out this unit with reflections on how a writer's manipulation of the passage of time in a story, or the creation of the illusion that time is passing, relates to the meaning a reader may find in a narrative.

The second section focuses on the element of "character," which is generally acknowledged by fiction writers to be the beginning and the end of good fiction. All other elements relate back to character and often grow out of character. R. V. Cassill shows how character is revealed by other elements, such as description, dialogue, and point of view. Robin Hemley goes into more detail than other writers in this chapter about the relationship between "real life" and fiction, especially between "real people" and fictional characters, illustrating how he "transforms" the stuff of life into art. David Huddle agrees that "character" is where fiction touches life most directly and gives both principles and examples from classic fiction of the ways in which characters are "brought to life" through masterful use of the elements of fiction.

If the writers in the first section avoid judgments on the uses and misuses of the elements of fiction, the writers in the third section have no such reservations. It sometimes seems that writers talk more about what can go wrong in a story than about what must go right. Much of their advice may be lists of warnings, caveats, and "thou-shalt-nots." Kit Reed lists "what to leave out and what to put in" based on her belief that beginning or amateur writers often provide information that is simply miscellaneous, unnecessary, and scattered, mostly because the stories they write lack any real "focus" or "consistency of intention." Ben Nyberg emphasizes that stories can "fail before they start" because of fatal flaws in the most basic planning of setting, character, plot, and theme. Jerome Stern presents a series of "don'ts," many of them hilarious, most without explanation, but qualifies what he says with a final "don't": "Don't believe any of the don'ts above." In other words, heed the warnings of these experienced writers (and readers) of fiction, but take these "thou-shalt-nots" for what they are worth, since, as Stern reminds us, "these don'ts can be your pleasure ground." Applying what you learn from these essays can help you not only avoid certain pitfalls in your own fiction but become a more insightful critic of the fiction of others. That is, you'll be able to express a more coherent idea about why a story is or isn't "working" for you.

The fourth section, in contrast to the third, offers positive rather than negative advice on revising stories to correct the inevitable weaknesses that creep into even the strongest early drafts. Jesse Lee Kercheval offers two checklists to use in examining your fiction on both the "macro" level (conflict, point of view, characterization) and the "micro" level (description, dialogue, transitions in time). David Madden focuses on point of view, agreeing with Wayne Booth that all the other basic features of fiction flow from this crucial element—and so revision should begin with it. David Michael Kaplan discusses what he considers the final step in revising fiction: attention to details of language. He, too, offers checklists, this time a list of "stylistic glitches."

Perhaps the most important lesson from the essays in this chapter is that the whole of a work of fiction is greater than the sum of its parts. A writer must learn, master, and apply the "craft" aspect of fiction, just as a painter must know paint and a chemist must know chemicals. But, as many of the writers in this chapter remind us, "craft" is constantly in the service of deeper artistic goals, especially the presentation of a meaningful view of life, and our use of craft is tutored by that imperative.

E. M. FORSTER

Aspects of Fiction
Homo Sapiens and Homo Fictus
Flat Characters and Round Characters
Stories and Plots

E. M. Forster (1879–1970) was a member of the storied Bloomsbury group that included novelist Virginia Woolf, biographer Lytton Strachey, art critic Roger Fry, and economist Maynard Keynes. His short stories are less popular than they once were, but his novels are still widely read, especially Where Angels Fear to Tread *(1905),* A Room with a View *(1908),* Howards End *(1910), and* A Passage to India *(1924). He also published dozens of books of nonfiction, including the essay collections* Abinger Harvest *(1936),* What I Believe *(1939), and* Two Cheers for Democracy *(1951). Undoubtedly his most famous work of nonfiction is the lecture series that became* Aspects of the Novel, *in which he creates the most basic vocabulary of the craft of fiction in use today.*

Homo Sapiens and Homo Fictus

. . . The main facts in human life are five: birth, food, sleep, love and death. One could increase the number—add breathing for instance—but these five are the most obvious. Let us briefly ask ourselves what part they play in our lives, and what in novels. Does the novelist tend to reproduce them accurately or does he tend to exaggerate, minimize, ignore, and to exhibit his characters going through processes which are not the same through which you and I go, though they bear the same names?

To consider the two strangest first: birth and death; strange because they are at the same time experiences and not experiences. We only know of them by report. We were all born, but we cannot remember what it was like. And death is coming even as birth has come, but, similarly, we do not know what it is like.

Our final experience, like our first, is conjectural. We move between two darknesses. Certain people pretend to tell us what birth and death are like: a mother, for instance, has her point of view about birth, a doctor, a religious, have their points of view about both. But it is all from the outside, and the two entities who might enlighten us, the baby and the corpse, cannot do so, because their apparatus for communicating their experiences is not attuned to our apparatus for reception.

So let us think of people as starting life with an experience they forget and ending it with one which they anticipate but cannot understand. These are the creatures whom the novelist proposes to introduce as characters into books; these, or creatures plausibly like them. The novelist is allowed to remember and understand everything, if it suits him. He knows all the hidden life. How soon will he pick up his characters after birth, how close to the grave will he follow them? And what will he say, or cause to be felt, about these two queer experiences?

Then food, the stoking up process, the keeping alive of an individual flame, the process that begins before birth and is continued after it by the mother, and finally taken over by the individual himself, who goes on day after day putting an assortment of objects into a hole in his face without becoming surprised or bored: food is a link between the known and the forgotten; closely connected with birth, which none of us remembers, and coming down to this morning's breakfast. Like sleep—which in many ways it resembles—food does not merely restore our strength, it has also an aesthetic side, it can taste good or bad. What will happen to this double-faced commodity in books?

And fourthly, sleep. On the average, about a third of our time is not spent in society or civilization or even in what is usually called solitude. We enter a world of which little is known and which seems to us after leaving it to have been partly oblivion, partly a caricature of this world and partly a revelation. "I dreamt of nothing" or "I dreamt of a ladder" or "I dreamt of heaven" we say when we wake. I do not want to discuss the nature of sleep and dreams—only to point out that they occupy much time and that what is called "History" only busies itself with about two-thirds of the human cycle, and theorizes accordingly. Does fiction take up a similar attitude?

And lastly, love. I am using this celebrated word in its widest and dullest sense. Let me be very dry and brief about sex in the first place. Some years after a human being is born, certain changes occur in it, as in other animals, which changes often lead to union with another human being, and to the production of more human beings. And our race goes on. Sex begins before adolescence, and survives sterility; it is indeed coeval with our lives, although at the mating age its effects are more obvious to society. And besides sex, there are other emotions, also strengthening towards maturity: the various upliftings of the spirit, such as affection, friendship, patriotism, mysticism—and as soon as we try to determine the relation between sex and these other emotions we shall of course begin to quarrel as violently as we ever could about Walter Scott, perhaps even more violently. Let me only tabulate the various points of view. Some people say that sex is basic and underlies all these other loves—love of friends, of God, of country. Others say that it is connected with them, but laterally, it is not their root. Others say that it is not connected at all. All I suggest is that we call the whole bundle of emotions love, and regard them as the fifth great experience through which human beings have to pass. When human beings love they try to get something. They also try to give something, and this double aim makes love more complicated than food or sleep. It is selfish and altruistic at the same time, and no amount of specialization in one direction quite atrophies the other. How much time does love take? This question sounds gross but it must be asked because it bears on our present enquiry. Sleep takes about eight hours out of the twenty-four, food about two more. Shall we put down love for another two? Surely that is a handsome allowance. Love may weave itself into our other activities—so may drowsiness and hunger. Love may start various secondary activities: for instance, a man's love for his family may cause him to spend a good deal of time on the Stock Exchange, or his love for God a good deal of time in church. But that he has emotional communion with any beloved object for more than two hours a day may be gravely doubted, and it is this emotional communion, this desire to give and to get, this mixture of generosity and expectation, that distinguishes love from the other experiences on our list.

That is the human make-up—or part of it. Made up like this himself, the novelist takes his pen in his hand, gets into the abnormal state which it is convenient to call "inspiration," and tries to create characters. Perhaps the characters have to fall in with something else in his novel: this often happens (the books of Henry James are an extreme case), and then the characters have, of course, to modify the make-up accordingly. However, we are considering now the more simple case of the novelist whose main passion is human beings and who will sacrifice a great deal to their convenience—story, plot, form, incidental beauty.

Well, in what senses do the nations of fiction differ from those of the earth? One cannot generalize about them, because they have nothing in common in the scientific sense; they need not have glands, for example, whereas all human beings have glands. Nevertheless, though incapable of strict definition, they tend to behave along the same lines.

In the first place, they come into the world more like parcels than human beings. When a baby arrives in a novel it usually has the air of having been posted. It is delivered "off"; one of the elder characters goes and picks it up and shows it to the reader, after which it is usually laid in cold storage until it can talk or otherwise assist in the action. There is both a good and a bad reason for this and for all other deviations from earthly practice; these we will note in a minute, but do just observe in what a very perfunctory way the population of noveldom is recruited. Between Sterne and James Joyce, scarcely any writer has tried either to use the facts of birth or to invent a new set of facts, and no one, except in a sort of auntish wistful way, has tried to work back towards the psychology of the baby's mind and to utilize the literary wealth that must lie there. Perhaps it cannot be done. We shall decide in a moment.

Death. The treatment of death, on the other hand, is nourished much more on observation, and has a variety about it which suggests that the novelist finds it congenial. He does, for the reason that death ends a book neatly, and for the less obvious reason that working as he does in time he finds it easier to work from the known towards the darkness rather than from the darkness of birth towards the known. By the time his characters die, he understands them, he can be both appropriate and imaginative about them—strongest of combinations. Take a little death—the death of Mrs. Proudie in the *Last Chronicle of Barset*. All is in keeping, yet the effect is terrifying, because Trollope has ambled Mrs. Proudie down many a diocesan bypath, showing her paces, making her snap, accustomed us, even to boredom, to her character and tricks, to her "Bishop, consider the souls of the people," and then she has a heart attack by the edge of her bed, she has ambled far enough,—end of Mrs. Proudie. There is scarcely anything that the novelist cannot borrow from "daily death"; scarcely anything he may not profitably invent. The doors of that darkness lie open to him and he can even follow his characters through it, provided he is shod with imagination and does not try to bring us back scraps of séance information about the "life beyond."

What of food, the third fact upon our list? Food in fiction is mainly social. It draws characters together, but they seldom require it physiologically, seldom enjoy it, and never digest it unless specially asked to do so. They hunger for each other, as we do in life, but our equally constant longing for breakfast and lunch does not get reflected. Even poetry has made more of it—at least of its aesthetic side. Milton and Keats have both come nearer to the sensuousness of swallowing than George Meredith.

Sleep. Also perfunctory. No attempt to indicate oblivion or the actual dream world. Dreams are either logical or else mosaics made out of hard little fragments of the past and future. They are introduced with a purpose and that purpose is not the character's life as a whole, but that part of it he lives while awake. He is never conceived as a creature a third of whose time is spent in the darkness. It is the limited daylight vision of the historian, which the novelist elsewhere avoids. Why should he not understand or reconstruct sleep? For remember, he has the right to invent, and we know when he is inventing truly, because his passion floats us over improbabilities. Yet he has neither copied sleep nor created it. It is just an amalgam.

Love. You all know how enormously love bulks in novels, and will probably agree with me that it has done them harm and made them monotonous. Why has this particular experience, especially in its sex form, been transplanted in such generous quantities? If you think of a novel in the vague you think of a love interest—of a man and woman who want to be united and perhaps succeed. If you think of your own life in the vague, or of a group of lives, you are left with a very different and a more complex impression. . . .

Here we must conclude our comparison of those two allied species, Homo Sapiens and Homo Fictus. Homo Fictus is more elusive than his cousin. He is created in the minds of hundreds of different novelists, who have conflicting methods of gestation, so one must not generalize. Still, one can say a little about him. He is generally born off, he is capable of dying on, he wants little food or sleep, he is tirelessly occupied with human relationships. And—most important—we can know more about him than we can know about any of our fellow creatures, because his creator and narrator are one. Were we equipped for hyperbole we might exclaim at this point: "If God could tell the story of the Universe, the Universe would become fictitious."

For this is the principle involved. . . .

Flat Characters and Round Characters

We may divide characters into flat and round.

Flat characters were called "humours" in the seventeenth century, and are sometimes called types, and sometimes caricatures. In their purest form, they are constructed round a single idea or quality: when there is more than one factor in them, we get the beginning of the curve towards the round. The really flat character can be expressed in one sentence such as "I never will desert Mr. Micawber." There is Mrs. Micawber—she says she won't desert Mr. Micawber, she doesn't, and there she is. Or: "I must conceal, even by subterfuges, the poverty of my master's house." There is Caleb Balderstone in *The Bride of Lammermoor*. He does not use the actual phrase, but it completely describes him; he has no existence outside it, no pleasures, none of the private lusts and aches that must complicate the most consistent of servitors. Whatever he does, wherever he goes, whatever lies he tells or plates he breaks, it is to conceal the poverty of his master's house. . . .

. . . [We] must admit that flat people are not in themselves as big achievements as round ones, and also that they are best when they are comic. A serious or tragic flat character is apt to be a bore. Each time he enters crying "Revenge!" or "My heart bleeds for humanity!" or whatever his formula is, our hearts sink. One of the romances of a popular contemporary writer is constructed round a Sussex farmer who says, "I'll plough up that bit of gorse." There is the farmer, there is the gorse; he says he'll plough it up, he does plough it up, but it is not like saying "I'll never desert Mr. Micawber," because we are so bored by his consistency that we do not care whether he succeeds with the gorse or fails. If his formula was analysed and connected up with the rest of the human outfit, we should not be bored any longer, the formula would cease to be the man and become an obsession in the man; that is to say he would have turned from a flat farmer into a round one. It is only round people who are fit to perform tragically for any length of time and can move us to any feelings except humour and appropriateness.

So now let us desert these two-dimensional people, and by way of transition to the round, let us go to *Mansfield Park*, and look at Lady Bertram, sitting on her sofa with pug. Pug is flat, like most animals in fiction. He is once represented as straying into a rose-bed in a cardboard kind of way, but that is all, and during most of the book his mistress seems to be cut out of the same simple material as her dog. Lady Bertram's formula is, "I am kindly, but must not be fatigued," and she functions out of it. But at the end there is a catastrophe. Her two daughters come to grief—to the worst grief known to Miss Austen's universe, far worse than the Napoleonic wars. Julia elopes; Maria, who is unhappily married, runs off with a lover. What is Lady Bertram's reaction? The sentence describing it is significant: "Lady Bertram did not think deeply, but, guided by Sir Thomas, she thought justly on all important points, and she saw therefore in all its enormity, what had happened, and neither endeavoured herself, nor required Fanny to advise her, to think little of guilt and infamy." These are strong words, and they used to worry me because I thought Jane Austen's moral sense was getting out of hand. She may, and of course does, deprecate guilt and infamy herself, and she duly causes all possible distress in the minds of Edmund and Fanny, but has she any right to agitate calm, consistent Lady Bertram? Is not it like giving Pug three faces and setting him to guard the gates of Hell? Ought not her ladyship to remain on the sofa saying, "This is a dreadful and sadly exhausting business about Julia and Maria, but where is Fanny gone? I have dropped another stitch"?

I used to think this, through misunderstanding Jane Austen's method— exactly as Scott misunderstood it when he congratulated her for painting on a square of ivory. She is a miniaturist, but never two-dimensional. All her characters are round, or capable of rotundity. Even Miss Bates has a mind, even Elizabeth Eliot a heart, and Lady Bertram's moral fervour ceases to vex us when we realize this: the disk has suddenly extended and become a little globe. When the novel is closed, Lady Bertram goes back to the flat, it is true; the dominant impression she leaves can be summed up in a formula. But that is not how Jane Austen conceived her, and the freshness of her reappearances are due to this. . . . Let us return to Lady Bertram and the crucial sentence. See how subtly it modulates from her formula into an area where the formula does not work. "Lady Bertram did not think deeply." Exactly: as per formula. "But guided by Sir Thomas she thought justly on all important points." Sir Thomas' guidance, which is part of the formula, remains, but it pushes her ladyship towards an independent and undesired morality. "She saw therefore in all its enormity what had happened." This is the moral fortissimo—very strong but carefully introduced. And then follows a most artful decrescendo, by means of negatives. "She neither endeavoured herself, nor required Fanny to advise her, to think little of guilt or infamy." The formula is reappearing, because as a rule she does try to minimize trouble, and does require Fanny to advise her how to do this; indeed Fanny has done nothing else for the last ten years. The words, though they are negative, remind us of this, her normal state is again in view, and she has in a single sentence been inflated into a round character and collapsed back into a flat one. How Jane Austen can write! . . .

As for the round characters proper, they have already been defined by implication and no more need be said. . . .

. . . The test of a round character is whether it is capable of surprising in a convincing way. If it never surprises, it is flat. If it does not convince, it is a flat pretending to be round. It has the incalculability of life about it—life within the pages of a book. And by using it sometimes alone, more often in combination with the other kind, the novelist achieves his task of acclimatization and harmonizes the human race with the other aspects of his work.

Stories and Plots

Let us define a plot. We have defined a story as a narrative of events arranged in their time-sequence. A plot is also a narrative of events, the emphasis falling on causality. "The king died and then the queen died," is a story. "The king died, and then the queen died of grief" is a plot. The time-sequence is preserved, but the sense of causality overshadows it. Or again: "The queen died, no one knew why, until it was discovered that it was through grief at the death of the king." This is a plot with a mystery in it, a form capable of high development. It suspends the time-sequence, it moves as far away from the story as its limitations will allow. Consider the death of the queen. If it is in a story we say "and then?" If it is in a plot we ask "why?" That is the fundamental difference between these two aspects of the novel. A plot cannot be told to a gaping audience of cave men or to a tyrannical sultan or to their modern descendant the movie-public. They can only be kept awake by "and then—and then——." They can only supply curiosity. But a plot demands intelligence and memory also. . . .

Intelligence first. The intelligent novel-reader, unlike the inquisitive one who just runs his eye over a new fact, mentally picks it up. He sees it from two points of view: isolated, and related to the other facts that he has read on previous pages. Probably he does not understand it, but he does not expect to do so yet awhile. The facts in a highly organized novel (like *The Egoist*) are often of the nature of cross-correspondences and the ideal spectator cannot expect to view them properly until he is sitting up on a hill at the end. This element of surprise or mystery—the detective element as it is sometimes rather emptily called—is of great importance in a plot. It occurs through a suspension of the time-sequence; a mystery is a pocket in time, and it occurs crudely, as in "Why did the queen die?" and more subtly in half-explained gestures and words, the true meaning of which only dawns pages ahead. Mystery is essential to a plot, and cannot be appreciated without intelligence. To the curious it is just another "and then——." To appreciate a mystery, part of the mind must be left behind, brooding, while the other part goes marching on.

That brings us to our second qualification: memory.

Memory and intelligence are closely connected, for unless we remember we cannot understand. If by the time the queen dies we have forgotten the existence of the king we shall never make out what killed her. The plot-maker expects us to remember, we expect him to leave no loose ends. Every action or word ought to count; it ought to be economical and spare; even when complicated it should be organic and free from dead matter. It may be difficult or easy, it may and should contain mysteries, but it ought not to mislead. And over it, as it unfolds, will hover the memory of the reader (that dull glow of the mind of which intelligence is the bright advancing edge) and will constantly rearrange and reconsider, seeing new clues, new chains of cause and effect, and the final sense (if the plot has been a fine one) will not be of clues or chains, but of something aesthetically compact, something which might have been shown by the novelist straight away, only if he had shown it straight away it would never have become beautiful. . . .

And now briefly to illustrate the mystery element in the plot: the formula of "The queen died, it was afterwards discovered through grief." I will take an example, not from Dickens (though *Great Expectations* provides a fine one), nor from Conan Doyle (whom my priggishness prevents me from enjoying), but again from Meredith: an example of a concealed emotion from the admirable plot of *The Egoist:* it occurs in the character of Laetitia Dale.

We are told, at first, all that passes in Laetitia's mind. Sir Willoughby has twice jilted her, she is sad, resigned. Then, for dramatic reasons, her mind is hidden from us, it develops naturally enough, but does not re-emerge until the great midnight scene where he asks her to marry him because he is not sure about Clara, and this time, a changed woman, Laetitia says "No." Meredith has concealed the change. It would have spoiled his high comedy if we had been kept in touch with it throughout. Sir Willoughby has to have a series of crashes, to catch at this and that, and find everything rickety. We should not enjoy the fun, in fact it would be boorish, if we saw the author preparing the booby traps beforehand, so Laetitia's apathy has been hidden from us. This is one of the countless examples in which either plot or character has to suffer, and Meredith with his unerring good sense here lets the plot triumph. . . .

Sometimes a plot triumphs too completely. The characters have to suspend their natures at every turn, or else are so swept away by the course of Fate that our sense of their reality is weakened. We shall find instances of this in a writer who is far greater than Meredith, and yet less successful as a novelist—Thomas Hardy. Hardy seems to me essentially a poet, who conceives of his novels from an enormous height. They are to be tragedies or tragi-comedies, they are to give out the sound of hammer-strokes as they proceed; in other words Hardy arranges events with emphasis on causality, the ground plan is a plot, and the characters are ordered to acquiesce in its requirements. Except in the person of Tess (who conveys the feeling that she is greater than destiny) this aspect of his work is unsatisfactory. His characters are involved in various snares, they are finally bound hand and foot, there is ceaseless emphasis on fate, and yet, for all the sacrifices made to it, we never see the action as a living thing as we see it in *Antigone* or *Berenice* or *The Cherry Orchard*. The fate above us, not the fate working through us—that is what is eminent and memorable in the Wessex novels. Egdon Heath before Eustacia Vye has set foot upon it. The woods without the Woodlanders. The downs above Budmouth Regis with the royal princesses, still asleep, driving across them through the dawn. Hardy's success in *The Dynasts* (where he uses another medium) is complete, there the hammer-strokes are heard, cause and effect enchain the characters despite their struggles, complete contact between the actors and the plot is established. But in the novels, though the same superb and terrible machine works, it never catches humanity in its teeth; there is some vital problem that has not been answered, or even posed, in the misfortunes of Jude the Obscure. In other words the characters have been required to contribute too much to the plot; except in their rustic humours, their vitality has been impoverished, they have gone dry and thin. This, as far as I can make out, is the flaw running through Hardy's novels: he has emphasized causality more strongly than his medium permits. As a poet and prophet and visualizer George Meredith is nothing by his side—just a suburban roarer—but Meredith did know what the novel could stand, where the plot could dun the characters for a contribution, where it must let them function as they liked. And the moral—well, I see no moral, because the work of Hardy is my home and that of Meredith cannot be: still the moral from the point of these lectures is again unfavourable to Aristotle. In the novel, all human happiness and misery does not take the form of action, it seeks means of expression other than through the plot, it must not be rigidly canalized. . . .

DISCUSSION QUESTIONS

1. How are real people ("homo sapiens") and fictional characters ("homo fictus") both similar to and different from each other? How does Forster account for the differences?
2. What is the difference between "flat" and "round" characters? What are the uses and purposes of each?
3. What's the difference between what Forster calls "story" and "plot"? Why must a piece of fiction have not only "story" but also "plot"?
4. All the elements Forster discusses—"homo fictus," "flat" and "round" characters, "plot"—are elements of fiction and not "real life." Why is this distortion of "real life" necessary if fiction is to succeed in communicating meaning?

ELIZABETH BOWEN

Notes on Writing a Novel

Elizabeth Bowen (1899–1973) was a prolific short story writer, novelist, playwright, and essayist. Her novels include Friends and Relations *(1931),* The House in Paris *(1935),* The Death of the Heart *(1938),* A World of Love *(1955), and* Eva Trout; or, Changing Scenes *(1968). Her nonfiction includes travel pieces, history, literary history, and memoirs of her Dublin childhood and later life. She was friends with or acquaintances of nearly every English novelist of her day, including Graham Greene and V. S. Pritchett, and together with E. M. Forster she has provided in her writing about the practice of fiction some of the most basic vocabulary of the craft.*

PLOT.

Essential. The Pre-Essential.

Plot might seem to be a matter of choice. It is not. The particular plot for the particular novel is something the novelist is driven to. It is what is left after the whittling-away of alternatives. The novelist is confronted, at a moment (or at what appears to be the moment: actually its extension may be indefinite) by the impossibility of saying what is to be said in any other way.

He is forced toward his plot. By what? By "what is to be said." What is "what is to be said?" A mass of subjective matter that has accumulated—impressions received, feelings about experience, distorted results of ordinary observation, and something else—*x*. This matter is *extra* matter. It is superfluous to the non-writing life of the writer. It is luggage left in the hall between two journeys, as opposed to the perpetual furniture of rooms. It is destined to be elsewhere. It cannot move till its destination is known. Plot is the knowing of destination.

Plot is diction. Action of language, language of action.

Plot is story. It is also "a story" in the nursery sense—lie. The novel lies, in saying that something happened that did not. It must, therefore, contain uncontradictable truth, to warrant the original lie.

Story involves action. Action towards an end not to be foreseen (by the reader) but also towards an end which, having *been* reached, must be seen to have been from the start inevitable.

Action by whom? The Characters (see CHARACTERS). Action in view of what, and because of what? The "what is to be said."

What about the idea that the function of action is to *express* the characters? This is wrong. The characters are there to provide the action. Each character is created, and must only be so created, as to give his or her action (or rather, contributory part in the novel's action) verisimilitude.

What about the idea that plot should be ingenious, complicated—a display of ingenuity remarkable enough to command attention? If more than such a display, what? Tension, or mystification towards tension, are good for emphasis. For their own sakes, bad.

Plot must further the novel towards its object. What object? The non-poetic statement of a poetic truth.

Have not all poetic truths been already stated? The essence of a poetic truth is that no statement of it can be final.

Plot, story, is in itself un-poetic. At best it can only be not anti-poetic. It cannot claim a single poetic licence. It must be reasoned—only from the moment when its none-otherness, its only-possibleness has become apparent. Novelist must always have one foot, sheer circumstantiality, to stand on, whatever the other foot may be doing. (N.B.—Much to be learnt from the detective story—especially non-irrelevance. (See RELEVANCE).)

Flaubert's "*Il faut interesser.*" Stress on manner of telling: keep in mind, "I will a tale *unfold.*" Interest of watching a dress that has been well packed unpacked from a dress-box. Interest of watching silk handkerchief drawn from conjuror's watch.

Plot must not cease to move forward. (See ADVANCE.) The *actual* speed of the movement must be even. *Apparent* variations in speed are good, necessary, but there must be no actual variations in speed. To obtain those apparent variations is part of the illusion-task of the novel. Variations in texture can be made to give the effect of variations in speed. Why are *apparent* variations in speed necessary? (*a*) For emphasis. (*b*) For non-resistance, or "give," to the nervous time-variations of the reader. Why is *actual* evenness, non-variation, of speed necessary? For the sake of internal evenness for its own sake. Perfection of evenness = perfection of control. The evenness of the speed should be the evenness inseparable from tautness. The tautness of the taut string is equal (or even) all along and at any part of the string's length.

CHARACTERS.

Are the characters, then, to be constructed to formula—the formula pre-decided by the plot? Are they to be drawn, cut out, jointed, wired, in order to be manipulated for the plot?

No. There is no question as to whether this would be right or wrong. It would be impossible. One cannot "make" characters, only marionettes. The manipulated movement of the marionette is not the "action" necessary for plot. Characterless action is not action at all, in the plot sense. It is the indivisibility of the act from the actor, and the inevitability of *that* act on the part of *that* actor, that gives action verisimilitude. Without that, action is without force or reason. Forceless, reasonless action disrupts plot. The term "creation of character" (or characters) is misleading. Characters pre-exist. They are *found*. They reveal themselves slowly to the novelist's perception—as might fellow-travellers seated opposite one in a very dimly-lit railway carriage.

The novelist's perceptions of his characters take place *in the course of the actual writing of the novel*. To an extent, the novelist is in the same position as the reader. But his perceptions should be always just in advance.

The ideal way of presenting character is to invite perception.

In what do the characters pre-exist? I should say, in the mass of matter (see PLOT) that had accumulated before the inception of the novel.

(N.B.—the unanswerability of the question, from an outsider: "Are the characters in your novel invented, or are they from real life?" Obviously, neither is true. The outsider's notion of "real life" and the novelist's are hopelessly apart.)

How, then, is the pre-existing character—with its own inner spring of action, its contrarieties—to be made to play a pre-assigned rôle? In relation to character, or characters, once these have been contemplated, *plot* must at once seem over-rigid, arbitrary.

What about the statement (in relation to PLOT) that "each character is created in order, and only in order, that he or she may supply the required action?" To begin with, strike out "created." Better, the character is *recognised* (by the novelist) by the signs he or she gives of unique capacity to act in a certain way, which "certain way" fulfills a need of the plot.

The character is there (in the novel) for the sake of the action he or she is to contribute to the plot. Yes. But also, he or she exists *outside* the action being contributed to the plot.

Without that existence of the character outside the (necessarily limited) action, the action itself would be invalid.

Action is the simplification (for story purposes) of complexity. For each one act, there are an x number of rejected alternatives. It is the palpable presence of the alternatives that gives action interest. Therefore, in each of the characters, while he or she is acting, the play and pull of alternatives must be felt. It is in being seen to be capable of alternatives that the character becomes, for their readers, valid.

Roughly, the action of a character should be unpredictable before it has been shown, inevitable when it has been shown. In the first half of a novel, the unpredictability should be the more striking. In the second half, the inevitability should be the more striking.

(Most exceptions to this are, however, masterpiece-novels. In *War and Peace, L'Education Sentimentale,* and *À la recherche du temps perdu,* unpredictability dominates up to the end.)

The character's prominence in the novel (pre-decided by the plot) decides the character's range—of alternatives. The novelist must allot (to the point of rationing) psychological space. The "hero," "heroine" and "villain" (if any) are, by agreement, allowed most range. They are entitled, for the portrayal of their alternatives, to time and space. Placing the characters in receding order to their importance to the plot, the number of their alternatives may be seen to diminish. What E. M. Forster has called the "flat" character has no alternatives at all.

The ideal novel is without "flat" characters.

Characters must *materialise*—i.e., must have a palpable physical reality. They must be not only see-able (visualisable); they must be felt. Power to give physical reality is probably a matter of the extent and nature of the novelist's physical sensibility, or susceptibility. In the main, English novelists weak in this, as compared to French and Russians. Why?

Hopelessness of categoric "description." Why? Because this is static. Physical personality belongs to action: cannot be separated from it. Pictures must be in movement. Eyes, hands, stature, etc., must appear, and only appear, *in play.* Reaction to physical personality is part of action—love, or sexual passages, only more marked application of this general rule.

(Conrad an example of strong, non-sexual use of physical personality.)

The materialisation (in the above sense) of the character for the novelist must be instantaneous. It happens. No effort of will—and obviously no effort of intellect—can induce it. The novelist can *use* a character that has not yet materialised. But the unmaterialised character represents an enemy pocket in an area that has been otherwise cleared. This cannot go on for long. It produces a halt in plot.

When the materialisation *has* happened, the chapters written before it happened will almost certainly have to be recast. From the plot point of view, they will be found invalid.

Also, it is essential that for the reader the materialisation of the character should begin early. I say begin, because for the *reader* it may, without harm, be gradual.

Is it from this failure, or tendency to fail, in materialisation that the English novelist depends so much on engaging emotional sympathy for his characters?

Ruling sympathy out, a novel must contain at least one *magnetic* character. At least one character capable of keying the reader up, as though he (the reader) were in the presence of someone he is in love with. This not a rule of salesmanship but a pre-essential of *interest*. The character must do to the reader what he has done to the novelist—magnetise towards himself perceptions, sense-impressions, desires.

The unfortunate case is, where the character has, obviously, acted magnetically upon the author, but fails to do so upon the reader.

There must be combustion. Plot depends for its movement on internal combustion.

Physically, characters are almost always copies, or composite copies. Traits, gestures, etc., are searched for in, and assembled from, the novelist's memory. Or, a picture, a photograph or the cinema screen may be drawn on. Nothing physical can be *invented*. (Invented physique stigmatises the inferior novel.) Proust (in last volume) speaks of this assemblage of traits. Though much may be lifted from a specific person in "real life," no person in "real life" could supply everything (physical) necessary for the character in the novel. No such person could have just that exact degree of physical intensity required for the character.

Greatness of characters is the measure of the unconscious greatness of the novelist's vision. They are "true" in so far as he is occupied with poetic truth. Their degrees in realness show the degrees of his concentration.

SCENE.

—Is a Derivative of Plot. Gives Actuality to Plot.

Nothing can happen nowhere. The locale of the happening always colours the happening, and often, to a degree, shapes it.

Plot having pre-decided what is to happen, scene, scenes, must be so found, so chosen, as to give happening the desired force.

Scene, being physical, is, like the physical traits of the characters, generally a copy, or a composite copy. It, too, is assembled—out of memories which, in the first place, may have had no rational connection with one another. Again, pictures, photographs, the screen are sources of supply. Also dreams.

Almost anything drawn from "real life"—house, town, room, park, landscape—will almost certainly be found to require *some* distortion for the purposes of the plot. Remote memories, already distorted by the imagination, are most useful for the purposes of scene. Unfamiliar or once-seen places yield more than do familiar, often-seen places.

Wholly invented scene is as unsatisfactory (thin) as wholly invented physique for a character.

Scene, much more than character, is inside the novelist's conscious power. More than any other constituent of the novel, it makes him conscious *of* his power.

This can be dangerous. The weak novelist is always, compensatorily, scene-minded. (Jane Austen's economy of scene-painting, and her abstentions from it in what might be expected contexts, could in itself be proof of her mastery of the novel.)

Scene is only justified in the novel where it can be shown, or at least felt, to act upon action or character. In fact, where it has dramatic use.

Where not intended for dramatic use, scene is a sheer slower-down. Its staticness is a dead weight. It cannot make part of the plot's movement by being shown *in play*. (Thunderstorms, the sea, landscape flying past car or railway-carriage windows are not scene but *happenings*.)

The deadeningness of straight and prolonged "description" is as apparent with regard to scene as it is with regard to character. Scene must he evoked. For its details relevance (see RELEVANCE) is essential. Scene must, like the characters, not fail to materialise. In this it follows the same law—instantaneous for the novelist, gradual for the reader.

In "setting a scene" the novelist directs, or attempts to direct, the reader's visual imagination. He must allow for the fact that the reader's memories will not correspond with his own. Or, at least, not at all far along the way.

DIALOGUE.

—Must (1) Further Plot. (2) Express Character.

Should not on any account be a vehicle for ideas for their own sake. Ideas only permissible where they provide a key to the character who expresses them.

Dialogue requires more art than does any other constituent of the novel. Art in the *celare artem* sense. Art in the trickery, self-justifying distortion sense. Why? Because dialogue must appear realistic without being so. Actual realism—the lifting, as it were, of passages from a stenographer's take-down of a "real life" conversation—would be disruptive. Of what? Of the illusion of the novel. In "real life" everything is diluted; in the novel everything is condensed.

What are the realistic qualities to be imitated (or faked) in novel dialogue?—Spontaneity. Artless or hit-or-miss arrival at words used. Ambiguity (speaker not sure, himself, what he means). Effect of choking (as in engine): more to be said than can come through. Irrelevance. Allusiveness. Erraticness: unpredictable course. Repercussion.

What must novel dialogue, behind mask of these faked realistic qualities, really be and do? It must be pointed, intentional, relevant. It must crystallise situation. It must express character. It must advance plot.

During dialogue, the characters confront one another. The confrontation is in itself an occasion. Each one of these occasions, throughout the novel, is unique. Since the last confrontation, something has changed, advanced. What is being said is the effect of something that has happened; at the same time, what is being said *is in itself something happening,* which will, in turn, leave its effect.

Dialogue is the ideal means of showing what is between the characters. It crystallises relationships. It *should,* ideally, so be effective as to make analysis or explanation of the relationships between the characters unnecessary.

Short of a small range of physical acts—a fight, murder, love-making—dialogue is the most vigorous and visible inter-action of which characters in a novel are capable. Speech is what the characters *do to each other.*

Dialogue provides means for the psychological materialisation of the characters. It should short-circuit description of mental traits. Every sentence in dialogue should be descriptive of the character who is speaking. Idiom, tempo, and shape of each spoken sentence should be calculated by novelist, towards this descriptive end.

Dialogue is the first case of the novelist's need for notation from real life. Remarks or turns of phrase indicatory of class, age, degree of intellectual pretension, *ideés reçues,* nature and strength of governing fantasy, sexual temperament, persecution-sense or acumen (fortuitous arrival at general or poetic truth) should be collected. (N.B.—Proust, example of this semi-conscious notation and putting to use of it.)

All the above, from *class* to *acumen,* may already have been established, with regard to each character, by a direct statement by the novelist to the reader. It is still, however, the business of dialogue to show these factors, or qualities in play.

There must be present in dialogue—i.e., in each sentence spoken by each character—*either* (*a*) calculation, or (*b*) involuntary self-revelation.

Each piece of dialogue *must* be "something happening." Dialogue *may* justify its presence by being "illustrative"—but this secondary use of it must be watched closely, challenged. Illustrativeness can be stretched too far. Like straight description, it then becomes static, a dead weight—halting the movement of the plot. The "amusing" for its *own* sake, should above all be censored. So should infatuation with any idiom.

The functional use of dialogue or the plot must be the first thing in the novelist's mind. Where functional usefulness cannot be established, dialogue must be left out.

What is this functional use? That of a bridge.

Dialogue is the thin bridge which must, from time to time, carry the entire weight of the novel. Two things to be kept in mind—(*a*) the bridge is there to permit *advance,* (*b*) the bridge must be strong enough for the weight.

Failure in any one piece of dialogue is a loss, at once to the continuity and the comprehensibility of the novel.

Characters should, on the whole, be under rather than over articulate. What they *intend* to say should be more evident, more striking (because of its greater inner importance to the plot) than what they arrive at *saying.*

ANGLE.

The question of *angle* comes up twice over in the novel.

Angle has two senses—(*a*) visual, (*b*) moral.

(*a*) *Visual Angle.*—This has been much discussed—particularly I think by Henry James. Where is the camera-eye to be located? (1) In the breast or brow of *one* of the characters? This is, of course, simplifying and integrating. But it imposes on the novel the limitations of the "I"—whether the first person is explicitly used or not. Also, with regard to any matter that the specific character does not (cannot) know, it involves the novelist in long cumbrous passages of cogitation, speculation and guesses. E.g.—of any character other than the specific or virtual "I" it must always be "he appeared to feel," "he could be seen to see," rather than "he felt," "he saw." (2) In the breast or brow of a succession of characters? This is better. It *must,* if used, involve very careful, considered division of the characters, by the novelist, in the *seeing* and the *seen.* Certain characters gain in importance and magnetism by being only *seen:* this makes them more romantic, fatal-seeming, sinister. In fact, no character in which these qualities are, for the plot, essential should be allowed to enter the *seeing* class. (3) In the breast or brow of omniscient story-teller (the novelist)? This, though appearing naive, would appear best. The novelist should retain right of entry, at will, into any of the characters: their memories, sensations and thought-processes should remain his, to requisition for appropriate use. What conditions "appropriateness"? The demands of the plot. Even so, the novelist must not lose sight of point made above—the gain in necessary effect, for some characters, of their remaining *seen*—their remaining closed, apparently, even to the omniscience of the novelist.

The cinema, with its actual camera-work, is interesting study for the novelist. In a good film, the camera's movement, angle and distance have all worked towards one thing—the fullest possible realisation of the director's idea, the completest possible surrounding of the subject. Any trick is justified if it adds a statement. With both film and novel, plot is the pre-imperative. The novelist's relation to the novel is that of the director's relation to the film. The cinema, cinema-going, has no doubt built up in novelists a great authoritarianism. This seems to me good.

(*b*) *Moral Angle.*—This too often means, pre-assumptions—social, political, sexual, national, aesthetic, and so on. These may all exist, sunk at different depths, in the same novelist. Their existence cannot fail to be palpable; and their nature determines, more than anything else, the sympatheticness or antipatheticness of a given novel to a given circle of readers.

Pre-assumptions are bad. They limit the novel to a given circle of readers. They cause the novel to act immorally *on* that given circle. (The lady asking the librarian for a "nice" novel to take home is, virtually, asking for a novel whose pre-assumptions will be identical with her own.) Outside the given circle, a novel's pre-assumptions must invalidate it for all other readers. The increasingly bad smell of most pre-assumptions probably accounts for the growing prestige of the detective story: the detective story works on the single, and universally acceptable, pre-assumption that an act of violence is anti-social, and that the doer, in the name of injured society, must be traced.

Great novelists write without pre-assumption. They write from outside their own nationality, class or sex.

To write thus should be the ambition of any novelist who wishes to state poetic truth.

Does this mean he must have no angle, no moral view-point? No, surely. Without these, he would be (*a*) incapable of maintaining the *conviction* necessary for the novel, (*b*) incapable of *lighting* the characters, who to be seen at all must necessarily be seen in a moral light.

From what source, then, must the conviction come? and from *what* morality is to come the light to be cast on the characters?

The conviction must come from certainty of the validity of the truth the novel is to present. The "moral light" is not, actually, a moral source; it is moral (morally powerful) according to the strength of its power of revelation. Revelation of what? The virtuousness or non-virtuousness of the action of the character. What is virtue in action? Truth in action. Truth by what ruling, in relation to what? Truth by the ruling of, and in relation to, the inherent poetic truth that the novel states.

The presence, and action, of the poetic truth is the motive (or motor) morality of the novel.

The direction of the action of the poetic truth provides—in fact, *is*—the moral angle of the novel. If he remains with that truth in view, the novelist has no option as to his angle.

The action, or continuous line of action, of a character is "bad" in so far as it runs counter to, resists, or attempts to deny, the action of the poetic truth. It is predisposition towards such action that constitutes "badness" in a character.

"Good" action, or "goodness" in the character from predisposition towards such action, is movement along with, expressive of and contributary to, the action of the poetic truth.

If the novelist's moral angle is (*a*) decided by recognition of the poetic truth, and (*b*) maintained by the necessity of stating the truth by showing the truth's action, it will be, as it should be, impersonal. It will be, and (from the "interest" point of view) will be able to stand being, pure of pre-assumptions—national, social, sexual, etc.

(N.B.—"Humour" is the weak point in the front against pre-assumptions. Almost all English humour shows social (sometimes, now, backed by political) pre-assumptions. Extreme cases—that the lower, or employed, classes are quaint or funny—that aristocrats, served by butlers, are absurd. National pre-assumptions show in treatment of foreigners.)

ADVANCE.

It has been said that plot must advance; that the underlying (or inner) speed of the advance must be even. How is this arrived at?

(1) Obviously, first, by the succession, the succeedingness, of events or happenings. It is to be remembered that *everything* put on record at all—an image, a

word spoken, an interior movement of thought or feeling on the part of a character—is an event or happening. These proceed out of one another, give birth to one another, in a continuity that must be (*a*) obvious, (*b*) unbroken.

(2) Every happening cannot be described, stated. The reader must be made to feel that what has not been described or stated has, none the less, happened. How? By the showing of subsequent events or happenings whose source *could* only have been in what has not actually been stated. Tuesday is Tuesday by virtue of being the day following Monday. The stated Tuesday must be shown as a derivative of the unstated Monday.

(3) For the sake of emphasis, time must be falsified. But the novelist's consciousness of the subjective, arbitrary and emotional nature of the falsification should be evident to the reader. Against this falsification—in fact, increasing the force of its effect by contrast—a clock should be heard always impassively ticking away at the same speed. The passage of time, and its demarcation, should be a factor in plot. The either concentration or even or uneven spacing-out of events along time is important.

The statement "Ten years had passed," or the statement, "It was now the next day"—each of these is an event.

(4) Characters most of all promote, by showing, the advance of the plot. How? By the advances, from act to act, in their action. By their showing (by emotional or physical changes) the effects both of action and of the passage of time. The diminution of the character's alternatives shows (because it is the work of) advance—by the end of a novel the character's alternatives, many at the beginning, have been reduced to almost none. In the novel, everything that happens happens either *to* or *because* of one of the characters. By the end of the novel, the character has, like the silk worm at work on the cocoon, spun itself out. Completed action is marked by the exhaustion (from one point of view) of the character. Throughout the novel, each character is expending potentiality. This expense of potentiality must be felt.

(5) Scene promotes, or contributes to, advance by its *freshness*. Generically, it is fresh, striking, from being unlike the scene before. It is the new "here and now." Once a scene ceases to offer freshness, it is a point-blank enemy to advance. Frequent change of scene *not* being an imperative of the novel—in fact, many novels by choice, and by wise choice, limiting themselves severely in this matter—how is there to continue to be freshness? By means of ever-differing presentation. Differing because of what? Season of year, time of year, effects of a happening (e.g., with house, rise or fall in family fortunes, an arrival, a departure, a death), beholding character's mood. At the first presentation, the *scene* has freshness; afterwards, the freshness must be in the *presentation*. The same scene can, by means of a series of presentations, each having freshness, be made to ripen, mature, to actually advance. The *static* properties in scene can be good for advance when so stressed as to show advance by contrast—advance on the part of the characters. Striking "unchangingness" gives useful emphasis to change. Change should not be a factor, at once, in *both* scene and character: either unchanged character should see, or be seen, against changed scene, or changed character should see, or be seen, against unchanged scene. *Two* changes, obvi-

ously cancel each other out, and would cancel each other's contribution to the advance of plot.

RELEVANCE.

Relevance—the question of it—is the headache of novel-writing.

As has been said, the model for relevance is the well-constructed detective story: nothing is "in" that does not tell. But the detective story is, or would appear to be, simplified by having *fact* as its kernel. The detective story makes towards concrete truth; the novel makes towards abstract truth.

With the detective story, the question "relevant to *what?*" can be answered by the intelligence. With the novel, the same question must constantly, and in every context, be referred to the intuition. The intelligence, in a subsequent check over, may detect, but cannot itself put right, blunders, lapses or false starts on the part of the intuition.

In the notes on Plot, Character, Scene and Dialogue, everything has come to turn, by the end, on relevance. It is seen that all other relevances are subsidiary to the relevance of the plot—i.e., the relevance to itself that the plot demands. It is as contributory, in fact relevant to plot that character, scene and dialogue are examined. To be perfectly contributory, these three must be perfectly relevant. If character, scene or dialogue has been weakened by anything irrelevant *to itself,* it can only be imperfectly relevant—which must mean, to a degree disruptive—to the plot.

The main hope for character (for each character) is that it should be magnetic—i.e., that it should *attract* its parts. This living propensity of the character to assemble itself, to integrate itself, to make itself in order to *be* itself will not, obviously, be resisted by the novelist. The magnetic, or magnetising, character can be trusted as to what is relevant *to itself.* The trouble comes when what is relevant to the character is found not to be relevant to the plot. At this point, the novelist must adjudicate. It is possible that the character may be right; it is possible that there may be some flaw in the novelist's sense of what is relevant to the plot.

Again, the character may, in fact must, decide one half of the question of relevance in dialogue. The character attracts to itself the right, in fact the only possible, idiom, tempo and phraseology for *that* particular character in speech. In so far as dialogue is *illustrative,* the character's, or characters', pull on it must not be resisted.

But in so far as dialogue must be "something happening"—part of action, a means of advancing plot—the other half of the question of dialogue-relevance comes up. Here, the pull from the characters may conflict with the pull from the plot. Here again the novelist must adjudicate. The recasting and recasting of dialogue that is so often necessary is, probably, the search for ideal compromise.

Relevance in scene is more straightforward. Chiefly, the novelist must control his infatuation with his own visual-power. *No* non-contributory image, must be the rule. Contributory to what? To the mood of the "now," the mood that either projects or reflects action. It is a good main rule that objects— chairs, trees, glasses, mountains, cushions—introduced into the novel should be stage-properties, necessary for "business." It will be also recalled that the well-set stage shows many objects *not* actually necessary for "business"—but that these have a right to place by being descriptive—explanatory. In a play, the absence of the narrating voice makes it necessary to establish the class, period and general psychology of the characters by means of objects that can be seen. In the novel, such putting of objects to a descriptive (explanatory) use is excellent—alternative to the narrator's voice.

In scene, then, relevance demands either usefulness for action or else explanatory power in what is shown. There is no doubt that with some writers (Balzac, sometimes Arnold Bennett) categoricalness, in the presentation of scene, is effective. The aim is, usually, to suggest, by multiplication and exactitude of detail, either a scene's material oppressiveness or its intrinsic authority. But in general, for the purposes of most novelists, the number of objects genuinely necessary for explanation will be found to be very small.

Irrelevance, in any part, is a cloud and a drag on, a weakener of, the novel. It dilutes meaning. Relevance crystallises meaning.

The novelist's—any writer's—object is, to whittle down his meaning to the exactest and finest possible point. What, of course, is fatal is when he does not know what he does mean: he has no point to sharpen.

Much irrelevance is introduced into novels by the writer's vague hope that at least some of this *may* turn out to be relevant, after all. A good deal of what might be called provisional writing goes to the first drafts of first chapters of most novels. At a point in the novel's progress, relevance becomes clearer. The provisional chapters are then recast.

The most striking fault in work by young or beginning novelists, submitted for criticism, is irrelevance—due either to infatuation or indecision. To direct such an author's attention to the imperative of relevance is certainly the most useful—and possibly the only—help that can be given.

DISCUSSION QUESTIONS

1. What might Bowen mean when she says that the object of fiction is "the non-poetic statement of a poetic truth"?
2. We usually think of being in conscious control of a plot: we *decide* where to start a story, where to end it, what happens in between and in what order. Bowen insists that the plot is not "a matter of choice," but instead "something the novelist is driven to." How might this be true?
3. Bowen says that characters are not "created" but are "found" by fiction writers. Has this been true of your experience writing fiction so far?
4. According to Bowen, what is the function of "scene" (or what is sometimes called "setting")?
5. Bowen includes "moral angle" in an essay that seems mostly focused on nuts-and-bolts "how-to" elements of fiction writing. What is "moral angle"? How does it fit and not fit with the other elements Bowen lists?

WAYNE C. BOOTH

Types of Narration

Wayne C. Booth (b. 1921) was a fixture at the University of Chicago, where he taught litera-
ture from 1962 to 1992, when he retired. He was co-editor of Critical Inquiry *for ten years*
(1974–1985) and has been a National Endowment for the Humanities fellow, a Guggenheim
fellow, and president of the Modern Language Association. His many works of literary theory
include The Rhetoric of Fiction *(1961),* The Company We Keep: An Ethics of
Fiction *(1988), and* The Writer Writing: Philosophic Acts in Literature *(1993),*
co-authored with Francis-Noel Thomas. Of all the literary critics, at least those who don't write
fiction themselves, Booth has the most to say to fiction writers about both the theory and the
practice of fiction.

"But he [the narrator] little knows what surprises lie in wait for him, if
someone were to set about analysing the mass of truths and falsehoods
which he has collected here."

—"Dr. S.," in *Confessions of Zeno*

"I give you notice betimes, because I design not to surprize you, as some
malicious Authors are wont to do, who aim at nothing else."

—Antoine Furetière, *Le Roman Bourgeois,* (1666)

"Perhaps I shall eliminate the preceding chapter. Among other reasons,
there is, in the last few lines, something that might be construed as an error
on my part. . . . Let us look into the future. Seventy years from now, a thin,
sallow, grey-haired fellow, who loves nothing but books, is bent over the
preceding page trying to find the error."

—Machado de Assis, *Epitaph of a Small Winner*

. . . If we think through the many narrative devices in the fiction we know, we
soon come to a sense of the embarrassing inadequacy of our traditional classification of "point of view" into three or four kinds, variables only of the "person"
and the degree of omniscience. If we name over three or four of the great narrators—say Cervantes' Cid Hamete Benengeli, Tristram Shandy, the "I" of *Middle-*
march, and Strether, through whose vision most of *The Ambassadors* comes to us,
we realize that to describe any of them with terms like "first-person" and "omniscient" tells us nothing about how they differ from each other, or why they succeed while others described in the same terms fail. . . .

PERSON

Perhaps the most overworked distinction is that of person. To say that a story is told in the first or the third person[1] will tell us nothing of importance unless we become more precise and describe how the particular qualities of the narrators relate to specific effects. It is true that choice of the first person is sometimes unduly limiting; if the "I" has inadequate access to necessary information, the author may be led into improbabilities. And there are other effects that may dictate a choice in some cases. But we can hardly expect to find useful criteria in a distinction that throws all fiction into two, or at most three, heaps. In this pile we see *Henry Esmond,* "A Cask of Amontillado," *Gulliver's Travels,* and *Tristram Shandy.* In that, we have *Vanity Fair, Tom Jones, The Ambassadors,* and *Brave New World.* But in *Vanity Fair* and *Tom Jones* the commentary is in the first person, often resembling more the intimate effect of *Tristram Shandy* than that of many third-person works. And again, the effect of *The Ambassadors* is much closer to that of the great first-person novels, since Strether in large part "narrates" his own story, even though he is always referred to in the third person.

Further evidence that this distinction is less important than has often been claimed is seen in the fact that all of the following functional distinctions apply to both first- and third-person narration alike.

DRAMATIZED AND UNDRAMATIZED NARRATORS

Perhaps the most important differences in narrative effect depend on whether the narrator is dramatized in his own right and on whether his beliefs and characteristics are shared by the author.

The Implied Author (the Author's "Second Self").—Even the novel in which no narrator is dramatized creates an implicit picture of an author who stands behind the scenes, whether as stage manager, as puppeteer, or as an indifferent God, silently paring his fingernails. This implied author is always distinct from the "real man"—whatever we may take him to be—who creates a superior of "himself," a "second self," as he creates his work. . . .

In so far as a novel does not refer directly to this author, there will be no distinction between him and the implied, undramatized narrator; in Hemingway's "The Killers," for example, there is no narrator other than the implicit second self that Hemingway creates as he writes.

Undramatized Narrators.—Stories are usually not so rigorously impersonal as "The Killers"; most tales are presented as passing through the consciousness of a teller, whether an "I" or a "he." Even in drama much of what we are given is narrated by someone, and we are often as much interested in the effect on the narrator's own mind and heart as we are in learning what *else* the author has to tell us. When Horatio tells of his first encounter with the ghost in *Hamlet,* his own character, though never mentioned, is important to us as we listen. In fiction, as soon as we encounter an "I," we are conscious of an experiencing mind whose views of the experience will come between us and the event. When there is no such "I," as in "The Killers," the inexperienced reader may make the mistake of thinking that the story comes to him unmediated. But no such mistake can be made from the moment that the author explicitly places a narrator into the tale, even if he is given no personal characteristics whatever.

Dramatized Narrators.—In a sense even the most reticent narrator has been dramatized as soon as he refers to himself as "I," or, like Flaubert, tells us that "we" were in the classroom when Charles Bovary entered. But many novels dramatize their narrators with great fullness, making them into characters who are as vivid as those they tell us about (*Tristram Shandy, Remembrance of Things Past, Heart of Darkness, Dr. Faustus*). In such works the narrator is often radically different from the implied author who creates him. The range of human types that have been dramatized as narrators is almost as great as the range of other fictional characters—one must say "almost" because there are some characters who are not fully qualified to narrate or "reflect" a story (Faulkner can use the idiot for *part* of his novel only because the other three parts exist to set off and clarify the idiot's jumble).

We should remind ourselves that many dramatized narrators are never explicitly labeled as narrators at all. In a sense, every speech, every gesture, narrates; most works contain disguised narrators who are used to tell the audience what it needs to know, while seeming merely to act out their roles.

Though disguised narrators of this kind are seldom labeled so explicitly as God in Job, they often speak with an authority as sure as God's. Messengers returning to tell what the oracle said, wives trying to convince their husbands that the business deal is unethical, old family retainers expostulating with wayward scions—these often have more effect on us than on their official auditors; the king goes ahead with his obstinate search, the husband carries out his deal, the hell-bound youth goes on toward hell as if nothing had been said, but *we* know what we know—and as surely as if the author himself or his official narrator had told us. "She's laughing at you to your face, brother," Cleante says to Orgon in *Tartuffe,* "and frankly, without meaning to anger you, I must say she's quite right. Has there ever been the like of such a whim? . . . You must be mad, brother, I swear." And in tragedy there is usually a chorus, a friend, or even a forthright villain, to speak truth in contrast to the tragic mistakes of the hero.

The most important unacknowledged narrators in modern fiction are the third-person "centers of consciousness" through whom authors have filtered their narratives. Whether such "reflectors," as James sometimes called them, are highly polished mirrors reflecting complex mental experience, or the rather turbid, sense-bound "camera eyes" of much fiction since James, they fill precisely the function of avowed narrators—though they can add intensities of their own.

> Gabriel had not gone to the door with the others. He was in a dark part of the hall gazing up the staircase. A woman was standing near the top of the first flight, in the shadow also. He could not see her face but he could see the terracotta and salmon-pink panels of her skirt which the shadow made appear black and white.

It was his wife. She was leaning on the banisters, listening to something. . . . He asked himself what is a woman standing on the stairs in the shadow, listening to distant music, a symbol of. [Joyce's "The Dead"]

The very real advantages of this method, for some purposes, have provided a dominant theme in modern criticism. Indeed, so long as our attention is on such qualities as naturalness and vividness, the advantages seem overwhelming. Only as we break out of the fashionable assumption that all good fiction tries for the same kind of vivid illusion in the same way are we forced to recognize disadvantages. The third-person reflector is only one mode among many, suitable for some effects but cumbersome and even harmful when other effects are desired. . . .

OBSERVERS AND NARRATOR-AGENTS

Among dramatized narrators there are mere observers (the "I" of *Tom Jones, The Egoist, Troilus and Criseyde*), and there are narrator-agents, who produce some measurable effect on the course of events (ranging from the minor involvement of Nick in *The Great Gatsby,* through the extensive give-and-take of Marlow in *Heart of Darkness,* to the central role of Tristram Shandy, Moll Flanders, Huckleberry Finn, and—in the third person—Paul Morel in *Sons and Lovers*). Clearly, any rules we might discover about observers may not apply to narrator-agents, yet the distinction is seldom made in talk about point of view. . . .

SCENE AND SUMMARY

All narrators and observers, whether first or third person, can relay their tales to us primarily as scene ("The Killers," *The Awkward Age,* the works of Ivy Compton-Burnett and Henry Green), primarily as summary or what Lubbock called "picture" (Addison's almost completely non-scenic tales in *The Spectator*), or, most commonly, as a combination of the two.

Like Aristotle's distinction between dramatic and narrative manners, the somewhat different modern distinction between showing and telling does cover the ground. But the trouble is that it pays for broad coverage with gross imprecision. Narrators of all shapes and shades must either report dialogue alone or support it with "stage directions" and description of setting. But when we think of the radically different effect of a scene reported by Huck Finn and a scene reported by Poe's Montresor, we see that the quality of being "scenic" suggests very little about literary effect. And compare the delightful summary of twelve years given in two pages of *Tom Jones* (Book III, chap. i) with the tedious showing of even ten minutes of uncurtailed conversation in the hands of a Sartre when he allows his passion for "durational realism" to dictate a scene when summary is called for. . . . The contrast between scene and summary, between showing and telling, is likely to be of little use until we specify the kind of narrator who is providing the scene or the summary.

COMMENTARY

Narrators who allow themselves to tell as well as show vary greatly depending on the amount and kind of commentary allowed in addition to a direct relating of events in scene and summary. Such commentary can, of course, range over any aspect of human experience, and it can be related to the main business in innumerable ways and degrees. To treat it as a single device is to ignore important differences between commentary that is merely ornamental, commentary that serves a rhetorical purpose but is not part of the dramatic structure, and commentary that is integral to the dramatic structure, as in *Tristram Shandy*. . . .

SELF-CONSCIOUS NARRATORS

Cutting across the distinction between observers and narrator-agents of all these kinds is the distinction between *self-conscious narrators* . . . , aware of themselves as writers (*Tom Jones, Tristram Shandy, Barchester Towers, The Catcher in the Rye, Remembrance of Things Past, Dr. Faustus*), and narrators or observers who rarely if ever discuss their writing chores (*Huckleberry Finn*) or who seem unaware that they are writing, thinking, speaking, or "reflecting" a literary work (Camus' *The Stranger,* Lardner's "Haircut," Bellow's *The Victim*).

VARIATIONS OF DISTANCE

Whether or not they are involved in the action as agents or as sufferers, narrators and third-person reflectors differ markedly according to the degree and kind of distance that separates them from the author, the reader, and the other characters of the story. In any reading experience there is an implied dialogue among author, narrator, the other characters, and the reader. Each of the four can range, in relation to each of the others, from identification to complete opposition, on any axis of value, moral, intellectual, aesthetic, and even physical. (Does the reader who stammers react to the stammering of H. C. Earwicker as I do? Surely not.) The elements usually discussed under "aesthetic distance" enter in of course; distance in time and space, differences of social class or conventions of speech or dress— these and many others serve to control our sense that we are dealing with an aesthetic object, just as the paper moons and other unrealistic stage effects of some modern drama have had an "alienation" effect. But we must not confuse these with the equally important effects of personal beliefs and qualities, in author, reader, narrator, and all others in the cast of characters.

1. The *narrator* may be more or less distant from the *implied author*. The distance may be moral (Jason vs. Faulkner, the barber vs. Lardner, the narrator vs. Fielding in *Jonathan Wild*). It may be intellectual (Twain and Huck Finn, Sterne and Tristram Shandy on the influence of noses, Richardson and Clarissa). It may be physical or temporal: most authors are distant from even the most

knowing narrator in that they presumably know how "everything turns out in the end." And so on.

2. The *narrator* also may be more or less distant from the *characters* in the story he tells. He may differ morally, intellectually, and temporally (the mature narrator and his younger self in *Great Expectations* or *Redburn*); morally and intellectually (Fowler the narrator and Pyle the American in Greene's *The Quiet American,* both departing radically from the author's norms but in different directions); morally and emotionally (Maupassant's "The Necklace," and Huxley's "Nuns at Luncheon," in which the narrators affect less emotional involvement than Maupassant and Huxley clearly expect from the reader); and thus on through every possible trait.

3. The *narrator* may be more or less distant from the reader's own norms; for example, physically and emotionally (Kafka's *The Metamorphosis*); morally and emotionally (Pinkie in *Brighton Rock,* the miser in Mauriac's *Knot of Vipers,* and the many other moral degenerates that modern fiction has managed to make into convincing human beings).

With the repudiation of omniscient narration, and in the face of inherent limitations in dramatized reliable narrators, it is hardly surprising that modern authors have experimented with unreliable narrators whose characteristics change in the course of the works they narrate. Ever since Shakespeare taught the modern world what the Greeks had overlooked in neglecting character change (compare *Macbeth* and *Lear* with *Oedipus*), stories of character development or degeneration have become more and more popular. But it was not until authors had discovered the full uses of the third-person reflector that they could effectively show a narrator changing *as he narrates*. The mature Pip, in *Great Expectations,* is presented as a generous man whose heart is where the reader's is supposed to be; he watches his young self move away from the reader, as it were, and then back again. But the third-person reflector can be shown, technically in the past tense but in effect present before our eyes, moving toward or away from values that the reader holds dear. Authors in the twentieth century have proceeded almost as if determined to work out all of the possible plot forms based on such shifts: start far and end near; start near, move far, and end near; start far and move farther; and so on. Perhaps the most characteristic, however, have been the astonishing achievements in the first of these, taking extremely unsympathetic characters like Faulkner's Mink Snopes and transforming them, both through character change and technical manipulation, into characters of dignity and power. We badly need thoroughgoing studies of the various plot forms that have resulted from this kind of shifting distance.

4. The *implied author* may be more or less distant from the *reader*. The distance may be intellectual (the implied author of *Tristram Shandy*, not of course to be identified with Tristram, more interested in and knowing more about recondite classical lore than any of his readers), moral (the works of Sade), or aesthetic. From the author's viewpoint, a successful reading of his book must eliminate all distance between the essential norms of his implied author and the norms of the postulated reader. Often enough, there is very little fundamental distance to begin with; Jane Austen does not have to convince us that pride and

prejudice are undesirable. A bad book, on the other hand, is often most clearly recognizable because the implied author asks that we judge according to norms that we cannot accept.

5. The *implied author* (carrying the reader with him) may be more or less distant from *other characters*. Again, the distance can be on any axis of value. Some successful authors keep most of their characters very far "away" in every respect (Ivy Compton-Burnett), and they may work very deliberately, as William Empson says of T. F. Powys, to maintain an artificiality that will keep their characters "at a great distance from the author." Others present a wider range from far to near, on a variety of axes. Jane Austen, for example, presents a broad range of moral judgment (from the almost complete approval of Jane Fairfax in *Emma* to the contempt for Wickham in *Pride and Prejudice*), of wisdom (from Knightley to Miss Bates or Mrs. Bennet), of taste, of tact, of sensibility.

It is obvious that on each of these scales my examples do not begin to cover the possibilities. What we call "involvement" or "sympathy" or "identification" is usually made up of many reactions to author, narrators, observers, and other characters. And narrators may differ from their authors or readers in various kinds of involvement or detachment, ranging from deep personal concern (Nick in *The Great Gatsby,* MacKellar in *The Master of Ballantrae,* Zeitblom in *Dr. Faustus*) to a bland or mildly amused or merely curious detachment (Waugh's *Decline and Fall*).

For practical criticism probably the most important of these kinds of distance is that between the fallible or unreliable narrator and the implied author who carries the reader with him in judging the narrator. If the reason for discussing point of view is to find how it relates to literary effects, then surely the moral and intellectual qualities of the narrator are more important to our judgment than whether he is referred to as "I" or "he," or whether he is privileged or limited. If he is discovered to be untrustworthy, then the total effect of the work he relays to us is transformed.

Our terminology for this kind of distance in narrators is almost hopelessly inadequate. For lack of better terms, I have called a narrator *reliable* when he speaks for or acts in accordance with the norms of the work (which is to say, the implied author's norms), *unreliable* when he does not. It is true that most of the great reliable narrators indulge in large amounts of incidental irony, and they are thus "unreliable" in the sense of being potentially deceptive. But difficult irony is not sufficient to make a narrator unreliable. Nor is unreliability ordinarily a matter of lying, although deliberately deceptive narrators have been a major resource of some modern novelists (Camus' *The Fall,* Calder Willingham's *Natural Child,* etc.). It is most often a matter of what James calls *inconscience;* the narrator is mistaken, or he believes himself to have qualities which the author denies him. Or, as in *Huckleberry Finn,* the narrator claims to be naturally wicked while the author silently praises his virtues behind his back.

Unreliable narrators thus differ markedly depending on how far and in what direction they depart from their author's norms; the older term "tone," like the currently fashionable terms "irony" and "distance," covers many effects that we should distinguish. Some narrators, like Barry Lyndon, are placed as far "away" from author and reader as possible, in respect to every virtue except a kind of interesting vitality. Some, like Fleda Vetch, the reflector in James's *The Spoils of Poynton,* come close to representing the author's ideal of taste, judgment, and moral sense. All of them make stronger demands on the reader's powers of inference than do reliable narrators.

VARIATIONS IN SUPPORT OR CORRECTION

Both reliable and unreliable narrators can be unsupported or uncorrected by other narrators (Gully Jimson in *The Horse's Mouth,* Henderson in Bellow's *Henderson the Rain King*) or supported or corrected (*The Master of Ballantrae, The Sound and the Fury*). Sometimes it is almost impossible to infer whether or to what degree a narrator is fallible; sometimes explicit corroborating or conflicting testimony makes the inference easy. Support or correction differs radically, it should be noted, depending on whether it is provided from within the action, so that the narrator-agent might benefit from it in sticking to the right line or in changing his own views (Faulkner's *Intruder in the Dust*), or is simply provided externally, to help the reader correct or reinforce his own views as against the narrator's (Graham Greene's *The Power and the Glory*). Obviously, the effects of isolation will be extremely different in the two cases.

PRIVILEGE

Observers and narrator-agents, whether self-conscious or not, reliable or not, commenting or silent, isolated or supported, can be either privileged to know what could not be learned by strictly natural means or limited to realistic vision and inference. Complete privilege is what we usually call omniscience. But there are many kinds of privilege, and very few "omniscient" narrators are allowed to know or show as much as their authors know.

We need a good study of the varieties of privilege and limitation and their function. Some limitations are only temporary, or even playful, like the ignorance Fielding sometimes imposes on his "I" (as when he doubts his own powers of narration and invokes the Muses for aid (*Tom Jones,* Book XIII, chap. i). Some are more nearly permanent but subject to momentary relaxation, like the generally limited, humanly realistic Ishmael in *Moby-Dick,* who can yet break through his human limitations when the story requires ("'He waxes brave, but nevertheless obeys; most careful bravery that!' murmured Ahab"—with no one present to report to the narrator). And some are confined to what their literal condition would allow them to know (first person, Huck Finn; third person, Miranda and Laura in Katherine Anne Porter's stories).

The most important single privilege is that of obtaining an inside view of another character, because of the rhetorical power that such a privilege conveys upon a narrator. There is a curious ambiguity in the term "omniscience." Many modern works that we usually classify as narrated dramatically, with everything relayed to us through the limited views of the characters, postulate fully as much omniscience in the silent author as Fielding claims for himself. Our roving visitation into the minds of sixteen characters in Faulkner's *As I Lay Dying,* seeing nothing but what those minds contain, may seem in one sense not to depend on an omniscient author. But this method is omniscience with teeth in it: the implied author demands our absolute faith in his powers of divination. We must never for a moment doubt that he knows everything about each of these sixteen minds or that he has chosen correctly how much to show of each. In short, impersonal narration is really no escape from omniscience—the true author is as "unnaturally" all-knowing as he ever was. If evident artificiality were a fault—which it is not—modern narration would be as faulty as Trollope's.

Another way of suggesting the same ambiguity is to look closely at the concept of "dramatic" storytelling. The author can present his characters in a dramatic situation without in the least presenting them in what we normally think of as a dramatic manner. When Joseph Andrews, who has been stripped and beaten by thieves, is overtaken by a stagecoach, Fielding presents the scene in what by some modern standards must seem an inconsistent and undramatic mode. "The poor wretch, who lay motionless a long time, just began to recover his senses as a stage-coach came by. The postilion, hearing a man's groans, stopped his horses, and told the coachman, he was certain there was a dead man lying in the ditch. . . . A lady, who heard what the postilion said, and likewise heard the groan, called eagerly to the coachman to stop and see what was the matter. Upon which he bid the postilion alight, and look into the ditch. He did so, and returned, 'That there was a man sitting upright, as naked as ever he was born.'" There follows a splendid description, hardly meriting the name of scene, in which are recorded the selfish reactions of each passenger. A young lawyer points out that they might be legally liable if they refuse to take Joseph up. "These words had a sensible effect on the coachman, who was well acquainted with the person who spoke them; and the old gentleman above mentioned, thinking the naked man would afford him frequent opportunities of showing his wit to the lady, offered to join with the company in giving a mug of beer for his fare; till, partly alarmed by the threats of the one, and partly by the promises of the other, and being perhaps a little moved with compassion at the poor creature's condition, who stood bleeding and shivering with the cold, he at length agreed." Once Joseph is in the coach, the same kind of indirect reporting of the "scene" continues, with frequent excursions, however superficial, into the minds and hearts of the assembly of fools and knaves, and occasional guesses when complete knowledge seems inadvisable. If to be dramatic is to show characters dramatically engaged with each other, motive clashing with motive, the outcome depending upon the resolution of motives, then this scene is dramatic. But if it is to give the impression that the story is taking place by itself, with the characters existing in a dramatic relationship vis-à-vis the spectator, unmediated by a narrator and decipherable only through inferential matching of word to word and word to deed, then this is a relatively undramatic scene.

On the other hand, an author can present a character in this latter kind of dramatic relationship with the reader without involving that character in any internal drama at all. Many lyric poems are dramatic in this sense and undramatic in any other. "That is no country for old men—" Who says? Yeats, or his "mask," says. To whom? To us. How do we know that it is Yeats and not some character as remote from him as Caliban is remote from Browning in "Caliban upon Setebos"? We infer it as the dramatized statement unfolds; the need for the inference is what makes the lyric dramatic in this sense. Caliban, in short, is dramatic in two senses; he is in a dramatic situation with other characters, and he is in a dramatic situation over against us. Yeats's poem is dramatic in only one sense.

The ambiguities of the word dramatic are even more complicated in fiction that attempts to dramatize states of consciousness directly. Is *A Portrait of the Artist as a Young Man* dramatic? In some respects, yes. We are not told about Stephen. He is placed on the stage before us, acting out his destiny with only disguised helps or comments from his author. But it is not his actions that are dramatized directly, not his speech that we hear unmediated. What is dramatized is his mental record of everything that happens. We see his consciousness at work on the world. Sometimes what it records is itself dramatic, as when Stephen observes himself in a scene with other characters. But the report itself, the internal record, is dramatic in the second sense only. The report we are given of what goes on in Stephen's mind is a monologue uninvolved in any modifying dramatic context. And it is an infallible report, even less subject to critical doubts than the typical Elizabethan soliloquy. We accept, by convention, the claim that what is reported as going on in Stephen's mind really goes on there, or in other words, that Joyce knows how Stephen's mind works. "The equation of the page of his scribbler began to spread out a widening tail, eyed and starred like a peacock's; and, when the eyes and stars of its indices had been eliminated, began slowly to fold itself together again. The indices appearing and disappearing were eyes opening and closing; the eyes opening and closing were stars. . . ." Who says so? Not Stephen, but the omniscient, infallible author. The report is direct, and it is clearly unmodified by any "dramatic" context—that is, unlike a speech in a dramatic scene, it does not lead us to suspect that the thoughts have been in any way aimed at an effect. We are thus in a dramatic relation with Stephen only in a limited sense—the sense in which a lyric poem is dramatic.

INSIDE VIEWS

Finally, narrators who provide inside views differ in the depth and the axis of their plunge. Boccaccio can give inside views, but they are extremely shallow. Jane Austen goes relatively deep morally, but scarcely skims the surface psychologically. All authors of stream-of-consciousness narration presumably attempt to go deep psychologically, but some of them deliberately remain shallow in the moral dimension.[2] We should remind ourselves that any sustained inside view, of whatever depth, temporarily turns the character whose mind is shown into a narrator; inside views are thus subject to variations in all of the qualities we have described above, and most importantly in the degree of unreliability. Generally speaking, the deeper our plunge, the more unreliability we will accept without loss of sympathy. . . .

Narration is an art, not a science, but this does not mean that we are necessarily doomed to fail when we attempt to formulate principles about it. There are systematic elements in every art, and criticism of fiction can never avoid the responsibility of trying to explain technical successes and failures by reference to general principles. But we must always ask where the general principles are to be found.

It is not surprising to hear practicing novelists report that they have never had any help from critics about point of view. In dealing with point of view the novelist must always deal with the individual work: which particular character shall tell this particular story, or part of a story, with what precise degree of reliability, privilege, freedom to comment, and so on. Shall he be given dramatic vividness? Even if the novelist has decided on a narrator who will fit one of the critic's classifications—"omniscient," "first person," "limited omniscient," "objective," "roving," "effaced," or whatever—his troubles have just begun. He simply cannot find answers to his immediate, precise, practical problems by referring to statements such as that the "omniscient is the most flexible method," or that "the objective is the most rapid or vivid." Even the soundest of generalizations at this level will be of little use to him in his page-by-page progress through his novel.

As Henry James's detailed records show, the novelist discovers his narrative technique as he tries to achieve for his readers the potentialities of his developing idea. The majority of his choices are consequently choices of degree, not kind. To decide that your narrator shall not be omniscient decides practically nothing. The hard question is: Just how *inconscient* shall he be? Again, to decide on first-person narration settles only a part of one's problem, perhaps the easiest part. What kind of first person? How fully characterized? How much aware of himself as narrator? How reliable? How much confined to realistic inference; how far privileged to go beyond realism? At what points shall he speak truth and at what points utter no judgment or even utter falsehood? These questions can be answered only by reference to the potentialities and necessities of particular works, not by reference to fiction in general, or the novel, or rules about point of view. . . .

NOTES

1. Efforts to use the second person have never been very successful, but it is astonishing how little real difference even this choice makes. When I am told, at the beginning of a book, "You have put your left foot. . . . You slide through the narrow opening. . . . Your eyes are only half open . . . ," the radical unnaturalness is, it is true, distracting for a time. But in reading Michel Butor's *La Modification* (Paris, 1957), from which this opening comes, it is surprising how quickly one is absorbed into the illusory "present" of the story, identifying one's vision with the "vous" almost as fully as with the "I" and "he" in other stories.

2. Discussion of the many devices covered by the loose term "stream-of-consciousness" has generally concentrated on their service to psychological realism, avoiding the moral effect of different degrees of depth. Even unfriendly critics—Mauriac in *Le romancier et ses personnages* (Paris, 1933), for example—have generally pointed to their amorphousness, their lack of clear control and their obvious artifice, not to their

moral implications. Too often, both attack and defense have assumed that there is a single device which can he assessed as good or bad, once and for all, for such-and-such general reasons. Melvin Friedman (*Stream of Consciousness* [New Haven, CT: 1955]) concludes that it is "almost axiomatic that no further work of the first order can be done within this tradition," since the method depended on a "certain literary mentality which died out with Joyce, Virginia Woolf, and the early Faulkner" (p. 261). But the works he treats make use of dozens of varieties of stream-of-consciousncss, some of which are now an established part of the novelist's repertoire. Most of them are likely to find new uses in the future.

DISCUSSION QUESTIONS

1. How does Booth complicate the usual categorizations of "point of view" into "first person" and "third person" (either "limited" or "omniscient")? In other words, how do these simple categories fail to account for all the possibilities for presenting information to a reader? What other categories does Booth create?
2. What are the "variations of distance" Booth discusses, and how do the various kinds of "distance" affect the presentation of information to the reader?
3. What is an unreliable narrator, and in what ways can a reader measure the degree of unreliability? Why would an author choose to use an unreliable narrator?
4. Explain the meaning of the three epigraphs at the beginning of this selection (from the *Confessions of Zeno*, *Le roman bourgeois*, and *Epitaph of a Small Winner*), relating them to specific passages from Booth's essay.
5. Locate as many of Booth's variations on "point of view" as you can in stories that you know. Quote passages that illustrate Booth's criteria for determining point of view, such as "dramatized" or "undramatized" narrator; various "distances" among implied author, narrator, and reader; "reliable" or "unreliable" narrator; and so on. (Booth himself provides many leads with the authors and works he mentions.)

LEON SURMELIAN

Scene and Summary

Leon Surmelian (b. 1907) has published the autobiography I Ask You, Ladies and Gentlemen *(1945), the novel* 98.6 *(1950), and the critical work* Techniques of Fiction Writing: Measure and Madness *(1968). In this selection, he fleshes out the traditional categories of "showing" and "telling" to explain their uses and misuses.*

SCENE

Scene Re-Creates a Single Incident

There are two ways of writing a story: scene and summary. Scene is the dramatic and summary the narrative method. Fiction is dramatic narration, neither wholly scene nor wholly summary, but scene-and-summary. If it were all scene, it would be a play; if all summary, more of a synopsis than a story.

The scene is a specific act, a single event that occurs at a certain time and place and lasts as long as there is no change of place and no break in the continuity of time. It is an incident acted out by the characters, a single episode or situation, vivid and immediate. The scene is the dramatic or play element in fiction, and a continuous present action while it lasts. The scene reproduces the movement of life, and life is action, motion. As a moving picture the scene is a closer imitation of what happens in life than a summary of it would be. It is not a narrator's report about it, but the event, the experience itself which unfolds before the eyes of the reader, with the actors caught in the act. . . .

Ernest Hemingway in *The Sun Also Rises* introduces Robert Cohn with a few paragraphs of summary, followed by a scene—a specific incident, that occurred one night after Jake Barnes, the narrator, had dinner with Cohn and his girl friend Frances. Later they went to the Café de Versailles for coffee, where he first became aware of the young woman's attitude toward Cohn, who after his divorce backed a review of the arts that started in Carmel, California, and finished in Provincetown, Massachusetts.

> Robert Cohn was a member, through his father, of one of the richest Jewish families in New York, and through his mother of one of the oldest. At the military school where he prepped for Princeton, and played a very good end on the football team, no one had made him race-conscious. No one had ever made him feel he was a Jew, and hence any different from anybody else, until he went to Princeton. He was a nice boy, a friendly boy, and very shy, and it made him bitter. He took it out in boxing, and he came out of Princeton with painful self-consciousness and the flattened nose, and was married by the first girl who was nice to him. He was married five years, had three children, lost most of the fifty thousand dollars his father left him, the balance of the estate having gone to his mother, hardened into a rather unattractive mould under domestic unhappiness with a rich wife; and just when he had made up his mind to leave his wife she left him and went off with a miniature-painter. . . .
>
> We had several *fines* after the coffee, and I said I must be going. Cohn had been talking about the two of us going off somewhere on a weekend trip. He wanted to get out of town and get in a good walk. I suggested we fly to Strasbourg and walk up to Saint Odile, or somewhere or other in Alsace. "I know a girl in Strasbourg who can show us the town," I said.
>
> Somebody kicked me under the table. I thought it was accidental and went on: "She's been there two years and knows everything there is to know about the town. She's a swell girl."

I was kicked again under the table and, looking, saw Frances, Robert's lady, her chin lifting and her face hardening.

"Hell," I said, "why go to Strasbourg? We could go up to Bruges, or to the Ardennes."

Cohn looked relieved. I was not kicked again. I said goodnight and went out. Cohn said he wanted to buy a paper and would walk to the corner with me. "For God's sake," he said, "why did you say that about that girl in Strasbourg for? Didn't you see Frances?"

"No, why should I? If I know an American girl that lives in Strasbourg what the hell is it to Frances?"

"It doesn't make any difference. Any girl. I couldn't go, that would be all."

The scene carries more weight with the reader. These are presumably the exact words spoken by Jake Barnes and Robert Cohn. This is the original event as it took place in Paris. A scene of course cannot go on indefinitely; it ends when another scene begins. A story happens in a certain time sequence. Each scene, by itself, is a continuous action, but a lapse in time would be a break, and so would a change of place. These breaks are minimized in modern fiction, and an impression of continuous present action, as there is on the screen, is given by writers who know their technique.

What the reader is told by the omniscient author may be illuminating, but it cannot have the same authority for him as what he sees himself, with his own eyes. "Seeing is believing." The reader prefers the living picture; he would rather have a direct view of the event, of the characters in action, with no narrator and guide coming between him and what is happening, not be forced to see the event through the eyes of somebody else. The scene in its pure form does not need a narrator, just as the playwright does not have to be on the stage with the actors, and with the exit of the author verisimilitude is gained. . . .

The scene shows us the actors in action, but some narration is usually mixed up in it, and we hear the narrator's voice also as he describes the gestures of the speakers and gives other stage directions which in a play would guide and inform the actors and not form part of the dialogue. In its pure form, with no stage directions, no commentary, the scene eliminates the narrator's voice and is, as in an acted play, only character voice or voices, and this heightens the illusion of reality. In the scene the burden of narration is shifted to the characters themselves and they do the work, they carry the ball.

It is useful for the writer to think of his story as a series of scenes and to visualize the whole story as so many "shots" in a motion picture. The scene is a close-up of the action, made with the writer's imaginative camera and microphone brought close to the actors as they play their parts, and as in a film, the scene records their dialogue and every significant detail of the action. It also records, in fiction, their unspoken speech or internal monologue. The thoughts and feelings of the characters are included.

By working in scenes the writer can spot in advance the weak points in his story, he can see better the incongruities and improbabilities in it that otherwise might escape his attention. The scene makes him the first perceptive reader of his tale. The scene moreover gives us durational realism. A scene on the stage or screen would take as much time to act as it would in real life, and this could be done in fiction too. Through scene we can capture the very process of living in its own time sequence. The scene shows *how* it happens and does not merely give the result after it has happened, and when we are shown how it happens, we might also have the answer to *why*. The reader is allowed to draw his own conclusions from the action, instead of accepting the writer's interpretation of it. . . .

There is nothing like scene for giving life and movement to the story. The writer who wants to produce an effect of the present will avoid summary as much as he can. Dialogue by itself—or internal monologue—will give an impression of immediacy. Usually the scene is not only acted out, but talked out, and where there is dialogue there is likely to be scene. But there may be scenes without dialogue, which is talk between two or more persons, or without monologue, spoken or silent. We may have only one person in a scene with his thoughts not given, silent pantomime.

Components of Scene

When the writer is organizing his material and blocking out his action, he can determine in advance the main events and choose these for scenic treatment. The three classic plot elements of discovery or recognition, reversal or peripety, and disaster or suffering may make exciting scenes. So would the climax of the story, as an obligatory scene. The scene may be an episode, in the more restricted sense of a separate incident or story within a larger story related to the main action but not an integral part of it. If such an episode is included then it is probably important enough to be dramatized. The scene may be a flashback. It may be an external or internal event; thought can be the highest action. The crucial incidents, the turning points, the climactic events, the advances or retreats in the attainment of a goal, pursuit and flight, various stratagems, crises and conflicts, the clash of human wills, arguments, quarrels, showdowns, trouble and misery, wounds, illness, death—these make good scenes.

But the scene need not be confined to the highlights of the plot. There is room also for small incidents, brief friendly meetings, a bit of conversation here and there. All kinds of significant acts, no matter how small, may make good scenes. The scenic or dramatic method can be used also for the apparently insignificant items in the story, and these, like secondary characters, can be extremely valuable in rounding out the picture and creating the necessary background for the principal actors and the main action. The scene is not always reserved for big moments.

A story need not be a series of dramatic explosions. The strength of fiction lies in depicting the slow, almost imperceptible changes, in re-creating the gradual growth and expansion of a consciousness with its consequent chaos or unity. We should not confuse method with content when we use the word scene as synonymous with drama. A dramatic subject with exciting situations may be written by the scenic method, and so may an undramatic subject. There are dramatic stories in non-dramatic form, and non-dramatic stories in dramatic form, scene throughout—as in much popular fiction. Here we are concerned with the method, and not with subject-matter or content, although content and method are by no means independent and content may well determine method. A dramatic subject naturally lends itself to scenic treatment. It is likely to have situations that can be shown and acted out. Some confusion is inevitable because of the various meanings of drama, and of scene, too. . . .

Dialogue

The scene then is a clear lucid image of action, revealing a life behind it. And since scene and dialogue go roughly together, and by scene we usually mean action and speech, short sharp sentences make not only for crisp dialogue, but contribute to the momentum of the scene. A staccato style accelerates the action. There is no need to describe repeatedly the gestures of the speakers (as Henry James does so often, and Hemingway does not), and usually "said" or "asked" or "answered" or some such simple word is enough. Gestures and other descriptions used for revealing character or explaining a situation bring in the author's voice and remind the reader he is being told a story. The author's voice should be heard as little as possible. In a dialogue scene the reader's attention should be drawn to what the characters are saying, and the words stand out better by themselves, as do the speakers, if the third person does not enter too often. When the speech is charged with emotional associations or significance, when it is loaded, as it should be, and requires the concentrated attention of the reader, stage directions might annoy, confuse and fatigue him, especially if more than three people are talking. The reader can supply the gesture and intonation himself. . . .

The dialogue should suggest, if not fully reproduce, the sharp, abrupt, disjointed nature of spoken English, with its stresses and slacks, its sudden bursts of explosive rhythm. English is a stress language and not a syllabic one in rhythm. A Frenchman who hears English spoken for the first time and is not used to such stresses and slacks would be impressed by its jerky up-and-down quality, by its long sustained vowels with abrupt breaks. In French the accent normally falls on the last syllable. We might say that while the story itself should be interconnected to make one whole, ideally a dramatic unity in structure, the speech of the characters should be somewhat disjointed, without too many connectives.

There are so many individual, class, regional, racial, cultural, period differences in spoken English that no statement about dialogue could apply to all of them, but our test again is mimesis—the closest imitation of actual speech, or thought-speech, expressive of character and emotion at any given moment in the action. In dialogue also the part stands for the whole.

Dialogue should be dramatic, as in a play; not written obviously for information or the history of the characters in quotation marks; not routine small talk; not too long, or a series of set speeches, but short, pointed, loaded.

No Anticipation of Future

As the scene is an event in progress, we cannot know in advance what is coming next, as we do not know in real life; we can only guess, make suppositions. This increases the suspense of the story. In the scene as it develops the result is still uncertain, and both character and reader are in a state of curiosity or anxiety about the outcome. "Paul was reading the paper in the college library when Mary came from behind him and blindfolded him with her hands" is the narrative method. "Paul was reading the paper in the college library when he felt two feminine hands blindfold him from behind, and as he pulled the hands away from his eyes and looked up over his shoulder he saw it was Mary" is the scenic method. Paul did not know it was Mary until he saw her, and the scenic method reproduces the original process with its sequence of motions and with the discovery of the girl's identity at the end. One tells us about a past action that has already occurred; it was Mary. The other is present action, scene, and we are shown how it happened.

A story like a poem may be an emotional experience recollected in tranquillity, but when written by the scenic method it is not retrospective; the unique event seems to be occurring for the first time, and this fresh impact makes the scene a more intense experience than recollections would be. The scene gives the story intensity, and intensity is a quality writers strive for. Poetry is more intense than prose. An intense imitation of life—an intense illusion of reality—this is what we want. It is gained through picture, point of view, plot, immediacy, inwardness, style, tone, etc. Intensity gives a tighter story line, drama and unity. . . .

Yet indispensable as it is, scene cannot do everything; it would take too much space to tell everything in scene, and certain other values in fiction might be lost. A short story, as a single dramatic episode, might conceivably be all scene, with no more than "said" added by the author, but in a novel, or in the longer tale, the incidents must be tied together. Other problems also arise, by no means absent in the short form, which are best met by another method of mimesis: summary.

SUMMARY AND DESCRIPTION

Not everything can, or need, be shown in fiction. The writer can also *tell* a story. Summary needs a teller, and this is admittedly a weakness; it does not have the seemingly spontaneous movement of the scene; it is not something acted out before the eyes of the reader, who is listening to somebody tell him about it. But summary has its rightful place in the structure of the story and can be extremely useful.

Summary brings in the author, or his alter ego, his spokesman, unless it is summary by character, in which case it becomes dramatic. There is a change in voice from scene to summary and from summary to scene, and the reader unconsciously prefers a character voice, because it means more mimetic writing. When the writer speaks through his own voice the all-important element of mimesis is definitely less and the reader's interest decreases. Hearing is substituted for seeing, and the ear is weaker than the eye in the creation of mental images. Nevertheless, no matter how scenic, a story requires a narrator. Omniscience may be eliminated, but not the narrator's voice. We still hear it. . . .

Summary, unlike scene, does not individualize characters through their actions and speech. It throws the whole burden of narration on the shoulders of the author or his narrator. It gives us experience secondhand. Scene is self-explanatory; in summary the narrator explains. Summary tends to be abstract, discursive, with something fanciful and "literary" clinging to it, in contrast to the concrete specific act of the scene. Scene at its best has the impact of life. In it, the characters are on their own (with an occasional assistance from the narrator); in summary they lack this independence. In scene, the reader also is on his own, judging the action for himself and interpreting it in his own way; in summary, the reader is guided by the narrator, who speaks in his own voice, whether or not the reader is directly addressed. Something is happening in the scene; in summary it has already happened.

Summary makes for distance. It does not give us a close-up of the action as it occurs; it is a long shot. We no longer have the words spoken by the characters to others or to themselves; the narrator summarizes their speech, spoken or silent, and he is the only speaker we hear. The dialogue or internal monologue is indirect, in third person, and dissolves in the general stream of the narrative. The third person itself makes for distance. Summary may reveal the characters, describe their actions and thoughts and feelings, but it is not a close re-creation as in the scene. It does not have the power of dramatic imitation, and the reader is deprived of the pleasure of viewing the event for himself.

Summary lacks the vividness of the scene, the immediacy, the presentness of the action acted out by the actors. There is obviously a difference between an event shown to us while it is taking place, and merely telling about it. Today's reader does not care to read synopses or outlines, but demands fully developed stories, told the way it really happened, and no rhetorical tricks will satisfy him if the concrete event is missing. The fiction writer speaks best through pictures, and in the imitation of life, there is no real substitute for the moving picture of the scene. Summary not only makes action distant in space and time, but also makes it abstract, unless written in highly visual prose, and even then some of the basic weakness of summary remains; style is burdened with greater responsibilities in the absence of scene, and there is a danger of overwriting and heightening the event through language, when it should be the other way around. . . .

We have then acknowledged the defects of summary. It lowers the mimetic quality of a story. When the author speaks, what he says is colored by his own sentiments and opinions, no matter how impersonal and objective he tries to be, even weeding out most of his adjectives and adverbs. There is inevitably some distortion of reality from the reader's point of view when he is forced to see events through someone else's eyes. The same distortion exists even when the narrator is one of the characters in the story, although the authority of an internal voice may be greater than the author's. Summary by character may be more credible, but the objection to summary is not entirely overcome; summary in character voice is still too general, not particular enough, and the specific incident is missing. Somebody in the story is describing it for us, while we are denied a direct view of the event.

Yet summary does many important things in a story. It links the scenes together and gives the story continuity and unity. If we consider scenes the main building blocks, summaries are the cement in creative construction. Summary may be reduced to the minimum, but that minimum is essential by the law of artistic economy if nothing else. Summary can span long periods of time when nothing of great importance happens, and the writer does not have to dwell at length upon them. . . .

Summary gives the writer freedom of movement from scene to scene, from one high point of the action to another. The skill with which the writer arranges his material into scene and summary shows his knowledge of story values and his sense of form. Henry Fielding boldly explained to the reader the necessity of not telling all in a much quoted passage.

> When any extraordinary scene presents itself (as we trust will often be the case), we shall spare no pains nor paper to open it at large to our readers; but if whole years should pass without producing anything worthy his notice, we shall not be afraid of chasm in our history, but shall hasten on to matters of conse-quence, and leave such periods of time totally unobserved.
> . . . My reader then is not to be surprised, if, in the course of this work, he shall find some chapters very short, and others altogether as long; some that con-tain only the time of a single day, and others that comprise years; in a word, if my history sometimes seems to stand still, and sometimes to fly.
>
> (*Tom Jones*, Book II, I)

A story is a dramatic concentration of life and the writer skips the detail of months and years in which nothing remarkable happens and re-creates the extraordinary rather than the ordinary. He sees the uncommon in the common, the general in the particular, and every good story is something of a wonder tale. It would be boring to tell the reader everything. The gaps in the action and char-acterization stimulate the reader's imagination; he fills them in himself.

The action moves by fits and starts; it does not proceed at a uniform rate of speed. Scene accelerates the movement, summary slows it down, and generally the longer the scene the greater its power over the reader, although length by itself cannot be the sole criterion of its effect. Short scenes, short chapters, chop up a story; long scenes unify it, and especially in an episodic plot, long scenes or long chapters give better continuity. Since the scene is a continuous act it has a natural unity of its own and makes for an unbroken story line, as long as it lasts. Contin-uous action is more lifelike. Film and fiction can do without curtains. The short story particularly is a unified event, and some novels, like *Mrs. Dalloway* by Vir-ginia Woolf, have no chapter divisions. The sustained scene heightens the illusion of reality and may be an excellent unifying and intensifying device, but what seems to be an unbroken story line is actually disconnected. Even in the cinema we do not have an uninterrupted sequence from beginning to end; scenes fade in and fade out or dissolve into the next scene, but it is done so unobtrusively we scarcely notice it (or do not mind it if we do). The same effect may be gained in fiction by short, skillful summaries carrying us from scene to scene, and the impression of one continuous movement is maintained. . . .

VERSATILITY OF SUMMARY

The weakness of summary may be turned to advantage. Beautiful economies may be achieved through summary and it is more versatile than scene. It gives a story depth, body, vividness, variety, freedom of movement, and brings out its full meaning, the philosophy of the tale. Summary may be narrative, descriptive, expository, or all three at once. We noted earlier that summary creates distance; it is a long shot. The long shot is as necessary as the close-up. Imagine a motion picture shot entirely in close-ups. The control of distance means among other things the control of intensities, of reader attention, and this may be done through summary. The writer changes the position of his camera to get certain effects.

In the scene we are sometimes too close to the action to understand it; summary gives perspective. As readers or writers, we see the situation better by withdrawing a little, just as a painter steps back to take a good look at what he is doing on the canvas, and the viewer of the finished painting regulates his distance to see it better. Then too, by supplying the connections between the incidents, summary is an aid to a better understanding of the story. We may go from the particular, scene, to the general, through summary.

Since summary favors a more detached spectator attitude, it may be used for giving the reader emotional relief when his nerves are frayed by the scenes. When a scene arouses too much anxiety, summary allays it. The reader's emotional tension relaxes when he comes to a summary, and as he moves back he is not so intimately involved in the events and can rest for a while—until the next scene. . . .

CONTROL OF EMOTION
AND AESTHETIC DISTANCE

The writer must regulate the reader's emotional reactions. He may intensify an emotional experience through scene just so much, after which, as indicated above, he has to establish a margin of safety through summary. Sophisticated fiction tends to a lower emotional tone, and the scene, unrelieved by summary, may be too much for any reader to take. We live in an age of social distances, and summary perhaps is a psychological necessity today.

It is largely through summary that the fiction writer piles up his details, and summary can cover a lot more territory than the scene. Scene excludes; summary includes. Its reach is longer. It is not confined to one particular incident at a particular place and time. Summary can range far and wide. We need summary for the slow march of years, for the erosions of time. We need it for recollection, for retrospect, for reflection and comment. The basic method of *À la recherche du temps perdu* by Marcel Proust is summary, as is the endless monologue in *Finnegans Wake*. Henry James wrote *The Awkward Age* in scenes, like a play, but it is not a very good novel and he did not repeat the experiment. The fiction writer should not deny himself the privilege of the general survey and the freedom of movement from peak to valley and from valley to peak, between present and past, that summary gives him. . . .

Scene is the foreground, summary the background, and without the background, the foreground appears thin and abstract. The scene by itself cannot give the movement of a wider life around it; that is the job of summary. The scene cuts off the immediate event from its surroundings, its tendency is to narrow it down, to detach and isolate it, just as a stage play is an isolated action, with its scenery and properties suggesting the wider life from which it is separated. On the stage the scenery and props are "summary." In fiction the writer has to supply the scenery and props himself. Sets are a later development in the theatre. The Elizabethan stage was practically bare.

Through summary the writer can give the social and geographical aspects of the story. Summary gives the action space, and even magnitude and grandeur. It is independent of time and place, and through it the writer can give the past, present and future of his characters, moving back and forth at will. . . .

By enlarging the scale, summary makes indirectly for greater realism, gives us the whole picture, even though as a method it is not a close mimesis of the action. The modern novel, and to a lesser extent the short story, is epic in structure. As we call summary the narrative method, we evidently believe it is natural to narration, and a story is a dramatic summary. The great novels are built on a large scale: this is important for beauty, the ultimate aim of technique. When the screen is widened, summary comes in, and with it, the complexity of life. Some of the intensity of drama may be lost, but the fiction writer can well afford this loss to gain other effects: the picture of a whole society, the imitation of places and manners, of a way of life, as in *Madame Bovary*. The scale is reduced in the short story, which lends itself more readily to close scenic treatment because it is short and can be more dramatic in structure, more like a play in method. Some successful novels are written like short stories or like plays with the whole action taking place in one day, but a subject may also be ruined by overdramatization. It is difficult to make changes in a character convincing if they occur within a few hours and much may be lost for the sake of intensity or unity.

Summary makes for density in writing, packs prose with concrete details of the setting, of the characters and their actions, and the story becomes richer and more significant through summary. By enlarging the scale to lifelike proportions, the writer gets the reader off the narrow stage of drama and out into the open as it were. Summary may be a counterpoise to theatrical effects, to quick turns of fortune, sudden reversals, swift changes in character and motive, which are not too convincing even on the stage. Lost tension may be recovered through the increasing suspense. Summary may be invaluable as a delaying maneuver, postponing the blow or the climax. Intensification is not always gained through speed. When a man speaks slowly in a tense situation, the tension increases; there is more power, more drama, in his speech. If there is no talk in summary, there may well be the drama of silence in it. Note how the music stops at a highly dramatic moment in the movies and the action is played in silence or largely in silence. Silence can be a powerful dramatic device.

Summary, then, widens and deepens the scope of the story and, by supplying the connective tissues, makes it an organic interrelated whole. It breaks up the monotonous sequence of scenes, making for variety and diversion, for change of pace. With the main action concentrated in a few big scenes, the events of other years and of peripheral actions, of incidental byplays, may be summarized, and the intervals between the main events need not be shown if they can be told, but the shorter these intervals the better. If we may risk another generalization here, let us say the safe rule for the writer to follow is summary in small amounts, here and there, without making the bridges from scene to scene too long. A lengthy summary in the midst of the action, with the story well on its way, and in prosaic prose, can be deadly. The craft-conscious writer avoids full stops and keeps the story moving, unless he has good reasons for not doing so. He knows that generally interest falls off when the reader comes to a summary. Crossing the bridge can be dull business, but it has to be done, and the quicker it is done the better, if there is no reason for lingering on the bridge.

SCENE OR SUMMARY

Usually the writer can tell in advance whether the subject he has chosen is dramatic or panoramic, a scene or summary kind of story, and always the best method is that which does the most for the particular subject. A novel crowded with hundreds of characters and covering a long span of time, like *War and Peace* or a family chronicle like *Buddenbrooks* by Thomas Mann, needs a lot of summary; so does a novel without a hero like *Vanity Fair,* in which there is no strict dramatic progression of events. Thackeray began as an essayist, and one can see in his writing the affinity that summary has with the essay and memoir. A story, grounded in its particular environment, which gives a picture of customs and costumes, one that is definitely located, in Russia, in Germany, in Mayfair, in Yonville, with the action extended over many years, cannot do without summaries.

One of the first things a writer must do in organizing his material is to place his scenes and summaries. He has to decide in advance what goes into scene and what goes into summary and work out his scene line, and summary line. The scene line is the main line of action, supported by the summary line, and the writer weaves scenes and summaries together into a pattern that makes a well-balanced whole. During the actual writing process some scenes will emerge as summaries and some summaries will break up into separate scenes, but the initial planning can save the writer false motions and wasted time and effort. Is it going to be a close-up, a medium shot, or a long panoramic shot? Essentially, the organization of a story on dramatic principles is a problem in distance, and not only scene and summary but point of view also have to do with the control of distance and the related problem of authority. . . .

The difference between scene and summary should be fairly clear by now. Each method has its strengths and weaknesses and they complement each other. We move in and out of scene and summary continuously when we read or write a story, and generally, as readers at least, we are not aware of it. Some people are astonished when they first learn about scene and summary and it becomes an important reading tool for them. It is the basic writing tool. Expository, or fact, writers become hardened in their habit of writing in summary and cannot write fiction until they learn to write in scene, shifting from explanation or commentary in one voice, their own, to imitation in several voices, from article or essay or editorial to moving pictures of life. . . .

DISCUSSION QUESTIONS

1. What is the difference between "scene" and "summary," according to Surmelian? Why does he seem to prefer the scene to summary, as a rule?
2. In spite of his emphasis on the crucial importance of scene, Surmelian also examines the role of summary. What functions does summary perform? Why is it necessary to mix scene and summary?
3. What are Surmelian's rules for scenic dialogue? How do they relate to the rules for scene generally?
4. Surmelian's bias in favor of "objective" scene over "omniscient" summary is characteristic of modern (especially twentieth-century) fiction. He reveals this bias in many ways, including explicit comparisons between writers (James and Hemingway, for example). Find several stories, both older and more modern, that illustrate older and more modern treatments of scene and summary, and explain the differences with specific examples from each story.

EUDORA WELTY

Some Notes on Time

Eudora Welty (b. 1909) has written a dozen collections of short stories and four novels in a dazzling variety of styles. From the stories in A Curtain of Green *(1941) and* The Bride of the Innisfallen *(1955) to the novels* Delta Wedding *(1946) and* The Optimist's Daughter *(1972), Welty delights us with voices ranging from "local color" first-person narration to a disembodied postmodern account. She has always written about the craft of fiction as well, from* Short Stories *(1949) to* Place in Fiction *(1957) to* Three Papers on Fiction *(1962). In these works, as in her fiction, she is concise, straightforward, and compelling.*

Time and place, the two bases of reference upon which the novel, in seeking to come to grips with human experience, must depend for its validity, operate together, of course. They might be taken for granted as ordinary factors, until the novelist at his work comes to scrutinize them apart.

Place, the accessible one, the inhabited one, has blessed identity—a proper name, a human history, a visible character. Time is anonymous; when we give it a face, it's the same face the world over. While place is in itself as informing as an old gossip, time tells us nothing about itself except by the signals that it is passing. It has never given anything away.

Unlike time, place has surface, which will take the imprint of man—his hand, his foot, his mind; it can be tamed, domesticized. It has shape, size, boundaries; man can measure himself against them. It has atmosphere and temperature, change of light and show of season, qualities to which man spontaneously responds. Place has always nursed, nourished and instructed man; he in return can rule it and ruin it, take it and lose it, suffer if he is exiled from it, and after living on it he goes to it in his grave. It is the stuff of fiction, as close to our living lives as the earth we can pick up and rub between our fingers, something we can feel and smell. But time is like the wind of the abstract. Beyond its all-pervasiveness, it has no quality that we apprehend but rate of speed, and our own acts and thoughts are said to give it that. Man can feel love for place; he is prone to regard time as something of an enemy.

Yet the novelist lives on closer terms with time than he does with place. The reasons for this are much older than any novel; they reach back into our oldest lore. How many of our proverbs are little nutshells to pack the meat of time in! ("He that diggeth a pit shall fall into it." "Pride goeth before destruction, and a haughty spirit before a fall.") The all-withstanding devices of myth and legend (the riddle of the Sphinx, Penelope's web, the Thousand and One Nights) are constructed of time. And time goes to make that most central device of all, the plot itself—as Scheherazade showed us in her own telling.

Indeed, these little ingots of time are ingots of plot too. Not only do they contain stories, they convey the stories—they speak of life-in-the-movement, with a beginning and an end. All that needed to be added was the middle; then the novel came along and saw to that.

Only the nursery fairy tale is not answerable to time, and time has no effect upon it; time winds up like a toy, and toy it is: when set to "Once upon a time" it spins till it runs down at "Happy ever after." Fairy tales don't come from old wisdom, they come from old foolishness—just as potent. They follow rules of their own that are quite as strict as time's (the magic of number and repetition, the governing of the spell); their fairy perfection forbids the existence of choices, and the telling always has to be the same. Their listener is the child, whose gratification comes of the fairy tale's having no suspense. The tale is about wishes, and thus grants a wish itself.

Real life is not wished, it is lived; stories and novels, whose subject is human beings in relationship with experience to undergo, make their own difficult way, struggle toward their own resolutions. Instead of fairy immunity to change, there is the vulnerability of human imperfection caught up in human emotion, and so there is growth, there is crisis, there is fulfillment, there is decay. Life moves toward death. The novel's progress is one of causality, and with that comes suspense. Suspense is a necessity in a novel because it is a main condition of our existence. Suspense is known only to mortals, and its agent and messenger is time.

The novel is time's child—"I could a tale *unfold*"—and bears all the earmarks, and all the consequences.

The novelist can never do otherwise than work with time, and nothing in his novel can escape it. The novel cannot begin without his starting of the clock; the characters then, and not until then, are seen to be alive, in motion; their situation can declare itself only by its unfolding. While place lies passive, time moves and is a mover. Time is the bringer-on of action, the instrument of change. If time should break down, the novel itself would lie in collapse, its meaning gone. For time has the closest possible connection with the novel's meaning, in being the chief conductor of the plot.

Thus time is not a simple length, on which to string beadlike the novel's episodes. Though it does join acts and events in a row, it's truer to say that it leads them in a direction, it induces each one out of the one before and into the one next. It is not only the story's "then—and then," it may also be a "but" or a "nevertheless"; and it is always a "thus" and a "therefore."

Why does a man do a certain thing now, what in the past has brought him to it, what in the future will come of it, and into what sequence will he set things moving now? Time, in which the characters behave and perform, alone and with others, through the changes rung by their situation, uncovers motive and develops the consequences. Time carries out a role of resolver. ("As a man soweth, so shall he reap.")

Clock time has an arbitrary, bullying power over daily affairs that of course can't be got around (the Mad Hatter's tea party). But it has not the same power in fiction that it has in life. Time is plot's right arm, indeed, but is always answerable to it. It can act only in accordance with the plot, lead only toward the plot's development and fulfillment.

Fiction does not hesitate to accelerate time, slow it down, project it forward or run it backward, cause it to skip over itself or repeat itself. It may require time to travel in a circle, to meet itself in coincidence. It can freeze an action in the middle of its performance. It can expand a single moment like the skin of a balloon or bite off a life like a thread. It can put time through the hoop of a dream, trap it inside an obsession. It can set a fragment of the past within a frame of the present and cause them to exist simultaneously. In Katherine Anne Porter's perfect short story "The Grave," a forgotten incident from her country-Texas childhood abruptly projects itself upon a woman's present; its meaning—too deep for the child's understanding—travels twenty years through time and strikes her full force on a city street in another country. In this story, time moves by metamorphosis, and in the flash it discloses another, earlier metamorphosis—the real one, which had lain there all the while in the past that the young woman had left behind her.

In going in the direction of meaning, time has to move through a mind. What it will bring about is an awakening there. Through whatever motions it goes through, it will call forth, in a mind or heart, some crucial recognition. ("I imagined that I bore my chalice safely through a throng of foes.")

What can a character come to know, of himself and others, by working through a given situation? This is what fiction asks, with an emotional urgency driving it all the way; and can he know it in time? Thus time becomes, as sharply as needed, an instrument of pressure. Any novel's situation must constitute some version of a matter of life or death. In the face of time, life is always at stake. This may or may not be the case in a literal sense; but it does need to be always the case as a matter of spiritual or moral survival. It may lie not so much in being rescued as in having learned what constitutes one's own danger, and one's own salvation. With the refinements of the danger involved, suspense is increased. Suspense has exactly the value of its own meaning.

In fiction, then, time can throb like a pulse, tick like a bomb, beat like the waves of a rising tide against the shore; it can be made out as the whisper of attrition, or come to an end with the explosion of a gun. For time is of course subjective, too. ("It tolls for thee.")

Time appears to do all these things in novels, but they are *effects*, necessary illusions performed by the novelist; and they make no alteration in the pace of the novel, which is one of a uniform steadiness and imperturbability. The novel might be told episodically, hovering over one section of time and skipping over the next; or by some eccentric method—Henry Green spoke of his as going crabwise; but however its style of moving, its own advance must remain smooth and unbroken, its own time all of a piece. The plot goes forward at the pace of its own necessity, its own heartbeat. Its way ahead, its line of meaning, is kept clear and unsnarled, stretched tight as a tuned string.

Time in a novel is the course through which, and by which, all things in their turn are brought forth in their significance—events, emotions, relationships in their changes, in their synchronized move toward resolution. It provides the order for the dramatic unfolding of the plot: revelation is not revelation until it is dramatically conceived and carried out.

The close three-way alliance of time, plot and significance can be seen clearly demonstrated in the well-written detective novel. We can learn from it that plot, by the very strength, spareness and boldness of its construction-in-motion, forms a kind of metaphor. I believe every well-made plot does, and needs to do so. But a living metaphor. From the simplest to the most awesomely complicated, a plot is a device organic to human struggle designed for the searching out of human truth. It is from inception highly sensitive to time, it acts within time, and it is in its time that we ourselves see it and follow it.

As readers, we accept more or less without blinking the novel's playing-free with time. Don't we by familiar practice accept discrepancies much like them in daily living? Fictional time bears a not too curious resemblance to our own interior clock; it is so by design. Fiction penetrates chronological time to reach our deeper version of time that's given to us by the way we think and feel. This is one of the reasons why even the first "stream-of-consciousness" novels, difficult as they must have been for their authors breaking new ground, were rather contrarily easy for the reader to follow.

Fictional time may be more congenial to us than clock time, precisely for human reasons. An awareness of time goes with us all our lives. Watch or no watch, we carry the awareness with us. It lies so deep, in the very grain of our characters, that who knows if it isn't as singular to each of us as our thumbprints.

In the sense of our own transience may lie the one irreducible urgency telling us to do, to understand, to love.

We are mortal: this is time's deepest meaning in the novel as it is to us alive. Fiction shows us the past as well as the present moment in mortal light; it is an art served by the indelibility of our memory, and one empowered by a sharp and prophetic awareness of what is ephemeral. It is by the ephemeral that our feeling is so strongly aroused for what endures, or strives to endure. One time compellingly calls up the other. Thus the ephemeral, being alive only in the present moment, must be made to live in the novel as *now*, while it transpires, in the transpiring.

Fiction's concern is with the ephemeral—that is, the human—effects of time, these alone. In action, scene and metaphor, these are set how unforgettably before our eyes! I believe the images of time may be the most indelible that fiction's art can produce. Miss Havisham's table in its spiderwebs still laid for her wedding feast; the "certain airs" in *To the Lighthouse* that "fumbled the petals of roses"— they come instantaneously to mind. And do you not see the movement of Gusev's body in the sea, after his burial from the hospital ship: see it go below the surface of the sea, moving on down and swaying rhythmically with the current, and then being met by the shark: "After playing a little with the body the shark nonchalantly puts its jaws under it, cautiously touches it with its teeth, and the sailcloth is rent its full length from head to foot." "Was it possible that such a thing might happen to anyone?" is the question Chekhov has asked as Gusev was slid into the sea, and in this chilling moment we look upon the story's answer, and we see not simply an act taking place in time; we are made, as witnesses, to see time happen. We look upon its answer as it occurs in time. This moment, this *rending,* is what might happen to anyone.

When passion comes into the telling, with a quickening of human meaning, changes take place in fictional time. Some of them are formidable.

I was recently lent a book by a student which had set itself to clear up *The Sound and the Fury* by means of a timetable; the characters' arrivals and departures, including births and deaths, were listed in schedule, with connections to and from the main points of action in the novel. What has defeated the compiler is that *The Sound and the Fury* remains, after his work as before it, approachable only as a novel. He was right, of course, in seeing time to be at the bottom of it. Time, though—not chronology.

Think of the timepieces alone. Think of only one timepiece: Dilsey has to use the Compson clock; it has only one hand. "The clock tick-tocked, solemn and profound. It might have been the dry pulse of the decaying house itself; after a while it whirred and cleared its throat and struck." It strikes five times. "Eight o'clock," says Dilsey. Even while the clock is striking, chronology is in the act of yielding to another sort of time.

Through the telling of the story three times in succession by three different Compsons in the first-person and then once again in the third-person, we are exposed to three different worlds of memory, each moving in its own orbit. "He thirty-three," Luster says of Benjy, "thirty-three this morning," and the reply comes, "You mean he been three years old thirty years." Benjy's memory is involuntary and not conscious of sequence or connections: a stick run along the palings of a fence. But time of whatever nature leaves a residue in passing, and out of Benjy comes a wail "hopeless and prolonged. It was nothing. Just sound. It might have been all time and injustice and sorrow become vocal for an instant by a conjunction of planets."

Time to Quentin is visible—his shadow; is audible—his grandfather's watch; and it is the heavy load that has to be carried inside him—his memory. Excruciatingly conscious, possessing him in torture, that memory works in spite of him and of all he can do, anywhere he can go, this last day of his life. The particular moment in time that links him forever to the past—his world—conditions *all* time. The future may be an extension of the past *where possible;* the future can include memory *if bearable.* But time will repeatedly assault what has been intact; which may be as frail as the virginity of Caddy. If experience is now, at every stage, a tragedy of association in the memory, how is the rememberer to survive? Quentin spends his last day, as he's spent his life, answering that he is already dead. He has willed the past some quality, some power, by which it can arrest the present, try to stop it from happening; can stop it.

Who, in the swirling time of this novel, knows the actual time, and can tell the story by it? Jason, of course. He keeps track of time to the second as he keeps track of money to the penny. Time is money, says Jason. And he cheats on both and is in turn cheated by both; we see him at the end a man "sitting quietly behind the wheel of a small car, with his invisible life ravelled out about him like a worn-out sock."

By all the interior evidence, we will come nearest to an understanding of this novel through the ways it speaks to us out of its total saturation with time. We read not in spite of the eccentric handling of time, but as well as we can by the aid of it. If a point is reached in fiction where chronology has to be torn down, it must be in order to admit and make room for what matters overwhelmingly more to the human beings who are its characters.

Faulkner has crowded chronology out of the way many times to make way for memory and the life of the past, as we know, and we know for what reason. "Memory believes before knowing remembers," he says (in *Light in August*). Remembering is so basic and vital a part of staying alive that it takes on the strength of an instinct of survival, and acquires the power of an art. Remembering is done through the blood, it is a bequeathment, it takes account of what happens before a man is born as if he were there taking part. It is a physical absorption through the living body, it is a spiritual heritage. It is also a life's work.

"There is no such thing as was," Faulkner remarked in answer to a student's question as to why he wrote long sentences. "To me, no man is himself, he is the sum of his past. There is no such thing really as was, because the past is. It is a part of every man, every woman, and every moment. All of his and her ancestry, background, is all a part of himself and herself at any moment. And so a man, a character in a story at any moment in action, is not just himself as he is then, he is all that made him; and the long sentence," he adds, "is an attempt to get his past and possibly his future into the instant in which he does something . . ."

Distortion of time is a deeply conscious part of any novel's conception, is an organic part of its dramatic procedure, and throughout the novel's course it matters continuously and increasingly, and exactly as the author gives it to us. The dilations, the freezing of moments, the persistent recurrences and proliferations, all the extraordinary tamperings with time in *The Sound and the Fury,* are answers to the meaning's questions, evolving on demand. For all Faulkner does to chronological time here—he explodes it—he does nothing that does not increase the dramatic power of his story. The distortions to time give the novel its deepest seriousness of meaning, and charge it with an intense emotional power that could come from nowhere else. Time, in the result, is the living essence of *The Sound and the Fury.* It appears to stand so extremely close to the plot that, in a most extraordinary way, it almost becomes the plot itself. It *is* the portentous part; it is the plot's long reverberation. Time has taken us through every degree of the long down-spiral to the novel's meaning—into the meaning; it has penetrated its way. It has searched out every convolution of a human predicament and brought us to the findings of tragedy.

Faulkner's work is, we know, magnetized to a core of time, to his conception of it as the continuing and continuousness of man. Faulknerian time is in the most profound and irrefutable sense *human* time. (*Corruption* is that which time brings to the Compsons' lives. *Progress* is the notion of those who are going to make something out of it: "What's in it for me?" ask the Snopeses.) His deepest felt and most often repeated convictions—"They endured." "Man will prevail"—are the long-reached and never-to-be-relinquished resolutions of his passionate idea of human time. And they contain, burned into them, all the plots of Faulkner's novels and stories.

Time, in a novel, may become the subject itself. Mann, attacking the subjectivity of man's knowledge of time, and Proust, discovering a way to make time give back all it has taken, through turning life by way of the memory into art, left masterpieces that are like clocks themselves, giant clocks stationed for always out in the world, sounding for us the high hours of our literature. But from greatest to least, don't most novels reflect that personal subjective time that lived for their writers throughout the writing?

There is the constant evidence of it in a writer's tempo, harmony, the inflections of his work, the symmetry and proportions of the parts in the whole; in the felt rhythms of his prose, his emotion is given its truest and most spontaneous voice; the cadence which is his alone tells us—it would almost do so in spite of him—his belief or disbelief in the story he intends us to hear. But I have in mind something more than this governing of a writer's style.

Faulkner has spoken for the record of his difficulties in writing *The Sound and the Fury,* the novel he loved best and considered his most imperfect; he spoke of its four parts as four attempts, and four failures, to tell his story. In their own degree, many other novels give evidence in themselves of what this difficulty suggests: the novel's duration is in part the measurable amount of time the novelist needs to apprehend and harness what is before him; time is part of the writing too. The novel finished and standing free of him is not the mirror-reflection of that writing-time, but is its equivalent. A novel's duration is, in some respect, exactly how long it takes the particular author of a particular novel to explore its emotional resources, and to give his full powers to learning their scope and meeting their demands, and finding out their truest procedure.

In the very imperfections of *The Sound and the Fury,* which come of a giant effort pushed to its limit and still trying, lies a strength we may set above perfection. They are the human quotient, and honorable as the marks left by the hand-held chisel in bringing the figure out of recalcitrant stone—which is another way of looking at time.

DISCUSSION QUESTIONS

1. Welty asserts that "time has the closest possible connection with the novel's meaning," in that it is not only a "then—and then," it is also a "thus" and a "therefore." How does this idea relate to Forster's idea about the difference between "story" and "plot"?
2. Welty notes that fiction "plays free" with time, doing things with it that are not true to our everyday experience of the passage of time. What things? Why do we accept fiction's distortion of "real" time?
3. Welty points to *The Sound and the Fury* as an example of a work that distorts time in various ways to achieve its purpose or meaning. Can you offer a similar example about any other piece of fiction you've read that deliberately "plays free" with time?

R. V. CASSILL

Character

R. V. Cassill (b. 1919) is Professor Emeritus at Brown University and has taught at the University of Iowa, Columbia University, and the New School for Social Research in New York City. He is the author of two dozen novels, a half dozen collections of short stories, several collections of poetry, several anthologies of literature, and the important textbook Writing Fiction *(1962). His best-known novel may be* La Vie Passionnée of Rodney Buckthorne: A Tale of the Great American's Last Rally and Curious Death *(1968), and other novels include* Clem Anderson *(1961),* The President *(1964),* The Goss Women *(1974),* Labors of Love *(1980), and* After Goliath *(1985).*

In real life, character is revealed to us; in fiction, character is created. *There* is the difference between experience and artifice.

One begins by drawing from life. The writer knows or has known some actual person whose qualities suit the role left open for someone in his general concept of a story.

We know that a great number of the best fictional characters have been drawn from life. Biographers delight in telling us which members of the family, which friends, and which enemies served as models for great authors. In *Anna Karenina* Kitty is drawn from Tolstoy's wife. Emily Brontë drew from her brother Branwell in creating the character of Heathcliff in *Wuthering Heights*. Surely Flaubert used his mistress Louise Colet as a model for the portrait called Madame Bovary. In the gallery of autobiographical characters, Levin is Tolstoy's self-portrait. Stephen Dedalus is Joyce's.

All this is true, as far as it goes—and it doesn't go far enough to satisfy the writer confronted with the problem of how to get Uncle Harry—or himself—onto the white sheets of paper lying beside his typewriter. You can't just press the old boy onto the paper, like a rose pressed between the pages of a book. And a typewriter isn't a camera. You can't get a portrait just by pressing one of the little nickeled levers.

We've got to ask what it means when we use the figurative expression "drawing from life." It means first of all observing a person, noting his history and his appearance, his bank roll and his mustache. It means achieving, to the extent we can, some sense of identification with that person so we know, intuitively, what it means to him when he says "I." Though scholarship has determined who is the principal model Flaubert used in writing of the adulterous wife of a country doctor, we would know much too little about the process of creation if we could not grasp what Flaubert meant by saying, *Madame Bovary, c'est moi.* ("I am Madame Bovary.") He meant that he had passed from observation of externals to a personal, intuitive knowledge of "I" as a desperate woman.

After observation and (when possible) a kind of identification, one still has to do more than feed the results of experience into a story like sand fed into a bag. We must not suppose that Louise Colet was the only model for Emma Bovary. Several other women contributed, including the unfortunate wife of a country doctor who had been, in reality, a student of Flaubert's father. From one woman the author drew mouth, eyes, insecurity, and the tendency to daydream, we suppose. From another he got those memorable fingernails and an unruly temper. From still another came the body and the outrageously trusting naiveté.

A fictional character—and particularly one who occupies a central position in a sizable work—is a composite, then, like so many of the other elements in fiction.

What determines which are suitable among all the characteristics available to a writer with a good memory and several models for a single character? Well, the plot, for one thing, gives some useful indications of what is required in a particular role and what is inappropriate. That is, if the plot requires a woman to cuckold her husband with a vain ladies' man, it must be obvious that the woman can't be given characteristics of tranquillity, obedience, or good sense. She has to emerge as the composite of those characteristics that would make such an action seem probable, and only those.

It is not necessary to think of plot as a dictatorial preconception imposed by the author to see that it always acts as a shaping and selecting influence in the development of characters. In some stories it is evident that characters have been mutilated to fit plot requirements. Obviously this is bad art. But even when it takes form at the same pace as the characters grow, plot restrains, limits, and gives definition to those characters.

The qualities of a character are also selected and shaded by the rest of the cast. The adulterous wife must be made to fit with the particular husband assigned her by the story, and with the particular seducer. In developing the whole cast of characters for his story, the author is a bit like a hostess planning a party, inviting guests who complement each other. The author has, though, the privilege and obligation of literally shaping the people he wants—not merely exercising a hostess's tact and judgment.

But, given an original conception of character and certain limiting requirements within the structure of the story, still more is required to make the artifice of fiction *seem* a true reflection of life. There ought to be in a story some quality of decision that will give the illusion that the characters are acting on their own volition. In "The Lady with the Pet Dog" Gurov is "already" bored with Anna after their first adultery. Yet the very naiveté and remorse that seem so boring in the woman are the qualities that will presently make him fall in love with her "really, truly—for the first time in his life." It amuses him that she considers him, at first, to be "kind, exceptional, high-minded" when he has treated her with the "coarse arrogance of a happy male . . . twice her age." Yet he will seek his own humility in an attempt to become what she erroneously thought him to be.

We can explain these expressive, ironic turns in the story by saying that the author's observation of life had shown him similar ironies. And we know that Chekhov "made things turn out" as he did to express the discrepancy between a man's superficial intentions and his underlying will. There is, beyond doubt, the imposition of a preconceived design on the material of this story. And yet it conveys to us the illusion of life because we feel that in the course of writing it Chekhov underwent the change of emotions that he attributes to Gurov—that the nice, bearded, passionate author at his desk must have said, "But after all *I* love Anna for the very qualities that amused me in the beginning."

One senses that almost magical (and yet common) submersion of the author's identity in the identity of his chief character. Logic and intellect and practice as a writer are all superseded while the author believes, "*I am Gurov.* What I have been doing in permitting him the action that has taken place thus far in my story is permitting myself that action. Next I will do this. . . ."

Of course no author ever completely gives up his own identity in the creative process. Chekhov knows he is Chekhov even when he chooses as Gurov. And when he has finished playing Gurov's role, he will look back over his work with the cold eye of the craftsman—striking out one passage and adding a calculated effect to polish his story. But unless he has known the moment of identification, when author and character are one, his labors of revision will be partly wasted.

It is probably these moments of identification that weld character and plot together in a perfect fusion, even if each has come from a separate process of thought, even if the plot was loosely determined a week before the character was settled on. Without such fusions, fiction is something less than art.

So, wouldn't it be wonderful if identification of author and character guaranteed perfect fiction? But it might mean only that the writer had perfected a way of daydreaming on paper. When the author is Chekhov—a conscious master of his craft who knows very well how to mesh the elements of his story before he yields conscious control—great fiction results. In the case of a writer who has not yet learned how to mingle character and action in a design of language, identification is often no better than self-indulgence.

Let's go back from the pinnacle of the art to some fundamentals. It is fundamental for the writer to remember that:

1. A character in a story is an artificial construction.
2. A character is composed by certain combinations of the basic elements of fiction—language, descriptions, actions, dialogue, and interaction with scene and other characters.
3. A fictional character is not alive in the same sense a human being is, but in a parallel sense. The character "lives" in the environment that the author builds for him, not in the limitless world of actuality.

Let's illustrate these points by reference to the stories included in this book.

Consider the weirdly stylized character of Miss Festner in "Us He Devours"—the spinster with "hard breasts" and "quick money-counting fingers." Accepting such details as being in accord with reality as he has experienced it, the reader still does not really ask, "*Was* there such a woman somewhere on this earth, once upon a time?" He believes that there *is* such a person because the author has temporarily forced him to accept the artificial world of the story as the only reality that concerns him.

Murphy's dumb, delicious Annie ("Murphy's Xmas") is not a real girl. We will never see her. We will only see words on a printed page. But we will remember her *as if* we had seen her because Mr. Costello built up an artificial association of girl with *shy skeleton, her thighs so cool, the pearl flick of her tongue,* and the way her fingers *make star-shafted wrinkles in the sheets* when a man presses her down onto a bed.

These words call to my mind images as moving as anything in my personal memory—but I know that if Costello had been making lilies out of crepe paper, wire, and wax he would not be producing objects more artificial than his story.

I stress the artificiality of fiction and the comparison with the flower maker because it is important to remember that writing fiction *ends* in a construction resembling nature, just as flower-making does. No one praises badly made artificial flowers just because their maker understood the horticulture of real plants. Similarly, a story cannot be praised merely because the author *started* from sound observation of human character.

Observation of character is structured into fiction by various kinds of description. In first person narration the narrator often defines himself and his motives. "I loved her ignorantly, impurely, and intermittently, sometimes unfurling toward her passions that . . . were, no doubt, more appropriate when directed toward building model airplanes . . . etc." ("In the Central Blue"). Such characterizations depend for their credibility on the general credibility of the narrator, and it is a nice trick to shape him so the reader may be aware of his biases.

Jones the preacher is "like an animal in a traveling show who, through some aberration, wears a vital organ outside the skin. . . ." His daughter's fingernails "were crudely bitten, some bleeding below the quick. She was tough and remote, wanting only to go on a trip for which she had a ticket." His wife is "no longer a woman, the woman whom he loves, but a situation." And his granddaughter's eyes "are a foal's eyes, navy-blue. She has grown in a few weeks to expect everything from Jones." ("Taking Care"). These descriptions, of course, do not tell us all we know about Jones and his dependents. But they supplement and heighten what we learn of them by taking in the situation and relationships of the story.

"'Isn't he funny?'" Grace's roommate says of her fiancé. "'He says "terlet." I didn't know people really said "terlet."'" ("The Best of Everything"). This scant and offhand description of Ralph by a girl who has had little chance to observe him may, indeed, do little by itself to characterize the husband-to-be for us. But, as it is structured into the story, it prepares us for the monstrous shock of revelation at the end. Then Ralph, in the full flowering of his callousness, will ask his bride, "'Mind if I use ya terlet?'"—and the shocked reader will see that this man regards his woman as no more than a vessel into which he can relieve himself. Then, I suppose, we are in a position to grasp and evaluate his character.

An author's knowledge of his character is built into the story by the actions he is called on to perform, whether these actions contribute directly to the plot or not. When Murphy bashes his fist against one solid surface after another, we get a measure of his inner fury and inability to find an appropriate target for it. The plot action—Murphy's self-destructive returns to the embrace of his wife—reveals his character even more forcefully.

When the boy on the way home from the movie ("In the Central Blue") tries to neck the girl his treacherous friend is necking, some sort of post-pubescent frenzy is revealed in its full enormity. The afterthoughts on this episode supplied by the adult narrator are intended to emphasize rather than minimize the absurdity involved.

Gurov's trip to Anna's home town ("The Lady with the Pet Dog") establishes the irrationality underlying his agile intelligence and prefigures the victory of love over the sterile self-image he has trusted so long. The trip is essential to the advancement of the plot—but we know the plot could have been forced to the same conclusion by the use of some other episode. Of course the other possible plot linkages would have done less to round out an image of a particular sort of man discovering his fate than the one the author chose.

Dialogue has always seemed to me one of the indispensable devices for shading and particularizing a character. In real life we like to see a person's face and hear his actual voice before we judge what he is up to. Fictional dialogue can be made to render very sensitively the mental and emotional ingredients in characters whose general outlines have already been accounted for. Although the dialogue in "Murphy's Xmas" is not conventionally punctuated, the following passage will serve to illustrate its fundamental fidelity to the characters involved.

The shattered family is driving home from the holiday visit when the young son points a toy pistol at his father's head and asks:

Why don't you come back Daddy?

Before he can think or excuse himself, Murphy says, *Because.*

Because why?

Because Mommy and I fight.

You're not fighting now.

In tears and on her knees, Murphy's wife lunges into the back seat and disarms her son. But he begins to cry and find his ultimatum: Daddy

I'm too shy to have a new daddy. I want you to be my daddy, and if you won't come back and be my daddy

I'm going to kill you.

Here the degree of pain felt by each of the three members of the family is measured out, along with the degree of restraint and responsibility the two adults can call up to master it and preserve a semblance of rational behavior against the uninhibited threat from the child.

Almost every story contains a number of characters. Some of them are little more than names. Others have things to say, bits of action to perform. Some—frequently one or two in each story—are the excuse for the story's existence. We see events through their eyes, or see them as if we were riding on their shoulders. What they do, see, and feel is the meaning of the story.

To accept the illusion of the story, the reader needs to know these central characters pretty well. Insofar as the design of the story permits, they should be made into "round" characters. That is, we need to show not merely their primary passions and motivations, but some of the hesitations and equivocations that are not altogether lined up with their principal drives. This character wants to make a fortune. Good. That's his main drive. But he won't cut throats to do it. That complicates things. He is relentless in his ambition. But susceptible to the diversions of love. That too complicates things—and is, very briefly, what is meant by showing a character in the round.

Rounding a character obviously makes him more lifelike, therefore more interesting. So it would seem at first thought that the thing to do is round out and complicate every character in a story. To the extent that this is done, the story would be improved, wouldn't it?

No. It would spoil the design of the story, destroy the overall unity. Round characters are part of the design of a good story, but so are flat ones, characters in whom there is no complexity.

In "The Best of Everything" it adds to the story that Gracie is dubious of the marriage *and* determined to go through with it. That Ralph is sexually attracted to her *and* unable to recognize her invitation. Without such degrees of roundness the story would mean little. At the same time, to keep proportion, to allow Gracie and Ralph their place in the center of the scene, it is necessary that Mr. Atwood be left flat as a stereotype and that Eddie should appear as the single-minded oaf, without the depth or variety within his character that such a person might have in real life.

Obviously the problem of flat and round characters is different in novels than it is in short stories. The novel simply offers more space for the author to show the variety within his characters and, if he wants to, to develop more of them in the round than he could in a short story. But basically the principle is the same. Flat characters are required as foils for the ones more fully rounded.

Needless to say, flat characters should not be dull characters. In "The Lady with the Pet Dog" Gurov's wife is a stereotype of the Russian intellectual female of her day. Anna's husband is a "flunkey." The two of them hardly appear on the scene of the story. Yet they are rendered with such sharp observation that they are a significant part of the whole unity. They are exactly what they have to be to help us see Anna and Gurov and their motives for adultery.

Sometimes it seems that the minor, flat characters in short stories amount to no more than a single epithet—"the fat man," or "Mr. Beaver, the timid boarder," or "Helen—the watchful eye." Seeing that they are only puppets made of a few words—and that still they may give a sense of lifelikeness within the whole unity of the story—the writer is reminded of the most important fact about his craft.

All fictional characters are made up of words. Observation begins the process. Identification—acting out the part—carries it along. But finally it is choice of language, the artifice of design and relationship to other fictional elements, that makes the character live for the reader.

DISCUSSION QUESTIONS

1. Cassill says that, just as fiction "draws on life," so fictional characters "draw on life"—that is, they are based on "real people." But in what way? Since, as Cassill puts it, if you want to base a character on Uncle Harry, "you can't just press the old boy onto paper, like a rose pressed between the pages of a book," how do fiction writers create characters out of people in their lives?

2. Fictional characters are never, strictly speaking, "true to life," since fiction is not biography (a form that has its own problems with "truth"). How, then, can a character express the "truth" of the lives of those we live with?

3. Cassill touches on the idea that all our characters contain at least some of our own personalities, quirks, weaknesses, and insights, just as Freud said that all the characters in a dream reveal aspects of the dreamer's psyche. In what ways can this be true, especially when a character is very unlike the author—when, as Booth might put it, there is a vast "distance" between the author and the character?

ROBIN HEMLEY

The Transformation Process

*Robin Hemley (b. 1958) teaches creative writing at Western Washington University. He has published two collections of short stories (*The Mouse Town*, 1987; and* All You Can Eat, *1992) and two novels (*The Big Ear, *1995; and* The Last Studebaker, *1992). In his textbook* Turning Life into Fiction *(1994), he has much to say about the relation of fiction to life, the transformation of life that fiction entails, and the resulting truths about life in fictional form.*

It's not the material. It's how you write it. A friend once told me an anecdote that I wrote in my journal, not once but twice. I guess I forgot about the first entry.

> Scott told me of a couple of children, one white, one black, who were no more than five years old, and they were running around Boston Commons with a pizza

box. They ran from one person to the next, saying, "You want a slice of pizza?" Then they opened the box. Inside, there was a squirrel that had been flattened by a car. They came up and did this to someone who was standing near Scott, and Scott yelled after them, "You kids should be ashamed of yourselves!"

I used this entry in a story, "Installations," about an unlikely affair between a conductor on the Chicago El and a fledgling performance artist named Ivy, who sees everything, all experience, as art. I have as much trouble with people like Ivy, who see everything as art, as I have with people who want "just the facts, ma'am," and feel that art is irrelevant.

I don't want to be self-aggrandizing here, but I want to show you how I transformed the passage. I used the basic idea of the squirrel in the pizza box, stretched it, dramatized it and altered it to fit the specifications of my story. In the following scene, my protagonist, the El conductor, has just been taken by Ivy to his first performance art exhibit, called an "installation," and he has no idea what to make of it. By the way, the description of the installation is a pretty accurate one of an actual installation I saw in Chicago while *I* was dating a fledgling performance artist, though her name wasn't Ivy and the similarities end there. I didn't, however, record the installation in my journal. It was so bizarre I knew I'd remember every detail for the rest of my life.

> We pass through a white curtain into this scene: a darkened room with a naked man and woman, thirtyish, lying like two sticks of old butter in the middle of the room. Either they're dead or mannequins. The music in the room sounds like the part in *The Wizard of Oz* where Dorothy and her boyfriends are looking at the witch's castle, and the soldiers march around singing: "O-li-o-eyohhh-oh."
>
> Ivy takes my hand and we approach the couple on the floor. A dozen other people saunter around as though nothing special's going on. We can't get any closer than five feet. The couple on the floor are surrounded by hundreds of apples in the shape of a cross. A ragged bat hangs above them, its ribbed wings stretching six feet. A sideways neon eight sways between the wings and glows pale blue.
>
> This is what Ivy calls an installation. This is what I call a fun house.
>
> Up close, I see their chests moving slightly, a small tremor from one of the woman's fingers touching the man's hand, a flickering eyelid. I study them and wonder if I've ever seen them on the El. I wonder if the woman's parents know this is what she does for a living.
>
> Candles burn on their chests. Luckily the candles are in jars, or the wax would be excruciating. Still, the heat must get to them. Not that I can tell. They're not exactly your liveliest couple. I can imagine showing up at Angel's Shortstop, my neighborhood bar, with them stiff as corpses on the bar stools, the candles still stuck on their chests. Angel would serve them up a couple of Old Styles, and squint at me and say, "They friends of yours?"
>
> Yeah, they're installations.
>
> We take the El back to Belmont and walk over to Clark Street. Everything seems strange tonight: a man waiting in the window of a tattoo parlor, the moan coming out of a storefront church.

Ivy asks me what I think about the installations. I don't know. I haven't thought about it. What are you supposed to think about a naked man and woman with candles on their chests?

"Everything," she says. "Adam and Eve lying in suspended animation beneath death and infinity. Christ figures surrounded by the forbidden fruit."

Yeah, well, I guess.

We turn the corner of Clark and Belmont, and two kids, one black and one white, not more than nine years old, slam into us as they tear through the parking lot of Dunkin' Donuts.

"Hey, watch where you're going," I say, touching the white one lightly on the shoulder.

"You watch where you're going, you fag," the kid tells me.

The black kid has a pizza box in his hands. He smiles and says, "You want some pizza?"

"Yeah, you want some pizza?" says the white kid.

The black kid opens up the box. Inside is a squirrel, its head smashed, its legs stretched out, its belly split open. At least a hundred cars have run over it. As flat as a pizza. A circle of dried tomato paste surrounds the carcass.

Before I can react, the kids run off shouting and laughing. They block one pedestrian after another yelling, "Hey, you want some pizza? Free pizza."

Ivy picks up a soft drink cup from the sidewalk and throws it after them. The cup, plastic lid and straw still attached, falls to the ground three feet away. "You brats," she screams. "Come back here."

Ivy takes off. The white kid trips. She chases the other one. I can't make out much through the distance and pedestrians. A few minutes later, she comes smiling back with the pizza box in her hands, the lid closed.

"What do you want *that* for?" I say.

"Stealing is the most sincere form of flattery," she says. "Picasso did it. Every great artist does it."

"Throw it away."

"Are you kidding?"

"Throw it away."

"Don't give me orders. I had to fight them for it."

I don't say a word. I'm tired of her. I was curious before, but now I'm just tired. I head for Angel's Shortstop and Ivy tags along. I figure it's Ivy's turn to feel out-of-place. Not many out-of-place people ever wander into Angel's. If they do, they wander back out again in a hurry. The crowd at Angel's is as tight as a VFW post.

Ignoring Ivy, I sit down on a stool at the bar. There isn't one for her, so she stands in between my stool and the next guy's, and places her pizza box on the counter. Angel gives her a look. Then she looks at me. I order a couple shots of Cuervo with Old Style chasers.

"I'll have to tap a new keg," says Angel. "How 'bout something else in the meantime?"

"How 'bout a mug of beefalo swill?" I say. "Come on, Angel. I'm talking brand loyalty."

"I'll go tap a new keg," she says. Angel is about sixty years old and has a white bubble hair-do. She comes to Chicago via the coal mines of Kentucky, and her husband's long-gone with black lung. Angel's jukebox has only the thickest country-and-western songs, with three exceptions: "A Cub Fan's Dying Prayer," Sinatra's version of "Chicago," and "Angel of the Morning." She's always pumping quarters painted with red fingernail polish into the jukebox and pushing those three tunes. I can't count the number of times I've come into The Shortstop and heard her belting, "Just call me angel of the morning, baby. Just one more kiss before you leave me, angel." She thinks of The Shortstop as a family establishment, even though I'd fall off my stool if I ever saw a family walk through the door. Maybe a family of cockroaches or sewer-bred alligators. Definitely not a family of mammals.

When Angel returns with the Old Styles, Ivy pushes hers away and says, "I don't drink alcohol."

"Angel, this is Ivy," I say. "She comes from Cody, Illinois, the beefalo capital of the Midwest. It's ten miles south of Beloit."

"Blech!" says Ivy.

"What?"

"Beloit. I grew up with the name. It sounds like a quarter being dropped in a toilet. Beloit . . . Besides, I live in Chicago now."

"Yeah, she's a performance artist," I tell Angel.

"Pleased to meet you," she says.

"You want some pizza?" Ivy says.

"No, she doesn't want any pizza," I say, and put my hand on the lid.

"Domino's?" Angel says.

"It's not pizza," I say. "It's a squirrel."

"A squirrel."

"Yeah, a dead one."

"Pepperoni," Ivy says. "You want to see it, Angel?"

"Sure, why not?"

"No, you don't want to see it," I say. My hand is still on the lid.

Ivy looks sideways at me and gives me a half-smile, a dare. Her look says "What's the big deal?" She's right. After all, Angel's not my mother.

With my job and all, I'm not easy to faze, but Ivy definitely fazes me. Not only her actions, but the way she dresses. An orange scarf as big as window drapes. Black fishnet stockings and metallic silver lipstick.

"You ever had squirrel?" says Angel. "Tastes just like chicken. Of course, there ain't as much meat on a squirrel."

"Do you always believe what you see, Angel?" Ivy says.

"Almost never," says Angel, leaning towards her, a look of concentration on her face. "A fella come in here the other day selling key chains. He had a metal man and a metal woman on the key chain, and when he wiggled a lever they started doing things. He said he had a whole trunkful in his car, and did I want to sell some on a card behind the counter? I said, 'Look around, this is a family place.' He said, 'You'd be surprised. People just love them. I've seen grandmas and young girls go crazy over them.' 'Yeah, well this is a gay bar, buddy,' I said.

'That's fine,' he said. 'I can take off the woman and put on another man. I already did that with one gay establishment. I'll put on dogs. I'll put on a man and a horse. Even two Japanese girls and a rhinoceros if that's what you want. Whatever turns you on.' Some people just want to shock you. I could have called the cops, but I ignored him. Eventually, he just slithered back under his rock."

"You want some pizza?" Ivy says.

"Yeah, why not?" says Angel.

I take my hand off the lid and wait for Ivy to open up the box, but she doesn't move. What's she waiting for? I wonder if I'm going nuts. If Ivy's brainwashing me. I've known her two days, and suddenly I want to show Angel the dead squirrel in the pizza box.

"One object can have many functions," Ivy says. "Consider this pizza box. For you and me, it signifies food. For Rocky the squirrel, it's his final resting place. When you put the two together, it's repulsive. Why? Because food and death are opposites, right? No, not at all. Food and death go hand in hand, but our escapist society allows us to blithely ignore that fact. Hold the mayo, hold the lettuce, special orders don't upset us. Right, Angel? Next time you go to an open casket funeral, don't be surprised if you see a pizza with the works lying there."

I have a strange feeling in my mouth. My tongue seems to be getting bigger. I've gone through my whole life barely noticing my tongue, and now, all of a sudden, it seems humongous. I can't figure out where to place it. I try to settle it down by my cheek. I stick it between my teeth.

Angel tucks her chin into her neck.

My tongue has swollen to the size of a blimp.

Still, I manage to say to Angel, "Ya wa thom peetha?"

"Sure, why not?" she says.

I open up the box and Angel shrinks back.

She gives me a look and I can already tell that she's canceled me out as a regular. Now, I'm just another bar story: "You remember Rick? He came in here with a squirrel in a pizza box. Yeah, it was dead."

Now is that stealing? I don't think so. I took a bare-boned anecdote from my journal and stretched it. You, undoubtedly, would have taken the squirrel in the pizza box and done something completely different with the image. You might have focused on the two children or a character based on yourself in that situation.

The writer and teacher George Garrett did something similar with the image of a wedding cake in the middle of the road, an image that one of his students, Beverly Goodrum, came up with in a class. Based on Goodrum's story, he and radio commentator Susan Stamberg asked twenty-three writers, both well known and not (including Garrett and Goodrum), to each write a story based on this image. Of course, a central question in each story was, "What is a wedding cake doing in the middle of the road?" Their versions were broadcast on NPR and collected in an anthology titled—what else?—*The Wedding Cake in the Middle of the Road* (Norton).

It's not the material. It's what you do with it.

A lot of the craft of writing fiction is in one's ability to order the material at hand, whether autobiographical or not. The content of the story itself means nothing. The form you give it, the way you shape the material, is everything.

Still, it might be helpful to know what from the above passage really happened—where it came from. As I mentioned, the installation itself was something I actually saw, though in this case, I had no need of recording it in my journal. When I lived in Chicago, there was a neighborhood bar called Kaye's Dugout, and a woman like Angel tended bar there. I never knew much about Kaye (if that woman behind the bar was indeed Kaye), where she came from, or whether she'd ever been married. But it's true that a lot of ex-coal miners from Kentucky have, over the years, moved to Chicago, and that a number of them suffer from black lung. When I was writing about Angel, I remembered this and so this is the history I decided to give her.

It's also true that at the corner of Clark and Belmont, you can still find a Dunkin' Donuts. I believe the storefront church is still there on Belmont, but the last time I visited Chicago I noticed the tattoo parlor was gone. The neighborhood is gentrifying.

Another real-life episode was the encounter with the man selling the funny key chains. That, too, happened, though not at Kaye's Dugout. It was at a more upscale fern bar in the area. This was something I recorded in my journal. It happened in midafternoon on a hot summer day in Chicago. I'd stopped in for a beer and was sitting at the bar when I overheard the man with the key chains trying to convince the bartender to sell some of them behind the bar.

I didn't record the conversation as it happened, but I wrote it down a short while later at my apartment. Almost everything Angel said in my story is verbatim what I overheard the man tell the bartender at the fern bar. However, there was more to that scene than what I chose to include in my story. Only the key chain episode fit in. Here's how the journal entry reads in its entirety.

6/10/86

Today, the humidity was about 70 percent. I walked all over town, and by the time I got off the Southport El I was drenched, so I stopped off for a beer at Justin's, a polished wood/ceiling fan kind of bar across from the station. An acquaintance, a guy named Carl, was tending bar, so I sat up at the counter, ordered an Augsburger. Carl started chatting with me, but as he was opening the bottle, it slipped out of his hands and he dropped it on the floor, beer splattering the front of his shirt. He said, "This hasn't been my day at all, man," and went to the rest room to wash the beer off. After he returned, neither of us had much to say to each other. Instead, he started flipping channels with the remote control for the two bar TVs, one at either end.

"Donahue," he said to me.

He kept the sound off one of the TVs, and that was the one I watched. I tried imagining the sound from the Donahue program to the other TV. The guests on Donahue were an unwed couple whose baby needed a heart transplant. The other TV had a burger commercial with talking burger cartons. Or, at least I assumed they were talking, since the burger boxes were flipping up and down in imitation of conversation. I listened to Donahue for a minute, placing the voices of the couple in the burger boxes. (Maybe I was suffering from heat stroke. I can't help editorializing there. Such a weird thing to do.)

After the commercial was over, I turned back to Carl, who wasn't looking at Donahue, but talking to three guys at the bar. The one closest to me had a long, stubbly face. The man in the middle was dark-skinned, Hispanic, and the guy at the end wore a green Justin's T-shirt with a dog mascot on front. This man looked large and boyish.

"So I guess I'm moving to North Carolina," I told Carl, loud enough for everyone to hear.

Carl turned toward me and said, "No kidding." He looked surprised.

For some reason, I thought I had mentioned it to him before.

"Yeah, I got a job there."

"You ever been to North Carolina?" the man with the stubble asked me. He had a hard tone in his voice, as though he was talking about prison.

"Yeah," I said.

"Oh," he said. He took a sip of his beer and said, "I've been there." The phone rang and the man with the stubble said, "I bet that's Justin."

"Justin hates me," said the Hispanic man.

Carl looked over at the man with the stubble, who said, "He's a real obnoxious son of a bitch, but he mellows out once you get to know him," and he pointed at the Hispanic guy.

Carl went to the phone and the Hispanic man laughed and yelled after him, "Tell Justin that Mexican son of a bitch is here. Yeah, he *hates* me."

Carl picked up the phone and took it around the corner, speaking softly. The three men at the counter looked at each other and broke out laughing.

"It *is* him," said the Hispanic man.

"Don't worry," said the guy with the stubble. "Carl can handle it. He's a good guy."

Carl hung up and started talking to the three guys again.

"Do you like working here?" I asked Carl.

"Yeah, I love it," he said. "But the hours are catching up with me. I opened this morning and closed last night."

Carl looked past me toward the door. A man in his fifties walked in wearing oily brown polyester pants.

Carl went to the middle of the bar and leaned forward.

"Can I help you?"

"Yeah, is Justin here?"

"No, he won't be in till six. Can I help you?"

"Well, I wanted to see if he'd be interested in buying some of these," and he took out a key chain from his pocket. The key chain had two metal figures attached to it, a man and a woman. The guy in the brown pants wiggled a little lever.

Carl took it from the man and wiggled the lever himself. Then he brought it to the end of the bar and showed it to the three guys there.

"Justin will love this," said the man with the stubble.

"How much you want for this?" asked the Hispanic man.

"Well, I'm asking three," said the man, who had now positioned himself between me and the other three men. "But I'll take two."

The Hispanic man who was holding the key chain laughed. The guy with the stubble whipped out his wallet and threw two dollars at the man.

"Justin'll love this," he said. "It's the perfect present for him."

"I got more in my car," said the man. "Who else wants one?"

"No, that's all," said the man with the stubble.

Then he took out another dollar bill and threw it at the man. "Here, it's worth three," he said.

"I got a whole load of them in my trunk," said the man. "It's right around the corner. I've got thousands."

"One's plenty," said the man with the stubble.

"But I was thinking of giving you a bunch to sell on a card behind the bar."

The four other guys laughed and the man with the stubble said, "Not here. That wouldn't go here."

"You'd be surprised," said the man. "People just love them. I've seen women and young girls go crazy over them."

"Yeah, well this is a gay bar," said the guy with the stubble, and the other guys laughed.

"That's fine," said the man. "I can take off the woman and put on another man. I already did that for one gay bar."

"What about dogs?" said the Hispanic man. "I want one with a man and a dog."

"Fine. I can put on anything."

"Well, I want two Japanese girls and a rhinoceros," said the Hispanic man.

"I want a man and a horse," said the guy with the stubble.

"Sure, whatever you want," said the man.

"This is all we want," said the man with the stubble. "You'll have to go somewhere else."

The man laughed and started walking out. "Anything you want," he said. "Well, I'll be back tonight to see Justin."

"No, don't come back," said the man with the stubble.

"Yeah, come back," said the Hispanic man. "Justin likes your element."

After the man was gone, the guy with the stubble said, "Did you see that guy's pants? I would have given him three dollars for those pants."

I love those characters, and I love some of their lines. I like the whole scene, in fact. The personalities seem pretty distinct to me. I love that line, "Justin likes your element." Too bad I couldn't use more of the scene in my story. Note, I referred to these guys as characters, not people. They *are* people. But the journal entry isn't flesh and blood. I couldn't reproduce real people in flesh and blood, in all their complexity, even if I wanted to. With the exception of Carl, I met them once and wouldn't know them again if I saw them. I can only imagine. That, again, is the key word. Imagine. Once you set pen to paper, even in your journal, your imagination plays an important role. There's no such thing as objectivity, as any basic philosophy course will tell you. Everything is a matter of perceptions. You'd write down the above incident in a different way from the way I wrote it. The words you'd choose would be different. What you thought was important would be different. You might not even see the scene as important at all. You might forget it entirely. But as soon as you started recording it, you'd be using your imagination.

That might sound like a great rationalization. Obviously, you can't go around thinking of everyone as a character. There are limits. All I'm saying is that your journal is your sketchbook. Don't think of it as a diary. As I mentioned, I wrote all of this down after I returned home. I have a good memory, but I can't swear that every word I recorded in my journal was exactly the way it was uttered. Does it matter? I don't think so. It's your journal. You're a fiction writer, not a reporter. Nineteenth-century English poet and critic Matthew Arnold said, "Journalism is literature in a hurry." Don't be in a hurry. Play around with it. You don't have to try to be faithful to reality in your journal. You couldn't be, even if you tried.

In any case, what I used from that journal entry was only a smidgen of the scene. Notice that in my journal entry I hardly paid any attention to the third guy, the one with the Justin's T-shirt. In a story, I'd probably cut him out or give him a larger role. Everything in fiction counts, and that's not always the case in real life. In real life, there are people who sit at the end of the bar without a role to play. In fiction, a character is either necessary to the story or extraneous.

In "Installations," none of those guys was necessary. I used the key chain incident itself and I condensed what the men at the bar said and attributed their whimsical requests to the key chain man. Then I further removed the scene from real life by filtering the dialogue through Angel's perceptions. As much as I liked some of those other passages in the journal, I had to be careful to use only what fit into my story, no more, no less.

What would have happened to the story if I'd simply lifted the entire journal entry into my story without transforming it? What would have happened if I'd included Carl, the Hispanic man, the guy with the stubble, the guy with the Justin's T-shirt *and* the key chain? Obviously, the story would have become unfocused. We'd forget about Ivy and Rick, not to mention Angel. . . . We'll discuss strategies for focusing stories like this that are based in real life.

One thing you must understand as a fiction writer: Real life matters only as a conduit for your imagination. As a fiction writer, your imagination takes precedence. As a human being, life takes precedence over your imagination, and it's best not to confuse the two.

One other journal entry found its way into the squirrel in the pizza box scene, and that was the mention of Rick's tongue suddenly seeming large. A friend once told me that an acquaintance of his had one day stopped midsentence and said, "You know, all of a sudden I'm noticing my tongue. I've gone through my whole life without noticing it, but now I can't figure out where to place it in my mouth. It keeps getting in the way." My friend laughed and said, "Maybe you should seek therapy."

When I came to the climax of the scene, when Rick finally decided to show Angel the squirrel in the pizza box, I wanted to show a change in him, a change in his perceptions, a hint that he was going through almost physical changes because of his association with Ivy. That's when I remembered the man who didn't know where to put his tongue.

Many passages in my journal are irrelevant and will never find their ways into stories. I don't even know what some of the passages mean.

At the end of the Justin's entry, there are three lines that make little sense to me:

> Maybe follows him out to car?
> Something about his move, his girlfriend.
> "Why are you trying to alienate me?" Mother asks.

I may have been thinking of a story. Judging from the strength of those lines, I wisely abandoned the idea.

Some of my journals contain these kinds of lines, indecipherable and abandoned ideas and passages. I also have grocery lists, quotes from other writers and artists, phone numbers, addresses. And, of course, I've included notes to myself on where to proceed in my novel or short stories, such as:

> Henry feels threatened by Gail, but he can't leave. He feels at home here. It *is*
> his home. Still, he feels compelled to redeem himself, to prove himself. Gail thinks
> Henry's clumsy, wimpish, impotent, unmasculine. He decides to take action. He
> needs to show Gail she's wrong.
> There used to be an element of the macho in Henry.
> Henry needs to be less passive.
> Bring back Sid.
> Henry and Willy have bidding war at auction. Henry suddenly gets aggressive,
> but the fact that he gets car might redeem himself in Gail's eyes.

Basically, stage directions. Then there are the story ideas:

> About Al at Our Place. How I thought he was brilliant and wanted to be just like
> him, but then we, the regulars of Our Place, decided he was really mad, and this
> diminished him as a human being.

This is more or less indecipherable to you and probably doesn't seem like much of an idea at all. But *I* know what I'm referring to, and in a journal that's all that counts.

I don't include anecdotes in my journals with the intention of putting them in future stories. It's not that calculated. I write something down because it grabs my attention, because I'd hate for it to be lost. For instance, there was the time a local theater critic came to one of my classes and told us about an amateur production of *Amadeus* in which everything went wrong:

> Perry Tannenbaum came to my Review Writing class today and he told us a
> story about reviewing a local production of *Amadeus*. Apparently, they got every-
> thing wrong. First of all, the guy playing Salieri had never acted before. Halfway

through the play, he forgot his lines and ran offstage. Then, during the scene in which *The Magic Flute* premieres, something went wrong with the sound and there was just silence as the courtiers applauded. Then, at the end of the play, as Mozart lay dying, he was supposed to have a vision of his father appearing in the door wearing his three-cornered hat while portentous music played. Instead, when they cued the sound, the light, airy music of *The Magic Flute* started playing when his father, dressed in black, appeared in the doorway and glowered.

I doubt this entry will ever find its way into a story of mine, but who knows? I wrote it down simply because it was funny. But now that I think about it, I can see it working into a story in a couple of ways. The way in which I'd incorporate the anecdote would depend entirely on whose point of view the story is told from. The haughty critic would view the episode differently from the unfortunate amateur thespian who played Salieri.

I keep a journal for a variety of reasons. Sometimes I want to chronicle, as in a diary. Sometimes I want to record a detail that otherwise would be lost forever. Like David Michael Kaplan, sometimes I record a dream, and a couple of these dreams have actually been the kernels for some short stories I've written.

Whatever the case, it's important to write in your journal before the event or image becomes stale. We've all had dreams that have awakened us in the middle of the night, that seem so striking we want to record them. But we're tired and want to go back to sleep. We say, "Oh, I'll write it down in the morning when I wake up." Almost invariably, when we awake in the morning, the dream has disappeared. So we rationalize further. "Oh, it probably wasn't that interesting anyway." But what if it was?

Of course, what's worth noting in your journal is up to you. But I'd suggest carrying a small notebook with you at all times, one that can fit in your pocket or purse. Don't go anywhere without it, and take along a pen that works. As Thoreau wrote, "The writer who postpones the recording of his thoughts uses an iron which has cooled to burn a hole with." That's a quote I wrote down in one of my journals.

Writers are spies, liars and thieves. Some, like Jean Genet, have been real criminals; some, like Graham Greene, have actually been spies. But most are spies and thieves in a more general sense. Your journal is basically your spy notebook. Don't let it fall into enemy hands. Greene used his journals extensively to write *The Heart of the Matter* (Viking Penguin) and *A Burnt-Out Case* (Viking Penguin). . . . . There's nothing wrong with borrowing from real life. It's neither crass nor unimaginative unless one goes about it in a crass or unimaginative way. *Imagination comes in the ordering of events, not in their source.*

WEAVING JOURNAL ENTRIES INTO FICTION

Writing is an associative process. And fiction writing is a kind of mosaic, a piecing together of memory and imagination. One's journal can come in handy in this way, but I don't want to give you the impression that I simply flip through my journal, filling in the blanks with fun-filled episodes from real life until I have enough pages to call it a story. It's not a matter of simply dropping overheard bits of conversation into a story. I wish it was that easy. One must attempt to weave in what one uses.

For instance, here's a bit of overheard dialogue from [F. Scott] Fitzgerald's notebook: "He wants to make a goddess out of me and I want to be Mickey Mouse."

In the completed story, "On Your Own," which was published posthumously, the Mickey Mouse quote isn't dropped in casually. On the contrary, it's woven seamlessly into the story, which concerns a young actress named Evelyn who's returning by boat to America after a five-year absence and some success on the British stage. On the voyage, she becomes entangled with a rich young lawyer named George Ives. The story was rejected seven times by various magazines, something Fitzgerald wasn't used to. Fitzgerald thought it was his one unpublished story with that "one little drop of something . . . the extra I had."

Early in the story, after the young couple meet, they walk the deck together:

> "You were a treat," he said. "You're like Mickey Mouse."
> She took his arm and bent double over it with laughter.
> "I like being Mickey Mouse . . ."

Later, after an on-again, off-again romance (and after Evelyn discovers George is rich), they have the following exchange:

> "Would you consider marrying me?"
> "Yes, I'd consider marrying you."
> "Of course if you married me we'd live in New York."
> "Call me Mickey Mouse," she said suddenly.
> "Why?"
> "I don't know—it was fun when you called me Mickey Mouse."

A little silly, but then, Evelyn is a little silly. That night, she wonders what she's gotten herself into:

> "He wants to make a goddess out of me and I want to be Mickey Mouse."

Finally, George's mother, a wealthy society matron, invites Evelyn to dinner. At the dinner party is a certain Colonel Cary, who Evelyn has met before—under slightly darker circumstances. It turns out that when she was a starving young actress on Broadway and had to go for days without eating, she survived by being a "party girl." Intimidated by Colonel Cary's presence, Evelyn gets drunk on champagne, blabs everything and lashes out at George's mother, who's properly horrified but tries to put a good face on things. Of course, George, under his mother's wing all along, tries to dump Evelyn, who, in her world-weary fashion, takes it all with philosophical aplomb.

> Ah, well, maybe she'd better go back to England—and be Mickey Mouse. He didn't know anything about women, anything about love, and to her that was the unforgivable sin.

Fiction, unlike real life, demands a kind of *symmetry,* or balance. No phrase or image or overheard bit of dialogue should be wasted or thrown carelessly into a story or novel. There's an old dramatic trick here that Fitzgerald has employed: If you want a reader to pay special attention to an image, put it in not once or twice, but three times. The first time you make a reference to Mickey Mouse, the reader will hardly notice. The second time, the reader's subconscious takes note, but it barely registers on the reader's conscious mind. The third time is the charm. In this case, Mickey Mouse becomes an organic symbol of Evelyn's frivolity, as well as her vacuousness. Fitzgerald has taken this overheard dialogue and fashioned it to suit his characters and their situation.

Fitzgerald also wrote ideas for short stories in his notebooks, including the following one, based on a true story:

> There once was a moving picture magnate who was shipwrecked on a desert island with nothing but two dozen cans of film (Herbert Howe).

As far as I know, Fitzgerald never did anything with the idea. I've thought about it myself. It's intriguing, but it's sort of a one-joke story, the idea of the creator stranded with nothing but potential, and without the means to do anything about it. The fact that Fitzgerald never did anything with the idea is all the more fitting. We all have canisters of film that we'll never develop.

The point is that a journal entry is little but a raw piece of information. What you do with it later is the tricky part. For the time being, enjoy yourself. Whoop it up. Have a party in your journal. Your journal entries can be more or less formless. They can be ungrammatical. You may misspell all the words you like. They can make no sense at all. There'll be enough time later for biting your fingernails to the quick, gnashing your teeth and beating your breast in frustration—once you decide to develop your ideas into a story or a novel.

DISCUSSION QUESTIONS

1. Hemley's slogan is, "It's not the material. It's what you do with it." What is it that you must "do" with "real-life" material to transform it into fiction?
2. In an extended example, Hemley shows how one incident—the two kids with a dead squirrel in a pizza box—is transformed into a central event in a story he wrote. How does he transform "the material"? How is the real-life event embedded into a completely different fictional setting? How does he transform an essentially "meaningless" little event from life into a fictional event that is full of meaning?

DAVID HUDDLE

Issues of Character
The Saint at the Typewriter

David Huddle (b. 1942) has taught at the University of Vermont and the Breadloaf School of English since 1971. For twenty-five years he has alternated publishing poetry (including Paper Boy, *1979;* Stopping by Home, *1988;* The Nature of Yearning, *1992; and* Summer Lake, *1999), short stories (including* The High Spirits, *1989; and* Intimates, *1993), and novels (including* Only the Little Bone, *1986; and* The Story of a Million Years, *1999). The essays on the craft and practice of fiction in* The Writing Habit *(1994) are widely read.*

Character has always been the element of fiction that interested me most. The other elements—language, structure, plot—seem to me clearly to belong to Art. Character is the company of other human beings, the experience of living.

I love gossip. I like to talk and hear and think about people. I like to have information about them. I like to see people, see their faces, their bodies, their gestures, their moves. I like to be told or to be able to guess what people are thinking and feeling. I am interested in the scandalous and the foolish, the brutal and fiendish, the brave and intelligent things people do. Of course I take pleasure in the sharing of sensory experience, the meal or the walk taken with a friend. And I am hungry to hear *talk* that seems to me especially true or serious or revealing or just plain pretty to listen to.

My desire to know other human beings and to have access to their experience isn't satisfied with my daily experience, and so I turn to fiction. A variety and an intimacy of experience are available to me in novels and stories. I must speculate about what even my dearest friends and closest relatives are thinking and feeling, but I am able to *know* what Anna Karenina and Emma Bovary think and feel.

Such knowledge as fiction gives me about its characters satisfies a yearning I have. I've never had much scientific curiosity. I've had a decent enough education, but I've forgotten almost every important fact I was ever taught. The kind of thing I've always wanted to know and to remember is the kind of thing that J. D. Salinger's Sergeant X experiences when he goes inside an English church to witness a children's choir at rehearsal:

> A dozen or so adults were among the pews, several of them bearing pairs of small-size rubbers, soles up, in their laps. I passed along and sat down in the front row. On the rostrum, seated in three compact rows of auditorium chairs, were about twenty children, mostly girls, ranging in age from about seven to thirteen. At the moment, their choir coach, an enormous woman in tweeds, was advising them to open their mouths wider when they sang. Had anyone, she asked, ever heard of a little dickeybird that dared to sing his charming song without first

opening his little beak wide, wide, wide? Apparently nobody ever had. She was given a steady, opaque look. She went on to say that she wanted *all* her children to absorb the *meaning* of the words they sang, not just *mouth* them like silly-billy parrots. She then blew a note on her pitch pipe, and the children, like so many underage weight-lifters, raised their hymnbooks.

They sang without instrumental accompaniment—or, more accurately in their case, without any interference. Their voices were melodious and unsentimental, almost to the point where a somewhat more denominational man than myself might, without straining, have experienced levitation. A couple of the very youngest children dragged the tempo a trifle, but in a way that only the composer's mother could have found fault with. I had never heard the hymn, but I kept hoping it was one with a dozen or more verses. Listening, I scanned all the children's faces but watched one in particular, that of the child nearest me, on the end seat in the first row. She was about thirteen, with straight ash-blond hair of ear-lobe length, an exquisite forehead, and blasé eyes that, I thought, might very possibly have counted the house. Her voice was distinctly separate from the other children's voices, and not just because she was seated nearest me. It had the best upper register, the sweetest-sounding, the surest, and it automatically led the way. The young lady, however, seemed slightly bored with her own singing ability, or perhaps just with the time and place; twice, between verses, I saw her yawn. It was a lady-like yawn, a closed-mouth yawn, but you couldn't miss it; her nostril wings gave her away.

Such knowledge as this passage offers a reader seems to me both deeply satisfying and wildly unpragmatic. It is only in writerly terms that I can speak of it practically. (The only difference between the fiction-writer and the town gossip, who are equally interested in this generally unnoticed area of human behavior, is that the writer *makes* something—namely, novels and stories—out of his interest.)

So down to practice: here are six ways to bring a character to life in a story:

1. **Information:** For example, here we know that Esmé, the character in this passage from Salinger's story, "For Esmé—With Love and Squalor," sings in a church choir, is "about thirteen," has the best voice of the singers, and is apparently bored.

2. **Physical appearance:** Esmé's "ash-blond hair of ear-lobe length, [her] exquisite forehead, and blasé eyes" are obviously exemplary details of this category of character-making. That her "nostril wings" give away her "lady-like . . . closed-mouth yawn[s]" is a less obvious and craftier example of character-making: the detail is minutely precise, it tells a great deal about the personality of the yawner, and it keeps a reader "seeing" the character. Beginning fiction-writers will often provide plenty of description of a character's looks in the paragraph in which they introduce that character. But then, having paid their dues to "details of appearance," they will forget all about what the character looks like for the rest of the story. Salinger is particularly good at using a character's physical presence throughout the whole story so that a reader has a sense of "seeing" the character for the whole story.

3. **Thoughts and feelings:** Because of this story's point of view, we don't have direct access to Esmé's mind and heart, but we are given powerful suggestions about what Esmé might be thinking and feeling—by way of her yawning between verses and her "blasé eyes that . . . might very possibly have counted the house," of our having heard the choir coach speak to her "little dickey-bird[s]" and "silly-billy parrots," and our having seen the children raise their hymnbooks "like so many underage weightlifters." So by some very strongly crafted implication we know what Esmé thinks and feels; we don't know it precisely—because she hasn't been able to tell us—but we know it more than generally. Through this whole middle section of the story in which Esmé appears, we know what Esmé thinks and feels, and we are given to know it by way of implication. I consider Esmé one of the dozen or so most vividly portrayed and memorable characters I have encountered in literature. Esmé has taught me a lot about character-making, and here's something new she's taught me on just this most recent reading of the story: when a character is fully realized, a reader knows—because the writer makes the reader know—what that character thinks and feels in whatever situations that character appears; if a reader doesn't know, then the character isn't "all there." This seems to me a principle that must be akin to actors' having to know what their characters are thinking and feeling on stage even when they are keeping quiet and standing off to the side.

4. **Actions:** In this scene, in which Salinger introduces Esmé into the story, there is no real need to have her *do* anything beyond singing; the only necessity here is for Sergeant X to *see* Esmé, perhaps to pick out her singing voice as being "distinctly separate." But Salinger chooses two small actions for Esmé that make her immediately remarkable: her eyes count the house, and she yawns between verses. These are not actions of high dramatic potency, nor are they especially comical or odd. These are actions that come out of the very center of Esmé's personality. I believe there's a lesson in that, too: characters have only to be themselves to be of interest to a reader; the trick is for the writer to know them so intimately that he can present them "as themselves." To hold a reader's attention a writer doesn't have to make his characters act strange or crazy.

5. **Sensory experience:** Again, because of the story's point of view, we don't really know what Esmé is smelling, hearing, touching, tasting, and seeing in this passage, though we could probably make some fairly accurate guesses. We know more precisely what she is experiencing intellectually and emotionally than what she is experiencing through her senses. Only occasionally is Salinger a writer for whom Sensory Experience is especially important. I wish he were more exemplary in this department, but since he isn't, the lesson I see here is that if some of a writer's powers of characterization are finely developed, he can get by without having all of them. Salinger is pretty good at five out of the six.

6. **Speech:** Speech is the characterizing power Salinger most relies upon. Esmé doesn't say anything in the passage I've been discussing, but in the next section she has plenty to say, beginning with "I thought Americans despised tea."

I'm going to be a professional singer. . . . I'm going to sing jazz on the radio and make heaps of money. Then, when I'm thirty, I shall retire and live on a ranch in Ohio. . . . Do you know Ohio? . . . You're the eleventh American I've met. . . . You seem quite intelligent for an American. . . . Most of the Americans I've seen act like animals. They're forever punching one another about, and insulting everyone, and—You know what one of them did? . . . One of them threw an empty whiskey bottle through my aunt's window. Fortunately, the window was open. But does that sound very intelligent to you? . . . My hair is soaking wet, . . . I look a fright. . . . I have quite wavy hair when it's dry. . . . Not actually curly but quite wavy. . . . Are you married? . . . Are you very deeply in love with your wife? Or am I being too personal? . . . Usually, I'm not terribly gregarious. . . . I purely came over because I thought you looked extremely lonely. You have an extremely sensitive face. . . . I'm training myself to be more compassionate. My aunt says I'm a terribly cold person. . . . I live with my aunt. She's an extremely kind person. Since the death of my mother, she's done everything within her power to make Charles and me feel adjusted. . . . Mother was an extremely intelligent person. Quite sensuous, in many ways. . . . Do you find me terribly cold? . . . My first name is Esmé. I don't think I shall tell you my full name, for the moment. I have a title and you may just be impressed by titles. Americans are, you know. . . . His name is Charles, . . . He's extremely brilliant for his age. . . . Sometimes he's brilliant and sometimes he's not, . . . Charles, do sit up! . . . He misses our father very much. He was s-l-a-i-n in North Africa. . . . Father adored him. . . . He looks very much like my mother—Charles, I mean. I look exactly like my father. . . . My mother was quite a passionate woman. She was an extrovert. Father was an introvert. They were quite well mated, though, in a superficial way. To be quite candid, Father really needed more of an intellectual companion than Mother was. He was an extremely gifted genius. . . . Charles misses him exceedingly, . . . He was an exceedingly lovable man. He was extremely handsome, too. Not that one's appearance matters greatly, but he was. He had terribly penetrating eyes, for a man who was intransically kind. . . . I'd be extremely flattered if you'd write a story exclusively for me sometime. I'm an avid reader. . . . It doesn't have to be terribly prolific! Just so that it isn't childish and silly. . . . I prefer stories about squalor. . . . I'm extremely interested in squalor. . . . *Il faut que je parte aussi,* . . . Do you know French? . . . I'm quite communicative for my age. . . . I'm dreadfully sorry about my hair, . . . I've probably been hideous to look at. . . . Would you like me to write to you? . . . I write extremely articulate letters for a person my— . . . I shall write to you first . . . so that you don't feel *compromised* in any way. . . . You're quite sure you won't forget to write that story for me. It doesn't have to be ex*clus*ively for me. It can— . . . Make it extremely squalid and moving. . . . Are you at all acquainted with squalor? . . . Isn't it a pity we didn't meet under less extenuating circumstances . . . Goodbye, . . . I hope you return from the war with all your faculties intact.

This monologue I've constructed to illustrate the power of Speech as a characterizing agent. Esmé says all these things in the course of an eleven-page scene. Salinger's writing has many charms, but for the moment I want to focus only on this business of Speech. What Esmé says shows, at the most immediate and engaging level, her intellectual, social, and linguistic precocity. At first glance, this writing might appear satirical, Salinger mocking the English, especially the upper class English, and mocking the young, especially thirteen year old girls. But for all the funniness of these lines of Esmé's and of the scene from which they are drawn, there isn't any mocking, and we readers can feel that in the tone, which is poignant, almost elegiac. What Esmé says, at its deepest level, comes out of grief, out of her reckoning with the loss of her parents: what she says has an outside of cheerfulness, snobbery, pluck, charm, naivete and an inside of sadness, courage, and that quality she's training herself to acquire more of, compassion. More than anything else, Esmé's speech here shows her to be, as she herself might put it, "extremely interesting." She's complicated. What she says shows her to be worthy of our attention and consideration. Fiction-writers who are strong on character first of all have to believe that individual human beings are "extremely interesting," and second of all have to discover and show what it is about them that is interesting. That people have exterior and interior lives which may be poignantly connected is one of the things Salinger's Esmé shows us.

Salinger has been accused of loving his characters more than God would love them, and I expect that's a fair charge. I expect that's one reason why his writing has such a powerful effect on so many of his readers, why his followers are so intense in their devotion to his work. And I expect it's one reason why Salinger's fiction became weaker in his later books and why he's apparently found it difficult to continue his work: love, of that magnitude, must be down-right impossible to sustain. "For Esmé—With Love and Squalor" was a kind of turning point in my life. I read it first in 1963 and was right powerfully disrupted by it. I cared about that story so much that I felt in some way as if I possessed it, as if it were mine. I suppose I should be grateful that I wasn't so moved by it that I tried to assassinate a President or something like that. I still have an inordinate affection for the story. I feel that the power it has on me is directly connected to the power of love the author must have invested in it. Love your characters, I could counsel would-be fiction-writers, but I know they'd know that was smarmy advice. Either you do or you don't. It's akin to being told by the store manager where you work as a window dresser, "You know, these mannequins will bring in more customers if you invest them with love when you dress them up"; or being told by the head embalmer you work for at the funeral home, "Love your cadavers, your funerals will be more successful." Anyone who would tell you what to do with your love merits your suspicion. Nevertheless, a useful fiction-writing principle can be extracted: if in doubt, treat your characters as if you loved them. If you've got to make some sort of adjustments with your character, try being generous, try letting that character—even if it's a treacherous, nasty-hearted character—be his or her best self, or maybe even *better* than his or her best self.

Speech is something most of us have an interest in and a talent for, if we could just unleash it properly. In a story it can hit a reader just right, can make characters come perfectly into focus like the right twist of a camera lens. Here's a couple in a Raymond Carver story called "Vitamins," a couple we've had some information about but one we really haven't seen clearly together by this point, which is about a quarter of the way into the story:

> Pattie said, "Vitamins." She picked up her glass and swirled the ice. "For shit's sake! I mean, when I was a girl this is the last thing I ever saw myself doing. Jesus, I never thought I'd grow up to sell vitamins. Door-to-door vitamins. This beats everything. This blows my mind."
>
> "I never thought so either, honey," I said.
>
> "That's right," she said. "You said it in a nutshell."
>
> "Honey."
>
> "Don't honey me," she said. "This is hard, brother. This life is not easy, any way you cut it."

That this talk sounds like real talk is one of its virtues. That it articulates the personalities of both characters and of their relationship with each other is another: after reading these lines, we're certain which one is the dominant personality, which one listens to the other and which one doesn't; we could predict with some accuracy what sort of problems this couple is likely to encounter. (Think about it a moment: when you are curious about the relationship between two people, what can tell you the most about it? If you're a romantic and you believe in "flashing eyes" and that sort of thing, you might say, "How they look at each other." But if you're a classicist, and you really want to know the answer to the question, you'll say, "How they talk with each other.") One final virtue of this "Ray Carver talk" is how the flatness of it, the triteness of it, works as a kind of pressure holding in the characters' emotion; the language contains the emotion, limits it in a way that's both sad and explosive.

Another writer who loves a good conversation and who can get the way people talk just exactly right is Eudora Welty. Here's this from "Why I Live at the P.O.":

> "Don't you notice anything different about Uncle Rondo?" asks Stella-Rondo.
>
> "Why, no, except he's got on some terrible-looking flesh-colored contraption I wouldn't be found dead in, is all I can see," I says.
>
> "Never mind, you won't be found dead in it, because it happens to be part of my trousseau, and Mr. Whitaker took several dozen photographs of me in it," says Stella-Rondo. "What on earth could Uncle Rondo *mean* by wearing part of my trousseau out in the road in open daylight without saying so much as 'Kiss my foot,' *knowing* I only got home this morning after my separation and hung my negligee up on the bathroom door, just as nervous as I could be?"

The quality of the talk in Eudora Welty's stories is both ordinary and extraordinary. What her people say seems like what somebody like that would say in that situation, and yet it also seems unusually musical, thingy (which is to say, full of the objects of the world), chirpy, and sociable. The talk in her stories affects me like money on the sidewalk: I want to pick it up and save it and jingle it in my pocket. Here's this from "Lily Daw and the Three Ladies":

> "Lily," said Mrs. Watts . . . , "we'll give you lots of gorgeous things if you'll only go to Ellisville instead of getting married."
> "What will you give me?" asked Lily.
> "I'll give you a pair of hemstitched pillowcases," said Mrs. Carson.
> "I'll give you a big caramel cake," said Mrs. Watts.
> "I'll give you a souvenir from Jackson—a little toy bank," said Aimee Slocum. "Now will you go?"
> "No," said Lily.
> "I'll give you a pretty little Bible with your name on it in real gold," said Mrs. Carson.
> "What if I was to give you a pink crêpe de Chine brassiére with adjustable shoulder straps?" asked Mrs. Watts grimly.
> "Oh, Etta."
> "Well, she needs it," said Mrs. Watts. . . .

When we speak casually about this kind of talk, we say that Eudora Welty writes "good dialogue." Reviewers will often remark a fiction-writer's "ear" for dialogue, as if all that's involved is to be able to listen carefully to people talking and to transcribe that talk onto the page. That Welty goes well beyond simply writing "good dialogue" or simply having a "good ear" ought to be evident in the *ordering* of the offerings to Lily to keep her from getting married and in how the offerings appeal to various of the human appetites: "a pair of hemstitched pillowcases . . . a big caramel cake . . . a souvenir from Jackson—a little toy bank . . . a pretty little Bible with your name on it in real gold . . ." And then consider the presentation of the ultimate temptation: "'What if I was to give you a pink crêpe de Chine brassiére with adjustable shoulder straps?' asked Mrs. Watts grimly." The *grimly* here is priceless. The *grimly*—the adverb that goes with a *said* or an *asked,* the little unit of grammar that bad writers love to use badly and that good writers learn not to use at all—here is evidence of this writer's being, as Esmé would put it, "an extremely gifted genius." Eudora Welty's great gift, the thing that sets her apart from her distinguished peers, Carson McCullers, Flannery O'Connor, and Katherine Anne Porter, is her range and agility with language. And one of her major contributions to story writing is that she has expanded the limits of what characters may say in a story; she is bold enough to allow her characters to speak as characters in stories have not heretofore spoken:

> "Listen!" whispers Powerhouse, looking into the ketchup bottle and slowly spreading his performer's hands over the damp, wrinkling cloth with red squares. "Listen how it is. My wife gets missing me. Gypsy. She goes to the window. She looks out and sees you know what. Street. Sign saying Hotel. People walking. Somebody looks up. Old man. She looks down, out the window. Well? . . . *Sssssst! Plooey!* What she do? Jump out and bust her brains all over the world."
> He opens his eyes.
> "That's it," agrees Valentine. "You gets a telegram."

"Sure she misses you," Little Brother adds.

"No, it's nighttime." How softly he tells them! "Sure, it's the nighttime. She say, What do I hear? Footsteps walking up the hall? That him? Footsteps go on off. It's not me. I'm in Alligator, Mississippi, she's crazy. Shaking all over. Listens till her ears and all grow out like old music-box horns but still she can't hear a thing. She says, All right! I'll jump out the window then. Got on her nightgown. I know that nightgown, and her thinking there. Says, Ho hum, all right, and jumps out the window. Is she mad at me! Is she crazy! She don't leave *nothing* behind her!"

"Ya! Ha!"

"Brains and insides everywhere, Lord, Lord."

All the watching Negroes stir in their delight, and to their higher delight he says affectionately, "Listen! Rats in here."

"That must be the way, boss."

"Only, naw, Powerhouse, that ain't true. That sound too *bad.*"

"Does? I even know who finds her," cries Powerhouse. "That no-good pussy-footed crooning creeper, that creeper that follow around after me, coming up like weeds behind me, following around after me everything I do and messing around on the trail I leave. Bets my numbers, sings my songs, gets close to my agent like a Betsy-bug; when I going out he just coming in. I got him now! I got my eye on him."

"Know who he is?"

"Why, it's that old Uranus Knockwood!"

"Ya Ha!"'

"Yeah, and he coming now, he going to find Gypsy. There he is, coming around that corner, and Gypsy kadoodling down, oh-oh, watch out! *Ssssst! Plooey!* See, there she is in her little old nightgown, and her insides and brains all scattered round."

A sigh fills the room.

"Hush about her brains. Hush about her insides."

"Ya! Ha! You talking about her brains and insides—old Uranus Knockwood," says Powerhouse, "look down and say Jesus! He say, Look here what I'm walking round in!"

They all burst into halloos of laughter. Powerhouse's face looks like a big hot iron stove.

"Why, he picks her up and carries her off!" he says.

"Ya! Ha!"

"Carries her *back* around the corner . . ."

"Oh, Powerhouse!"

"You know him."

"Uranus Knockwood!"

"Yeahhh!"

"He take our wives when we gone!"

"He come in when we goes out!"

"Uh-huh!"

"He go out when we comes in!"

"Yeahhh!"
"He standing behind the door!"
"Old Uranus Knockwood."
"You know him."
"Middle-size man."
"Wears a hat."
"That's him."
Everyone in the room moans with pleasure . . .

Powerhouse has exotic powers of speech that enable him to say everything from "Boogers" to the words of the despairing tale of his wife, Gypsy, who "jumps out the window" and "bust[s] her brains all over the world." Powerhouse, in the joyful noise he makes out of his powerful gloom, is at the center of this music, this scene, this story, but the others in that bar in "Alligator, Mississippi," on that rainy night, are given charming, intricate riffs of language; they all contribute to the sound of that fantastic conversation. The experimental aspect of "Powerhouse" is the way the limits of language have been extended so as to make words—and in particular, human speech—evoke music, jazz music, blues, improvisation in which various people contribute various elements of the whole musical sound. But this is experiment in the service of the entirely traditional element of the story, character; the story "presents" Powerhouse, demonstrates his extraordinariness.

What we casually call "dialogue," what I am trying to elevate in significance by calling it "Speech" here, is the quintessential human act. As Faulkner says in his Nobel Prize acceptance speech,

> . . . when the last ding-dong of doom has clanged and faded from the last worthless rock hanging tideless in the last red and dying evening, . . . even then there will be one more sound: that of [man's] puny inexhaustible voice, still talking.

And John Cheever, in the admirable ending of his not-especially admired novel, *Falconer,* accomplishes the final steps of his main character's figurative resurrection through the "drunken palaver" of a stranger. Farragut manages to escape from Falconer prison by substituting himself for a dead man and zipping himself into a burial sack. Outside, unzipping himself from the death of his prison existence, Farragut makes his way back to life with this encounter:

> The stranger was utterly inconsequential, beginning with his lanky hair, his piecemeal face, his spare, piecemeal frame and his highly fermented breath. "Hi," he said. "What you see here is a man who is being evicted. This ain't everything I own in the world. I'm making my third trip. I'm moving in with my sister until I find another place. You can't find nothing this late at night. I ain't been evicted because of non-payment of rent. Money I got. Money's the one thing I don't have to worry about. I got plenty of money. I been evicted because I'm a human being, that's why. I make noises like a human being. I close doors, I cough sometimes in the night, I have friends in now and then, sometimes I sing, sometimes I whistle, sometimes I do yoga, and because I'm human and make a little noise, a little

human noise going up and down the stairs, I'm being evicted. I'm a disturber of the peace."

"That's terrible," said Farragut.

"You hit the nail on the head," said the stranger, "you hit the nail on the head. My landlady is one of those smelly old widows—they're widows even when they got a husband drinking beer in the kitchen—one of those smelly old widows who can't stand life in any form, fashion, or flavor. I'm being evicted because I'm alive and healthy. This ain't all I own, by a long shot. I took my TV over on the first trip. I got a beauty. It's four years old, color, but when I had a little snow and asked the repairman to come in, he told me never, never turn this set in for a new one. They don't make them like this any more, he said. He got rid of the snow and all he charged me was two dollars. He said it was a pleasure to work on a set like mine. It's over to my sister's now. Christ, I hate my sister and she hates my guts, but I'll spend the night there and find a beautiful place in the morning. They have some beautiful places on the south side, places with views of the river. You wouldn't want to share a place with me, would you, if I found something beautiful?"

That Cheever locates redemption in the speech of this nutty, drunken stranger is of course ironic, but it seems to me a special, fiction-writer's kind of irony. To accomplish the work of fiction-writing, the writer must become the ultimate democrat, the ultimate Christian: the fiction-writer can't condemn anybody. A state of suspended moral sensibility is necessary to take on the business of character-making. The fiction-writer's motto must be, as Stanley Elkin puts it, "Everybody has his reasons." In our regular, walking-around, gum-chewing lives, we're used to proceeding with all of humanity divided into *them* and *us*. *They* are everybody we don't know, don't understand, don't like, don't approve of; *they* aren't kin to us; *they* have less money than we do or more money than we do; *they* do and think and say and feel things differently. However, when we sit down to write fiction, everybody has to become us. We must imagine the lives of people who are *other* than ourselves, and to do so we must become them, they must become us.

This transformation that must come about in a fiction-writer's moral attitude is not one that is consciously elected. It begins, as many of the larger issues of fiction-writing begin, with a technical problem, in this case the problem of getting the details right: the cold-blooded murderer whose story we mean to tell will not become real for us as writers or as readers unless we can see many of the details of his life with precision; once we begin to imagine the details, we begin to see things his way, we begin to understand his reasons. The more we make this character come alive in our story—the more we fill in the details of information about him, his physical appearance, his thoughts and feelings, his actions, his sensory experience, and his speech, the more we *become* this character. The transformation is a given dynamic of fiction-writing. But I do not mean to say that anybody who attempts to write fiction will undergo such a transformation. If a writer does not give himself or herself over to the material and to the characters, then the transformation will not come about and the fiction will fail. If the writer keeps that distance between himself or herself and the murderer, the murderer will not become a living, convincing character, and the story won't work.

So the fiction-writer must be open to experience other than his or her own. As a result of such opening up, the writer will usually manage to avoid certain mistaken attitudes that result in shallow characterization or obviously manipulative plotting. The transformed fiction-writer won't try to condemn a character or a type of character. The transformed writer won't condescend, or write down, to his characters. The transformed writer will avoid simplifying his characters in order to make some abstract point, will ignore the boring limitations of stereotype. The transformed fiction-writer will be more likely to choose characters who are at least his or her equal. The transformed writer carries his characters' burdens, takes responsibility for their actions, forgives them their trespasses, and fights for their rights. This miracle of the transformed writer occurs, I assert, because in the conscientious making of characters and their fictional world, the saint at the typewriter tries to get the details right.

DISCUSSION QUESTIONS

1. Huddle points to one of the ironies of the difference between "real life" and fiction: we can know the motivations and ethics and psychology of fictional characters with much more certainty than we can those of "real people." Why?

2. Huddle emphasizes that "speech" (also known as dialogue) may be the best way to bring characters to life. In what ways? What can be revealed in speech that is revealed in no other way? Choose one passage of dialogue quoted by Huddle, and discuss what it reveals about the characters who speak in it.

3. Following Huddle's example, choose one brief passage from a short story (as he did with "For Esmé—With Love and Squalor"), and show how the writer reveals character through its details.

KIT REED

What to Leave Out and What to Put In

Kit Reed (b. 1932) has published over two dozen novels, collections of short stories, and works of young adult fiction and science fiction, including At War as Children *(1964),* Cry of the Daughter *(1971),* Tiger Rag *(1973),* Captain Grown-Up *(1976),* Fort Privilege *(1985),* The Revenge of the Senior Citizens *(1986),* Catholic Girls *(1987),* Thief of Lives *(1992), and* Weird Women, Wired Women *(1998). She has also produced the fiction-writing textbooks* Story First: The Writer as Insider *(1982) and* Revision *(1989). Currently, working with Wesleyan University, she teaches a class on the World Wide Web called StoryMOO.*

It's easier to talk about what to leave out of a short story than what to put in.

You leave out everything that doesn't belong.

The inner logic of a given story will determine this to a large extent. Each choice you make will focus and channel your work. Everything: the words you choose, ideas, characters, belong in a particular story *only as they function in that story* and you as writer are going to have to be ruthless about getting rid of anything that doesn't belong.

Short fiction is particularly demanding. Novelists are permitted occasional indulgences because the stage they occupy may be as intimate as a theater-in-the-round or large enough to accommodate a cast of thousands including elephants, but a writer of short stories has a relative space the approximate size of a puppet stage, and if he lets things get out of control he will end up knocking over scenery and threatening the entire arrangement with collapse.

The business of a short story of three to ten thousand words must be accomplished in such a limited compass that any misstep can throw the entire story out of proportion. At every point the writer needs to resist the temptations to digression: falling in love with the sound of his own voice, or following a lesser character for too long because he happens to be interesting. If he is that interesting, either the story is focused in the wrong place or else the writer is backing into something larger, a novella or a novel. If the landscape takes over then maybe the story is about the landscape and not the people in the foreground; in either case the story is out of control and you are going to have to make sacrifices to bring it into focus.

If you are working with some concern for inner logic, you'll discover before long that most of the major problems solve themselves. Given a specific set of choices, or givens, you have already excluded a great many things, beginning with anything that disrupts the mood. A comic story may be a number of things besides funny, and almost anything can happen, but it had better be told in a way that maintains the reader's sense of comedy, and a story which is essentially serious in tone will go haywire if you try to tack on a funny ending unless you have prepared for it. If you're going to throw a custard pie at the end, you'd better have it behind your back the whole time.

Given a certain point of view and a specific place to stand, you've already excluded other kinds of points of view and places to stand. Given a set of characters, you know by their nature which kinds of things they will do and which they won't, and which of these actions belong in the story. Each defining choice will strengthen your sense of what belongs and what doesn't.

The simple rule of thumb is: *everything you put in a story had better function in the story.* If it doesn't function it doesn't belong.

Beyond the built-in understanding supplied by inner logic, you may find some use for a simple set of rules.

Here are some things to leave out of short stories.

1. What characters do between scenes. If two people have a fight at the office and then they go to their respective homes and have supper and pay the bills or make some phone calls and go to the movies and go back home to their respective beds and get ready for bed and get in bed and go to sleep and wake up and have breakfast and go to the office and meet again and have another fight, it is quite likely that we don't need to know about it. All that extraneous information can be implied by dropping them at the end of the fight:

"All right, dammit, I don't care if I never see you again," and picking them up in the next scene:

> Naturally the next morning they saw each other again, as they had every
> morning; after all, their desks were side by side in the same corner of the office.

If, on the other hand, one of them has gone home and constructed a pistol out of some cotton wadding and gunpowder and a length of pipe, we had probably better hear about it.

This is a gross example of an extremely complicated matter: all that eating and sleeping didn't belong in the story, but anything that grew out of the fight, anything that would affect the outcome, did belong. Anything that serves character or development belongs, but the things characters do *between* things can simply be skipped. We as readers are familiar enough with quick cuts and dissolves in the movies to be able to fill in the blanks for ourselves, and, furthermore, to assume with very little prompting that a scene has shifted.

2. Unnecessary dialog must go. Only the important business stays, and although you can hint that people are having a boring discussion about the weather, you had better not give it in full. Another gross example:

> "Good morning Mr. Ransom," Higgins said.
>
> "Good morning, Higgins."
>
> "Nice day we're having."
>
> "Yes it is, isn't it, Higgins?"
>
> "Yes I think so, as a matter of fact it was so lovely out that I walked."
>
> "Did you really?"
>
> "Yes, it only took another ten minutes, and the sun felt so good on my back. Everything is in bloom."
>
> "I know, my dahlias are out already, and Mrs. Ransom is very excited about the marigolds, we're going to have thousands of them this year, but by the way, Higgins."
>
> "Yes, Mr. Ransom."
>
> "You're late."
>
> "I know I'm late sir, but I thought you would understand, you know, how beautiful it was out and all, how lovely the flowers were . . ."
>
> "I love flowers just as much as you do, Higgins, but if it hadn't been the flowers it would have been your car stalled, or you found an injured pussycat, you're late today because you're always late and I'm getting damn sick and tired of you being late."

OK. The business of the scene is that Higgins takes his sweet time getting to the office and for Ransom today is the last straw. Unless their fight is going to culminate in Higgins going over and poisoning Ransom's garden, or something that happened on Higgins's walk to the office is going to function in the story later on, all you really need is:

> "Good morning, Mr. Ransom," Higgins said. "It was so beautiful out I decided to walk."
>
> "Late again, Higgins."
>
> "The sun was so warm on my back, all the flowers are out . . ."
>
> "Forget the flowers, Higgins, you are late."

We have arrived at the confrontation without any detours.

3. You can leave out anything you had to write to get from one point to another. Sometimes this is a scene which you, as writer, had to work through in order to know what was going to happen next. Sometimes, as in the weather dialog above, it's what you had to make your characters say in order to discover for yourself what the true business of the scene was. If the business is the one man being late and the other man being angry, we as readers might like to know that the one is late because of the weather, but that's all we need to know, and it can be done in a single line. Character descriptions written to help the author discover character, or extensive physical descriptions written to help the author

discover setting or action, should be combed relentlessly. Anything that does not enhance the finished story, anything that distracts or bores the reader has to go.

4. You can leave out elapsed time. This is so logical and obvious, the process is so simple that many beginning writers don't see it at first. Faced with a gap of days or weeks or years between one crucial event and another, they will find themselves writing in summers and snowfalls from a compulsion to *fill the space between events*. Movies and television have educated this generation of readers and writers to the quick cut, the flashback and flash forward, the shock cut and any number of other techniques; we have absorbed them by osmosis and whether we realize it or not, they are a natural part of our equipment. You already know these things; you can put them to use in fiction. IF NOTHING GOES ON BETWEEN ONE SCENE AND ANOTHER, CUT DIRECTLY. Most of us as readers have become so sophisticated about filmmakers' cuts from one scene to another, from one location to another, that we are more than ready to make any leap an author asks. We can be moved from one scene to another, from one location to another so swiftly that we walk into the next moment without stopping to ask how we got there.

5. You can leave out most explanations. You can assume that your reader knows almost as much as you do about your setting, or the occupation of your central character. Naturally he doesn't, but for complicated reasons which I'll attempt to get at here, he'll think it's his fault. There is a mysterious authority to the printed word. One of the most important things you as writer will learn is how to exercise that authority. The reader who does not know everything about offices, or newspaper city rooms or steamfitting or long-distance running seldom blames the writer for not filling him in. Instead he will feel faintly guilty in the face of your assumption that he does know, because in assuming that he knows, you are also implying that it is his business to know. What's more he will resent you if you assume he is ignorant and slow down a story in order to explain.

If it is important to the story he'll find some way to supply the missing details as best he can, and if you, as writer, choose to give him a few clues or crumbs of information to head him in the right direction, he will fall on them with gratitude. Depending on who he is, the reader will fill in the details in one of three ways:

a. He will put in what you have left out, using his own store of knowledge to create the setting. The newsroom you see may not necessarily be the one he furnishes in his own mind, but it will function for him. He'll use everything he's read or heard or seen on film or TV to put together a functioning background for your story. He will do the same for a story whether it takes place in an insane asylum or Alaska or the army.

b. Or he will read carefully for context, and figure out the details from what you have given him, combining what you give with what he already knows to fill in the picture. In *A Clockwork Orange* Anthony Burgess imposes an entire vocabulary on his readers by the relentless use of new words in familiar contexts. After a few pages readers know that tolchoks are blows and peeting is drinking and they accept an alien vocabulary for the same reason. Burgess doesn't explain; reader doesn't refer to his glossary. Reading swiftly and for context, reader figures it out. The same goes for Ernest Hemingway and his *cojones*.

    c. Or, if the reader feels guilty enough about his ignorance, he'll find some way to find out what he doesn't know. He'll look it up or ask somebody. He'll do this because he knows you are assuming he is just as smart as you are, and he is moved to live up to your expectations. He will, furthermore, be pathetically grateful for whatever he learns from context and he'll absorb whatever details you have given him into his memory banks for use the next time he's faced with a similar problem. Thanks to you, he gets wise; the next time he is faced with a newspaper city room or a steamfitting shop or a long distance race he'll nod sagely. Yup, yup, I know about this one; uh-huh, uh-huh, yeah.

    Here's an example. It would be possible to begin a story about a reporter as follows:

> The city room of an evening newspaper is organized according to function. There is a U-shaped arrangement of desks with the city editor sitting at the center of the U and the rewrite man sitting next to him. On the paper in this story he is responsible for everything that goes into the paper that day; he will decide which stories to send reporters out on and which stories already written are important. He may also make the dummy (showing the composing room which headlines belong on which stories in which size type face) and mark this on top of the copy before passing it on to the men who sit around him in the U. They are called desk men and they read the copy for errors and write the headlines. The reporters all sit at desks ranged around this central U. They have certain regular assignments, but if anything important happens the city editor will make them drop everything to go out and cover the story. They will telephone the rewrite man with the details and he will put on his headphones and type out the information as fast as it comes in because the deadline is coming and they have to get the story set up in type as quickly as they can so it will be on the front page of the first edition. On an evening paper, the first edition goes to press around noon. Ralph Carlson was a reporter on an evening paper, and he was having his lunch one day when the phone rang and Henderson, the city editor, answered it . . .

Although all that information is background, there is no real reason to give it. All the writer needs to give is what functions:

> Henderson was in the slot that day and when the first call came he listened for a minute and then turned it over to Casey, who was on rewrite. Then he bellowed, "Carson, Williams, there's a hell of a fire at Wooster Square. Get on over there."
>
> "Right." Carson dropped his sandwich onto his story about the Fresh Air Fund and left the newsroom on the run.
>
> Henderson was already on the phone to the composing room. "Tell Ray to hold Page One."

If gentle reader doesn't already know he's in a newspaper office, he'll find out quickly. He will, furthermore, feel stupid for not catching on sooner. "In the slot" implies a position of responsibility and the reader will figure out that Henderson is an editor and in passing that he's learned a new phrase. By the end of the story he will know what the rewrite man does, as the embattled Casey takes in bits of information on the phone and gets the story in shape for Henderson. There is a sense of urgency about ripping up Page One to accommodate this new disaster, and if the sandwich doesn't indicate it's lunchtime, it doesn't much matter. Any real insider will know it's accurate. Meanwhile we as readers are being treated like insiders. By the time the story is over we'll have a pretty good idea what newspaper work is like without ever being instructed. We are involved because the writer assumes we are on the inside of what's going on; even though we may not know exactly where the writer has put us, we're grateful for being considered smart enough to be along on the trip. What's more, we're learning all the time.

Remember that readers hate being condescended to. We all like to think we've been around, and if you insist on explaining at length we will resent that, and, strangely, we will begin to question your authority. Who is this writer trying to convince? Is it really us, or is it himself? Look for the right details to put your reader in the picture and do it with authority. Never apologize for knowing more than he does, and never stop to explain.

6. Leave out loving descriptions unless they function. You can give the reader a room, a landscape, any kind of a setting, using as wide a sweep of prose as the subject commands, but you can do so only if this room, or landscape, or setting, or object is going to function in the story. That ormolu clock on the mantel in the old man's sitting room may be a marvel of workmanship, but unless you are going to use it to signify time passing or as an emblem of the grandeur of the old man's past or his regrets, or unless somebody is going to come in and brain him with it, there is no need to describe it in detail. That autumn landscape that so takes your imagination is suspect too. No matter how beautifully you describe it, it must assert its function in the story in order to belong. You may use it as background, or as the first frame in a sequence that will narrow down to a certain piece of property, the house on the property, a given room in the house, the people in the room. You may set it against the moods of the people in the story or use it in any number of other ways, but if it is there simply because you liked the way you wrote about it, you are going to need to be ruthless. Beautiful as it is, it is going to have to go. Otherwise it is going to stand between the reader and the story like a misplaced flat in an amateur theatrical.

Deciding what to leave out, you will test everything you put in, discarding everything that does not belong. Once you have finished a story you will need to go back and look again, paring, amputating if necessary, until everything that is in the story serves the story.

Once you have developed a relatively sure sense of what to leave out of a short story, you have yet another responsibility: deciding how much to put in. Short stories written by beginners are often sketchy at best, and a new writer dealing in subtleties may assume that because he knows what is going on, the reader is going to know too. He may respond with surprise or resentment when the story fails to come across, saying huffily that it's the reader's fault if he doesn't get it.

This is not necessarily the case.

Writing, you need to put in enough to make a functioning story. You may be as sensitive and subtle as you like, but, working, you must be clear in your own mind about what you are attempting. You need to know what is the center of your story, and you have to be able to focus, to give the reader enough information so that he will know it too.

This is subtle and complex territory. Attempting to write short fiction, you have to supply the indefinable and elusive element which distinguishes story from non-story, and if there is any way to learn about it from the outside it is by reading short stories by the hundreds with some attempt to understand what the writer is doing to you as reader, and how. Having done so you will still have to write stories by the dozens, perhaps even by the hundreds until you as insider feel the movement, the extraordinary number of possibilities for different kinds of movements, and understand at least one of them well enough to convey it to the reader.

I have suggested that as writer, you are already rich in resources, that every word, object, name, action or reaction or speech or stylistic device you choose shapes what you are doing, and that in addition to its more or less universal associations and meanings, each of these has accumulated accretions in the alluvial sludge at the back of your mind, so that every element takes on added value as you use it *according to what it means to you*. If you are good at what you are doing the reader will take all these enriched elements, perhaps enriching them further with his own emotional baggage but at the same time receiving what you intended to give him.

It is here that you must take the most care.

You have to put in enough for the reader to go on.

Using your intensely personal store of references, you can be as subtle or experimental or ambiguous as you like, but there had better be something there to reward close scrutiny and it had better be precisely what you intended. If your meaning is private you can't take it for granted that a good reader is necessarily going to get it, and you'd better not be angry with him if he doesn't. It's probably your fault.

Within the framework of what you are doing, there has to be that focus, that consistency of intention or meaning that a close reading will reveal to the reader who is scrupulous enough to track it down. If the careful reader doesn't get it, don't be too quick to blame him; look at the work again and be at least as quick to question your own judgment as you are to question his. If he couldn't figure out what you meant, could it be in part because you weren't precisely sure? Or were you sure, but careless or imprecise in the way you gave it? Obscurity coming out of authorial uncertainty and imprecision is just as damaging to short stories as a monkey wrench thrown into the electric fan.

There is no easy way to talk about this.

Our friend the electrical engineer introduced me to the information theory, which was developed during a study of military cables transmitted during World War II. Since he used to talk about analog computers with a condescending aside ("giant electronic brains to you"), I have to assume that his explanation was simplistic, and there is also the possibility that I got it wrong. What I extracted has been useful to me and so I offer it here.

As I understand it, the good folks with the computers were engaged in discovering just exactly what percent of a given message had to be transmitted for the intent of the message to get through. If wartime cables were too garbled in transmission, if too many parts were left out, the whole intent was lost. Either the message was misconstrued or it didn't get through. If a certain crucial percentage of the message was presented, the mind would supply whatever was missing and the message would go through.

The writer needs to supply enough to give the reader the meaning he, the writer, intends. This can be done with great subtlety; the reader is capable of supplying enormous amounts for himself, doing a large part of the work, and so sharing in the excitement of discovery. On the other hand, as writer, you want him to make the discovery you intended him to make. You don't want him to invent some wild story loosely based on the sparse elements you have given him. The delicate balance, then, is to give the reader enough to carry him through to your intended meaning, or moment of discovery, without having to spell it out word for word.

This means that although his mind is going to supply whatever is missing, he is going to supply a wrong meaning unless you give him enough details or information to point him in the right direction. If you write a story without a center, the reader is going to try and find one; after all, he has trusted you this far, and because he trusted you enough to come this far with you, he has to assume you brought him here to some purpose. If he emerges from your story without discovering the center, he still assumes you are telling him all this for some reason and unless he has given up in disgust, he will supply one. Nine times out of ten, you as writer aren't going to like the construction he puts on your story, and whether or not he gives up on the meaning or supplies a wrong meaning, your work is wasted.

This means that it is extremely important for you, as writer, to know what you are trying to do in a story; where you pick the reader up and where you want to leave him. Then it is your business to put in *enough* detail, or action, or information or a combination of all those to reward the close reader and prevent gross misinterpretation.

You must write like an insider, because you have to be an insider to write. Having done so, you need to re-read like an outsider, and adjust accordingly.

DISCUSSION QUESTIONS

1. What do you think Reed means when she says that some things "belong" in a story and others don't, that some things "function" in a story and others don't, that a story must have "focus" or "consistency of intention"? (She admits that such considerations are "subtle and complex territory.")

2. Reed mentions the influence of film technique on fiction writing (for example, the quick cut and the flashback). If we are living in the "video age," how must fiction writers consider the "video literacy" of their readers? How might the

style and technique of your own stories be influenced by your exposure (and your audience's exposure) to thousands of hours of TV and movie viewing?

3. Do you accept all of Reed's principles? Can you think of valid exceptions to any of them? When might it actually benefit a story to break one of her rules, and why?

4. Reed's list of "what to leave out" may not be exhaustive. Try to add to it, brainstorming other things that might be left out of stories because, according to Reed, they "don't belong" or "don't function" in the larger interests of the story.

5. Try making an alternative list of "what to put in" a story, what is absolutely necessary to make a story function. Start by thinking about contrasts to Reed's list of what to leave out, and examine her essay for hints of what she thinks does belong in a story, what helps make it function. Consider too your own instincts as a writer. What elements do you consider to be necessary in your stories?

6. Try examining two or three stories by writers with different styles to see if you can find Reed's principles at work, and describe your findings.

BEN NYBERG

Why Stories Fail

Ben Nyberg (b. 1933) has taught for over thirty years at Kansas State University, where he edited the Kansas Quarterly *and where he is now Emeritus Professor of English and creative writing. He has published several short stories, and, he says, written many more, though he is "not prepared to say why—or whether—any of them fail."*

A few years ago I set down my impressions of why stories succeed, or at least what makes literary magazine editors (like myself) take and publish the stories they do. The resulting essay, "The Serious Business of Choosing Literary Fiction," took up only seven pages in the 1986 *Fiction Writer's Market*. I could cover so large a subject in so few pages because I wasn't trying to do much more than identify the qualities and describe the effects that nearly all well-crafted short fiction shares.

For all their diversity, successful stories, like Tolstoy's happy families, have a lot in common—to quote myself: Honesty, Efficiency, Complexity, Authority, Originality. Whereas every single unsuccessful fiction is "unhappy" in its own unique way, so that even listing all the separate reasons short stories fail becomes a hopeless task. Still, after reading a thousand-plus story manuscripts every year for twenty-five years, I've come to recognize some family resemblances among the failed faces in the mixed crowd of hopefuls I screen daily, enough of them that it should be possible to sort most of the specific flaws by kin or kind into larger categories of style and strategy and perhaps come up with some generalizations that may help writers avoid a few of the most common pitfalls of their chosen genre.

Of course any system of classification is bound to be flawed by blind caprice and unwitting bias. When the question is how to codify something as complicated as the whole range of error in handling the grammar and rhetoric of fiction, the task is formidable. I may be thought foolhardy even to try it. But I proceed in the assurance that I seek to propose neither a formulaic paradigm for writers nor a Procrustean set of standards for editors. Rather my intent is to lay out as clearly and completely as possible what I've learned in my editing career about what makes stories fail, in the conviction that seeing what's wrong must always be the first step toward getting it right.

Since I can't, in 1992, improve on those criteria of success I proposed back in 1986, I'll use them—or rather the *lack* of them—to outline the causes of failure as well. But as successful stories all share the virtue of winning the races they run, and many unsuccessful ones seem to drop out long before they can break their finish-line tape, I'll also look at deficiencies in terms of what stage in a story's progress flaws normally appear and take their toll. Some problems, like genetic birth defects, date back to a story's conception and keep it from running its race at all, whereas others—equally crucial but more subtle—don't show up till the run is almost over and victory seems all but certain.

So I've taken the familiar three phase division of a story into beginning (exposition), middle (complication/crisis), and end (resolution/denouement), added a "pre-story" fourth division, and considered each division in the light of my five basic criteria, which gives me twenty categories to consider, each with its special pitfalls. To clarify focus I've also sorted my remarks into subsections labeled according to fiction's traditional elements: setting, plot, character, and theme. Marginal extracts from actual letters I've sent writers over the years complete the format.

HOW STORIES FAIL BEFORE THEY START

To begin at the beginning, let's consider how stories can fail even before they get going. Impossible? Hardly. In fact, probably more stories are disabled by mistakes during advance planning, by conceptual errors made before the writer pens a single line than at any other stage of construction.

Pre-Story Lapses in Honesty

By honesty in fiction I mean knowing what one is writing about and writing only about what one knows. Most of the world's great fiction is grounded, one way

Dear ——,
We'd like to believe what you ask us to see here, but you've got to see it first.

Dear ——,
A wild adventure, but it just didn't take us along.

Dear ——,
We respect your need to catch the reader's eye, but readers need more than rapid eye movement to keep them interested.

or another, in real life. Yet not all knowledge is life-based. It is possible through research to learn enough about places and times outside one's own autobiographical history to make their other-worldly settings feel as familiar and "lived-in" as firsthand experience. Obviously historical fiction requires writers to reach beyond their "natural" time frame.

Even more so do the futuristic speculations of s-f writers. No library has research materials on alien life forms, history yet to happen. True, this only makes the task of becoming knowledgeable more interesting: s-f writers learn about their worlds by creating them. Not quite from scratch, to be sure. Frank Herbert had earth ecology to work from when he was building *Dune*. And George Orwell had a grim post-WWII view of fascism to help him depict *1984*. The point is, s-f writers are no freer than others to make it up as they go along. Just as surely as authors of "autobiographical" stories, they're responsible for the validity of what they record.

Which is what fictive honesty comes down to: making so "real" an "eye-witness" report of what you "see" and "hear" that readers get a feel for what being there was like. So what matters, finally, isn't whether the events of writers' accounts are real, but whether those events "happen" for their readers. A writer who believes what he sees and brings that sureness of vision to his readers is being honest.

So how, specifically, do writers fall short of honesty in the planning stage of stories?

Setting

Surprisingly often, writers seem to give no thought whatsoever to where the action of a story is to take place. Instead of imagining a complete context with solid ground for their people to walk on, they content themselves with putting a character in motion who can only perish from a lack of breathable air. Setting is a story's life-support system, and without it everything dies.

When it isn't entirely ignored, setting is sometimes daubed in dutifully but without conviction, by writers who seem to know that it's supposed to be useful, but whose hastily painted backdrops merely force the characters to act out their scenes on an amateur-hour stage. The quality of life in a story can't exceed the quality of

Dear ——,
Life on other worlds has to be different from life on earth, but the differences must mean something to earthly readers if you're going to tell them as a story.

Dear ——,
Your alien world is spooky and zany, but without cause and effect, it's just not possible to lay out an earth-relevant plot.

Dear ——,
Sorry. You just didn't take us into your world. You seemed to be discussing what happened rather than describing it.

Dear ——,
Interesting enough story idea, but the presentation is so detached and remote and uninvolved that you don't seem to have any stake in how it all comes out.

Dear ——,
Ingenious scenario, delightfully quirky narrator, but you just don't make any space for it all to happen in.

Dear ——,
It may happen in a desert, but it can't happen in a void.

Dear ——,
The "Paris" of your story is pretty well documented, but the data has a travel-brochure feel to it, as if you hadn't ever been there in person.

its sustaining environment; to cut corners on setting is to degrade the whole picture.

Finally, just as setting can be underconceived and executed, it is also possible (though this happens less often) for setting to be over-deliberated to the point that its use becomes suspect. Some writers persist in ignoring Ruskin's famous warning against the "pathetic fallacy" (portraying natural forces as responding in sympathy to human events, e.g., rain = Heaven weeping at someone's death). But obtrusive settings need not be "empathic" to be manipulative, hence dishonest. Except for allegory, where visible action is supposed to serve symbolic sense, setting should stay modestly in the background, not push forward to guide readers' understanding or interpret the author's message.

Character

Dishonesty in conceiving characters is one of the most common planning errors story writers make. And it's a mistake made by many who ought to know better. I myself should have known better, even thirty-some years ago, when I concocted a flimsy high school romance featuring a bespectacled goofball intellectual who falls for a devastatingly cute cheerleader, and sent it off to *Good Housekeeping* as proof that I could do better stuff than their readers were used to getting. My characters were cardboard cutouts, my story a travesty of real-life drama, a mockery of true feeling, and my reward was a well-deserved non-personalized rejection slip.

Such unconvincing characters are usually a result of thinking in generic rather than specific terms. The hero of my silly story had no individual personality because I hadn't bothered to think about him as a person. He was only a function, a means to an end, a stereotype nerd, a big brain drunk with infatuation. All I was after was a picturesque contrast; I didn't really care whether or not he or his cheerleader heroine had any feelings that might disturb the easy flow of a nifty little tale. It wasn't *their* story, after all, it was *mine*. Such is the error of prideful dishonesty.

But many a more famous writer than I has committed this sin. No need to name names here, just consider all the sleazy "pot-boiler" bestsellers cranked out by reputable authors who either knew better or ought to

Dear ——,
Why set your story in Greece? Nothing occurs that couldn't just as well happen in Peoria.

Dear ——,
The weather in your story is too heavy, especially when it tries to clue us in on how to understand Donna's motives.

Dear ——,
We appreciate your desire to give this "Old West" saga the sand-in-the-eye feel of 19th-century Tombstone; but setting laid on this thick is pure mud in the eye of anyone trying to watch the action.

Dear ——,
Probably there are "real" people like these characters, and maybe you know what makes them tick. But unless you let us in on it, they're nothing but so many "scary" Halloween "Costume goblins."

Dear ——,
If you want us to care about and respect your main character in the end, you have to care about and respect him from the beginning. As is, you don't seem to take him seriously till you've already turned him into a cliché.

Dear ——,
Poor Jake acts like a windup toy man that walks off a cliff only because "somebody" set him down and pointed him that way. If he did his own thinking, he might not obey orders.

have. I'm not saying writers shouldn't want to earn money. I *am* saying that bad practice is bad practice, especially when name authors stoop to pander. Because they can get away with it, they cause great harm by encouraging crowds of would-be get-rich-quick imitators to waste time trying their hands at the same sort of tripe.

But what makes such fiction "character-flawed"? Actually, it's both character- and plot-flawed, but the plot errors usually stem from faulty character conception. Years ago I read a very bad novel by Mary Elizabeth Braddon titled *Rupert Godwin*. I now recall little of the wild story line, but it did give me enduring evidence of how devastating an error it is to send a character off on an assignment he's not equipped to tackle. If a mission really is impossible, the story won't sell because readers won't buy it.

Put another way, one of the defining qualities of dramatic tragedy is that it presents a situation that tests the weak spot ("Achilles' heel") of its hero. Thus, Othello would have no trouble coping with Hamlet's problems, and vice versa. But the power of tragedy derives from our sense that, were circumstances just slightly different or our hero's psycho-emotional makeup altered only marginally, the heroic fall would be averted. In other words, the hero's "failure" is the story's intended point. Had it happened by accident, merely because the writer neglected to give his character the strengths or talents needed to cope effectively with the challenges he faces, that would be exactly the sort of planning error I mean.

Characters are sometimes forced into unnatural behavior by writers who are out to prove a point, take revenge, or just vent frustrations. Of course story writers are teachers (even at times preachers) with deeply held beliefs whose fictions convey strong value statements, and they have every right to employ any character they need to tell their tale effectively. But the godlike power to create people carries the equally large responsibility to understand them, to present them as fairly and compassionately as possible. To understand all may not quite be to forgive all, but honest writers always *try* to forgive. Certainly they never treat any of their characters as straw monsters whose only job is to terrify and/or be blown away, or straw wimps and fools who live only to be bullied and humiliated.

Dear ——,
But *why* is Leon such a woman-hating swine? Only to give readers a character to hate?

Dear ——,
Your title character is a "femme fatale," but does she have to be "dumb blonde" too? Makes it too easy for you to push her into cheap no-win scrapes.

Dear ——,
Feels like plot leading character to us, which always gives a story a rigged, "predestined" quality.

Dear ——,
Of course life's full of disappointments, but this story reads like a stacked deck. Your "hero" is subjected to Job-like ordeals, but for all the pain you inflict on him, he doesn't learn much and neither do we.

Dear ——,
Zoe's misfortunes all result from either incredibly bad luck or her own unbelievable stupidity—both of which you seem to inflict on her.

Dear ——,
When Ned gets worked up, he starts spouting such batty claptrap he might as well carry a sign saying "Don't believe me—I'm a wild-eyed radical!"

Dear ——,
Why make Doug such a pushover? Marge could get the better of a smarter cad, so why not let her win a better fight?

So I deny the existence of real, live monsters? Not at all. In life most things are possible, many of them not very interesting. Because it's "real," life may be forgiven some dullness, but fiction can't afford to be dull or pointless. So fiction's successful ogres are its Scrooges, Raskolnikovs, Ahabs—depraved and tormented souls whose spiritual night journeys we watch with a personal involvement born of recognition that somehow or other we share their struggles. The totally, irredeemably evil monster holds no real interest for human readers because its motives don't compute in human terms. A Bad Terminator android is scary; but, lacking the complexity of human motivation, it can't become a truly interesting character.

So even monsters need something driving them more than wicked hearts. However deep are his profligates' or philanderers' villainy, a good writer will explain such behavior well enough to "justify" it in human terms. Criminals' crimes need not be excused, nor their souls redeemed, but an honest story will clarify the reasoning even of sociopaths like Poe's "Tell-Tale Heart" narrator or O'Connor's Misfit in "A Good Man Is Hard to Find."

Which leads to another all-too-common abuse of writer's "license": copping a plea on the basis of insanity. However fair a defense it may be in the real world, it's nothing but a dodge in fiction's court. It's the central difference between life and art: life must acknowledge mental derangement that we mortals can't explain, whereas fiction's "madness" always has its "method." If Hamlet be truly insane, rather than pretending madness as part of a shrewd revenge strategy, his moves are deprived of calculation (and interest!) and his final triumph is reduced to no more than a random shot in the dark, pure fluke. The fictional author of "Diary of a Madman" comes unglued before our eyes, but Gogol's artistry lets readers make sense of even his craziest outbursts.

The bottom line on character invention: people in fiction must have intelligible, supportable reasons for what they do and say, which is possible only if their behavior is motivated by factors a reader can understand and verify from evidence in the story. Unlike flesh-and-blood humans, story personae, however weird,

Dear ——,
This would be lots more gripping if you gave us something scarier than a freak-show ogre to worry about.

Dear ——,
We print psychological thrillers, but not "situational suspense drama." Even by category horror (Stephen King) standards, your grisly night stalker seems undermotivated to "justify" it in human terms.

Dear ——,
We don't have to love your protagonist, but he needs to have a "nature" human enough for us to relate to.

Dear ——,
Your wild and crazy monologue is amusing, but we get no clue to where this guy is coming from or where he thinks he's taking us.

Dear ——,
Earl keeps telling us he's not insane, and since he's got an author vouching for him we're ready to believe it, but then he goes on not making sense.

Dear ——,
Interesting, but you direct our attention to the abnormalities that divide her from us rather than the qualities she shares with us.

must behave in ways that make some kind of sense; if they don't, their "mystery" stays unsolved, unsolvable, pointless.

Plot

As noted above, many faulty plots are caused by trying to force characters to play out a script they are unqualified for. But of course plot doesn't always follow character, and when it leads it can sometimes take characters for quite a ride. Of particular concern is the plot idea that makes impossible demands on its characters. It may be said that, by this rule, many a famous story premise would have been doomed in advance to certain failure. A man wakes up and finds himself turned into a cockroach? Come on, get real! Or how about basing a novella-length story on the idea that a man wastes his whole life waiting for some event to pounce on him, and doesn't even notice when it bites him on the leg (Henry James's "The Beast in the Jungle")? Don't these scenarios all but guarantee failing stories?

Yes, all but. If I received query letters about either of them as possible material for the magazine I edit, I doubt I'd be interested. I can even imagine myself groaning over the first sentence of Kafka's "Metamorphosis," knowing that I was about to suffer through a hopelessly stupid story. But genius has a way of proving rules by violating them. For every successful tour de force achieved by breaking rules, thousands of experiments fail. Those who defy the odds should be aware of the risks.

Then too, Kafka and James didn't come up with these ideas just to prove they could pull a fast one. They were master craftsmen with a keen awareness of their art's demands who chose story materials not because they were flashy, but because they could be grounded in theme, so that both character and plot obey the dictates of thesis. Those determined to run the risks associated with "incredible" tales should know that theme-powered fiction, being cousin to allegory, does stand a better chance of surviving ventures into the absurd or the surreal.

Plots can also be "well-made" to the point of dishonesty. To be sure, fiction is artifice, and all storylines

Dear ——,
The geyser of disjunctive revelation that spews from your narrator may be meant to fit together, but it was too incoherent for us to follow.

Dear ——,
Maybe, if you had a whole novel to deal with all the issues your plot poses your characters, they might be up to their job.

Dear ——,
It's not enough to startle readers; they expect some food for thought as well.

Dear ——,
We can follow the events of your story, but not the motivation of your characters.

Dear ——,
It takes daring to try something this difficult, and genius to succeed. You come close, but a miss is still a miss.

Dear ——,
We admired the well-decorated corridors of your plot, but ended up feeling that there was more glitter than gold in the story.

Dear ——,
The machinery of your plot is so elaborate that it can't help but draw attention to itself, and once we notice it the illusion of reality is gone.

are accordingly conjectural narrative schemes. But some schemes are so rigid they turn characters into marbles rolling and bumping their way along a set of pre-cut grooves so deep nobody could conceivably get off track.

This sort of "idiot plot" is beautifully illustrated by the cliché film chase in which someone in a car tries to run down someone on foot. In order to make the scene last, two things must happen: 1) the car must not catch up with the runner; 2) the runner must not outrun the car. In order to achieve both these ends, it's necessary to put severe restrictions on both runner and driver. The driver must drive so as to appear to be really trying to catch the runner, and the runner must not run anywhere that a car can't follow. The result is a thoroughly dishonest piece of plotting: runner runs only in streets, parking lots and other open places; driver makes his car roar and buck frantically but without ever closing distance on the fleeing runner.

So most dishonest plot-planning comes down to thinking up adventures that overtax a character's ability or will to accomplish what's asked of him. He must do what he can't (in some cases, what nobody could) or what no one of sound mind would agree to do. But sometimes plot ideas are more innocently dishonest: writers often undermine their credibility by getting historical facts wrong or out of order (anachronism) or contravening established physical or biological laws, or casually contradicting themselves (scrambling natural time by having corn ripen in October), forgetting that a character did something (like walk to a party) that prevents his doing something else (like driving home in his car), etc. Gaffes like these may not seem serious, but for the reader who notices them they can easily destroy a story's illusion of reality. At the least they say that an author isn't really watching his story unfold.

Theme

As noted earlier, theme-dominant fiction leans toward allegory, is by nature more abstract, more overtly symbolic, more concerned about subtextual meaning than is ordinary garden-variety mimetic fiction. But writers of theme stories sometimes get so caught up in "message" they forget that they still need to show as well as tell.

Dear ——,
Verdi wrote a good opera called *The Force of Destiny*, but in a short story fatalism is usually a recipe for melodrama.

Dear ——,
Serious plots are more than obstacle courses improvised ad hoc by authors intent on keeping the action going.

Dear ——,
You seem more concerned with thwarting Dave's progress toward his goal than with understanding why he wants to reach it.

Dear ——,
You seem to want us to believe that John is really a skilled fly fisherman, yet you commit so many errors in describing basic technical skills that we began to wonder if it was deliberate, and if so, why.

Dear ——,
For a 1960s "period piece," your story contains far too many slang terms from more recent decades (and several bits of consumer goods as well).

Dear ——,
Your story arrives like a Delphic pronouncement, abstract and lacking clear contextual references, leaving us to puzzle away at its riddles as best we can.

No matter how thesis-driven, fiction never "sells direct" in the manner of essays, always presents meaning obliquely, implicitly, for readers to infer.

Ironically, it's usually when writers work too hard at making their intended statements clear and emphatic that they lose their grip on the dramatic illusion necessary to sustain their case. In their desire to spell things out so unambiguously no reader will mistake them, they may be tempted to thrust a more-or-less explicit message into the story's text, sometimes even putting wise words in the mouth of a "spokesman" character—whether he can speak them or not. The impression left may be earnest and intense, but it always has a hollow, unconvincing ring to it, because the writer has resorted to "special pleading" in support of a shaky argument.

Strange to say, one of the most common failings of theme fiction is thematic insincerity. Stories by writers with a point to prove might be expected to burn with even greater zeal than most, but in fact theme fiction seems to be the medium of choice for those who simply want to impress the world with their ability. Like my story mentioned earlier, condescendingly written to show the editors of *Good Housekeeping* what they were missing, too many apprentice-level theme stories have an attitude problem. Most of the time what makes such scenarios dishonest is that their authors are trying to argue for (or against) causes that they lack the knowledge to discuss. I must have rejected hundreds of stories that were nothing but shallow diatribes against abortion, capital punishment, police brutality, political corruption, spouse abuse, and other hot topics by writers more concerned with attracting attention to themselves than stirring reader concern about anything.

Sadly, sincerity is itself no guarantee of thematic honesty. Often a theme story author's subjective dedication to a pet cause actually spawns other sorts of dishonesty: selective documentation, which gives the argument an unconvincing slant; distorted evidence, rotten apples that can spoil a whole barrel of sound ones; and skewed logic, which turns authors into con artists.

It's probably fair to say of theme stories that, though they are the rarest of fiction's usual birds, they are also the ones most likely to crash and burn. Taking flight from a perch removed from visible reality, they seem to meet with more problems in fictional aerodynamics.

Dear ——,
You make your point forcefully and cogently, but the story feels over-argued, pushed at to make its own way.

Dear ——,
Ben sounds suspiciously like a "mouthpiece." If you want us to "buy" what he says, better not let him say it.

Dear ——,
This isn't so much a story as a dramatized debate with Ms. Pro and Mr. Con duking it out for ten bloody rounds.

Dear ——,
If you really want to write tracts, maybe you ought to switch to propaganda's natural essay genre rather than trying to twist fiction to your ends.

Dear ——,
We approve the passionate commitment you bring to your writing, but the "blood in your eye" keeps you from seeing your characters and their story fairly and truly enough to make us trust your account.

1. What does Nyberg mean by "honesty" in a story? How can a story fail due to lack of honesty?
2. What fatal mistakes can writers make with setting? Character? Plot?
3. How does "theme-dominant" fiction present special problems? How might too much emphasis on presenting a clear "thesis" to the reader sabotage a story?
4. Can you imagine any reasons for breaking any of Nyberg's rules? If so, under what circumstances and for what purposes?
5. Try stating Nyberg's principles as positives rather than negatives, as "thou-shalts" rather than "thou-shalt-nots." In other words, using his guidelines, try writing "Why Stories Succeed," especially with reference to the planning stages.

JEROME STERN

Don't Do This
A Short Guide to What Not to Do

Jerome Stern (1938–1996) taught at Florida State University for thirty years, where he directed the writing program. He was the father of "microfiction," stories of 250 words or less, which he championed in the collection Micro Fiction: An Anthology of Really Short Stories *(1996). He also published the textbook* Making Shapely Fiction *(1991).*

DON'T TRY TO TELL TOO MANY STORIES AT ONCE.

Some writers, full of ideas and excitement, try to do too much in a single story, have too many incidents, too many plots. They want to tell about little Ilena, lost in the supermarket, but also about her mother, who is crying because she was arrested for shoplifting, and also about the dad, who's a manic-depressive who disappears for days but then shows up with beautiful toys, and about the new neighbors next door, who scream at each other all night—and the reader is soon as confused as little Ilena.

A story that's too complicated uses up its energy just to explain what's happening. Complication is not complexity. A story that renders a single moment convincingly is a complex accomplishment. The complexity lies in the richness, the rendering, the texture, the subtlety of observation, the experience created for readers.

A beautifully complex story is often complex not because of a complicated surface but because of an impressive depth.

DON'T WRITE STORIES
IN WHICH THE LAST LINES ARE:

And then I woke up.

And then the alarm rang.

Well, they're bringing my supper now, steak and french fries they promised me. I guess they'll shave my head later, when the padre comes.

He realized he was alone, and slowly blinked his third eye.

It's not a bad place to live—warm, dry, and nice padded walls.

The guillotine blade fell swiftly, severing my head from my body.

"Doris, I'm gay."

He slowly drew the thin razor across his wrists.

He slowly shook out the whole bottle of pills in his hand.

He slowly put the muzzle of the gun against his forehead.

He slowly walked deeper into the water. He did not look back.

He pulled the sheet of paper out of the typewriter. The story was done.

What's wrong with these terrific last lines? They're all based on the same principle—surprise the reader. But who wants to read a whole story just for a punch line, especially ones that are this old?

DON'T WRITE ABOUT THINGS
YOU DON'T KNOW ABOUT.

Some beginnings make readers instantly suspicious.

"Mush, mush," Nooknook shouted, as he threw bits of meat to make his dogs bound across the ice floe.

Chichen Itza was especially beautiful on coronation day, thought Uxmalki as he carved on his chacmool.

If you don't know much about huskies or Mayans, basing your fiction on them will probably lead to trouble.

DON'T WRITE A STORY WHOSE MAIN POINT IS THAT
IT IS FROM SOME UNEXPECTED POINT OF VIEW.

Such stories often end this way:

I can't help it if that's all I understand. After all, I'm just a dachshund.

(Or "just a parakeet," "just a teddy bear," etc.)

I've seen stories from the point of view of raccoons, roaches, deer, chairs, and, once, a pet rock. Writers have, of course, written fine stories from various points of view—animate and inanimate, human and nonhuman—but that's just their starting premise. The question is what is achieved by the device. An odd point of view may seem too cute, too contrived. It can seem to be nothing but a joke on the reader: you never guessed it was all being told by an eggbeater! Or it could be too sentimental and didactic (stories told by dog hit-and-run victims, foxes in traps, and caged chickens).

DON'T WRITE STORIES THAT
ARE SIMPLY IDEA-DRIVEN.

When you have an idea—"Abortions are bad," "Alcoholism destroys homes," "Old people are neglected"—and you write a story mainly to exemplify that idea, you're giving your readers an *exemplum,* a little sermon that preaches by example. In a good story, however, the experience is primary, not a message. If you think of a story you admire, and someone asks you what its point is, you're likely to answer, "Well, it's about a lot of things." In other words, you felt that the story wasn't reducible to a single idea—it probably raised more questions that it answered.

DON'T LET YOUR STORIES
HAVE POPULATION EXPLOSIONS.

Readers lose track if there are too many names to retain. You must determine who is necessary to the story and remove everyone else from the set, forcibly if necessary.

> Arlo swung his mallet at Arlene's ball while Uncle Claude looked on admiringly. Arlo had a nice swing for a young man. Wilson was too easily distracted, and Roger was hopeless. If anything, Roger should really be paying attention to Arlene, not standing by the wicket snickering with Frederick and Carl about Benita falling off her big sorrel, Elena.

By this time, readers are looking for their own croquet mallets.

DON'T GIVE YOUR CHARACTERS NAMES
THAT ARE PHONETICALLY SIMILAR
UNLESS YOU ARE DELIBERATELY TRYING
TO MAKE A POINT.

Characters with names like Jack and Kirk, Winston and Kingston, tend to run together in readers' minds. Jim and Susquehanna don't. Two-syllable names with diminutive endings have the same confusing effect: Vicky and Teddy and Cindy and Danny blur phonetically.

DON'T PREFACE YOUR STORY WITH EXPLANATORY MATERIAL THAT MAKES YOUR READERS IMPATIENT FOR THE STORY TO BEGIN.

Don't be like the guy who starts telling you an anecdote:

> This girl, I met her last Thursday, no it was Wednesday . . . wait, it *was* Thursday. I remember because I was getting the laundry. Well really I was coming back with the laundry, and I had to stop for gas. My car doesn't hold but ten gallons, but I usually only buy two dollars at a time anyway. So I stopped at this little self-service place because I always pump my own—I mean I'm not a mechanic but I can pump my own gas . . .

Don't paint elaborate stage sets, don't have long overtures, don't have lengthy preambles, don't do formal introductions, don't keep readers wondering What is this about? When is this thing going to begin?

Good stories intrigue readers from the first words of the first sentence.

DON'T WRITE THE FOLLOWING STORIES:

The Banging-Shutter Story

This is a story based on anticlimax. A perceived threat is built up by describing mysterious and frightening noises, sights, and sensations. The character's terror is developed by describing various fears and possibilities, and perhaps recent atrocities in the vicinity. The end reveals that it was all caused by a cat, a raccoon, a possum, a shutter, a loud clock, wind in the trees, moonlight in the mirror, a child's wind-up toy, one's own heartbeat. (Also known as the *I am der viper, I am der vindow viper story.*)

The Bathtub Story

In the bathtub story a character stays in a single, relatively confined space for the whole story. While in that space the character thinks, remembers, worries, plans, whatever. Before long, readers realize that the character is not going to do anything. Nothing is going to happen in terms of action. The character is not interacting with other people, but is just thinking about past interactions. Problems will not be faced but thought about. Troubles will not occur but will be remembered. That's the problem with the bathtub story: The character is never going to get out of the bathtub.

Can a good bathtub story be written? Are there good bathtub stories? Of course, especially if the claustrophobia and lack of movement are exploited for suspense and tension. Bernard Malamud's *The Fixer* never gets out of prison. Samuel Beckett's character in *Malone Dies* never gets out of bed. But often the lack of motion signifies a failure of imagination. You must find a way to make up for the lack of plot, of action, and of momentum. The missing kinetic energy must be generated by particular daring, wit, or ingenuity. And even then, someone might say, "It's funny all right, but it's really just a bathtub story."

The Hobos-in-Space Story

Here a small number of characters, perhaps only two, isolated from ordinary society, talk a lot about life while not doing very much. They tend to comment about civilization, philosophize about meanings, and squabble a bit among themselves. One of them says, "It's cold." Another answers, "It's always been cold."

Perhaps this is all Samuel Beckett's fault. But it's really not fair to blame him. It *is* fair to blame those who don't realize that giving portentous dialogue to philosophizing outcasts (in a world gone mad) is self-indulgent, sentimental, and heavy-handed. The stylized setting makes all actions seem weightily symbolic, and the characters generally seem to stand for some major idea about the nature of man. Stories of this sort tend to end with either a bang (punching, knifing, hitting with a plank) or a whimper (staring into embers, staring into an empty pot, staring into nothing).

The I-Can-Hardly-Wait Story

An I-can-hardly-wait sets up a character who will have his expectations dashed. A grandfather is depicted joyfully anticipating the arrival of a granddaughter. A woman is preparing an elaborate meal for the man of her dreams. A man is looking forward to his evening with the long-sought perfect woman. A child is waiting for her daddy to come home. The I-can-hardly-wait dwells on the joys expected and then deprives the central character of whatever is desired. The beloved one— man, woman, child, dog, or cat—inexplicably never shows up or is killed on the road or drunkenly calls from a bar or runs away with someone else or has really been dead for years.

It's true that life can be cruel, but this sort of story trivializes sad occurrences by focusing on the simple plot device of disappointed expectations. It's an easy way to manipulate readers, but it's too familiar a formula. Unless it brings readers to an insight beyond "Gee, you never know, do you? That was so sad," you haven't really created a story.

A variant of this is the *I-knew-the-last-line-when-I-read-the-first-line story.* That starts with the banker in a hurry knocking the bag lady into the gutter, the bully humiliating the defective child, the selfish man killing the good collie's half-breed puppies—pain is inflicted on some apparently helpless victim. Then we wait for the inevitable end. The bag lady has a secret mortgage and forecloses on the banker, the defective child ignores the screams of the bully imploring him to push the STOP button and lets the garbage compactor have its way with his tormentor, and the collie eats its owner in a lightning storm.

The I-Cried-Because-I-Had-No-Shoes- Till-I-Met-a-Man-Who-Had-No-Feet Story

This story is primarily designed to teach a lesson. Writers tell these to impart a moral, rather than to create an experience.

In these stories, characters do not have the idiosyncrasies of individuals. They have stereotyped traits—we have the unloving grandfather, the careless mother, or the ungrateful young girl. Events are set up to show the harmful consequences of bad behavior (or the beneficial results of good behavior), and the plot seems mechanical. If the effect of the ending is that this is the moral, this is the bottom line, the work will seem only like a lesson, a sermon, a homily.

Fine stories are written about characters learning, coming to understand, and having insights, but the I-cried-because story doesn't care about rendering psychological and emotional complexity. Instead, it tries to tell readers how to behave.

The-Last-Line-Should-Be-the-First-Line Story

There's a story that keeps getting told, a kind of urban legend, about a shy little guy who falls in love with a mysterious, lovely woman. They plan to get married, and the man's office friends throw a bachelor party, get him drunk, take him to a brothel, push him into a room, where he finds . . . guess who?

Now the question is, where should this story begin? It's just a long lead-up to a nasty surprise ending. It could be interesting if its ending was its beginning. How would two people behave in such a situation? Stories that lead up to revelations and odd situations really quit just where they should begin. An arrest, a compromising position, or a shocking discovery about a loved one will likely make a better opening than a closing. As an opening, there is high tension, interest, and momentum—readers want to know what happened next. As a conclusion, the revelation doesn't deal with the issue it raises.

The Weird Harold Story

Weird Harolds are stories focused on a character who is strange and different. Readers are given many examples of the character's behavior, but no insight into the character. Writers of Weird Harold stories are fascinated with a character who certainly seems worthy of fictional representation. However, they haven't figured out a shape that gives readers what they need in order to know the character from the inside, what might be driving him, what he might be searching for, what might be missing that makes him do what he does.

This does not mean you should go in for overt psychologizing, or provide a secret reason to explain complex behavior. But there has to be a sense of how the character perceives and thinks. If you can embed information in an evocative anecdote—include the story about the time the character's older brothers stuffed him into a laundry bag and left him on the sidewalk—we can begin to feel the character's emotional processes, see the world through his eyes. We may not fully understand what's going on, but we don't expect a character to be fully explained. If a character is wholly inexplicable, though, readers can only say, "That's weird," or "That's really strange." And that doesn't make a story. (Or it does—a Weird Harold.)

The Zero-to-Zero Story

If the beginning of a story presents a character who appears rigid and dull and the story simply demonstrates that the character is rigid and dull, readers and the story haven't gone anywhere. Zero-to-zero lends itself to heavy-handed ironies:

the story of the loser who tries but loses once more; the chronic cheater who, when presented with a moral choice, cheats again; the alcoholic who goes back to the bottle; the suicide who finally succeeds. These stories also tend to dwell on one characteristic, usually a weakness or a vice.

This type of story just acts out what readers learned right at the beginning. A variant teases readers with the possibility that there is more to the person than is first presented, but the story returns to zero with an ending that corroborates the beginning. Readers still haven't been taken anywhere. The longer the story, the further they haven't gone.

The Zero-to-One-Hundred Story

In this story, a character totally overcomes some character problem. But a major, permanent change in personality is difficult to make plausible in a short story.

Behavior lies deep and is rooted in habits and responses that cannot simply vanish in a wish or a phrase. The way a person has behaved or the way people have behaved toward a person affects everyone for a long time, whether they like it or not. You cannot eradicate the past merely by saying so. To write otherwise is to be simplistic.

Massive character change is a staple of commercial entertainment. Half-hour situation comedies or one-hour mystery shows rely over and over again on a formula in which various family members finally realize they love each other or have behaved badly, but now everything is all right. These endings are emotionally attractive but, deep down, we know they just aren't true.

DON'T BELIEVE ANY OF THE DON'TS ABOVE.

Art is made out of broken rules. Art pushes at the envelope of the never-done, but also constantly recycles the forever-done. Clichés are the compost of art. Transformations, inversions, reversions, and conversions continually revive fiction. If you dare, these don'ts can be your pleasure ground.

DISCUSSION QUESTIONS

1. What do all or most of the prohibited last lines Stern lists ("And then I woke up," "And then the alarm rang," etc.) seem to have in common? What might be wrong with ending a story with any of these lines?
2. What is "didacticism," and why does Stern feel that it's fatal to a story?
3. Much of what Stern feels should be forbidden to story writers is presented without explanation or justification, but here and there he does explain what's wrong with the things he doesn't want fiction writers to do. Collect his scattered explanations and try to create a coherent approach out of them. What, in general, does Stern feel ruins stories?
4. Have you been guilty of writing any of the stories that Stern frowns on—the Banging-Shutter Story, the Bathtub Story, and so on? Looking at the story, do you feel that his criticism of that story pattern is valid?

5. Add your own items to any of Stern's lists of amusing "don'ts": bad last lines, plots not to write, etc. Be prepared to explain why, for example, the last line is indicative of an awful story or why the plot is doomed to failure.

6. Stern himself invites us to disobey any of his rules ("Don't believe any of the don'ts above"), and he also qualifies many of them with examples of writers who have done just that, including Malamud in *The Fixer* and Beckett in *Malone Dies*. Identify other successful pieces of fiction that violate any of Stern's rules, and explain how they succeed in spite of it.

A MORE NURTURING
APPROACH TO REVISION

JESSE LEE KERCHEVAL

Revision

Jesse Lee Kercheval (b. 1956) has taught at the University of Wisconsin at Madison since 1987. Her short story collection The Dogeater *(1987) won first place in the annual AWP Award series in short fiction. She has also published a novel,* The Museum of Happiness *(1993), and a textbook,* Building Fiction *(1997).*

Most serious writers believe revision is what separates real writers from those who only think they want to write, the dedicated and talented from the merely talented. When I was at the Iowa Writers' Workshop, we fiction writers liked to think of ourselves as craftsmen, not because we didn't think we were artists, but because the word *craftsmen* implied long hours of painstaking work by people who really knew what they were doing.

This was partly defensive. The poets, our opposite numbers in that particular little world, always seemed to dress better, have wilder parties, and really know how to dance. We suspected them of living on pure inspiration, the poems effortlessly flowing out of their pens five minutes before class. So we took a perverse pride in the hours we spent hunched over word processors and typewriters. Some fiction writers even kept track of the number of drafts they put a short story through, the way a weight lifter counts reps. Revision was a cult of masochism, and we took pride in self-imposed pain of the kind that keeps athletes reciting the mantra *no pain, no gain.*

That is the wrong way to look at revision. Most writers who have been at it awhile will tell you with a straight face that revision is their favorite part of the writing process, and they mean it. They see revision as a time when the hard work of raising the framework and getting the roof on the story is done, and they can take pleasure in the finish work, the cabinetry and decorative details that make reading a pleasure.

Bernard Malamud said, "Revision is one of the true pleasures of writing." Whether you learn to love revision or dread it with the intensity most people reserve for trips to the dentist, all fiction deserving of the time and effort it took to write it in the first place also deserves careful, serious, and thorough revision.

In some ways it's an artificial distinction to think of revision as a separate stage in the writing process. When I am writing a short story or chapter, I am revising all the time. I write a sentence, glance back, and change a word or two. Write a paragraph, look it over, and cut a line or add one. My usual method is to write my way as far into a story as I can, stretching for the end. Inevitably I get stopped at some point by what I don't know or pulled back by the mistakes that have accumulated behind me. I may have discovered in writing the story that I need to tell it from a different point of view or that I want to turn a character from a landlord into a landlady. So I go back and make changes. Then I start forward again. The process is circular rather than linear. Sometimes I imagine my writing self as an old hound dog turning around and around before lying down.

There comes a stage, however, when I have made it through to what I hope is the perfect end to a perfect story. I allow myself to sigh with happiness, to sit for a moment awash in the golden glow of my successfully completed work. Then I come back to reality, and the real process of revision begins.

THE RHYTHM OF REVISION

The rhythm of revision is rather like marching: left brain, right brain, left brain, right brain. Your critical sense alternates with your creative sense. You assess the work with a cold eye, then reenter the creative world where all things are possible. It's important to learn to make these transitions. If you can't look at your work critically, you will be stuck forever with half-realized first drafts. If the pure unedited flow of thought and language is your only goal, keep a diary. If you keep it long enough and live in interesting times, you may earn a place in literary history without ever revising or publishing a word. This is what happened to the great diarist Samuel Pepys, chronicler of English life in the seventeenth century. At least you would leave a record of your life for your children and grandchildren. However, most writers aim for a larger audience, one that will read their work in their own lifetimes.

On the other hand, if you do not learn to separate the critical from the creative, you are setting the stage for an inevitable case of writer's block. If every time you look at a word, a line of dialogue, or a transition in a rough draft, you think, *This is crap,* and cross it out, you will never be able to finish, let alone publish, anything. When you are in the creative mode, you have to give yourself room to discover what it is you want to say even if it means giving yourself a license to write badly until you do.

THE CRITICAL EYE

When I finish a draft, I read it with a cold, hard eye, trying to see the story as it actually exists. This can be a discouraging experience. The stories on the pages never match the perfection of the ones in our heads. The trick at this stage is to remember we get to fix our mistakes, to bring the work closer and closer to our ideals. To do that we have to be rather ruthless in diagnosing what is working and what isn't.

All writers have their own quirks when it comes to the stages of writing, and revision is no exception. My own habits have changed over time. When I began I wrote drafts longhand on legal pads and typed the finished stories. Eventually I graduated to typing first drafts, and now I work on a computer. In addition to these technological changes, my approach varies from story to story and novel to novel. Still when I have completed a draft, I print out a clean copy and read it from beginning to end. I read it through at least once without marking anything. If I had a pen in one hand I would spend all my time marking typos and misplaced commas and not enough time asking myself the important question, *Does this story work?*

If it works well enough, I take the story and find a few good readers for their sage, or at least honest, advice. Even after all the years I have been writing, I find it hard to conduct a completely dispassionate and thorough exam myself (doctors are rarely capable of operating on themselves). Like most writers I have cultivated a small group of first readers, people who will take the time and care to give me useful and detailed responses, people who have a good sense of what my fiction tries to do.

Even in a room filled with writers, however, how do you know whose advice is good advice? Even very good writers can be poor critics. If someone praises your style and wit, the comments will seem brilliant. If she criticizes your flat characters and dull prose, the great temptation is to dismiss her as all wrong. But good writers learn to take a deep breath and think again. While their work is being discussed, I encourage my students to clear their minds, think Zen, and listen to what's being said. Imagine your critics are on the other side of a one-way mirror, I say. Pretend your story is a new snack food and you have paid these experienced snack food eaters to taste your product and tell you what they honestly think. Be quiet, let them talk, and take notes. If you waste your time and mental energy defending yourself, you will inhibit them from saying what they really think, and you will not be able to hear them anyway. If you can do it graciously, ask a few questions at the end if you don't understand quite what you are being told. Then go off and think about what's been said.

Not all criticism is valid. Even worse, not all of it is useful. Some of it will be silly, the result of sloppy reading. (These are people you won't be coming back to for more response.) Some is wonderful advice but for another story. Writers have a tendency to want all fiction to resemble their own. An experimental writer might ask you to make a story more experimental, and a more traditional writer to make your story less offbeat. Also readers bring their own interests to a story. Some might want a story to be about the father instead of the mother, but if that is not the story you want to write, it is not advice you can take. Usually good advice echoes doubts you had already. Good critics have a way of sticking their fingers right in those soft spots you hoped no one would notice. The best criticism is very specific. General complaints, like, "Gee, I just got bored after a while," are hard to respond to. A good critic will point to the place in a story where a scene or a stretch of dialogue went on half a page too long. Readers are also great for spotting a minor confusion that you had no idea was a problem, such as the names *Tim* and *Tom,* characters they couldn't keep straight. That's easy to fix: *Tim* and *Alfonse.*

If you find a writer in a workshop or a friend whose criticism is thorough and helpful, take that person to dinner, stay in touch. This is how you build a network of reliable first readers.

MAJOR REVISION

Whether you are the critic, reading your own work with an analytical eye, or someone else is, all criticism breaks down into two categories:

1. Problems of a larger structural nature that may require serious rethinking before you know what to do to fix them

2. Smaller problems that show up line by line and word by word, the sort that can usually be marked on the story itself

Both are important and connected. If you look only at the smaller issues, you risk not seeing the forest for the trees. It's like worrying about wallpaper when the wall itself is about to fall down, or rearranging furniture when the real problem is a gaping hole in the floor. You could struggle trying to get a line of dialogue right, not realizing that you don't know what the character should say because you don't know what she wants. Instead you should first establish her external and internal conflicts more clearly. On the other hand, if you only look at the story from a distance, only at the forest and not at the trees, you risk losing sight of the place on the page where the larger actions happen. A conflict that's muddy now could be made clear by a single good line of dialogue. A story is not made up of abstractions but of words, the very leaves on the trees.

Still it's best to consider the major renovations that need to be done (the macro questions) before dealing with minor remodeling (the micro questions). Over the years I've developed revision checklists for these two categories. I use them on every piece of fiction I finish.

Macro Revision Checklist

1. Check your external conflict.
   - Does the story have an immediate and gripping external conflict?
   - Does the external conflict keep tension alive throughout the story?
   - If the first external conflict is resolved and its place taken by successive external conflicts, check each for conflict, crisis, and resolution to ensure that the parts are working.
   - Is there a final crisis action bringing all the outstanding external conflicts together as the glass slipper fitting does in *Cinderella*?
   - If there is more than one final crisis action (Cinderella puts her foot in the slipper and then takes it out), you are divided about how the story should end. Decide now.

2. Check your internal conflict.

   - Is the internal conflict well established after one page of the short story or one chapter of the novel?

   - Trace the internal conflict as it heats up and cools down throughout the story to make sure the flame doesn't burn out.

   - When the internal conflict is finally resolved, do you use a dream or an image, or the character's thoughts and memories to make the moment significant and convincing?

   - Which type of resolution is it, comes-to-realize or fails-to-realize? Decide now.

3. Check your point of view. If you are having trouble with developing external and internal conflicts, you may have chosen the wrong viewpoint.

   - Is your third-person point-of-view character or first-person narrator well situated to tell the story either by participation or observation in the central conflict?

   - Does your point-of-view character have the personality and skills to be an effective storyteller? Shyness, stupidity, inexperience, or dishonesty may make the character unsuitable for the job, although using a third-person authorial voice can overcome these problems.

   - If you're using first person, check the effectiveness and consistency of the narrator's voice by comparing how it sounds in the first paragraph and the last. It must seem like the same person.

   - If you're using third person, check the effectiveness of your use of the point-of-view character's thoughts, especially at critical moments like the resolution of the internal conflict.

   - If you're using an authorial voice, is it effective or even necessary?

   - If you're using a single narrator or point-of-view character, could you tell the story better with more?

   - If you're using multiple points of view, could you tell the story better with fewer?

4. Check your characters.

   - If readers don't understand your central character, but you're certain you're using the right point of view, see if you can put more of the character on the page by adding action, thought, dialogue, and memories.

   - If other major characters seem flat and underdeveloped, be sure that each has an internal conflict.

   - If a character seems enigmatic, try putting her in a scene with others to draw out her personality and motivations.

   - Check the development of your minor characters. They can lack internal conflict, but they should be clearly and vividly drawn.

- Count lines to see if the space the characters take up is proportional to their importance in the story.
- If a character has become too good for a minor role, make him more important. If he is superfluous, cut him entirely.
- If the story seems depopulated, add more characters.

5. Check your opening.
   - Cut the first paragraph, page, or chapter to see if the story can stand without it. If it can, cut it.
   - If you moved a scene from the middle to the beginning, or if you moved the end to the beginning, would it make a better opening than the one you have now?

6. Check your ending.
   - If you removed the last paragraph, page, or chapter, would it make a difference? If not, cut.
   - If the story continued for another paragraph, page, or chapter, would something happen to resolve the conflict more thoroughly, interestingly, or beautifully?

REVISION

After you and perhaps others have turned critical eyes on your poor, naked piece of fiction and it's been run through the mill of my Macro Revision Checklist, what comes next? You may have a pile of notes and a marked copy or two of your first draft. Looking over the accumulated evidence of your doubts and your readers' complaints, you may be tempted to just give up. At this stage it often seems easier to start another short story or another novel than to deal with the mess this one has turned out to be. A new idea may start glowing in the back of your mind, the proverbial grass that is always greener. Take a deep breath, and know that all fiction and all great writers have passed this way before. Read your notes and comments, and then take a hot bath or a long walk or make a huge batch of lentil soup. While your hands and body are occupied, count on your mind and your imagination to start back to work. Mull it over. (If there is a problem with that first scene, I could . . . and maybe the ending would work better if . . .)

The important thing now is to *stop* being critical and to start letting your creative self take over and come up with the solutions to the problems your analytical self discovered. If you say, *Forget it, that will never work,* your story is going to stay in pieces. If you go back to the story while still in a negative mood, cutting and adding and half-heartedly patching it together using the criticism you've received, you will end up with a story with as many ugly, highly visible scars as Frankenstein's creature. Nothing is more discouraging to me as a writer, an editor, or a teacher than to reread a story I critiqued and find that revision has made it worse. The writer has surrendered his story, given up his vision for it, his hope of perfecting it, and that is a sad, sickening sight.

You have to get back into the story and remember the dream that made you want to write it in the first place. I think of this stage as *re-vision*. You need to re-see your work with fresh eyes. It is easy for someone to suggest cuts, but only you can dream up wonderful new scenes, characters, conflicts, and images that were not there before. My students groan when I point to a spot in a story that I think needs something and I say, "Right here, add something brilliant." But really, that is all anyone can say to the author in the end. Go, be brilliant. I know you can do it. And you can.

LIFE IS REVISION

When I finished a first draft of my novel, *The Museum of Happiness,* I read it from start to finish and fell quite thoroughly out of love with it. The draft was told completely from Ginny's point of view, the American in Paris. Seen only through Ginny's inexperienced and foreign eyes, Roland, the other major character, didn't make sense. There was just too much Ginny couldn't know about Roland, his family, and his past. In other words, I checked my point of view (number three on my Macro Revision Checklist) and found that it did not work.

I decided to tell the story again, this time from Roland's point of view, intercutting these new chapters with the ones I had already written. It was a big decision. It meant writing hundreds of new pages, essentially writing a second book, but it worked. The novel became what I had dreamed it could be. It took the analytical half of my writing brain to realize the novel didn't work as it stood. But it took re-vision by my creative half to see how the problem could be fixed and get excited enough to plunge back in and do the work.

An excellent example of this kind of major revision can be found in a comparison of Raymond Carver's short story "The Bath," which appeared in his early collection *What We Talk About When We Talk About Love,* and "A Small, Good Thing," from his last collection, *Cathedral.* "A Small, Good Thing" is a revised version of "The Bath." Carver made changes in language from the original short story, but also larger, structural changes. Since both are published short stories, the usually private record of a writer's process of revision is there for all to see.

Both open with a mother ordering a birthday cake for her son. But the birthday boy is struck by a car, and though he walks home, something is clearly wrong. In "The Bath" the prose is more tightly controlled, the style more minimalist.

> The birthday boy told his mother what had happened. They sat together on the sofa. She held his hands in her lap. This is what she was doing when the boy pulled his hands away and lay down on his back.

In "A Small, Good Thing" the birthday boy has a name, and his mother a voice.

> But after the birthday boy was inside his house and was telling his mother about it, she sitting beside him on the sofa, holding his hands in her lap, saying, "Scotty, honey, are you sure you feel all right, baby?" thinking she would call the doctor anyway, he suddenly lay back on the sofa, closed his eyes, and went limp.

In both stories the boy remains in a coma at the hospital while the parents suffer in the waiting room anxious for word. In both, the baker, unaware of what has happened, keeps calling the house, angry the birthday cake hasn't been picked up. "The Bath" ends when the mother, momentarily home to take the bath in the title, answers the phone. A man's voice says, "It has to do with Scotty." Readers are left to wonder whether this last call is bad news from the hospital or the disgruntled baker calling yet again.

In "A Small, Good Thing," the boy dies suddenly of a hidden brain occlusion. The parents return home only to receive another call from the angry baker. The mother demands to be driven to the shopping center and confronts the baker working in his bakery in the middle of the night. When she tells him Scotty is dead, he clears a place for the parents to sit and insists they eat some of his hot rolls, saying, "You have to eat and keep going. Eating is a small, good thing in a time like this." The story ends with the baker and the parents talking and eating under fluorescent lights as bright as day. It is a very different ending from that of "The Bath," a more humane one, the work of an older, perhaps wiser, writer. And the product of revision.

MINOR REVISION

When you've finished the major revision, go through the items of the Macro Revision Checklist again just to make certain you haven't forgotten anything. If your short story or novel passes all the tests, it is in good shape in the ways that matter most. But your writing deserves attention to detail that goes even farther. Vladimir Nabokov was famous for writing each word on a separate index card so he could compose his sentences with exquisite and painstaking care. I have never done that in my revision, but I do apply the following steps to polish and shine my finished work.

I begin by slowly reading my short story or novel aloud to myself. Wherever something seems questionable in any way, I make a mark and continue reading. When I am done with the short story or have finished a chapter or two of the novel, I go back and move through word by word and sentence by sentence reworking the passages I marked and checking for the items below.

Micro Revision Checklist

1. Check your words.

   - If each word you used cost a dollar, could you find some your story didn't need?

   - If you got paid by the word, what would you add to make your language denser, richer, more beautiful and effective?

   - Jot down a list of words and phrases that you overuse, and weed them from your writing. The *find* or *search* function of a computer word processor makes this easy.

- Question any phrase that reminds you of something constantly repeated on television, in movies, or in books and magazines. Use your own language instead.

2. Check your descriptions.

- If your characters were suspects in a robbery, would your readers be able to describe their ages, appearances, clothing, heights, weights, mannerisms, and attitudes to the police?

- Is the physical setting for your story so consistent and believable and the relationship between different places so clear that you can sketch the floor plan of a house, the streets of a town, or the route of a cross-country trip that is important in your story? (Or at least so that the details of the setting aren't contradictory.)

- Do you account for the time that passes, or do unexpected jumps, shifts, and discontinuities make your story hard to follow?

3. Check your dialogue.

- Does each conversation do at least two of the following: advance the plot, develop the character who's speaking, help set the time and place?

- Can you eliminate some unnecessary dialogue tags?

- Can you insert some dialogue tags when it's unclear who's speaking?

- Can you tell which characters are speaking from what they say?

- Is the language characters use believable and consistent?

- Do the characters breathe, cough, scratch, and in other ways act like human beings while they speak to each other?

- Are your characters standing or sitting someplace while they speak, rather than floating in space?

- Have you generated tension by having characters avoid speaking about what concerns them most, for example, arguing about their mother's lasagna recipe instead of her love?

4. Check your transitions.

- If you move from one place to another, from one time to another, or from one character's consciousness to another, are the clues sufficient to keep readers from being confused?

- Are you consistent in your use of paragraphing, extra white space, subheadings, chapter breaks, and other typographical signals of transition?

5. Check the first and the last, again.

- Reread, polish, and primp your opening so that no readers will escape its attraction. (There is no catch if the fish doesn't take the bait.)

- Reread, polish, and primp your ending. Endings of great stories and novels often have a heightened poetic quality about them that readers cannot forget. Is your language as good as your idea for the ending?

LETTING GO

At some point, revision must stop. Humans are not perfect, nor is the fiction they create. In his *Paris Review* interview, William Faulkner explains his view of our imperfectability.

> In my opinion, if I could write all my work again, I am convinced that I would do it better, which is the healthiest condition for an artist. That's why he keeps on working, trying again; he believes each time that this time he will do it, bring it off. Of course, he won't, which is why this condition is healthy. Once he did it, once he matched the work to the image, the dream, nothing would remain but to cut his throat, jump off the other side of that pinnacle of perfection into suicide.

One problem with writing on computers is that you can revise endlessly, change a word, change it back. It's easy to get stuck. You may spend precious and limited writing time fiddling with a line, paragraph, or chapter that you end up cutting later. When this happens to me, I force myself to move on. If I am writing new material, I set an egg timer and make myself write for twenty minutes without stopping or going back to revise. If I am revising, I try to leave questions I can't answer for the time being and move forward, trusting the creative half of my brain to keep working on the problem while my mind is elsewhere.

I may go through many drafts before I send a short story to a magazine. I might edit again before it appears in print. I might revise before it appears in a book of stories, but at some point I have to call a halt, and you will too. If you don't, you risk revising a single short story or novel into the many other ones you might have written. Start a novel when you are happily married, and the point of it might be love saves us all. Keep working on it through a bitter divorce, and it won't be the same novel. Part of this is unavoidable. We are different people today than we will be tomorrow. If you work long enough, the piece can become impossible to finish, something that never will be. When the writer and professional celebrity Truman Capote died, all anyone found of his much-touted last novel was a handful of pages. When noted novelist Ralph Ellison died at eighty, his long-awaited second novel, the follow-up to his classic *The Invisible Man,* was still uncompleted after four decades.

At some point writers have to move on. Leave whatever doubts you still have about a single word or a whole book to the critics and scholars. Start something new.

EXERCISES

1. Use the Macro and Micro Revision Checklists on a piece of fiction you have written. Make notes of what you think works or doesn't work in your piece. Put question marks next to things you are not sure about.

2. Show the piece to a friend, fellow writer, or group of writers. Make careful notes about what they say. Compare them to the notes you made after using the checklists. Make a combined chore list of things that need

to be fixed. Concentrate on the larger structural questions, the macro concerns. Don't worry too much yet about how you will fix them.

3. Now go for a long walk or just live your life for a few days or weeks, but keep thinking about your piece. When you feel restless with ideas, return to your desk or computer and begin revising.

4. After you have finished revising, let the piece sit for a while, then read it beginning to end, preferably aloud. If you have any doubts, go through exercises one, two, and three again.

5. When you are as sure as you can be that you are finished revising, use the Micro Checklist one last time, and always be sure to proofread your final copy carefully. Then start something new.

DISCUSSION QUESTIONS

1. What is the difference, according to Kercheval, between the kind of revision that goes on while a writer is still in the process of finishing a draft and the kind of revision that goes on after a draft has been completed?

2. Kercheval points to the importance of feedback in revising fictions. What are the worst and best kinds of feedback? Are her estimations true to your own experience of receiving feedback? What feedback has been particularly useful or useless to you? Has your feedback to other writers always been the best kind?

3. Recent revelations about the relationship between writer Raymond Carver and editor Gordon Lish indicate that Lish may have had a heavy hand in creating Carver's famous "minimalist" style and that Carver later returned to a more expansive style. Therefore, the "revision" of "The Bath" that Kercheval discusses may be less a revision than a revival of an old story. Have you ever received advice on a story that you initially took but subsequently rejected (or felt like rejecting)?

DAVID MADDEN

Point of View

David Madden (b. 1933), best known for his novel The Suicide's Wife, *which was nominated for a Pulitzer Prize (1978), has taught at Louisiana State University since 1968, where he has also directed the Creative Writing Program. He is the author of eight other novels, including* Bijou *(1974),* On the Big Wind *(1980), and* Sharpshooter *(1996, also nominated for a Pulitzer Prize). In addition to volumes of literary criticism and literature textbooks, he has*

written on the craft of fiction in Revising Fiction (*1988*) *and* The Fiction Tutor:
The Art of Writing and Reading Fiction (*1990*).

1. CONSIDERING THE EXPERIENCE YOU WANT THE READER TO HAVE IN THIS STORY, HAVE YOU USED A POINT OF VIEW THAT IS <u>INEFFECTIVE</u>?

All the reader's experiences flow from the point-of-view technique you employ. When the point of view is gratuitous, the writer loses control of other elements. Because it most directly affects the choice and use of all elements, point of view is the most important technical choice. Because the choice of an ineffective point-of-view technique produces so many other problems, it is the only technical choice you need to make *before* plunging into the first draft.

In the revision process, you may ask yourself:

What is the best point of view for the effects I want to have on the reader?

How does the point of view affect style, characterization, conflict, theme, structure?

What is the psychological effect on the reader of presenting this story through the mind of the main character in the third person as opposed to letting him tell it in his own voice?

What are other possible points of view for this story and what are their particular effects?

The major fallacy, from which all other fallacies spring, is the point-of-view fallacy. If the writer uses poor judgment in his choice of the point of view through which the elements of the story are presented, or if he mishandles the one he chooses, he sets up a chain reaction that demolishes most of his carefully prepared effects. A story told in the third person will differ radically—in style, content, even structure—from the same story told in the first person.

The reader must feel that the point of view through which all elements reach him is the inevitable one for this story. In every story, the reader responds to a voice of authority as the source of everything—words, phrases, sentences, etc.— presented in the story. The writer creates that voice: sometimes the voice is the writer's own voice; sometimes he lets a character tell the story in the first person; sometimes he filters the story through the mind of a character, using the third person. For both writers and readers, point of view is the most difficult concept to understand and keep in focus.

"The whole question of the point of view," said Mary McCarthy, ". . . tortures everybody." Choosing the most effective point of view, as we can see in *The Notebooks for "Crime and Punishment,"* tortured Dostoyevsky. "The decision on narrative point-of-view," said Ross Macdonald, "is a key one for any novelist. It determines shape and tone, and even the class of detail that can be used."

The major point-of-view techniques are described . . . next. . . .

2. IF YOU HAVE USED THE <u>OMNISCIENT</u> POINT OF VIEW, HAVE YOU REALIZED ALL ITS POTENTIALS?

In the omniscient point of view, the author narrates the story in the third person, although he may speak now and then in his own first-person voice. The all-knowing omniscient narrator is godlike, for he sees, hears, feels, knows all; he may move from one character to another; he may move anywhere he wishes in time and space, giving the reader objective views of his characters' actions, or subjective views of their thoughts. The roving, omniscient narrator strives for a balance between interior and exterior views of his characters. He has a godlike control of all the elements.

You may get a very good sense of the characteristics of the omniscient point of view by reading the opening passages of novels using that technique. Charles Dickens's novels exhibit the entire range from extremely remote from, to close to a character. In the opening of *Bleak House,* a metaphor pervades, like the creator's own consciousness, the scene.

> London. . . . Fog everywhere. Fog up the river, where it flows among green aits and meadows; fog down the river, where it rolls defiled among the tiers of shipping, and the waterside pollutions of a great (and dirty) city. Fog on the Essex marshes, fog on the Kentish heights. Fog creeping into the cabooses of collier-brigs; fog lying out on the yards, and hovering in the rigging of great ships; fog drooping on the gunwales of barges and small boats. Fog in the eyes and throats of ancient Greenwich pensioners, wheezing by the firesides of their wards. . . . Chance people on the bridges peeping over the parapets into a nether sky of fog, with fog all round them, as if they were up in a balloon, and hanging in the misty clouds.

Now, to see the range of characteristics of the omniscient point of view, read, in order, the openings of Dickens's *The Life and Adventures of Martin Chuzzlewit, Our Mutual Friend,* and *The Life and Adventures of Nicholas Nickleby.* The openings of Dickens's chapters in these and his other novels also demonstrate the range of omniscience.

Each type of point-of-view technique allows the writer its own particular freedoms and imposes its own particular limitations. The omniscient narrator is the freest, but his freedom may lead to excess, lack of focus, loss of control. The reader may feel that the omniscient narrator, because he sees and knows all and can go anywhere, ought to tell all, that he should not withhold information (arbitrarily, it sometimes seems), that he should not fail to render a scene which the reader knows he can render.

The omniscient narrator is free to speak directly to the reader, to tell him what he will or will not do in a particular story. Or because he speaks in his own voice, he may so ingratiate himself with the reader that he is not reproached for withholding information or for failing to present an expected scene. And he knows that the reader knows that he cannot, after all, tell everything. The omniscient narrator may use his freedom to manipulate the reader intellectually or emotionally; he may intrude to make explicit authorial comments, to analyze, philosophize, to render judgments on his characters. He may tell about his characters in generalized commentary or summary narrative passages, or he may show them in dramatic scenes.

Authorial commentary can provide relief from dramatic pacing, and it can perform many other functions, such as enabling the author to cover a great deal of important but nondramatic territory through panoramic narrative, enlivened sometimes with the author's own distinctive first-person voice. Henry Fielding's "Farewell to the Reader," after 750 pages of *The History of Tom Jones, a Foundling,* gives an impression of the engaging personality of the author, of which the reader is almost always conscious:

> We are now, reader, arrived at the last stage of our long journey. As we have, therefore, travelled together through so many pages, let us behave to one another like fellow-travellers in a stagecoach, who have passed several days in the company of each other; and who, notwithstanding any bickerings or little animosities which may have occurred on the road, generally make all up at last. . . . As I have taken up this simile, give me leave to carry it a little further.

Modern writers, critics, and readers generally object to commentary direct from the author because it shatters the illusion that real people are involved in real events; unity is also shattered when a reader must reorient himself with each shift from dramatic scene to panoramic narration, conveying a sense of events happening now, not told as having happened in the past.

To solve the problems of classic omniscient narration, and to achieve dramatic immediacy, some writers create an objective narrator. The author is invisible; his voice is silent or neutral. As much as is humanly possible, he does not take sides with one character against another; he is impartial, impersonal, disinterested. He refrains from expressing attitudes about every passing controversy or social issue. The reader feels as if there were no narrator, as if he were watching a play or a movie. This camera-eye objectivity can never be total, of course; words have too many uncontrollable connotations. Ernest Hemingway's "The Killers" sets the scene:

> Outside it was getting dark. The street-light came on outside the window. The two men at the counter read the menu. From the other end of the counter Nick Adams watched them. He had been talking to George when they came in.

The possibilities for the omniscient point of view have not yet been fully enough realized. It was uniquely employed by Jules Romains as long ago as 1911 when his novella *The Death of a Nobody* appeared. He wanted to express the collective behavior and consciousness of social groups as they were affected by the death of a man who when he was alive was nobody and did nothing. See his introduction to the American edition, in which he describes his method; its implications for use by other writers are exciting but have so far been unrealized.

Here are some works in which the omniscient point of view functions especially well: Thackeray, *Vanity Fair;* Gogol, *Dead Souls;* Turgenev, *Fathers and Sons;* Trollope, *The Eustace Diamonds;* Balzac, *Eugénie Grandet;* George Eliot,

The Mill on the Floss; Henry James, *The Bostonians;* E. M. Forster, *Howards End;* Virginia Woolf, *To the Lighthouse* and *Orlando;* D. H. Lawrence, "The Blind Man"; Thomas Wolfe, *Look Homeward, Angel;* John Hawkes, *The Cannibal;* William Gaddis, *The Recognitions;* Michel Tournier, *The Ogre* (Part II, etc.). Wayne C. Booth's *The Rhetoric of Fiction* provides a very readable explanation of the working of the omniscient point of view.

3. IF YOU HAVE USED THE FIRST-PERSON POINT OF VIEW, HAVE YOU REALIZED ALL ITS POTENTIALS?

Traditionally, the author either narrated the story directly to the reader or allowed one of his characters to tell or write it. In a way, the first-person narrator has as much mobility and freedom and as much license to comment on the action as the omniscient narrator. The omniscient narrator's freedom limits him in some ways, but the first-person narrator is even more limited. The first-person narrator cannot get into the minds of other characters as the omniscient, godlike, all-knowing narrator can; first-person narration is limited to those things that the narrating character sees, hears, feels, knows himself or that have been reported to him by other witnesses. But the advantage of first-person narration is that it is dramatically immediate, as all quoted speech is, and thus has great authority. Here is the narrative voice of *Huckleberry Finn:*

> So somebody started on a run. I walked down the street a ways and stopped. In about five or ten minutes here comes Boggs again but not on his horse. He was a-reeling across the street towards me, bare headed, with a friend on both sides of him a-holt of his arms and hurrying him along. He was quiet and looked uneasy and he warn't hanging back any but was doing some of the hurrying himself. Somebody sings out:
>
> "Boggs!"
>
> I looked over there to see who said it, and it was that Colonel Sherburn. He was standing perfectly still in the street and had a pistol raised in his right hand— not aiming it but holding it out with the barrel tilted up towards the sky. The same second I see a young girl coming on the run, and two men with her. Boggs and the men turned round to see who called him, and when they see the pistol the men jumped to one side, and the pistol-barrel come down slow and steady to a level—both barrels cocked. Boggs throws up both of his hands and says, "O Lord, don't shoot!" Bang! goes the first shot and he staggers back, clawing at the air—bang! goes the second one and he tumbles backwards onto the ground, heavy and solid, and with his arms spread out. That young girl screamed out and comes rushing, and down she throws herself on her father, crying and saying, "Oh, he's killed him, he's killed him!" The crowd closed up around them and shouldered and jammed one another, with their necks stretched, trying to see, and people on the inside trying to shove them back and shouting, "Back, back! give him air, give him air!"

Colonel Sherburn he tossed his pistol onto the ground, and turned around on his heels and walked off.

Huck's "I was there, I was a witness" tone has an appeal that is characteristic of first-person narratives. By allowing one of his characters to narrate, the author surrenders part of his control over the elements of the story. He must achieve his own purposes, which may be very different from those of his character, through implication, irony, and other devices. For instance, suppose the author hates war, but the character telling the story loves war. How can the author convey his own attitude to the reader? The reader must remember that the first-person narrator is not the author.

The first-person narrator may be a major participant, a minor participant, or a witness to the story he tells; or he may simply retell a story he has heard. In effect, he is saying, "This happened to me," or "This happened mainly to someone else." He may tell the story to a clearly identified listener, or to an implied or to an ambiguous audience. Or he may write his story for a particular reader-character (as in a story told through letters) or for readers generally, as a kind of autobiography or memoir. The form of writing may be a report, a diary, a journal. In many first-person stories, whether the story is spoken or written is unspecified; we simply accept it as a literary convention. But each of these possibilities affects the story and thus the reader in different ways; they are not incidental, arbitrary elements; they are vital.

Here is an example of the *literary* first-person, written style, from William Faulkner's "That Evening Sun":

> Monday is no different from any other weekday in Jefferson now. The streets are paved now, and the telephone and electric companies are cutting down more and more of the shade trees—the water oaks, the maples and locusts and elms—to make room for iron poles bearing clusters of bloated and ghostly and bloodless grapes, and we have a city laundry which makes the rounds on Monday morning, gathering the bundles of clothes into bright-colored, specially made motor cars: the soiled wearing of a whole week now flees apparitionlike behind alert and irritable electric horns, with a long diminishing noise of rubber and asphalt like tearing silk, and even the Negro women who still take in white people's washing after the old custom, fetch and deliver it in automobiles.

The first-person narrator combines the subjective (how he feels about what he sees) with the objective (he wants to *show* the reader). He is both omniscient storyteller and subject of his story. Perception is an act of self-discovery for him. First-person narration is probably the most favored technique used today. . . .

Here are a variety of first-person voices: Defoe, *Moll Flanders;* Brontë, *Wuthering Heights;* Ford Madox Ford, *The Good Soldier;* Hemingway, *A Farewell to Arms;* James M. Cain, *The Postman Always Rings Twice;* Sherwood Anderson, "The Egg"; Ralph Ellison, *Invisible Man;* Ernest Gaines, "Just like a Tree"; Jack Kerouac, *On the Road.* The narrator of some first-person novels achieves a kind of omniscience: Fitzgerald, *The Great Gatsby;* Henry Miller, *The Tropic of Cancer;* Ken Kesey, *One Flew over the Cuckoo's Nest;* Robert Penn

Warren, *All the King's Men.* See Wayne C. Booth, *The Rhetoric of Fiction,* for an excellent explanation of the unreliable first-person narrator.

4. IF YOU HAVE USED THE <u>THIRD-PERSON</u>, <u>CENTRAL-INTELLIGENCE</u> POINT OF VIEW, HAVE YOU REALIZED ALL ITS POTENTIALS?

In the third-person, central-intelligence point of view, the author filters the story through the perceptions of a character. The character is the center of consciousness. In both the first-person point-of-view technique and the third-person, central-intelligence point-of-view technique, the author removes himself from the story and works from inside the character outward. In central-intelligence narration, the story is presented in the third person, but all the elements of the story are filtered through the perceptions of a single character (the central intelligence), revealing his personality. The writer presents only what that character sees, hears, feels, thinks, knows. To use Henry James's phrase, the character "reflects" events; he is not a straight teller of events as the first-person narrator is. It is as if the author were paraphrasing in the third person what the character would say *if* he were telling the story in the first person. Usually, the author adjusts his style and vocabulary to the age, mentality, and social situation of the point-of-view character. Katherine Mansfield's "Miss Brill" is a near-perfect example:

> Although it was so brilliantly fine—the blue sky powdered with gold and great spots of light like white wine splashed over the Jardins Publiques—Miss Brill was glad that she had decided on her fur. The air was motionless, but when you opened your mouth there was just a faint chill, like a chill from a glass of iced water before you sip, and now and again a leaf came drifting—from nowhere, from the sky. Miss Brill put up her hand and touched her fur. Dear little thing! It was nice to feel it again. She had taken it out of its box that afternoon, shaken out the moth-powder, given it a good brush, and rubbed the life back into the dim little eyes. "What has been happening to me?" said the sad little eyes. Oh, how sweet it was to see them snap at her again from the red eiderdown! . . . But the nose, which was of some black composition, wasn't at all firm. It must have had a knock, somehow. Never mind—a little dab of black sealing-wax when the time came—when it was absolutely necessary. . . . Little rogue! yes, she really felt like that about it. She felt a tingling in her hands and arms, but that came from walking, she supposed. And when she breathed, something light and sad—no, not sad, exactly—something gentle seemed to move in her bosom.

"In 'Miss Brill,'" Katherine Mansfield said, "I chose not only the length of every sentence, but even the sound of every sentence. I chose the rise and fall of every paragraph to fit her, and to fit her on that day, at that very moment."

Many writers favor the third-person, central-intelligence point of view. Its great advantage is that the reader consistently experiences everything through the character's own mind and emotions with the greatest intimacy and intensity. The limitation of this method is that it is a little weak dramatically, because we cannot see the character himself in action; he often remains physically passive, almost invisible.

The focus may be primarily upon the experiences of the point-of-view character or upon his responses to the experiences of a character more dramatic than himself. In important ways, the focus determines the reader's responses to the elements being developed in the story.

Just as readers sometimes mistakenly attribute to the author the attitudes of his first-person narrator, readers often forget that in third-person, central-intelligence narration, every perception is to be attributed to the point-of-view character. As in first-person narration, the immediate authority for everything in the story is the character (although the author is, of course, the ultimate authority).

Because nothing goes into the story that the point-of-view character has not experienced, the author is more likely to include only what is truly relevant. Because his character's perceptions may be limited, the writer must be very adroit in the use of such devices as implication, irony, and symbolism as ways of communicating to the reader more than the character himself can perceive.

You can do many things in the omniscient point of view that you cannot do through the third-person, central-intelligence point of view. The omniscient point of view was most appropriate and effective in times when the author might pretend to know all, to be the creator of the world he described, as Dickens could. Today's writers, feeling that to pretend to know all is an impertinence in a world so complex, specialize in select areas of human experience, and more often use the mind of a single character through which to reveal those selected areas to the reader.

The third-person, central-intelligence point of view is effectively illustrated in these novels: Henry James, *The Ambassadors;* Joyce, *A Portrait of the Artist as a Young Man;* Truman Capote, *Other Voices, Other Rooms;* Frederick Buechner, *A Long Day's Dying;* John Cheever, *Falconer* (with a few shifts for contrast); Wright Morris, *The Field of Vision* (alternate focus on five characters) and the sequel *Ceremony in Lone Tree.* . . .

5. WHAT ARE THE NEGATIVE EFFECTS IN STYLE OF THE POINT-OF-VIEW TECHNIQUE YOU EMPLOYED IN YOUR FIRST DRAFT?

This question assumes you have decided to change in revision the point of view you used in the first draft. Such a change will have positive and negative effects on character conflict, structure, theme. The focus in this entry is on style.

Point of view determines style. With a change in point of view comes major changes in style, as you can see in two versions of a scene in Barry Hannah's first novel, *Geronimo Rex.* The first version appeared in *Intro* as "The Crowd Punk Season Drew":

> Now, as a punk, he chose not to steal; he thought that would be begging. Sometimes, if he was waiting around the campus for any time at all, he would sneak up and efface the fender of one of the better cars parked in front of the administration

building, Provine Hall. This he would do by crushing the heel of his boot against the car while no one was around. Buicks, Pontiacs, and Fords with eccentric horsepower and conveniences—he scarred them all. He sat on a fender until the campus depopulated, then ruined it with a flurry of his legs.

In this version, the omniscient point of view produces a rather formal, stilted style, despite the author's own slangy direct comments about his protagonist. Hannah *may* have decided the voice and its tone were not working in the omniscient, that it put the protagonist at too great a distance from both the author and the reader. He would retain some of that tone and style when he changed to the protagonist's first-person narration, but it is enhanced in the revision by dramatic immediacy, and a kind of frenzy, and a certain obnoxious aggressiveness that catches and holds the reader's attention. A possible factor in the success of the first-person voice in *Geronimo Rex* is that the narrator already thinks of himself as Geronimo, whereas in the short-story version, someone calls him Geronimo *after* the passage quoted above. Here is the scene in the novel:

> I was standing beside a skyblue Cadillac. You pretentious whale, you Cadillac, I thought.
> I jumped up on the hood of it. I did a shuffle on the hood. I felt my boots sinking into the metal. "Ah!" I pounced up and down, weighted by the books. It amazed me that I was taking such effect on the body. I leaped on the roof and hurled myself up and pierced it with my heels coming down . . . again, again. I flung outward after the last blow and landed on the sidewalk, congratulating myself like an artist of the trampoline.

6. HAVE YOU FAILED TO IMAGINE <u>OTHER POINT-OF-VIEW</u> TECHNIQUES AND THEIR POSSIBLE EFFECTS ON THE READER?

Because the characters, the style, and all other elements are so vitally affected by the point of view you have used, test it by reimagining the story from all possible points of view.

To test the first-draft point of view on paper, identify the scene in your story that is giving you the most trouble. Try rewriting that scene from two other points of view. If the first draft is third-person, avoid simply transposing "she" to "I." Imagine the possibilities posed by each point of view; explore the possibility of using multiple point-of-view techniques. You may see clearly that technique is a mode of discovery; you may find the true emotive and thematic center of your story.

Taking all elements into consideration, what is lost and what is gained by changing the point of view? What happens to the story's elements and effects as you tell it from each of the other two points of view? How are conflict, characterization, and theme handled differently in the three different point-of-view techniques? What are some differences in techniques? In emotional effect?

Although the point of view of Faulkner's *Sanctuary* in the two major published versions is omniscient, he moves in and out of the third-person central intelligences of several characters. When he decided in the galley stage to revise the novel radically, it was a point-of-view restructuring that he performed, as we see in two versions of this well-known scene, in which Horace Benbow first sees Popeye, the impotent two-bit gangster.

> When he rose, the surface of the water broken into a myriad glints by the dripping aftermath of his drinking, he saw among them the shattered reflections of the straw hat.
> The man was standing beyond the spring, his hands in his coat pockets, a cigarette slanted from his pallid chin.

That scene appears on p. 21 of the recently published original text, but it appears on p. 1 of the novel as readers knew it for half a century. Now the point of view is reversed: it is Popeye who sees Benbow.

> From beyond the screen of bushes which surrounded the spring, Popeye watched the man drinking. A faint path led from the road to the spring. Popeye watched the man—a tall, thin man, hatless, in worn gray flannel trousers and carrying a tweed coat over his arm—emerge from the path and kneel to drink from the spring.

Having opened with this scene, from Popeye's point of view, Faulkner restructured the novel, and created new relationships among the characters through whose perceptions he presented events: Gowan Stevens, Popeye, Temple Drake, and Horace Benbow (whose point of view had dominated the novel's galley version). If you read the first version and then the second, you will have two very different experiences—traceable to the differences in Faulkner's handling of point of view.

In revising *The Mysterious Stranger,* Mark Twain tested the possibilities of various point-of-view strategies; for him, explorations in point-of-view techniques were discovery ventures. In *Mark Twain, the "Mysterious Stranger" Manuscripts,* William Gibson publishes all versions except the one readers knew and which is readily available. . . .

7. HAVE YOU NOT YET ACHIEVED THE PROPER <u>DISTANCE</u> BETWEEN YOURSELF AND YOUR MATERIAL?

The question of the author's distance arises on several levels, making the problem very complex. The problem begins with the source of ideas for fictions, . . . The spectrum of possibilities extends from the deeply subconscious origin of ideas to the extremely objective (an idea found in reading a textbook, for instance). The degree of distance on that level of origin usually bears little relation to the degree or kind of distance the reader senses that the author has in relation to the finished work.

As you interrogate your first draft, however, ask whether you have achieved the kind of distance that is needed to make the story effective. For instance, if the idea arose suddenly out of your subconscious, it just may be that to make it work you need great objectivity, and the reader needs to feel that objectivity in the work. On the other hand, and rather paradoxically, an idea gleaned from a casual reading of some technical work may justify the most lyrical subjectivity in your treatment of the idea.

Ask yourself, What is the depth or level of my involvement in this story? Does my emotional involvement show in every paragraph, and if so, is that good for *this* story's intended effect, or detrimental? Or am I an impartial, impersonal, detached, objective, invisible, disinterested narrator (I've listed most of the terms used in discussing this problem)? If so, is that objectivity working for or against all my intentions? A third general possibility is that you want a rhythmic alternation between modulations of subjectivity and objectivity. All the devices and techniques of fiction come into play, especially point of view and style, to enable you to achieve the degree and kind of distance you want for each story.

Distance in relation to what? To the characters, first of all, to the narrative generally, and to the reader. Do you want your reader to feel that you are intimate with your character? If so, it does not follow that the reader will share your intimacy; experiencing *your* intimacy, the reader may feel distant from the character. Paradoxically, it is often the effect that when the author is most distant (in his style, not in his personal feelings) from the main character (Flaubert from Madame Bovary), the reader is most intimate. "As to making known my own opinion about the characters I produce," said Flaubert, "no, no, a thousand times no!"

Do you comment thematically by intruding as the author to editorialize upon the narrative? Do you show partiality for one character over another, or are you neutral? Does your attitude come across in the *tone* conveyed by your style? There is no best answer to these questions except in terms of all your conscious intentions in each work. Revision poses the question of whether you should expand or lessen the distance between you and the character and/or you and the reader.

Again, the very techniques you have at your command enable you to discover an answer. For instance, if the point of view is third-person, central-intelligence, it follows logically that any word, phrase, or sentence that reveals your own attitudes, especially negative ones about the point-of-view character, should be cut, because the purpose of that point of view is to limit yourself entirely to the perceptions of that character. The style, then, must be appropriate to that character; where the style violates the character point of view, it may be cut, as being, for instance, too formal.

Here, as with most technical matters, it is impossible to deal with one technical question without considering it in relation to others. That is fortunate, because just as a problem in one area creates or worsens problems in others, each solution has beneficial ramifications. . . .

As you read fiction, notice the degree to which the writer is involved, as an omniscient "I" or as a felt presence. Trollope, Thackeray, Fielding, Eliot, and Forster offer varieties of omniscient involvement; Kerouac, Henry Miller, and Thomas Wolfe varieties of subjectivity; Joyce, Hemingway, and Flaubert varieties of objectivity.

8. DO PASSAGES THAT REFLECT YOUR OWN BIASES OR JUDGMENTS <u>INTRUDE</u>?

This question is one aspect of the question of author distance, but it is such a common problem that it needs special attention. Consideration of point of view helps you to answer the question. If it is omniscient, you are free to intrude as often as you like to express your own biases toward characters ("We will tell the story of Lizzie Greystock from the beginning, but we will not dwell over it at great length, as we might do if we loved her") or to set humankind straight on philosophical matters ("There is no end to man's inhumanity to man!"). Such comments work in first person, but only if they are in character; if they are not, you have made your narrator a mouthpiece for your own ideas. Such passages are impossible in third-person, central-intelligence; if they are there in your first draft, you will want to cut them as violations of the point-of-view technique you have decided to use.

Revising *Watch and Ward,* Henry James realized that he had violated the central-intelligence point of view of Nora by intruding with his own judgments. Early version: "There he tossed, himself a living instance, if need were, of the furious irresponsibility of passion; loving in the teeth of reason, of hope, of justice almost, in blind obedience to a reckless personal need. Why, if *his* passion scorned counsel, was Nora's bound to take it?" James's revision places the reader back in Nora's point of view: "There was no discretion in his own love; why should there be in Nora's?"

Is your style appropriate to the point of view? Your answers to that question enable you to answer Question 8. Sometimes, your own biases and judgments come through in rhetorical maneuvers. ". . . but, dear me," wrote George Eliot in *Middlemarch*, "has it not by this time ceased to be remarkable—is it not rather the very thing we expect in men that they should have numerous strands of experience lying side by side and never compare them with each other?" The dubious occasion for this intrusion is Eliot's description of Lydgate's way of life. Once started, Eliot can't seem to stop; she continues for almost half a page, but keeps only what I have quoted, except for the phrase "the very thing."

If the point of view is omniscient, do you fail to distinguish clearly your perspective from that of your characters? Who, at any given moment, is the authority? This appears to be, but is not, a restatement of the question posed above. The writer does not allow his reader to become confused as to whose evaluation of events he is getting. For instance, in the omniscient point of view, he avoids jumping from one character's mind to another's without careful transition or without reorienting the reader. An example of clear and firm control is Evelyn Scott's *The Narrow House.*

When Dickens, Eliot, Thackeray, Stendhal, and Trollope, using the overall omniscient point of view, weave in and out of the minds of several characters within a novel, within a scene, sometimes within a single sentence, it is sometimes difficult for the reader to distinguish the author's perspective from that of a character. Rosamond's words "fell like a mortal chill on Lydgate's roused tenderness," wrote George Eliot in one version of *Middlemarch*. "It was a fatal sign that h—"

Eliot stopped in midword, realizing she was being unclear as to whom it was "a fatal sign." It would not seem so to Lydgate himself; we are in his perception here, so Eliot cut that line. "He did not storm in indignation," she continued. The revisions of these and other omniscient authors show many instances where adjustments are made to make clear to the reader who the authority is. Authority confusion is not quite the same problem as author intrusion.

The careful reader will not accept the authority of the narrator too literally or too fully. Your knowing that will affect the way you revise. When you use the omniscient point of view, you are usually a reliable authority for what the reader is told. But human perception is limited and faulty; therefore, what the first-person narrator tells or writes or what the central-intelligence character experiences will be carefully evaluated by the reader. In such stories, the essence of your reader's experience lies in the differences between the way the reader perceives the story's elements and the way the point-of-view character perceives them. The reader has, in a sense, a certain omniscience.

In *The Rhetoric of Fiction* Wayne C. Booth discusses degrees of reliability among the various types of narrators.

9. ARE THERE <u>INCONSISTENCIES</u> IN YOUR USE OF POINT OF VIEW?

Strive to employ the point of view consistently and to make all elements consistent with the point of view as your major means of controlling the elements of your story.

It is unlikely that you will employ the first person inconsistently; if by chance you drift, in the first draft, from first person into third, you will see that immediately as a mistake. But maintaining consistency in the third-person, central-intelligence and in the omniscient point of view is a common problem throughout the revision process.

The reader does not want to have the experience of feeling that the point of view is arbitrarily handled, that the omniscient author simply happened to shift to a focus on this character, then that one, without fulfilling some expressive and meaningful pattern. Sometimes what may seem a violation of the author's own pattern may be deliberate, to achieve an effect that can be achieved no other way. For instance, James Joyce's "The Dead" is an excellent example of third-person, central-intelligence point of view (Gabriel Conroy's), but Joyce deliberately opens with an omniscient view of many people gathering, gradually focusing on Gabriel; at the end, he returns to omniscience for an even larger view than in the opening.

D. H. Lawrence provides another example of expressive inconsistency. The point of view in "Odour of Chrysanthemums" is omniscient, with a dominant focus on Elizabeth, wife of an alcoholic miner who is killed. In the scene in which his comrades bring his body home, the focus is very scattered, especially with the shift into the point of view of the men ("they"). But Lawrence's revisions do not drop the men to keep the focus on Elizabeth; rather they shift the focus *to* the men. He makes the inconsistency meaningful. The deliberateness of this odd solution to inconsistency in point of view is seen in Lawrence's further revisions for the version included in the collection *The Prussian Officer.* Lawrence's emphasis on the pronoun "they" has a mysterious quality, as if it includes not only the dead miner's comrades but his family as well, and so the community of the living as it responds to the dead. . . .

The problem of inconsistency in point of view has a second dimension: What elements are inconsistent with the point of view? Is the style inconsistent? Suppose, for instance, your central intelligence is a young woman with a limited education who works in a towel factory in a small southern town. As you present everything through her perceptions, is your style too complex? If the point of view is first-person, do you allow your narrator to use a vocabulary she is not likely to have? Sometimes the way exposition or information is presented is inconsistent with the point of view. Do you attribute information, ideas, or emotions to a character that, given the point of view, she cannot know, think, or feel?

10. DOES THE POINT OF VIEW YOU HAVE USED FAIL TO <u>EXPRESS</u>, IN ITSELF, SOME MAJOR ASPECT OF THE EXPERIENCE YOU ARE RENDERING?

The point of view you employ should express something in itself—it should not seem to the reader to have been arbitrarily chosen, or chosen as the easiest one for you to use. Your choice should be, in every way, so effective that the reader feels it is the only possible choice, the inevitable choice.

This question may help to put into clearer perspective other questions about point of view and to stress the overall importance of point of view.

In several major novels, for instance, the relationship between a kind of hero and characters who witness his behavior produces the point-of-view structure for the works. Fitzgerald's *The Great Gatsby* offers an example that is simple in structure but complex in its various ramifications: Nick Carroway tells the story of Gatsby; what makes Gatsby a hero is his effect on Nick's storytelling consciousness.

There is a similar hero-witness relationship in Robert Penn Warren's *All the King's Men;* Jack Burden, a reporter, feels a compulsion to tell the story of Governor Willie Stark, but it is Stark's effect on other people and on Jack that most commands our interest. Jack's first-person voice is that of a tough guy like Raymond Chandler's private eye Philip Marlowe. But Jack is also a historian obsessed with the past; when he is telling the reader about events in the historical past, his voice becomes very lyrical and philosophical. The tone of these two voices and their juxtaposition to each other throughout the book become the reader's major experience, not the narrative in itself about Willie Stark's rise and fall, interesting though it is.

Wright Morris combines first-person narrative with third-person central intelligence in *The Huge Season.* Chapters from Peter Foley's first-person autobiographical novel, about the relationship between a hero and his witnesses in the twenties, alternate with chapters presenting Peter Foley's thoughts and perceptions one day in the fifties as he goes to a reunion with surviving witnesses. The juxtaposition and contrast of the two point-of-view techniques express facets of this hero-witness relationship. I know of no instance in which a writer makes exclusive use of the third-person, central-intelligence point of view throughout a hero-witness novel; that point of view would not lend itself as readily, as effectively, to the expression of this hero-witness relationship as do the first-person and the omniscient. . . .

In *The Heart Is a Lonely Hunter,* Carson McCullers employs an overall omniscient point of view, but she alternates chapters that focus on the thoughts and feelings of the mute hero, Mr. Singer, with chapters that focus on his four witnesses. McCullers expresses in this omniscient-point-of-view strategy the paradox that these four very different people, each isolated in his own psyche, crave communication with others at the same time that they do not want a reciprocal relationship—that's why they are hostile to each other and why each tells his deepest feelings to a mute. The bitter irony, best expressed in this omniscient point of view, is that none of the four characters know what the author, the hero, and the reader know—that Mr. Singer doesn't understand a word any of them are saying. Thomas Hardy revised *The Return of the Native* to express, through his unique use of omniscience, a similar vision: each person, no matter how passionate his love for another person may be, is always and finally alone in an indifferent universe.

Both Virginia Woolf in *Mrs. Dalloway* and William Faulkner in *Absalom, Absalom!* express facets of a hero-witness relationship through the omniscient point of view, but they do it very differently.

Woolf uses the omniscient point of view to enable her to move rapidly in and out of several consciousnesses many times throughout the novel. Most of the witness characters either talk with or think about Mrs. Dalloway, the heroine, or they parallel in some way the reader's concern with her. The omniscient point of view expresses in itself the simultaneous separateness of the characters at a given moment and the way that fact relates them all to each other; though none know it, the reader does.

All these writers express through their various point-of-view strategies and through the thematic pattern of the hero-witness relationship the irony of an unconsciously shared community of vision. That concept is especially powerful in Faulkner's *Absalom, Absalom!* A great many of Faulkner's revisions were made in an effort to orchestrate, within an overall omniscient point of view, the first-person narratives of five characters, and most important, to make Quentin Compson's the most expressive. To express his concept that the telling of the story of Colonel Sutpen by various interacting voices creates a community of vision, Faulkner made all his narrators sound alike; he even assigned to them, in quotation marks but without stylistic changes, passages he had originally written in his own omniscient voice. In this case, all the witnesses share with each other their fixation on the hero. The effect is best observed at a point when most of the voices converge in a single passage. . . .

DISCUSSION QUESTIONS

1. Using a "how-to" approach, Madden covers much of the same territory that Wayne Booth covers in *The Rhetoric of Fiction* (and, in fact, Madden mentions Booth by name). How do Madden's categorizations of the possibilities of point of view compare to Booth's?
2. What are the connections, according to Madden, between point of view and other basic elements of fiction, such as characterization, plot, and meaning?
3. Which of the possible points of view defined by Madden have you used most often? Why, in each case? That is, how did you take advantage of the strengths of that point of view as they are explained by Madden? How might you have used that point of view more effectively?

DAVID MICHAEL KAPLAN

Revising Your Prose for Power and Punch

David Michael Kaplan (b. 1956), a fiction writer, is best known for his textbook Revision: A Creative Approach to Writing and Rewriting Fiction *(1997), which offers practical techniques for improving stories.*

You've got the main dramatic elements of your story—character, conflict, plot, pacing—under control. It's working. You like it. You feel you're nearing the end of your revision efforts. Now it's time to tidy and polish and make it absolutely perfect. We come to that part of revision that many beginning writers assume to be the whole; namely, stylistics, or fine-tuning your prose for power and punch. Under this rubric fall all sorts of rules/quasi-rules/thoughts/suggestions about making your prose read fluidly and forcefully, so that it helps create that "vivid, continuous imaginative dream" John Gardner deems fiction to be. . . . You should be concerned with stylistics only *after* you've addressed the first concerns in revision—getting the story and characters straight, arranging events in proper sequence, expanding what needs expansion and deleting what needs deletion, and so on. Only then are you ready to dot your *i*'s and cross your *t*'s and make your prose sing.

Before we go into specifics, consider for a moment what you're doing when you "fine-tune" your prose. You're really removing the sense of a "writer" from the work, so that the only thing of which a reader is aware is the imaginative world of the story. You're removing any stylistic "glitches" or infelicities that could interfere with this and make your reader uncomfortably aware that these are *only* words on paper and not a living imaginative reality. "Glitches"—like those you see on television when there's interference—is a good metaphor here. The occasional glitch is not going to interfere with your involvement in a show. But if there's a lot of them, you start to become distracted. You start noticing glitches more than show. If there are too many, you just can't see the show anymore. You give up and turn the channel. Just so in reading a story. One or two stylistic glitches or infelicities are not going to bother a reader. He can still stay imaginatively involved in the story. But the more that occur, the more a reader notices them, and the less he's involved. The imaginative illusion—the vivid, continuous imaginative dream—is broken, and the reader becomes all too aware that there's a *writer* there, and not a very skilled one. Remember *The Wizard of Oz,* when the curtain is pulled back to reveal a little old man at the controls of Oz? We writers, like the Wizard, usually want to keep that curtain closed. If we do want to part it and show the writer/wizard at work, as in certain kinds of metafiction, we want to do so on our terms, with full skill and control. We don't want to ruin the illusion through easily remedied stylistic glitches.

So what are these stylistic glitches? How do we best fine-tune our prose?

First of all, I'm assuming that you're perfectly capable of making the obvious revisions of grammar, capitalization and punctuation. Those are the province of grammar books, not this one. And I'm assuming you will correct any misspelled words. That's what a spell checker, or a good dictionary, is for. What follows is something else: a laundry list, culled from years of teaching fiction writing as well as revising my own work, of the more common stylistic "glitches." They pop up over and over again. Watch out for them. Without exception they are to be carefully considered, if not outright avoided. Trust me.

KAPLAN'S LAUNDRY LIST OF STYLISTIC GLITCHES

Abstract or Imprecise Language

The more specific and concrete your language is, the more powerful. Note the difference between

> He picked up something heavy and hit James on the face. James cried out, and fell.

and

> He snatched up a rock and smashed it against James' nose. James groaned, and sank to his knees.

"Snatched" is both more concrete and more exact than the vague "picked up," just as "smashed," "groaned," and "sank to his knees" are more specific and vivid than the words they replace. And "nose" is much more exact than the vaguer "face."

Unnecessary Words and Phrases, Especially Unnecessary Adjectives

Sometimes called overwriting. It's ironic. Beginning writers are taught to write exactly and vividly—what I noted above—but then sometimes they go overboard and start describing things too minutely and too vividly. Every noun starts to have a modifier, maybe two or three. Unwittingly, the writer is drawing attention to herself: Look, Ma, I'm really *writing!* Consider the following (words suggested for deletion italicized):

> The morning sun's *silent rays* burned Julia's skin as she walked from the grassy, *open* field into the deeply *forested* woods. Immediately the late spring air felt cooler. She sat down on *a gray* rock, took off her *Cordura nylon* backpack, pulled open the *sticky Velcro* fastener from a side pocket, and took out a *plastic* bottle of soda water. She opened *the blue screw-type top,* and drank *thirstily.* Her *green and gold speckled* kerchief felt sticky *against her sweaty skin,* so she loosened it. Crows cackled wickedly from somewhere in the dark woods. A *small* ladybug with one wing torn off was crawling on the rock's *rough surface* . . .

Here, every noun and verb seems to have an adjective or adverb attached to it. We feel there's a writer *really writing.* What the writer should be doing is making you forget that. Eliminating about half the adjectives and adverbs here will help a lot. The trick is to decide which ones are essential and which are fluff. Do we need to know that it's the sun's rays burning her? Isn't that what usually burns? Do we need to know the field is open and the woods forested? Aren't they usually? And aren't most ladybugs small and most Velcro fasteners sticky? For that matter, do we really need to know that it's a Velcro fastener, or that the backpack is made from Cordura nylon, or that the bottle top is a screw type, or that the rock is gray and her kerchief green and gold? Are all of these details really advancing the story or slowing it down?

On the other hand, it does seem important to know that it's late spring—this situates us in time. And it's important to know that her kerchief feels sticky, the ladybug has one wing torn off, the crows' cackling is wicked, and the woods are dark. These descriptive details are unique and add important sensory information *and* emotional atmosphere to the scene. When an adjective or adverb or descriptive phrase is doing both, it's essential and should be kept. If not, consider deleting it. If we eliminate the nonessential words, we have:

> The morning sun burned Julia's skin as she walked from the grassy field into the deep woods. Immediately the late spring air felt cooler. She sat down on a rock, took off her backpack, pulled open the fastener from a side pocket, and took out a bottle of soda water. She opened it and drank. Her kerchief felt sticky,

so she loosened it. Crows cackled wickedly from somewhere in the dark woods. A
ladybug with one wing torn off was crawling on the rock . . .

Now we can see the scene, not the writer.

Kaplan's Law of Words: Any words that aren't working for you are working
against you. So weed them out. If a word—yes, any single word—isn't adding
something we don't know *and need to know,* it's adding nothing. Worse, it's distracting. It's slowing down the prose. Too much, and the reader—consciously or
unconsciously—feels she is plodding through thick prosey muck.

Words and Phrases of Unnecessary Specificity

We touched on this somewhat in the section above. Sometimes we belabor the
obvious, as in the following:

> Elwood turned off the ignition, opened the *driver's side* door, picked up the
> gun *with his left hand,* got out, and walked up the concrete sidewalk to the house.
> He pushed the doorbell *with his finger,* and waited. He pressed his *right* ear
> against the door. Hearing no one come *from inside the house,* Elwood pushed
> open the *front* door.

The words in italics are all unnecessarily specific. If you're driving, what other
door will you open to get out but the driver's side door? Does it really matter
whether Elwood picks up the gun with his left or right hand? For that matter, how
else do you pick up something than with your hand? And what else do you push
a doorbell with but your finger? If Elwood's going to push it with his nose, surely
the writer would tell us this! Why bother us with the obvious? Similarly, if we're
not told differently—that it's made out of pebbles or alabaster—we probably
assume the sidewalk's concrete. Most are. And what other door would Elwood be
walking toward, with a sidewalk and doorbell and all, but the front one, unless
we're told differently? Where else would he be listening for people coming than
from "inside the house"? And is it really important to know that it's his right ear,
not his left, that he's pressing against the door? Too many of these unnecessary
words, and the prose starts to slow . . . down . . . and readers feel as if they're
again slogging through verbal molasses.

This issue is important enough to warrant a few more examples. Examine
the following sentences, all of which contain words or phrases of unnecessary
specificity:

> A small frown appeared on her face. *(Where else do frowns appear?)*
>
> He squinted his eyes. *(With what else do you squint?)*
>
> She shrugged her shoulders. *(With what else do you shrug?)*
>
> The child nodded her head. *(With what else do you nod?)*
>
> After he pulled up the chair, he sat down on the seat. *(Where else?)*
>
> He held the bird in his hand. *(Unless he's holding it with something like fire
> tongs, he's probably using his hand.)*
>
> An unknown stranger appeared at the door. *(Are there any* known *strangers?)*

Their voices echoed back and forth through the canyon. *(That's what an echo does: it goes back and forth.)*

When he was alone again, he muttered to himself, "I'll get even."
(If it's established that a character is alone, do you need to say that he muttered/spoke/whispered/yelled "to himself"? Who else is there?)

"P-please . . . c-c-come in," she stammered with difficulty. *(Are there any easy stammers?)*

"Come into my parlor," the spider whispered in a soft voice. *(Whispers are by definition soft.)*

That's right, she thought to herself. *(Who else do you think to, unless you're telepathic?)*

The horsemen disappeared from sight. *(How else?)*

A black and white penguin was trundling across the snow. *(Are there penguins that aren't black and white?)*

"I'm through with you!" Joyce yelled. "You—"

"Don't say that," Kevin interrupted. *(We've just seen him interrupt— why tell us too?)*

"I'm through with you!" Joyce yelled.

"You can't say that," Kevin said to her. *(If it's been established Joyce is the only one he's talking to, then "to her" is superfluous.)*

Weasel Words

There are some unnecessary words that aren't ones of undue specificity or overdescription; they're more outrightly unnecessary. They're the written equivalent to the "uhs" and "wells" and "you knows" in conversation—space fillers. They convey no useful information and add to the sense of mushy, imprecise prose. I call them "weasel words." They seem innocent enough, but should *always* be regarded with suspicion. The following list includes some of the most common ones:

about	exactly	simply
actually	finally	somehow
almost	here	somewhat
almost like	just	somewhat like
already	just then	sort of
appears	kind of	suddenly
approximately	nearly	then
basically	now	there
close to	practically	truly
even	really	utterly
eventually	seems	

How do these work as "weasel words"? Consider the following paragraph:

> The man was *there* in the bushes, waiting. When Joan was *just* three feet away,
> he *kind of* tensed, *then* leaped out and grabbed her. Joan struggled, but *it seemed*
> he was *just* too strong for her, and *finally* they fell down. She *actually* screamed,
> and *even* scratched his face.

All the italicized words aren't necessary. They create mushy prose. They show a
writer insecure about what he's describing. Take them out, and see how much
more vigorous the writing becomes:

> The man was in the bushes, waiting. When Joan was three feet away, he
> tensed, leaped out, and grabbed her. Joan struggled, but he was too strong for her,
> and they fell down. She screamed, and scratched his face.

Overusing Adverbs

As in the following example:

> She slammed the phone down *forcefully* and muttered, "Damn." She *quickly*
> jumped to her feet and strode over to the china cabinet. She *hurriedly* riffled
> through the papers in the top drawer.

An adverb well chosen is a wondrous thing. But too many in a row (because of
the "-ly" ending that most adverbs have) create a singsong, clickety-clack effect
that draws attention to itself. Also, many adverbs are unnecessary because they're
already denoted or connoted by the verbs they modify. How else do you slam a
phone down but "forcefully"? How else do you jump to your feet but "quickly"?
How else do you riffle but "hurriedly"? And so on. Why belabor the obvious?
Take them out. Remember—words that aren't working for you are working
against you.

Overuse of the Conditional or Past Perfect Verb Tense

We're talking here about "would" and "had" verb constructions, as in the
following:

> Every morning that summer, John *would get* up around six. He *would smell*
> the bacon and pancakes his mother *would be making* in the kitchen, and his
> stomach *would give* a little hungry flip. He *would jump* out of bed and *would*
> *rush* to the bathroom. The tile floor *would be* cool against his bare feet. He *would*
> *wash* his face quickly.

Or in the past perfect tense:

> Every morning that summer, John *had gotten* up around six. He *had smelled*
> the bacon and pancakes his mother *had made* in the kitchen, and his stomach *had*
> *given* a little hungry flip. He *had jumped* out of bed and *had rushed* to the bath-
> room. The tile floor *had been* cool against his bare feet. He *had washed* his face
> quickly.

Again, as in overusing adverbs, the "would" and "had" constructions start to grate. How do you solve this? Very simply. Introduce the conditional or past perfect tense at the beginning of the passage, then slip into the simple past. It works, and makes for less intrusive, more graceful prose:

> Every morning that summer, John had gotten up around six. He smelled the bacon and pancakes his mother was making in the kitchen, and his stomach gave a little hungry flip. He jumped out of bed and rushed to the bathroom. The tile floor was cool against his bare feet. He quickly washed his face.

Strict grammatical tense agreement is a wonderful thing, but agreeable prose is even better.

Overusing Participial Phrases

One of the most common errors in beginning writing. They are often overused with verbal tags, as in the following:

> "This is a really boring movie," Susanna said, *fidgeting* in her seat.
> "You said it," Bob agreed, *handing* her the popcorn. *Considering* for a moment, Susanna took a big handful.
> "I really shouldn't be eating this stuff," she said, her voice *dropping*.

I don't know what it is about dialogue tags, but participial phrases just seem to fly to them, like bees to honey. Again, the "-ing" construction creates that self-conscious, clickety-clack rhythm. What to do? Transform some of the participial phrases into sentences in their own right. So:

> Susanna fidgeted in her seat. "This is a really boring movie."
> "You said it." Bob handed her the bag of popcorn. Susanna considered for a moment, then took a big handful.
> "I really shouldn't be eating this stuff," she said, her voice dropping.

Keeping *one* participial phrase is fine. But get two or more close together, and they start to draw attention to themselves.

Illogical Use of "As" or "While" Adverbial Constructions

Consider the following examples:

> "Hey Jim! How about another for this guy, and give me a Tequila Sunrise." While she said this, Anna leaned forward and dropped one leg to the floor.
>
> Jennifer's head shot up as she looked above her.
>
> "Damned lighter," Jack said as the dash lighter dropped onto the floor.

The problem with "as" and "while" constructions is often one of logic. It's unlikely someone would be able to notice a lighter falling and say "Damned lighter" in the half-second it takes one to drop. And how could Jennifer already be looking up at the same time her head shoots up? And isn't it unlikely that Anna would be giving that long drink order, all the while dropping to one knee? It would have to be a slow-motion drop!

The solution, of course, is to turn each into the discrete actions they really are. Thus:

"Hey, Jim!" Anna leaned forward and dropped one leg to the floor. "How about another for this guy, and give me a Tequila Sunrise."

Jennifer's head shot up. She looked above her.

The dash lighter dropped onto the floor. "Damned lighter," Jack said.

Run-On Prepositional Phrases

As in:

He hardly moved except to puff on his cigar which burned judiciously *in* the ashtray *next to* a red glass lantern *with* a small fluttering candle *in front of* him.

Clickety-clack, clickety-clack. The prepositional phrases all in a row create a monotonous rhythm and at the same time make the geography of the scene almost impossible to visualize. The solution, of course, is to eliminate or replace phrases that aren't important, or to rearrange phrases so they don't all fall in a row, or to think of simple words to replace prepositional phrases, or to break the sentence up into several smaller sentences:

He hardly moved except to puff on his cigar which burned judiciously in the ashtray. In front of him, a small candle fluttered in a red glass lantern.

Repetitious Words or Phrases

Another case of the unnecessary, as in the following:

By the time Gabe arrived at Ellsworth's apartment with Angela, his girlfriend, *there* were several other friends *there*. Now that the master of ceremonies was *there,* the party was all set and the tradition would continue. *There* was the strangest feeling in the air that night.

Or:

Jay instinctively headed for the *back* seat of Sarah's car. He always sat in *back* on long road trips. This was his time to sit *back* and gaze out at the landscape.

The solution for both of these is either elimination of some of the repetitious words or substitution of other words for them. Thus:

By the time Gabe arrived at Ellsworth's apartment with Angela, his girlfriend, several other friends were there. Now that the master of ceremonies had arrived, the party was all set and the tradition would continue. The strangest feeling was in the air that night.

Jay instinctively headed for the back seat of Sarah's car. He always sat there on long road trips. This was his time to sit and gaze out at the landscape.

Tortured, Convoluted Phrasing

Brevity is the soul of wit, and often of writing too. Sometimes less *is* more. Consider the difference between "Jesus felt tears falling from his eyes" and "Jesus wept." Or between "You no longer are going to be working here" and "You're fired." Or between "I feel a strong affection for you" and "I love you." Tortured phraseology is used by bureaucrats, but it has little place in fiction, except for effect (a character who speaks or thinks in bureaucratese, for example). Short, pungent, concrete and specific are key here. So instead of:

> The place turned out to be a laundromat.
>
> She launched herself forward at him.
>
> He raised himself from the chair and came to stand by the bar.

Say more simply:

> The place was a laundromat.
>
> She jumped at him.
>
> He rose from the chair and stood by the bar.

Weak Sentence Structure

Powerful prose is created sentence by sentence, not paragraph by paragraph or page by page. When revising, you should make sure each sentence is written in the most powerful way possible. Keep in mind that the most important part of the sentence is its end—that's what echoes in the reader's mind. Ending sentences with prepositional, adverbial or participial phrases is often weak. Look at these:

> Chris and Aaron high-fived outside on the back patio.
>
> George knocked after a moment's hesitation.
>
> Annette saw the accident as she was looking out the window.
>
> "I hate you," Julia said while picking at her nails.

These sentences end weakly, without punch, with subordinate phrases or clauses. The power words in the first two sentences are the verbs "high-fived" and "knocked." The prepositional phrases are but modifiers to those verbs; putting them at the end weakens the sentences' force. The power word in the third sentence is the noun "accident"; in the last one, it's the statement "I hate you." Look how much more forceful each becomes when these power words or phrases end the following sentences.

> Outside on the back patio, Chris and Aaron high-fived.
>
> After a moment's hesitation, George knocked.
>
> As she was looking out the window, Annette saw the accident.
>
> Julia picked at her fingernails and said, "I hate you."

Too picky, you say? Not at all. Anything, no matter how small, affects the imaginative illusion and emotional power of a story. It's all held together, like the strands of a spider's web, by each individual word and sentence. Weaken one strand, and the whole intricate lacelike pattern can start swaying dangerously. Weaken two, and the beauty of the design may collapse.

If you're having trouble developing a good inner ear for sentence strength, the best thing you can do is read your sentences aloud as if they were individual lines of poetry. This will give you a better feel for each sentence's rhythm and dynamism.

Dialogue Tag Problems

Here's a snatch of dialogue between Mary and her friend Jeanette:

> "Did you see that dress that Jezebel was wearing?" asked Mary, disbelievingly.
> "Did I ever! It looked like some penguin outfit. A very fat, black penguin!" said Jeanette.
> "I'm surprised her mother let her out of the house like that," said Mary, reaching for another blueberry muffin.
> "Well, the way her mother dresses . . . ," replied Jeanette. "I don't know."
> "Yeah," said Mary, nibbling on her muffin. "I guess you're right."

This dialogue needs polishing. First, there are only two people here, Mary and Jeanette. Why do we need to keep identifying them with verbal tags? We can keep them straight. Don't overuse tags—use as few as you can get away with. A second problem is the dangling verbal tag in the second paragraph. It's only after three sentences that we finally see who's speaking, which is way too long to wait for this information. It seems like an afterthought to boot. Don't tack on tags at the end of a string of sentences, or God forbid, a lengthy paragraph. Put them near the beginning, even if you have to break up a sentence. A third problem is the overuse of participial phrases, which I've discussed before. Either get rid of them, or (better yet) condense a verbal tag and a participial phrase together into a separate sentence, thus solving two problems at once.

Doing all these, our revised dialogue might look like this:

> "Did you see that dress that Jezebel was wearing?" Mary asked in disbelief.
> "Did I ever," said Jeanette. "It looked like some penguin outfit. A very fat, black penguin!"
> "I'm surprised her mother let her out of the house like that." Mary reached for another blueberry muffin.
> "Well, the way her mother dresses . . . I don't know."
> "Yeah." Mary nibbled at the muffin. "I guess you're right."

Impossible, Overinflated, Hyperbolic Imagery

In prose a good simile, metaphor or personification adds texture and emotional layering to its referent. A bad image only calls undue attention to itself and to a writer straining to be "literary." Worse, it almost always produces an unintentionally comic effect:

Doubt overwhelmed him, like a plane circling an airport in a storm which grew louder and stronger, until the thunder and lightning drowned out the sound of the engines and no planes could land.

The smells hit him like a swarm of wasps, buzzing and vengeful, ready to fly into his nose and sting him.

The first example is ludicrous. Homer could get away with extended similes, but they were carefully constructed and always came from the same world as their referent. They sustained their logic. But this simile just breaks down. We get lost somewhere in the storm. And the imaginative connection between a nonsubstantial thought and very physical airplanes, with fuselages, wings, engines and so on is strained at best. The second example has some potential, even though it's straining a bit to connect the sound of wasps with smells. But it falls off the deep end when it also asks the reader to think of smells as something visual and kinesthetic too ("ready to fly into his nose and sting"). Better would have been to keep the image simple, and confined to only one sensory paradox: "The smells hit him like a swarm of wasps." Short, sweet and punchy.

Unnecessary Phrases of Realization and Discernment

Look at the following constructions, quite common in unpolished writing:

He saw that there were three men running over the hill.

He discovered he was not alone in the room.

Barbara realized a sound was coming from the closet.

Tammy noticed that the man had long, dirty blond hair.

He could see that George hadn't shaved in days. *He also saw that* he was whispering to himself.

It seemed she was lost.

Most sentences of this ilk can be strengthened simply by eliminating the phrase of discernment (in italics above). It's often not needed, especially if the point of view has already been established. And the sentence automatically becomes punchier:

Three men were running over the hill.

He was not alone in the room.

A sound was coming from the closet.

The man had long, dirty blond hair.

George hadn't shaved in days and was whispering to himself.

She was lost.

Overuse of the Passive Voice

I know, this isn't news. It's something all creative writing instructors and texts emphasize. We all know that "He heard gunshots" is stronger than "Gunshots were heard by him," and that "She threw off the covers" is stronger than "The covers were thrown off." But there are also two *hidden* passive constructions that are often overused, but overlooked: "there are/were/is/was" constructions and self-reflexive constructions. Look at these examples:

There was a hush that fell over the party.

There were two men stumbling down the street.

John found himself trembling.

She thought of herself as a strong person.

These are not as strong as:

A hush fell over the party.

Two men were stumbling down the street.

John trembled.

She thought she was a strong person.

or even better:

I'm a strong person, she thought.

Unnecessary Telling

Consider the following paragraph:

Fascinated, Sarah watched Mrs. McQuade take the book in her hands, open it, remove the bookmark, and smooth the pages. The teacher adjusted her glasses. Her every movement seemed precise and pure, Sarah thought. Mrs. McQuade began reading the poem by Byron, and Sarah was lulled again by the teacher's soft warm burr of a voice. She wasn't listening to the words at all. She was just listening to their sound, and watching the way Mrs. McQuade's thin, delicate finger traced the lines on the page, the way her eyebrows rose and fell, the slight quiver to her nostril as if the words gave off a fragrance. *She was completely hypnotized by the teacher.*

We've already seen very vividly that Sarah is entranced by her teacher. We don't need to be told, as in the italicized sentence. Similarly:

If he tries to call me again, Jean thought, I'll tell him to kiss off. She imagined him saying he was sorry and how this would be the last time he'd ever cheat on her, but this time she wouldn't give in. "Kiss off," she'd tell him, or "Go cheat on her, I've had enough." *Jean was fantasizing.* If he comes to the door, she thought, I'll slam it in his face. He could stand and talk to it. In fact, he probably would. And she'd just slip out the back door and down the stairs.

We *see* Jean's fantasies; we don't need to be told that's what she's doing. In both cases, take out the unnecessary explanatory sentences.

Monotonous Sentence Rhythm

We've already seen an example of this with the overuse of participial phrases. Monotonous sentence rhythm happens when one or both of two things happens:

Sentences are always of the same length without a specific aesthetic reason, and/or sentences are always constructed in a similar way. Often the two occur together, like Tweedledum and Tweedledee. An example:

> Dan looked at his watch. It said three o'clock. He looked down the street. The street was empty and silent. A neon sign was blinking over a bar. Dan rubbed his chin. A man walked out of the bar. Dan sighed.

The prose sets up that old clickety-clack monotony because the sentences are all of similar length—here, short—and because they're all similarly constructed: subject/verb/object or adjective/adjectival clause. That example is fairly obvious, but here's one with the same problems, a bit more disguised:

> Pulling back the sleeve of his sweater, Dan looked at his watch. It said three o'clock. When he looked down the street, Dan saw it was empty and silent. Blinking over a bar was a neon sign. As Dan was rubbing his chin, a man walked out of the bar. Dan sighed.

Here, we see more variety in sentence length, but too many too close together feature the same construction: They begin with a participial or adverbial phrase or clause. And again monotony creeps over the prose.

Okay—quiz time. Let's put what we've learned to work. Here's a sentence ready for polishing. What's wrong with it, and how can it be revised?

> He saw that there were two men just dashing quickly across the field, screaming "Fire!" in loud voices.

We examine. We read aloud. We consider. We realize "He saw that . . ." is an unnecessary phrase of discernment. "There were" is a hidden passive. "Just" is a weasel word. "Quickly" is unnecessarily specific ("dashing" denotes moving quickly), as is the phrase "in loud voices" (how else do you scream?). Also, that prepositional phrase makes the sentence end weakly. A revised sentence might read like this: Two men were dashing across the field screaming "Fire!"

Punchier, right? But too easy, you say? Let's look at a more extended example, a section from a story by a student, . . . before revision and after. In the draft below, I've indicated by underline and interlinear comment the particular stylistic glitch involved.

> St. Nicholas Church was just like Mary remembered. She walked up the
>
> concrete steps to the huge, oak doors and reached for the brass handle.
> *repetition*
> The handle was cold, sending a chill up Mary's arm. She pulled on the
>   *repetition* *unnecessary word*   *weasel word*
> handle of the solid, heavy door and couldn't even crack it open a couple
>   *unnecessary specificity*
> of inches. Mary pushed the sleeves of her sweater up toward her forearm
>   *convoluted phrasing*   *convoluted*   *repetition*
> exposing a melted patch of flesh. She caught sight of the burn scar and

unnecessary specificity   *unnecessary specificity*

quickly pulled the <u>one</u> sleeve back down <u>to her wrist</u>. Mary used both

convoluted phrasing

hands to open the door, just as she did <u>when she was</u> a little girl. The weight

repetition   *unnecessary specificity*

<u>of the church doors</u> always seemed oppressively heavy <u>to her</u>, sometimes

convoluted phrasing

making her feel <u>as though she weren't really welcome</u>. She stepped inside

unnecessary word   *repetition*

the vestibule and let the <u>heavy</u> doors shut behind her. <u>The doors</u> shut out the

unnecessary word   *repetition*

<u>outside</u> world with one great thump, and entombed her <u>in her childhood</u>

unnecessary phrase of realization   *weak sentence structure*

<u>church</u>. <u>Mary discovered</u> this old church had not changed. <u>It still had</u> two

run-on prepositional phrases; unnecessary phrases

marble basins filled <u>with holy water on each side of the double doors</u>

<u>leading from the vestibule to the inside of the church.</u> The basins stood like

unnecessary words   *unnecessary words*

sentinels <u>guarding royalty</u>. You were not to pass <u>their post</u> without their

unnecessary word   *repetition*   *overusing adverbs*

blessing <u>first</u>. She walked toward the <u>double</u> doors <u>slowly</u> peering into the

weak sentence structure   *overusing adverbs*   *repetition*

church <u>nervously</u>. She stopped <u>momentarily</u> at one of the <u>marble</u> basins

unnecessary specificity

and gently dipped her <u>middle</u> finger into the cool, calm water and blessed

weak sentence structure; unnecessary phrase

herself <u>before entering the church</u>.

Behind the stylistic glitches, there's good, strong prose here. If we correct the glitches, we have a paragraph that could read:

> St. Nicholas Church was just like Mary remembered. She walked up the concrete steps to the huge, oak doors and reached for the brass handle. It was cold, sending a chill up Mary's arm. She pulled on the heavy door and couldn't crack it open a couple of inches. Mary pushed up the sleeves of her sweater, exposing a scar from a burn. She looked at it and quickly pulled the sleeve back down. Mary used both hands to open the doors, just as she did as a little girl. Their weight always seemed oppressively heavy, sometimes making her feel unwelcome. She stepped inside the vestibule and let the doors shut behind her. They shut out the world with one great thump, and entombed her there. The old church had not changed. Two marble basins filled with holy water stood like sentinels on either side of the double doors. You were not to pass without their blessing. She walked toward the doors, nervously peering into the church. She stopped at one of the basins and gently dipped her finger into the cool, calm water and blessed herself.

Better, right? You see how it works? Cut away everything that isn't the strong prose. Say exactly what you mean, and no more. Polish, polish, polish.

THE KEY CONCEPTS

This discussion of stylistic glitches is by no means complete. I've described several that pop up frequently. There are many others. The important point is that you grasp a few crucial concepts behind all of this fine-tuning:

1. Don't worry about fine-tuning your prose until you've got the bigger problems of your story under control. You can't polish a silver bowl until it's been smelted and cast. Just so with a story. Of course, you can't help doing some fine-tuning at the same time you're solving the other, bigger problems. That's natural. But don't make it your focus in early revisions. You'll start seeing trees instead of the forest. Map out the forest first, then start trimming trees.

2. When you're fine-tuning, every sentence, every word, counts. Everything has an effect. Words and sentences are the building blocks of your fictional universe. They're either working for you or against you. A weasel word here, a passive construction there, and you've got a limp, mushy sentence. A few of those sentences, and you've got a limp, mushy paragraph. Enough of those paragraphs, and you've got a limp, mushy story—and a disinterested reader. Just as you are what you eat, your story *is* what you write. If you think that's a tautology, think about it again.

3. So, when you're fine-tuning, go over your prose with the idea of making *each and every* sentence as strong as possible.

4. Go over it again.

5. Go over it again. A story is finished only when it's perfect, each and every word. Don't be in a hurry. Don't "finish" it before it really is finished. . . . Unpolished prose is a sure sign of an early draft.

6. Most importantly, start becoming aware of your own particular stylistic quirks and glitches, so that you can watch out for them upon revision. You may be prone to overusing the passive voice, for example, or to overusing adverbs. If so, you must become especially sensitive to these infelicities and watch out for them. Every writer has stylistic weaknesses, and it's no shame to indulge them in early drafts. But only bad writers live with them through the final draft.

DISCUSSION QUESTIONS

1. Kaplan asserts that the final revision of a story's language is a process of "removing the sense of a 'writer' from the work." What does he mean by that, and how can it be true that good fiction hides its author as the curtain hid the man pulling the levers in *The Wizard of Oz*?

2. In what ways do each of the "stylistic glitches" Kaplan mentions keep "the sense of a 'writer'" present before the reader's eyes?

3. Are you guilty of any of Kaplan's "stylistic glitches"? Why do you suppose you (along with many other writers) commit these errors? That is, how are stylistic choices (and missteps) tied inextricably to the other elements of fiction rather than being simply a matter of editing?

WRITING ACTIVITIES

1. Write a scene that has both a "flat" and a "round" character. Be prepared to explain how they obey the principles laid out by Forster for these two types of characters.

2. Summarize the "stories" of several published short stories. Then summarize the "plots," using the rule of "causality" that Forster posits as the necessary element of a plot.

3. Write a passage of dialogue that possesses the properties Bowen says are important for good dialogue.

4. The last of Bowen's basic elements of fiction is "relevance." Analyze a draft of one of your own stories for the "relevance" of all its elements, as Bowen explains the concept. Draft a plan for rewriting the story to tighten the relevance of its elements, and then do the rewrite.

5. Write a scene from several different "points of view" as defined by Booth. Determine which version of the scene presents information in the best way, communicating what you feel is important about the scene.

6. Experiment with distorting time in the ways discussed by Welty and exemplified by Faulkner's *The Sound and the Fury*. Try writing a story, in other words, that is anything but linear, that "plays free" by stretching time out, collapsing time, and reshuffling events in time.

7. Write a summary of a story you intend to write, from beginning to end. Make a list of scenes to dramatize in the "scenic" presentation of the same story. Write one of the scenes, leading into and out of the scene with summary.

8. Write a scene containing a character based very closely on someone you know. Use dramatic action ("scene" rather than "summary") to communicate the character's personality, attitudes, and values.

9. Write an outline for a story with a main character who is a composite of several people you know, possibly including yourself. Explain what qualities you have borrowed from which people. Write a scene from the story in which the character displays some of these qualities.

10. Like many fiction writers, Hemley keeps a journal of events and observations from life that sometimes make it into his fiction. (See Joan Didion's essay "On Keeping a Notebook" for another take on recording "real-life" events that become fiction.) If you don't already do so, try keeping a journal for a week, making notes on unusual events, bits of

overheard dialogue, faces, clothes, and so on. Then, following Hemley's example, transform some part of your journal into a fictional scene.

11. Hemley tells about an anthology of stories based on a single image from real life: a wedding cake in the middle of the road. Discuss with some classmates or fellow writers an image from real life observed by one of you that might fuel a similar experiment. After you settle on an image, write and share with the others a brief story in which the image appears.

12. If you have already written a story inspired by real life, perform the exercise that Hemley did in discussing the dead squirrel in the pizza box. First, narrate the real-life events that eventually were transformed into fiction; then present the passages from the story that relate to the real-life events, explaining how you changed them to fit into the story.

13. Huddle asserts that, in at least a small way, we must "become" our characters, as we inhabit their minds and hearts in order to understand them and make them real to the reader—a process that he refers to as a "transformation . . . in a fiction writer's moral attitude." Write a scene or even an entire story from the point of view of a character very unlike yourself, perhaps a character not particularly likable (or worse). Write in total sympathy with the character's outlook on life, trying more to present its reasonableness than to criticize it.

14. Using Huddle's example from Salinger as a model, write a scene that communicates what a character is all about through his "six ways to bring a character to life": information, physical appearance, thoughts and feelings, actions, sensory appearance, and speech.

15. Write a short scene (or a series of short scenes) that observes all of Reed's rules explicitly.

16. Examine one of your own stories for items on Reed's list of "what to leave out." Try the experiment of cutting the story to the bone and see what you have left. Did this exercise help you find (or at least think about) a "focus" or "consistency of intention" in the story?

17. Write an outline of a story that breaks every one of Nyberg's rules— a really awful story, in other words, one that fails before it has even started.

18. Examine your own notes or outline for a story that you have been thinking about but haven't drafted yet. Think about each of Nyberg's categories (honesty, setting, character, plot, theme) and his principles for success and failure in each category. How would Nyberg assess the possible success or failure of your story before it has even been written? How can you strengthen your story before you have even begun to write it?

19. Try using Kercheval's checklists to work on a story you've drafted. Make a note of which items on her lists seem most useful and which

items you might add to her lists. When you've revised the story, make your own checklists for future use.

20. Try rewriting a story from a different point of view, changing from third-person omniscient to first-person, for example, or from the point of view of one character to the point of view of another.

21. Try experimenting with multiple points of view. Draft a story that breaks the rules of "consistency" in point of view, as Madden explains that writers like William Faulkner and Wright Morris do. What are the difficulties of such an experiment? What are the rewards? Are the rewards worth the problems?

22. Use Kaplan's "laundry list of stylistic glitches" to revise a few pages of your own fiction. Which "glitches" do you find most often? Revise the rest of the story with attention solely to those errors.

A Workshop for Writers:
Invention and Revision*

GUIDED WRITING EXERCISES—INVENTION

The elements of craft discussed previously are useful not only as analytical categories but also as generative categories, as specific "means of representation" available to the fiction writer. Aristotle, in his *Rhetoric,* describes the elements of persuasive speaking and goes on to list, exhaustively, specific strategies for developing proofs in support of an argument. A rhetoric for fiction writers, which these exercises are intended to be a part of, aims to teach fiction writers to be more persuasive in their representations of human experience, providing proofs in the sense that John Gardner and Flannery O'Connor outline in their pieces in Chapter 1. Remember that these exercises should not shackle your imagination; think of them as guiding your imagination, helping you to form the habits of art that are essential to writing convincing, compelling fiction.

The first set of exercises focuses on invention and should be most useful as you begin working on a story. These exercises can help you see and understand your characters and their relationships, help you imagine the settings through which they move, and help you perceive how they see these settings and the people around them.

Story Structure

Plot/Relationship   Many short stories can be considered "relationship stories," with the plot growing out of a central conflict involving two people whose lives are intertwined. One such story is Anton Chekhov's "The Lady with the Pet Dog," which illuminates the meeting and subsequent relationship of Gurov and

---

*Many of the exercises in this workshop owe a debt to exercises collected in earlier books, particularly Wendy Bishop's *Working Words: The Process of Creative Writing* (Mayfield, 1992) and Anne Bernays and Pamela Painter's *What If? Writing Exercises for Fiction Writers,* rev. ed. (HarperCollins, 1995). Teachers of writing often borrow and adapt exercises from each other; the intent here is to build on the examples of others, developing this particular sequence of exercises as part of an informal rhetoric of fiction.

Anna. This exercise is derived from the shape of Chekhov's story; after you sketch out the moments/scenes of the relationship, though, you may find that you want to change the order or delete some and add others.

Think of a relationship between two characters that is an important part of your story. This relationship doesn't have to be *the* core of the story, but it should be a relationship that affects the story. Write briefly about the following moments/scenes in the relationship:

1. First meeting of the characters
2. First "click" (when one or both realize something important about the relationship)
3. First conflict
4. First pattern
5. Challenge to the pattern
6. Response to the challenge
7. Establishing of new pattern or end of the relationship

Spectrum of Settings   Think of one of the central characters in your story. Write briefly about this character in each type of setting listed here. You may work with settings that are already part of how you imagine the story will unfold, but you should also try to imagine the character in settings you haven't imagined yet. Use the first- or third-person limited point of view, emphasizing specific details and the character's perceptions of each setting.

1. A domestic setting, either inside or just outside (garden, yard, patio, driveway, porch) where the character lives
2. Someone else's domestic setting, either inside or just outside where that character lives
3. A social setting, in which the character is observing or interacting with a group of people
4. A setting connected in some way to travel (a road, a train station, an airport), in which the character is going on or returning from a journey or interacting with another character who is leaving or returning
5. A public setting that has a ceremonial (church, cemetery) or cultural (the Washington Monument, Wall Street, the Golden Gate Bridge) meaning
6. A domestic setting that the character is returning to after an absence, with the focus on the character's sense that something has changed, that something is different (this could be the setting you used in items 1 or 2, or it could be another domestic setting)

After writing about your character in each of these settings, arrange the pieces in a way that generates a plot, a sequence of scenes. Consider how the settings reveal your character's conflicts and desires. How does arranging the settings in different ways suggest different kinds of story movement, different emphases for the plot?

Making Scenes

Scene/Specification   To begin, think of two of your characters in a particular setting. (You may choose to work with the characters from the "Plot/Relationship" exercise and one of the settings from the "Spectrum of Settings" exercise.) Write some notes about the two characters (their names, their ages, the nature of their relationship) and the setting. Then write at least one sentence in response to each of the following prompts. Write quickly; don't think too much about whether each sentence works. While the exercise will result in the drafting of a scene, don't decide in advance exactly how the scene will develop. Open yourself up to the possibilities that the prompts offer. If you want to write more than one sentence in response to a prompt, do so. If you blank on a prompt, skip it and go on to the next one.

Before beginning the exercise, you should decide on a particular point of view, such as third-person objective, third-person limited, or first-person. Consider repeating the exercise, writing about the same characters in the same setting from different points of view; this shifting perspective can help you understand and illuminate the relationships and conflicts in your story.

1. A sentence with a wall or boundary in it
2. A sentence with weather (temperature, wind, air) in it
3. A sentence with a sound in it
4. A sentence with a gesture in it
5. A line of dialogue of six words or less
6. A sentence with light in it
7. A line of dialogue of ten words or more
8. A sentence with a ceiling or floor in it
9. A sentence with a texture (the feel of something) in it
10. A sentence with an object smaller than a hand in it
11. A sentence with an allusion to literature or art in it
12. A sentence fragment
13. A sentence with a piece of furniture in it
14. A line of dialogue that is a question
15. Another line of dialogue that is a question
16. A sentence with a hand or fingers in it
17. A sentence with a dash in it
18. A sentence with an allusion to a current event in it
19. A sentence with a metaphor in it
20. A line of dialogue that is whispered

After completing the exercise, read what you've written, making notes in the margins of sentences that surprise you, sentences that suggest new insight into the characters, and sentences that have energy or emotion compelling you to write more. Again, consider repeating the exercise from a different point of view, such as the first-person perspective of the other character in the scene or the third-person objective stance.

This exercise can get you started on a story, and doing the exercise several times in quick succession can help you generate a complete draft of a story.

Observation/Perspective   Think of two of your characters in a domestic setting; the setting can be one that they share or one that belongs mostly to one of the characters. For each of the activities listed here, describe one character doing the activity from the perspective of the other character. What does the observing character notice? How does the observing character interpret or judge the actions of the other?

First, describe Character B doing the following things from Character A's perspective:

1. Watering a plant
2. Watching the news on television
3. Putting away groceries
4. Getting dressed on a Sunday morning
5. Sweeping the porch or patio or driveway
6. Talking on the telephone
7. Washing the dishes
8. Drying hair after a bath or shower

Second, describe Character A doing the following things from Character B's perspective:

1. Putting on shoes
2. Vacuuming
3. Reading the newspaper
4. Chopping vegetables to make a salad
5. Making the bed
6. Looking in a mirror before going to work
7. Folding laundry
8. Playing with the family pet

Dialogue   Think of two of your characters in a particular setting, one that allows them to talk to each other, though they may be involved in another activity too (eating, reading, working out, gardening, walking in the park). Use the third-person objective point of view, with the narrator limited to observing the characters' actions and hearing their words.

Character A: a line of dialogue of six words or less

Character B: no spoken response—the narrator describes a gesture by B

A: a line of dialogue of six words or less

B: two complete sentences of dialogue

A: two words of dialogue

B: a line of dialogue of ten words or more

A: no spoken response—the narrator describes a noise made by A

B: a line of dialogue of six words or less

Narrator: a description of the body language of A and B in relation to each other

A: a line of dialogue beginning with "I remember . . ."

B: a line of dialogue commenting on something in the setting

A: a line of dialogue that is a question

B: a line of dialogue beginning with "I used to believe . . ."

Narrator: a description of an object that is part of the setting

A: a line of dialogue that is a question

B: no spoken response—the narrator describes B handling an object in the setting

A: tells a story in dialogue

B: a line of dialogue beginning with "You never . . ." or "I never . . ."

A: no spoken response—the narrator describes a gesture by A

Variation: You may wish to repeat this exercise using a different point of view, such as first-person or third-person limited. Shifting the perspective can illuminate the differences in the characters' perceptions of the same events. Or you might reverse the order of the prompts, so that the story A tells comes early in the scene.

Developing a Character's Inner Life

Character Development/Associative Thinking*   To begin, think of two of your characters in a particular setting. Imagine that the two characters are thinking about each other. Then write in response to each of the following prompts, using either a first-person or third-person point of view. (You may also wish to do this exercise from a third-person omniscient point of view, to explore your own sense of the characters.) Don't try to write complete sentences or logical sequences. Write quickly, without too much conscious thought.

Before beginning, write all of the names that these characters have been known by. Note by whom and at what period in the characters' lives each name was used. Consider as well what name each character uses when thinking about

---

*This exercise is derived from the "Metaphorical Character Exercise" in Wendy Bishop, *Working Words: The Process of Creative Writing* (Mountain View, CA: Mayfield, 1992).

her- or himself, and what name Character A uses when thinking about Character B, and vice versa.

First, describe Character A thinking about/describing Character B:

1. As a season
2. As a food
3. As a game or a sport
4. As a movie
5. As a country (e.g., What are the geographical features of this country? What are the major imports and exports? What does the flag look like?)
6. As a song or piece of music
7. As a form of transportation
8. As a magazine

Second, describe Character B thinking about/describing Character A:

1. As a city
2. As a language (e.g., How does it sound? Is it difficult or easy to speak and understand?)
3. As a garden
4. As a field of study or course at a university
5. As a dance
6. As a form of government
7. As something to drink
8. As a vacation destination

Variation: In exploring the relationships of characters, you can return to these prompts, reversing the order, perhaps, or having the characters think about themselves in associative or metaphorical ways. Note the contrast between the characters' perceptions and the way these contrasts can lead to misunderstanding and conflict.

Inner Life/Interior Landscape   Think of one of your characters whom you want to understand more fully. This could be the point-of-view character or another character whose motivations are important to the story. In the first or third person, describe past events from the character's life that embody the following abstractions; these should be events that are part of the character's inner landscape, that live in the character's mind from day to day. But don't name the abstractions themselves in describing the events.

1. Shame
2. Contentment
3. Despair
4. Rage

5. Desire
6. Fear
7. Joy
8. Belonging
9. Accomplishment
10. Failure
11. Mental images of heaven and hell
12. The character's dream of where he or she will be in five years and then the picture of what the character thinks that future will really be like
13. A crime that the character can imagine committing
14. An action that the character cannot imagine performing despite its common occurrence

Inner Life/Interior Voice   Think of one of your characters whom you want to understand more fully and whose inner voice you want to hear more clearly. In the first-person or close-third-person point of view, complete the following prompts, writing up to a paragraph for each one. (The version of the prompt in parentheses is a third-person variant of the first-person prompt.) Work to hear the character's interior voice, the way the character explains the world to her- or himself. If you decide to work in the third person, note how the character's voice influences the narrative voice.

1. "When I hear my voice on tape, I . . ." (When she heard her voice on tape, she . . .)
2. "I still don't understand why I . . ." (He still didn't understand why . . .)
3. "The best birthday I ever had was . . ." (The best birthday she ever had was . . .)
4. "Someone knocked on the door, so I . . ." (Someone knocked on the door, so he . . .)
5. "I'd like to look good in . . ." (He'd like to look good in . . .)
6. "When it storms, I think about . . ." (When it stormed, she thought about . . .)
7. "In elevators I always stand . . ." (In elevators he always stood . . .)
8. "Hearing that song on the radio, . . ."
9. "I'll never get caught . . ." (She'd never get caught . . .)
10. "I used to be sure that . . ." (He used to be sure that . . .)
11. "When I imagine the world ending . . ." (When she imagined the world ending, . . .)
12. "By this time next year . . ."
13. "A little thing I couldn't do without . . ." (A little thing he couldn't do without . . .)

14. "What tells me I'm different from everyone else is . . ." (What told her she was different from everyone else was . . .)

15. "I'm afraid of getting what I want because . . ." (He was afraid of getting what he wanted because . . .)

16. "One thing I remember from school is . . ." (One thing she remembered from school was . . .)

17. "What tells me I'm just like everyone else is . . ." (What told him he was just like everyone else was . . .)

18. "The one question I'd like an honest answer to is . . ." (The one question she'd like an honest answer to was . . .)

19. "The first time I stopped loving someone . . ." (The first time he stopped loving someone . . .)

20. "Most people don't see the beauty of . . ."

Developing a Character's World

External Landscape   Think of one of your characters whom you want to under-stand more fully. This could be the point-of-view character or another character who plays an important role in the story. In the first or third person, describe the character's pantheon of important figures from history and contemporary culture. These figures may represent heroes, villains, or role models, or they may embody particular values or qualities. Use these prompts to understand how your charac-ter imagines him- or herself in relation to the external world.

1. A historical figure
2. A political figure from the past
3. A current political figure
4. A literary or artistic figure
5. A literary character
6. A figure from popular culture (music, sports, movies, TV)
7. A mythological figure
8. A religious figure

In developing the character's connections to the external world, try several approaches. For example, have the character engage in conversation with the fig-ure, share some everyday activity with the figure, or replace the figure at some key moment in the figure's life. Which of these situations is your character most likely to imagine when thinking about his or her role in the world? In other words, if your character is drawn to Elvis, is the character most likely to imagine talking to Elvis, hanging out with Elvis at Graceland, or being Elvis on stage in Las Vegas?

Newspaper Prompts   Think of one of your characters whom you want to under-stand more fully. Imagine the character in a particular setting reading the daily newspaper. If your character habitually reads the paper, place him or her in the usual setting for this activity. If your character does not often read the paper, imagine a situation (a bus ride, a doctor's waiting room, the lobby of a hair salon) in which she or he picks up a paper to pass the time. In the first or third person, explore the character's reactons to the headlines and the opening sentences of the day's top stories. Also consider the order in which the character would read the newspaper, and start the exercise there. (If your character is not living in a contemporary setting, you may wish—if possible—to find a newspaper from the character's time to help develop your understanding of his or her external world.)

(Note: *USA Today* works well for this exercise, as it bills itself as "the Nation's Newspaper" and includes one page of brief stories from all fifty states in each edition. If your character absolutely never reads the newspaper, imagine a situation in which she or he is hearing a series of news stories—such as through TV or the conversation of other characters or an Internet news service. The key to the exercise is exploring your character's thinking about the external world.)

Character Experiencing Art   Write about your character doing the following things, which all involve experiencing various forms of art. Include physical details from the setting, the character's sensory experience and actions, and the character's thoughts about the experience.

1. Visiting a museum (What kind of museum would the character be likely to visit? What would the character go to see first?)
2. Attending a concert (What kind of music would the character want to hear? Where would the character want to sit or stand?)
3. Watching a play (What kind of play would the character go to see? How would the character react to the performers breaking the invisible fourth wall of the stage?)
4. Watching a movie (What kind of movie would the character go to see? Where does the character like to sit?)
5. Hanging a picture in a domestic setting (What kind of picture is it? Has it been framed? Where is it being placed?)
6. Listening to music at home or in the car (What kind of music does the character listen to? Does the character sing along, tap feet, dance?)

Variation: Try this exercise with specifics that the character doesn't choose willingly; for instance, the character can be required to go to a museum by parents or teachers, or can go to a movie to please a date or a friend.

Character Making Art   While not all characters are artists, most have some kind of imaginative or creative life. In this exercise, imagine your character doing the following things, all of which involve making art in some form. For each prompt, you may choose to write about the character performing these acts, or you can try to draw/write/design as the character.

1. Doodling
2. Drawing

3. Writing a poem
4. Singing
5. Playing an instrument
6. Writing and delivering a speech
7. Taking a photograph
8. Designing a website

Character Riffs

Personal Ad   Your character is writing a personal ad. To help you decide what to include in the ad, divide a piece of paper with a line down the middle. On one side, list the descriptive phrases the character is considering for the ad. On the other, write the character's inner monologue about the phrase—what it hides about the character, what has to be left out of the character's history for the phrase to be even nominally true, and what the character fears anyone responding to the ad would immediately find out if they were to meet.

Feature Story   Your character is being interviewed by the local newspaper—about what? Decide what your character could be interviewed about for a general interest feature—not some heroic rescue story about saving an infant from a fire, but something for the Living or Metro section. This could be some unusual hobby, some family history, or some form of public service. Write about the interview itself, the feature story, and the character's reaction when reading the story in the newspaper.

Paralysis   Write a scene in which your character is paralyzed by some insight about his or her experience. Set the scene. Make the character's inability to move physically palpable. The inner experience of the insight can be as active and chaotic as you want, but the character cannot move during the scene.

Imagined Children   Write about your character imagining the children she or he will have someday. What does the character want to give the children in terms of traits (physical, intellectual, emotional)? What does the character *not* want the children to inherit? What is most frightening to the character about what the children may or may not inherit?

The Lord of All Surveyed   Often writers are advised not to begin or end stories with a character waking up. For this exercise, though, begin with the character waking up in his or her perfect world. Focus on the details of this world, writing in a hyper-realistic mode. Then describe how the perfect world might get complicated, messy, imperfect. Where does conflict come from in this perfect world?

Work History   List the character's employment history in resume form. If your character is too young to have a work history, be inventive: make up a child's employment history (e.g., play, eat, cry, do chores, sleep). Then write a scene dramatizing each item in the resume, including the work itself, the setting, and interaction with others.

Money History   Write the history of your character's experience with money. When/how did the character become aware of the importance/unimportance and the presence/absence of money? What form of money (quarters, crisp bills, jars of pennies, paychecks) does the character most like the look or feel of?

CRAFT EXERCISES—REVISION

This set of exercises focuses on revision. Once you have a complete draft of a story, you can do several things to help illuminate the shape and structure of your story and, more importantly, the possibilities for developing it further. Remember that the process of crafting your story has only just begun when you have a full draft in front of you. Many writers assert that the real writing—the real crafting —begins at this point. Although some of these exercises ask you to think analytically about your story, the intent is to return you to invention, to the available means of representation foregrounded in the previous exercises.

Revising Within and Outside the Shell

A useful methaphor for thinking about revision is that of breaking or not breaking the shell of the draft. You can revise within the shell—working within the basic boundaries established by the draft—or you can break the shell, writing beyond the boundaries, even to the extent of radically re-imagining the characters and plot. The following exercises should help you see the shell—how the draft has set up boundaries of setting, action, and interaction. Analyze your draft for narrative structure, temporal structure, and character dynamics.

Time Line—Scene/Summary   Draw a line across the piece of paper to represent your story. Mark off a section of the line for each scene or narrative summary, writing a key word or phrase under the line to remind you of what that scene or summary focuses on. The section marked off should represent how much of the story that scene or narrative summary takes up. Looking at your story this way can show you how well you've balanced scene and summary, and how much attention you're giving to each scene in relation to the rest of the story. Sometimes you will find that you're narrating, or telling, too much, or that one of the longer scenes does not really deserve that much space. Conversely, you may find that a crucial moment or interaction is quickly summarized, suggesting that the scene/specification exercise might help you imagine and dramatize that moment more effectively.

Time Line—Present and Past Action   Again, draw a line across a piece of paper to represent your story. This time, though, you will mark off sections in two temporal dimensions: the present action and the past action of the story. As before, mark off sections of the line to represent how much of the story each scene takes up. For present-action scene and summary, write the key word or phrase describing the scene above the line; for past-action scene and summary (dramatized or narrated flashback), write the key word or phrase below the line. You may find that the heart of the story is in the past action, below the line, and that the present-action material is nothing more than a frame that may detract from the real story. You may find that all or most of your story is present action and that your characters' motivations are thus less fully developed than they could be. This could lead you to the inner-life exercise to help you explore what past events in your characters' lives are part of their motivation.

Setting Map/Constellation   Draw a constellation or map of the settings you use in your story. Don't try to do an exact rendering of the settings; instead, do an impressionistic sketch of each setting, including material objects (furniture, articles of clothing, paintings or other artworks) that distinguish the setting in your or the characters' minds. You might make each point in the constellation a bubble, with the size of the bubble determined by how much of the story takes place in that setting. You may notice that the small bubble of one setting is the site of lots of emotional baggage, lots of loaded objects of great importance to your characters. This may lead you to write more about the characters in this setting. You might draw lines between different points or bubbles in the constellation to represent the gravitational pull of the settings on each other. You might find that one point or bubble dominates the constellation and that the dominant setting doesn't really deserve that much story space.

Character Groupings   Make a list of all the characters who appear in your story; this list should include characters who are thought about by other characters even if they haven't been shown yet. Then make another list of each scene in your story, noting the characters who interact in each scene. This exercise can show you groupings that you haven't explored yet; you might find that you have been avoiding certain groupings, keeping characters apart because you're not sure how they will behave with each other. These avoided interactions are often the key to moving the story forward in the next draft.

Listening to Voices

Letters from Your Characters   Imagine a magical realm in which you and all of your characters exist in an omniscient state, a kind of metaphysical workshop. That is, all of your characters have read the draft of the story too. Have each of the characters write you a letter responding to the draft. How does the character feel about how you've told the story? About how you've portrayed her or him? About what you've included and what you've left out, and what you've emphasized and what you've glossed over? What does the character know about the story that you don't know? What advice and demands does the character have related to the revision of the story?

You may also have the characters write letters to each other. What do they want to know from each other? What puzzles or confuses them about each other?

(The epistolary genre, featuring letters as the narrative mode, is a staple of fiction, although in contemporary fiction the letters may appear in the form of e-mail or faxes; you may find that the characters' letters to each other warrant a place in the revision in some form.)

Finally, you may want to write letters to the characters yourself, asking them questions about their motivations and feelings and choices. They may answer— then again they may not.

Letters to Yourself   Write a letter or memo to yourself about ways to revise the story within the shell. Write another letter or memo about ways to break the shell of the draft. Although many stories can be effectively revised within the shell, we sometimes resist breaking the shell because we know that the story, at least initially, will look messier—less complete—than we thought it was when we completed the draft. That's a part of the process that writers need to learn to accept— craft requires time and patience, a willingness to explore and re-explore the available means of telling the story.

PART TWO

Contexts for Fiction Writing

CHAPTER 3

The Writer's Life

We are curious about writers' lives: how they got to be writers, how they write, what else they do, how they keep a roof over their heads. We want to know what they did when they weren't being famous or exercising their genius. We want to know if their lives are like our lives, or if our lives can yield the kind of writing we admire. Fortunately, writers write about their lives with some frequency and at length—in essays, autobiographies, diaries, and letters. They tutor us in the relation between art and life, in making a place for art within a life, in devoting a life to art. They also tell us about the ways in which the fiction a writer produces can be not only a piece of art but also a cultural artifact, or a political statement, or an expression of pop culture—in other words, a unit in a much broader social, political, and economic system.

In the first section of this chapter, "Writers' Lives," three well-known writers explain how, for them, there is no difference between life and art. In the first selection, Ernest Hemingway reconstructs the life he lived before he was famous, when he arranged his meager income around the need to write. There is little doubt that in passages like this the old Hemingway personal-myth-making machine is at work; at the same time, he does give a sense of the single-minded focus with which he pursued his art. Like many writers, James Baldwin cannot remember a time when he did not write, or a time when his life did not feed his writing with language and experience. Specifically, his inspiration is the life and language of his African-American community in Harlem, which continued to inform his sensibility even after decades of expatriate life in France. Finally, Virginia Woolf chronicles personal ambition and crippling doubt with an honesty that should reassure any of us who have ever felt pride, envy, and insecurity with regard to our own writing. The highs and lows she captures so tellingly as she drafts, revises, and publishes should be familiar to any writer who has been through the experience.

The second section, "Growing Up and Growing into the Writing Life," begins with Bernard Malamud's memoir, "Long Work, Short Life." Malamud writes of his slow progress toward becoming what he strives to be, a "very good writer." He offers a portrait of the dedicated artist who regrets that he doesn't have two lives to lead: one to devote to the demands of art, the other to more common joys and challenges of a life apart from writing. Carol Bly, in "Writing Whole Literature," addresses the early experiences of an imagined protagonist, Jill. Bly explores the importance of psychological nurturing in the life of the young writer, illuminating how a lack of encouragement and validation may lead to cynicism and emotionally constricted writing. Bly also addresses the young writer's relationship to the wider world of politics and social issues, positing that writers must be aware of public concerns and should learn to contextualize their characters' actions in "the widest possible periphery." Dorothy Allison, in "Believing in Literature," writes of the potential for literature to effect social change, citing her own early belief that "our writing was better than we were." Allison describes her experiences as an activist, feminist, and lesbian, tracing her role in the development of an inclusive literature that can alter both the definition of literature and the readers' sense of the world. Allison suggests that judgments about stories and other literary works are always subjective and political, and she asks writers to balance their loyalties to craft and social progress. Anne Lamott's introduction to her book *Bird by Bird* chronicles her childhood and her relationship to her father, a writer who was not like the other fathers in the neighborhood. Lamott benefits from having a supportive role model in the house, and she pursues writing from an early age. Observing and reacting to her father's actions, she develops a complex, ambivalent attitude toward the risks and rewards of the writer's life.

The third section, "Metaphors for the Writing Life," begins with Annie Dillard's collage of analogies from her book *The Writing Life*. Most of the metaphors in this piece illuminate the courage and commitment a writer must have in order to keep writing at all. She notes that the process of writing is "epistemological," that writing is a way of knowing the world, and not simply of expressing oneself. While the writer has the heady freedom to work—to probe, to build, to hover in a magical creative space created by words—Dillard notes that the writer's efforts are not guaranteed a place in the world. In "The Master-Slave Relationship," Victoria Nelson focuses more intensely on the psychology of the writer at work. Reiterating the idea that the "whole person" must participate in writing, Nelson analyzes how trying to control the process through the conscious mind may result in a shutdown, a refusal of the unconscious to join in the creative act. Nelson offers us ways to understand the dynamic of such writer's blocks (a common metaphor itself) and provides advice designed to bring our conscious and unconscious selves into harmony. For Tim O'Brien, the best metaphor for writing is "magic," in at least two senses of the word. In one sense, fiction is trickery, sleight of hand, the creation of an illusion of reality. In another sense, however, the magic of fiction partakes of the deepest mysteries of human life and even a kind of spiritual faith; O'Brien points out that in some cultures the magician and the storyteller are often the same person. The creation of a magical reality, in both senses, enables us to reflect on the "reality" and mystery of our own lives.

The fourth section examines the idea that fiction may have political content, purposes, and uses. E. L. Doctorow, a novelist known for creating fiction that does have explicit political meanings, traces the ways in which all narratives, both fiction and nonfiction, are "false documents," and also the obligations that this idea places on all writers. In "Dysfunctional Narratives," Charles Baxter asserts that the Watergate ethic of total "deniability" has infected the world of fiction writing, bringing with it the corrupt political values of the Nixon White House. He proposes a complex counterethic of responsibility, in which narratives would posit not that "mistakes were made" but that "so-and-so made such-and-such mistakes, and here's what it means." Nadine Gordimer, whose stories and novels set in apartheid-era South Africa are unabashedly political, discusses how fiction, morals, and politics end up as "strange bedfellows" no matter how hard we may try to write "for art's sake" alone. The choice, she implies, is not between instilling politics into our fiction or not doing so, but between ignorance and conscious use of its inevitable political content.

The last section, "The Fiction Writer and Popular Culture," focuses on the effects of mass media, particularly television, and digital communication on fiction writers and their work. Jonathan Franzen, in "Perchance to Dream," explores how the traditionally "solitary work" of the writer has been intruded upon by the ever-shifting, alluring images of film and television. He also suggests that today's "therapeutic society"—in which personal, formerly private conflicts become grist for the media mill—undermines the writer's careful examination of the individual in relation to society, thus threatening the tradition of the social novel. David Foster Wallace, in "E Unibus Pluram," analyzes the "nexus where television and fiction converse and consort," assessing the effects of the mode of "self-conscious irony" that dominates television and much contemporary fiction. Wallace also illuminates historical connections between metafiction (and more recent work he labels "image-fiction") and the spread of television in the 1950s and 1960s. He claims that the youthful irreverence and rebellion of those days have been co-opted by the ironic, "spectatorial" stance fostered by postmodern techniques. Janet Murray, in "The Cyberbard and the Multi-form Plot," offers a more hopeful view of the future of narrative. She asserts that the "multi-form" stories facilitated by digital environments link back to bardic traditions of oral storytelling, in which "singers of tales" worked creatively with conventions and structures familiar to their audiences. For Murray, cyberspace provides such a creative frame for the "cyberbard," who can use technology to build compelling narratives out of human experience within a digital context.

In some ways, writers' lives are like any lives: They are consumed by work, love, worry, grief, and joy. In other ways, writers' lives are unique: They are consumed by language. Writers are self-consciously aware of perceiving life through the lens of language as they collect and categorize and make sense of experience, and as they read how other writers have done the same. They watch themselves creating versions of life with language and sometimes come to feel that life is real only insofar as it can be expressed in language. They share the urgency of the task of reaching out to readers with their stories, the sense of inadequacy in communicating what they think they know, the awe at being able to say more than they thought they could, and the devotion to a life that is often exasperating, some-times rewarding, but never boring. At the same time, they share a consciousness that fiction can never be "in and of itself," but is always a product, a reflection, and a creator of the social order in which it is embedded. Our own fiction writing can be enhanced by an awareness of the forces at work on us as we sit down to our task, forces that are certainly artistic or psychological but also social, cultural, and political.

WRITERS' LIVES

ERNEST HEMINGWAY

Hunger Was Good Discipline

Ernest Hemingway (1899–1961) was one of the most important writers of the twentieth century, a recipient of the Nobel Prize for literature (1954), and a prolific short story writer, novelist, travel writer, and journalist. His story collections and novels are American monuments: In Our Time (1924), The Sun Also Rises (1926), A Farewell to Arms (1929), To Have and Have Not (1937), For Whom the Bell Tolls (1940), and The Old Man and the Sea (1952). Fiction writers today may love him or hate him, but nobody can ignore his influence. In his nonfiction (which sometimes borders on fiction) and his thinly veiled autobiographical fiction, he has much to say about his technique, his inspiration, and his goals as a fiction writer.

You got very hungry when you did not eat enough in Paris because all the bakery shops had such good things in the windows and people ate outside at tables on the sidewalk so that you saw and smelled the food. When you had given up journalism and were writing nothing that anyone in America would buy, explaining at home that you were lunching out with someone, the best place to go was the Luxembourg gardens where you saw and smelled nothing to eat all the way from the Place de l'Observatoire to the rue de Vaugirard. There you could always go into the Luxembourg museum and all the paintings were sharpened and clearer and more beautiful if you were belly-empty, hollow-hungry. I learned to understand Cézanne much better and to see truly how he made landscapes when I was hungry. I used to wonder if he were hungry too when he painted; but I thought possibly it was only that he had forgotten to eat. It was one of those unsound but illuminating thoughts you have when you have been sleepless or hungry. Later I thought Cézanne was probably hungry in a different way.

After you came out of the Luxembourg you could walk down the narrow rue Férou to the Place St.-Sulpice and there were still no restaurants, only the quiet square with its benches and trees. There was a fountain with lions, and pigeons walked on the pavement and perched on the statues of the bishops. There was the church and there were shops selling religious objects and vestments on the north side of the square.

From this square you could not go further toward the river without passing shops selling fruits, vegetables, wines, or bakery and pastry shops. But by choosing your way carefully you could work to your right around the grey and white stone church and reach the rue de l'Odéon and turn up to your right toward Sylvia Beach's bookshop and on your way you did not pass too many places where things to eat were sold. The rue de l'Odéon was bare of eating places until you reached the square where there were three restaurants.

By the time you reached 12 rue de l'Odéon your hunger was contained but all of your perceptions were heightened again. The photographs looked different and you saw books that you had never seen before.

"You're too thin, Hemingway," Sylvia would say. "Are you eating enough?"

"Sure."

"What did you eat for lunch?"

My stomach would turn over and I would say, "I'm going home for lunch now."

"At three o'clock?"

"I didn't know it was that late."

"Adrienne said the other night she wanted to have you and Hadley for dinner. We'd ask Fargue. You like Fargue, don't you? Or Larbaud. You like him. I know you like him. Or anyone you really like. Will you speak to Hadley?"

"I know she'd love to come."

"I'll send her a *pneu*. Don't you work so hard now that you don't eat properly."

"I won't."

"Get home now before it's too late for lunch."

"They'll save it."

"Don't eat cold food either. Eat a good hot lunch."

"Did I have any mail?"

"I don't think so. But let me look."

She looked and found a note and looked up happily and then opened a closed door in her desk.

"This came while I was out," she said. It was a letter and it felt as though it had money in it. "Wedderkop," Sylvia said.

"It must be from *Der Querschnitt*. Did you see Wedderkop?"

"No. But he was here with George. He'll see you. Don't worry. Perhaps he wanted to pay you first."

"It's six hundred francs. He says there will be more."

"I'm awfully glad you reminded me to look. Dear Mr. Awfully Nice."

"It's damned funny that Germany is the only place I can sell anything. To him and the *Frankfurter Zeitung*."

"Isn't it? But don't you worry ever. You can sell stories to Ford," she teased me.

"Thirty francs a page. Say one story every three months in *The Transatlantic*. Story five pages long makes one hundred and fifty francs a quarter. Six hundred francs a year."

"But, Hemingway, don't worry about what they bring now. The point is that you can write them."

"I know. I can write them. But nobody will buy them. There is no money coming in since I quit journalism."

"They will sell. Look. You have the money for one right there."

"I'm sorry, Sylvia. Forgive me for speaking about it."

"Forgive you for what? Always talk about it or about anything. Don't you know all writers ever talk about is their troubles? But promise me you won't worry and that you'll eat enough."

"I promise."

"Then get home now and have lunch."

Outside on the rue de l'Odéon I was disgusted with myself for having complained about things. I was doing what I did of my own free will and I was doing it stupidly. I should have bought a large piece of bread and eaten it instead of skipping a meal. I could taste the brown lovely crust. But it is dry in your mouth without something to drink. You God damn complainer. You dirty phony saint and martyr, I said to myself. You quit journalism of your own accord. You have credit and Sylvia would have loaned you money. She has plenty of times. Sure. And then the next thing you would be compromising on something else. Hunger is healthy and the pictures do look better when you are hungry. Eating is wonderful too and do you know where you are going to eat right now?

Lipp's is where you are going to eat and drink too.

It was a quick walk to Lipp's and every place I passed that my stomach noticed as quickly as my eyes or my nose made the walk an added pleasure. There were few people in the *brasserie* and when I sat down on the bench against the wall with the mirror in back and a table in front and the waiter asked if I wanted beer I asked for a *distingué*, the big glass mug that held a liter, and for potato salad.

The beer was very cold and wonderful to drink. The *pommes à l'huile* were firm and marinated and the olive oil delicious. I ground black pepper over the potatoes and moistened the bread in the olive oil. After the first heavy draft of beer I drank and ate very slowly. When the *pommes à l'huile* were gone I ordered another serving and a *cervelas*. This was a sausage like a heavy, wide frankfurter split in two and covered with a special mustard sauce.

I mopped up all the oil and all of the sauce with bread and drank the beer slowly until it began to lose its coldness and then I finished it and ordered a *demi* and watched it drawn. It seemed colder than the *distingué* and I drank half of it.

I had not been worrying, I thought. I knew the stories were good and someone would publish them finally at home. When I stopped doing newspaper work I was sure the stories were going to be published. But every one I sent out came back. What had made me so confident was Edward O'Brien's taking the "My Old Man" story for the *Best Short Stories* book and then dedicating the book for that year to me. Then I laughed and drank some more beer. The story had never been published in a magazine and he had broken all his rules to take it for the book. I laughed again and the waiter glanced at me. It was funny because, after all that, he had spelled the name wrong. It was one of two stories I had left when everything I had written was stolen in Hadley's suitcase that time at the Gare de Lyon when she was bringing the manuscripts down to me to Lausanne as a surprise, so

I could work on them on our holidays in the mountains. She had put in the originals, the typescripts and the carbons, all in manila folders. The only reason I had the one story was that Lincoln Steffens had sent it out to some editor who sent it back. It was in the mail while everything else was stolen. The other story that I had was the one called "Up in Michigan" written before Miss Stein had come to our flat. I had never had it copied because she said it was *inaccrochable*. It had been in a drawer somewhere.

So after we had left Lausanne and gone down to Italy I showed the racing story to O'Brien, a gentle, shy man, pale, with pale blue eyes, and straight lanky hair he cut himself, who lived then as a boarder in a monastery up above Rapallo. It was a bad time and I did not think I could write any more then, and I showed the story to him as a curiosity, as you might show, stupidly, the binnacle of a ship you had lost in some incredible way, or as you might pick up your booted foot and make some joke about it if it had been amputated after a crash. Then, when he read the story, I saw he was hurt far more than I was. I had never seen anyone hurt by a thing other than death or unbearable suffering except Hadley when she told me about the things being gone. She had cried and cried and could not tell me. I told her that no matter what the dreadful thing was that had happened nothing could be that bad, and whatever it was, it was all right and not to worry. We would work it out. Then, finally, she told me. I was sure she could not have brought the carbons too and I hired someone to cover for me on my newspaper job. I was making good money then at journalism, and took the train for Paris. It was true all right and I remember what I did in the night after I let myself into the flat and found it was true. That was over now and Chink had taught me never to discuss casualties; so I told O'Brien not to feel so bad. It was probably good for me to lose early work and I told him all that stuff you feed the troops. I was going to start writing stories again I said and, as I said it, only trying to lie so that he would not feel so bad, I knew that it was true.

Then I started to think in Lipp's about when I had first been able to write a story after losing everything. It was up in Cortina d'Ampezzo when I had come back to join Hadley there after the spring skiing which I had to interrupt to go on assignment to the Rhineland and the Ruhr. It was a very simple story called "Out of Season" and I had omitted the real end of it which was that the old man hanged himself. This was omitted on my new theory that you could omit anything if you knew that you omitted and the omitted part would strengthen the story and make people feel something more than they understood.

Well, I thought, now I have them so they do not understand them. There cannot be much doubt about that. There is most certainly no demand for them. But they will understand the same way that they always do in painting. It only takes time and it only needs confidence.

It is necessary to handle yourself better when you have to cut down on food so you will not get too much hunger-thinking. Hunger is good discipline and you learn from it. And as long as they do not understand it you are ahead of them. Oh sure, I thought, I'm so far ahead of them now that I can't afford to eat regularly. It would not be bad if they caught up a little.

I knew I must write a novel. But it seemed an impossible thing to do when I had been trying with great difficulty to write paragraphs that would be the distillation of what made a novel. It was necessary to write longer stories now as you would train for a longer race. When I had written a novel before, the one that had been lost in the bag stolen at the Gare de Lyon, I still had the lyric facility of boyhood that was as perishable and as deceptive as youth was. I knew it was probably a good thing that it was lost, but I knew too that I must write a novel. I would put it off though until I could not help doing it. I was damned if I would write one because it was what I should do if we were to eat regularly. When I had to write it, then it would be the only thing to do and there would be no choice. Let the pressure build. In the meantime I would write a long story about whatever I knew best.

By this time I had paid the check and gone out and turned to the right and crossed the rue de Rennes so that I would not go to the Deux-Magots for coffee and was walking up the rue Bonaparte on the shortest way home.

What did I know best that I had not written about and lost? What did I know about truly and care for the most? There was no choice at all. There was only the choice of streets to take you back fastest to where you worked. I went up Bonaparte to Guynemer, then to the rue d'Assas, up the rue Notre-Dame-des-Champs to the Closerie des Lilas.

I sat in a corner with the afternoon light coming in over my shoulder and wrote in the notebook. The waiter brought me a *café crème* and I drank half of it when it cooled and left it on the table while I wrote. When I stopped writing I did not want to leave the river where I could see the trout in the pool, its surface pushing and swelling smooth against the resistance of the log-driven piles of the bridge. The story was about coming back from the war but there was no mention of the war in it.

But in the morning the river would be there and I must make it and the country and all that would happen. There were days ahead to be doing that each day. No other thing mattered. In my pocket was the money from Germany so there was no problem. When that was gone some other money would come in.

All I must do now was stay sound and good in my head until morning when I would start to work again.

DISCUSSION QUESTIONS

1. Hemingway alternates in his references to himself between second person ("You got very hungry . . .") and first person ("I learned to understand Cezanne . . ."). Why do you suppose he uses second person at all? What effect does it help him create? Why does he then alternate?

2. Some readers feel that Hemingway's later prose (this selection is an example) displays so many of his stylistic affectations that it's almost a parody of his earlier groundbreaking work. What features of the "Hemingway style" does this selection display? Do you find them powerful, as some readers do, or irritating, as others do? Why?

3. One of the most remarked-upon features of Hemingway's style is its minimalistic suppression of important information, information that is only hinted at and must be discovered by the reader. As he puts it himself, his "new theory" was "that you could omit anything if you knew that you omitted and the omitted part would strengthen the story and make people feel something more than they understood." Later he mentions working on a story that is about "coming back from the war but there was no mention of the war in it." In the selection here, what information do you suspect Hemingway is omitting? What is he leaving you to guess at, and how are you guessing?

4. One theme of this selection is the poverty experienced by many writers. How does Hemingway discuss poverty and its advantages and disadvantages for a writer?

JAMES BALDWIN

Autobiographical Notes

James Baldwin (1924–1987) was a novelist, playwright, memoirist, social critic, and civil rights activist. His widely read novels include Go Tell It on the Mountain *(1953),* Giovanni's Room *(1956),* Another Country *(1962), and* If Beale Street Could Talk *(1974). The essays in* Notes of a Native Son *(1955) and* The Fire Next Time *(1963) taught America a new vocabulary for the discussion of race and insisted that his race be recognized as essential to his identity as a writer.*

I was born in Harlem thirty-one years ago. I began plotting novels at about the time I learned to read. The story of my childhood is the usual bleak fantasy, and we can dismiss it with the restrained observation that I certainly would not consider living it again. In those days my mother was given to the exasperating and mysterious habit of having babies. As they were born, I took them over with one hand and held a book with the other. The children probably suffered, though they have since been kind enough to deny it, and in this way I read *Uncle Tom's Cabin* and *A Tale of Two Cities* over and over and over again; in this way, in fact, I read just about everything I could get my hands on—except the Bible, probably because it was the only book I was encouraged to read. I must also confess that I wrote—a great deal—and my first professional triumph, in any case, the first effort of mine to be seen in print, occurred at the age of twelve or thereabouts, when a short story I had written about the Spanish revolution won some sort of prize in an extremely short-lived church newspaper. I remember the story was censored by the lady editor, though I don't remember why, and I was outraged.

Also wrote plays, and songs, for one of which I received a letter of congratulations from Mayor La Guardia, and poetry, about which the less said, the better.

My mother was delighted by all these goings-on, but my father wasn't; he wanted me to be a preacher. When I was fourteen I became a preacher, and when I was seventeen I stopped. Very shortly thereafter I left home. For God knows how long I struggled with the world of commerce and industry—I guess they would say they struggled with *me*—and when I was about twenty-one I had enough done of a novel to get a Saxton Fellowship. When I was twenty-two the fellowship was over, the novel turned out to be unsalable, and I started waiting on tables in a Village restaurant and writing book reviews—mostly, as it turned out, about the Negro problem, concerning which the color of my skin made me automatically an expert. Did another book, in company with photographer Theodore Pelatowski, about the store-front churches in Harlem. This book met exactly the same fate as my first—fellowship, but no sale. (It was a Rosenwald Fellowship.) By the time I was twenty-four I had decided to stop reviewing books about the Negro problem —which, by this time, was only slightly less horrible in print than it was in life— and I packed my bags and went to France, where I finished, God knows how, *Go Tell It on the Mountain.*

Any writer, I suppose, feels that the world into which he was born is nothing less than a conspiracy against the cultivation of his talent—which attitude certainly has a great deal to support it. On the other hand, it is only because the world looks on his talent with such a frightening indifference that the artist is compelled to make his talent important. So that any writer, looking back over even so short a span of time as I am here forced to assess, finds that the things which hurt him and the things which helped him cannot be divorced from each other; he could be helped in a certain way only because he was hurt in a certain way; and his help is simply to be enabled to move from one conundrum to the next—one is tempted to say that he moves from one disaster to the next. When one begins looking for influences one finds them by the score. I haven't thought much about my own, not enough anyway; I hazard that the King James Bible, the rhetoric of the store-front church, something ironic and violent and perpetually understated in Negro speech—and something of Dickens' love for bravura—have something to do with me today; but I wouldn't stake my life on it. Likewise, innumerable people have helped me in many ways; but finally, I suppose, the most difficult (and most rewarding) thing in my life has been the fact that I was born a Negro and was forced, therefore, to effect some kind of truce with this reality. (Truce, by the way, is the best one can hope for.)

One of the difficulties about being a Negro writer (and this is not special pleading, since I don't mean to suggest that he has it worse than anybody else) is that the Negro problem is written about so widely. The bookshelves groan under the weight of information, and everyone therefore considers himself informed. And this information, furthermore, operates usually (generally, popularly) to reinforce traditional attitudes. Of traditional attitudes there are only two—For or Against—and I, personally, find it difficult to say which attitude has caused me the most pain. I am speaking as a writer; from a social point of view I am perfectly aware that the change from ill-will to good-will, however motivated, however imperfect, however expressed, is better than no change at all.

But it is part of the business of the writer—as I see it—to examine attitudes, to go beneath the surface, to tap the source. From this point of view the Negro problem is nearly inaccessible. It is not only written about so widely; it is written about so badly. It is quite possible to say that the price a Negro pays for becoming articulate is to find himself, at length, with nothing to be articulate about. ("You taught me language," says Caliban to Prospero, "and my profit on't is I know how to curse.") Consider: the tremendous social activity that this problem generates imposes on whites and Negroes alike the necessity of looking forward, of working to bring about a better day. This is fine, it keeps the waters troubled; it is all, indeed, that has made possible the Negro's progress. Nevertheless, social affairs are not generally speaking the writer's prime concern, whether they ought to be or not; it is absolutely necessary that he establish between himself and these affairs a distance which will allow, at least, for clarity, so that before he can look forward in any meaningful sense, he must first be allowed to take a long look back. In the context of the Negro problem neither whites nor blacks, for excellent reasons of their own, have the faintest desire to look back; but I think that the past is all that makes the present coherent, and further, that the past will remain horrible for exactly as long as we refuse to assess it honestly.

I know, in any case, that the most crucial time in my own development came when I was forced to recognize that I was a kind of bastard of the West; when I followed the line of my past I did not find myself in Europe but in Africa. And this meant that in some subtle way, in a really profound way, I brought to Shakespeare, Bach, Rembrandt, to the stones of Paris, to the cathedral at Chartres, and to the Empire State Building, a special attitude. These were not really my creations, they did not contain my history; I might search in them in vain forever for any reflection of myself. I was an interloper; this was not my heritage. At the same time I had no other heritage which I could possibly hope to use—I had certainly been unfitted for the jungle or the tribe. I would have to appropriate these white centuries, I would have to make them mine—I would have to accept my special attitude, my special place in this scheme—otherwise I would have no place in *any* scheme. What was the most difficult was the fact that I was forced to admit something I had always hidden from myself, which the American Negro has had to hide from himself as the price of his public progress; that I hated and feared white people. This did not mean that I loved black people; on the contrary, I despised them, possibly because they failed to produce Rembrandt. In effect, I hated and feared the world. And this meant, not only that I thus gave the world an altogether murderous power over me, but also that in such a self-destroying limbo I could never hope to write.

One writes out of one thing only—one's own experience. Everything depends on how relentlessly one forces from this experience the last drop, sweet or bitter, it can possibly give. This is the only real concern of the artist, to recreate out of the disorder of life that order which is art. The difficulty then, for me, of being a Negro writer was the fact that I was, in effect, prohibited from examining my own experience too closely by the tremendous demands and the very real dangers of my social situation.

I don't think the dilemma outlined above is uncommon. I do think, since writers work in the disastrously explicit medium of language, that it goes a little way towards explaining why, out of the enormous resources of Negro speech and life, and despite the example of Negro music, prose written by Negroes has been generally speaking so pallid and so harsh. I have not written about being a Negro at such length because I expect that to be my only subject, but only because it was the gate I had to unlock before I could hope to write about anything else. I don't think that the Negro problem in America can be even discussed coherently without bearing in mind its context; its context being the history, traditions, customs, the moral assumptions and preoccupations of the country; in short, the general social fabric. Appearances to the contrary, no one in America escapes its effects and everyone in America bears some responsibility for it. I believe this the more firmly because it is the overwhelming tendency to speak of this problem as though it were a thing apart. But in the work of Faulkner, in the general attitude and certain specific passages in Robert Penn Warren, and, most significantly, in the advent of Ralph Ellison, one sees the beginnings—at least—of a more genuinely penetrating search. Mr. Ellison, by the way, is the first Negro novelist I have ever read to utilize in language, and brilliantly, some of the ambiguity and irony of Negro life.

About my interests: I don't know if I have any, unless the morbid desire to own a sixteen-millimeter camera and make experimental movies can be so classified. Otherwise, I love to eat and drink—it's my melancholy conviction that I've scarcely ever had enough to eat (this is because it's *impossible* to eat enough if you're worried about the next meal)—and I love to argue with people who do not disagree with me too profoundly, and I love to laugh. I do *not* like bohemia, or bohemians, I do not like people whose principal aim is pleasure, and I do not like people who are *earnest* about anything. I don't like people who like me because I'm a Negro; neither do I like people who find in the same accident grounds for contempt. I love America more than any other country in the world, and, exactly for this reason, I insist on the right to criticize her perpetually. I think all theories are suspect, that the finest principles may have to be modified, or may even be pulverized by the demands of life, and that one must find, therefore, one's own moral center and move through the world hoping that this center will guide one aright. I consider that I have many responsibilities but none greater than this: to last, as Hemingway says, and get my work done.

I want to be an honest man and a good writer.

DISCUSSION QUESTIONS

1. Baldwin says that, on the one hand, "any writer . . . feels that the world into which he was born is nothing less than a conspiracy against the cultivation of his talent," while on the other hand, "the things which hurt him and the things which helped him cannot be divorced from each other." What does Baldwin say "hurt" and "helped" him in his life, and in what ways?
2. What in Baldwin's life influenced the language with which he creates his fiction, and in what ways?
3. Baldwin discusses the expectations imposed on him as a "Negro writer" and the problems these expectations create for him as a writer. What are the expectations, and what problems do they create? Do you feel the weight of any

expectations on you as a writer because of perceptions about who you are or ought to be?

4. Baldwin's last line is, "I want to be an honest man and a good writer." Throughout the essay, he conflates who he is "as a man" and who he is "as a writer." How are the two identities intermingled?

VIRGINIA WOOLF

A Writer's Diary

Virginia Woolf (1882–1941), with her sister, the painter Vanessa Bell, was the center of the storied Bloomsbury group, whose members included novelist E. M. Forster, biographer Lytton Strachey, art critic Roger Fry, and economist Maynard Keynes. She is a monumental modern novelist who, together with James Joyce, D. H. Lawrence, William Faulkner, and Ernest Hemingway, experimented with form in ways that transformed the face of fiction. Her challenging novels include Jacob's Room *(1922),* Mrs. Dalloway *(1925),* To the Lighthouse *(1927),* Orlando *(1928), and* The Waves *(1931). Her book-length essays* A Room of One's Own *(1929) and* Three Guineas *(1938) are also widely read. She wrote hundreds of essays, reviews, and sketches that were collected into dozens of volumes after her death. She kept voluminous diaries detailing her day-to-day struggle to create fiction, and they offer invaluable insight into the insecurities and the triumphs of a working writer. These diary entries show Woolf worrying about critical reception of one book (the story collection* Monday or Tuesday) *as she struggles to finish another (the experimental novel* Jacob's Room*), then worrying about that book's reception as she begins still another (*Mrs. Dalloway*), and all the while reading literature classic and modern, writing reviews and articles, and managing the business of the Hogarth Press.*

Tuesday, March 1st [1921]

I am not satisfied that this book [*Jacob's Room*] is in a healthy way. Suppose one of my myriad changes of style is antipathetic to the material? or does my style remain fixed? To my mind it changes always. But no one notices. Nor can I give it a name myself. The truth is that I have an internal, automatic scale of values; which decides what I had better do with my time. It dictates "this half hour must be spent on Russian." "This must be given to Wordsworth." Or "Now I'd better darn my brown stockings." How I come by this code of values I don't know. Perhaps it's the legacy of puritan grandfathers. I suspect pleasure slightly. God knows. And the truth is also that writing, even here, needs screwing of the brain —not so much as Russian, but then half the time I learn Russian I look in the fire and think what I shall write tomorrow. Mrs. Flanders is in the orchard. If I were at Rodmell I should have thought it all out walking on the flats. I should be in fine writing trim. As it is Ralph,* Carrington† and Brett‡ have this moment gone; I'm dissipated; we dine and go out to the Guild. I can't settle as I should to think of Mrs. Flanders in the orchard.

Sunday, March 6th

Nessa approves of *Monday or Tuesday*—mercifully; and thus somewhat redeems it in my eyes. But I now wonder a little what the reviewers will make of it—this time next month. Let me try to prophesy. Well, *The Times* will be kindly, a little cautious. Mrs. Woolf, they will say, must beware of virtuosity. She must beware of obscurity. Her great natural gifts etc. . . . . She is at her best in the simple lyric, or in *Kew Gardens. An Unwritten Novel* is hardly a success. And as for *A Society,* though spirited, it is too one-sided. Still Mrs. Woolf can always be read with pleasure. Then, in the *Westminster, Pall Mall* and other serious evening papers I shall be treated very shortly with sarcasm. The general line will be that I am becoming too much in love with the sound of my own voice; not much in what I write; indecently affected; a disagreeable woman. The truth is, I expect, that I shan't get very much attention anywhere. Yet, I become rather well known.

Friday, April 8th. 10 minutes to 11 a.m.

And I ought to be writing *Jacob's Room;* and I can't, and instead I shall write down the reason why I can't—this diary being a kindly blankfaced old confidante. Well, you see, I'm a failure as a writer. I'm out of fashion: old: shan't do any better: have no headpiece: the spring is everywhere: my book [*Monday or Tuesday*] out (prematurely) and nipped, a damp firework. Now the solid grain of fact is that Ralph sent my book out to *The Times* for review without date of publication in it. Thus a short notice is scrambled through to be in "on Monday at latest," put in an obscure place, rather scrappy, complimentary enough, but quite unintelligent. I mean by that they don't see that I'm after something interesting. So that makes me suspect that I'm not. And thus I can't get on with *Jacob.* . . .

Well, this question of praise and fame must be faced. (I forgot to say that Doran has refused the book in America.) How much difference does popularity make? (I'm putting clearly, I may add, after a pause in which Lottie has brought in the milk and the sun has ceased to eclipse itself, that I'm writing a good deal of nonsense.) One wants, as Roger said very truly yesterday, to be kept up to the mark; that people should be interested and watch one's work. What depresses me is the thought that I have ceased to interest people—at the very moment when, by the help of the press, I thought I was becoming more myself. One does *not* want an established reputation, such as I think I was getting, as one of our leading female novelists. I have still, of course, to gather in all the private criticism, which is the real test. When I have weighed this I shall be able to say whether I am

---

*Ralph Partridge.
†Mrs. Partridge.
‡Dorothy Brett.

"interesting" or obsolete. Anyhow, I feel quite alert enough to stop, if I'm obsolete. I shan't become a machine, unless a machine for grinding articles. As I write, there rises somewhere in my head that queer and very pleasant sense of something which I want to write; my own point of view. I wonder, though, whether this feeling that I write for half a dozen instead of 1500 will pervert this?—make me eccentric—no, I think not. But, as I said, one must face the despicable vanity which is at the root of all this niggling and haggling. I think the only prescription for me is to have a thousand interests—if one is damaged, to be able instantly to let my energy flow into Russian, or Greek, or the press, or the garden, or people, or some activity disconnected with my own writing.

Sunday, April 9th

I must note the symptoms of the disease, so as to know it next time. The first day one's miserable; the second happy. There was an Affable Hawk* on me in the *New Statesman* which at any rate made me feel important (and it's that that one wants) and Simpkin Marshall rang up for a second fifty copies. So they must be selling. Now I have to stand all the twitching and teasing of private criticism which I shan't enjoy. There'll be Roger tomorrow. What a bore it all is!—and then one begins to wish one had put in other stories and left out the *Haunted House,* which may be sentimental.

Tuesday, April 12th

I must hurriedly note more symptoms of the disease, so that I can turn back here and medicine myself next time. Well; I'd worn through the acute stage and come to the philosophic semi-depressed, indifferent, spent the afternoon taking parcels round the shops, going to Scotland Yard for my purse, when L. [Woolf's husband Leonard] met me at tea and dropped into my ear the astonishing news that Lytton thinks the *String Quartet* "marvellous." This came through Ralph, who doesn't exaggerate, to whom Lytton [Strachey] need not lie; and did for a moment flood every nerve with pleasure, so much so that I forgot to buy my coffee and walked over Hungerford Bridge twanging and vibrating. A lovely blue evening too, the river sky colour. And then there was Roger [Fry] who thinks I'm on the track of real discoveries and certainly not a fake. And we've broken the record of sales, so far. And I'm not nearly so pleased as I was depressed; and yet in a state of security; fate cannot touch me; the reviewers may snap; and the sales decrease. What I had feared was that I was dismissed as negligible.

Friday, June 23rd [1922]

Jacob, as I say, is being typed by Miss Green, and crosses the Atlantic on July 14th. Then will begin my season of doubts and ups and downs. I am guarding myself in this way. I am going to be well on with a story for Eliot, lives for Squire, and *Reading;* so that I can vary the side of the pillow as fortune inclines. If they say this is all a clever experiment, I shall produce *Mrs. Dalloway* in Bond Street as

---

*Desmond MacCarthy's pseudonym.

the finished product. If they say your fiction is impossible, I shall say what about Miss Ormerod, a fantasy. If they say "You can't make us care a damn for any of your figures," I shall say read my criticism then. Now what *will* they say about *Jacob?* Mad, I suppose: a disconnected rhapsody; I don't know. I will confide my view to this book on re-reading. On re-reading novels is the title of a very laborious, yet rather gifted article, for the *Supt.*

Wednesday, July 26th

On Sunday L. read through *Jacob's Room.* He thinks it my best work. But his first remark was that it was amazingly well written. We argued about it. He calls it a work of genius; he thinks it unlike any other novel; he says that the people are ghosts; he says it is very strange: I have no philosophy of life he says; my people are puppets, moved hither and thither by fate. He doesn't agree that fate works in this way. Thinks I should use my "method" on one or two characters next time; and he found it very interesting and beautiful, and without lapse (save perhaps the party) and quite intelligible. Pocky has so disturbed my mind that I cannot write this as formally as it deserves, for I was anxious and excited. But I am on the whole pleased. Neither of us knows what the public will think. There's no doubt in my mind that I have found out how to begin (at 40) to say something in my own voice; and that interests me so that I feel I can go ahead without praise.

Wednesday, August 16th

I should be reading *Ulysses,* and fabricating my case for and against. I have read 200 pages so far—not a third; and have been amused, stimulated, charmed, interested, by the first 2 or 3 chapters—to the end of the cemetery scene; and then puzzled, bored, irritated and disillusioned by a queasy undergraduate scratching his pimples. And Tom [T. S. Eliot], great Tom, thinks this on a par with *War and Peace!* An illiterate, underbred book it seems to me; the book of a self taught working man, and we all know how distressing they are, how egotistic, insistent, raw, striking, and ultimately nauseating. When one can have the cooked flesh, why have the raw? But I think if you are anaemic, as Tom is, there is a glory in blood. Being fairly normal myself I am soon ready for the classics again. I may revise this later. I do not compromise my critical sagacity. I plant a stick in the ground to mark page 200.

For my own part I am laboriously dredging my mind for *Mrs. Dalloway* and bringing up light buckets. I don't like the feeling. I'm writing too quickly. I must press it together. I wrote 4 thousand words of *Reading* in record time, 10 days; but then it was merely a quick sketch of Pastons, supplied by books. Now I break off, according to my quick change theory, to write *Mrs. D.* (who ushers in a host of others, I begin to perceive). Then I do Chaucer; and finish the first chapter early in September. By that time, I have my Greek beginning perhaps, in my head; and so the future is all pegged out; and when *Jacob* is rejected in America and ignored in England, I shall be philosophically driving my plough fields away. They are cutting the corn all over the country, which supplies that metaphor, and perhaps excuses it. But I need no excuses, since I am not writing for the *Lit. Sup.* Shall I ever write for them again?

Tuesday, August 22nd

The way to rock oneself back into writing is this. First gentle exercise in the air. Second the reading of good literature. It is a mistake to think that literature can be produced from the raw. One must get out of life—yes, that's why I disliked so much the irruption of Sydney—one must become externalised; very, very concentrated, all at one point, not having to draw upon the scattered parts of one's character, living in the brain. Sydney comes and I'm Virginia; when I write I'm merely a sensibility. Sometimes I like being Virginia, but only when I'm scattered and various and gregarious. Now, so long as we are here, I'd like to be only a sensibility. By the way, Thackeray is good reading, very vivacious, with "touches" as they call them over the way at the Shanks', of astonishing insight.

Monday, August 28th

I am beginning Greek again, and must really make out some plan: today 28th: *Mrs. Dalloway* finished on Saturday 2nd Sept.: Sunday 3rd to Friday 8th; start Chaucer. Chaucer—that chapter, I mean, should be finished by Sept. 22nd. And then? Shall I write the next chapter of *Mrs. D.*—if she is to have a next chapter; and shall it be *The Prime Minister*? which will last till the week after we get back—say October 12th. Then I must be ready to start my Greek chapter. So I have from today, 28th, till 12th—which is just over 6 weeks—but I must allow for some interruptions. Now what have I to read? Some Homer: one Greek play: some Plato: Zimmern: Shepphard, as textbook: Bentley's Life: if done thoroughly, this will be enough. But which Greek play? and how about Homer, and what Plato? Then there's the anthology. All to end upon the Odyssey because of the Elizabethans. And I must read a little Ibsen to compare with Euripides—Racine with Sophocles—perhaps Marlowe with Aeschylus. Sounds very learned; but really might amuse me; and if it doesn't, no need to go on.

Wednesday, September 6th

My proofs* come every other day and I could depress myself adequately if I went into that. The thing now reads thin and pointless; the words scarcely dint the paper; and I expect to be told I've written a graceful fantasy, without much bearing upon real life. Can one tell? Anyhow, nature obligingly supplies me with the illusion that I am about to write something good; something rich and deep and fluent, and hard as nails, while bright as diamonds.

I finished *Ulysses* and think it a mis-fire. Genius it has, I think; but of the inferior water. The book is diffuse. It is brackish. It is pretentious. It is underbred, not only in the obvious sense, but in the literary sense. A first rate writer, I mean, respects writing too much to be tricky; startling; doing stunts. I'm reminded all the time of some callow board school boy, full of wits and powers, but so self-conscious and egotistical that he loses his head, becomes extravagant, mannered, uproarious, ill at ease, makes kindly people feel sorry for him and stern ones merely annoyed; and one hopes he'll grow out of it; but as Joyce is 40 this

---

*Of *Jacob's Room*.

scarcely seems likely. I have not read it carefully; and only once; and it is very obscure; so no doubt I have scamped the virtue of it more than is fair. I feel that myriads of tiny bullets pepper one and spatter one; but one does not get one deadly wound straight in the face—as from Tolstoy, for instance; but it is entirely absurd to compare him with Tolstoy.

Thursday, September 7th

Having written this, L. put into my hands a very intelligent review of *Ulysses,* in the American *Nation;* which, for the first time, analyses the meaning; and certainly makes it very much more impressive than I judged. Still I think there is virtue and some lasting truth in first impressions; so I don't cancel mine. I must read some of the chapters again. Probably the final beauty of writing is never felt by contemporaries; but they ought, I think, to be bowled over; and this I was not. Then again, I had my back up on purpose; then again I was over stimulated by Tom's praises.

Wednesday, October 4th

I am a little uppish, though, and self assertive, because Brace wrote to me yesterday, "We think *Jacob's Room* an extraordinarily distinguished and beautiful work. You have, of course, your own method, and it is not easy to foretell how many readers it will have; surely it will have enthusiastic ones, and we delight in publishing it," or words to that effect. As this is my first testimony from an impartial person I am pleased. For one thing it must make *some* impression, as a whole; and cannot be wholly frigid fireworks. We think of publishing on October 27th. I daresay Duckworth is a little cross with me. I snuff my freedom. It is I think true, soberly and not artificially for the public, that I shall go on unconcernedly whatever people say. At last, I like reading my own writing. It seems to me to fit me closer than it did before. I have done my task here better than I expected. *Mrs. Dalloway* and the Chaucer chapter are finished: I have read 5 books of the Odyssey; *Ulysses;* and now begin Proust. I also read Chaucer and the Pastons. So evidently my plan of the two books running side by side is practicable and certainly I enjoy my reading with a purpose. I am committed to only one *Supt.* article—on essays—and that at my own time; so I am free. I shall read Greek now steadily and begin *The Prime Minister* on Friday morning. I shall read the Trilogy and some Sophocles and Euripides and a Plato dialogue: also the lives of Bentley and Jebb. At forty I am beginning to learn the mechanism of my own brain—how to get the greatest amount of pleasure and work out of it. The secret is I think always so to contrive that work is pleasant.

Saturday, October 14th

I have had two letters, from Lytton and Carrington, about *Jacob's Room,* and written I don't know how many envelopes; and here we are on the verge of publication. I must sit for my portrait to *John o' London's* on Monday. Richmond writes to ask that date of publication may be put ahead, so that they may notice it on Thursday. My sensations? they remain calm. Yet how could Lytton have praised me more highly? prophesies immortality for it as poetry; is afraid of my romance; but the beauty of the writing, etc. Lytton praises me too highly for it to give me exquisite pleasure; or perhaps that nerve grows dulled. I want to be through the splash and swimming in calm water again. I want to be writing unobserved. *Mrs. Dalloway* has branched into a book; and I adumbrate here a study of insanity and suicide; the world seen by the sane and the insane side by side— something like that. Septimus Smith? is that a good name? and to be more close to the fact than *Jacob:* but I think *Jacob* was a necessary step, for me, in working free. . . .

As for my views about the success of *Jacob,* what are they? I think we shall sell 500; it will then go slowly and reach 800 by June. It will be highly praised in some places for "beauty"; will be crabbed by people who want human character. The only review I am anxious about is the one in the *Supt:* not that it will be the most intelligent, but it will be the most read and I can't bear people to see me clowned in public. The *W.G.** will be hostile; so, very likely, the *Nation.* But I am perfectly serious in saying that nothing budges me from my determination to go on, or alters my pleasure; so whatever happens, though the surface may be agitated, the centre is secure.

Tuesday, October 17th

As this is to be a chart of my progress I enter hastily here: one, a letter from Desmond [MacCarthy] who is halfway through, says "You have never written so well . . . I marvel and am puzzled"—or words to that effect: two, Bunny† rings up enthusiastic; says it is superb, far my best, has great vitality and importance: also he takes 36 copies, and says people already "clamour." This is not confirmed by the bookshops, visited by Ralph. I have sold under 50 today; but the libraries remain and Simpkin Marshall.

Sunday, October 29th

Miss Mary Butts being gone, and my head too stupid for reading, I may as well write here, for my amusement later perhaps. I mean I'm too riddled with talk and harassed with the usual worry of people who like and people who don't like *J.R.* to concentrate. There was *The Times* review on Thursday—long, a little tepid, I think—saying that one can't make characters in this way; flattering enough. Of course, I had a letter from Morgan in the opposite sense—the letter I've liked best of all. We have sold 650, I think; and have ordered a second edition. My sensations? as usual—mixed. I shall never write a book that is an entire success. This time the reviews are against me and the private people enthusiastic. Either I am a great writer or a nincompoop. "An elderly sensualist," the *Daily News* calls me. *Pall Mall* passes me over as negligible. I expect to be neglected and sneered at. And what will be the fate of our second thousand then? So far of course the success is much more than we expected. I think I am better pleased so

---

* *Westminster Gazette.*
†David Garnett.

far than I have ever been. Morgan, Lytton, Bunny, Violet, Logan,* Philip,† have all written enthusiastically. But I want to be quit of all this. It hangs about me like Mary Butts' scent. I don't want to be totting up compliments, and comparing reviews. I want to think out *Mrs. Dalloway.* I want to foresee this book better than the others and get the utmost out of it. I expect I could have screwed *Jacob* up tighter, if I had foreseen; but I had to make my path as I went.

DISCUSSION QUESTIONS

1. Though she had her critics, Woolf at the time she was writing these passages in her diary was a well-known and well-respected writer. In spite of her success, what worries did she continue to have about her writing and its reception?
2. In the passages from April 9 and April 12, Woolf writes about "the symptoms of the disease." What does she mean? What is "the disease," and what are its "symptoms"?
3. Woolf was notoriously competitive with other writers. What was her objection to Joyce's *Ulysses*?
4. What might Woolf mean when she says (on August 22), "It is a mistake to think that literature can be produced from the raw. One must get out of life . . ."?
5. If you have read either of the novels Woolf mentions here, *Jacob's Room* and *Mrs. Dalloway,* how does her explanation of how she worked on them illuminate the book in any way for you?

---

*Logan Pearsall Smith.
†Philip Morrell.

BERNARD MALAMUD

Long Work, Short Life*

Bernard Malamud (1914–1986) wrote some of the most enduring American fiction of the twentieth century, including the short story collections The Magic Barrel *(1958) and* Rembrandt's Hat *(1973) and the novels* The Natural *(1952),* The Assistant *(1957),* A New Life *(1961),* The Fixer *(1966), and* Dubin's Lives *(1979). He received countless honors, including a National Book Award and a Pulitzer Prize. In writing about his own writing life, he is typically laconic, ironic, and powerful.*

I intend to say something about my life as a writer. Since I shan't go into a formal replay of the life, this will read more like a selective short memoir.

The beginning was slow, and perhaps not quite a beginning. Some beginnings promise a start that may take years to induce a commencement. Before the first word strikes the page, or the first decent idea occurs, there is the complicated matter of breaking the silence. Some throw up before they can breathe. Not all can run to the door at the knock of announcement—granted one hears it. Not all know what it means. Simply, not always is the gift of talent given free and clear. Some who are marvelously passionate to write may have to spend half their lives learning what their proper subject matter may be.

Not even geniuses know themselves in their youth. For years Emily Dickinson was diverted from her poetry by men she felt she loved, until one day she drew the shutters in her sunlit room and sat in loneliness at her table. She had at last unearthed a way of beginning. Those who loved her appeared in her home from time to time, perhaps less to love than to cause her to write her wondrous poems of intricate feeling and intricate love.

I began to write at an early age, yet it took me years actually to begin writing. Much diverted me. As a child I told stories for praise. I went for inspiration to the

---

*This memoir was originally delivered at Bennington College, in the Ben Belitt Lectureship Series, on October 13, 1984, and thereafter published in a limited edition as one of The Bennington Chapbooks in Literature, 1985.

movies. I remember my mother delivering me, against her will, on a wet Sunday, to a movie house to see Charlie Chaplin, whose comedy haunted my soul. After being at the pictures I recounted their plots to school friends who would listen at dreadfully long length as I retold them. The pleasure, in the beginning, was in retelling the impossible tale.

When I overcontrived or otherwise spoiled a plot, I would substitute another of my own. I could on occasion be a good little liar who sometimes found it a burden to tell the truth. Once my father called me a "bluffer," enraging me because I had meant to tell him a simple story, not one that had elaborated itself into a lie.

In grammar school, where I lived in a state of self-enhancing discovery, I turned school assignments into stories. Once I married off Roger Williams in Rhode Island to an Indian maiden, mainly because I had worked up an early feeling for the romantic. When I was ten, I wrote a story about a ship lost in the Sargasso Sea. The vessel appeared in dreams, about to undertake a long voyage in stagnant seas. This sort of thing, to begin with, was the nature of my "gift" as a child, that I had awakened to one day, and it remained with me many years before I began to use it well. Throughout my life I struggled to define it, and to write with originality. However, once it had pointed at me and signaled the way, it kept me going even when I wasn't writing. For years it was a blessing that could bleed as a wound.

Thus began an era of long waiting.

I had hoped to start writing short stories after graduation from City College during the depression, but they were long in coming. I had ideas and felt I was on the verge of sustained work. But at that time I had no regular means of earning a living; and as the son of a poor man, a poor grocer, I could not stand the thought of living off him, a generous and self-denying person. However, I thought the writing would take care of itself once I found steady work. I needed decent clothes; I would dream of new suits. Any work I found would make life different, I thought, and I could begin writing day or night. Yet I adamantly would not consider applying, in excess of pride, to the WPA. Years later, I judged that to have been a foolish act, or non-act.

I considered various things I might do to have time for writing, like getting up at 5:00 A.M. to work for an hour or two each morning before hitting the dreadful Sixth Avenue agencies in Manhattan to scrounge around for jobs. More often than not there were none, especially for someone with no work experience. And where there was no work there were no words.

The Second World War had begun in 1939. I was born at the beginning of the First World War, in 1914. The Second was being called "The Phony War." The French and German armies sat solemnly, eyeing each other over the Maginot Line, yet almost not moving except for night forays. No one seemed about to launch a major attack. Neville Chamberlain, after Munich, was on his way out. He had rolled up his umbrella and was hastening away from the frightful future; Churchill came to power and was eloquently growling that Britain would never be conquered. Possibly diplomacy was in progress. Perhaps there would be no renewed conflict. Many Americans seemed to think the threat of war might expire. Many of us hoped so, though hoping was hard work; nor did it make too much sense, given the aberrations of Adolf Hitler. We worried about the inevitable world war but tried not to think of it.

Often young writers do not truly know what is happening in their lives and world. They know and they don't know. They are not sure what, in essence, is going on and are years in learning. Recently I was reading Ernst Pawel's book of the life of Kafka, and the author speaks of Kafka's "all-encompassing goal in which the writer searches for his own truth." Truth or no truth, I felt the years go by without accomplishment. Occasionally I wrote a short story that no one bought. I called myself a writer though I had no true subject matter. Yet from time to time I sat at a table and wrote, although it took years for my work to impress me.

By now I had registered at Columbia University for an M.A. in English, on a government loan. The work was not demanding. I told myself what I was doing was worthwhile; for no one who spends his nights and days devoted to great works of literature will be wasting his time as a writer, if he is passionate to write.

But when did I expect to begin writing?

My answer was unchanged: when I found a job that would support my habit: the self's enduring needs. I registered for a teachers' examination and afterwards worked a year at $4.50 a day as a teacher-in-training in a high school in Brooklyn. I was also applying for, and took, several civil service examinations, including those leading to jobs of postal clerk and letter carrier. This is mad, I thought, or I am. Yet I told myself the kind of work I might get didn't matter so long as I was working for time to write. Throughout these unsatisfying years, writing was still my gift and persuasion.

It was now four years after my graduation from college, but the four felt like fifty when I was counting. However, in the spring of 1940 I was offered work in Washington, D.C., as a clerk in the Census Bureau. I accepted at once, though I soon realized the "work" was a laugh. All morning I conscientiously checked estimates of drainage ditch statistics as they appeared in various counties of the United States. Although the job hardly thrilled me, I worked diligently and was promoted, at the end of three months, to receive a salary of $1,800 per annum. That, in those times, was "good money." What was better was that I had begun to write seriously on company time. No one seemed to care what I was doing so long as the record showed I had finished a full day's work; therefore, after lunchtime I kept my head bent low while I was writing short stories at my desk.

At about this time I wrote a piece for the *Washington Post,* mourning the fall of France after the German Army had broken through the Maginot Line and was obscenely jubilant in conquered Paris. I felt unhappy, as though mourning the death of a civilization I loved; yet somehow I managed to celebrate ongoing life and related acts.

Although my writing seemed less than inspiring to me, I stayed with it and tried to breathe into it fresh life and beauty, hoping that the gift was still in my possession, if by some magic act I could see life whole. And though I was often lonely, I stayed in the rooming house night after night trying to invent stories I needn't be ashamed of.

One night, after laboring in vain for hours attempting to bring a short story to life, I sat up in bed at an open window looking at the stars after a rainfall. Then I experienced a wave of feeling, of heartfelt emotion bespeaking commitment to life and art, so deeply it brought tears to my eyes. For the hundredth time I promised myself that I would someday be a very good writer. This renewal, and others like it, kept me alive in art years from fulfillment. I must have been about twenty-five then, and was still waiting, in my fashion, for the true writing life to begin. I'm reminded of Kafka's remark in his midtwenties: "God doesn't want me to write, but I must write."

There were other matters to consider. What about marriage—should I, shouldn't I? I sometimes felt that the young writers I knew were too much concerned with staying out of marriage, whereas they might have used it, among other things, to order their lives and get on with their work. I wondered whether I could make it a necessary adjunct of my writing. But marriage was not easy: wouldn't it hurt my career if I urged on myself a way of life I could hardly be sure of? One has his gift—the donnée—therefore he'd better protect it from those who seem to be without a compelling purpose in life. Many young women I met had no clear idea what they wanted to do with their lives. If such a woman became a writer's wife, would she, for instance, know what was going on in his thoughts as he worked in his sleep? Would she do her part in keeping the family going? I was often asking myself these and related questions—though not necessarily of someone who might answer them. And I was spending too much time being in love, as an uneasy way of feeling good when I wasn't writing. I needed someone to love and live with, but I wasn't going out of my way to find her.

Meanwhile, I had nailed down an evening-school job in September of 1940; I then completed an M.A. thesis and began to think of writing a novel. By now I had finished about a dozen stories, a few of which began to appear in university quarterlies. One of these, "The Place Is Different Now," was the forerunner of *The Assistant*. And a novel I had started while I was teaching in Erasmus Hall Evening High School in Brooklyn was called *The Light Sleeper*. It was completed but not sold. Later, I burned it one night in Oregon because I felt I could do better. My son, who was about four at that time, watched me burning the book. As we looked at the sparks fly upward I was telling him about death; but he denied the concept.

Several years before that, not long after Pearl Harbor, while I was teaching at night and writing this novel, I met a warm, pretty young woman at a party. I was told she was of Italian descent and lived in a hotel with her mother and stepfather, who was a musician. I observed my future wife for a while before we talked.

Soon we began to meet. Some nights she would come to Flatbush to watch me teach. We ate at Sears, or Oetgen's, and sometimes walked across the Parade Grounds to my room. We wrote each other during the week. Her letters were intense and witty, revealing an informed interest in politics and literature; in love and marriage. After the death of my own mother, I had had a stepmother and a thin family life; my wife, the child of a woman divorced young, had experienced a richer cultural life than I. And since we both wanted children we wondered how we would fare in a mixed marriage. She had been Catholic. I defined myself as Jewish.

Life in New York City was not easy or pleasant during the Second World War. Our friends Rose and James Lechay, the painter, had rented a small walk-up flat on King Street, in the Village, which we took over when they went off to live in Iowa, Jim to take Grant Wood's place as professor of painting at the university. After we were married, we both continued working until my wife was pregnant. I taught day and evening classes, with practically no time to write. A few years later I left the evening high school and spent a year teaching in Harlem, incidentally picking up ideas for short stories like "Black Is My Favorite Color," before we decided to go west. I had now received an offer to teach at Oregon State College though I had no Ph.D. degree. In 1949, when my son was two, we moved to Corvallis, Oregon, where I taught three days a week and wrote four. In my own eyes I had become seriously a writer earning his living, though certainly not from his writing.

I think I discovered the Far West and some subject matter of my earlier fiction at almost the same time, an interesting conjunction, in imagination, of Oregon and the streets of New York. One's fantasy goes for a walk and returns with a bride.

During my first year at Oregon State I wrote *The Natural,* begun before leaving New York City. Baseball had interested me, especially its comic aspects, but I wasn't able to write about the game until I transformed game into myth via Jessie Weston's Percival legend with an assist by T. S. Eliot's "The Waste Land" plus the lives of several ballplayers I had read, in particular Babe Ruth's and Bobby Feller's. The myth enriched the baseball lore as feats of magic transformed the game.

Soon we were making plans to go abroad. We had wanted to go earlier but could not afford it until we experienced the fortunate coincidence of a sabbatical leave from Oregon State with a *Partisan Review*–Rockefeller Foundation grant.

We left in late August 1956 for Italy. On board the SS *Constitution* I spent hours studying the horizon, enjoying the sight of ocean as the beginning of more profound adventure, amid thoughts of new writing. One night we passed our sister ship, the SS *America,* steaming along in the mid-Atlantic, all decks alight. I felt I was on the verge of a long celebration.

Previously, my wife had been abroad twice, once at age eight, for a year in Italy, and at another time for her college junior year, in France.

I was ready for a broader kind of living with as much range in writing as I could manage. Before leaving Oregon to go abroad, I had completed *The Assistant,* and had begun to develop several of the stories that became *The Magic Barrel,* some of which I wrote in Rome.

Italy unrolled like a foreign film; what was going on before my eyes seemed close to unreality. An ancient city seemed to be alive in present time. It was larger than life, yet defined itself as our new life. I felt the need to live in a world that was more than my world to live in. I walked all over the city. I walked in the ghetto. I met Italian Jews who had been tortured by the Nazis; one man held up his hand to show his finger-shorn fist. I felt I was too much an innocent American. I wandered along Roman streets and studied Roman faces, hoping to see what they saw when they looked; I wanted to know more of what they seemed to know. On All Souls', I walked in the Campo Verano cemetery. I visited the Ardeatine Caves where the Nazis had slaughtered Italians and Jews. Rome had its own sad way of sharing Jewish experience.

Mornings I walked my eight-year-old son to Piazza Bologna where he took his bus to the American school. At noon, after finishing my morning's work, I picked up my four-year-old daughter at her kindergarten. She would hand me her drawings as we walked home. Home was 88 Via Michelo Di Lando, not far from where Mussolini had lived with Clara Petacci, his mistress. We had made friends of our landlords. Mr. Gianolla was an old Socialist who had been forced to swallow castor oil by Mussolini's fascist thugs. His wife, thin and energetic, talkative, courteous, was one of the rare women university graduates of her time.

I returned to Oregon to an improved situation after our year abroad. From a teacher of freshman grammar and technical report writing, I was transformed into a teacher of English literature, as though a new talent had been discovered in a surprised self. What had happened was that the two gentlemen who administered the English department had heard I was acquiring a small reputation as a serious writer of fiction, and therefore I was no longer required to teach composition only, but might be allowed, even without a doctoral degree, to teach unsuspecting sophomores a little poetry, with even a touch of Shakespeare in the night. For this relief I gave happy thanks.

Let me, at this point, say a short word about the yeas and nays of a writer teaching what is called Creative Writing. I have done it because I teach decently well, but I wouldn't recommend that anyone devote his life to teaching writing if he takes little pleasure in informing others. Elsewhere I've said about teaching creative writing that one ought to keep in mind he is not so much teaching the art of imaginative writing as he is encouraging people with talent how to work as writers. Writing courses are of limited value, although in certain cases they may encourage young writers to read good fiction with the care it deserves. However, I think about a year of these courses should be enough for any serious student. Thereafter writing must become a way of life.

When my Western-born daughter appeared, my father sent us $350 for a washing machine. Once when I was twenty, he trudged up the hall stairs from his grocery store one morning. I had a summer cold and was stretched out in bed. I had been looking for a job without success. My father reached for my foot and grasped it with his hand.

"I wish it was me with that cold instead of you."

What does a writer need most? When I ask the question, I think of my father.

I had already begun to receive literary awards. It seemed to me that I did nothing to get them other than stay at the writing table, and the prizes would mysteriously appear. One day I had a phone call from New York. My publisher, Roger Straus, asked me whether I was sitting down. I said I was. He told me I had just won the National Book Award for *The Magic Barrel.*

I must know how to write, I told myself, almost surprised.

I was in a happy mood when I began to work on *A New Life,* my fourth book. Once, at Yaddo, while I was writing it, a visitor knocked at my door. I had just written something that moved me. He saw my wet eyes. I told him I was enjoying writing my book. Later the legend grew that I had wept my way through it.

During my early years at Oregon State I had gone nowhere, with the exception of our trip abroad, and a ten-day visit to Montana, when Leslie Fiedler was there in the 1950s. He had sent me a copy of an article he had published in *Folio,* in Indiana. His was the first appreciation of *The Natural* that I had read by someone who knew how to read. Fiedler was always *sui generis,* but on the whole generous in his judgment of my work. I shan't forget that he appreciated the quality of my imaginative writing before anyone else wrote about it. That was long before Robert Redford, in his sad hat of failure, appeared on the scene, socking away at a ball that went up in the lights.

Not long after our return to Corvallis from Italy, I had a telephone call from Howard Nemerov at Bennington College, where I was invited to teach a year. I was glad to go. After our year abroad, stimulated by the life and art I had seen, I wasn't very patient with my experience in a small town, though my wife, after a difficult start, now enjoyed her Western life. I seized the opportunity to return to the East. She would have liked living in San Francisco, but there were no job offers. So we traveled to Vermont by way of Harvard Summer School, where I substituted for Albert Guérard. When the class filled quickly, someone at Harvard asked John Hawkes, the novelist at Brown University, to teach a second section of the course. Before long we were walking together in Cambridge streets, talking about fiction. Hawkes is a gallant man and imaginative writer. His work should be better known than it is.

In September 1961, my wife and I arrived with our kids in Bennington, Vermont. The college, an unusual place to work and learn, soon became a continuing source of education for me. My teachers were my new colleagues: Howard Nemerov, poet and faithful friend; Stanley Edgar Hyman, a unique scholar and fine critic; and Ben Belitt, a daring, original poet and excellent teacher—from all of whom I learned. My other teachers were my students, whom I taught to teach me.

Stanley Hyman reminded me of Leslie Fiedler in more ways than one. They both knew a great deal about literature, and neither found it difficult to say what. Hyman was an excellent theoretician of myth and literature. His humor kept him young and so did his appetite. Once my wife and I invited him and his wife, the writer Shirley Jackson, to a restaurant, to help us celebrate our wedding anniversary. Stanley ordered the champagne. He and Shirley lived hard, and—I think they thought—well; and almost did not regret dying young. Flannery O'Connor once described them as two large people in a small car, when they came to call on her in Milledgeville, Georgia. She showed them her peacocks.

When I think of Hyman as a critic of literature, what stands out was his honesty of self and standards. One of his favorite words was *standards,* and you weren't in his league if you didn't know what he meant. He defined and explicated. He was proud of what he knew, though I remember his saying, speaking of himself, "knowledge is not wisdom." He enjoyed the fun of wit, merriment, poker, horseplay, continuous laughter. He died young.

Before I come to the end of this casual memoir, perhaps I ought to say that I served as president of American PEN (Poets, Editors, and Novelists) from 1979 to 1981. PEN had come to life in 1921 as an international organization founded in London by John Galsworthy, the British novelist and dramatist. Basically, PEN brings together writers from all over the world to meet as a fraternity, to foster literature, and to defend the written word wherever threatened.

When I was president, I began to deal more frequently with publishers after the difficult period that followed a time of consolidation in the book industry. The consolidation I refer to was not always helpful to those who wrote, and much remains to be done to improve the situation of writers, dealing in whatever way with their own publishers.

Though my publisher is a good one, I fear that too many of them are much more concerned with making money than with publishing good books that will seriously influence generations of writers in the future. Stanley Hyman had preached standards, but one tendency in publishing today is that standards are forgotten. I can't tell you how badly some books are edited these days; one excuse given is "We can't afford too much time on one book. We've got to make our profit." I'm all for profit from the work of writers, but the simple fact is that we have begun to pay more in a loss of quality in publishing than our culture can afford. Happily, many people of good will, dissatisfied with present-day publishing, are trying to find new ways to improve the industry. And some of the new presses that have begun to publish are quite good, a few even daring.

If I may, I would at this point urge young writers not to be too much concerned with the vagaries of the marketplace. Not everyone can make a first-rate living as a writer, but a writer who is serious and responsible about his work, and life, will probably find a way to earn a decent living, if he or she writes well. And there's great pleasure in writing, if one writes well. A good writer will be strengthened by his good writing at a time, let us say, of the resurgence of ignorance in our culture. I think I have been saying that the writer must never compromise with what is best in him in a world defined as free.

I have written almost all my life. My writing has drawn, out of a reluctant soul, a measure of astonishment at the nature of life. And the more I wrote well, the better I felt I had to write.

In writing I had to say what had happened to me, yet present it as though it had been magically revealed. I began to write seriously when I had taught myself the discipline necessary to achieve what I wanted. When I touched that time, my words announced themselves to me. I have given my life to writing without regret, except when I consider what in my work I might have done better. I wanted my writing to be as good as it must be, and on the whole I think it is. I would write a book or a short story at least three times—once to understand it, the second time to improve the prose, and a third to compel it to say what it still must say.

Somewhere I put it this way: first drafts are for learning what one's fiction wants him to say. Revision works with that knowledge to enlarge and enhance an idea, to re-form it. Revision is one of the exquisite pleasures of writing: "The men and things of today are wont to lie fairer and truer in tomorrow's meadow," Henry Thoreau said.

I don't regret the years I put into my work. Perhaps I regret the fact that I was not two men, one who could live a full life apart from writing; and one who lived in art, exploring all he had to experience and know how to make his work right; yet not regretting that he had put his life into the art of perfecting the work.

DISCUSSION QUESTIONS

1. What does Malamud mean by "the complicated matter of breaking the silence" in relation to a writer's development?
2. Malamud offers this paradoxical sentence: "I began to write at an early age, yet it took me years actually to begin writing." What does he mean? What kind of definition of what it means to write is he working toward?
3. Another paradoxical assertion Malamud offers about young writers is that they "do not truly know what is happening in their lives and world. They know and they don't know." What accounts for this paradox? What kind of temperament and perspective does Malamud assume a writer will have?
4. Malamud promises himself that he will "someday be a very good writer." What does this phrase mean to him? What does it mean to you?
5. Malamud describes himself burning the manuscript of his first novel. Why? Have you ever destroyed, or do you think you could destroy, your own work for the reason that Malamud describes?
6. What is the significance of the anecdote Malamud includes about his father? What does this story suggest about what a writer needs in relation to character?
7. Malamud ends his memoir by regretting that he didn't have two lives, one apart from writing and the other devoted to art. Do you also feel this desire to be two people, to lead two lives?

CAROL BLY

Writing Whole Literature

Carol Bly (b. 1930) writes fiction and nonfiction about small-town and rural life, usually in her native Minnesota. As an activist, she helped found the Prairie Arts Center in Madison, Wisconsin, and has published Soil and Survival *(1986) with Joe Paddock and Nancy Paddock.*

Her story collections include The Tomcat's Wife and Other Stories *(1991) and* My Lord Bag of Rice: New and Selected Stories *(2000). She is also the author of the text-book* The Passionate, Accurate Story *(1990), which reflects her belief that life and fiction are (or should be) intimately connected, and that the concerns of life should be the concerns of fiction.*

JILL'S WRATH: HOW WE TREAT YOUNG WRITERS

The greatest beauty in a short story mainly floats towards us from its plot. That is not a fashionable idea just at the moment, but it is true. In Charles Baxter's "Scheherazade," an old woman is healing her husband. He is in the hospital, after a stroke.[1] She tells him tall stories which he experiences as empowering. We see what he needs: he needs to see himself as the ever-seductive male patrolling the range of does and mares, cutting his swath, a man with no consideration of any human being other than himself. His wife's stories are designed to reassure him that all that starry selfishness is intact. There is beauty in the language and structure, because Baxter is one of the most passionate and most subtle short-story writers of our time—but what makes me say, "What a beautiful story!" is Baxter's plot. This wife is not under threat of being killed if she can't amuse her husband, yet she is an echo of the original Scheherazade because she sacrifices her own psychological health—the sense of what is *fair and decent*—in order to return her husband to his health. The story has beauty of plot.

All beauty isn't in plot. There are two psychological disciplines authors exercise which make stories beautiful in tone and language: The first is the determination not to be embittered—at the same time as one avoids denial of the evil that people do. That is very difficult. It is hard to describe wretched behavior in even the tiniest corner of life without cynicism, perhaps because people will likely continue to behave in the bad ways. The second is using language of consequence, because how writer talks to reader and how characters talk to each other depend on psychological circumstances.

Let's imagine a writer whose circumstances, from age eight to age twenty-four, lead her again and again to write stories whose style is either noncommittal or cynical. Jill is a twenty-four-year-old graduate student at a snappy writing workshop. She does not write beautiful literature. Jill is not a horrible person. Why is she deliberately writing ugliness?

I pretend I am a social worker and Jill has been sent to "see someone." She is a writer, and here is her story, the story of why Americans go out of their way to make ugly literature.

Jill was born in Lawrencetown, Massachusetts, the daughter of civilized parents who had stable notions and a safe house. She always wanted to be a writer.

She wrote her first official short story in the third grade. It was about the town dump, with its wheel spokes, bedsprings, moribund kittens in their gunny sack, rusting kitchen pots—all of which tell one another their stories. Dogs, cats, all domestic refugees come to the dump and tell all the ways they have been cruelly used. (Jill had imagination.) When she got her story back from the teacher, she found written on the bottom: "Jill, we have been studying sentences now for two years. You know perfectly well that a sentence begins with a capital letter and you need a period at the end."

What Jill learned from that comment was that psychological content in literature does not count. What counts is mechanics. Maybe that's right! her half-conscious mind says. After all, whenever you try to tell your stories at home, your mother says, "Boy, do kids have imagination!" to your dad. Both of them, mysteriously, in the next second, notice that you have tracked in mud, too.

When Jill was in fifth grade, she wrote another story for her English class. Unfortunately her school had not elected to get in a poet or storyteller from the Writers-in-the-Schools movement.[2] Her new story was about parents who were rude to their children—gratuitously rude. For interesting insights on parental rudeness to children, see Alice Miller's work, especially *For Your Own Good*.[3] Jill's parents were forever adjuring her to behave, but they were rude. This story came back with the comment that Jill's spelling was improved: the teacher had even drawn a smiling face at the bottom, with radiating lines coming out from it, indicating, I think, sunshine.

In the seventh grade, Jill happened to get an English teacher who herself did not read through any of the papers regarded as "creative writing" since creative writing was humanities fluff.

So Jill's third try at a story about rude parents was channelled like lock water into the peer-criticism pond. The peers, Jill's classmates, had now spent five years or more being told to respect mechanics more than content, mechanics more than content, mechanics more than content. It never crossed any of their minds to remark on anything more inner in Jill's work than her "effective sentences." If they had talked about Jill's content—the rudeness of her parents to her—it wouldn't have helped Jill much: empathy is ineffective between young peers. Its marvelous use for giving people confidence and verve works only when the empathizing is by an authority (parent or teacher or other wise adult)—not by other kids.

Jill did a well-imagined story in the tenth grade. Here is the plot: a tenth-grade girl came home from school to her parents' clean but uncultivated house in an industrial town near Andover, Massachusetts. The author tells us the house had wall-to-wall carpeting, which ran from the hallways into all the rooms, even her room. The previous owners had built a full-wall bookcase in the living room, but that didn't bother this girl's parents: they put their copy of *Reach Out* and their other book, *We Never Would Have Made It Without Him,* in the center of the eye-level shelf, and then placed glass bricks on both sides so the books stayed put. The girl threw one leg over the lounge-chair arm and listened to the baseboard heating for a while. Then she took down one of the books and studied the photo on the back jacket. It showed a woman sitting upright in a chair, and her husband sat on its arm, smiling. Both had excellent teeth. "Mom? Mom?" the girl said. Her mother appeared. "Mom, how much mousse do you suppose that lady's got on there to get that 360° look, anyhow?" The girl held up the book. "And those eyes, hey, Mom, like the dials on Dad's safe!" "Let me tell *you* something, young lady," the mother said, "before you make any more fun of those people of Jesus. You get this very straight. If we hear any more smart remarks from you about Jesus or the people of Jesus, your father will take it up with you. This is a Christ-centered home. You know what Christ-centered means? It means that if a certain young lady can't learn to love our Lord and Saviour, maybe she would like to just pick up and live somewhere else and see how *that* feels!"

Jill's teacher wrote on her story, "You don't give us any idea of the colors of the house. You say wall-to-wall carpeting, but we can't see it because we can't see the colors of it. You need to offer more physical description." She did not comment on the author's disdain for the religious parents and the Born-Again authors, nor on the mother's offering to throw the girl out if she couldn't get filled with the spirit. Religion is a chancy subject in American public schools, and, anyway, she had been teaching for twenty-four years and she knew her job: it was to tell Jill how to *polish her skills,* and *only* to polish her skills.

Jill read her comment. She felt the way you would if you went to a psychotherapist and cried, "I am in psychological pain!" and the therapist replied, "One thing sure—get that athlete's foot taken care of, pronto!"

Jill's parents' religion, and Jill's disdain for it, are *content.* By now, at sixteen, that part of Jill's personality which wants to feel disdain for parents and do either a little or a lot of "parent bashing" supposes that it can't be done in literature. That part of Jill balls itself up in its own fetal position, so to speak, and rolls away somewhere underneath the surface of Jill's mind, flattening other feelings as it goes. When you "negatively reinforce" one kind of expression in young people, you negatively reinforce several other kinds of expressiveness as well. We know that: look at the people who are "rigid and judgmental": it isn't just sensuality they can't praise; they find it very hard to praise anything. It is because the psychological muscle which praises got hurt some time in their past.

How one does a thing, Jill has now learned, *how* one does just the *surface* of it, is more important than *what* one does. She has learned that lesson three times over. She does not, therefore, major in English, as she once had wanted to. She majors in Business Administration, as do 25%–75% of undergraduates of small liberal-arts colleges and universities, who have been told that college is a tool for money-making, not learning for a good life.

Finally, the gorgeous day comes when she is relieved of college. She had a marvelous love affair, but college had been mostly boring.

After a year or two, Jill decides to try once more: she enters a graduate creative-writing workshop. She puts together a short fiction about two young adults who are fundamentalist in religion. They truck away all broken or dirty items from their house. They decide not to have a pet because you know pets. Jill, not skilled or disciplined enough to eschew Author Intrusions and Interior Monologue, tells us these two characters are vulgar, facile, evasive, and given to totalitarian ideas, although they talk about *koinonia* and *agape.* Jill gives us a sex scene. It is wretched sex.

Jill's teacher has, alas, seen so many such angry and stereotyping short stories that he is exasperated. He writes at the foot of the page, "You make your point all right, slam bang, but we can't get interested because we can't feel either love or pity for your characters."

This time Jill's development is not just balked: it is stunted. Likely Jill will now not become a writer, even a bad one. Jill's disgust for those characters was a genuine passion which in the course of twenty years she had nursed along under the surface. Her third-grade teacher discounted it without noticing it. Her tenth-grade teacher tried to distract her from it by asking, what color was the carpeting? instead of, what were some other meannesses about those parents? any kind things at all? Here then are the psychological suppressants which Jill has experienced so far:

1. No one who counts has "reflected back" Jill's fret about mean parents. She, therefore, thinks she was wrong to have such feelings. (This is a well-documented, very common response to psychological abuse of children.) Jill's disdain never gets refined.

2. Truth learnt in solitude and quiet insight itself apparently has no value: the only truth which gets respect appears to be what you learn from the powers that be.

3. Finally, Jill turns outward and asks, since my heart's truth apparently isn't much, what does count in literature? She sees our usual panoply—silvery little stories made up of shards of experience, quickly picked up, experienced by the reader the way a jogger sees the glitter of mica in clay. Well, that's one thing they want, Jill thinks, logically examining the technical surfaces of the stories she reads. Put it in the present tense, she thinks, to make *The New Yorker.* Have a misery going on under the surface without cure, but only small objects get discussed as properties of the drama—grass from the mower blade, oil spitting in a pan, congealed eggs on one's plate (that one's Hemingway's—a nice, miserable sort of parallel to the story content), and, of course, the crocodile of the American short story, narratives of male bonding through drinking and casual humping—done raucously by young writers, with nostalgia by the middle-aged, from habit and fear of change by the old.

The great stories are out there to be seen, too: Charles Baxter, Mark Helprin, Alice Munro, Margaret Atwood, Susan Lowell—but Jill's eyes are half-closed to them by now. There is a particular reason why she will not learn to write from these authors. She was never allowed to develop her own disdainful feelings, so she rolled them under. It means she never moved to the step which can follow disdain (in stage development): the stage of refining one's original feeling. Refining takes place only when a feeling has been heard by another human being:

INTERVIEWER (or creative-writing teacher): "Jill, you show clearly about four or five ways in which your parents were cruel. Anything else?"
JILL: "What do you mean, anything else? Any other ways they were mean?"
INTERVIEWER: "Yes—for starters. Yes. How else? Can you tuck anything else into this autobiographical piece of writing?"

JILL murmurs, "No—I think that's about it."

INTERVIEWER (casually): "Well, anything else you want in here about the parents?" The interviewer is deliberately asking the question twice.

JILL: "They were great airplane-model-maker helpers. God, they were great. Hour after hour, Dad would hold the prop of the left engine of the P-38 while I wound up the starboard engine—you know, on a rubber band— then together we'd go out the door trying not to bang the plane. Mom rushed to the door and pulled the hydraulic stay-opener on the screen door, and Dad and I kind of shouldered each other out into the yard; Dad just got into the thing so goddamned well. 'This is M for Mongoose,' he would say, as we were hobbling to a good, open place to fly the plane. 'M for Mongoose, calling J for Jill, signal, J for Jill, when you are ready for take off.' He wouldn't be laughing either—looking fatherly. He would squint over the meadow, dead serious, with a perfect Southern accent like what you need for intercom talk in warplanes, dead serious, 'J for Jill, come in J for Jill, crissake come in, are you guys all right?'"

INTERVIEWER: "Fantastic!"

JILL: "Well—yeah—yeah, so here's the thing—then he beat me up, because he said I closed my heart to Christ, you see, but when he was being the Control Tower, he was terrific."

INTERVIEWER: "Complicated, you mean?"

JILL: "Both things going on in the same man at the same time."

INTERVIEWER: "Listen, Jill—it's a wonderful, *wonderful,* complicated story. Think it through and do another draft. I'll read it. Just list everything about the man—don't say, he was this or he was that. A person is a lot of things. Also—just for fun—I want to see the P-38, too. If you get stuck, call. If you don't, good luck. See you Monday."

If Jill had at any point in her writing participated in a conversation like this one, she would have learned you can talk frankly about evil, yet recognize that it sits next to good. She would have learned to see that one's first dash of judging human character is too simple: you can refine it.

But Jill is still left with a lot of unexpressed disdain.

Further, since she never got her disdain all written out, she will keep unconsciously circling round it. It will hide inside her, wrecking otherwise good, clean, new inspirations, wanting its way into her consciousness. It cries for attention, its *cris d'enfance* make such a racket inside her she doesn't hear happier voices, whose messages deserve at least as much attention.

When unconscious anger joins low self-esteem, an inexperienced author generally bends to write stories with jeering or chill feelings. The many American short stories in print which have low-life plots and obvious language work as role models for further cold-hearted narration. If one is, like the perfect C.I.A. recruit, "externalized," one will feel convinced that flip or chill writing is *de rigueur* in the short story.

Jill wrote a story in which a couple drink and carp at one another in a dump-yard, although Jill herself was having a gorgeous love affair with a fellow grad student named Henry. She and Henry spent some of their time on stepladders in the back aisles of Barnes & Noble, looking at photographs of our planet in a geology text or two. In one text, Figure 24 showed a pen-and-ink-drawn section of our world's crust. Some of the flat, generally horizontal strata were filled with regularly placed plus-signs, looking for all the world like a military graveyard. Other layers were filled with dozens of regularly placed hyphens. There were wonderful words in the captions: *extrusions, lobes, dolomite.* On the right-hand page, Figure 25 was a b/w photograph of flat land strewn with greenstone and some peaked-looking little lakes: Northern Minnesota, the caption explained, abraded by glaciers—and under its chill and scarified flesh, rockmolt still shoving about, meeting lenient or stubborn strata. All that lay under Henry's and Jill's feet: the cheerful moral of that story is that little of what counts makes it to the surface. The passers-by in Barnes & Noble got no glimpse of Jill's and Henry's caring: they were so close to one another they felt as if all the geomorphology of twelve thousand years (at least what they knew of it from Figures 24 and 25!) were part of their life together.

If Jill's own young-adult life was so pleasant, why did she choose to write a story about a night watchman for an old people's home who made out with his girl in the gravel pit and later crept into the home residents' rooms to steal? Why would Jill choose savagery for her subject?

We have seen how various teachers blocked her from handling the cruelties she observed. Further, she came, let's say, from a nonliterary family. Jill's family thought of reading as something you do to find out what's rotten going on somewhere, the way one reads a newspaper. Most people who don't read serious literature suppose that literature is exposé. Their mindset when reading or writing is to expose some evil or other. This is the mindset of junior high-schoolers, too: all their lives they haven't been allowed to talk back to parents. Then they get a creative-writing assignment: it's the first chance of their lifetimes to conduct some parent bashing without reprisal.

UGLY FACTS OF OUR TIME
AND OUR SENSE OF THE PUBLIC CONCERN

Because our Jill's and other jacks' and jills' work is ugly, journal- and diary-writers hunch their shoulders against it. Alas, this wraps them further in their own lives and delays their taking on some care for the *res publica.* This just when the world desperately needs public-minded literature. Here is Tom Wolfe arguing for literature taking on the public issues:

> Young writers are constantly told, "Write about what you know." There is nothing wrong with that rule as a starting point, but it seems to get quickly magnified into an unspoken maxim: The only valid experience is personal experience . . .

Dickens, Dostoyevsky, Balzac, Zola, and Sinclair Lewis assumed that the novelist had to go beyond his personal experience and head out into society as a reporter.[4]

Christa Wolff (in *Accident/A Day's News*) recognizes how much anyone wants not to worry over the public world. People "want to sit back in their armchairs after a hard day's work like me and have their beer—wine in my case, what of it—and they want to be presented (on TV) with something that makes them happy, a complicated murder plot, for example, but nothing which affects them too much and that is the normal behavior we have been taught so that it would be unjust to reproach them for this behavior merely because it contributes to our deaths."[5] Morally speaking, that is one of the fastest-moving long sentences I've read! It explains why for every Susan Lowell who makes herself focus on how the United States irradiated an entire family in her story "White Canyon,"[6] there are thousands of writers who practice what therapists call "pain avoidance." Crimes by government and scientists are so painful to think of, most writers, most readers, stay clear of them.

One cure for Jill, even for many jills, is to remember that at any one time there are at least two injustices being perpetrated somewhere. Such awareness gives you perspective without making you shrill: the two injustices can be far off. Tolstoy's greatest gift to modern literature is moral scope. The notion is this: while you are absorbed in your provincial affairs, elsewhere some evil is being forwarded by courteous people who belong to a financially powerful group. While you are fixing a man's buttonhole so he and his friend may stand together at his marriage, you see from the vestry window someone hunting deeply in the garbage can across the street. Tolstoy always brought in such perspective:

> During an interval in the Melvinski trial, in the large building of the Law Courts, the members and the public prosecutor met . . . while Peter Ivanovich, not having entered into the discussion at the start, took no part in it but looked through the Gazette which had just been handed in. "Gentleman," he said, "Ivan Ilyich has died!"[7]

Since Tolstoy knows we all live our lives in the shadow of laws, governments, either inside or outside the right clubs, he bothers to mention such things. We know from the paragraph above that he will tell us a story in which justice, law, establishment, and death will each share some time onstage. Once we know that our hobbies and love affairs and job hunting and funeral arrangements are all going to take place in a world which also has governments and corporations, we mustn't pretend otherwise—not if we're serious. As Christa Wolff says, "We have pushed off from the animal kingdom for good."[8]

We can do any number of grimy narratives like those Jill feels driven to write, and still turn them into beautiful literature by *giving them their full setting*. If the *major considerations* are present in a work, then some low-intensity realism can come in without foundering the whole piece. Even such a disdainful passage as the one below, in which the author looks down on the protagonist, can take place in a short story provided the general scope is big enough:

He told me to take them back before I'd lose the papers. Now, Sears will let you exchange, all right, without you got the papers, but they do always ask you to have the papers when you exchange, if you can remember. God, when I think of the number of times I've brought back stuff to Sears! Things I bought in good faith, or worse, his things! Machinery, workgloves, cloth, tools—things in the cat-alogue he thought he wanted and no sooner do I get home from picking them up then he wants me to take them back and exchange them!

The paragraph shows us a workingman's wife expressing irritation: because we see her focus on minutia, we take her for not only tiresome or ill-tempered, but petty as well. A whole short story about her and the people she consorts with might well end up a peevish tale without a sympathetic protagonist.

Yet all one has to do to make the dullest people sympathetic is set them in their periphery. There are two psychological reasons for that: first, as every inter-vention consultant knows, to get some level of a) tolerance and then b) under-standing going between people or between a person's idea of self and the real self, you widen the conversation to include as much of the person's anecdotes as you can. As the circle of events in that person's life is mentioned, widening, including more events, the way the wave goes outward from the stone thrown in the pond, some of the events mentioned will be of universal interest. At some point, since we live in a finite world, one comes across things which the more boring people have in common with the most interesting people. Spouses of diplomats are con-stantly forced to have superficial, cordial conversations. If they have been diplo-mats' spouses long enough, they know how to race through the "And how is the family?" punctilio as fast as they can and get to a shared hobby. The same thing works in fiction. In the passage on the next page, the hobbies are used-car-lot dealing, boring support groups, and getting drunk.

The second psychological reason for setting people in the widest possible periphery of their lives is that it increases our affection for them. Human beings are rather too much like the watchdogs Plato talked about in Book II of *The Republic:* we don't like what we don't know (two-year-old children loathe may-onnaise because they have never tasted it) and we do like—just as inappropriately —what we do know. The most astounding case of this I ever knew of had to do with a high-school teacher who threw pencils at the students in his French class. I heard about it and called the principal to ask if he was firing the French teacher. Well, no, I guess not, the principal said, because if we fire him, we'd have to hire someone else, and while he isn't the greatest, at least we know him, and if we hire someone new, he'd be an unknown factor.

It is easy to jeer at such a stupid allowance made to a bully, but a grimmer look at the same mindset reminds us of the hundreds and thousands of human beings who have been equable about

child labor

slavery

sadistic behavior of males to females

the disparity between rich people's fun and poor people's desperation

only because those evils are familiar. Familiarity may occasionally breed the contempt Bolingbroke spoke of: most of the time it breeds what John Kenneth Gal-
braith called "accommodation" to injustice.

In literature, telling the whole story about some deplorable person or situation breeds a good kind of accommodation in both reader and author. The more
we know about a character, the more like one of us the character appears. Jill, the
young writer with the poor creative-writing background, could exchange her
over-all cynicism for a combination of general affection and specific wrath if she
would drop the practice of minimalism. When she writes her dumpyard relationship as a minimalist narrative, she starts with disaffection and ends with disaffection. If she pulled in all kinds of peripheral life for the dumpyard couple, she
could still do a story disdaining their inchoate relationship, but the moral tone
would brighten.

Here is an example of how a grungy passage can change into a human
predicament worth bothering putting into story, just by the author's listing more
about the person. First, she needs a name: it will be Kate.

> Kate got disgusted with Donny about the Sears purchases. Donny beat her
> some. She guessed she was a battered wife. Their town was beautiful. Halfway
> between St. Fursey Lake, Minnesota, and St. Paul.
>
> She liked getting juiced with Donny. She didn't see him as your average wife-
> beater. She saw him as someone who can't read a Sears catalogue with enough
> imagination to know if he wants something or what.
>
> This one time she got to meet what she guessed was a real idealist. Some guy
> had lost his job because he refused to work on chemical warfare. His buddy
> explained to Kate he was a whistleblower. Kate had never met any of those types
> before.
>
> Then the whistle-blower's buddy slugged Donny right there in the booth.
>
> Once Kate talked Donny into letting her keep a kitten she and their daughter
> found at the dump.
>
> Their daughter got in trouble, but that was a lot later.
>
> Every so often, Donny did something so charming and funny, she would decide
> he was a wonderful man and she was crazy to listen to those support-group
> women talking about shelters. The funniest time was when he took her and their
> daughter to the used-car dealer in St. Fursey and said "Here we go, girls! Here we
> go! Don't talk, either of you! Don't show you like a car; let me do the talking."
> Then he and the dealer gave them rides in various Honda Civic Wagons, of '84,
> '85, '86, and '87, the years Donny was interested in. Donny made a lot of jokes.
> Usually the dealer could see the joke, too. Sometimes the jokes seemed mean at
> first, but everyone laughed and you got to have fun. "She don't say nothing,"
> Donny would laugh, jerking his head over towards Kate. "Can't tell if you like the
> car." Kate giggled. Or Donny would say, "Well, old lady, what do you think?"

and the dealer would smile at Kate but she kept her mouth shut good and Donny turned to the dealer. "No deal," Donny would say, "She don't like it." This went on for an hour and a half anyway. Finally Donny got $850 off an '84 and a real tire thrown in instead of that shrinkeroo spare the car came with . . . It takes a man.

The leader of Kate's support group didn't know how to tell her she was boring the group, taking up too much air time.

Donny said as long as that kitten grew up male, o.k., but if it was female it had to go to Doc Buchwald and that was the end of it.

Kate once met a real whistle-blower whose friend slugged her husband in the face and Donny never broke her jaw again.

I like Kate better now. Her style is still U.S.A.-Casual, and what's more, she not only is peevish about minutia, as we knew from the Sears passage, but she likes being drunk and she bores her support group. But now we know three universal and not despicable qualities in her: first, she has met and taken cognizance of a whistle-blower. She therefore joins, however tangentially, the world of shall-we-or-shall-we-not-do-evil-work-for-our-boss. Second, Kate shares at least one major value with the [former] First Lady of the United States. Like Mrs. Bush, Kate "would regret time not spent with a husband, a child, a friend or a parent." She would more than agree with Mrs. Bush's warning not "to lose the most important investment you will ever make." (All over the world, of course, there are social workers and psychotherapists who wish that the concept of husband-as-investment would not reach the ears of battered women: fear of losing that investment is one of the powerful forces which keeps battered women battered.) Leaving aside how inappropriately Kate would apply Mrs. Bush's strictures to her own life, we have at least got our female protagonist linked to a decent, major idea. And finally, Kate has a decent, major emotion as well: she is capable of simple, cheerful admiration, whether or not Donny's aplomb in the used-car lot deserves it.

America has a good deal of ugly-hearted fiction about. Some of the violence in it is salacious: that is, the author gets a kick out of thinking about it and knows the reader will, too. But some is a mistake in calculation: the author thinks that exposing the reader to this or that specific grunge or evil will teach the reader not to participate in that grunge or evil. In fact, people imitate what they see most sensually put before them—rather than learning from the moral brought out at the end of anything. We know this from television: people are imitating the violence they see, quarter-hour by quarter-hour; the police dramas do not teach them that crime doesn't pay, no matter how many last thirty seconds are given to showing the criminals being caught. In literature, shabby emotions or evil emotions inform the work if they take up all its pages. There will always be salacious writers. Let's set their work aside. Our question is: how can anxious Americans put evil or dingy situations into short stories without rotting the tone? I think Tolstoy's method is best: put in so much else of the characters' lives that the periphery of their worlds overlaps the periphery of all our worlds.

NOTES

1. Charles Baxter, "Scheherazade," *Harper's,* June 1989.
2. Writers-in-the-Schools Program, founded by COMPAS, the St. Paul, Minnesota-based arts organization.
3. Alice Miller, *For Your Own Good: Hidden Cruelty in Child-Rearing and the Roots of Violence,* trans. by Hildegarde and Hunter Hannum (New York: Farrar, Straus & Giroux, 1983). Early works by Alice Miller: *Prisoners of Childhood* (reissued in paperback as *The Drama of the Gifted Child*), *Thou Shall Not Be Aware: Societies' Betrayal of the Child,* and *Pictures of a Childhood: 66 Watercolors and an Essay.*
4. Tom Wolfe, "Stalking the Billion-Footed Beast: A Literary Manifesto, for the New Social Novel," *Harper's,* Nov. 1989, p. 45.
5. Christa Wolff, *Accident/A Day's News,* trans. by Heike Schwarzbauer and Rick Takvorian (New York: Farrar, Straus & Giroux, 1989).
6. Susan Lowell, *Ganado Red* (Minneapolis: Milkweed Editions, 1989). Also of interest, *The New York Times,* 7 June 1990, reports that the House of Representatives has approved a bill to give financial compensation and a government apology to uranium miners and to people downwind of the Nevada Nuclear Testing Site who now suffer from radiation sickness. *The Times* reports: "From 1945 to 1963, the Federal Government tested atomic weapons in the atmosphere, exposing about 220,000 military personnel and 150,000 civilians to radiation."
7. Leo Tolstoy, "The Death of Ivan Ilyich," trans. by Louise and Aylmer Maude, *Fiction 100: An Anthology of Short Stories,* 4th ed., ed. James H. Pickering (New York: Macmillan, 1985), p. 1034.
8. Christa Wolff, *Accident/A Day's News,* p. 90.

DISCUSSION QUESTIONS

1. Bly recommends a couple of disciplines she feels may lead to the creation of "beauty" in fiction: Writers should not be "embittered" by the evil they see in life, and they should use "language of consequence" in their work. What does Bly mean by each of these? Why are these disciplines important?
2. Why does Bly tell Jill's story? What is the connection between this case study of a young writer and the "ugly" or cynical literature Bly decries in contemporary writing?
3. Does Jill's life experience seem familiar to you? In what ways? What experiences have you had that parallel or reinforce Jill's?
4. What does Bly mean when she asserts that Jill's disdain for her parents and their beliefs "never gets refined"? Why would this refining of emotions be important for the development of a writer?
5. Do you agree with Bly that writers practice "pain avoidance" by refusing to write about public issues such as governmental and corporate misconduct? Why must writers be aware of injustices beyond their own immediate lives, according to Bly?
6. What does Bly mean when she encourages writers to set their characters in "the widest possible periphery," or context? What are the benefits of this widened perspective for writers? For readers?

Believing in Literature

Dorothy Allison (b. 1949) is the author of short stories, novels, memoirs, and essays. Her story collection Trash *(1988) won two Lambda Literary awards, Best Small Press Book and Best Lesbian Book. Her novel* Bastard Out of Carolina *(1992) was nominated for a National Book Award. Her most recent novel is* Cavedweller *(1998). Her fiction draws on powerful personal sources and delivers a powerful emotional punch.*

I have always passionately loved good books—good stories and beautiful writing, and most of all, books that seemed to me to be intrinsically important, books that told the truth, painful truths sometimes, in a voice that made eloquent the need for human justice. That is what I have meant when I have used the word *literature*. It has seemed to me that literature, as I meant it, was embattled, that it was increasingly difficult to find writing doing what I thought literature should do— which was simply to push people into changing their ideas about the world, and to go further, to encourage us in the work of changing the world, to making it more just and more truly human.

All my life I have hated clichés, the clichés applied to people like me and those I love. Every time I pick up a book that purports to be about either poor people or queers or Southern women, I do so with a conscious anxiety, an awareness that the books about us have often been cruel, small, and false. I have wanted our lives taken seriously and represented fully—with power and honesty and sympathy— to be hated or loved, or to terrify and obsess, but to be real, to have the power of the whole and the complex. I have never wanted politically correct parables made out of my grief, simpleminded rote speeches made from my rage, simplifications that reduce me to cardboard dimensions. But mostly that is what I have found. We are the ones they make fiction of—we queer and disenfranchised and female —and we have the right to demand our full, nasty, complicated lives, if only to justify all the times our reality has been stolen, mismade, and dishonored.

That our true stories may be violent, distasteful, painful, stunning, and haunting, I do not doubt. But our true stories will be literature. No one will be able to forget them, and though it will not always make us happy to read of the dark and dangerous places in our lives, the impact of our reality is the best we can ask of our literature.

Literature, and my own dream of writing, has shaped my system of belief—a kind of atheist's religion. I gave up God and the church early on, choosing instead to place all my hopes in direct-action politics. But the backbone of my convictions has been a belief in the progress of human society as demonstrated in its fiction. Even as a girl I believed that our writing was better than we were. There were, after all, those many novels of good and evil, of working-class children shown to be valuable and sympathetic human beings, of social criticism and subtle education—books that insisted we could be better than we were. I used my belief in the power of good writing as a way of giving meaning to some of the injustices I saw around me.

When I was very young, still in high school, I thought about writing the way Fay Weldon outlined in her essay, "The City of Imagination," in *Letters to My Niece on First Reading Jane Austen*. I imagined that Literature was, as she named it, a city with many districts, or was like a great library of the human mind that included all the books ever written. But what was most important was the enormous diversity contained in that library of the mind, that imaginary city. I cruised that city and dreamed of being part of it, but I was fearful that anything I wrote would be relegated to unimportance—no matter how finely crafted my writing might be, no matter how hard I worked and how much I risked. I knew I was a lesbian, and I believed that meant I would always be a stranger in the city—unless I performed the self-defeating trick of disguising my imagination, hiding my class origin and sexual orientation, writing, perhaps, a comic novel about the poor or the sexually dysfunctional. If that was the only way in, it made sense to me how many of the writers I loved drank or did drugs or went slowly crazy, trying to appear to be something they were not. It was enough to convince me that there was no use in writing at all.

When feminism exploded in my life, it gave me a vision of the world totally different from everything I had ever assumed or hoped. The concept of a feminist literature offered the possibility of pride in my sexuality. It saved me from either giving up writing entirely, or the worse prospect of writing lies in order to achieve some measure of grudging acceptance. But at the same time, Feminism destroyed all my illusions about Literature. Feminism revealed the city as an armed compound to which I would never be admitted. It forced me to understand, suddenly and completely, that literature was written by men, judged by men. The city itself was a city of Man, a male mind even when housed in a female body. If that was so, all my assumptions about the worth of writing, particularly working-class writing, were false. Literature was a lie, a system of lies, the creation of liars, some of them sincere and unaware of the lies they retold, but all acting in the service of a Great Lie—what the system itself labeled Universal Truth. If that truth erased me and all those like me, then my hopes to change the world through writing were illusions. I lost my faith. I became a feminist activist propelled in part by outrage and despair, and a stubborn determination to shape a life, and create a literature, that was not a lie.

I think many lesbian and feminist writers my age had a similar experience. The realizations of feminist criticism made me feel as if the very ground on which I stood had become unsteady. Some of that shake-up was welcome and hopeful, but it also meant I had to make a kind of life raft for myself out of political conviction, which is why I desperately needed a feminist community and so feared being driven out of the one I found. I know many other women who felt the same way, who grew up in poverty and got their ideas of what might be possible from novels of social criticism, believing those books were about us even when they were obviously not. What the feminist critique of patriarchal literature meant was not only that all we had believed about the power of writing to change the world was not possible, but that to be true to our own vision, we had to create a new canon, a new literature. Believing in literature—a feminist literature—became a reason to spend my life in that pursuit.

There are times I have wondered if that loss of faith was really generational, or only my own. I have seen evidence of a similar attitude in the writing of many working-class lesbians who are my age peers, the sense of having been driven out of the garden of life, and a painful pride in that exile though still mourning the dream of worth and meaning. The feminist small press movement was created out of that failed belief and the hope of reestablishing a literature that we could believe in. Daughters, Inc., Know, Inc., Diana Press, *Amazon Quarterly, Quest, Conditions* . . . right down to *OUT/LOOK*. All those magazines and presses—the ones I have worked with and supported even when I found some of the writing tedious or embarrassing—were begun in that spirit of rejecting the false ideal for a true one. This was a very mixed enterprise at its core, because creating honest work in which we did not have to mask our actual experiences, or our sexuality and gender, was absolutely the right thing to do, but rejecting the established literary canon was not simple, and throwing out the patriarchy put so much else in question. Many of us lost all sense of what could be said to be good or bad writing, or how to think about being writers while bypassing the presses, grants, and teaching programs that might have helped us devote the majority of our time to writing, to creating a body of work.

The difficulty faced by lesbian and feminist writers of my generation becomes somewhat more understandable if we think about the fact that almost no lesbian-feminist writer my age was able to make a living as a writer. Most of us wrote late at night after exhausting and demanding day jobs, after evenings and weekends of political activism, meetings, and demonstrations. Most of us also devoted enormous amounts of time and energy to creating presses and journals that embodied our political ideals, giving up the time and energy we might have used to actually do our own writing. During my involvement with *Quest,* I wrote one article. The rest of my writing time was given over to grant applications and fund-raising letters. I did a little better with *Conditions,* beginning to actually publish short stories, but the vast majority of work I did there was editing other people's writing and again, writing grants and raising money. Imagine how few paintings or sculptures would be created if the artists all had to collectively organize the creation of canvas and paint, build and staff the galleries, and turn back all the money earned from sales into the maintenance of the system. Add to that the difficulty of creating completely new philosophies about what would be suitable subjects for art, what approaches would be valid for artists to take to their work, who, in fact, would be allowed to say what was valuable and what was not, or more tellingly, what could be sold and to whom. Imagine that system and you have the outlines of some of the difficulties faced by lesbian writers of my generation.

As a writer, I think I lost at least a decade in which I might have done more significant work because I had no independent sense of my work's worth. If Literature was a dishonest system by which the work of mediocre men and women could be praised for how it fit into a belief system that devalued women, queers, people of color, and the poor, then how could I try to become part of it? Worse, how could I judge any piece of writing, how could I know what was good or bad, worthwhile or a waste of time? To write for that system was to cooperate in your own destruction, certainly in your misrepresentation. I never imagined that what we were creating was also limited, that it, too, reflected an unrealistic or dishonest vision. But that's what we did, at least in part, making an ethical system that insists a lightweight romance has the same worth as a serious piece of fiction, that there is no good or bad, no "objective" craft or standards of excellence.

I began to teach because I had something I wanted to say, opinions that seemed to me rare and important and arguable. I wanted to be part of the conversation I saw going on all around, the one about the meaning and use of writing. The first literature classes I taught were not-for-credit workshops in a continuing education program in Tallahassee, Florida. When I moved to Washington, D.C. to work on *Quest* in 1975, I volunteered to help teach similar workshops through the women's center, and in Brooklyn in 1980 I joined with some of the women of *Conditions* to participate in a series of classes organized to specifically examine class and race issues in writing. Working as an editor, talking with other lesbian and gay writers, arguing about how fiction relates to real life—all of that helped me to systematically work out what I truly believed about literature, about writing, about its use and meaning, and the problematic relationship of writing to literature.

Starting in 1988 in San Francisco, I began to teach writing workshops because it was one of the ways I could earn rent and grocery money without taking a full-time job and still be able to write as much as possible. But teaching full time taught me how much I loved teaching itself, at least teaching writing, and how good I could be at it. Sometimes my writing classes gave me a great deal more than rent or groceries; sometimes they gave me a reason to believe in writing itself.

If you want to write good fiction, I am convinced you have to first decide what that means. This is what I always tell my students. They think I'm being obvious at the outset, and that the exercise is a waste of time, as it could be if I did not require that they apply their newly determined standards to their own work. Figure it out for yourself, I tell them. Your lovers will try to make you feel good, your friends will just lie, and your critics can only be trusted so far as they have in mind the same standards and goals that you do.

I have used one exercise in every writing class that is designed to provoke the students into thinking about what they really believe about the use of literature. In the beginning, I did not realize how much it would also challenge my own convictions. I require my students to spend the first weeks collecting examples of stories they can categorically label *good* and *bad*. I make them spend those weeks researching and arguing, exchanging favorite stories, and talking about what they have actually read, not pretend to have read. I want them to be excited and inspired by sharing stories they love, and to learn to read critically at the same time, to begin to see the qualities that make a story good and determine for themselves what makes a story bad. Near the end of the class they are asked to bring in what they think is the best and worst story they have ever read, along with a list of what constitutes a good story, and what a bad one, and to support their ideas from their examples. I tell my students to keep in mind that all such judgments, including those about craft and technique, are both passionately subjective and slyly political.

The difficult thing about this exercise is that young writers love to talk about bad writing, to make catty jokes about this writer or that, but only so long as none of that nastiness is turned on them. It is always a struggle to get students to confront what is flawed in their stories without losing heart for the struggles of writing, to help them develop a critical standard without destroying their confidence in their own work, or what their work can become. I encourage young writers to find truly remarkable work by people like them, writers who share something of their background or core identity, because I have discovered that every young writer fears that they and their community are the ones who are not as good as the more successful mainstream writing community. I prod young lesbians and gay men to find work by other queers from the small and experimental presses. Then I try to make them think about what they could be writing that they haven't even thought about before. They become depressed and scared when it is difficult for them to locate queer stories they believe are really good, but I am ruthless about making them see what hides behind some of their easy assumptions about the nature of good literature. Sometimes I feel like a literary evangelist, preaching the gospel of truth and craft. I tell them they are the generation that might be able to do something truly different, write the stories that future readers will call unqualifiedly good, but only if they understand what can make that possible, and always, that part of the struggle is a necessity to learn their own history.

In one of my most extraordinary classes the exercise worked better than I had hoped when one of the women brought in a "best" selection that was another woman's choice for "worst." The situation was made more difficult for me because her bad story was one I loved, a painful but beautifully written account of a female survival after rape in a wilderness setting. It was bad, said my student, because of how well-written and carefully done it was. It stayed in her mind, disturbed her, made her nervous and unhappy every time she went into the woods. She didn't want those ideas in her head, had enough violence and struggle in her life, enough bad thoughts to confront all the time. I understood exactly what she was saying. She was, after all, a lesbian-feminist activist of my generation, and both of us were familiar with the kind of feminist literary criticism that supported her response to the story. But many of the students were younger and frankly confused.

Subjective, I reminded myself then. We had agreed that essentially judgments about fiction are subjective—mine as well as my students'. But the storyteller seized up inside me. I thought of my stories, my characters, the albino child I murdered in "Gospel Song," the gay man who kills his lover in "Interesting Death," the little girl who tries to seduce her uncle in "Private Rituals." Bad characters, bad acts, bad thoughts—as well-written as I can make them because I want my people to be believable, my stories to haunt and obsess my readers. I want, in fact, to startle my readers, shock and terrify sometimes, to fascinate and surprise. To show them something they have not imagined, people and tales they will feel strongly about in spite of themselves, or what they would prefer to feel, or not feel. I want my stories to be so good they are unforgettable, to make my ideas live, my memories sing, and my own terrors real for people I will never meet. It is a completely amoral writer's lust, and I know that the author of that "bad" story felt it too. We all do, and if we begin to agree that some ideas are too dangerous, too bad to invite inside our heads, then we stop the storyteller completely. We silence everyone who would tell us something that might be painful in our vulnerable moments.

Everything I know, everything I put in my fiction, will hurt someone somewhere as surely as it will comfort and enlighten someone else. What then is my responsibility? What am I to restrain? What am I to fear and alter—my own nakedness or the grief of the reader?

My students are invariably determined that their stories will be powerful, effective, crafted, and unforgettable, not the crap that so embarrasses them. "Uh-huh," I nod at them, not wanting to be patronizing but remembering when I was twenty-four and determined to start my own magazine, to change how people thought about women, poor people, lesbians, and literature itself. Maybe it will be different in their lifetimes, I think, though part of me does believe it is different already. But more is possible than has yet been accomplished, and what I have done with my students is plant a seed that I expect to blossom in a new generation.

Once in a while one of my students will ask me, "Why have there been no great lesbian novels?" I do not pretend that they are wrong, do not tell them how many of the great writers of history were lesbians. They and I know that a lesbian author does not necessarily write a lesbian novel. Most often I simply disagree and offer a list of what I believe to be good lesbian writing. It is remarkable to me that as soon as I describe some wonderful story as being by a lesbian, there is always someone who wants to argue whether the individual involved really deserves that label. I no longer participate in this pointless argument. I feel that as a lesbian I have a perfect right to identify some writing as lesbian regardless of whether the academy or contemporary political theorists would agree with me.

What I find much more interesting is that so many of my gay and lesbian and feminist students are unaware of their own community's history. They may have read *Common Lives/Lesbian Lives, On Our Backs,* or various 'zines, and joke about any magazine that could publish such trivial fiction, believing the magazines contemptible because they do not edit badly written polemics and true confessions. But few of them know anything about the ideology that made many of us in the 1970s abandon the existing literary criterion to create our own.

We believed that editing itself was a political act, and we questioned what was silenced when raw and rough work by women outside the accepted literary canon was rewritten or edited in such a way that the authentic voices were erased. My students have no sense of how important it was to let real women tell their stories in their own words. I try to explain, drawing their attention to ethnographies and oral histories, techniques that reveal what is so rarely shown in traditionally edited fiction—powerful, unusual voices not recognized by the mainstream. I tell them how much could not be published or even written before the creation of the queer and lesbian presses which honored that politic. I bring in old copies of Daughters books, not *Rubyfruit Jungle,* which they know, but *The True Story of a Drunken Mother* by Nancy Hall, which mostly they haven't seen. I make it personal and tell them bluntly that I would never have begun to write anything of worth without the example of those presses and magazines reassuring me that my life, and my family's life, was a fit subject for literature.

As I drag my poor students through my own version of the history of lesbian and gay publishing, I am painfully aware that the arguments I make—that I pretend are so clear and obvious—are still completely unresolved. I pretend to my students that there is no question about the value of writing, even though I know I have gone back and forth from believing totally in it to being convinced that books never really change anything and are only published if they don't offend people's dearly held prejudices too much. So affecting confidence, I still worry about what I truly believe about literature and my writing.

Throughout my work with the lesbian and gay, feminist, and small press movements, I went on reading the enemy—mainstream literature—with a sense of guilt and uncertainty that I might be in some way poisoning my mind, and wondering, worrying, trying to develop some sense of worth outside purely political judgments. I felt like an apostate who still mumbles prayers in moments of crisis. I wanted to hear again the equivalent of the still, small voice of God telling me: Yes, Dorothy, books are important. Fiction is a piece of truth that turns lies to meaning. Even outcasts can write great books. I wanted to be told that it is only the form that has failed, that the content was still there—like a Catholic who returns to God but never the church.

The result has been that after years of apostasy, I have come to make distinctions between what I call the academy and literature, the moral equivalents of the church and God. The academy may lie, but literature tries to tell the truth. The academy is the market—university courses in contemporary literature that never get past Faulkner, reviewers who pepper their opinions with the ideas of the great men, and editors who think something is good because it says the same thing everyone has always said. Literature is the lie that tells the truth, that shows us human beings in pain and makes us love them, and does so in a spirit of honest revelation. That's radical enough, and more effective than only publishing unedited oral history. It is the stance I assumed when I decided I could not live without writing fiction and trying to publish it for the widest possible audience. It is the stance I maintain as I try to make a living by writing, supplemented with teaching, and to publish with both a mainstream publishing house and a small lesbian press. What has been extraordinarily educational and difficult to accept these past few years of doing both has been the recognition that the distinction between the two processes is nowhere near as simple or as easily categorized as I had once thought.

In 1989, when I made the decision to take my novel *Bastard Out of Carolina* to a mainstream press, I did so in part because I did not believe I could finish it without financial help. I was broke, sick, and exhausted. My vision had become so bad I could no longer assume I could go back at any time to doing computer work or part-time clerical jobs. I had to either find a completely new way to make a living and devote myself to that enterprise, or accept the fact that I was going to have to try to get an advance that would buy me at least two years to finish the book. Finally, I also knew that this book had become so important to me that I *had* to finish it, even if it meant doing something I had never assumed I would do. Reluctantly, I told Nancy Bereano what I was doing with *Bastard,* and then approached a friend to ask him to act as my agent. I had never worked with an agent before, but all my political convictions convinced me I could not trust mainstream presses and did not know enough to be able to deal with them. In fact, I learned while doing journalism in New York in the 1980s that I was terrible at the business end of writing, rotten at understanding the arcane language of contracts. In some ways my worst fears were realized. Selling a manuscript to strangers is scary.

What most surprised me, however, was learning that mainstream publishing was not a monolith, and finding there not only people who believed in literature the way I did, but lesbians and gay men who worked within mainstream publishing because of their belief in the importance of good writing and how it can change the world. Mostly younger, and without my experience of the lesbian and gay small presses, they talked in much the same way as I did about their own convictions, the jobs they took that demanded long hours and paid very poorly but let them work, at least in part, with writing and writers they felt vindicated their sacrifices. Talking to those men and women shook up a lot of my assumptions, particularly when I began to work with heterosexuals who did not seem uniformly homophobic or deluded or crassly obsessed with getting rich as quickly as possible. I found within mainstream publishing a great many sincere and hopeful people of conviction and high standards who forced me to reexamine some of my most ingrained prejudices. If I was going to continue to reject the ideology and standards of mainstream literature, I had to become a lot more clear and specific about the distinction between the patriarchal literature I had been trying to challenge all my life and the good-hearted individuals I encountered within those institutions.

As I was finishing the copyediting of *Bastard,* I found myself thinking about all I had read when Kate Millett published *Flying:* her stated conviction that telling the truth was what feminist writers were supposed to do. That telling the truth—your side of it anyway, knowing that there were truths other than your own—was a moral act, a courageous act, an act of rebellion that would encourage other such acts. Like Kate Millett, I knew that what I wanted to do as a lesbian and a feminist writer was to remake the world into a place where the truth would be hallowed, not held in contempt, where silence would be impossible.

Sometimes it seems that all I want to add to her philosophy is the significance of craft, a restatement of the importance of deeply felt, powerful writing versus a concentration on ethnography, or even a political concentration on adding certain information to the canon—information about our real lives that would make it possible for lesbians, working-class runaways, incest survivors, and stigmatized and vilified social outlaws to recognize themselves and their experiences. If I throw everything out and start over without rhetoric or a body of theory behind my words, I am left with the simple fact that what I want as a writer is to be able to tell the truth so well and so powerfully that it will have to be heard, understood, and acted on. It's why I have worked for years on lesbian, feminist, and gay publishing, for no money and without much hope, and why my greatest sorrow has been watching young writers do less than their best because they have no concept of what good writing can be and what it can accomplish.

I started this whole process—forcing my students' discussion of the good and the bad—in order to work on my own judgment, to hold it up to outside view. I can take nothing for granted with these twenty-year-olds, and there is always at least one old-line feminist there to keep me honest, to ask why and make me say out loud all the things I have questioned and tried to understand. Sometimes it helps a lot. Sometimes it drives me back down inside myself, convincing me all over again that Literature belongs to the Other—either the recognized institutions or my innocent students who have never known my self-conscious sense of sin, my old loss of faith. They question so little, don't even know they have a faith to lose. There are times I look at my writing and despair. I cannot always make it the story I think should be told, cannot make it an affirmation or anything predictable or easy or sometimes even explainable. The story tells itself, banal or not. What, then, is the point of literary criticism that tells writers what they should be writing rather than addressing what is on the page?

The novel I am working on now seems to be driving me more crazy in the actual writing of it than it ever did when I was trying to get around to the writing of it. I don't understand if it is just me or the process itself, since many other writers I have talked to are noncommunicative about the work of writing itself. Everyone discusses day jobs, teaching, what they read, music, being interviewed, groups they work with, things they want to do when this project is finished.

But over here, I am halfway done with the thing and feel like I have nothing, know nothing, am nothing. Can't sleep, and part of the time I can't even work, staying up till 4:00 or 5:00 in the morning. Thinking. About what, people ask, the book? I stare blankly, sometimes unable to explain and other times too embarrassed. I think about the book, yes, but also about my childhood, my family, and about sex, violence, what people will ask me when they read this book, about my ex-girlfriends and what they will say, about my hips and how wide they have become, my eyesight that is steadily growing worse, the friends who have somehow become strangers, even enemies, the friends who have died without ever managing to do the things they wanted to do, how old I have gotten not recognizing that time was actually passing, about why I am a lesbian and not heterosexual, about children and whether the kind of writing I do will endanger my relationship to my son—allow someone to take him away from me or accuse me of being a bad mother—and about all the things I was not told as a child that I had to make up for myself. When I am writing I sink down into myself, my memory, dreams, shames, and terrors. I answer questions no one has asked but me, avoid issues no one else has raised, and puzzle out just where my responsibility to the real begins and ends. Morality and ethics are the heart of what I fear, that I might fail in one or the other, that people like me cannot help but fail to show true ethical insight or moral concern. Then I turn my head and fall into the story, and all that thinking becomes background to the novel writing itself, the voices that are only partly my own. What I can tell my students is that the theory and philosophy they take so seriously and pick apart with such angst and determination is still only accompaniment to the work of writing, and that process, thankfully, no matter what they may imagine, is still not subject to rational determined construction.

A few years ago I gave a copy of a piece of "fiction" I had written about incest and adult sexual desire to a friend of mine, a respected feminist editor and activist. "What," she asked me, "do you want from me about this? An editorial response, a personal one, literary or political?" I did not know what to say to her, never having thought about sorting out reading in that way. Certainly, I wanted my story to move her, to show her something about incest survivors, something previously unimaginable and astounding—and not actually just one thing either, as I did not want one thing from her. The piece had not been easy for me, not simple to write or think about afterward. It had walked so close to my own personal history, my nightsweats, shame, and stubborn endurance. What did I want? I wanted the thing all writers want—for the world to break open in response to my story. I wanted to be understood finally for who I believe myself to be, for the difficulty and grief of using my own pain to be justified. I wanted my story to be unique and yet part of something greater than myself. I wanted to be seen for who I am and still appreciated—not denied, not simplified, not lied about or refused or minimized. The same thing I have always wanted.

I have wanted everything as a writer and a woman, but most of all a world changed utterly by my revelations. Absurd, arrogant, and presumptuous to imagine that fiction could manage that—even the fiction I write which is never wholly fictive. I change things. I lie, I embroider, make over, and reuse the truth of my life, my family, lovers, and friends. Acknowledging this, I make no apologies, knowing that what I create is as crafted and deliberate as the work of any other poet, novelist, or short story writer. I choose what to tell and what to conceal. I design and calculate the impact I want to have. When I sit down to make my stories I know very well that I want to take the reader by the throat, break her heart, and heal it again. With that intention I cannot sort out myself, say this part is for the theorist, this for the poet, this for the editor, and this for the wayward ethnographer who only wants to document my experience.

"Tell me what you really think," I told my friend. "Be personal. Be honest." Part of me wanted to whisper, Take it seriously, but be kind. I did not say that out loud, however. I could not admit to my friend how truly terrified I was that my story did none of what I had wanted—not and be true to the standard I have set for myself. Writing terrible stories has meaning only if we hold ourselves to the same standard we set for our readers. Every time I sit down to write, I have a great fear that anything I write will reveal me as the monster I was always told I would be, but that fear is personal, something I must face in everything I do, every act I contemplate. It is the whisper of death and denial. Writing is an act that claims courage and meaning, and turns back denial, breaks open fear, and heals me as it makes possible some measure of healing for all those like me.

Some things never change. There is a place where we are always alone with our own mortality, where we must simply have something greater than ourselves to hold onto—God or history or politics or literature or a belief in the healing power of love, or even righteous anger. Sometimes I think they are all the same. A reason to believe, a way to take the world by the throat and insist that there is more to this life than we have ever imagined.

DISCUSSION QUESTIONS

1. Allison connects her youthful desire for social progress to fiction: "Even as a girl I believed that our writing was better than we were." Do you share this sense of writing's potential role in driving social change? Why? How can fiction, or literature in general, have this effect?
2. Allison, later in her life, encounters literature as "a city of Man," and she worries that she may not be allowed a place in this city. Now, in an age that some have labeled "postfeminist," do you feel that the city of literature has evolved to include all writers within its boundaries? How?
3. Allison claims that judgments about stories "are both passionately subjective and slyly political." What does this mean? Can you see this blend of the subjective and political in your own opinions of whether stories are good or bad?
4. Allison, like Bly in "Writing Whole Literature," discusses the challenge of writing about evil: "bad character, bad acts, bad thoughts," in Allison's phrasing. How is Allison's approach to this predicament in the writer's life like and unlike Bly's?
5. Allison, an activist, states her belief in the "significance of craft," asserting its importance even when the writer is politically motivated to illuminate the lives of people formerly left out of literature. How can craft and politics get in each other's way? What social and aesthetic realities might keep a writer from being able to serve both political beliefs and art equally?

ANNE LAMOTT

Introduction to *Bird by Bird*

Anne Lamott (b. 1954) has written fiction and essays about writing fiction throughout a life that has included working in restaurants, appearing on the radio show West Coast Live, *writing book reviews for* Mademoiselle *magazine, and serving as a staff writer for* Women's Sports. *Her novels include* Hard Laughter *(1980),* Rosie *(1983),* Joe Jones *(1985),* All New People *(1989), and* Crooked Little Heart *(1997). Her textbook* Bird by Bird: Some Instructions on Writing and Life *(1994) reflects the intertwining of "real" and fictional experiences in her own life.*

I grew up around a father and a mother who read every chance they got, who took us to the library every Thursday night to load up on books for the coming week. Most nights after dinner my father stretched out on the couch to read, while my mother sat with her book in the easy chair and the three of us kids each retired to our own private reading stations. Our house was very quiet after dinner —unless, that is, some of my father's writer friends were over. My father was a writer, as were most of the men with whom he hung out. They were not the quietest people on earth, but they were mostly very masculine and kind. Usually in the afternoons, when that day's work was done, they hung out at the no name bar in Sausalito, but sometimes they came to our house for drinks and ended up staying for supper. I loved them, but every so often one of them would pass out at the dinner table. I was an anxious child to begin with, and I found this unnerving.

Every morning, no matter how late he had been up, my father rose at 5:30, went to his study, wrote for a couple of hours, made us all breakfast, read the paper with my mother, and then went back to work for the rest of the morning. Many years passed before I realized that he did this by choice, for a living, and that he was not unemployed or mentally ill. I wanted him to have a regular job where he put on a necktie and went off somewhere with the other fathers and sat in a little office and smoked. But the idea of spending entire days in someone else's office doing someone else's work did not suit my father's soul. I think it would have killed him. He did end up dying rather early, in his mid-fifties, but at least he had lived on his own terms.

So I grew up around this man who sat at his desk in the study all day and wrote books and articles about the places and people he had seen and known. He read a lot of poetry. Sometimes he traveled. He could go anyplace he wanted with a sense of purpose. One of the gifts of being a writer is that it gives you an excuse to do things, to go places and explore. Another is that writing motivates you to look closely at life, at life as it lurches by and tramps around.

Writing taught my father to pay attention; my father in turn taught other people to pay attention and then to write down their thoughts and observations. His students were the prisoners at San Quentin who took part in the creative-writing program. But he taught me, too, mostly by example. He taught the prisoners and me to put a little bit down on paper every day, and to read all the great books and plays we could get our hands on. He taught us to read poetry. He taught us to be bold and original and to let ourselves make mistakes, and that Thurber was right when he said, "You might as well fall flat on your face as lean over too far backwards." But while he helped the prisoners and me to discover that we had a lot of feelings and observations and memories and dreams and (God knows) opinions we wanted to share, we all ended up just the tiniest bit resentful when we found the one fly in the ointment: that at some point we had to actually sit down and write.

I believe writing was easier for me than for the prisoners because I was still a child. But I always found it hard. I started writing when I was seven or eight. I was very shy and strange-looking, loved reading above everything else, weighed about forty pounds at the time, and was so tense that I walked around with my shoulders up to my ears, like Richard Nixon. I saw a home movie once of a birthday party I went to in the first grade, with all these cute little boys and girls playing together like puppies, and all of a sudden I scuttled across the screen like Prufrock's crab. I was very clearly the one who was going to grow up to be a serial killer, or keep dozens and dozens of cats. Instead, I got funny. I got funny because boys, older boys I didn't even know, would ride by on their bicycles and taunt me about my weird looks. Each time felt like a drive-by shooting. I think this is why I walked like Nixon: I think I was trying to plug my ears with my shoulders, but they wouldn't quite reach. So first I got funny and then I started to write, although I did not always write funny things.

The first poem I wrote that got any attention was about John Glenn. The first stanza went, "Colonel John Glenn went up to heaven / in his spaceship, *Friendship Seven*." There were many, many verses. It was like one of the old English ballads my mother taught us to sing while she played the piano. Each song had thirty or forty verses, which would leave my male relatives flattened to our couches and armchairs as if by centrifugal force, staring unblinking up at the ceiling.

The teacher read the John Glenn poem to my second-grade class. It was a great moment; the other children looked at me as though I had learned to drive. It turned out that the teacher had submitted the poem to a California state schools competition, and it had won some sort of award. It appeared in a mimeographed collection. I understood immediately the thrill of seeing oneself in print. It provides some sort of primal verification: you are in print; therefore you exist. Who knows what this urge is all about, to appear somewhere outside yourself, instead of feeling stuck inside your muddled but stroboscopic mind, peering out like a little undersea animal—a spiny blenny, for instance—from inside your tiny cave? Seeing yourself in print is such an amazing concept: you can get so much attention without having to actually show up somewhere. While others who have something to say or who want to be effectual, like musicians or baseball players or politicians, have to get out there in front of people, writers, who tend to be shy, get to stay home and still be public. There are many obvious advantages to this. You don't have to dress up, for instance, and you can't hear them boo you right away.

Sometimes I got to sit on the floor of my father's study and write my poems while he sat at his desk writing his books. Every couple of years, another book of his was published. Books were revered in our house, and great writers admired above everyone else. Special books got displayed prominently: on the coffee table, on the radio, on the back of the john. I grew up reading the blurbs on dust jackets and the reviews of my father's books in the papers. All of this made me start wanting to be a writer when I grew up—to be artistic, a free spirit, and yet also to be the rare working-class person in charge of her own life.

Still, I worried that there was never quite enough money at our house. I worried that my father was going to turn into a bum like some of his writer friends. I remember when I was ten years old, my father published a piece in a magazine that mentioned his having spent an afternoon on a porch at Stinson Beach with a bunch of other writers and that they had all been drinking lots of red wine and smoking marijuana. No one smoked marijuana in those days except jazz musicians, and they were all also heroin addicts. Nice white middle-class fathers were not supposed to be smoking marijuana; they were supposed to be sailing or playing tennis. My friends' fathers, who were teachers and doctors and fire fighters and lawyers, did not smoke marijuana. Most of them didn't even drink, and they certainly did not have colleagues who came over and passed out at the table over the tuna casserole. Reading my father's article, I could only imagine that the world was breaking down, that the next time I burst into my dad's study to show him my report card he'd be crouched under the desk, with one of my mother's nylon stockings knotted around his upper arm, looking up at me like a cornered wolf. I felt that this was going to be a problem; I was sure that we would be ostracized in our community.

All I ever wanted was to belong, to wear that hat of belonging.

In seventh and eighth grades I still weighed about forty pounds. I was twelve years old and had been getting teased about my strange looks for most of my life. This is a difficult country to look too different in—the United States of Advertising, as Paul Krassner puts it—and if you are too skinny or too tall or dark or weird or short or frizzy or homely or poor or nearsighted, you get crucified. I did.

But I was funny. So the popular kids let me hang out with them, go to their parties, and watch them neck with each other. This, as you might imagine, did not help my self-esteem a great deal. I thought I was a total loser. But one day I took a notebook and a pen when I went to Bolinas Beach with my father (who was not, as far as I could tell, shooting drugs yet). With the writer's equivalent of canvas and brush, I wrote a description of what I saw: "I walked to the lip of the water and let the foamy tongue of the rushing liquid lick my toes. A sand crab burrowed a hole a few inches from my foot and then disappeared into the damp sand. . . ." I will spare you the rest. It goes on for quite a while. My father convinced me to show it to a teacher, and it ended up being included in a real textbook. This deeply impressed my teachers and parents and a few kids, even some of the popular kids, who invited me to more parties so I could watch them all make out even more frequently.

One of the popular girls came home with me after school one day, to spend the night. We found my parents rejoicing over the arrival of my dad's new novel, the first copy off the press. We were all so thrilled and proud, and this girl seemed to think I had the coolest possible father: a writer. (Her father sold cars.) We went out to dinner, where we all toasted one another. Things in the family just couldn't have been better, and here was a friend to witness it.

Then that night, before we went to sleep, I picked up the new novel and began to read the first page to my friend. We were lying side by side in sleeping bags on my floor. The first page turned out to be about a man and a woman in bed together, having sex. The man was playing with the woman's nipple. I began to giggle with mounting hysteria. Oh, this is great, I thought, beaming jocularly at my friend. I covered my mouth with one hand, like a blushing Charlie Chaplin, and pantomimed that I was about to toss that silly book over my shoulder. This is wonderful, I thought, throwing back my head to laugh jovially; my father writes pornography.

In the dark, I glowed like a light bulb with shame. You could have read by me. I never mentioned the book to my father, although over the next couple of years, I went through it late at night, looking for more sexy parts, of which there were a number. It was very confusing. It made me feel very scared and sad.

Then a strange thing happened. My father wrote an article for a magazine, called "A Lousy Place to Raise Kids," and it was about Marin County and specifically the community where we lived, which is as beautiful a place as one can imagine. Yet the people on our peninsula were second only to the Native Americans in the slums of Oakland in the rate of alcoholism, and the drug abuse among teenagers was, as my father wrote, soul chilling, and there was rampant divorce and mental breakdown and wayward sexual behavior. My father wrote disparagingly about the men in the community, their values and materialistic frenzy, and about their wives, "these estimable women, the wives of doctors, architects, and lawyers, in tennis dresses and cotton frocks, tanned and well preserved, wandering the aisles of our supermarkets with glints of madness in their eyes." No one in our town came off looking great. "This is the great tragedy of California," he wrote in the last paragraph, "for a life oriented to leisure is in the end a life oriented to death—the greatest leisure of all."

There was just one problem: I was an avid tennis player. The tennis ladies were my friends. I practiced every afternoon at the same tennis club as they; I sat with them on the weekends and waited for the men (who had priority) to be done so we could get on the courts. And now my father had made them look like decadent zombies.

I thought we were ruined. But my older brother came home from school that week with a photocopy of my father's article that his teachers in both social studies and English had passed out to their classes; John was a hero to his classmates. There was an enormous response in the community: in the next few months I was snubbed by a number of men and women at the tennis club, but at the same time, people stopped my father on the street when we were walking together, and took his hand in both of theirs, as if he had done them some personal favor. Later that summer I came to know how they felt, when I read *Catcher in the Rye* for the first time and knew what it was like to have someone speak for me, to close a book with a sense of both triumph and relief, one lonely isolated social animal finally making contact.

I started writing a lot in high school: journals, impassioned antiwar pieces, parodies of the writers I loved. And I began to notice something important. The other kids always wanted me to tell them stories of what had happened, even—or especially—when they had been there. Parties that got away from us, blowups in the classroom or on the school yard, scenes involving their parents that we had witnessed—I could make the story happen. I could make it vivid and funny, and even exaggerate some of it so that the event became almost mythical, and the people involved seemed larger, and there was a sense of larger significance, of meaning.

I'm sure my father was the person on whom his friends relied to tell their stories, in school and college. I know for sure that he was later, in the town where he was raising his children. He could take major events or small episodes from daily life and shade or exaggerate things in such a way as to capture their shape and substance, capture what life felt like in the society in which he and his friends lived and worked and bred. People looked to him to put into words what was going on.

I suspect that he was a child who thought differently than his peers, who may have had serious conversations with grown-ups, who as a young person, like me, accepted being alone quite a lot. I think that this sort of person often becomes either a writer or a career criminal. Throughout my childhood I believed that what I thought about was different from what other kids thought about. It was not necessarily more profound, but there was a struggle going on inside me to find some sort of creative or spiritual or aesthetic way of seeing the world and organizing it in my head. I read more than other kids; I luxuriated in books. Books were my refuge. I sat in corners with my little finger hooked over my bottom lip, reading, in a trance, lost in the places and times to which books took me. And there was a moment during my junior year in high school when I began to believe that I could do what other writers were doing. I came to believe that I might be able to put a pencil in my hand and make something magical happen.

Then I wrote some terrible, terrible stories.

In college the whole world opened up, and the books and poets being taught in my English and philosophy classes gave me the feeling for the first time in my life that there was hope, hope that I might find my place in a community. I felt that in my strange new friends and in certain new books, I was meeting my other half. Some people wanted to get rich or famous, but my friends and I wanted to get real. We wanted to get deep. (Also, I suppose, we wanted to get laid.) I devoured books like a person taking vitamins, afraid that otherwise I would remain this gelatinous narcissist, with no possibility of ever becoming thoughtful, of ever being taken seriously. I became a socialist, for five weeks. Then the bus ride to my socialist meetings wore me out. I was drawn to oddballs, ethnic people, theater people, poets, radicals, gays and lesbians—and somehow they all helped me become some of those things I wanted so desperately to become: political, intellectual, artistic.

My friends turned me on to Kierkegaard, Beckett, Doris Lessing. I swooned with the excitement and nourishment of it all. I remember reading C. S. Lewis for the first time, *Surprised by Joy,* and how, looking inside himself, he found "a zoo of lusts, a bedlam of ambitions, a nursery of fears, a harem of fondled hatreds." I felt elated and absolved. I had thought that the people one admired, the kind, smart people of the world, were not like that on the inside, were different from me and, say, Toulouse-Lautrec.

I started writing sophomoric articles for the college paper. Luckily, I was a sophomore. I was incompetent in all college ways except one—I got the best grades in English. I wrote the best papers. But I was ambitious; I wanted to be recognized on a larger scale. So I dropped out at nineteen to become a famous writer.

I moved back to San Francisco and became a famous Kelly Girl instead. I was famous for my incompetence and weepiness. I wept with boredom and disbelief. Then I landed a job as a clerk-typist at a huge engineering and construction firm in the city, in the nuclear quality-assurance department, where I labored under a tsunami wave of triplicate forms and memos. It was very upsetting. It was also so boring that it made my eyes feel ringed with dark circles, like Lurch. I finally figured out that most of this paperwork could be tossed without there being any real . . . well . . . fallout, and this freed me up to write short stories instead.

"Do it every day for a while," my father kept saying. "Do it as you would do scales on the piano. Do it by prearrangement with yourself. Do it as a debt of honor. And make a commitment to finishing things."

So in addition to writing furtively at the office, I wrote every night for an hour or more, often in coffeehouses with a notepad and my pen, drinking great quantities of wine because this is what writers do; this was what my father and all his friends did. It worked for them, although there was now a new and disturbing trend—they had started committing suicide. This was very painful for my father, of course. But we both kept writing.

I eventually moved out to Bolinas, where my father and younger brother had moved the year before when my parents split up. I began to teach tennis and clean houses for a living. Every day for a couple of years I wrote little snippets and vignettes, but mainly I concentrated on my magnum opus, a short story called "Arnold." A bald, bearded psychiatrist named Arnold is hanging out one day with a slightly depressed young female writer and her slightly depressed younger brother. Arnold gives them all sorts of helpful psychological advice but then, at the end, gives up, gets down on his haunches, and waddles around quacking like a duck to amuse them. This is a theme I have always loved, where a couple of totally hopeless cases run into someone, like a clown or a foreigner, who gives them a little spin for a while and who says in effect, "I'm lost, too! But look—I know how to catch rabbits!"

It was a terrible story.

I wrote a lot of other things, too. I took notes on the people around me, in my town, in my family, in my memory. I took notes on my own state of mind, my grandiosity, the low self-esteem. I wrote down the funny stuff I overheard. I learned to be like a ship's rat, veined ears trembling, and I learned to scribble it all down.

But mostly I worked on my short story "Arnold." Every few months I would send it to my father's agent in New York, Elizabeth McKee.

"Well," she'd write back, "it's really coming along now."

I did this for several years. I wanted to be published so badly. I heard a preacher say recently that hope is a revolutionary patience; let me add that so is being a writer. Hope begins in the dark, the stubborn hope that if you just show up and try to do the right thing, the dawn will come. You wait and watch and work: you don't give up.

I didn't give up, largely because of my father's faith in me. And then, unfortunately, when I was twenty-three, I suddenly had a story to tell. My father was diagnosed with brain cancer. He and my brothers and I were devastated, but somehow we managed, just barely, to keep our heads above water. My father told me to pay attention and to take notes. "You tell your version," he said, "and I am going to tell mine."'

I began to write about what my father was going through, and then began to shape these writings into connected short stories. I wove in all the vignettes and snippets I'd been working on in the year before Dad's diagnosis, and came up with five chapters that sort of hung together. My father, who was too sick to write his own rendition, loved them, and had me ship them off to Elizabeth, our agent. And then I waited and waited and waited, growing old and withered in the course of a month. But I think she must have read them in a state of near euphoria, thrilled to find herself not reading "Arnold." She is not a religious woman by any stretch, but I always picture her clutching those stories to her chest, eyes closed, swaying slightly, moaning, "Thank ya, Lord."

So she sent them around New York, and Viking made us an offer. And thus the process began. The book came out when I was twenty-six, when my father had been dead for a year. God! I had a book published! It was everything I had ever dreamed of. And I had reached nirvana, right? Well.

I believed, before I sold my first book, that publication would be instantly and automatically gratifying, an affirming and romantic experience, a Hallmark commercial where one runs and leaps in slow motion across a meadow filled with wildflowers into the arms of acclaim and self-esteem.

This did not happen for me.

The months before a book comes out of the chute are, for most writers, right up there with the worst life has to offer, pretty much like the first twenty minutes of *Apocalypse Now*, with Martin Sheen in the motel room in Saigon, totally decompensating. The waiting and the fantasies, both happy and grim, wear you down. Plus there is the matter of the early reviews that come out about two months before publication. The first two notices I got on this tender book I'd written about my dying, now dead father said that my book was a total waste of time, a boring, sentimental, self-indulgent sack of spider puke.

This is not verbatim.

I was a little edgy for the next six weeks, as you can imagine. I had lots and lots of drinks every night, and told lots of strangers at the bar about how my dad had died and I'd written this book about it, and how the early reviewers had criticized it, and then I'd start to cry and need a few more drinks, and then I'd end up telling them about this great dog we'd had named Llewelyn who had to be put to sleep when I was twelve, which still made me so sad even to think about, I'd tell my audience, that it was all I could do not to go into the rest room and blow my brains out.

Then the book came out. I got some terrific reviews in important places, and a few bad ones. There were a few book-signing parties, a few interviews, and a number of important people claimed to love it. But overall it seemed that I was not in fact going to be taking early retirement. I had secretly believed that trumpets would blare, major reviewers would proclaim that not since *Moby-Dick* had an American novel so captured life in all of its dizzying complexity. And this is what I thought when my second book came out, and my third, and my fourth, and my fifth. And each time I was wrong.

But I still encourage anyone who feels at all compelled to write to do so. I just try to warn people who hope to get published that publication is not all that it is cracked up to be. But writing is. Writing has so much to give, so much to teach, so many surprises. That thing you had to force yourself to do—the actual act of writing—turns out to be the best part. It's like discovering that while you thought you needed the tea ceremony for the caffeine, what you really needed was the tea ceremony. The act of writing turns out to be its own reward.

I've managed to get some work done nearly every day of my adult life, without impressive financial success. Yet I would do it all over again in a hot second, mistakes and doldrums and breakdowns and all. Sometimes I could not tell you exactly why, especially when it feels pointless and pitiful, like Sisyphus with cash-flow problems. Other days, though, my writing is like a person to me—the person who, after all these years, still makes sense to me. It reminds me of "The Wild Rose," a poem Wendell Berry wrote for his wife:

> Sometimes hidden from me
> in daily custom and in trust,
> so that I live by you unaware
> as by the beating of my heart,
>
> Suddenly you flare in my sight,
> a wild rose blooming at the edge
> of thicket, grace and light
> where yesterday was only shade,
>
> and once again I am blessed, choosing
> again what I chose before.

Ever since I was a little kid, I've thought that there was something noble and mysterious about writing, about the people who could do it well, who could create a world as if they were little gods or sorcerers. All my life I've felt that there was something magical about people who could get into other people's minds and skin, who could take people like me out of ourselves and then take us back to ourselves. And you know what? I still do.

So now I teach. This just sort of happened. Someone offered me a gig teaching a writing workshop about ten years ago, and I've been teaching writing classes ever since. But you can't *teach* writing, people tell me. And I say, 'Who the hell are you, God's dean of admissions?'"

If people show up in one of my classes and want to learn to write, or to write better, I can tell them everything that has helped me along the way and what it is like for me on a daily basis. I can teach them little things that may not be in any of the great books on writing. For instance, I'm not sure if anyone else has mentioned that December is traditionally a bad month for writing. It is a month of Mondays. Mondays are not good writing days. One has had all that freedom over the weekend, all that authenticity, all those dreamy dreams, and then your angry mute Slavic Uncle Monday arrives, and it is time to sit down at your desk. So I would simply recommend to the people in my workshops that they never start a large writing project on any Monday in December. Why set yourself up for failure?

Interviewers ask famous writers why they write, and it was (if I remember correctly) the poet John Ashbery who answered, "Because I want to." Flannery O'Connor answered, "Because I'm good at it," and when the occasional interviewer asks me, I quote them both. Then I add that other than writing, I am completely unemployable. But really, secretly, when I'm not being smart-alecky, it's because I want to and I'm good at it. I always mention a scene from the movie *Chariots of Fire* in which, as I remember it, the Scottish runner, Eric Liddell, who is the hero, is walking along with his missionary sister on a gorgeous heathery hillside in Scotland. She is nagging him to give up training for the Olympics and to get back to doing his missionary work at their church's mission in China. And he replies that he wants to go to China because he feels it is God's will for him, but that first he is going to train with all of his heart, because God also made him very, very fast.

So God made some of us fast in this area of working with words, and he gave us the gift of loving to read with the same kind of passion with which we love nature. My students at the writing workshops have this gift of loving to read, and some of them are really fast, really good with words, and some of them aren't really fast and don't write all that well, but they still love good writing, and they just want to write. And I say, "Hey! That is good enough for me. Come on *down.*"

So I tell them what it will be like for me at the desk the next morning when I sit down to work, with a few ideas and a lot of blank paper, with hideous conceit and low self-esteem in equal measure, fingers poised on the keyboard. I tell them they'll want to be really good right off, and they may not be, but they *might* be good someday if they just keep the faith and keep practicing. And they may even go from wanting to have written something to just wanting to be writing, wanting to be working on something, like they'd want to be playing the piano or tennis, because writing brings with it so much joy, so much challenge. It is work and play together. When they are working on their books or stories, their heads will spin with ideas and invention. They'll see the world through new eyes. Everything they see and hear and learn will become grist for the mill. At cocktail parties or in line at the post office, they will be gleaning small moments and overheard expressions: they'll sneak away to scribble these things down. They will have days at the desk of frantic boredom, of angry hopelessness, of wanting to quit forever, and there will be days when it feels like they have caught and are riding a wave.

And then I tell my students that the odds of their getting published and of it bringing them financial security, peace of mind, and even joy are probably not that great. Ruin, hysteria, bad skin, unsightly tics, ugly financial problems, maybe; but probably not peace of mind. I tell them that I think they ought to write anyway. But I try to make sure they understand that writing, and even getting good at it, and having books and stories and articles published, will not open the doors that most of them hope for. It will not make them well. It will not give them the feeling that the world has finally validated their parking tickets, that they have in fact finally arrived. My writer friends, and they are legion, do not go around beaming with quiet feelings of contentment. Most of them go around with haunted, abused, surprised looks on their faces, like lab dogs on whom very personal deodorant sprays have been tested.

My students do not want to hear this. Nor do they want to hear that it wasn't until my fourth book came out that I stopped being a starving artist. They do not want to hear that most of them probably won't get published and that even fewer will make enough to live on. But their fantasy of what it means to be published has very little to do with reality. So I tell them about my four-year-old son Sam, who goes to a little Christian preschool where he recently learned the story of Thanksgiving. A friend of his, who is also named Sam but who is twelve years old and very political, asked my Sam to tell him everything he knew about the holiday. So my Sam told him this lovely Christian-preschool version of Thanksgiving, with the pilgrims and the Native Americans and lots of lovely food and feelings. At which point Big Sam turned to me and said, somewhat bitterly, "I guess he hasn't heard about the small-pox-infected blankets yet."

Now, maybe we weren't handing out those blankets yet; maybe we were still on our good behavior. But the point is that my students, who so want to be published, have not yet heard about the small-pox-infected blankets of getting published. So that's one of the things I tell them.

But I also tell them that sometimes when my writer friends are working, they feel better and more alive than they do at any other time. And sometimes when they are writing well, they feel that they are living up to something. It is as if the right words, the true words, are already inside them, and they just want to help them get out. Writing this way is a little like milking a cow: the milk is so rich and delicious, and the cow is so glad you did it. I want the people who come to my classes to have this feeling, too. . . .

DISCUSSION QUESTIONS

1. What are Lamott's earliest impressions of the writer's life, as embodied by her father? What does she notice about his habits, about how he differs from other fathers?

2. Lamott humorously paraphrases Descartes with her version of "primal verification: you are in print; therefore you exist." What are the benefits and possible disadvantages of living by such a motto?

3. As she gets older, Lamott continues to look to her father as a role model and mentor. How do details about him (his marijuana use, the sex scenes in his novel, his exposé of Marin County lifestyles) make Lamott's sense of the writer's life more complex and ambivalent?

4. How does Lamott's account of her youth contrast with Bly's fictional biography of Jill in "Writing Whole Literature"? Which experience seems more representative of life in the United States? Of your own experiences?
5. What is the role of "revolutionary patience" in the writer's life? How can a writer cultivate such a character trait? What works against this quality in contemporary life?
6. Lamott concludes that "the act of writing turns out to be its own reward." Are you convinced that this is so? Why or why not?

ANNIE DILLARD

The Writing Life

Annie Dillard (b. 1943) has been Writer in Residence at Wesleyan University since 1987. She won the Pulitzer Prize for Pilgrim at Tinker Creek (1974), was nominated for a Los Angeles Times Book Prize for Living by Fiction (1982), and was nominated for a National Book Critics Circle Award for An American Childhood (1987). In addition to her nonfiction, she has published poetry (most recently, Mornings like This, 1995) and a novel (The Living, 1992). Many of her essays reflect on the meaning of viewing life through a writer's eye.

When you write, you lay out a line of words. The line of words is a miner's pick, a woodcarver's gouge, a surgeon's probe. You wield it, and it digs a path you follow. Soon you find yourself deep in new territory. Is it a dead end, or have you located the real subject? You will know tomorrow, or this time next year.

You make the path boldly and follow it fearfully. You go where the path leads. At the end of the path, you find a box canyon. You hammer out reports, dispatch bulletins.

The writing has changed, in your hands, and in a twinkling, from an expression of your notions to an epistemological tool. The new place interests you because it is not clear. You attend. In your humility, you lay down the words carefully, watching all the angles. Now the earlier writing looks soft and careless. Process is nothing; erase your tracks. The path is not the work. I hope your tracks have grown over; I hope birds ate the crumbs; I hope you will toss it all and not look back.

The line of words is a hammer. You hammer against the walls of your house. You tap the walls, lightly, everywhere. After giving many years' attention to these things, you know what to listen for. Some of the walls are bearing walls; they have to stay, or everything will fall down. Other walls can go with impunity; you can hear the difference. Unfortunately, it is often a bearing wall that has to go. It cannot be helped. There is only one solution, which appalls you, but there it is. Knock it out. Duck.

Courage utterly opposes the bold hope that this is such fine stuff the work needs it, or the world. Courage, exhausted, stands on bare reality: this writing weakens the work. You must demolish the work and start over. You can save some of the sentences, like bricks. It will be a miracle if you can save some of the paragraphs, no matter how excellent in themselves or hard-won. You can waste a year worrying about it, or you can get it over with now. (Are you a woman, or a mouse?)

The part you must jettison is not only the best-written part; it is also, oddly, that part which was to have been the very point. It is the original key passage, the passage on which the rest was to hang, and from which you yourself drew the courage to begin. Henry James knew it well, and said it best. In his preface to *The Spoils of Poynton,* he pities the writer, in a comical pair of sentences that rises to a howl: "Which is the work in which he hasn't surrendered, under dire difficulty, the best thing he meant to have kept? In which indeed, before the dreadful *done,* doesn't he ask himself what has become of the thing all for the sweet sake of which it was to proceed to that extremity?"

So it is that a writer writes many books. In each book, he intended several urgent and vivid points, many of which he sacrificed as the book's form hardened. "The youth gets together his materials to build a bridge to the moon," Thoreau noted mournfully, "or perchance a palace or temple on the earth, and at length the middle-aged man concludes to build a wood-shed with them." The writer returns to these materials, these passionate subjects, as to unfinished business, for they are his life's work.

It is the beginning of a work that the writer throws away.

A painting covers its tracks. Painters work from the ground up. The latest version of a painting overlays earlier versions, and obliterates them. Writers, on the other hand, work from left to right. The discardable chapters are on the left. The latest version of a literary work begins somewhere in the work's middle, and hardens toward the end. The earlier version remains lumpishly on the left; the work's beginning greets the reader with the wrong hand. In those early pages and chapters anyone may find bold leaps to nowhere, read the brave beginnings of dropped themes, hear a tone since abandoned, discover blind alleys, track red herrings, and laboriously learn a setting now false.

Several delusions weaken the writer's resolve to throw away work. If he has read his pages too often, those pages will have a necessary quality, the ring of the inevitable, like poetry known by heart; they will perfectly answer their own familiar rhythms. He will retain them. He may retain those pages if they possess some virtues, such as power in themselves, though they lack the cardinal virtue, which is pertinence to, and unity with, the book's thrust. Sometimes the writer leaves his early chapters in place from gratitude; he cannot contemplate them or read them without feeling again the blessed relief that exalted him when the words first appeared—relief that he was writing anything at all. That beginning served to get him where he was going, after all; surely the reader needs it, too, as groundwork. But no.

Every year the aspiring photographer brought a stack of his best prints to an old, honored photographer, seeking his judgment. Every year the old man studied the prints and painstakingly ordered them into two piles, bad and good. Every year the old man moved a certain landscape print into the bad stack. At length he turned to the young man: "You submit this same landscape every year, and every year I put it on the bad stack. Why do you like it so much?" The young photographer said, "Because I had to climb a mountain to get it."

A cabdriver sang his songs to me, in New York. Some we sang together. He had turned the meter off; he drove around midtown, singing. One long song he sang twice; it was the only dull one. I said, "You already sang that one; let's sing something else." And he said, "You don't know how long it took me to get that one together."

How many books do we read from which the writer lacked courage to tie off the umbilical cord? How many gifts do we open from which the writer neglected to remove the price tag? Is it pertinent, is it courteous, for us to learn what it cost the writer personally?

You write it all, discovering it at the end of the line of words. The line of words is a fiber optic, flexible as wire; it illumines the path just before its fragile tip. You probe with it, delicate as a worm.

Few sights are so absurd as that of an inchworm leading its dimwit life. Inchworms are the caterpillar larvae of several moths or butterflies. The cabbage looper, for example, is an inchworm. I often see an inchworm: it is a skinny bright green thing, pale and thin as a vein, an inch long, and apparently totally unfit for life in this world. It wears out its days in constant panic.

Every inchworm I have seen was stuck in long grasses. The wretched inchworm hangs from the side of a grassblade and throws its head around from side to side, seeming to wail. What! No further? Its back pair of nubby feet clasps the grass stem; its front three pair of nubs rear back and flail in the air, apparently in search of a footing. What! No further? What? It searches everywhere in the wide world for the rest of the grass, which is right under its nose. By dumb luck it touches the grass. Its front legs hang on; it lifts and buckles its green inch, and places its hind legs just behind its front legs. Its body makes a loop, a bight. All it has to do now is slide its front legs up the grass stem. Instead it gets lost. It throws up its head and front legs, flings its upper body out into the void, and panics again. What! No further? End of world? And so forth, until it actually reaches the grasshead's tip. By then its wee weight may be bending the grass toward some other grass plant. Its davening, apocalyptic prayers sway the grasshead and bump it into something. I have seen it many times. The blind and frantic numbskull makes it off one grassblade and onto another one, which it will climb in virtual hysteria for several hours. Every step brings it to the universe's rim. And now— What! No further? End of world? Ah, here's ground. What! No further? Yike!

"Why don't you just jump?" I tell it, disgusted. "Put yourself out of your misery."

I admire those eighteenth-century Hasids who understood the risk of prayer. Rabbi Uri of Strelisk took sorrowful leave of his household every morning because he was setting off to his prayers. He told his family how to dispose of his manuscripts if praying should kill him. A ritual slaughterer, similarly, every morning bade goodbye to his wife and children and wept as if he would never see them again. His friend asked him why. Because, he answered, when I begin I call out to the Lord. Then I pray, "Have mercy on us." Who knows what the Lord's power will do to me in that moment after I have invoked it and before I beg for mercy?

When you are stuck in a book; when you are well into writing it, and know what comes next, and yet cannot go on; when every morning for a week or a month you enter its room and turn your back on it; then the trouble is either of two things. Either the structure has forked, so the narrative, or the logic, has developed a hairline fracture that will shortly split it up the middle—or you are approaching a fatal mistake. What you had planned will not do. If you pursue your present course, the book will explode or collapse, and you do not know about it yet, quite.

In Bridgeport, Connecticut, one morning in April 1987, a six-story concrete-slab building under construction collapsed, and killed twenty-eight men. Just before it collapsed, a woman across the street leaned from her window and said to a passerby, "That building is starting to shake." "Lady," he said, according to the Hartford *Courant,* "you got rocks in your head."

You notice only this: your worker—your one and only, your prized, coddled, and driven worker—is not going out on that job. Will not budge, not even for you, boss. Has been at it long enough to know when the air smells wrong; can sense a tremor through boot soles. Nonsense, you say; it is perfectly safe. But the worker will not go. Will not even look at the site. Just developed heart trouble. Would rather starve. Sorry.

What do you do? Acknowledge, first, that you cannot do nothing. Lay out the structure you already have, x-ray it for a hairline fracture, find it, and think about it for a week or a year; solve the insoluble problem. Or subject the next part, the part at which the worker balks, to harsh tests. It harbors an unexamined and wrong premise. Something completely necessary is false or fatal. Once you find it, and if you can accept the finding, of course it will mean starting again. This is why many experienced writers urge young men and women to learn a useful trade.

Every morning you climb several flights of stairs, enter your study, open the French doors, and slide your desk and chair out into the middle of the air. The desk and chair float thirty feet from the ground, between the crowns of maple trees. The furniture is in place; you go back for your thermos of coffee. Then, wincing, you step out again through the French doors and sit down on the chair and look over the desktop. You can see clear to the river from here in winter. You pour yourself a cup of coffee.

Birds fly under your chair. In spring, when the leaves open in the maples' crowns, your view stops in the treetops just beyond the desk; yellow warblers hiss and whisper on the high twigs, and catch flies. Get to work. Your work is to keep cranking the flywheel that turns the gears that spin the belt in the engine of belief that keeps you and your desk in midair.

Putting a book together is interesting and exhilarating. It is sufficiently difficult and complex that it engages all your intelligence. It is life at its most free. Your freedom as a writer is not freedom of expression in the sense of wild blurting; you may not let rip. It is life at its most free, if you are fortunate enough to be able to try it, because you select your materials, invent your task, and pace yourself. In the democracies, you may even write and publish anything you please about any governments or institutions, even if what you write is demonstrably false.

The obverse of this freedom, of course, is that your work is so meaningless, so fully for yourself alone, and so worthless to the world, that no one except you cares whether you do it well, or ever. You are free to make several thousand close judgment calls a day. Your freedom is a by-product of your days' triviality. A shoe salesman—who is doing others' tasks, who must answer to two or three bosses, who must do his job their way, and must put himself in their hands, at their place, during their hours—is nevertheless working usefully. Further, if the shoe salesman fails to appear one morning, someone will notice and miss him. Your manuscript, on which you lavish such care, has no needs or wishes; it knows you not. Nor does anyone need your manuscript; everyone needs shoes more. There are many manuscripts already—worthy ones, most edifying and moving ones, intelligent and powerful ones. If you believed *Paradise Lost* to be excellent, would you buy it? Why not shoot yourself, actually, rather than finish one more excellent manuscript on which to gag the world?

To find a honey tree, first catch a bee. Catch a bee when its legs are heavy with pollen; then it is ready for home. It is simple enough to catch a bee on a flower: hold a cup or glass above the bee, and when it flies up, cap the cup with a piece of cardboard. Carry the bee to a nearby open spot—best an elevated one—release it, and watch where it goes. Keep your eyes on it as long as you can see it, and hie you to that last known place. Wait there until you see another bee; catch it, release it, and watch. Bee after bee will lead toward the honey tree, until you see the final bee enter the tree. Thoreau describes this process in his journals. So a book leads its writer.

You may wonder how you start, how you catch the first one. What do you use for bait?

You have no choice. One bad winter in the Arctic, and not too long ago, an Algonquin woman and her baby were left alone after everyone else in their winter camp had starved. Ernest Thompson Seton tells it. The woman walked from the camp where everyone had died, and found at a lake a cache. The cache contained one small fishhook. It was simple to rig a line, but she had no bait, and no hope of bait. The baby cried. She took a knife and cut a strip from her own thigh. She fished with the worm of her own flesh and caught a jackfish; she fed the child and herself. Of course she saved the fish gut for bait. She lived alone at the lake, on fish, until spring, when she walked out again and found people. Seton's informant had seen the scar on her thigh.

It takes years to write a book—between two and ten years. Less is so rare as to be statistically insignificant. One American writer has written a dozen major books over six decades. He wrote one of those books, a perfect novel, in three months. He speaks of it, still, with awe, almost whispering. Who wants to offend the spirit that hands out such books?

Faulkner wrote *As I Lay Dying* in six weeks; he claimed he knocked it off in his spare time from a twelve-hour-a-day job performing manual labor. There are other examples from other continents and centuries, just as albinos, assassins, saints, big people, and little people show up from time to time in large populations. Out of a human population on earth of four and a half billion, perhaps twenty people can write a book in a year. Some people lift cars, too. Some people enter week-long sled-dog races, go over Niagara Falls in barrels, fly planes through the Arc de Triomphe. Some people feel no pain in childbirth. Some people eat cars. There is no call to take human extremes as norms.

Writing a book, full time, takes between two and ten years. The long poem, John Berryman said, takes between five and ten years. Thomas Mann was a prodigy of production. Working full time, he wrote a page a day. That is 365 pages a year, for he did write every day—a good-sized book a year. At a page a day, he was one of the most prolific writers who ever lived. Flaubert wrote steadily, with only the usual, appalling, strains. For twenty-five years he finished a big book every five to seven years. My guess is that full-time writers average a book every five years: seventy-three usable pages a year, or a usable fifth of a page a day. The years that biographers and other nonfiction writers spend amassing and mastering materials are well matched by the years novelists and short-story writers spend fabricating solid worlds that answer to immaterial truths. On plenty of days the writer can write three or four pages, and on plenty of other days he concludes he must throw them away.

Octavio Paz cites the example of "Saint-Pol-Roux, who used to hang the inscription 'The poet is working' from his door while he slept."

The notion that one can write better during one season of the year than another Samuel Johnson labeled, "Imagination operating upon luxury." Another luxury for an idle imagination is the writer's own feeling about the work. There is neither a proportional relationship, nor an inverse one, between a writer's estimation of a work in progress and its actual quality. The feeling that the work is magnificent, and the feeling that it is abominable, are both mosquitoes to be repelled, ignored, or killed, but not indulged.

The reason to perfect a piece of prose as it progresses—to secure each sentence before building on it—is that original writing fashions a form. It unrolls out into nothingness. It grows cell to cell, bole to bough to twig to leaf; any careful word may suggest a route, may begin a strand of metaphor or event out of which much, or all, will develop. Perfecting the work inch by inch, writing from the first word toward the last, displays the courage and fear this method induces. The strain, like Giacometti's penciled search for precision and honesty, enlivens the work and impels it toward its truest end. A pile of decent work behind him, no matter how small, fuels the writer's hope, too; his pride emboldens and impels him. One Washington writer—Charlie Butts—so prizes momentum, and so fears self-consciousness, that he writes fiction in a rush of his own devising. He leaves his house on distracting errands, hurries in the door, and without taking off his coat, sits at a typewriter and retypes in a blur of speed all of the story he has written to date. Impetus propels him to add another sentence or two before he notices he is writing and seizes up. Then he leaves the house and repeats the process; he runs in the door and retypes the entire story, hoping to squeeze out another sentence the way some car engines turn over after the ignition is off, or the way Warner Bros.' Wile E. Coyote continues running for several yards beyond the edge of a cliff, until he notices.

The reason not to perfect a work as it progresses is that, concomitantly, original work fashions a form the true shape of which it discovers only as it proceeds, so the early strokes are useless, however fine their sheen. Only when a paragraph's role in the context of the whole work is clear can the envisioning writer direct its complexity of detail to strengthen the work's ends.

Fiction writers who toss up their arms helplessly because their characters "take over"—powerful rascals, what is a god to do?—refer, I think, to these structural mysteries that seize any serious work, whether or not it possesses fifth-column characters who wreak havoc from within. Sometimes part of a book simply gets up and walks away. The writer cannot force it back in place. It wanders off to die. It is like the astonishing—and common—starfish called the sea star. A sea star is a starfish with many arms; each arm is called a ray. From time to time a sea star breaks itself, and no one knows why. One of the rays twists itself off and walks away. Dr. S. P. Monks describes one species, which lives on rocky Pacific shores:

"I am inclined to think that *Phataria* . . . always breaks itself, no matter what may be the impulse. They make breaks when conditions are changed, sometimes within a few hours after being placed in jars. . . . Whatever may be the stimulus, the animal can and does break of itself. . . . The ordinary method is for the main portion of the starfish to remain fixed and passive with the tube feet set on the side of the departing ray, and for this ray to walk slowly away at right angles to the body, to change position, twist, and do all the active labor necessary to the breakage." Marine biologist Ed Ricketts comments on this: "It would seem that in an animal that deliberately pulls itself apart we have the very acme of something or other."

The written word is weak. Many people prefer life to it. Life gets your blood going, and it smells good. Writing is mere writing, literature is mere. It appeals only to the subtlest senses—the imagination's vision, and the imagination's hearing—and the moral sense, and the intellect. This writing that you do, that so thrills you, that so rocks and exhilarates you, as if you were dancing next to the band, is barely audible to anyone else. The reader's ear must adjust down from loud life to the subtle, imaginary sounds of the written word. An ordinary reader picking up a book can't yet hear a thing; it will take half an hour to pick up the writing's modulations, its ups and downs and louds and softs.

An intriguing entomological experiment shows that a male butterfly will ignore a living female butterfly of his own species in favor of a painted cardboard one, if the cardboard one is big. If the cardboard one is bigger than he is, bigger than any female butterfly ever could be. He jumps the piece of cardboard. Over and over again, he jumps the piece of cardboard. Nearby, the real, living female butterfly opens and closes her wings in vain.

Films and television stimulate the body's senses too, in big ways. A nine-foot handsome face, and its three-foot-wide smile, are irresistible. Look at the long legs on that man, as high as a wall, and coming straight toward you. The music builds. The moving, lighted screen fills your brain. You do not like filmed car chases? See if you can turn away. Try not to watch. Even knowing you are manipulated, you are still as helpless as the male butterfly drawn to painted cardboard.

That is the movies. That is their ground. The printed word cannot compete with the movies on their ground, and should not. You can describe beautiful faces, car chases, or valleys full of Indians on horseback until you run out of words, and you will not approach the movies' spectacle. Novels written with film contracts in mind have a faint but unmistakable, and ruinous, odor. I cannot name what, in the text, alerts the reader to suspect the writer of mixed motives; I cannot specify which sentences, in several books, have caused me to read on with increasing dismay, and finally close the books because I smelled a rat. Such books seem uneasy being books; they seem eager to fling off their disguises and jump onto screens.

Why would anyone read a book instead of watching big people move on a screen? Because a book can be literature. It is a subtle thing—a poor thing, but our own. In my view, the more literary the book—the more purely verbal, crafted sentence by sentence, the more imaginative, reasoned, and deep—the more likely people are to read it. The people who read are the people who like literature, after all, whatever that might be. They like, or require, what books alone have. If they want to see films that evening, they will find films. If they do not like to read, they will not. People who read are not too lazy to flip on the television; they prefer books. I cannot imagine a sorrier pursuit than struggling for years to write a book that attempts to appeal to people who do not read in the first place.

You climb a long ladder until you can see over the roof, or over the clouds. You are writing a book. You watch your shod feet step on each round rung, one at a time; you do not hurry and do not rest. Your feet feel the steep ladder's balance; the long muscles in your thighs check its sway. You climb steadily, doing your job in the dark. When you reach the end, there is nothing more to climb. The sun hits you. The bright wideness surprises you; you had forgotten there was an end. You look back at the ladder's two feet on the distant grass, astonished.

The line of words fingers your own heart. It invades arteries, and enters the heart on a flood of breath; it presses the moving rims of thick valves; it palpates the dark muscle strong as horses, feeling for something, it knows not what. A queer picture beds in the muscle like a worm encysted—some film of feeling, some song forgotten, a scene in a dark bedroom, a corner of the woodlot, a terrible dining room, that exalting sidewalk; these fragments are heavy with meaning. The line of words peels them back, dissects them out. Will the bared tissue burn? Do you want to expose these scenes to the light? You may locate them and leave them, or poke the spot hard till the sore bleeds on your finger, and write with that blood. If the sore spot is not fatal, if it does not grow and block something, you can use its power for many years, until the heart resorbs it.

The line of words feels for cracks in the firmament.

The line of words is heading out past Jupiter this morning. Traveling 150 kilometers a second, it makes no sound. The big yellow planet and its white moons spin. The line of words speeds past Jupiter and its cumbrous, dizzying orbit; it looks neither to the right nor to the left. It will be leaving the solar system soon, single-minded, rapt, rushing heaven like a soul. You are in Houston, Texas, watching the monitor. You saw a simulation: the line of words waited still, hushed, pointed with longing. The big yellow planet spun toward it like a pitched ball and passed beside it, low and outside. Jupiter was so large, the arc of its edge at the screen's bottom looked flat. The probe twined on; its wild path passed between white suns small as dots; these stars fell away on either side, like the lights on a tunnel's walls.

Now you watch symbols move on your monitor; you stare at the signals the probe sends back, transmits in your own tongue, numbers. Maybe later you can guess at what they mean—what they might mean about space at the edge of the solar system, or about your instruments. Right now, you are flying. Right now, your job is to hold your breath.

DISCUSSION QUESTIONS

1. What does Dillard mean when she describes writing as changing "from an expression of your notions to an epistemological tool"?
2. In one of the many metaphors in this piece, Dillard writes of the courage necessary to demolish a "bearing wall" in order to start over. What does she mean by this? How is a piece of writing like a house? What are the indicators that some element of the work is a "bearing wall"?
3. Dillard's quotations from Henry James and Thoreau illustrate that writers must often sacrifice, or surrender, their most grandiose aims for their work. Why is this so? Why do writers continue to write if this is so regularly their fate?
4. What is Dillard's definition of the freedom of the writer? What is the trapdoor built into this freedom that Dillard describes?
5. One two-pronged line of exploration that Dillard lays out is whether a writer should strive "to perfect a piece of prose as it progresses." What are the pros

and cons of each method, as Dillard describes them? Which method do you
prefer? Why?

6. What distinction does Dillard make between movies and literature? Why does
she assert that the more "literary" the book, "the more likely people are to
read it"?

VICTORIA NELSON

The Master-Slave Relationship

Victoria Nelson (b. 1945) has been published in The New Yorker *and many other magazines. She is the author of* On Writer's Block: A New Approach to Creativity *(1993),
which has been praised for its understanding of the psychology of writing and for its practical
advice for overcoming the anxiety associated with writing.*

All work and no play make Jack a dull boy.

In Stanley Kubrick's film of Stephen King's *The Shining* as adapted by Diane
Johnson, this sentence, typed over and over, comprises the three-hundred-odd
pages of manuscript the deranged writer Jack Torrance has pecked out in that
classic last resort of blocked writers, a deserted mountain hotel. It is an eloquent
telegram of protest from his enslaved unconscious. (Later Torrance takes an ax to
his family, a less wholesome form of revolt.)

Works of art do require work to come into being. But unlike most of the jobs
and chores that occupy our lives, the act of creating art involves the whole person.
That is at once its great blessing and its curse. In the same way that clouds pass
before and then uncover the sun, deep self-awareness is a state that comes and
goes. The burden of imaginative writers is to be dependent much of the time on
their level of self-awareness, for this state has an immediate effect on the ability to
dream up something and put it down on paper. It is relatively easy, even desirable,
to mow the lawn or balance a checkbook while on automatic pilot. But it is usually (though not always) very hard to write when not in a state of heightened
awareness. Then comes the doodling, the forcing, the lack of concentration, the
guilt—all work and no play.

Being in touch with oneself is elusive and maddening, because it is a state that
cannot be *controlled* but only *allowed*. Adjusting oneself to the demands of the
unconscious, not the other way around, is the best way to "regulate" creativity.
Of all the psychologies emerging in our era, the Gestaltists have paid the most

attention to this problem of defusing ego control to allow for the spontaneous encounter with self. In the words of Fritz Perls:

> You don't drive a car according to a program like, "I want to drive 65 miles per hour." You drive according to the situation. You drive a different speed at night, you drive a different speed when there is traffic there, you drive differently when you are tired. You listen to the situation. The less confident we are in ourselves, the less we are in touch with ourselves and the world, the more we want to control.

"Listening to the situation" is something a tyrant, intent on asserting will at all costs, finds hard to do. Imposing on yourself an ego-conceived framework of duty, schedule, and appropriate topics of composition is an attempt to dam, channel, and otherwise divert the stream of spontaneous creation in directions it does not wish to follow and in which it would not naturally flow. This invariably triggers the unconscious reaction we call writer's block.

The creative experience can and must be guided, but it cannot be controlled. Control in its extreme form represents the attempt of one small segment of the psyche to declare absolute power over the rest. These strange fellow citizens of ours, as we all come painfully to realize in the course of a lifetime, are highly independent, egalitarian souls. They will not stand for any kind of dictatorship, and the forms their rebellion takes are as varied and devious as the human heart itself. Primary among these inner cotenants is that proud creature who likes to play. Every word a writer puts down is the product of a dialogue between the conscious self and the unconscious, and with every word the two move closer to fruitful partnership or war. If it comes to war, both sides will lose. If they cannot cooperate, they will destroy each other as well as their common undertaking.

You (here I address the conscious self, the side we all identify with) have the responsibility of guiding the spontaneous uprushings of the unconscious. But the minute you try to exert excessive control over the flow of unconscious ideas, the flow stops. You may get away with it in outside life, but within your heart that side of you *refuses* to be your slave. When this palace rebellion of the soul occurs, you have the choice of responding in one of several ways.

You may entrench yourself behind your bogus authority and issue an even stricter command, trying to compel obedience. "I said *create,* damn you! We'll sit here all day until you do it!" This overused response is not an option for chronically blocked writers, because they have typically abused the privilege of self-command with *too much* will. (In a milder form, however, this method does work for that small number of writers who have been gentle with themselves and rarely resort to barking out orders.)

The other, pleasanter option is to relax the will, unclench the muscles of your mind. You might take a walk, listen to music—then, if all parties agree, cautiously proceed with writing. Remember always to start with what you most *want* to write, as a hook to draw you into the process. Once you've gotten started, it's often not hard to shift course back to the project at hand.

If your resistance persists, you may be obliged to put aside the project for a longer period. Keeping your mind completely open and nonjudgmental, you can allow whatever doubts, hesitations, or other feelings you may be having about the work to enter consciousness. This may take days or weeks or even longer. Awareness of what is going wrong or right with your project takes its own time in emerging into consciousness, especially if you are not accustomed to listening to yourself. Such awareness will never break through at all if it encounters only a fortified stone wall.

The most desperate blocked writers should consider the back-door discipline of actively letting their fields lie fallow. Resolving entrenched writer's block often means having the courage to make a conscious decision not to write for a period of time. As long as that is happening anyway, why not risk a *positive* silence for a change? Dare to aim for less, and you will write more in the long run. Your long-term productivity will increase in direct proportion to the care and acceptance you lavish on your short-term silences.

Here is one way you might go about doing this. Make a decision not to do any creative work for a week or other definite time. Make this an active, positive choice that leaves you to enjoy all the rest of your life activities free from nagging guilt. The more energy you put into enjoying the state of not writing, the more successful this experiment will be. At the end of your week of nonwriting, take your pulse. Would you like to extend your grace period, or would you like to try some writing? Absolute honesty is essential here, for there is no "right" choice except the one you most incline toward. If you deeply prefer to have another week without writing, *give it to yourself* and enjoy it to the hilt. If you deeply prefer to start creative work, do so—but not on a production-quota basis.

At the end of your second week, test your true inclinations again—another week of the same (whichever it was), or is it time to switch? Again, either choice is right if you are basing your decision on what you truly want to do, not on what you *ought* to do. A set amount of time when you are actively not writing allows you to build momentum and anticipation toward doing some creative work.

Many blocked writers experience the week free of work as an enormous relief. To choose consciously not to work increases the sense of self-mastery and decreases self-blame, feelings of helplessness, and the like. Sincerely practiced, this exercise gradually helps blur the barriers between creating and noncreating until the week of creative work begins to feel like the holiday instead of the other way around.

In these calculated delays and postponements, which are actually one of the most vital parts of the creative process, may be recognized our *bête noire* procrastination in its true, transfigured form. A consciously taken rest period allows the unconscious either to let you know something is out of kilter in your approach or simply to proceed in various necessary but inaccessible activities that, though they lie outside your sphere of consciousness, will nonetheless allow the work in progress to carry on. What most chronically blocked writers lack is the gut faith in themselves that allows these needed intervals of silence to occur. Overcontrolling, self-distrustful personalities find the period of quiescence intolerable and interpret it as further proof of failure. For such writers the rest period may prove futile because their minds are closed off to the important information about the writing process or the nature of the project that the unconscious may be trying to communicate by temporarily halting the production of words.

Yet no work of art was ever completed without inscrutable pauses, unexplained hiatuses. The rewards of such deliberate procrastination, of complete and trusting surrender to the needs of that other side of the self, have been summed up by Eugène Delacroix: "When one yields oneself completely to one's soul, it opens itself completely to one."

OUGHT VERSUS WANT

The key symptom of the controlling personality is the *oughts* and *shoulds* that crowd his or her life. "I ought to go to exercise class." "I shouldn't eat chocolate again." "I should be able to write ten pages a day." If you were to make a list of all your most persistent *oughts* in life, you would probably note two striking characteristics of your list: the severity (often unrealistic) of the expectations, and the glaring, inescapable truth that the things you ought to do, you *don't*. The existential truth about oughts is that we don't do them. That's why they're oughts to begin with.

This is the classic dynamic of the master-slave relationship. Any command made by the ego that the unconscious finds unpalatable, it will not perform. Period. Almost anything we set up as an ought we are doomed never to accomplish. No matter how much the ego desires it, the rest of the psyche takes perverse pleasure in denying gratification. Though the master may stubbornly insist on staying the boss, the slave refuses to be the slave.

The Gestaltists characterized this personality conundrum as a split between two parts of the psyche characterized as the "topdog" and the "underdog." Here is Perls again:

> The topdog usually is righteous and authoritarian; he knows best. He is sometimes right, but always righteous. The topdog is a bully, and works with "You should" and "You should not." The topdog manipulates with demands and threats of catastrophe. . . .
>
> The underdog manipulates with being defensive, apologetic, wheedling, playing the cry-baby, and such. . . . The underdog is cunning, and usually gets the better of the topdog because the underdog is not as primitive as the topdog. So the topdog and underdog strive for control. Like every parent and child, they strive with each other for control. The person is fragmented into controller and controlled.
>
> This is the basis for the famous self-torture game. We usually take for granted that the topdog is right, and in many cases the topdog makes impossible perfectionistic demands. So if you are cursed with perfectionism, then you are absolutely sunk. This ideal is a yardstick which always gives you the opportunity to browbeat yourself, to berate yourself and others. Since this ideal is an impossibility, you can never live up to it.

I will return to the double-edged nature of perfectionism later. For now it's enough to note the distortion of perfectionism into a weapon we direct against our underdog unconscious self, who, as Perls points out, always wins in any inner conflict of this sort, though not in a productive way. By sabotaging orders, the slave becomes the true master. That is why we don't stick to our diets, exercise every day, or turn out ten pages of deathless prose like clockwork every morning. That other, unacknowledged side of ourselves prefers thumbing its nose—or, more accurately, cutting it off—to following orders.

Because it's so important to raise up the inner relationship from this level of hooligan brawling, you must begin to make a more conscious acquaintance with what lies within. One way to begin is to compose a completely spontaneous dialogue between your conscious self ("I") and your unconscious (give it a separate identity and name, or let one emerge from the dialogue). When you finish your dialogue, describe the personalities of the two speakers. What kind of person is the "I"? What kind of person is the unconscious? (Individuals are highly variable; you may find creatures other than topdogs and underdogs.) Are they opposites, or are they kindred spirits? Are they at loggerheads, or do they achieve resolution? (Don't try to force a resolution; that is your ego taking charge. Be absolutely honest about where you are at the moment.) You might consider rewriting this dialogue whenever you experience a new resistance, as a way of focusing on exactly what about the project is bothering your other side at a given time.

But, some will still argue, goals like exercising or dieting or writing ten pages a day are modest, healthy ones to aim for. They are not examples of impossible perfectionism; they lie easily within the realm of human achievement. *Other* people achieve these goals, certainly; the world is full of slender people, athletic people, prolific writers. Yes, because most of these people (masochistic overachievers excluded) do what they do by preference, not command. They *like* to exercise, for example, and it fits their natural rhythm; no unnatural effort is required. But chances are that these same well-exercised people are tormenting themselves for not doing enough of something else—reading, for example—that the exercise-blocked individual feels not a shred of resistance to doing. These other people believe that reading is a wholesome, self-improving activity they would do a great deal more of were they not so spineless and undisciplined.

Behind the word "ought," then, lies a hideous tangle of autocratic attitudes and superstitions that can strangle the joy of writing. These are some standard oughts the demon puts into the beginning writer's mind: (1) If I'm ever going to be famous, I ought to be writing a lot more than I do. (2) I ought to write like (pick any well-known writer) Ernest Hemingway did, up before daybreak, standing at his desk, always stopping when he still knew what would happen next so he'd have a starting place the next day. (3) I ought to be writing every night and weekend instead of using this time to relax.

It is easy, once they are dragged into the daylight of consciousness, to counter each of these assumptions. First, you can only write to write, not to be famous. Expectations of future glory extinguish creativity. As for following the Master's Example, his first two bits of wisdom are almost certainly major embellishments of the truth, and I suspect the last one is, too—Hemingway, for most of his later writing life, was severely blocked by alcoholism. Even if it were all true, though, beware always the fallacy of modeling yourself after a famous author. Every writer, by heeding her own deepest instincts, spins a unique web of idiosyncratic habits that make up a writing routine. At best, it's helpful to know there's so much individual variation. But what worked for Kafka is not necessarily going to work for you.

As for the third ought, do not use writing as an excuse to ruin your life.

Now if writing itself is on a writer's list of oughts, this does not necessarily mean—especially if she has already written a great deal—that her ego has shoehorned her into a profession for which she has no great desire or avocation. What it probably indicates is that over the years she has moved away from her initial childlike and playful joy in writing. It is now a duty-bound and ego-ridden chore. And no activity, viewed from this perspective, is very enticing.

Think of a project you have been struggling to write, with no success. Make a list of thoughts about the project, beginning each item on the list in the following manner:

1. I *ought* to write X because . . .

Now write a new list:

1. I *refuse* to write X because . . .

Notice that your inability to get into your project means that your second list of reasons is more powerful than your first. Can you learn to value your refusals consciously as much as you do unconsciously—that is, take them seriously enough to *act* on them instead of trying to steamroll over them?

Now write a third list:

1. I would *love* to write X.

List everything you would feel eager and enthusiastic about starting, no matter how trivial or silly your ego judges them to be. And you might consider trying one of these items, just for the fun of it.

One way that even experienced writers get caught in the "ought/refuse" conflict without considering the easy "love and prefer" solution is by overidentifying with an image of themselves as a certain kind of author, usually of the "serious" variety. The phoniness of this image is enough by itself to cause a temporary or permanent shutdown of creative powers, but it often leads to the further error of choosing writing projects geared to the image instead of to deep preference. It is one of the pervasive ironies of the creative life that integrity often operates only on the unconscious level, as a writer's block.

Most writers who have struggled through the beginning and intermediate stages of their apprenticeship have had at least some of this inflation knocked out of them by the enormous amounts of rejection and frustration they have had to endure. During the long struggle to gain a regular writing rhythm, they are more likely to find they have reached for the brass ring of discipline but have grasped instead the nettle of control.

DISCIPLINE AND CONTROL

I have already stressed that creative discipline is based on spontaneous, pleasurable play, not a Spartan regime of stern self-control. From the Latin *disciplina*, meaning instruction or knowledge (a disciple is literally a "learner"), discipline is training that produces a certain pattern of behavior. The grim connotation the word has come to carry reflects the austerity of our culture rather than the true nature of this enjoyable, life-enhancing experience. Discipline is not the same as forcing oneself to do distasteful tasks. Tasks, in fact, tend to become distasteful only to the degree to which they are forced. That we usually mistake control for discipline is a measure of our personal as well as societal rigidity. Only a writing routine that has the consent of the total psyche can provide a foundation solid enough to sustain a writer through the years of drudgery and tedium all creative effort requires.

How does one free discipline from the killing grip of control? Here is the therapist Muriel Schiffman's solution:

> I used to struggle anew each day with the problem, "Should I write now or later, or maybe skip this one day?" until I began to treat myself exactly as I did my small children.
>
> Now at a specific hour each morning I stop whatever I am doing and sit down at the typewriter. No need for the daily conflict between "want" and "should." . . . I write for exactly one hour each morning, no more, no less. Writing for one hour seems a natural creative activity for me. Ideas flow smoothly without stress or strain. But after an hour the work becomes an effort of will, a forced assignment, performed with much physical tension (clenched teeth, etc.), like swimming upstream.
>
> I learned by trial and error that morning is the best time for me to write: words come easily. Later in the day I get bogged down in a compulsive search for the "perfect" word. I torture myself with inhibiting thoughts. . . .
>
> I do not *know* why this happens in the afternoon and not in the morning. . . . My Adult self avoids frustrating the Child in me by choosing a time which is most comfortable for writing, just as it chooses the most satisfying menu when I diet. I never forced my children to eat foods they disliked just because they were "good" for them.

Schiffman established her discipline by trusting the organism, not her ego. She guided herself only to the extent of setting aside that hour to allow the writing to happen; that was her conscious self's productive input in this partnership. Her trust in her innate creative rhythms (instead of the judgmental "Only *one* hour?") was rewarded by a free and uninterrupted flow of writing for the allotted period every day. And an hour a day can produce a lot of writing.

Here the Devil may tempt you with the thought: "If I do this much in an hour, think how much I could do if I worked eight hours every day!" This kind of falsely rational conclusion will only get you into trouble. Most blocked writers have a conscious expectation of results that far exceeds their unconscious preference, and the "block" is nothing more than the gap between these two opposing perspectives. The nature of your deep inner inclinations, their rhythms and direction, can be determined only by patiently *allowing* a pattern to emerge. Once the pattern has surfaced, your conscious self can step in cautiously to guide it, exploit it, and build on it. Each time you attempt to work faster than your inner rhythm, it will break down. That is your signal to let up and allow the unconscious once again to set the pace. You determine your limits by testing them gently but repeatedly, then respecting them—no matter how unlike anybody else's they are.

This can be a time-consuming process, even for a person who does not tend to be overcontrolling. For the blocked writer who has spent years mistreating himself in a master-slave struggle, it is likely to take even longer. Freedom to develop a true discipline does not come overnight. The abused organism needs time to heal its wounds, to recover from the all too familiar pattern of command-rebellion-punishment and to begin to establish a new one. Such a gentle reorganization can indeed occur. And it is a far pleasanter process than whipping oneself. The key is to be able to give up pain for pleasure, and most people find this very hard to do.

Donald Newlove, a fiction writer and recovered alcoholic, recounts the agonies he experienced when he was blocked by ambitious plans for a nine-hundred-page novel:

> For three months I sat around my fellowship table [at Alcoholics Anonymous meetings] and complained of my fears and paralysis. . . . I'd explain carefully that my method of writing was to write a first draft in longhand, type that up, correct and retype it from start to finish, then again correct and totally retype it. Since the novel was set at NINE HUNDRED PAGES, this meant that when done I'd have filled THIRTY-SIX HUNDRED PAGES with my writing. This was daunting. The idea that I would have to fill 3600 pages with my imagination was now a black mountain of work that had kept me stoned with weakness for three months.

Then came the epiphany:

> This dumb phrase suddenly filled me with light. It was: One Day at a Time. . . . To write it I had only to write one word at a time, one phrase at a time, one sentence at a time, one paragraph at a time, one page at a time, one day at a time—and if I wrote four pages a day I'd be done in three years. The magnitude of the results of this simpleminded approach to boating my white whale sent me home like a shot after the meeting and I jumped at the dining room table with a blank sheet and began.

What Newlove describes is the conversion experience of a man who stopped wanting to punish himself and started wanting to be kind to himself. It is perhaps significant that this change occurred in a therapeutic setting.

To gain true discipline, it is necessary to learn to treat yourself with at least the same courtesy, respect, and affection you accord your spouse, friends, and even the grocery store bagger. This sounds easy, but it is not. The urge to hate and tyrannize yourself does not go away by itself; *real* effort is required to dispel it. Even in fairy tales, frogs don't change back into princes until a ritual period of time (a year and a day, seven years) has passed and certain tasks have been performed. We have already seen the importance of time; the task of gaining self-respect is a lifework.

And there is one thing always to remember. The long-afflicted writer who suddenly feels the joy of a spontaneous flow of words wants to say at once,

"That's it! I'm cured. I'll never have writer's block again." But all you have done is reap the benefits of a friendly dialogue, instead of a hostile engagement, with your resistance. As an essential part of the creative process, the resistance was, is, and will be a constant; the only thing that has changed is your attitude toward it. Without resistance one can do nothing.

RESPECTING THE EGO

In these pages you will frequently find a villainous, punishing ego contrasted with a noble, put-upon unconscious. The distorted emphasis is necessary to right the balance between these two components of the psyche in writers who experience a block. Such writers have habitually attempted to dominate their unconscious instead of establishing a true relationship with it. Art, as Cocteau said, is a "marriage of the conscious and the unconscious"; it does not spring from an unequal relationship. Finding ways of relaxing the iron grip on self is the main purpose of this book, which suggests that the path back to writing is, by definition, free of effort.

Once the imbalance is righted, however, we must recognize that the ego is obviously a powerful player in the writing process whose important function is to guide and structure the inchoate outpourings of the unconscious. The unconscious, in turn, is by no means always the "better half" of this duo; unregulated, it can sweep a person into a crushing depression or even psychosis. There is sometimes a fine line between the spontaneous desires of the playful child and the infantile destructiveness of some unconscious impulses. The crucial issue here is restoring the natural equilibrium of these forces.

Sometimes—blocked writers be wary here—the only way out of an impasse is to exert the ego, not the unconscious. As Christopher Isherwood noted, "Even the tiniest act of the will towards a thing is better than not doing it at all." And tiny acts of will, as we shall see, get you where you want to go much more efficiently than great big acts of will that are hollow and unsupported by desire. Contrary to stereotype, art lives in the modest effort, not the grandiose one.

The last word on successfully exerting an act of will against resistance should go, by way of contrast, to a highly prolific writer, Joyce Carol Oates:

> One must be pitiless about this matter of "mood." In a sense, the writing will
> *create* the mood. . . . Generally I've found this to be true: I have forced myself to
> begin writing when I've been utterly exhausted, when I've felt my soul as thin as
> a playing card, when nothing has seemed worth enduring for another five minutes
> . . . and somehow the activity of writing changes everything.

To use the act of writing itself to cancel out resistance and render it irrelevant is a powerful strategy, and one that fluent writers employ as a matter of course. To use this strategy exclusively, however, is to risk missing the important messages, personal and aesthetic, that certain resistances may be trying to communicate. Think twice about burying your friend the block—even when you have the shovelful of words to do it—before you listen to what he has to say.

DISCUSSION QUESTIONS

1. Nelson further explores a concept introduced earlier in the book, most notably by Flannery O'Connor: Writing fiction requires the involvement of the whole person, not any magical fiction-writing facet of a person. How does Nelson develop this idea, providing reasons this is so? What does she emphasize about creativity and human nature?
2. What does Nelson mean by distinguishing between allowing oneself to be creative and trying to control the creative process? To what degree do you identify with her description of the dialogue between the conscious self and the unconscious mind?
3. Why does Nelson recommend "positive silence" as an alternative to writer's block in a writer's life? How can this ritual help writers change their attitude toward periods when they aren't writing? Toward procrastination?
4. Are the "oughts" listed by Nelson similar to your "oughts"? Make a list of your own, and assess how they function in your writing life.
5. How does Nelson try to reclaim the word "discipline" from its negative connotations? How does this relate to O'Connor's discussion of the "habits of art" necessary in a fiction writer's life?

TIM O'BRIEN

The Magic Show

Tim O'Brien (b. 1946) won the National Book Award for Going After Cacciato *(1978), considered by many to be the best work of literature to come out of the Vietnam experience. He has also published five other novels, including* The Things They Carried *(1990), which was nominated for the National Book Critics Circle Award and the Pulitzer Prize, as well as the memoir* If I Die in a Combat Zone, Box Me Up and Send Me Home *(1973). His fiction can tend toward the surreal, and he sees in that tendency a property shared by all fiction.*

As a kid, through grade school and into high school, my hobby was magic. I enjoyed the power; I liked making miracles happen. In the basement, where I practiced in front of a stand-up mirror, I caused my mother's silk scarves to change color. I used a scissors to cut my father's best tie in half, displaying the pieces, and then restored it whole. I placed a penny in the palm of my hand, made my hand into a fist, made the penny into a white mouse. This was not true magic. It was trickery. But I sometimes pretended otherwise, because I was a kid then, and because pretending was the thrill of magic, and because for a time what seemed to happen became a happening in itself. I was a dreamer. I liked watching my hands in the mirror, imagining how someday I might perform much grander magic, tigers becoming giraffes, beautiful girls levitating like angels in the high yellow spotlights, naked maybe, no wires or strings, just floating.

It was illusion, of course—the creation of a new and improved reality. What I enjoyed about this peculiar hobby, at least in part, was the craft of it: learning the techniques of magic and then practicing those techniques, alone in the basement, for many hours and days. That was another thing about magic. I liked the aloneness, as God and other miracle makers must also like it—not lonely, just alone. I liked shaping the universe around me. I liked the power. I liked the tension and suspense when, for example, the magician displays a guillotine to the audience, demonstrating its cutting power by slicing a carrot in half; the edgy delight when a member of the audience is asked to place his hand in the guillotine hole; the hollow silence when, very slowly, the magician raises up the blade. Believe me, *there* is drama. And when the blade slams down, if it's *your* hand in the hole, you have no choice but to believe in miracles.

When practiced well, however, magic goes beyond a mere sequence of illusions. It becomes art. In the art of magic, as opposed to just doing tricks, there is a sense of theater and drama and continuity and beauty and wholeness. Take an example. Someone in the audience randomly selects a card from a shuffled deck—the Ace of Diamonds. The card is made to vanish, then a rabbit is pulled out of a hat, and the hat collapses into a fan, and the magician uses the fan to fan the rabbit, and the rabbit is transformed into a white dove, and the dove flies into the spotlights and returns a moment later with a playing card in its beak—the Ace of Diamonds. With such unity and flow, with each element contributing as both cause and effect, individual tricks are blended into something whole and unified, something indivisible, which is in the nature of true art.

Beyond anything, though, what appealed to me about this hobby was the abiding mystery at its heart. Mystery everywhere—permeating mystery—even in the most ordinary objects of the world: a penny becomes a white mouse. The universe seemed both infinite and inexplicable. Anything was possible. The old rules were no longer binding, the old truths no longer true. If my father's tie could be restored whole, why not someday use my wand to wake up the dead?

It's pretty clear, I suppose, where all this is headed. I stopped doing magic—at least of that sort. I took up a new hobby, writing stories. But without straining too much, I can suggest that the fundamentals seemed very much the same. Writing fiction is a solitary endeavor. You shape your own universe. You practice all the time, then practice some more. You pay attention to craft. You aim for tension and suspense, a sense of drama, displaying in concrete terms the actions and reactions of human beings contesting problems of the heart. You try to make art. You strive for wholeness, seeking continuity and flow, each element performing both as cause and effect, always hoping to create, or to re-create, the great illusions of life.

Above all, writing fiction involves a desire to enter the mystery of things: that human craving to know what cannot be known. In the ordinary world, for instance, we have no direct access to the thoughts of other human beings—we cannot *hear* those thoughts—yet even in the most "realistic" piece of fiction we listen as if through a stethoscope to the innermost musings of Anna Karenina and

Lord Jim and Huck Finn. We know, in these stories, what cannot be known. It's a trick, of course. (And the tricks in these stories have been elevated into art.) In the ordinary sense, there *is* no Huck Finn, and yet in the extraordinary sense, which is the sense of magic, there most certainly *is* a Huck Finn and always will be. When writing or reading a work of fiction, we are seeking access to a kind of enigmatic "otherness"—other people and places, other worlds, other sciences, other souls. We give ourselves over to what is by nature mysterious, imagining the unknowable, and then miraculously knowing by virtue of what is imagined. There are new standards of knowing, new standards of reality. (Is Huck Finn real? No, we would say, by ordinary standards. Yes, by extraordinary standards.) For a writer, and for a reader, the process of imaginative knowing does not depend upon the scientific method. Fictional characters are not constructed of flesh and blood, but rather of words, and those words serve as explicit incantations that invite us into and guide us through the universe of the imagination. Language is the apparatus —the magic dust—by which a writer performs his miracles. Words are uttered: "By and by," Huck says, and we hear him. Words are uttered: "We went tiptoeing along a path amongst the trees," and we see it. Beyond anything, I think, a writer is someone entranced by the power of language to create a magic show of the imagination, to make the dead sit up and talk, to shine light into the darkness of the great human mysteries.

In many cultures, including our own, the magician and the storyteller are often embodied in a single person. This seems most obvious, I suppose, in religion, which seeks to penetrate into the greatest mysteries of all. The healer, or the miracle worker, is also the teller of stories about prior miracles, or about miracles still to come. In Christianity, the personage of Jesus is presented as a doer of both earthly miracles and the ultimate heavenly miracle of salvation. At the same time Jesus is a teller of miraculous stories—the parables, for instance, or the larger story about damnation and redemption. The performance of miracles and the telling of stories become part of a whole. One aspect serves the other. In the culture of the North American Kiowa tribes, the shaman or witch doctor was believed to have access to an unseen world, a world of demons and gods and ancestral spirits, and these spirits were invoked in rites of healing and exorcism and divine intervention. But the shaman also told stories *about* those spirits: their wars, their loves, their treacheries, their defeats, their victories. The shaman's earthly claims upon his people were at once validated and legitimized by heavenly stories.

My point, of course, has to do with the interpenetration of magic and stories. In part, at least, storytelling involves the conjuring up of spirits—Huck Finn or Lord Jim. And those spirits, in turn, make implicit moral claims on us, serving as models of a sort, suggesting by implication how we might or might not lead our own lives. Stories encourage and discourage. Stories affirm and negate. In the tales of the Kiowa shaman, as in those of the modern New York novelist, spirits of virtue struggle against spirits of evil, heroes go up against villains, antiheroes confront antivillains, and in the course of the narrative a spirit's spirit is both defined and refined in moral terms. But these terms are not absolute. Stories are rooted in particulars—this village, this time, this character—and it strikes me that storytelling represents one form of what we now call situational ethics. The spirits in a story cast moral shadow and moral light. By example, through drama, stories display our own potential for good and evil: the range of moral possibility is extended.

There is also, I think, an incorporeal but nonetheless genuine "aliveness" to the characters, or ghosts, that are conjured up by good stories. In *The Sun Also Rises,* Jake Barnes and Brett Ashley and Bill Gorton and Mike Campbell are identities—spirits of a sort—that live between the covers of that book. They are not embodied, of course, and never were. They have no flesh and never did. Yet these characters live in the way spirits live, in the memory and imagination of the reader, as a dead father lives in the memory of his son or in the imagination of his daughter. The storyteller evokes, and invokes, this spirit world not with potions or pixie dust, but, as I suggested earlier, with the magic of language—those potent nouns, those levitating verbs, those tricky little adverbs, those amazing conjunctions, the whole spectacular show of clauses becoming sentences and sentences becoming paragraphs and paragraphs becoming stories. The Kiowa shaman achieves a similar effect by inducing in his tribe a trancelike state, summoning a collective dream with the language of incantation and narrative drama. The writer of fiction, like the shaman, serves as a medium of sorts between two different worlds—the world of ordinary reality and the extraordinary world of the imagination. In this capacity, the writer often enters a trancelike state of his own. Certainly this is my own experience. When I am writing well, invoking well, there is a dreamlike sense of gazing through the page as if it were the thinnest onionskin parchment, watching the spirits beyond, quietly looking on as the various characters go about their peculiar business. This is the sensation I get—both physical and emotional—as a waking dream unfolds into words and as the words unfold into a piece of fiction. Half in the embodied world, half in a world where bodies are superfluous. I realize, as this semitrance occurs, that the page before me is only paper, the typescript only ink, and yet there is also a powerful awareness of those ghostly characters in motion just behind the page, just beyond the boundaries of the mundane. Whatever we call this process—imagination, fantasy, self-hypnosis, creativity—I know from my own life that it is both magical and real. And I think other writers of fiction would offer similar testimony. In any case, to complete the parallel with which I began, it is reported that the Kiowa shaman, too, enters the trance of his own dream, partly as a way of inducing that dream in his tribe, partly to serve as a guide into and through the other, fictional world. The more I write and the more I dream, the more I accept this notion of the writer as a medium between two planes of being—the ordinary and the extraordinary—the embodied world of flesh, the disembodied world of idea and morality and spirit.

In this sense, then, I must also believe that writing is essentially an act of faith. Faith in the heuristic power of the imagination. Faith in the fertility of dream. Faith that as writers we might discover that which cannot be known through empirical means. (The notions of right and wrong, for instance. Good and evil. Ugliness and beauty.) Faith in story itself. Faith that a story will lead, in some way, to epiphany or understanding or enlightenment. In the most practical sense, just to *begin* a story involves a great leap of faith that the first imagined event will somehow lead to the next, that chapter two will somehow follow upon chapter one. Faith that language will continue to serve us from day to day. Faith that a story will take us somewhere—in the plot sense, in the thematic sense—and that the destination will be worth the journey. And just as faith seems essential to me as a writer, and maybe to all of us, it seems also true that crises of faith are common to the vocation of the storyteller: writer's block, lapses of confidence, the terror of aesthetic subjectivity as the final arbiter of excellence. For all of us, I would guess, there is, at least on occasion, a terrible sense of howling in the dark. I would suppose that many of us have experienced more than one crisis of faith—in our talents, in our lives—and yet because we are still at work, still writing, I would also suppose that we have at some point undergone a renewal of that faith.

So far I've been discussing, in a less than systematic way, a set of "mysteries" inherent in the *process* of writing fiction. But it seems to me that the fiction itself —the story, the novel—must ultimately represent and explore those same mysteries. Or to say it bluntly: it is my view that good storytelling involves, in a substantive sense, a plunge into mystery of the grandest order. Briefly, almost in summary form, I want to examine this notion through two different windows of craft—plot and character.

It is my belief that plot revolves around certain mysteries of fact, or what a story represents as fact. What happened? What will happen? Huck and Jim hop on a raft (fact) and embark on a journey (fact) and numerous events occur along the way (facts). On the level of plot, this narrative appeals to our curiosity about where the various facts will lead. As readers, we wonder and worry about what may befall these two human beings as they float down a river in violation of the ordinary social conventions. We are curious about facts still to come. In this sense, plot involves the inherent and riveting mystery of the *future*. What next? What are the coming facts? By its very nature, the future compels and intrigues us —it holds promise, it holds terror—and plot relies for its power on the essential cloudiness of things to come. We don't know. We want to know.

In a magic act, as in a story, there is the reporting (or purporting) of certain facts. The guillotine *is* sharp, it *does* cut the carrot, the man's hand *does* enter the guillotine's hole, the blade *does* slam down. For an audience, the mystery has entirely to do with future facts. What will become of this poor man? Will he lose his hand? Will he weep? Will the stump bleed as stumps tend to do?

Without some concept of the future, these questions would be both impossible and irrelevant. It is the mystery of the future, at least in part, that compels us to turn the pages of a novel, or of a story, or of our own lives. Unlike the animals, we conceive of tomorrow. And tomorrow fascinates us. Tomorrow matters— maybe too much—and we spend a great portion of our lives adjusting the present in hope of shaping the future. In any case, we are driven to care and to be curious about questions of fate and destiny: we can't help it, we're human.

On one level, then, I am arguing in defense of old-fashioned plot—or in defense of plot in general—which is so often discredited as a sop to some unsophisticated and base human instinct. But I see nothing base in the question,

"What will happen next?" I'm suggesting that plot is grounded in a high—even noble—human craving to *know,* a craving to push into the mystery of tomorrow.

This is not to argue, however, that plot need give an impression of finality. A good plot does not tie up the loose ends of the future in a tidy little knot. The plot of my own life has not often, so far as I can tell, resolved itself in any neat and final way. Death itself, when it comes, dissolves into enigma. Maybe this, maybe that. But who knows? Who really *knows?* The plot mystery of life—what will happen to us, to all of us, to the human race—is unresolved and must remain that way if it is to endure as a compelling story. As a species, I believe, we are beguiled by uncertainty. It is both a gift and a burden. We crave knowledge, yes, but we also crave its absence, for the absence alone makes possible the joy of discovery. Once the factual curtain falls—for instance, if we were to know beyond doubt that Lee Harvey Oswald acted on his own to assassinate President Kennedy—that ticklish sense of uncertainty vanishes and the puzzle no longer puzzles and the story is both finished and boring. Nothing remains to ignite curiosity. Nothing beckons, nothing tantalizes. As Edmund Wilson suggests in his famous comment, "Who cares who killed Cock Robin," there is something both false and trivial about a story that arrives at absolute closure. With closure, the facts of today have no bearing on the facts of tomorrow. (It seems ironic that most so-called mystery stories conclude with no mystery whatsoever. The killer's methods and motives are exposed. Ah, we think, no *wonder.* All is explicable, all is settled. The case is closed.) A satisfying plot, I believe, involves not a diminution of mystery but rather a fundamental enlargement. As in scientific endeavor, the solution to one set of problems must open out into another and even greater set. The future must still matter. The unknown must still issue its call. One tomorrow must imply the next.

About real people, we sometimes say: "Well, she's a mystery to me," or "I wonder what makes him tick." Such comments represent, I think, a deep and specific desire for the miraculous: to enter another human soul, to read other minds and hearts, to find access to what is by nature inaccessible. A person lives in his own skin. All else is other, and otherness is suspect. If we see a man laugh, for instance, we might guess that he is experiencing elation or giddiness or joy of some sort. But perhaps not. Maybe it's ironic laughter, or nervous laughter, or the laughter of the insane. Again, who knows? In a story called *The Lady with the Pet Dog,* Chekhov has one of his characters muse as follows: "Judging others by himself, he did not believe what he saw, and always fancied that every man led his real, most interesting life under cover of secrecy as under cover of night." It is easy to sympathize with this view. Like Chekhov's character, we can "judge others by ourselves," but we cannot directly experience their loves and pains and joys. We know our own thoughts—we know by the act of thinking—but we cannot think those "other" thoughts. The mystery of otherness seems permanent and binding, a law of the universe, and yet *because* it is a mystery, *because* it binds, we find ourselves clawing at the darkness of human nature in an effort to know what cannot be known. "I love you," someone says, and we begin to wonder. "Well, how much?" we say, and when the answer comes, "With my whole heart," we then wonder about the wholeness of that heart. We probe and probe again. Along with Chekhov, we fancy that there is some secret lodged inside a human personality, hidden as if under cover of night, and that if light could be cast into the darkness of another's heart, we would find there the "real" human being. Such curiosity seems to me both inevitable and misdirected. Judging from what I know of myself, the human "character," if there is such a thing, seems far too complex and fluid and contradictory ever to pin down with much solidity or specificity. To really know a human character, to expose a single "secret," strikes me as beyond reach. In a sense, we "know" human character—maybe even our own—in the same way we know black holes: by their effects on the external world. The source of the light is sucked up by the nature of nature.

My focus here is on the construction of literary character, and my general argument is that characterization is achieved not through a "pinning down" process but rather through a process that opens up and releases mysteries of the human spirit. The object is not to "solve" a character—to expose some hidden secret—but instead to deepen and enlarge the riddle itself. Too often, I believe, characterization fails precisely *because* it attempts to characterize. It narrows; it pins down; it explicates; it solves. The nasty miser is actually quite sweet and generous. The harlot has a heart of gold. The gunfighter is a peaceable guy who yearns to own a small cattle ranch. The failure here is twofold. For me, at least, such solutions do not square with my sense of the immense complexity of man's spirit. The human life seems cheapened. Beyond that, however, this sort of characterization has the effect of diminishing the very mystery that makes us care so passionately about other human beings. There is false and arbitrary closure. A "solved" character ceases to be mysterious, hence becomes less than human. As with plot, I believe that successful characterization requires an enhancement of mystery: not shrinkage, but expansion. To beguile, to bewitch, to cause lasting wonder—these are the aims of characterization. Think of Kurtz in *Heart of Darkness*. He has witnessed profound savagery, has immersed himself in it, and as he lies dying, we hear him whisper, "The horror, the horror." There is no solution here. Rather, the reverse. The heart *is* dark. We gape into the tangle of this man's soul, which has the quality of a huge black hole, ever widening, ever mysterious, its gravity sucking us back into the book itself. What intrigues us, ultimately, is not what we know but what we do not know and yearn to discover.

The magician's credo is this: don't give away your secrets. Once a trick is explained—once a secret is divulged—the world moves from the magical to the mechanical. Similarly, with plot and character, the depletion of mystery robs a story of the very quality that brings us to pursue fiction in the first place. We might admire the cleverness of the writer. But we forget the story. Because there is no miracle to remember. The object of storytelling, like the object of magic, is not to explain or to resolve, but rather to create and to perform miracles of the imagination. To extend the boundaries of the mysterious. To push into the unknown in pursuit of still other unknowns. To reach into one's own heart, down into that place where the stories are, bringing up the mystery of oneself.

DISCUSSION QUESTIONS

1. O'Brien lists the fundamental similarities of magic and story writing. Which of these similarities do you consider most persuasive? To what degree do you feel drawn to writing stories for these features?

2. O'Brien describes language as the "magic dust" through which a writer explores "great human mysteries." What can you say about this process in terms of your own writing experience?

3. Culturally, "the magician and the storyteller are often embodied in the same person," O'Brien states. What is your sense of this link between magic and storytelling? What memories do you have of the magic of storytelling in your family, among your friends, or in the wider culture?

4. Do you share O'Brien's experience of entering a dream or trance when you're writing stories? How does this feel? Do you agree that writing is an "act of faith" in the power of imagination and story?

5. O'Brien argues that plot should not lessen mystery but rather should enlarge it. What does he mean by this? What consequences does this view have for how you think about resolving your plots and ending your stories?

6. O'Brien also challenges the idea that characters in fiction can or should be fully explained, or solved. In relation to character, how might you put into practice his assertion that stories should "extend the boundaries of the mysterious"?

THE FICTION WRITER
AND POLITICS

E. L. DOCTOROW

False Documents

E. L. Doctorow (b. 1931) has taught at New York University since 1982. Among his many widely read novels are Welcome to Hard Times *(1960),* The Book of Daniel *(1971, nominated for a National Book Award),* Ragtime *(1975, National Book Critics Circle Award),* Loon Lake *(1980),* World's Fair *(1985, National Book Award),* Billy Bathgate *(1989, National Book Critics Circle Award),* The Waterworks *(1994), and* City of God *(2000). He has also written plays, screenplays, and essays on literature and politics. The selection we've chosen reflects his thoughts on the interplay of literature and politics.*

Fiction is a not entirely rational means of discourse. It gives to the reader something more than information. Complex understandings, indirect, intuitive, and nonverbal, arise from the words of the story, and by a ritual transaction between reader and writer, instructive emotion is generated in the reader from the illusion of suffering an experience not his own. A novel is a printed circuit through which flows the force of a reader's own life.

Sartre in his essay "Literature and Existentialism" says: ". . . each book is a recovery of the totality of being . . . For this is quite the final goal of art: to recover this world by giving it to be seen as it is, but as if it had its source in human freedom."

Certainly I know that I would rather read a sentence such as this from Nabokov's *The Gift*—

> As he crossed toward the pharmacy at the corner he involuntarily turned his head because of a burst of light that had ricocheted from his temple, and saw, with that quick smile with which we greet a rainbow or a rose, a blindingly white parallelogram of sky being unloaded from the van—a dresser with mirror, across which, as across a cinema screen, passed a flawlessly clear reflection of boughs, sliding and swaying not arboreally, but with a human vascillation, produced by the nature of those who were carrying this sky, these boughs, this gliding facade.

—whose occasion is in question, whose truth I cannot test, than a sentence such as this from the rational mentality of *The New York Times*—

> The Navy has announced base consolidations and other actions that it said would eliminate 500 civilian jobs and 16 military positions at an annual savings of about five million dollars.

—whose purposes are immediately clear, and with regard to whose truth I am completely credulous.

As a writer of fiction I could make the claim that a sentence spun from the imagination, i.e., a sentence composed as a lie, confers upon the writer a degree of perception or acuity or heightened awareness, but in any event some additional usefulness, that a sentence composed with the most strict reverence for fact does not. In any event, what can surely be distinguished here are two kinds of power in language, the power of the Navy's announcement residing in its manifest reference to the verifiable world—let us call that *the power of the regime*—and the power of Nabokov's description inhering in a private or ideal world that cannot be easily corroborated or verified—let us call that *the power of freedom*.

Immediately I have to wonder if this formulation is too grandiose—the power of the regime and the power of freedom. But it is true that we live in an industrial society which counts its achievements from the discoveries of science and which runs on empirical thinking and precise calculations. In such a society language is conceived primarily as the means by which facts are communicated. Language is seen as a property of facts themselves—their persuasive property. We are taught that facts are to be distinguished from feeling and that feeling is what we are permitted for our rest and relaxation when the facts get us down. This is the bias of scientific method and empiricism by which the world reveals itself and gives itself over to our control insofar as we recognize the primacy of fact-reality. We all kick the rock to refute Berkeley.

So what I suppose I mean by *the power of the regime* is first of all the modern consensus of sensibility that could be called *realism,* which, since there is more than epistemology to this question of knowing the world, may be defined as the business of getting on and producing for ourselves what we construe as the satisfaction of our needs—and doing it with standards of measure, market studies, contracts, tests, polls, training manuals, office memos, press releases, and headlines.

But I shall go further: if we are able to recognize and name any broad consensus of sensibility we are acknowledging its rule. Anything which governs us must by necessity be self-interested and organized to continue itself. Therefore I have to conclude that the regime of facts is not from God but man-made, and, as such, infinitely violable. For instance, it used to be proposed as a biological fact that women were emotionally less stable and intellectually less capable than men. What we proclaim as the discovered factual world can be challenged as the questionable world we ourselves have painted—the cultural museum of our values, dogmas, assumptions, that prescribes for us not only what we may like and dislike, believe and disbelieve, but also what we may be permitted to see and not to see.

And so I am led to an acceptance of my phraseology. There is a regime language that derives its strength from what we are supposed to be and a language of freedom whose power consists in what we threaten to become. And I'm justified in giving a political character to the nonfictive and fictive uses of language because there is conflict between them.

It is possible there was a time in which the designative and evocative functions of language were one and the same. I remember being taught that in school. The sun was Zeus' chariot in fact as well as fiction—the chariot was metaphor and operative science at one and the same time. The gods have very particular names and powers and emotions in Homer. They go about deflecting arrows, bringing on human rages, turning hearts, and controlling history. Nevertheless there really was a Troy and a Trojan war. Alone among the arts, literature confuses fact and fiction. In the Bible the natural and supernatural flow into each other, man and God go hand in hand. Even so, there are visible to our own time volcanoes that are pillars of fire by night and pillars of cloud by day.

I conclude there must have been a world once in which the act of telling a story was in itself a presumption of truth. It was not necessarily a better world than our own, but as a writer of fiction I can see the advantages to my craft of not having a reader question me and ask if what I've written is true—that is, if it really happened. In our society there is no presumption of truth in the act of storytelling except in the minds of children. We have complex understandings of the different functions of language and we can all recognize the esthetic occasion and differentiate it from a "real" one. This means to me that literature is less a tool for survival than it once was. In ancient times, presumably, the storyteller got a spot near the fire because the story he told defined the powers to which the listener was subject and suggested how to live with them. Literature was as valuable as a club or a sharpened bone. It bound the present to the past, the visible with the invisible, and it helped to compose the community necessary for the continuing life of its members.

In Walter Benjamin's brilliant essay "The Story Teller: Reflections on the Works of Nikolai Leskov," I read that storytelling in the Middle Ages was primarily a means of giving counsel. The resident master craftsmen and traveling journeyman worked together in the same room and stories passed between them in the rhythm of their work. Thus each story was honed by time and many tellers. If the story was good the counsel was valuable and therefore the story was true. "The art of story telling is coming to an end," Benjamin says, writing in 1936. "Less and less frequently do we encounter people with the ability to tell a tale properly. . . . one reason for this is obvious: experience has fallen in value . . . we are not richer but poorer in communicable experience."

For our sins, Benjamin implies, we have the novelist, an isolated individual who gives birth to his novel whole, himself uncounseled and without the ability to counsel others. "In the midst of life's fullness, the novel gives evidence of the profound perplexity of the living," he says. "The first great novel, *Don Quixote,* teaches how the spiritual greatness, the boldness, the helpfulness, of one of the noblest of men, Don Quixote, are completely devoid of counsel and do not contain the slightest scintilla of wisdom."

But I am interested in the ways, not peculiar to itself, that *Don Quixote* does its teaching. And of special significance I think is Cervantes' odd claim that he cannot be considered the author of his book. In Chapter 9, Part One, for instance, he introduces the Don's adventures that follow by claiming to have come across an account of them, on parchment, by an Arab historian, in a marketplace in Toledo. "I bought all the parchments for half a *real*," he confides. "But if the merchant had any sense and known how much I wanted them he might have demanded and got more than six reals from the sale."

I look at another great early fiction, *Robinson Crusoe,* and see that it is treated by its author in much the same way. There is a Robinson Crusoe and this is his memoir, and Daniel Defoe has only edited this book for him. As editor, Defoe can assure us, with all the integrity naturally falling to his profession, that the story is true. "The editor believes the thing to be a just history of fact," he says. "Neither is there any appearance of fiction in it."

So both of these classic practitioners dissociate themselves from the work apparently as a means of gaining authority for the narrative. They use other voices than their own in the composition and present themselves not as authors but as literary executors. In the excellent phrase of Kenneth Rexroth, they adopt the device of the "false document."

I'm not familiar enough with their publishing histories to know the degree of gullibility with which these false documents were originally received by their readers. Certainly the parodic intentions of *Don Quixote* were explicit. But the romances of chivalry and pastoral love that punctuate the narrative stand in contrast to the realistic humiliations of the Don. Cervantes complains at the beginning of Part Two of *Don Quixote* that other writers have, subsequent to the great success of Part One, written their own histories of the same person. In fact, he has Quixote and Sancho Panza review their representations in the piratical works, thus conferring upon themselves an additional falsely documented reality. But let us grant Cervantes' audience, and Defoe's as well, a gullibility no greater than ironic appreciation: in order to have its effect, a false document need only be possibly true. The transparency of the pretense does not damage it. A man named Alexander Selkirk who had been a castaway was famous in Defoe's London and all the English readers needed to know to read *Crusoe* and to believe it, was that there were others who could have had Selkirk's experience . . . .

Of course every fiction is a false document in that compositions of words are not life. But I speak specifically of the novelist's act of creative disavowal by which the text he offers takes on some additional authority because he did not write it, or latterly, because he claims it was impossible to write it.

Come back for a moment to *Robinson Crusoe.* As a false document it interests me enormously. It was published at a time when the life adventures of Alexander Selkirk had been well broadcast in London for several years. In fact Selkirk's autobiography had been published and there is reason to believe Defoe actually interviewed him. Selkirk was a clearly unstable, tormented individual. His months alone on an island had so wrecked what equanimity he had that when he was restored to London he immediately built himself a cave in his garden, and he lived in the cave and sulked and raged, an embarrassment to his family and a menace to his neighbors. Defoe turned this disturbed person into the stout, resolute Englishman (Crusoe), a genius at survival by the grace of his belief in God and in the white European race.

And inevitably, Crusoe the composition has obscured Selkirk the man, whose great gift to civilization, we see now, was in providing Daniel Defoe the idea for a story. The story tells what happens when an urban Englishman is removed from his environment and plunked down in nature. What happens is that he defines the national character.

But the point about this first of the great false documents in English is that at the moment of its publication there was an indwelling of the art in the real life, everyone in London who read *Crusoe* knew about Selkirk, there was intravention, a mixing-up of the historic and the esthetic, the real and the possibly real. And what was recovered was the state of wisdom that existed, for Walter Benjamin, before fact and fiction became ontologically differentiated—that is, when it was possible for fiction to give counsel.

The novelist deals with his isolation by splitting himself in two, creator and documentarian, teller and listener, conspiring to pass on the collective wisdom in its own language, disguised in its own enlightened bias, that of the factual world.

It is not a bad system, but it gets the writer into trouble. To offer facts to the witness of the imagination and pretend they are real is to commit a kind of regressive heresy. The language of politicians, historians, journalists and social scientists always presumes a world of fact discovered, and like a religious tenet the presumption is held more fiercely the more it is seen to be illusory.

Fiction writers are at best inconvenient, like some old relative in mismatching pants and jacket who knocks on our door during a dinner party to remind us from what we come. Society has several ways of dealing with this inconvenience. The writer is given most leeway in the Western democracies which are the most industrially advanced. In these countries, where empiricism works so well as to be virtually unassailable, the writer-nuisance is relegated to the shadow world of modern esthetics or culture, a nonintegral antiuniverse with reflections of power rather than power, with a kind of shamanistic potence at best, subject to the whims of gods and spirits, an imitation with words of the tangible real world of act and event and thunder.

In those countries which are not advanced industrial democracies the writer is treated with more respect. In Uganda or Iran or Chile or Indonesia or the Soviet Union, a writer using the common coin of the political speech or the press release or the newspaper editorial to compose facts in play is accorded the power to do harm. He is recognized to have discovered the secret the politician is born knowing: that good and evil are construed, that there is no outrage, no monstrousness that cannot be made reasonable and logical and virtuous, and no shining act that cannot be turned to disgrace—with language.

Thus the American Center of PEN, the organization of novelists, poets, essayists, editors, and publishers, finds it necessary to distribute each year a poster entitled WRITERS IN PRISON. This poster, which is very large, simply lists the writers who are currently locked in cells or insane asylums or torture chambers in various countries around the world—who are by their being and profession threats to the security of political regimes. The imprisonment of writers is common in countries of the right and of the left, it doesn't seem to matter what the ideology. I know from the novelist Alexander Solzhenitsyn about the Gulag Archipelago, the network of Soviet prison camps and secret police in Siberia, but I know too from Reza Baraheni, the Iranian novelist and poet now living in this country, about the Iranian secret police, SAVAK, and the hideous torture of artists and intellectuals in Iranian prisons. Wherever citizens are seen routinely as enemies of their own government, writers are routinely seen to be the most dangerous enemies.

So that in most countries of the world literature is politics. All writers are by definition *engagé*. Even if they are timid gentle souls who write pastoral verses on remote farms, the searchlight will seek them out.

In this country we are embarrassed or angered by the excesses of repression of foreign petty tyrants and murderous bureaucracies. But forgetting the excesses the point of view is hardly unprecedented. Elizabethan writers lived in the shadow of the Tower and when Plato proposed his ideal republic he decreed that poets were to be outlawed. Part of our problem, as Americans, in failing to apprehend the relationship of art and politics is, of course, our national good fortune. . . . Our primary control of writers in the United States does not have to be violent— it operates on the assumption that esthetics is a limited arena where according to the rules we may be shocked or threatened, but only in fun. The novelist need not be taken seriously because his work is a taste of young people, women, intellectuals, and other pampered minorities, and, lacking any real currency, is not part of the relevant business of the nation.

If these thoughts were a story the story would tell of a real tangible world and the writer's witness of that world in which some writers occasionally, by the grace of God, cause the real world to compose itself according to the witness, as our faces compose themselves in our mirrors.

However I detect a faint presumption of romance in my attitude, and I have to wonder why I suspect myself of being less than hospitable to the forms of nonfictive discourse, as if they were a team from another city. Nonfiction enjoys the sort of authority that has not easily been granted fiction since Walter Benjamin's storytellers traded their last tales. On the other hand it does give up something for the privilege, it is dulled by the obligation to be factual. This is acknowledged by the same people who would not pick up a novel, but who say of a particularly good biography or history that it reads like one.

Perhaps I feel that the nonfictive premise of a discoverable factual world is in itself a convention no less hoary than Cervantes' Arab historian.

Consider those occasions—criminal trials in courts of law—when society arranges with all its investigative apparatus to apprehend factual reality. Using the tested rules of evidence and the accrued wisdom of our system of laws we determine the guilt or innocence of defendants and come to judgment. Yet the most important trials in our history, those which reverberate in our lives and have most meaning for our future, are those in which the judgment is called into question:

Scopes, Sacco and Vanzetti, the Rosenbergs. Facts are buried, exhumed, deposed, contradicted, recanted. There is a decision by the jury and, when the historical and prejudicial context of the decision is examined, a subsequent judgment by history. And the trial shimmers forever with just that perplexing ambiguity characteristic of a true novel. . . .

"There are no facts in themselves," said Nietzsche. "For a fact to exist we must first introduce meaning." When a physicist invents an incredibly sophisticated instrument to investigate subatomic phenomena, he must wonder to what degree the instrument changes or creates the phenomena it reports. This problem was elucidated by Werner Heisenberg as the Principle of Uncertainty. At the highest level of scruple and reportorial disinterest there is the intrusive factor of an organized consciousness. At lower levels, in law, in political history, the intrusion is not instrumental but moral: meaning must be introduced, and no judgment does not carry the passion of the judge.

We all know examples of history that doesn't exist. We used to laugh at the Russians who in their encyclopedias attributed every major industrial invention to themselves. We knew how their great leaders who had fallen out of favor were erased from their history texts. We were innocent then: our own school and university historians had done just the same thing to whole peoples who lived and died in this country but were seriously absent from our texts: black people, Indians, Chinese. There is no history except as it is composed. There are no failed revolutions, only lawless conspiracies. All history is contemporary history, says Croce in *History, as the Story of Liberty:* "However remote in time events may seem to be, every historical judgment refers to present needs and situations." That is why history has to be written and rewritten from one generation to another. The act of composition can never end.

What is an historical fact? A spent shell? A bombed-out building? A pile of shoes? A victory parade? A long march? Once it has been suffered it maintains itself in the mind of witness or victim, and if it is to reach anyone else it is transmitted in words or on film and it becomes an image, which, with other images, constitutes a judgment. I am well aware that some facts, for instance the Nazi extermination of the Jews, are so indisputably monstrous as to seem to stand alone. But history shares with fiction a mode of mediating the world for the purpose of introducing meaning, and it is the cultural authority from which they both derive that illuminates those facts so that they can be perceived.

Facts are the images of history, just as images are the data of fiction.

Of course it happens that the people most skeptical of history as a nonfictive discipline are the historians themselves. E. H. Carr, in his famous essay, "The Historian and His Facts," speaks of history "as a continuous process of interaction" between the writer of history and his facts. Carr also quotes the American historian Carl Becker, who said: "The facts of history do not exist for any historian until he has created them." Neither man would be surprised by the tentative conclusions of the structuralist critic Roland Barthes who, in an essay entitled "Historical Discourse," attempts to find the specific linguistic features that differentiate factual and imaginary narrative. "By structures alone," Barthes concludes, "historical discourse is essentially a product of ideology, or rather of imagination." In other words a visitor from another planet could not by study of the techniques of discourse distinguish composed fiction from composed history. The important stylistic device of composed history, the chaste or objective voice, one that gives no clues to the personality of the narrator, Barthes says, "turns out to be a particular form of fiction." (Teachers of English know that form well: they call it Realism.)

So that as a novelist considering this particular non-fictive discipline I could claim that history is a kind of fiction in which we live and hope to survive, and fiction is a kind of speculative history, perhaps a superhistory, by which the available data for the composition is seen to be greater and more various in its sources than the historian supposes.

At issue is the human mind, which has to be shocked, seduced, or otherwise provoked out of its habitual stupor. Even the Biblical prophets knew they had to make it new. They shouted and pointed their fingers to heaven, but they were poets too, and dramatists. Isaiah walked abroad naked and Jeremiah wore a yoke around his neck to prophesy deportation and slavery, respectively, to their soon to be deported and enslaved countrymen. Moral values are inescapably esthetic. In the modern world it is the moral regime of factual reality that impinges on the provinces of art. News magazines present the events of the world as an ongoing weekly serial. Weather reports are constructed on television with exact attention to conflict (high pressure areas clashing with lows), suspense (the climax of tomorrow's weather prediction coming after the commercial), and other basic elements of narrative. The creating, advertising, packaging, and marketing of factual products is unquestionably a fictional enterprise. The novelist looking around him has inevitably to wonder why he is isolated by a profession when everywhere the factualists have appropriated his techniques and even brought a kind of exhaustion to the dramatic modes by the incessant exploitation of them.

Nevertheless, there is something we honor in the character of a journalist—whatever it is that makes him value reportorial objectivity and assure us at the same time that it is an unattainable ideal. We recognize and trust that combination of passion and humility. It is the religious temperament.

The virtues of the social sciences are even more appealing to us. Sociologists and social psychologists not only make communion with facts but in addition display the scientific method of dealing with them. The tale told by the social scientists, the counsel given, is nonspecific, collated, and subject to verification. Because they revise each other's work constantly and monitor themselves as novelists do not, and are like a democracy in that the rule of this or that elevated theorist is subject to new elections every few years, we find them ingenuous and trustworthy. Today we read the empirical fictions of Konrad Lorenz or Oscar Lewis, B. F. Skinner or Eric Erikson, as we used to read Dickens and Balzac, for pleasure and instruction. The psychologists' and sociologists' compositions of facts seem less individualistic and thus more dependable than any random stubborn vision of which the novelist is capable. They propose to understand human character or to define it as a function of ethnic background, sexuality, age, economic class, and they produce composite portraits like those done in a police station—bad art, but we think we see someone we recognize. It is at least a possibility that the idea of human beings as demographic collections of traits, or as loci of cultural and racial and economic events, is exactly what is needed in our industrial society to keep the machines going. We have in such concepts as "complex," "sublimation," "repression," "identity crisis," "object relations," "borderline," and so on, the interchangeable parts of all of us. In this sense modern psychology is the industrialization of storytelling.

I am thus led to the proposition that there is no fiction or nonfiction as we commonly understand the distinction: there is only narrative.

But it is a novelist's proposition, I can see that very well. It is in my interest to claim that there is no difference between what I do and what everyone else does. I claim as I pull everyone else over to my side of the mirror that there is nothing between the given universe and our attempt to mediate it, there is no real power, only some hope that we might deny our own contingency.

And I am led to an even more pugnacious view—that the development of civilizations is essentially a progression of metaphors.

The novelist's opportunity to do his work today is increased by the power of the regime to which he finds himself in opposition. As clowns in the circus imitate the aerialists and tightrope walkers, first for laughs and then so that it can be seen that they do it better, we have it in us to compose false documents more valid, more real, more truthful than the "true" documents of the politicians or the journalists or the psychologists. Novelists know explicitly that the world in which we live is still to be formed and that reality is amenable to any construction that is placed upon it. It is a world made for liars and we are born liars. But we are to be trusted because ours is the only profession forced to admit that it lies—and that bestows upon us the mantle of honesty. "In a writer's eyes," said Emerson, "anything which can be thought can be written; the writer is the faculty of reporting and the universe is the possibility of being reported." By our independence of all institutions, from the family to the government, and with no responsibility to defend them from their own hypocrisy and murderousness, we are a valuable resource and an instrument of survival. There is no nonfictive discipline that does not rule out some element of the human psyche, that does not restrict some human energy and imprison it, that does not exclude some monstrous phantom of human existence. Unlike the politicians we take office first and then create our constituencies and that is to be a shade more arrogant than the politicians. But our right and our justification and redemption is in emulating the false documents that we universally call our dreams. For dreams are the first false documents, of course: they are never real, they are never factual; nevertheless they control us, purge us, mediate our baser natures, and prophesy our fate.

DISCUSSION QUESTIONS

1. What distinction does Doctorow make between "the power of the regime" and "the power of freedom"?
2. In what way does Doctorow feel "justified in giving a political character to the nonfictive and fictive uses of language because there is conflict between them"? In other words, in what way is fiction writing a political use of language?
3. In most countries other than the United States, how is literature quite literally a political act? What prevents fiction from becoming truly political in the United States?
4. In what way can it be true that fiction, which is technically "a lie, confers upon the writer a degree of perception or acuity or heightened awareness, but in any event some additional usefulness, that a sentence composed with the most strict reverence for fact does not"?
5. From where does Doctorow borrow his metaphor of "false documents"? What does all fiction share, metaphorically, with a "false document" such as *Don Quixote* or *Robinson Crusoe*?
6. In what ways are all "narratives" (including fiction, history, sociology, and science) "false documents"?

CHARLES BAXTER

Dysfunctional Narratives
Or "Mistakes Were Made"

Charles Baxter (b. 1947) teaches fiction writing at the University of Michigan, where he has also been director of the MFA program. He has published five collections of short stories including A Relative Stranger *(1990) and* Believers *(1997); three novels, most recently* The Feast of Love *(2000); a volume of essays,* Burning Down the House: Essays on Fiction *(1997); and a book of poetry,* Imaginary Paintings and Other Poems *(1990). He won the O'Henry Prize in 1995.*

Here are some sentences of distinctive American prose from our era.

> From a combination of hypersensitivity and a desire not to know the truth in case it turned out to be unpleasant, I had spent the last ten months putting off a confrontation with John Mitchell. . . . I listened to more tapes. . . . I heard Haldeman tell me that Dean and Mitchell had come up with a plan to handle the problem of the investigation's going into areas we didn't want it to go. The plan was to call in Helms and Walters of the CIA and have them restrain the FBI. . . .

> Haldeman and I discussed [on the "smoking gun" tape] having the CIA limit the
> FBI investigation for political rather than the national security reasons I had given
> in my public statements. . . . On June 13, while I was in Egypt, Fred Buzhardt had
> suffered a heart attack. Once I was assured that he was going to pull through, I
> tried to assess the impact his illness would have on our legal situation.

These sentences are *almost* enough to make one nostalgic for an adversary
with a claim upon our attention. There he is, the late lawyer-President setting
forth the brief for the defense, practicing the dogged art of the disclaimer in *RN:
The Memoirs of Richard Nixon*. (I've done some cut-and-pasting, but the sentences I've quoted are the sentences he wrote.) And what sentences! Leaden and
dulling, juridical-minded to the last, impersonal but not without savor—the hap-
less Buzhardt and his heart attack factored into the "legal situation," and that
wonderful "hypersensitivity" combined with a desire "not to know the truth"
that makes one think of Henry James's Lambert Strether or an epicene character
in Huysmans—they present the reader with camouflage masked as objective
thought.

In his memoir, Richard Nixon does not admit that he lied, exactly, or that he
betrayed his oath of office. In his "public comments," he did a bit of false
accounting, that was all. One should expect this, he suggests, from heads of state.

Indeed, the only surprise this reader had, trudging gamely through *RN*, looking for clues to a badly defined mystery, was the author's report of a sentence
uttered by Jacqueline Kennedy. Touring the White House after *RN*'s election, she
said, "I always live in a dream world." Funny that she would say so; funny that
he would notice.

Lately, I've been possessed of a singularly unhappy idea: the greatest influence
on American fiction for the last twenty years may have been the author of *RN*,
not in his writing but in his public character. He is the inventor, for our purposes
and for our time, of the concept of *deniability*. Deniability is the almost complete
disavowal of intention in relation to bad consequences. This is a made-up word,
and it reeks of the landfill-scented landscape of lawyers and litigation and high
school. Following Richard Nixon in influence on recent fiction would be two run-
ners-up, Ronald Reagan and George Bush. Their administrations put the passive
voice, politically, on the rhetorical map. In their efforts to acquire deniability on
the arms-for-hostages deal with Iran, their administrations managed to achieve
considerable notoriety for self-righteousness, public befuddlement about facts,
forgetfulness under oath, and constant disavowals of political error and criminal-
ity, culminating in the quasi-confessional, passive voice–mode sentence, "Mistakes were made."

Contrast this with Robert E. Lee's statement after the battle of Gettysburg,
the third day and the calamity of Pickett's Charge: "All this has been my fault,"
Lee said. "I asked more of men than should have been asked of them."

These sentences have a slightly antique ring. People just don't say such things
anymore.

What difference does it make to writers of stories if public figures are denying their responsibility for their own actions? So what if they are, in effect, refusing to tell their own stories accurately? So what if the President of the United States is making himself out to be, of all things, a *victim*? Well, to make an obvious point, they create a climate in which social narratives are designed to be deliberately incoherent and misleading. Such narratives humiliate the act of storytelling. You can argue that only a coherent narrative can manage to explain public events, and you can reconstruct a story if someone says, "I made a mistake," or "We did that," but you can't reconstruct a story—you can't even know what the story *is*— if everyone is saying, "Mistakes were made." Who made them? Well, everybody made them and no one did, and it's history anyway, so we should forget about it. Every story is a history, however, and when there is no comprehensible story, there is, in some sense, no history; the past, under those circumstances, becomes an unreadable mess. When we hear words like "deniability," we are in the presence of narrative dysfunction, a phrase employed by the poet C. K. Williams to describe the process by which we lose track of the story of ourselves, the story that tells us who we are supposed to be and how we are supposed to act.

One spiritual godfather of the contemporary disavowal movement, the author of *RN*, set the tenor for the times and reflected the times as well in his life-long denial of responsibility for the Watergate break-in and coverup. He claimed that misjudgments were made, though not necessarily by him; mistakes were made, though they were by no means his own, and the crimes that were committed were only crimes if you define "crime" in a certain way, in the way, for example, that his enemies liked to define the word, in a manner that would be unfavorable to him, that would give him, to use a word derived from the Latin, some culpability. It wasn't the law, he claims; it was all just politics.

A curious parallel: the Kennedy assassination may be *the* narratively dysfunctional event of our era: no one really knows who's responsible for it. One of the signs of a dysfunctional narrative is that we cannot leave it behind, and we cannot put it to rest, because it does not, finally, give us the explanation we need to enclose it. We don't know who the agent of the action is. We don't even know why it was done. Instead of achieving closure, the story spreads over the landscape like a stain as we struggle to find a source of responsibility. In our time, responsibility within narratives has been consistently displaced by its enigmatic counterpart, conspiracy. Conspiracy works in tandem with narrative repression, the repression state of who-has-done-what. We go back over the Kennedy assassination second by second, frame by frame, but there is a truth to it that we cannot get at because we can't be sure who really did it or what the motivations were. Everyone who claims to have closed the case simply establishes that the case will stay open. The result of dysfunctional narrative, as the poet Lawrence Joseph has suggested to me, is sorrow; I would argue that it is sorrow mixed with depression, the condition of the abject, but in any case we are talking about the psychic landscape of trauma and paralysis, the landscape of, for example, two outwardly different writers, Don DeLillo (in most of *Libra*) and Jane Smiley (in the last one hundred pages of *A Thousand Acres*).

A parenthesis: Jane Smiley's novel has been compared to *King Lear,* and its plot invites the comparison, but its real ancestors in fiction are the novels of Emile Zola. *A Thousand Acres* is Zola on the plains. Like Zola, Jane Smiley assembles precisely and carefully a collection of facts, a Naturalistic pile-up of details about —in this case—farming and land use. As for characters, the reader encounters articulate women (including the narrator, Rose) and mostly frustrated inarticulate men driven by blank desires, like Larry, the Lear figure. Lear, however, is articulate. Larry is not. He is like one of Zola's male characters, driven by urges he does not understand or even acknowledge.

Somewhat in the manner of other Naturalistic narratives, *A Thousand Acres* causes its characters to behave like mechanisms, under obscure orders. Wry but humorless, shorn of poetry or any lyric outburst, and brilliantly observant and relentless, the novel at first seems to be about 1980s greed and the destruction of resources that we now associate with Reaganism, a literally exploitative husbandry. Such a story would reveal clear if deplorable motives in its various characters. Instead, with the revelation of Larry's sexual abuse of his daughters, including the narrator, it shifts direction toward an account of conspiracy and repressed memory, sorrow and depression, in which several of the major characters are acting out rather than acting.

The characters' emotions are thus preordained, and the narrator herself gathers around herself a cloak of unreliability as the novel goes on. It is a moody novel, but the mood itself often seems impenetrable because the characters, even the men, are not acting upon events in present narrative time but are reacting obscurely to harms done to them in the psychic past, from unthinkable impulses that will go forever unexplained. Enacting greed at least involves making some decisions, but in this novel, the urge to enact incest upon one's daughter is beyond thought, and, in turn, creates consequences that are beyond thought. Rose herself lives in the shadow of thought (throughout much of the book she is unaccountable, even to herself) by virtue of her having been molested by her father. This is dysfunctional narrative as literary art, a novel that is also very much an artifact of *this* American era.

Watergate itself would have remained narratively dysfunctional if the tapes hadn't turned up, and, with them, the "smoking gun"—notice, by the way, the metaphors that we employ to designate narrative responsibility, the naming and placing of the phallically inopportune protagonist at the center. The arms-for-hostages deal is still a muddled narrative because various political functionaries are taking the fall for what the commander-in-chief is supposed to have decided himself. However, the commander-in-chief was not told; or he forgot; or he was out of the loop. The buck stops here? In recent history, the buck doesn't stop anywhere. The buck keeps moving, endlessly; perhaps we are in the era of the endlessly traveling buck, the buck seeking a place to stop, like a story that cannot find its own ending.

We have been living, it seems, in a political culture of disavowals. Disavowals follow from crimes for which no one is capable of claiming responsibility. Mistakes and crimes tend to create narratives, however, and they have done so from the time of the Greek tragedies. How can the contemporary disavowal movement

not affect those of us who tell stories? We begin to move away from fiction of protagonists and antagonists into another mode, another model. It is hard to describe
this model but I think it might be called the fiction of finger-pointing, the fiction of
the quest for blame.

In such fiction, people and events are often accused of turning the protagonist
into the kind of person the protagonist is, usually an unhappy person. That's the
whole story. When blame has been assigned, the story is over. (In writing workshops, this kind of story is often the rule rather than the exception.) Probably this
model of storytelling has arisen because, for many reasons, large population
groups in our time feel confused and powerless, as they often do in mass societies
when the mechanisms of power are carefully masked. For people with bad jobs
and mounting debts and faithless partners and abusive parents, the most interesting feature of life is its unhappiness, its dull constant weight. But in a commodity
culture, people are *supposed* to be happy; this is the one tireless myth of advertising. In such a consumerist climate, the perplexed and unhappy don't know what
their lives are telling them, and they don't feel as if they are in charge of their own
existence. No action they have ever taken is half as interesting to them as the consistency of their unhappiness.

Natural disasters, by contrast—earthquakes and floods—have a quality of
narrative relief: we know what caused the misery, and we usually know what we
can do to repair the damage, no matter how long it takes.

But corporate and social power, any power carefully masked, puts its victims
into a state of frenzy, the frenzy of the *Oprah* show, of *Geraldo,* and Montel
Williams. Somebody must be responsible for my pain. Someone *will* be found;
someone, usually close to home, will be blamed. TV loves dysfunctional families.
Dysfunctional S&L's and banks and corporate structures are not loved quite so
much. In this sense we have moved away from the Naturalism of Zola or Frank
Norris or Dreiser. Like them, we believe that people are often helpless, but we
don't blame the corporations so much anymore; we blame the family.

Afternoon talk shows have only apparent antagonists. Their sparring partners are not real antagonists because the bad guys usually confess and then immediately disavow. The trouble with narratives like this without antagonists or a
counterpoint to the central character—stories in which no one ever seems to be
deciding anything or acting upon any motive except the search for a source of dis-
content—is that they tend formally to mirror the protagonists' unhappiness and
confusion. Stories about being put-upon almost literally do not know what to
look at; the visual details are muddled or indifferently described or excessively
specific in nonpertinent situations. In any particular scene, everything is significant, and nothing is. The story is trying to find a source of meaning, but in the
story, everyone is disclaiming responsibility. Things have just happened.

When I hear the adjective "dysfunctional" now, I cringe. But I have to use it
here to describe a structural unit (like the banking system, or the family, or narrative) whose outward appearance is intact but whose structural integrity may have
collapsed, so that no one is answerable within it—every event, every calamity, is
unanswered, from the S&L collapse to the Exxon *Valdez* oil spill.

So we have created for ourselves a paradise of lawyers: we have an orgy of blame-finding on the one hand and disavowals of responsibility on the other.

All the recent debates and quarrels about taking responsibility as opposed to being a victim reflect some bewilderment about whether in real life protagonists still exist or whether we are all, in some sense, minor characters, the objects of terrible forces. Of course, we are often both. But look at *Oprah*. (I have, I do, I can't help it.) For all the variety of the situations, the unwritten scripts are often similar: someone is testifying because s/he's been hurt by someone else. The pain-inflicter is invariably present and accounted for onstage, and sometimes this person admits, abashedly, to inflicting the ruin: cheating, leaving, abusing, or murdering. Usually, however, there's no remorse, because some other factor caused it: bad genes, alcoholism, drugs, or—the cause of last resort—Satan. For intellectuals it may be the patriarchy: some devil or other—but an *abstract* devil. In any case, the malefactor may be secretly pleased: s/he's on television and will be famous for fifteen minutes.

The audience's role in all this is to comment on what the story means and to make a judgment about the players. Usually the audience members disagree and get into fights. The audience's judgment is required because the dramatis personae are incapable of judging themselves. They generally will not say that they did what they did because they wanted to, or because they had *decided* to do it. The story is shocking. You hear gasps. But the participants are as baffled and bewildered as everyone else. So we have the spectacle of utterly perplexed villains deprived of their villainy. Villainy, properly understood, gives someone a largeness, a sense of scale. It seems to me that that sense of scale has probably abandoned us.

What we have instead is not exactly drama and not exactly therapy. It exists in that twilight world between the two, very much of our time, where deniability reigns. Call it therapeutic narration. No verdict ever comes in. No one is in a position to judge. It makes the mind itch as if from an ideological rash. It is the spectacle, hour after hour, week after week, of dysfunctional narratives, interrupted by commercials (in Detroit, for lawyers).

Here is a koan for the 1990s: what is the relation between the dysfunctional narratives and the commercials that interrupt them?

But wait: isn't there something deeply interesting and moving and sometimes even beautiful when a character *acknowledges* an error? And isn't this narrative mode becoming something of a rarity?

Most young writers have this experience: they create characters who are an imaginative projection of themselves, minus the flaws. They put this character into a fictional world, wanting that character to be successful and—to use that word from high school—"popular." They don't want these imaginative projections of themselves to make any mistakes, wittingly or, even better, unwittingly, or to demonstrate what Aristotle thought was the core of stories, flaws of character that produce intelligent misjudgments for which someone must take the responsibility.

What's an unwitting action? It's what we do when we have to act so quickly, or under so much pressure, that we can't stop to take thought. It's not the same as an urge, which may well have a brooding and inscrutable quality. For some reason, such moments of unwitting action in life and in fiction feel enormously charged with energy and meaning.

It's difficult for fictional characters to acknowledge their mistakes, because then they become definitive: they *are* that person who did *that* thing. The only people who like to see characters performing such actions are readers. They love to see characters getting themselves into interesting trouble and defining themselves.

Lately, thinking about the nature of drama and our resistance to certain forms of it, I have been reading Aristotle's *Poetics* again and mulling over his definition of what makes a poet. A poet, Aristotle says, is first and foremost a maker, not of verses, but of plots. The poet creates an imitation, and what he imitates is an action.

It might be useful to make a distinction here between what I might call "me" protagonists and "I" protagonists. "Me" protagonists are largely objects—objects of impersonal forces or the actions of other people. They are central characters to whom things happen. They do not initiate action so much as receive it. For this reason, they are largely reactionary, in the old sense of that term, and passive. They are figures of fate and destiny, and they tend to appear during periods of accelerated social change, such as the American 1880s and 1890s, and again in the 1980s.

The "I" protagonist, by contrast, makes certain decisions and takes some responsibility for them and for the actions that follow from them. This does not make the "I" protagonist admirable by any means. It's this kind of protagonist that Aristotle is talking about. Such a person, Aristotle says, is not outstanding for virtue or justice, and she or he arrives at ill fortune not because of any wickedness or vice, but because of some mistake that s/he makes. There's that word again, "mistake."

Sometimes—if we are writers—we have to talk to our characters. We have to try to persuade them to do what they've only imagined doing. We have to nudge but not force them toward situations where they will get into interesting trouble, where they will make interesting mistakes that they may take responsibility for. When we allow our characters to make mistakes, we release them from the grip of our own authorial narcissism. That's wonderful for them, it's wonderful for us, but it's best of all for the story.

A few instances: I once had a friend in graduate school who gave long, loud, and unpleasantly exciting parties in the middle of winter; he and his girlfriend usually considered these parties unsuccessful unless someone did something shocking or embarrassing or both—*something you could talk about later.* He lived on the third floor of an old house in Buffalo, New York, and his acquaintances regularly fell down the front and back stairs.

I thought of him recently when I was reading about Mary Butts, an English writer of short fiction who lived from 1890 to 1937. Her stories have now been reissued in a collection called *From Altar to Chimneypiece*. Virgil Thomson, who was gay, once proposed marriage to her. That tells us something about the power of her personality. This is what Thomson says about her in his autobiography:

> I used to call her the "storm goddess," because she was at her best surrounded by cataclysm. She could stir up others with drink and drugs and magic incantations, and then when the cyclone was at its most intense, sit down at calm center and glow. All of her stories are of moments when the persons observed are caught up by something, inner or outer, so irresistible that their highest powers and all their lowest conditionings are exposed. The resulting action therefore is definitive, an ultimate clarification arrived at through ecstasy.

As it happens, I do not think that this is an accurate representation of Mary Butts's stories, which tend to be about crossing thresholds and stumbling into very strange spiritual dimensions. But I am interested in Thomson's thought concerning definitive action, because I think the whole concept of definitive action is meeting up with a considerable cultural resistance these days.

Thomson, describing his storm goddess, shows us a temptress, a joyful, worldly woman, quite possibly brilliant and bad to the bone. In real life people like this can be insufferable. Marriage to such a person would be a relentless adventure. They're constantly pushing their friends and acquaintances to lower their defenses and drop their masks and do something for which they will probably be sorry later. They like it when anyone blurts out a sudden admission, or acts on an impulse and messes up conventional arrangements. They like to see people squirm. They're *gleeful*. They prefer Bizet to Wagner; they're more Carmen than Sieglinde. They like it when people lunge at a desired object, and cacophony and wreckage are the result.

The morning after, you can say, "Mistakes were made," but at least with the people I've spent time with, a phrase like "Mistakes were made" won't even buy you a cup of coffee. There is such a thing as the poetry of a mistake, and when you say, "Mistakes were made," you deprive an action of its poetry, and you sound like a weasel. When you say, "I fucked up," the action retains its meaning, its sordid origin, its obscenity, and its poetry.

Chekhov says about this, in two of his letters, ". . . shun all descriptions of the characters' spiritual state. You must try to have that state emerge from their actions. . . . The artist must be only an impartial witness of his characters and what they said, not their judge." In Chekhov's view, a writer must try to release the story's characters from the aura of judgment that they've acquired simply because they're fictional. It's as if fiction has a great deal of trouble shedding its moral/pedagogical origins in fable and allegory.

In an atmosphere of constant moral judgment, characters are not often permitted to make interesting and intelligent mistakes and then to acknowledge them. It's as if the whole idea of the "intelligent mistake," the importance of the mistake made on an impulse, had gone out the window. Or, if fictional characters do make such mistakes, they're judged immediately and without appeal. One thinks of the attitudes of the aging Tolstoy here, and of his hatred of Shakespeare's and Chekhov's plays, and of his obsessive moralizing. He especially hated

King Lear. He called it stupid, verbose, and incredible, and thought the craze for Shakespeare was like the tulip craze, a matter of mass hypnosis and "epidemic suggestion."

In the absence of any clear moral vision, we get moralizing. There's quite a lot of it around, and I think it has been inhibiting writers and making them nervous and irritable. Here is Mary Gaitskill, commenting on one of her own short stories, "The Girl on the Plane," in a recent *Best American Short Stories.* It's a story about a gang rape, and it apparently upset quite a few readers.

> In my opinion, most of us have not been taught how to be responsible for our thoughts and feelings. I see this strongly in the widespread tendency to read books and stories as if they exist to confirm how we are supposed to be, think, and feel. I'm not talking wacky political correctness, I'm talking mainstream. . . . Ladies and gentlemen, please. Stop asking "What am I supposed to feel?" Why would an adult look to me or to any other writer to tell him or her what to feel? You're not *supposed* to feel anything. You feel what you feel.

Behind the writer's loss of patience one can just manage to make out a literary culture begging for an authority figure, the same sort of figure that Chekhov refused for himself. Mary Gaitskill's interest in bad behavior is that of the observer, not the judge. Unhappy readers want her to be both, as if stories should come prepackaged with discursive authorial opinions about her own characters. Her exasperation is a reflection of C. K. Williams's observation that in a period of dysfunctional narratives, the illogic of feeling erodes the logic of stories. When people can't make any narrative sense out of their own feelings, readers start to ask writers what they are supposed to feel. Reading begins to be understood as a form of therapy. In such an atmosphere, already-moralized stories are more comforting than stories in which characters are making intelligent or unwitting mistakes.

Marilynne Robinson, in her essay "Hearing Silence: Western Myth Reconsidered," calls the already-moralized story, the therapeutic narrative, part of a "mean little myth" of our time. She notes, however, that "we have ceased to encode our myths in narrative as that word is traditionally understood. Now they shield themselves from our skepticism by taking on the appearance of scientific or political or economic discourse. . . ." And what is this "mean little myth"?

> One is born and in passage through childhood suffers some grave harm. Subsequent good fortune is meaningless because of this injury, while subsequent misfortune is highly significant as the consequence of this injury. The work of one's life is to discover and name the harm one has suffered.

As long as this myth is operational, one cannot act, in stories or anywhere else, in a meaningful way. The injury takes for itself all the meaning. The injury *is* the meaning, though it is, itself, opaque. All achievements, and all mistakes, are finessed. There is no free will. There is only acting out, the acting out of one's destiny. But acting out is not the same as acting. Acting out is behavior that proceeds according to a predetermined, invisible pattern created by the injury. The injury becomes the unmoved mover, the replacement for the mind's capacity to judge and to decide. One thinks of Nixon here: the obscure wounds, the vindictiveness, the obsession with enemies, the acting out.

It has a feeling of Calvinism to it, of predetermination, this myth of injury and predestination. In its kingdom, sorrow and depression rule. Marilynne Robinson calls this mode of thought "bungled Freudianism." It's both that and something else: an effort to make pain acquire some comprehensibility so that those who feel helpless can at least be illuminated. But unlike Freudianism it asserts that the source of the pain can *never be expunged.* There is no working-through of this injury. It has no tragic joy because within it, all personal decisions have been made meaningless, deniable. It is a life-fate, like a character disorder. Its politics cannot get much further than gender-injury; it cannot take on the corporate state.

Confronted with this mode, I feel like an Old Leftist. I want to say: the Bosses are happy when you feel helpless. They're pleased when you think the source of your trouble is your family. They're delighted when you give up the idea that you should band together for political action. They love helplessness (in you). They even like addicts, as long as they're mostly out of sight: after all, *addiction is just the last stage of consumerism.*

And I suppose I am nostalgic—as a writer, of course—for stories with mindful villainy, villainy with clear motives that any adult would understand, bad behavior with a sense of *scale,* that would give back to us our imaginative grip on the despicable and the admirable and our capacity to have some opinions about the two. Most of us are interested in characters who willingly give up their innocence and decide to act badly. I myself am fascinated when they not only do that but admit that they did it, that they had good reasons for doing so. At such moments wrongdoing becomes intelligible. It also becomes legibly political. If this is the liberal fallacy, this sense of choice, then so be it. (I know that people *do* get caught inside systems of harm and cannot maneuver themselves out—I have written about such situations myself—but that story is hardly the only one worth telling.)

It does seem curious that in contemporary America—a place of considerable good fortune and privilege—one of the most favored narrative modes, from high to low, has to do with disavowals, passivity, and the disarmed protagonist. Possibly we have never gotten over our American romance with innocence. We would rather be innocent than worldly and unshockable. Innocence is continually shocked and disarmed. But there is something wrong with this. No one can go through life perpetually shocked. It's disingenuous. Writing in his journals, Thornton Wilder notes, "I think that it can be assumed that no adults are ever really 'shocked'—that being shocked is always a pose." If so, there is some failure of adulthood in contemporary American life. Our interest in victims and victimization has finally to do with our constant ambivalence about power, about being powerful, about wanting to be powerful but not having to acknowledge the buck stopping on our desk.

What I am arguing against is *not* political or social action against abusers of power, corporate or familial. I am registering my uneasiness with the Romance of Victimization, especially in this culture, and the constant disavowal of responsibility by the abuser. Romantic victims and disavowing perpetrators land us in a peculiar territory, a sort of neo-Puritanism without the backbone of theology and philosophy. After all, *The Scarlet Letter* is about disavowals, specifically Dimmesdale's, and the supposed "shock" of a minister of God being guilty of adultery. Dimmesdale's inability to admit publicly what he's done has something to do with the community—i.e., a culture of "shock"—and something to do with his own pusillanimous character.

The dialectics of innocence and worldliness have a different emotional coloration in British literature, or perhaps I simply am unable to get Elizabeth Bowen's *The Death of the Heart* (1938) out of my mind in this context. Portia, the perpetual innocent and stepchild, sixteen years old, in love with Eddie, twenty-three, has been writing a diary, and her guardian, Anna, has been reading it. Anna tells St. Quentin, her novelist friend, that she has been reading it. St. Quentin tells Portia what Anna has done. As it happens, Portia has been writing poisonously accurate observations about Anna and her husband, Thomas, in the diary. Anna is a bit pained to find herself so neatly skewered.

Bowen's portrait of Portia is beautifully managed, but it's her portrayal of Anna that fascinates me. Anna cannot be shocked. Everything she has done, she admits. In the sixth chapter of the novel's final section, she really blossoms: worldly, witty, rather mean, and absolutely clear about her own faults, she recognizes the situation and her own complicity in it. She may be sorry, but she doesn't promise to do better. Portia is the one who is innocent, who commands the superior virtues, not she herself. Speaking of reading private diaries, she says, "It's the sort of thing I do do. Her diary's very good—you see, she has got us taped. . . . I don't say it has changed the course of my life, but it's given me a rather more disagreeable feeling about being alive—or, at least, about being me."

That "disagreeable feeling" seems to arise not only from the diary but also from Anna's wish to read it, to violate it. Anna may feel disagreeable about being the person she is, but she does not say that she could be otherwise. She is the person who does what she admits to. As a result, there is a clarity, a functionality to Bowen's narrative, that becomes apparent because everybody admits everything in it and then gives their reasons for doing what they've done. It's as if their actions have found a frame, a size, a scale. As bad as Anna may be, she is honest.

Anna defines herself, not in the American way of reciting inward virtues, but in a rather prideful litany of mistakes. In her view, we define ourselves at least as much by our mistakes as by our achievements. The grace and honor of fiction is that in stories, mistakes are every bit as interesting as achievements are; they have an equal claim upon truth. Perhaps they have a greater one, because they are harder to show, harder to hear, harder to say. For that reason, they are rarer and more precious.

Speaking of a library book that is eighteen years overdue, but which she has just returned, the narrator of Grace Paley's story "Wants" says, "I didn't deny anything." She pays the thirty-two-dollar fine, and that's it. One of the pleasures of Paley's stories is that the stories, as narrated, are remarkably free of denial and subterfuge. Their characters explain themselves but don't bother to excuse themselves. City dwellers, they don't particularly like innocence, and they don't expect to be shocked. When there's blame, they take it. When they fall, there's a good reason. They don't rise; they just get back on their feet, and when they think about reform, it's typically political rather than personal. For one of her characters, this is the "powerful last-half-of-the-century way." Well, it's nice to think so. Free of the therapeutic impulse, and of the recovery movement, and of Protestantism generally, her characters nevertheless *like* to imagine various social improvements in the lives of the members of their community.

Dysfunctional narratives tend to begin in solitude and they tend to resist their own forms of communication. They don't have communities so much as audiences of fellow victims. There is no polite way for their narratives to end. Richard Nixon, disgraced, resigned, still flashing the V-for-victory from the helicopter on the White House lawn, cognitively dissonant to the end, went off to his enforced retirement, where, tirelessly, year after year, in solitude, he wrote his accounts, every one of them meant to justify and to excuse. His last book, as of this writing not yet published, is entitled *Beyond Peace*.

DISCUSSION QUESTIONS

1. How does Baxter answer his own question: "What difference does it make to writers of stories if public figures are denying their responsibility for their own actions"?
2. What does Baxter mean by "deniability" and "disavowal"? What do these terms, made famous in the Watergate scandal, have to do with contemporary fiction?
3. What is a "dysfunctional narrative," according to Baxter? What examples does he offer from history, and what examples from fiction?
4. What is the connection between Baxter's overall thesis and his analysis of afternoon talk shows such as *Oprah* and *Geraldo*?
5. Would you agree with Baxter that "most young writers . . . create characters who are an imaginative projection of themselves, minus the flaws. . . . They don't want these imaginative projections of themselves to make any mistakes, wittingly or, even better, unwittingly . . ."?
6. Explain what impact on your own fiction the following assertion might have: "The grace and honor of fiction is that in stories, mistakes are every bit as interesting as achievements are; they have an equal claim upon truth. Perhaps they have a greater one . . ."

NADINE GORDIMER

Three in a Bed: Fiction, Morals and Politics

Nadine Gordimer (b. 1923), South African short story writer, novelist, and essayist, won the Nobel Prize for literature in 1991. Among her novels are Occasion for Loving *(1963), The*

Conservationist (*1974*), Burger's Daughter (*1979*), *and* July's People (*1981*). *In her fiction as in her lectures and essays, Gordimer is frankly political, in the sense that her characters find themselves living in a world where their possibilities are dictated not only by their individual personalities but also by their social identities. Before the abolition of apartheid, she frequently ran afoul of the South African authorities; she describes this experience in* What Happened to Burger's Daughter; or, How South African Censorship Works (*1980*). *Her essays on fiction and politics appear in* The Essential Gesture: Writing, Politics, and Places (*1988*).

Three in a bed: it's a kinky cultural affair. I had better identify the partners.

Politics and morals, as concepts, need no introduction, although their relationship is shadily ambiguous. But fiction has defining responsibilities I shall be questioning, so I shall begin right away with the basic, dictionary definition of what fiction is supposed to be.

Fiction, says the Oxford English Dictionary, is 'the action of feigning or inventing imaginary existences, events, states of things'. Fiction, collectively, is prose novels and stories. So poetry, according to the OED, is not fiction. The more I ponder this, the more it amazes me; the more I challenge it. Does the poet not invent imaginary existences, events, states of things?

Now what is politics doing in bed with fiction? Morals have bedded with story-telling since the magic of the imaginative capacity developed in the human brain—and in my ignorance of a scientific explanation of changes in the cerebrum or whatever, to account for this faculty, I believe it was the inkling development that here was somewhere where the truth about being alive might lie. The harsh lessons of daily existence, co-existence between human and human, with animals and nature, could be made sense of in the ordering of properties of the transforming imagination, working on the 'states of things'. With this faculty fully developed, great art in fiction can evolve in imaginative revelation to fit the crises of an age that comes after its own, undreamt of when it was written. *Moby-Dick* can now be seen as an allegory of environmental tragedy. 'The whale is the agent of cosmic retribution':* we have sought to destroy the splendid creature that is nature, believing we could survive only by 'winning' a battle against nature; now we see our death in the death of nature, brought about by ourselves.

Morals are the husband/wife of fiction. And politics? Politics somehow followed morals in, picking the lock and immobilizing the alarm system. At first it was in the dark, perhaps, and fiction thought the embrace of politics was that of morals, didn't know the difference . . . And this is understandable. Morals and politics have a family connection. Politics' ancestry is morality—way back, and generally accepted as forgotten. The resemblance is faded. In the light of morning, if fiction accepts the third presence within the sheets it is soon in full cognizance of who and what politics is.

---

* '. . . to Ahab, the whale is the agent of cosmic retribution.' Harry Levin, 'The Jonah Complex', from *The Power of Blackness* (New York: Vintage Books, 1960), p. 215.

The relationship of fiction with politics has not had the kind of husbandly/fatherly authoritarian sanction that morals, with their religious origins, lingeringly has. No literary critic I know of suggests that *moralizing* as opposed to 'immorality' has no place in fiction, whereas many works of fiction are declared 'spoiled' by the writer's recognition of politics as a motivation of character as great as sex or religion. Of course, this lack of sanction is characteristic of an affair, a wild affair in which great tensions arise, embraces and repulsions succeed one another, distress and celebration are confused, loyalty and betrayal change place, accusations fly. And whether the fiction writer gets involved with politics initially through his/her convictions as a citizen pushing within against the necessary detachment of the writer, or whether by the pressure of seduction from without, the same problems in the relationship arise and have to be dealt with in the fiction as well as in the life.

For when have writers not lived in times of political conflict? Whose Golden Age, whose *belle époque,* whose Roaring Twenties were these so-named lovely times? The time of slave and peasant misery, while sculptors sought perfect proportions of the human torso? The time of revolutionaries in Czar Alexander's prisons, while Grand Dukes built mansions in Nice? The time of the hungry and unemployed offered the salvation of growing Fascism, while playboys and girls danced balancing glasses of pink champagne?

When, overtly or implicitly, could writers evade politics? Even those writers who have seen fiction as the pure exploration of language, as music is the exploration of sound—the babbling of Dada and the page-shuffling attempts of Burroughs have been in reaction to what each revolted against in the politically imposed spirit of their respective times; literary movements which were an act—however far-out—of acknowledgement of a relationship between politics and fiction.

It seems there is no getting away from the relationship. On the one hand, we live in what Seamus Heaney* calls a world where the 'undirected play of the imagination is regarded at best as luxury or licentiousness, at worst as heresy or treason. In ideal republics . . . it is a common expectation that the writer will sign over his or her venturesome and potentially disruptive activity into the keeping of official doctrine, traditional system, a party line, whatever . . .'

We are shocked by such clear cases of creativity outlawed. But things are not always so drastically simple. Not every fiction writer entering a relation with politics trades imagination for the hair shirt of the party hack. There is also the case of the writer whose imaginative powers are genuinely roused by and involved with the spirit of politics as she or he personally experiences it. This may be virtually inescapable in times and places of socially seismic upheaval. Society shakes, the walls of entities fall; the writer has known the evil, indifference or cupidity of the old order, and the spirit of creativity naturally pushes towards new growth. The writer is moved to fashion an expression of a new order, accepted on trust as

---

*Seamus Heaney, *The Government of the Tongue* (Faber and Faber, 1988), p. 96.

an advance in human freedom that therefore also will be the release of a greater creativity.

'Russia became a garden of nightingales. Poets sprang up as never before. People barely had the strength to live but they were all singing'—so wrote Andrey Bely in the early days of the Russian revolution. One of Pasternak's latest biographers, Peter Levi,* notes that Pasternak—popularly known to the West on the evidence of his disillusioned *Dr Zhivago* as *the* anti-Communist writer—in his young days contributed manifestos to the 'infighting of the day'. In his poem to Stalin† he sang:

> We want the glorious. We want the good.
> We want to see things free from fear.
> Unlike some fancy fop, the spendthrift
> of his bright, brief span, we yearn
> for labour shared by everyone,
> for the common discipline of law.

This yearning is addressed by writers in different ways, as fiction seeks a proper relation with politics. In the Soviet Union of Pasternak's day, some fell into what the Italian contemporary writer, Claudio Magris,‡ in a different context, calls with devastating cynicism 'A sincere but perverted passion for freedom, which led . . . into mechanical servitude; as is the way with sin'. The noble passion deteriorated to the tragically shabby, as in the 1930s the Writers' Union turned on itself to beat out all but mediocrity mouthing platitudes, driving Mayakovsky to suicide and turning down Pasternak's plea to be granted a place where he would have somewhere other than a freezing partitioned slice of a room in which to write and live. Yet Pasternak had not abandoned belief—never did—in the original noble purpose of revolution, although for him the writing of this period became, by the edicts of the State and the Writers' Union, 'a train derailed and lying at the bottom of an embankment'.

Politics is not always the murderer of fiction. The Brechts and Nerudas survive, keeping the revolutionary vision. But the relation, like all vital ones, always implies some danger. The first dismaying discovery for the writer is once again best expressed by Magris's§ cynicism: 'the lie is quite as real as the truth, it works upon the world, transforms it'; whereas the fiction writer, in pursuit of truth beyond the guise of reasoning, has believed that truth, however elusive, is the only reality. Yet we have seen the lie transforming; we have had Goebbels. And his international descendants, practising that transformation on the people of a number of countries, including the white people of my own country, who accepted the lie that apartheid was both divinely decreed and secularly just, and created a society on it.

---

*Peter Levi, *Boris Pasternak* (Hutchinson, 1990), p. 77.
†Boris Pasternak, quoted by Evgeny Pasternak in *Boris Pasternak, the Tragic Years 1930–60* (Collins Harvill, 1990), p. 38.
‡Claudio Magris, *Inferences on a Sabre,* trans. from the Italian by Mark Thompson (Polygon, 1990), p. 43.
§Ibid., 63.

To be aware that the lie also can transform the world places an enormous responsibility on art to counter this with its own transformations. The *knowledge* that the writer's searching and intuition gain instinctively contradicts the lie.

> We page through each other's faces
> we read each looking eye . . .
> It has taken lives to be able to do so

writes the South African poet, Mongane Wally Serote.* We may refuse to write according to any orthodoxy, we may refuse to toe any party line, even that drawn by the cause we know to be just, and our own, but we cannot refuse the responsibility of what we know. What we know beyond surface reality has to become what, again in Serote's words, 'We want the world to know'; we must in this, our inescapable relation with politics, 'page for wisdom through the stubborn night'.

DISCUSSION QUESTIONS

1. Would you agree with Gordimer that, while most readers and critics accept the "moralizing" content of fiction, "many works of fiction are declared 'spoiled' by the writer's recognition of politics as a motivation of character as great as sex or religion"?
2. How does Gordimer answer the criticism that political content "spoils" fiction?
3. Is "politics" in fiction "inescapable," as Gordimer asserts? In what ways?
4. Test Gordimer's ideas against an example of fiction with "political" content or purpose. An obvious candidate would be one of Gordimer's own short stories or novels.

---

*Mongane Wally Serote, *A Tough Tale* (Kliptown Books, 1987), p. 7.

THE FICTION WRITER AND POPULAR CULTURE

JONATHAN FRANZEN

Perchance to Dream

Jonathan Franzen (b. 1959) won the Whiting Writers Award for his novel The Twenty-Seventh City *(1988) and has been a Massachusetts Artists Fellow (1986). Once a research assistant in earth and planetary sciences at Harvard (1983–87), he brings a scientist's sensibility to the plots that his characters live. In this essay, he reflects on the role of "serious" fiction in a culture increasingly impatient with the slow pleasures of reading literary works.*

. . . A century ago, the novel was the preeminent medium of social instruction. A new book by William Dean Howells was anticipated with the kind of fever that today a new Pearl Jam release inspires. The big, obvious reason that the social novel has become so scarce is that modern technologies do a better job of social instruction. Television, radio, and photographs are vivid, instantaneous media. Print journalism, too, in the wake of *In Cold Blood,* has become a viable creative alternative to the novel. Because they command large audiences, TV and magazines can afford to gather vast quantities of information quickly. Few serious novelists can pay for a quick trip to Singapore, or for the mass of expert consulting that gives serial TV dramas like *E.R.* and *NYPD Blue* their veneer of authenticity.

Instead of an age in which Dickens, Darwin, and Disraeli all read one another's work, therefore, we live in an age in which our presidents, if they read fiction at all, read Louis L'Amour or Walter Mosley, and vital social news comes to us mainly via pollsters. A recent *USA Today* survey of twenty-four hours in the life of American culture contained twenty-three references to television, six to film, six to popular music, three to radio, and one to fiction (*The Bridges of Madison County*). The writer of average talent who wants to report on, say, the plight of illegal aliens would be foolish to choose the novel as a vehicle. Ditto the writer who wants to offend prevailing sensibilities. *Portnoy's Complaint,* which even my mother once heard enough about to disapprove of, was probably the last American novel that could have appeared on Bob Dole's radar as a nightmare of depravity. When the Ayatollah Khomeini placed a bounty on Salman Rushdie's head, what seemed archaic to Americans was not his Muslim fanaticism but the simple fact that he'd become so exercised about a *book.*

In the season when I began "My Obsolescence" and then abandoned it in midsentence, I let myself become involved with Hollywood. I had naively supposed that a person with a gift for story structure might be able, by writing screenplays, to support his private fiction habit and simultaneously take the edge off his hunger for a large audience. My Hollywood agent, whom I'll call Dicky, had told me that I could sell a treatment, not even a finished script, if the concept were sufficiently high. He was enthusiastic about the treatment I submitted six months later (I had the concept down to five words, one of which was "sex"), but unfortunately, he said, the market had changed, and I would need to produce a complete script. This I managed to do in fifteen days. I was feeling very smart, and Dicky was nearly apoplectic with enthusiasm. Just a few small changes, he said, and we were looking at a very hot property.

The next six months were the most hellish of my life. I now *needed* money, and despite a growing sense of throwing good work after bad ("Enthusiasm is free," a friend warned me), I produced a second draft, a third draft, and a fourth-and-absolutely-final draft. Dicky's enthusiasm was unabated when he reported to me that my fourth draft had finally shown him the light: we needed to keep the three main characters and the opening sequence, and then completely recast the remaining 115 pages. I said I didn't think I was up to the job. He replied, "You've done wonderful work in developing the characters, so now let's find another writer and offer him a fifty percent stake."

When I got off the phone, I couldn't stop laughing. I felt peculiarly restored to myself. The people who succeed in Hollywood are the ones who want it badly enough, and I not only didn't want it badly enough, I didn't want it at all. When I refused to let another writer take over, I ensured that I would never see a penny for my work; Dicky, understandably, dropped me like medical waste. But I couldn't imagine not *owning* what I'd written. I would have no problem with seeing one of my novels butchered onscreen, provided I was paid, because the book itself would always belong to me. But to let another person "do creative" on an unfinished text of mine was unthinkable. Solitary work—the work of writing, the work of reading—is the essence of fiction, and what distinguishes the novel from more visual entertainments is the interior collaboration of writer and reader in building and peopling an imagined world. I'm able to know Sophie Bentwood intimately, and to refer to her as casually as if she were a good friend, because I poured my own feelings of fear and estrangement into my construction of her. If I knew her only through a video of *Desperate Characters* (Shirley MacLaine made the movie in 1971, as a vehicle for herself), Sophie would remain an Other, divided from me by the screen on which I viewed her, by the ineluctable surficiality of film, and by MacLaine's star presence. At most, I might feel I knew MacLaine a little better.

Knowing MacLaine a little better, however, is what the country seems to want. We live under a tyranny of the literal. The daily unfolding stories of Steve Forbes, Magic Johnson, Timothy McVeigh, and Hillary Clinton have an intense, iconic presence that relegates to a subordinate shadow-world our own untelevised lives. In order to justify their claim on our attention, the organs of mass culture and information are compelled to offer something "new" on a daily, indeed hourly, basis. The resulting ephemerality of every story or trend or fashion or issue is a form of planned obsolescence more impressive than a Detroit car's problems after 60,000 miles, since it generally takes a driver four or five years to reach that limit and, after all, a car actually has some use.

Although good novelists don't deliberately seek out trends, they do feel a responsibility to dramatize important issues of the day, and they now confront a culture in which almost all of the issues are burned out almost all of the time. The writer who wants to tell a story about society that's true not just in 1996 but in 1997 as well finds herself at a loss for solid cultural referents. I'm not advancing some hoary notion of literary "timelessness" here. But since art offers no objective standards by which to validate itself, it follows that the only practical standard—the only means of distinguishing yourself from the schlock that is your enemy—is whether anybody is willing to put effort into reading you ten years down the line. This test of time has become a test of the times, and it's a test the times are failing. How can you achieve topical "relevance" without drawing on an up-to-the-minute vocabulary of icons and attitudes and thereby, far from challenging the hegemony of overnight obsolescence, confirming and furthering it?

Since even in the Nineties cultural commentators persist in blaming novelists for their retreat from public affairs, it's worth saying one more time: Just as the camera drove a stake through the heart of serious portraiture and landscape painting, television has killed the novel of social reportage.[1] Truly committed social novelists may still find cracks in the monolith to sink their pitons into. But they do so with the understanding that they can no longer depend on their material, as William Dean Howells and Upton Sinclair and Harriet Beecher Stowe did, but only on their own sensibilities, and with the expectation that no one will be reading them for *news*.

This much, at least, was visible to Philip Roth in 1961. Noting that "for a writer of fiction to feel that he does not really live in his own country—as represented by *Life* or by what he experiences when he steps out the front door—must seem a serious occupational impediment," he rather plaintively asked: "what will his subject be? His landscape?" In the intervening years, however, the screw has taken another turn. Our obsolescence now goes further than television's usurpation of the role as news-bringer, and deeper than its displacement of the imagined with the literal. Flannery O'Connor, writing around the time that Roth made his remarks, insisted that the "business of fiction" is "to embody mystery through manners." Like the poetics that Poe derived from his "Raven," O'Connor's formulation particularly flatters her own work, but there's little question that "mystery" (how human beings avoid or confront the meaning of existence) and "manners" (the nuts and bolts of how human beings behave) have always been primary concerns of fiction writers. What's frightening for a novelist today is how the technological consumerism that rules our world specifically aims to render both of these concerns moot.

O'Connor's response to the problem Roth articulated, to the sense that there is little in the national mediascape that novelists can feel they *own*, was to insist that the best American fiction has always been regional. This was somewhat awkward, since her hero was the cosmopolitan Henry James. But what she meant was that fiction feeds on specificity, and that the manners of a particular region have always provided especially fertile ground for its practitioners. Superficially, at least, regionalism is still thriving. In fact it's fashionable on college campuses nowadays to say that there is no America anymore, only Americas; that the only things a black lesbian New Yorker and a Southern Baptist Georgian have in common are the English language and the federal income tax. The likelihood, however, is that both the New Yorker and the Georgian watch *Letterman* every night, both are struggling to find health insurance, both have jobs that are threatened by the migration of employment overseas, both go to discount superstores to purchase *Pocahontas* tie-in products for their children, both are being pummeled into cynicism by commercial advertising, both play Lotto, both dream of fifteen minutes of fame, both are taking a serotonin reuptake inhibitor, and both have a guilty crush on Uma Thurman. The world of the present is a world in which the rich lateral dramas of local manners have been replaced by a single vertical drama, the drama of regional specificity succumbing to a commercial generality. The American writer today faces a totalitarianism analogous to the one with which two generations of Eastern bloc writers had to contend. To ignore it is to court nostalgia. To engage with it, however, is to risk writing fiction that makes the same point over and over: technological consumerism is an infernal machine, technological consumerism is an infernal machine . . .

Equally discouraging is the fate of "manners" in the word's more common sense. Rudeness, irresponsibility, duplicity, and stupidity are hallmarks of real human interaction: the stuff of conversation, the stuff of sleepless nights. But in the world of consumer advertising and consumer purchasing, no evil is moral. The evils consist of high prices, inconvenience, lack of choice, lack of privacy, heartburn, hair loss, slippery roads. This is no surprise, since the only problems worth advertising solutions for are problems treatable through the spending of money. But money cannot solve the problem of bad manners—the chatterer in the darkened movie theater, the patronizing sister-in-law, the selfish sex partner— except by offering refuge in an atomized privacy. And such privacy is exactly what the American Century has tended toward. First there was mass suburbanization, then the perfection of at-home entertainment, and finally the creation of virtual communities whose most striking feature is that interaction within them is entirely optional—terminable the instant the experience ceases to gratify the user.

That all these trends are infantilizing has been widely noted. Less often remarked is the way in which they are changing both our expectations of entertainment (the book must bring something to us, rather than our bringing something to the book) and the very content of that entertainment. What story is there to tell, Sven Birkerts asks in *The Gutenberg Elegies,* about the average American whose day consists of sleeping, working at a computer screen, watching TV, and talking on the phone? The problem for the novelist is not just that the average man or woman spends so little time F2F with his or her fellows; there is, after all, a rich tradition of epistolary novels, and Robinson Crusoe's condition approximates the solitude of today's suburban bachelor. The real problem is that the average man or woman's entire life is increasingly structured to avoid precisely the kinds of conflicts on which fiction, preoccupied with manners, has always thrived.

Here, indeed, we are up against what truly seems like the obsolescence of serious art in general. Imagine that human existence is defined by an Ache: the Ache of our not being, each of us, the center of the universe; of our desires forever outnumbering our means of satisfying them. If we see religion and art as the historically preferred methods of coming to terms with this Ache, then what happens to art when our technological and economic systems and even our commercialized religions become sufficiently sophisticated to make each of us the center of our own universe of choices and gratifications? Fiction's response to the sting of poor manners, for example, is to render them comic. The reader laughs with the writer, feels less alone with the sting. This is a delicate transaction, and it takes some work. How can it compete with a system that spares you the sting in the first place?

In the long run, the breakdown of communitarianism is likely to have all sorts of nasty consequences. In the short run, however, in this century of amazing prosperity and health, the breakdown displaces the ancient methods of dealing with the Ache. As for the sense of loneliness and pointlessness and loss that social atomization may produce—stuff that can be lumped under O'Connor's general heading of mystery—it's already enough to label it a disease. A disease has causes: abnormal brain chemistry, childhood sexual abuse, welfare queens, the patriarchy, social dysfunction. It also has cures: Zoloft, recovered-memory therapy, the Contract with America, multiculturalism, virtual reality.[2] A partial cure or, better yet, an endless succession of partial cures, but failing that, even just the consolation of knowing you have a disease—anything is better than mystery. Science attacked religious mystery a long time ago. But it was not until applied science, in the form of technology, changed both the demand for fiction and the social context in which fiction is written that we novelists fully felt its effects.

Even now, even when I carefully locate my despair in the past tense, it's difficult for me to confess to all these doubts. In publishing circles, confessions of doubt are commonly referred to as "whining"—the idea being that cultural complaint is pathetic and self-serving in writers who don't sell, ungracious in writers who do. For people as protective of their privacy and as fiercely competitive as writers are, mute suffering would seem to be the safest course. However sick with foreboding you feel inside, it's best to radiate confidence and to hope that it's infectious. When a writer says publicly that the novel is doomed, it's a sure bet his new book isn't going well; in terms of his reputation, it's like bleeding in shark-infested waters.

Even harder to admit is how depressed I was. As the social stigma of depression disappears, the aesthetic stigma increases. It's not just that depression has become fashionable to the point of banality. It's the sense that we live in a reductively binary culture: you're either healthy or you're sick, you either function or you don't. And if that flattening of the field of possibilities is precisely what's depressing you, you're inclined to resist participating in the flattening by calling yourself depressed. You decide that it's the world that's sick, and that the resistance of refusing to function in such a world is healthy. You embrace what clinicians call "depressive realism." It's what the chorus in *Oedipus Rex* sings: "Alas, ye generations of men, how mere a shadow do I count your life! Where, where is the mortal who wins more of happiness than just the seeming, and, after the semblance, a falling away?" You are, after all, just protoplasm, and some day you'll be dead. The invitation to leave your depression behind, whether through medication or therapy or effort of will, seems like an invitation to turn your back on all your dark insights into the corruption and infantilism and self-delusion of the brave new McWorld. And these insights are the sole legacy of the social novelist, who desires to represent the world not simply in its detail but in its essence, to shine light on the morally blind eye of the virtual whirlwind, and who believes that human beings deserve better than the future of attractively priced electronic panderings that is even now being conspired for them. Instead of saying *I am depressed,* you want to say *I am right!*

But all the available evidence suggests that you have become a person who's impossible to live with and no fun to talk to. And as you increasingly feel, as a novelist, that you are one of the last remaining repositories of depressive realism and of the radical critique of the therapeutic society that it represents, the burden of newsbringing that is placed on your art becomes overwhelming. You ask yourself, why am I bothering to write these books? I can't pretend the mainstream will listen to the news I have to bring. I can't pretend I'm subverting anything, because any reader capable of decoding my subversive messages does not need to hear them (and the contemporary art scene is a constant reminder of how silly things get when artists start preaching to the choir). I can't stomach any kind of notion that serious fiction is *good for us,* because I don't believe that everything that's wrong with the world has a cure, and even if I did, what business would I, who feel like the sick one, have in offering it? It's hard to consider literature a medicine, in any case, when reading it serves mainly to deepen your depressing estrangement from the mainstream; sooner or later the therapeutically minded reader will end up fingering reading itself as the sickness. Sophie Bentwood, for instance, has "candidate for Prozac" written all over her. No matter how gorgeous and comic her torments are, and no matter how profoundly human she appears in light of those torments, a reader who loves her can't help wondering whether perhaps treatment by a mental-health-care provider wouldn't be the best course all around.

I resist, finally, the notion of literature as a noble higher calling, because elitism doesn't sit well with my American nature, and because even if my belief in mystery didn't incline me to distrust feelings of superiority, my belief in manners would make it difficult for me to explain to my brother, who is a fan of Michael Crichton, that the work I'm doing is simply *better* than Crichton's. Not even the French poststructuralists, with their philosophically unassailable celebration of the "pleasure of the text," can help me out here, because I know that no matter how metaphorically rich and linguistically sophisticated *Desperate Characters* is, what I experienced when I first read it was not some erotically joyous lateral slide of endless associations but something coherent and deadly pertinent. I know there's a reason I loved reading and loved writing. But every apology and every defense seems to dissolve in the sugar water of contemporary culture, and before long it becomes difficult indeed to get out of bed in the morning.

Two quick generalizations about novelists: we don't like to poke too deeply into the question of audience, and we don't like the social sciences. How awkward, then, that for me the beacon in the murk—the person who inadvertently did the most to get me back on track as a writer—should have been a social scientist who was studying the audience for serious fiction in America.

Shirley Brice Heath is a former MacArthur Fellow, a linguistic anthropologist, and a professor of English and linguistics at Stanford; she's a stylish, twiggy, white-haired lady with no discernible tolerance for small talk. Throughout the Eighties, Heath haunted what she calls "enforced transition zones"—places where people are held captive without recourse to television or other comforting pursuits. She rode public transportation in twenty-seven different cities. She lurked in airports (at least before the arrival of CNN). She took her notebook into bookstores and seaside resorts. Whenever she saw people reading or buying "substantive works of fiction" (meaning, roughly, trade-paperback fiction), she asked for a few minutes of their time. She visited summer writers conferences and creative-writing programs to grill ephebes. She interviewed novelists. Three years ago she interviewed me, and last summer I had lunch with her in Palo Alto.

To the extent that novelists think about audience at all, we like to imagine a "general audience"—a large, eclectic pool of decently educated people who can be induced, by strong enough reviews or aggressive enough marketing, to treat themselves to a good, serious book. We do our best not to notice that among adults with similar educations and similarly complicated lives some read a lot of novels while others read few or none.

Heath has noticed this circumstance, and although she emphasized to me that she has not polled everybody in America, her research effectively demolishes the myth of the general audience. For a person to sustain an interest in literature, she told me, two things have to be in place. First, the habit of reading works of substance must have been "heavily modeled" when he or she was very young. In other words, one or both of the parents must have been reading serious books and must have encouraged the child to do the same. On the East Coast, Heath found a strong element of class in this. Parents in the privileged classes encourage reading out of a sense of what Louis Auchincloss calls "entitlement": just as the civilized person ought to be able to appreciate caviar and a good Burgundy, she ought to be able to enjoy Henry James. Class matters less in other parts of the country, especially in the Protestant Midwest, where literature is seen as a way to exercise the mind. As Heath put it, "Part of the exercise of being a good person is not using your free time frivolously. You have to be able to account for yourself through the work ethic *and* through the wise use of your leisure time." For a century after the Civil War, the Midwest was home to thousands of small-town literary societies in which, Heath found, the wife of a janitor was as likely to be active as the wife of a doctor.

Simply having a parent who reads is not enough, however, to produce a life-long dedicated reader. According to Heath, young readers also need to find a person with whom they can share their interest. "A child who's got the habit will start reading under the covers with a flashlight," she said. "If the parents are smart, they'll forbid the child to do this, and thereby encourage her. Otherwise she'll find a peer who also has the habit, and the two of them will keep it a secret between them. Finding a peer can take place as late as college. In high school, especially, there's a social penalty to be paid for being a reader. Lots of kids who have been lone readers get to college and suddenly discover, 'Oh my God, there are other people here who read.'"

As Heath unpacked her findings for me, I was remembering the joy with which I'd discovered two friends in junior high with whom I could talk about J.R.R. Tolkien. I was also considering that for me, today, there is nothing sexier than a reader. But then it occurred to me that I didn't even meet Heath's first precondition. I told her I didn't remember either of my parents ever reading a book when I was a child, except aloud to me.

Without missing a beat Heath replied: "Yes, but there's a second kind of reader. There's the social isolate—the child who from an early age felt very different from everyone around him. This is very, very difficult to uncover in an interview. People don't like to admit that they were social isolates as children. What happens is you take that sense of being different into an imaginary world. But that world, then, is a world you can't share with the people around you—because it's imaginary. And so the important dialogue in your life is with the *authors* of the books you read. Though they aren't present, they become your community."

Pride compels me, here, to draw a distinction between young fiction readers and young nerds. The classic nerd, who finds a home in facts or technology or numbers, is marked not by a displaced sociability but by an *anti*sociability. Reading does resemble more nerdy pursuits in that it's a habit that both feeds on a sense of isolation and aggravates it. Simply being a "social isolate" as a child does not, however, doom you to bad breath and poor party skills as an adult. In fact, it can make you hypersocial. It's just that at some point you'll begin to feel a gnawing, almost remorseful need to be alone and do some reading—to reconnect to that community.

According to Heath, readers of the social-isolate variety are much more likely to become writers than those of the modeled-habit variety. If writing was the medium of communication within the community of childhood, it makes sense that when writers grow up they continue to find writing vital to their sense of connectedness. What's perceived as the antisocial nature of "substantive" authors, whether it's James Joyce's exile or J. D. Salinger's reclusion, derives in large part from the social isolation that's necessary for inhabiting an imagined world. Looking me in the eye, Heath said: "You are a socially isolated individual who desperately wants to communicate with a substantive imaginary world."

I knew she was using the word "you" in its impersonal sense. Nevertheless, I felt as if she were looking straight into my soul. And the exhilaration I felt at her accidental description of me, in unpoetic polysyllables, was my confirmation of that description's truth. Simply to be recognized for what I was, simply not to be misunderstood: these had revealed themselves, suddenly, as reasons to write.

By the spring of 1994 I was a socially isolated individual whose desperate wish was mainly to make some money. I took a job teaching undergraduate fiction-writing at a small liberal arts college, and although I spent way too much time on it, I loved the work. I was heartened by the skill and ambition of my students, who had not even been born when *Rowan and Martin's Laugh-In* first aired. I was depressed, however, to learn that several of my best writers, repelled by the violence done to their personal experience of reading, had vowed never to take a literature class again. One evening a student reported that his contemporary fiction class had been encouraged to spend an entire hour debating whether the novelist Leslie Marmon Silko was a homophobe. Another evening when I came to class three women students were hooting with laughter at the patently awful utopian-feminist novel they were being forced to read for an honors seminar in Women and Fiction.

It goes without saying that a book as dark as *Desperate Characters* would never be taught in such a seminar, however demonstrably female its author may be. Sophie and Otto Bentwood treat each other both badly and tenderly; there's no way to fit such three-dimensionality into the procrustean beds of victim and victimizer. But the therapeutic optimism now raging in English literature departments insists that novels be sorted into two boxes: Symptoms of Disease (canonical work from the Dark Ages before 1950), and Medicine for a Happier and Healthier World (the work of women and of people from nonwhite or non-hetero cultures). That you can now easily get a B.A. in English literature without reading Shakespeare—that students are encouraged to read the literature that is most "meaningful" to them personally, and even if they do read Shakespeare to read him as they "choose" (say, for his (mis)representations of the Other)—reflects a notion of culture that resembles nothing so much as a menu to be pointed at and clicked.

It does seem strange that with all the Marxists on college campuses, more is not made of the resemblance that multiculturalism and the new politics of identity bear to corporate specialty-marketing—to the national sales apparatus that can target your tastes by your zip code and supply you with products appropriate to your demographics. Strange, too, that postmodernism, which is multiculturalism's counterpart among the tenured creative-writing avant-garde, should celebrate as "subversive" the same blending of Hi and Lo culture that *The New York Times Magazine* performs every Sunday between ads for Tiffany's and Lancôme.[3] Stranger yet that all these academic Che Guevaras have targeted as "monolithic" and "repressive" certain traditional modes of serious fiction that in fact are fighting television and therapy for their very life. Strangest of all, perhaps, that such heroic subversives, lecturing on the patriarchal evil *du jour* while their TIAA-CREF accounts grow fat on Wall Street, manage to keep a straight face.

Then again, there has always been a gulf between ideologues, whose ideas abound with implicit optimism, and novelists, whose pessimism reflects their helplessness to ignore the human beings behind ideas. The contemporary fiction writers whose work is being put to such optimistic use in the academy are seldom, themselves, to blame. To the extent that the American novel still has cultural authority—an appeal beyond the academy, a presence in household conversations —it's largely the work of women. Knowledgeable booksellers estimate that 70 percent of all fiction is bought by women, and so perhaps it's no surprise that in recent years so many crossover novels, the good books that find an audience, have been written by women: fictional mothers turning a sober eye on their children in the work of Jane Smiley and Rosellen Brown; fictional daughters listening to their Chinese mothers (Amy Tan) or Sioux grandmothers (Louise Erdrich); a fictional freedwoman conversing with the spirit of the daughter she killed to save her from slavery (Toni Morrison). The darkness of these novels is not a political darkness, banishable by the enlightenment of contemporary critical theory; it's the darkness of sorrows that have no easy cure.

The current flourishing of novels by women and cultural minorities may in part represent a movement, in the face of a hyperkinetic televised reality, to anchor fiction in the only ground that doesn't shift every six months: the author's membership in a tribe. If nothing else, the new cultural diversity of fiction shows the chauvinism of judging the vitality of American letters by the fortunes of the traditional social novel. It's often argued, in fact, that the country's literary culture is *healthier* for having disconnected from mainstream culture; that a universal "American" culture was little more than an instrument for the perpetuation of a white, male, heterosexual elite, and that its decline is the just desert of an exhausted tradition. (Joseph Heller's depiction of women in *Catch-22* is so embarrassing, certainly, that I hesitated to recommend the book to my students.) There's little doubt that many of the new novels are at some level dramas of assimilation, which are broadening our conception of the national culture just as Roth's novels of Jewish-American life did a generation ago.

Unfortunately, there's also evidence that young writers today feel ghettoized in their ethnic or gender identities—discouraged from speaking across boundaries by a culture that has been conditioned by television to accept only the literal testimony of the Self.[4] The problem is aggravated, or so it's frequently argued, by the degree to which fiction writers, both successful ones and ephebes, have taken refuge from a hostile culture in university creative-writing programs. Any given issue of the typical small literary magazine, edited by MFA candidates aware that the MFA candidates submitting manuscripts need to publish in order to obtain or hold on to teaching jobs, reliably contains variations on three generic short stories: "My Interesting Childhood," "My Interesting Life in a College Town," and "My Interesting Year Abroad." Of all the arts, fiction writing would seem to be the least suited to the monotony of academic sequestration. Poets draw their material from their own subjectivities, composers from God knows where. Even painters, though they inhale at their own risk the theoretical miasma emanating from art history and English departments (and the only thing more harmful to a working artist than neglect is idiotic encouragement), do not depend on *manners,* on eavesdropped conversations and surmounted quotidian obstacles, the way novelists do. For a long time, I rationalized my own gut aversion to the university with the idea that a novelist has a responsibility to stay close to life in the mainstream, to walk the streets, rub shoulders with the teeming masses, etc.—the better to be able, in Sven Birkerts's words, to bring readers "meaningful news about what it means to live in the world of the present."

Now, however, I think my gut aversion is just that: a gut aversion. Novelists within the academy serve the important function of teaching literature for its own sake; some of them also produce interesting work while teaching. As for the much greater volume of impeccably competent work that's manufactured in and around the workshops, no one is forcing me to read it. The competitor in me, in fact, is glad that so many of my peers have chosen not to rough it in the free-market world. I happen to enjoy living within subway distance of Wall Street and keeping close tabs on the country's shadow government. But the world of the present is accessible to anyone with cable TV, a modem, and transportation to a mall; and as far as I'm concerned, any writer who wants to revel in that life is welcome to it. Although the rise of identity-based fiction has coincided with the American novel's retreat from the mainstream, Shirley Heath's observations have reinforced my conviction that bringing "meaningful news" is no longer so much a defining function of the novel as an accidental by-product.

The value of Heath's work, and the reason I'm citing her so liberally, is that she has bothered to study empirically what nobody else has, and that she has brought to bear on the problem of reading a vocabulary that is neutral enough to survive in our value-free cultural environment. Readers aren't "better" or "healthier" or, conversely, "sicker" than non-readers. We just happen to belong to a rather strange kind of community.

For Heath, a defining feature of "substantive works of fiction" is *unpredictability*. She arrived at this definition after discovering that most of the hundreds of serious readers she interviewed have had to deal, one way or another, with personal unpredictability. Therapists and ministers who counsel troubled people tend to read the hard stuff. So do people whose lives have not followed the course they were expected to: merchant-caste Koreans who don't become merchants, ghetto kids who go to college, men from conservative families who lead openly gay lives, and women whose lives have turned out to be radically different from their mothers'. This last group is particularly large. There are, today, millions of American women whose lives do not resemble the lives they might have projected from their mothers', and all of them, in Heath's model, are potentially susceptible to substantive fiction.[5]

In her interviews, Heath uncovered a "wide unanimity" among serious readers that literature "'makes me a better person.'" She hastened to assure me that, rather than straightening them out in a self-help way, "reading serious literature impinges on the embedded circumstances in people's lives in such a way that they have to deal with them. And, in so dealing, they come to see themselves as deeper and more capable of handling their inability to have a totally predictable life." Again and again, readers told Heath the same thing: "Reading enables me to maintain a sense of something *substantive*—my ethical integrity, my intellectual integrity. 'Substance' is more than 'this weighty book.' Reading that book gives *me* substance." This substance, Heath added, is most often transmitted verbally, and is felt to have permanence. "Which is why," she said, "computers won't do it for readers."

With near unanimity, Heath's respondents described substantive works of fiction as "the only places where there was some civic, public hope of coming to grips with the ethical, philosophical, and sociopolitical dimensions of life that were elsewhere treated so simplistically. From Agamemnon forward, for example, we've been having to deal with the conflict between loyalty to one's family and loyalty to the state. And strong works of fiction are what refuse to give easy answers to the conflict, to paint things as black and white, good guys versus bad guys. They're everything that pop psychology is not."

"And religions themselves are substantive works of fiction," I said.

She nodded. "This is precisely what readers are saying: that reading good fiction is like reading a particularly rich section of a religious text. What religion and good fiction have in common is that the answers aren't there, there isn't closure. The language of literary works gives forth something different with each reading. But unpredictability doesn't mean total relativism. Instead it highlights the persistence with which writers keep coming back to fundamental problems. Your family versus your country, your wife versus your girlfriend."

"Being alive versus having to die," I said.

"Exactly," Heath said. "Of course, there is a certain predictability to literature's unpredictability. It's the one thing that all substantive works have in common. And that predictability is what readers tell me they hang on to—a sense of having company in this great human enterprise, in the continuity, in the persistence, of the great conflicts." . . .

One of the cherished notions of cybervisionaries is that literary culture is anti-democratic—that the reading of good books is primarily a pursuit of the leisured white male—and that our republic will therefore be healthier for abandoning itself to computers. As Shirley Heath's research (or even a casual visit to a bookstore) makes clear, the cybervisionaries are lying. Reading is an ethnically diverse, socially skeptical activity. The wealthy white men who today have powerful notebook computers are the ones who form this country's most salient elite. The word "elitist" is the club with which they bash those for whom purchasing technology fails to constitute a life.

That a distrust or an outright hatred of what we now call "literature" has always been a mark of social visionaries, whether Plato or Stalin or today's free-market technocrats, can lead us to think that literature has a function, beyond entertainment, as a form of social opposition. Novels, after all, do sometimes ignite political debates or become embroiled in them. And since the one modest favor that any writer asks of a society is freedom of expression, a country's poets and novelists are often the ones obliged to serve as voices of conscience in times of religious or political fanaticism. Literature's aura of oppositionality is especially intense in America, where the low status of art has a way of turning resistant child readers into supremely alienated grown-up writers. What's more, since the making of money has always been of absolute centrality to the culture, and since the people who make a lot of it are seldom very interesting, the most memorable characters in U.S. fiction have tended to be socially marginal: Twain's Huck Finn and Hurston's Janie Crawford, O'Connor's Hazel Motes and Pynchon's Tyrone Slothrop. Finally, the feeling of oppositionality is compounded in an age when simply picking up a novel after dinner represents a kind of cultural *Je refuse!*

It's all too easy, therefore, to forget how frequently good artists through the ages have insisted, as W. H. Auden put it, that "art makes nothing happen." It's all too easy to jump from the knowledge that the novel *can* have agency to the conviction that it *must* have agency. Nabokov pretty well summed up the political platform that every novelist can endorse: no censorship, good universal education, no portraits of heads of state larger than a postage stamp. If we go any further than that, our agendas begin to diverge radically. What emerges as the belief that unifies us is not that a novel can change anything but that it can *preserve* something. The thing being preserved depends on the writer; it may be as private as "My Interesting Childhood." But as the country grows ever more distracted and mesmerized by popular culture, the stakes rise even for authors whose primary ambition is to land a teaching job. Whether they think about it or not, novelists are preserving a tradition of precise, expressive language; a habit of looking past surfaces into interiors; maybe an understanding of private experience and public context as distinct but interpenetrating; maybe mystery, maybe manners. Above all, they are preserving a community of readers and writers, and the way in which members of this community recognize each other is that nothing in the world seems simple to them.

Shirley Heath uses the bland word "unpredictability" to describe this conviction of complexity; Flannery O'Connor called it "mystery." In *Desperate Characters,* Fox captures it like this: "Ticking away inside the carapace of ordinary life and its sketchy agreements was anarchy." For me, the word that best describes the novelist's view of the world is "tragic." In Nietzsche's account of the "birth of tragedy," which remains pretty much unbeatable as a theory of why people enjoy sad narratives, an anarchic "Dionysian" insight into the darkness and unpredictability of life is wedded to an "Apollonian" clarity and beauty of form to produce an experience that's religious in its intensity. Even for people who don't believe in anything that they can't see with their own two eyes, the formal aesthetic rendering of the human plight can be (though I'm afraid we novelists are rightly mocked for overusing the word) redemptive.

It's possible to locate various morals in *Oedipus Rex*—"Heed oracles," say, or "Expect the unexpected," or "Marry in haste, repent at leisure"—and their existence confirms in us a sense of the universe's underlying orderliness. But what makes Oedipus human is that of course he doesn't heed the Oracle. And though Sophie Bentwood, 2,500 years later, "shouldn't" try to insulate herself from the rabid society around her, of course she tries to anyway. But then, as Fox writes: "How quickly the husk of adult life, its *importance,* was shattered by the thrust of what was, all at once, real and imperative and absurd."

The most reliable indicator of a tragic perspective in a work of fiction is comedy. I think there's very little good fiction that isn't funny. I'm still waiting for the non-German-speaking world to get the news that Kafka, for example, is a comic writer. Truer words were never spoken than when Clarence Thomas responded to Anita Hill's accusations by intoning: "This is Kafkaesque." A man who probably is guilty—a man whose twisted private problems with women have become public property—indignantly protesting his innocence? If Kafka had been alive, he would have been laughing. Given the prospect of Thomas on the bench for another thirty years, what else is there to do?

I hope it's clear that by "tragic" I mean just about any fiction that raises more questions than it answers: anything in which conflict doesn't resolve into cant. The point of calling serious fiction tragic is simply to highlight its distance from the rhetoric of optimism that so pervades our culture. The necessary lie of every successful regime, including the upbeat techno-corporatism under which we now live, is that the regime has made the world a better place. Tragic realism preserves the recognition that improvement always comes at a cost; that nothing lasts forever; that if the good in the world outweighs the bad, it's by the slimmest of margins. I suspect that art has always had a particularly tenuous purchase on the American imagination because ours is a country to which hardly anything really terrible has ever happened. The only genuine tragedies to befall us were slavery and the Civil War, and it's probably no accident that the tradition of Southern literature has been strikingly rich and productive of geniuses. (Compare the literature of the sunny, fertile, peaceful West Coast.) Superficially at least, for the great white majority, the history of this country has consisted of success and more success. Tragic realism preserves access to the dirt behind the dream of Chosenness—to the human difficulty beneath the technological ease, to the sorrow behind the pop-cultural narcosis: to all those portents on the margins of our existence.

> People without hope not only don't write novels, but what is more to the point, they don't read them. They don't take long looks at anything, because they lack the courage. The way to despair is to refuse to have any kind of experience, and the novel, of course, is a way to have experience.
>
> —Flannery O'Connor

Depression, when it's clinical, is not a metaphor. It runs in families, and it's known to respond to medication and to counseling. However truly you believe there's a sickness to existence that can never be cured, if you're depressed you will sooner or later surrender and say: I just don't want to feel bad anymore. The shift from depressive realism to tragic realism, from being immobilized by darkness to being sustained by it, thus strangely seems to require believing in the possibility of a cure, though this "cure" is anything but straightforward.

I spent the early Nineties trapped in a double singularity. Not only did I feel different from everyone around me, but the age I lived in felt utterly different from any age that had come before. For me the work of regaining a tragic perspective has therefore involved a dual kind of reaching-out: both the reconnection with a community of readers and writers, and the reclamation of a sense of history.

It's possible to have a general sense of history's darkness, a mystical Dionysian conviction that the game ain't over till it's over, without having enough of an

Apollonian grasp of the details to appreciate its consolations. Until a year ago, for example, it would never have occurred to me to assert that this country has *always* been dominated by commerce.[6] I saw only the ugliness of the commercial present, and naturally I raged at the betrayal of an earlier America that I presumed to have been truer, less venal, less hostile to the enterprise of fiction. But how ridiculous the self-pity of the writer in the late twentieth century can seem in light, say, of Herman Melville's life. How familiar his life is: the first novel that makes his reputation, the painful discovery of how little his vision appeals to prevailing popular tastes, the growing sense of having no place in a sentimental republic, the horrible money troubles, the abandonment by his publisher, the disastrous commercial failure of his finest and most ambitious work, the reputed mental illness (his melancholy, his *depression*), and finally the retreat into writing purely for his own satisfaction.

Reading Melville's biography, I wish that he'd been granted the example of someone like himself, from an earlier century, to make him feel less singularly cursed. I wish, too, that he'd been able to say to himself, when he was struggling to support Lizzie and their kids: hey, if worst comes to worst, I can always teach writing. In his lifetime, Melville made about $10,500 from his books. Even today, he can't catch a break. On its first printing, the title page of the second Library of America volume of Melville's collected works bore the name, in 24-point display type, HERMAN MEVILLE.

Last summer, as I began to acquaint myself with American history, and as I talked to readers and writers and pondered the Heathian "social isolate," there was growing inside me a realization that my condition was not a disease but a nature. How could I *not* feel estranged? I was a *reader*. My nature had been waiting for me all along, and now it welcomed me. All of a sudden I became aware of how starved I was to construct and inhabit an imagined world. The hunger felt like a loneliness of which I'd been dying. How could I have thought that I needed to cure myself in order to fit into the "real" world? I didn't need curing, and the world didn't, either; the only thing that did need curing was my understanding of my place in it. Without that understanding—without a sense of *belonging* to the real world—it was impossible to thrive in an imagined one.

At the heart of my despair about the novel had been a conflict between my feeling that I should Address the Culture and Bring News to the Mainstream, and my desire to write about the things closest to me, to lose myself in the characters and locales I loved. Writing, and reading too, had become a grim duty, and considering the poor pay, there is seriously no point in doing either if you're not having fun. As soon as I jettisoned my perceived obligation to the chimerical mainstream, my third book began to move again. I'm amazed, now, that I'd trusted myself so little for so long, that I'd felt such a crushing imperative to engage explicitly with all the forces impinging on the pleasure of reading and writing: as if, in peopling and arranging my own little alternate world, I could ignore the bigger social picture even if I wanted to.

As I was figuring all this out, I got a letter from Don DeLillo, to whom I'd written in distress. This, in part, is what he said:

The novel is whatever novelists are doing at a given time. If we're not doing the big social novel fifteen years from now, it'll probably mean our sensibilities have changed in ways that make such work less compelling to us—we won't stop because the market dried up. The writer leads, he doesn't follow. The dynamic lives in the writer's mind, not in the size of the audience. And if the social novel lives, but only barely, surviving in the cracks and ruts of the culture, maybe it will be taken more seriously, as an endangered spectacle. A reduced context but a more intense one.

Writing is a form of personal freedom. It frees us from the mass identity we see in the making all around us. In the end, writers will write not to be outlaw heroes of some underculture but mainly to save themselves, to survive as individuals.

DeLillo added a postscript: "If serious reading dwindles to near nothingness, it will probably mean that the thing we're talking about when we use the word 'identity' has reached an end."

The strange thing about this postscript is that I can't read it without experiencing a surge of hope. Tragic realism has the perverse effect of making its adherents into qualified optimists. "I am very much afraid," O'Connor once wrote, "that to the fiction writer the fact that we shall always have the poor with us is a source of satisfaction, for it means, essentially, that he will always be able to find someone like himself. His concern with poverty is with a poverty fundamental to man." Even if Silicon Valley manages to plant a virtual-reality helmet in every American household, even if serious reading dwindles to near nothingness, there remains a hungry world beyond our borders, a national debt that government-by-television can do little more than wring its hands over, and the good old apocalyptic horsemen of war, disease, and environmental degradation. If real wages keep falling, the suburbs of "My Interesting Childhood" won't offer much protection. And if multiculturalism succeeds in making us a nation of independently empowered tribes, each tribe will be deprived of the comfort of victimhood and be forced to confront human limitation for what it is: a fixture of life. History is the rabid thing from which we all, like Sophie Bentwood, would like to hide. But there's no bubble that can stay unburst. On whether this is a good thing or a bad thing, tragic realists offer no opinion. They simply represent it. A generation ago, by paying close attention, Paula Fox could discern in a broken ink bottle both perdition and salvation. The world was ending then, it's ending still, and I'm happy to belong to it again.

NOTES

1. Tom Wolfe's manifesto for the "New Social Novel" (*Harper's*, November 1989) was probably the high-water mark of sublime incomprehension. What was most striking about Wolfe's essay—more than his uncannily perfect ignorance of the many excellent socially engaged novels published between 1960 and 1989, more, even, than his colossal self-regard—was his failure to explain why his ideal New Social Novelist should not be writing scripts for Hollywood.

2. Here is cyberphilosopher Brenda Laurel, speaking to the *Times:* "In the V. R. field, there's kind of a naive belief that once we're able to do . . . what Tim Leary calls screen each other's mind, we'll suddenly get a whole lot better at understanding each other. I know this sounds squishy, but I really believe it."

3. Last fall the word "literature" appeared twice on the magazine's cover: "The Roseanne of Literature" (profile of Dorothy Allison) and "Want Literature? Stay Tuned!" ("The Triumph of the Prime-Time Novel").

4. The popularity of role-playing in on-line MUDs (multiple-user dialogues) and chat rooms, which enthusiastic theorists extol for their liberating diffractions of selfhood, in fact merely confirms how obsessed we all are with a superficially defined "identity." Identity as a mystery (the continuity of a conscious I-ness from your childhood through the present) or as manners (how kind you are, how direct, how funny, how snobbish, how self-deceptive, how ironic; how you behave) is evidently weightless in comparison to the assertion: "I am a twenty-five-year old bi female in fishnet stockings."

5. If the rolls of nineteenth-century literary societies are any indication, women have always done the bulk of fiction reading. But in a society where a majority of women both work and take care of their families, it's significant that, even today, two out of every three novels purchased are purchased by women. The vastly increased presence of women in serious American writing probably has explanations on both the supply side and the demand side. An expanded pool of readers with unexpected lives inevitably produces an expanded pool of writers. And sometime around 1973, when American women entered the workplace in earnest, they began to demand fiction that wasn't written from a male perspective. Writers like Jane Smiley and Amy Tan today seem conscious and confident of an attentive audience. Whereas all the male novelists I know, including myself, are clueless as to who could possibly be buying our books.

6. I realize that this is a dismal confession, and that my managing to slip through college without ever taking a course in either American history or American literature is hardly an excuse.

DISCUSSION QUESTIONS

1. Why does Franzen assert that a writer who wants to report on topical issues as primary subject matter "would be foolish to choose the novel as a vehicle" for this purpose? How has the world changed, according to Franzen, to make such social fiction "obsolete"?

2. How has the traditionally "solitary work" of writing and reading been undermined by other forms of communication, particularly film and television?

3. How does Franzen see the "manners" of particular regions being destroyed by the forces of "technological consumerism"? Further, how does this cultural trend limit face-to-face communication and thus change the drama of human interaction?

4. What does Franzen mean by "depressive realism"? How does he see the "therapeutic society" working against the traditional aims of fiction that examines the individual in relation to society?

5. What attitudes toward literature does Franzen find when he teaches fiction writing at a liberal arts college? What flaws and limitations does he point out in his assessment of how literary works are assigned and analyzed?

6. How does fiction that grows out of "the author's membership in a tribe" challenge the homogenizing effects of mass culture? Must fiction, according to Franzen, be disconnected from mainstream consumer culture to retain its power and integrity?

7. What pressures does the literary marketplace, now linked to television interviews and media tours, exert on the "social isolate" who writes fiction?

DAVID FOSTER WALLACE

E Unibus Pluram: Television and U.S. Fiction

David Foster Wallace (b. 1967) has published the novels and story collections The Broom of the System *(1987),* Girl with Curious Hair *(1988),* Infinite Jest *(1996), and* Brief Interviews with Hideous Men *(1999). Sometimes called the Gen X Thomas Pynchon, he has taught at Illinois State University at Bloomington-Normal since 1993. His essays, which showcase a keen satirical eye and talent for cultural analysis, are collected in* A Supposedly Fun Thing I'll Never Do Again *(1997).*

METAWATCHING

It's not like self-reference is new to U.S. entertainment. How many old radio shows—Jack Benny, Burns and Allen, Abbott and Costello—were mostly about themselves as shows? "So, Lou, and you said I couldn't get a big star like Miss Lucille Ball to be a guest on our show, you little twerp." Etc. But once television introduces the element of watching, and once it informs an economy and culture like radio never could have, the referential stakes go way up. Six hours a day is more time than most people (consciously) do any other one thing. How human beings who absorb such high doses understand themselves will naturally change, become vastly more spectatorial, self-conscious. Because the practice of "watching" is expansive. Exponential. We spend enough time watching, pretty soon we start watching ourselves watching. Pretty soon we start to "feel" ourselves feeling, yearn to experience "experiences." And that American subspecies into fiction writing starts writing more and more about . . .

The emergence of something called Metafiction in the American '60s was hailed by academic critics as a radical aesthetic, a whole new literary form, literature unshackled from the cultural cinctures of mimetic narrative and free to plunge into reflexivity and self-conscious meditations on aboutness. Radical it may have been, but thinking that postmodern Metafiction evolved unconscious of prior changes in readerly taste is about as innocent as thinking that all those college students we saw on television protesting the Vietnam war were protesting only because they hated the Vietnam war. (They may have hated the war, but they also wanted to be seen protesting on television. TV was where they'd *seen* this war, after all. Why wouldn't they go about hating it on the very medium that made their hate possible?) Metafictionists may have had aesthetic theories out the bazoo, but they were also sentient citizens of a community that was exchanging an old idea of itself as a nation of doers and be-ers for a new vision of the U.S.A. as an atomized mass of self-conscious watchers and appearers. For Metafiction, in its ascendant and most important phases, was really nothing more than a single-order expansion of its own great theoretical nemesis, Realism: if Realism called it like it saw it, Metafiction simply called it as it saw itself seeing itself see it. This high-cultural postmodern genre, in other words, was deeply informed by the emergence of television and the metastasis of self-conscious watching. And (I claim) American fiction remains deeply informed by television . . . especially those strains of fiction with roots in postmodernism, which even at its rebellious Metafictional zenith was less a "response to" televisual culture than a kind of abiding-in-TV. Even back then, the borders were starting to come down.

It's strange that it took television itself so long to wake up to watching's potent reflexivity. Television shows about the business of television shows were rare for a long time. *The Dick van Dyke Show* was prescient, and Mary [Tyler] Moore carried its insight into her own decade-long exploration of local-market angst. Now, of course, there's been everything from *Murphy Brown* to *Max Headroom* to *Entertainment Tonight*. And with Letterman, Miller, Shandling, and Leno's battery of hip, sardonic, this-is-just-TV schticks, the circle back to the days of "We've just got to get Miss Ball on our show, Bud" has closed and come spiral, television's power to jettison connection and castrate protest fueled by the very ironic postmodern self-consciousness it had first helped fashion.

It will take a while, but I'm going to prove to you that the nexus where television and fiction converse and consort is self-conscious irony. Irony is, of course, a turf fictionists have long worked with zeal. And irony is important for understanding TV because "TV," now that it's gotten powerful enough to move from acronym to way of life, revolves off just the sorts of absurd contradictions irony's all about exposing. It is ironic that television is a syncretic, homogenizing force that derives much of its power from diversity and various affirmations thereof. It is ironic that an extremely canny and unattractive self-consciousness is necessary to create TV performers' illusion of unconscious appeal. That products presented as helping you express individuality can afford to be advertised on television only because they sell to enormous numbers of people. And so on.

Television regards irony sort of the way educated lonely people regard television. Television both fears irony's capacity to expose, and needs it. It needs irony because television was practically *made* for irony. For TV is a bisensuous medium. Its displacement of radio wasn't picture displacing sound; it was picture added. Since the tension between what's said and what's seen is irony's whole sales territory, classic televisual irony works via the conflicting juxtaposition of pictures and sounds. What's seen undercuts what's said. A scholarly article on network news describes a famous interview with a corporate guy from United Fruit on a CBS special about Guatemala: "I sure don't know of anybody being so-called 'oppressed,'" this guy, in a '70s leisure suit and bad comb-over, tells Ed Rabel. "I think this is just something that some reporters have thought up."[1] The whole interview is intercut with commentless footage of big-bellied kids in Guatemalan slums and union organizers lying in the mud with cut throats.

Television's classic irony function came into its own in the summer of 1974, as remorseless lenses opened to view the fertile "credibility gap" between the image of official disclaimer and the reality of high-level shenanigans. A nation was changed, as Audience. If even the president lies to you, whom are you supposed to trust to deliver the real? Television, that summer, got to present itself as the earnest, worried eye on the reality behind all images. The irony that television is itself a river of image, however, was apparent even to a twelve-year-old, sitting there, rapt. After '74 there seemed to be no way out. Images and ironies all over the place. It's not a coincidence that *Saturday Night Live,* that Athens of irreverent cynicism, specializing in parodies of (1) politics and (2) television, premiered the next fall (on television).

I'm worried when I say things like "television fears . . ." and "television presents itself . . ." because, even though it's kind of a necessary abstraction, talking about television as if it were an entity can easily slip into the worst sort of anti-TV paranoia, treating of TV as some autonomous diabolical corrupter of personal agency and community gumption. I am concerned to avoid anti-TV paranoia here. Though I'm convinced that television today lies, with a potency somewhere between symptom and synecdoche, behind a genuine crisis for U.S. culture and literature, I do not agree with reactionaries who regard TV as some malignancy visited on an innocent populace, sapping IQs and compromising SAT scores while we all sit there on ever fatter bottoms with little mesmerized spirals revolving in our eyes. Critics like Samuel Huntington and Barbara Tuchman who try to claim that TV's lowering of our aesthetic standards is responsible for a "contemporary culture taken over by commercialism directed to the mass market and necessarily to mass taste"[2] can be refuted by observing that their Propter Hoc isn't even Post Hoc: by 1830, de Tocqueville had already diagnosed American culture as peculiarly devoted to easy sensation and mass-marketed entertainment, "spectacles vehement and untutored and rude" that aimed "to stir the passions more than to gratify the taste."[3] Treating television as evil is just as reductive and silly as treating it like a toaster w/pictures.

It is of course undeniable that television is an example of Low Art, the sort of art that has to please people in order to get their money. Because of the economics of nationally broadcast, advertiser-subsidized entertainment, television's one goal—never denied by anybody in or around TV since RCA first authorized field tests in 1936—is to ensure as much watching as possible. TV is the epitome of Low Art in its desire to appeal to and enjoy the attention of unprecedented numbers of people. But it is not Low because it is vulgar or prurient or dumb. Television is often all these things, but this is a logical function of its need to attract and please Audience. And I'm not saying that television is vulgar and dumb because the people who compose Audience are vulgar and dumb. Television is the way it is simply because people tend to be extremely similar in their vulgar and prurient and dumb interests and wildly different in their refined and aesthetic and noble interests. It's all about syncretic diversity: neither medium nor Audience is fault-able for quality.

Still, for the fact that individual American human beings are consuming vul-gar, prurient, dumb stuff at the astounding average per-household dose of six hours a day—for this both TV and we need to answer. We are responsible basi-cally because nobody is holding any weapons on us forcing us to spend amounts of time second only to sleep doing something that is, when you come right down to it, not good for us. Sorry to be a killjoy, but there it is: six hours a day is not good.

Television's greatest minute-by-minute appeal is that it engages without de-manding. One can rest while undergoing stimulation. Receive without giving. In this respect, television resembles certain other things one might call Special Treats (e.g. candy, liquor), i.e. treats that are basically fine and fun in small amounts but bad for us in large amounts and *really* bad for us if consumed in the massive reg-ular amounts reserved for nutritive staples. One can only guess at what volume of gin or poundage of Toblerone six hours of Special Treat a day would convert to.

On the surface of the problem, television is responsible for our rate of its con-sumption only in that it's become so terribly successful at its acknowledged job of ensuring prodigious amounts of watching. Its social accountability seems sort of like that of designers of military weapons: unculpable right up until they get a lit-tle too good at their job.

But the analogy between television and liquor is best, I think. Because (bear with me a second) I'm afraid good old average Joe Briefcase might be a teleholic. I.e., watching TV can become malignantly addictive. It may become malignantly addictive only once a certain threshold of quantity is habitually passed, but then the same is true of Wild Turkey. And by "malignant" and "addictive" I again do not mean evil or hypnotizing. An activity is addictive if one's relationship to it lies on that downward-sloping continuum between liking it a little too much and really needing it. Many addictions, from exercise to letter-writing, are pretty benign. But something is *malignantly* addictive if (1) it causes real problems for the addict, and (2) it offers itself as a relief from the very problems it causes.[4] A malignant addiction is also distinguished for spreading the problems of the addic-tion out and in in interference patterns, creating difficulties for relationships, com-munities, and the addict's very sense of self and spirit. In the abstract, some of this hyperbole might strain the analogy for you, but concrete illustrations of malig-nantly addictive TV-watching cycles aren't hard to come by. If it's true that many Americans are lonely, and if it's true that many lonely people are prodigious TV-watchers, and it's true that lonely people find in television's 2-D images relief from their stressful reluctance to be around real human beings, then it's also obvious that the more time spent at home alone watching TV, the less time spent in the world of real human beings, and that the less time spent in the real human world, the harder it becomes not to feel inadequate to the tasks involved in being a part of the world, thus fundamentally apart from it, alienated from it, solipsistic, lonely. It's also true that to the extent one begins to view pseudo-relationships with Bud Bundy or Jane Pauley as acceptable alternatives to relationships with real people, one will have commensurately less conscious incentive even to try to connect with real 3-D persons, connections that seem pretty important to basic mental health. For Joe Briefcase, as for many addicts, the Special Treat begins to substitute for something nourishing and needed, and the original genuine hunger —less satisfied than bludgeoned—subsides to a strange objectless unease.

TV-watching as a malignant cycle doesn't even require special preconditions like writerly self-consciousness or neuroallergic loneliness. Let's for a second imagine Joe Briefcase as now just an average U.S. male, relatively unlonely, adjusted, married, blessed with 2.3 apple-cheeked issue, utterly normal, home from hard work at 5:30, starting his average six-hour stint in front of the television. Since Joe B. is average, he'll shrug at pollsters' questions and answer averagely that he most often watches television to "unwind" from those elements of his day and life he finds unpleasant. It's tempting to suppose that TV enables this unwinding simply because it offers a . . . "distraction," something to divert the mind from quotidian troubles. But would mere distraction ensure continual massive watching? Television offers way more than distraction. In lots of ways, television purveys and enables *dreams,* and most of these dreams involve some sort of transcendence of average daily life. The modes of presentation that work best for TV—stuff like "action," with shoot-outs and car wrecks, or the rapid-fire "collage" of commercials, news, and music videos, or the "hysteria" of prime-time soap and sitcom with broad gestures, high voices, too much laughter—are unsubtle in their whispers that, somewhere, life is quicker, denser, more interesting, more . . . well, *lively* than contemporary life as Joe Briefcase knows it. This might seem benign until we consider that what good old average Joe Briefcase does more than almost anything else in contemporary life is watch television, an activity which anyone with an average brain can see does not make for a very dense and lively life. Since television must seek to attract viewers by offering a dreamy promise of escape from daily life, and since stats confirm that so grossly much of ordinary U.S. life is watching TV, TV's whispered promises must somehow undercut television-watching in theory ("Joe, Joe, there's a world where life is lively, where nobody spends six hours a day unwinding before a piece of furniture") while reinforcing television-watching in practice ("Joe, Joe, your best and only access to this world is TV").

Well, average Joe Briefcase has an OK brain, and deep down inside he knows, as we do, that there's some kind of psychic shell-game going on in this system of conflicting whispers. But if it's so bald a delusion, why do he and we keep watching in such high doses? Part of the answer—a part which requires discretion lest it slip into anti-TV paranoia—is that the phenomenon of television somehow trains or conditions our viewership. Television has become able not only to ensure that we watch but somehow to inform our deepest responses to what's watched. Take jaded TV-critics, or our acquaintances who sneer at the numbing sameness of all the television they sit still for. I always want to grab these unhappy guys by the lapels and shake them until their teeth rattle and point to the absence of guns to their heads and ask why the hell they keep watching, then. But the truth is that there's some complex high-dose psychic transaction between TV and Audience whereby Audience gets trained to respond to and then like and then *expect* trite, hackneyed, numbing television shows, and to expect them to such an extent that when networks do occasionally abandon time-tested formulas the Audience usually punishes them for it by not watching novel shows in sufficient numbers to let them get off the ground. Hence the networks' bland response to its critics that in the majority of cases—and until the rise of hip metatelevision you could count the exceptions on one hand—"different" or "high-concept" programming simply doesn't get ratings. High-quality television cannot stand up to the gaze of millions, somehow.

Now, it is true that certain PR techniques—e.g. shock, grotesquerie, or irreverence—can ease novel sorts of shows' rise to national demographic viability. Examples here might be the "shocking" *A Current Affair,* the "grotesque" *Real People,* the "irreverent" *Married . . . with Children.* But these programs, like most of those touted by the industry as "fresh" or "outrageous," turn out to be just tiny transparent variations on old formulas.

It's not fair to blame television's shortage of originality on any lack of creativity among network talent. The truth is that we seldom get a chance to know whether anybody behind any TV show is creative, or more accurately that they seldom get a chance to show us. Despite the unquestioned assumption on the part of pop-culture critics that television's poor old Audience, deep down, "craves novelty," all available evidence suggests, rather, that the Audience *really* craves sameness but thinks, deep down, that it *ought* to crave novelty. Hence the mixture of devotion and sneer on so many viewerly faces. Hence also the weird viewer complicity behind TV's sham "breakthrough programs": Joe Briefcase needs that PR-patina of "freshness" and "outrageousness" to quiet his conscience while he goes about getting from television what we've all been trained to want from it: some strangely American, profoundly shallow, and eternally temporary *reassurance.*

Particularly in the last decade, this tension in the Audience between what we do want and what we think we ought to want has been television's breath and bread. TV's self-mocking invitation to itself as indulgence, transgression, a glorious "giving in" (again, not exactly foreign to addictive cycles) is one of two ingenious ways it's consolidated its six-hour hold on my generation's cojones. The other is postmodern irony. The commercials for *Alf*'s Boston debut in a syndicated package feature the fat, cynical, gloriously decadent puppet (so much like Snoopy, like Garfield, like Bart, like Butt-Head) advising me to "Eat a whole lot of food and stare at the TV." His pitch is an ironic permission-slip to do what I do best whenever I feel confused and guilty: assume, inside, a sort of fetal position, a pose of passive reception to comfort, escape, reassurance. The cycle is self-nourishing. . . .

I DO HAVE A THESIS

I want to persuade you that irony, poker-faced silence, and fear of ridicule are distinctive of those features of contemporary U.S. culture (of which cutting-edge fiction is a part) that enjoy any significant relation to the television whose weird pretty hand has my generation by the throat. I'm going to argue that irony and ridicule are entertaining and effective, and that at the same time they are agents of a great despair and stasis in U.S. culture, and that for aspiring fiction writers they pose especially terrible problems.

My two big premises are that, on the one hand, a certain subgenre of pop-conscious postmodern fiction, written mostly by young Americans, has lately arisen and made a real attempt to transfigure a world of and for appearance, mass appeal, and television; and that, on the other hand, televisual culture has somehow evolved to a point where it seems invulnerable to any such transfiguring assault. Television, in other words, has become able to capture and neutralize any attempt to change or even protest the attitudes of passive unease and cynicism that television requires of Audience in order to be commercially and psychologically viable at doses of several hours per day.

IMAGE-FICTION

The particular fictional subgenre I have in mind has been called by some editors post-postmodernism and by some critics Hyperrealism. Some of the younger readers and writers I know call it Image-Fiction. Image-Fiction is basically a further involution of the relations between lit and pop that blossomed with the '60s' postmodernists. If the postmodern church fathers found pop images valid *referents* and *symbols* in fiction, and if in the '70s and early '80s this appeal to the features of mass culture shifted from use to mention—i.e. certain avant-gardists starting to treat of pop and TV-watching as themselves fertile *subjects*—the new Fiction of Image uses the transient received myths of popular culture as a *world* in which to imagine fictions about "real," albeit pop-mediated, characters. Early uses of Imagist tactics can be seen in the DeLillo of *Great Jones Street,* the Coover of *Burning,* and in Max Apple, whose '70s short story "The Oranging of America" projects an interior life onto the figure of Howard Johnson.

But in the late '80s, despite publisher unease over the legalities of imagining private lives for public figures, a real bumper crop of this behind-the-glass stuff started appearing, authored largely by writers who didn't know or cross-fertilize one another. Apple's *Propheteers,* Jay Cantor's *Krazy Kat,* Coover's *A Night at the Movies, or You Must Remember This,* William T. Vollmann's *You Bright and Risen Angels,* Stephen Dixon's *Movies: Seventeen Stories,* and DeLillo's own fictional hologram of Oswald in *Libra* are all notable post-'85 instances. (Observe too that, in another '80s medium, the arty *Zelig, Purple Rose of Cairo,* and *sex, lies, and videotape,* plus the low-budget *Scanners* and *Videodrome* and *Shockers,* all began to treat of mass-entertainment screens as permeable.)

It's in the last year that the Image-Fiction scene has really taken off. A. M. Homes's 1990 *The Safety of Objects* features a stormy love affair between a boy and a Barbie doll. Vollmann's 1989 *The Rainbow Stories* has Sonys as characters in Heideggerian parables. Michael Martone's 1990 *Fort Wayne Is Seventh on Hitler's List* is a tight cycle of stories about the Midwest's pop-culture giants—James Dean, Colonel Sanders, Dillinger—the whole project of which, spelled out in a preface about Image-Fiction's legal woes, involves "questioning the border between fact and fiction when in the presence of fame."[5] And Mark Leyner's

1990 campus smash *My Cousin, My Gastroenterologist,* less a novel than what the book's jacket copy describes as "a fiction analogue of the best drug you ever took," features everything from meditations on the color of Carefree Panty Shield wrappers to "Big Squirrel, the TV kiddie-show host and kung fu mercenary" to NFL instant replays in an "X-ray vision which shows leaping skeletons in a bluish void surrounded by 75,000 roaring skulls."[6]

One thing I have to insist you realize about this new subgenre is that it's distinguishable not just by a certain neo-postmodern technique but by a genuine socio-artistic agenda. The Fiction of Image is not just a use or mention of televisual culture but an actual *response* to it, an effort to impose some sort of accountability on a state of affairs in which more Americans get their news from television than from newspapers and in which more Americans every evening watch *Wheel of Fortune* than all three network news programs combined.

And please see that Image-Fiction, far from being a trendy avant-garde novelty, is almost atavistic. It is a natural adaptation of the hoary techniques of literary Realism to a '90s world whose defining boundaries have been deformed by electric signal. For one of realistic fiction's big jobs used to be to afford easements across borders, to help readers leap over the walls of self and locale and show us unseen or -dreamed-of people and cultures and ways to be. Realism made the strange familiar. Today, when we can eat Tex-Mex with chopsticks while listening to reggae and watching a Soviet-satellite newscast of the Berlin Wall's fall—i.e., when damn near *everything* presents itself as familiar—it's not a surprise that some of today's most ambitious Realist fiction is going about trying to *make the familiar strange.* In so doing, in demanding fictional access behind lenses and screens and headlines and reimagining what human life might truly be like over there across the chasms of illusion, mediation, demographics, marketing, imago, and appearance, Image-Fiction is paradoxically trying to restore what's taken for "real" to three whole dimensions, to reconstruct a univocally round world out of disparate streams of flat sights.

That's the good news.

The bad news is that, almost without exception, Image-Fiction doesn't satisfy its own agenda. Instead, it most often degenerates into a kind of jeering, surfacey look "behind the scenes" of the very televisual front people already jeer at, a front they can already get behind the scenes of via *Entertainment Tonight* and *Remote Control.*

The reason why today's Image-Fiction isn't the rescue from a passive, addictive TV-psychology that it tries so hard to be is that most Image-Fiction writers render their material with the same tone of irony and self-consciousness that their ancestors, the literary insurgents of Beat and postmodernism, used so effectively to rebel against their own world and context. And the reason why this irreverent postmodern approach fails to help the new Imagists transfigure TV is simply that TV has beaten the new Imagists to the punch. The fact is that for at least ten years now, television has been ingeniously absorbing, homogenizing, and re-presenting the very same cynical postmodern aesthetic that was once the best alternative to the appeal of Low, over-easy, mass-marketed narrative. How TV's done this is blackly fascinating to see.

A quick intermission contra paranoia. By saying that Image-Fiction aims to "rescue" us from TV, I again am not suggesting that television has diabolic designs, or wants souls, or brainwashes people. I'm just referring again to the kind of natural Audience-conditioning consequent to high daily doses, a conditioning so subtle it can be observed best obliquely, through examples. And so if a term like "conditioning" still seems hyperbolic or hysterical to you, I'll ask you to consider for a moment the exemplary issue of prettiness. One of the things that makes the people on television fit to stand the Megagaze is that they are, by ordinary human standards, extremely pretty. I suspect that this, like most television conventions, is set up with no motive more sinister than to appeal to the largest possible Audience—pretty people tend to be more appealing to look at than nonpretty people. But when we're talking about television, the combination of sheer Audience size and quiet psychic intercourse between images and oglers starts a cycle that both enhances pretty people's appeal and erodes us viewers' own security in the face of gazes. Because of the way human beings relate to narrative, we tend to identify with those characters we find appealing. We try to see ourselves in them. The same I.D.-relation, however, also means that we try to see them in ourselves. When everybody we seek to identify with for six hours a day is pretty, it naturally becomes more important to us to be pretty, to be viewed as pretty. Because prettiness becomes a priority for us, the pretty people on TV become all the more attractive, a cycle which is obviously great for TV. But it's less great for us civilians, who tend to own mirrors, and who also tend not to be anywhere near as pretty as the TV-images we want to identify with. Not only does this cause some angst personally, but the angst increases because, nationally, everybody else is absorbing six-hour doses and identifying with pretty people and valuing prettiness more, too. This very personal anxiety about our prettiness has become a national phenomenon with national consequences. The whole U.S.A. gets different about things it values and fears. The boom in diet aids, health and fitness clubs, neighborhood tanning parlors, cosmetic surgery, anorexia, bulimia, steroid-use among boys, girls throwing acid at each other because one girl's hair looks more like Farrah Fawcett's than another . . . are these supposed to be unrelated to each other? to the apotheosis of prettiness in a televisual culture?

It's not paranoid or hysterical to acknowledge that television in enormous doses affects people's values and self-perception in deep ways. Nor that televisual conditioning influences the whole psychology of one's relation to himself, his mirror, his loved ones, and a world of real people and real gazes. No one's going to claim that a culture all about watching and appearing is fatally compromised by unreal standards of beauty and fitness. But other facets of TV-training reveal themselves as more rapacious, more serious, than any irreverent fiction writer would want to take seriously. . . .

What does TV's institutionalization of hip irony have to do with U.S. fiction? Well, for one thing, American literary fiction tends to be about U.S. culture and the people who inhabit it. Culture-wise, shall I spend much of your time pointing out the degree to which televisual values influence the contemporary mood of jaded weltschmerz, self-mocking materialism, blank indifference, and the delusion that cynicism and naïveté are mutually exclusive? Can we deny connections between an unprecedentedly powerful consensual medium that suggests no real difference between image and substance, on one hand, and stuff like the rise of Teflon presidencies, the establishment of nationwide tanning and liposuction industries, the popularity of "Vogueing" to a cynical synthesized command to "Strike a Pose"? Or, in contemporary art, that televisual disdain for "hypocritical" retrovalues like originality, depth, and integrity has no truck with those recombinant "appropriation" styles of art and architecture in which "past becomes pastiche," or with the repetitive solmizations of a Glass or a Reich, or with the self-conscious catatonia of a platoon of Raymond Carver wannabes?

In fact, the numb blank bored demeanor—what one friend calls the "girl-who's-dancing-with-you-but-would-obviously-rather-be-dancing-with-somebody-else" expression—that has become my generation's version of cool is all about TV. "Television," after all, literally means "seeing far"; and our six hours daily not only helps us feel up-close and personal at like the Pan-Am Games or Operation Desert Shield but also, inversely, trains us to relate to real live personal up-close stuff the same way we relate to the distant and exotic, as if separated from us by physics and glass, extant only as performance, awaiting our cool review. Indifference is actually just the '90s' version of frugality for U.S. young people: wooed several gorgeous hours a day for nothing but our attention, we regard that attention as our chief commodity, our social capital, and we are loath to fritter it. In the same regard, see that in 1990, flatness, numbness, and cynicism in one's demeanor are clear ways to transmit the televisual attitude of stand-out-transcendence—flatness and numbness transcend sentimentality, and cynicism announces that one knows the score, was last naïve about something at maybe like age four.

Whether or not 1990s' youth culture seems as grim to you as it does to me, surely we can agree that the culture's TV-defined pop ethic has pulled a marvelous touché on the postmodern aesthetic that originally sought to co-opt and redeem the pop. Television has pulled the old dynamic of reference and redemption inside-out: it is now *television* that takes elements of the *postmodern*—the involution, the absurdity, the sardonic fatigue, the iconoclasm and rebellion—and bends them to the ends of spectation and consumption. This has been going on for a while. As early as '84, critics of capitalism were warning that "What began as a mood of the avant-garde has surged into mass culture."[7]

But postmodernism didn't just all of a sudden "surge" into television in 1984. Nor have the vectors of influence between the postmodern and the televisual been one-way. The chief connection between today's television and today's fiction is historical. The two share roots. For postmodern fiction—authored almost exclusively by young white overeducated males—clearly evolved as an intellectual expression of the "rebellious youth culture" of the '60s and '70s. And since the whole gestalt of youthful U.S. rebellion was made possible by a national medium that erased communicative boundaries between regions and replaced a society segmented by location and ethnicity with what rock music critics have called "a national self-consciousness stratified by generation,"[8] the phenomenon of TV had as much to do with postmodernism's rebellious irony as it did with Peaceniks' protest rallies.

In fact, by offering young, overeducated fiction writers a comprehensive view of how hypocritically the U.S.A. saw itself circa 1960, early television helped legitimize absurdism and irony as not just literary devices but sensible responses to a ridiculous world. For irony—exploiting gaps between what's said and what's meant, between how things try to appear and how they really are—is the time-honored way artists seek to illuminate and explode hypocrisy. And the television of lone-gunman westerns, paternalistic sitcoms, and jut-jawed law enforcement circa 1960 celebrated what by then was a deeply hypocritical American self-image. Miller describes nicely how the 1960s sitcom, like the westerns that pre-ceded them,

> negated the increasing powerlessness of white-collar males with images of paternal strength and manly individualism. Yet by the time these sit-coms were produced, the world of small business [whose virtues were the Hugh Beaumontish ones of "self-possession, probity, and sound judgment"] had been . . . superseded by what C. Wright Mills called "the managerial demi-urge," and the virtues per-sonified by . . . Dad were in fact passé.[9]

In other words, early U.S. TV was a hypocritical apologist for values whose reality had become attenuated in a period of corporate ascendancy, bureaucratic entrenchment, foreign adventurism, racial conflict, secret bombing, assassination, wiretaps, etc. It's not one bit accidental that postmodern fiction aimed its ironic crosshairs at the banal, the naïve, the sentimental and simplistic and conservative, for these qualities were just what '60s' TV seemed to celebrate as distinctively American.

And the rebellious irony in the best postmodern fiction wasn't just credible as art; it seemed downright socially useful in its capacity for what counterculture critics called "a *critical negation* that would make it self-evident to everyone that the world is not as it seems."[10] Kesey's black parody of asylums suggested that our arbiters of sanity were often crazier than their patients; Pynchon reoriented our view of paranoia from deviant psychic fringe to central thread in the corporo-bureaucratic weave; DeLillo exposed image, signal, data and tech as agents of spiritual chaos and not social order. Burroughs's icky explorations of American narcosis exploded hypocrisy; Gaddis's exposure of abstract capital as deforming exploded hypocrisy; Coover's repulsive political farces exploded hypocrisy.

Irony in postwar art and culture started out the same way youthful rebellion did. It was difficult and painful, and productive—a grim diagnosis of a long-denied disease. The assumptions behind early postmodern irony, on the other hand, were still frankly idealistic: it was assumed that etiology and diagnosis pointed toward cure, that a revelation of imprisonment led to freedom.

So then how have irony, irreverence, and rebellion come to be not liberating but enfeebling in the culture today's avant-garde tries to write about? One clue's to be found in the fact that irony is *still around,* bigger than ever after 30 long years as the dominant mode of hip expression. It's not a rhetorical mode that wears well. As Hyde (whom I pretty obviously like) puts it, "Irony has only emer-gency use. Carried over time, it is the voice of the trapped who have come to enjoy their cage."[11] This is because irony, entertaining as it is, serves an almost exclusively negative function. It's critical and destructive, a ground-clearing. Surely this is the way our postmodern fathers saw it. But irony's singularly unuseful when it comes to constructing anything to replace the hypocrisies it debunks. This is why Hyde seems right about persistent irony being tiresome. It is unmeaty. Even gifted ironists work best in sound bites. I find gifted ironists sort of wickedly fun to listen to at parties, but I always walk away feeling like I've had several radical surgical procedures. And as for actually driving cross-country with a gifted ironist, or sitting through a 300-page novel full of nothing but trendy sardonic exhaustion, one ends up feeling not only empty but somehow . . . oppressed.

Think, for a moment, of Third World rebels and coups. Third World rebels are great at exposing and overthrowing corrupt hypocritical regimes, but they seem noticeably less great at the mundane non-negative task of then establishing a superior governing alternative. Victorious rebels, in fact, seem best at using their tough, cynical rebel-skills to avoid being rebelled against themselves—in other words, they just become better tyrants.

And make no mistake: irony tyrannizes us. The reason why our pervasive cultural irony is at once so powerful and so unsatisfying is that an ironist is *impossible to pin down*. All U.S. irony is based on an implicit "I don't really mean what I'm saying." So what *does* irony as a cultural norm mean to say? That it's impossible to mean what you say? That maybe it's too bad it's impossible, but wake up and smell the coffee already? Most likely, I think, today's irony ends up saying: "How totally *banal* of you to ask what I really mean." Anyone with the heretical gall to ask an ironist what he actually stands for ends up looking like an hysteric or a prig. And herein lies the oppressiveness of institutionalized irony, the too-successful rebel: the ability to interdict the *question* without attending to its *subject* is, when exercised, tyranny. It is the new junta, using the very tool that exposed its enemy to insulate itself.

This is why our educated teleholic friends' use of weary cynicism to try to seem superior to TV is so pathetic. And this is why the fiction-writing citizen of our televisual culture is in such very deep shit. What do you do when postmodern rebellion becomes a pop-cultural institution? For this of course is the second answer to why avant-garde irony and rebellion have become dilute and malign. They have been absorbed, emptied, and redeployed by the very televisual establishment they had originally set themselves athwart.

Not that television is culpable for any evil here. Just for immoderate success. This is, after all, what TV *does*: it discerns, decocts, and re-presents what it thinks U.S. culture wants to see and hear about itself. No one and everyone is at fault for the fact that television started gleaning rebellion and cynicism as the hip upscale Baby-Boomer *imago populi*. But the harvest has been dark: the forms of our best rebellious art have become mere gestures, schticks, not only sterile but perversely enslaving. How can even the idea of rebellion against corporate culture stay meaningful when Chrysler Inc. advertises trucks by invoking "The Dodge Rebellion"? How is one to be a bona fide iconoclast when Burger King sells onion rings with "Sometimes You Gotta Break the Rules"? How can an Image-Fiction writer hope to make people more critical of televisual culture by parodying television as a self-serving commercial enterprise when Pepsi and Subaru and FedEx parodies of self-serving commercials are already doing big business? It's almost a history lesson: I'm starting to see just why turn-of-the-last-century Americans' biggest fear was of anarchists and anarchy. For if anarchy actually *wins*, if rulelessness becomes the *rule*, then protest and change become not just impossible but incoherent. It'd be like casting a ballot for Stalin: you are voting for an end to all voting.

So here's the stumper for the U.S. writer who both breathes our cultural atmosphere and sees himself heir to whatever was neat and valuable in avant-garde literature: how to rebel against TV's aesthetic of rebellion, how to snap readers awake to the fact that our televisual culture has become a cynical, narcissistic, essentially empty phenomenon, when television regularly *celebrates* just these features in itself and its viewers? These are the very questions DeLillo's poor schmuck of a popologist was asking back in '85 about America, that most photographed of barns:

> "What was the barn like before it was photographed?" he said. "What did it
> look like, how was it different from other barns, how was it similar to other
> barns? We can't answer these questions because we've read the signs, seen the
> people snapping the pictures. We can't get outside the aura. We're part of the
> aura. We're here, we're now."

He seemed immensely pleased by this.[12]

NOTES

1. Daniel Hallin, "We Keep America On Top of the World," in Todd Gitlin, *Watching Television* (New York: Random House/Pantheon, 1987).
2. Barbara Tuchman, "The Decline of Quality," *New York Times Magazine,* 2 Nov. 1980.
3. M. Alexis de Tocqueville, *Democracy in America* (New York: Vintage, 1945), pp. 57, 73.
4. I didn't get this definition from any sort of authoritative source, but it seems pretty modest and commonsensical.
5. Martone, *Fort Wayne Is Seventh on Hitler's List* (Indiana University Press, 1990), p. ix.
6. Leyner, *My Cousin, My Gastroenterologist* (Harmony/Crown, 1990), p. 82.
7. Fredric Jameson, "Postmodernism, or the Cultural Logic of Late Capitalism," *New Left Review* 146 (Summer 1984):60–66.
8. Pat Auferhode, "The Look of the Sound," in good old Gitlin's anthology, p. 113.
9. Mark Crispin Miller, "Deride and Conquer," in Gitlin's anthology, p. 199.
10. Greil Marcus, *Mystery Train* (New York: Dutton, 1976).
11. Lewis Hyde, "Alcohol and Poetry: John Berryman and the Booze Talking," *American Poetry Review,* reprinted in the *Pushcart Prize* anthology for 1987.
12. Don DeLillo, *White Noise* (New York: Penguin Books, 1985), p. 13.

DISCUSSION QUESTIONS

1. How does Wallace connect the development of metafiction (fiction that explicitly comments on its own devices and fictional nature) in the 1960s to the "spectatorial" and "self-conscious" elements of watching television? What

would inspire writers to write fiction that "called it as it saw itself seeing itself see it"?

2. Wallace aims to prove that "the nexus where television and fiction converse and consort is self-conscious irony." What does he mean by this? What are the elements of the totalizing ironic stance that Wallace describes as central to television and fiction influenced by television?

3. What are the problems that irony and ridicule pose for fiction writers and their work when they become dominant strategies?

4. How does Wallace define "Image-Fiction"? How does this genre function as a form of "Hyperrealism"? Why does Wallace see this subgenre of postmodernism as fueled by a "genuine socio-artistic agenda"? Why does Wallace believe that "Image-Fiction" generally doesn't achieve its aims?

5. What are the historical connections between television and postmodernist techniques in fiction that Wallace describes? How did postmodernist fiction originally relate to youthful rebelliousness and criticism of adult conformity and hypocrisy? How have "irony, irreverence, and rebellion" become enfeebled since the 1960s, according to Wallace?

6. What does Wallace, quoting from Don DeLillo's *White Noise*, mean by the image of the "aura"? How can fiction writers "get outside the aura"?

JANET H. MURRAY

The Cyberbard and the Multiform Plot

Janet Murray (b. 1946), a Harvard Ph.D. in English literature, has worked as an IBM systems programmer and taught at MIT and Georgia Tech, where she designs and produces interactive multimedia projects. In addition to many essays of literary criticism and the book-length study Courtship and the English Novel: Feminist Readings in the Fiction of George Meredith *(1987), she has written* Hamlet on the Holodeck: The Future of Narrative in Cyberspace *(1997), from which we chose this selection.*

A plot is . . . a narrative of events, the emphasis falling on causality. "The king died and then the queen died" is a story. "The king died and then the queen died of grief" is a plot.

—E. M. FORSTER, *Aspects of the Novel*

What will it take for authors to create rich and satisfying stories that exploit the characteristic properties of digital environments and deliver the aesthetic pleasures the new medium seems to promise us? We would have to find some way to allow them to write procedurally; to anticipate all the twists of the kaleidoscope, all the actions of the interactor; and to specify not just the events of the plot but also the rules by which those events would occur. Writers would need a concrete way to structure a coherent story not as a single sequence of events but as a multiform plot open to the collaborative participation of the interactor. At first this kaleidoscopic composition seems like a violent break with tradition, but when we look at how stories have historically developed, we find techniques of pattern and variation that seem very suggestive for computer-based narrative.

From the nineteenth century on, there has been considerable interest in the striking similarities found between stories from vastly different cultures. Carl Jung hypothesized that these similarities offer proof of a collective unconscious, a set of archetypal tales (the journey, the quest, the rebirth) and archetypal figures (the hero, the trickster, the earth mother) that together define what it is to be human. Some have argued that all of the world's great wisdom stories express the same religious and psychological truths and therefore are just variant versions of a single tale. Joseph Campbell, one of the most passionate and eloquent proponents of the unity of human narrative traditions, saw in stories as diverse as those of Prometheus and Buddha a single "monomyth" about a "hero with a thousand faces" who sets off from the common world, encounters fantastic dangers, and returns to bestow gifts on his society.[1] Although such totalizing views of human culture have fallen out of fashion, the enduring appeal of mythic patterns is indisputable. We have only to look at George Lucas's ubiquitous Star Wars series (which was directly inspired by Campbell's research) to see that age-old story epic formulas remain compelling even in our postmodern and antiheroic era.

But it is not only folktales and adventure stories that have formulaic patterns. Many narrative theorists and writers have insisted that there are a limited number of plots in the world, corresponding to the basic patterns of desire, fulfillment, and loss in human life. Rudyard Kipling counted sixty-nine basic plots, and Borges thought that there were less than a dozen. Ronald B. Tobias, in one of the more competent of the many guidebooks for writers, suggests there are twenty "master plots" in all of literature. Here is his list:[2]

- Quest
- Adventure
- Pursuit
- Rescue
- Escape
- Revenge
- The Riddle
- Rivalry
- Underdog
- Temptation
- Metamorphosis
- Transformation
- Maturation

- Love
- Forbidden Love
- Sacrifice
- Discovery
- Wretched Excess
- Ascension
- Descension

One would be hard put to name any story that did not belong, at least in part, to one of these categories, whether it is *The Incredible Hulk* (metamorphosis), *King Lear* (descension), or *Seinfeld* (refused maturation). The patterns are constant because human experience is constant, and though cultural differences may inflect these patterns differently from one place to another and one historical period to another, the basic events out of which we tell stories are the same for all of us.

The formulaic nature of storytelling makes it particularly appropriate for the computer, which is made for modeling and reproducing patterns of all sorts. But no one would want to hear a story that was a mere mechanical shuffling of patterns. How do we tell the computer which to use and how to use them? How can the author retain control over the story yet still offer interactors the freedom of action, the sense of agency, that makes electronic engagement so pleasurable? To answer these questions we have to look back at an earlier storytelling technology, the community of oral bards.

THE ORAL BARD AS A STORYTELLING SYSTEM

We now know that densely plotted, encyclopedic works like the *Iliad* and the *Odyssey* were produced not by a single creative genius but by the collective effort of an oral storytelling culture that employed a highly formulaic narrative system. From the Renaissance through the beginning of the twentieth century, Homer was considered to be a great *writer,* rather than a preliterate singer, and his epics were taken as the height of Western literature. It was therefore disconcerting when the Harvard classicist Milman Parry and his student, Alfred Lord, documented the similarities between the Homeric poems and those they heard performed by oral bards still active in Yugoslavia earlier in this century. Lord's book, *The Singer of Tales,* published in 1960, describes the actual composition and performance process of the bards and argues from internal evidence that Homer's poems are the result of similar methods.

Oral story composition, as Lord describes it, relies on what we in a literate era devalue as repetition, redundancy, and cliché, devices for patterning language into units that make it easier for bards to memorize and recall. The stories are composed anew for each recitation and are therefore multiform, with no single canonical version. Every performance of a story varies from all others, reflecting the interests of the audience and the dramatic interpretation of the storyteller. Lord's research gives us a detailed picture of these multiform stories and how they achieved a coherency of plot across many varied tellings.[3]

The bardic tradition is a set of formulas within formulas, starting at the level of the phrase and moving through the organization of the story as a whole. Singers of tales had a repertoire of formulaic ways to describe common people, things, and events, descriptions that could be rearranged and plugged into a template of the chanted line in a way that made for pleasurable variation within an overall pattern of regular rhythms and sounds. Major characters were associated with familiar epithets that helped recall them to the audience and fill out the poetic line; for instance, Homer could refer to Zeus as "the counselor" or "son of Chronos" or "the cloud-gatherer." Lord discovered that a hero might have one typical epithet when invoked in the beginning of a line and another one more commonly used after the caesura in the middle of the line. The appellation would therefore have less to do with how the hero was behaving at a particular moment in the narrative than with where his name fell in the rhythm.

Lord refers to the bard's stock of variant phrases as a "substitution system." This is similar to the Mad Libs parlor game, where a paragraph is given with words missing and players are asked to contribute words based on syntactic or category descriptions (a noun, a body part, a furry animal, etc.) with hilarious results. Early attempts at computer-based literature tried to use similar methods of simple substitution, with equally incongruous results. For instance, here are two of the millions of possible stories based on a language substitution system devised by the French experimental writer Raymond Queneau:

> *A Story As You Like It, version #1:*
> Do you wish to hear the story of the three big skinny beanpoles?
> The three big beanpoles were watching them.
>
> *A Story As You Like It, version #2:*
> Do you wish to hear the story of the three middling mediocre bushes?
> The three middling mediocre bushes were watching them.
> Seeing themselves voyeurized in this fashion, the three alert peas, who were
> very modest, fled.[4]

Although such compositions are provocative as artifacts that play with the theoretical concepts of literature, machines, and originality, no one would read such stories for the sheer pleasure of it. But Web surfers can now visit many entertaining sites where they can generate endless parodies of corporate home pages, candidate's speeches, and even love letters by using substitution programs stocked with the appropriate buzzwords. These pages provide the same pleasure as ELIZA . . . ; they use the rote utterances of the machine to expose the meaninglessness of such formulaic writing.

But even if a verbal substitution system cannot by itself produce satisfying and coherent digital narratives, it is a useful model for establishing the "primitives" or basic building blocks of a story construction system. In computer programming systems the "primitives" are the smallest components (such as simple arithmetical calculations) upon which the larger operations (such as complex calculus functions) are built. In an interactive narrative the key primitives are the actions of the interactors themselves, as structured by the author. Currently, the most complex sets of primitives are the icon palettes in puzzle games, which contain items like a magnifying glass, a set of objects picked up on the way (tools, treasure, food), communications devices, a way to select who should be speaking or acting, and perhaps an icon for a hand or a foot to allow the interactor to pick things up or move around. Such a palette constitutes an iconographic substitution system, since the interactor can substitute one tool for another, or one item for another as the object of the tool, in order to build up more complex possibilities of action, in the same way that the epic singer could substitute phrases in making up his poetic line.

In order for the medium to mature, storytellers will have to develop more expressive primitives, simple actions that will allow ever-subtler input by the interactor. For instance, game designers have already progressed from an interface that requires the user to type "go north" or even "n" to one that allows users to point and click in three-dimensional space, which changes the interaction from a command structure to a dramatic gesture. The easier these primitives are to learn and the less they call attention to the computer itself—that is, the more transparent they are—the deeper our immersion and the stronger our sense of dramatic enactment. Today's interaction conventions are equivalent to the invention of a few useful epithets for the gods and heroes, basic tools that every storyteller needs but not enough to get you very far with a particular tale.

One of the chief stumbling blocks to mature digital storytelling is the difficulty of establishing expressive conventions for the interactor's use of language. If we give the interactor complete freedom to improvise, we lose control of the plot. But if we ask the interactor to pick from a menu of things to say, we limit agency and remind them of the fourth wall. Some CD-ROM stories give the interactor the task of deciding the mood or tone of a spoken response rather than picking a statement from a list of possible things to say. This is a more promising route because it seems less mechanical, although the mood selector is often a menu or slider bar that is outside the frame of the story. A more immersive set of primitives might be applied to character gesture. Gestures like placing a hand on the shoulder of another character, making a fist, raising both hands with palms turned up in exasperation—these could become part of an emotional repertoire similar to the supply of epithets used by the bards. Alternately, interactors could be given a limited vocabulary of separate words or perhaps preformed phrases, like the bardic epithets, that could be assembled in many different ways. Such an artificial interface would work best if it is motivated by the situation, as, for example, in a visit to another country or in a conversation in restricted circumstances where things have to be said according to a strict protocol or secret code. But whether a writer creates the set of primitives out of gestures or phrases or a combination of the two, the challenge will be to make them as transparently expressive of emotion and intention as joystick fighting and link-navigation are in the current environment.

The next level of patterning after the stock phrase in the bardic storytelling method is what Lord refers to as the theme, that is, a generic narrative unit that can be fit into multiple narratives, a unit such as the departure of a hero, the catalog of ships, the dressing of a hero for battle, the boast of a hero before battle, and the death of a hero. The theme functions like a scene in a play or a chapter in a book. This is the key unit of segmentation that the poet focused on when memorizing a new story from the recital of another bard. Like the folksinger who concentrates on the chord sequence and the general rhyme scheme of the verses rather than on the exact words of a newly acquired song, the bardic performer did not think about line accuracy but focused instead on reproducing the order of the component themes. With no system of writing or recording with which to compare two renditions, bardic performers repeated the poem with perhaps only 70 percent accuracy of words but with exactly the same order of themes.

The plot events in electronic games and MUDs closely resemble these epic themes, because they draw their material from genres like fantasy, science fiction, and comic book heroics that are very close to the folktale tradition. The more filmic CD-ROMs rely on later formulaic genres such as the murder mystery or the horror film. Genre fiction is appropriate for electronic narrative because it scripts the interactor. When I begin a CD-ROM murder mystery, I know I am supposed to question all the characters I meet about what they were doing at the time of the murder and keep track of all the suspects' alibis. I will use whatever primitives I am given (navigation through the space, conducting an interview, picking up pieces of evidence and looking at them under a microscope, etc.) for enacting these prescripted scenes. In a Western adventure I can be counted on to try to shoot at the bad guys, and in a horror story I will always enter the haunted house. I perform these actions not because I have read a rule book but because I have been prepared to do so by exposure to thousands of stories that follow these patterns.

A mature narrative tradition will take advantage of this common base of formulas to refine the scripts, to offer the interactor a richer range of behaviors. For instance, since within the conventions of a mystery story it is already customary to send the detective to a mystery bar, CD-ROMs already include bars and the interrogation of bartenders. A refinement of this convention might mean offering well-lit booths and dark corners for the detective to choose from. A well-lit table might be safer in a confrontation, whereas a dark corner might invite more revealing disclosures. Or we might discover in a more domestic story that bringing breakfast to a lover or a box of crayons to a child will deepen a relationship and move the plot forward. Patterned activities like these could grow into new thematic units (like making friends or winning trust or showing loyalty) in new genres of electronic stories that focus on textured relationships rather than on puzzle solving and gunfights.

At the highest level of organization, Lord's bardic singers assembled their thematic units into plots. One very common pattern for the Yugoslavian poets was the story of the hero's return, which exhibited both constant and variable elements. The most constant part of the story was the return itself, which always included thematic units detailing disguise, deception, and recognition. Usually the return was preceded by an account of the hero's release from prison and was followed by an account of his return to prison to rescue someone else; often it included a recollection of a much earlier event in which the hero was summoned to war on his wedding day. The wedding story might be told as the beginning of the whole tale or just as a flashback from later events. Sometimes the prison part of the story did not end in the hero's release but in a refusal of release, followed by rescue of the hero by someone else. Sometimes the rescue tale elements were rearranged into a story of a bride being rescued from the enemy.

Lord realized that all the stories that center on rescue and release intertwined with marriage and battle were "basically one song" with many different plot possibilities. Both listeners and performers were constantly aware of other narrative possibilities growing out of the same thematic elements. Therefore, whenever the singer reached a thematic event that belonged to multiple story patterns, he would be "drawn in one direction or another" by "similarities with related groups" of songs:

> The intensity of that pull may differ from performance to performance, but it is always there and the singer always relives that tense moment. Even though the pattern of the song he intends to sing is set early in the performance, forces moving in other directions will still be felt at critical junctures, simply because the theme involved can lead in more than one path.[5]

The singer's "tense moment" is a consciousness of a branching point in the formulaic composition process. Lord points out that the *Odyssey,* which is a similar "return" story, includes significant vestigial elements of another potential plot —in which Telemachus starts to set off to rescue his father—showing that Homer also felt this pull. Although the written tradition is based on a fixed set of events, the oral tradition is much more "fluid" and is based on what Lord calls a multiform story.

> Unlike the oral poet, we are not accustomed to thinking in terms of fluidity [of text]. We find it difficult to grasp something that is multiform. It seems to us necessary to construct an ideal text or to seek an original, and we remain dissatisfied with an ever-changing phenomenon. I believe that once we know the facts of oral composition we must cease trying to find an original of any traditional song. From one point of view each performance is an original. From another point of view it is impossible to retrace the work of generations of singers to that moment when some singer first sang a particular song.[6]

The bardic system is fundamentally conservative; it serves to transmit a fixed story from teller to teller and from generation to generation. But what it conserves is not a single particular performance but the underlying patterns from which the bards can create multiple varied performances. Their success in combining the satisfactions of a coherent plot with the pleasures of endless variation is therefore a provocative model of what we might hope to achieve in cyberspace. To do so we must reconceptualize authorship, in the same way Lord did, and think of it not as the inscribing of a fixed written text but as the invention and arrangement of the expressive patterns that constitute a multiform story.

VLADIMIR PROPP AND THE BARDIC ALGORITHM

Oral composition can even provide us with a specific algorithm for producing multiform stories. Around the same time that Milman Parry first began to notice the oral character of Greek epic, the Russian formalist Vladimir Propp set out to analyze a body of Russian oral narrative in order to arrive at a "morphology of the folktale." He was quite successful in his efforts at reducing a seeming "labyrinth of the tale's multiformity" to an "amazing uniformity." The set of 450 fairy tales Propp studied, though very different from one another on the surface, resolved themselves into variants of a single core tale composed of twenty-five basic "functions," or plot events, which we can think of as Propp's essential morphemes.[7] (Propp gave each of these morphemes its own symbol, which appears in parentheses to the left of each example below.)

After a brief introductory section (with its own distinctive morphemes, including the following: a family member absents himself from home, an interdiction is violated, a villain attempts reconnaissance, the hero is deceived, and so on), the first element of the story is one of these:

(A)   The villain causes harm or injury to a member of the family (nineteen variants ranging from threats to abduction and murder).

(a)   One member of the family either lacks something or desires something.

These elements are familiar to us from other fairy tales, even if we have never heard the Russian ones Propp studied. Here are some of the key story elements and their symbols:

($\uparrow$)   The hero leaves home.

(D)   The hero is tested (ten variants ranging from requests for help to challenges to fight).

(F)   The hero acquires a magical agent (a magic hen, a magic horse, magic foods, etc.).

(H)   The hero and the villain join in direct combat.

(I)   The hero defeats the villain.

(J)   The hero is branded.

(K)   The initial misfortune or lack is "liquidated," or resolved (eleven variants).

(L)   A false hero presents unfounded claims.

(M)   The hero is given a difficult task.

(N)   The hero successfully performs the task.

($\downarrow$)   The hero returns.

(Ex)   The false hero is exposed.

(U)   The villain is punished.

(W)   The hero is married and ascends the throne.

In addition to identifying the elements, Propp tried to establish the rules by which these morphemes are combined. He found that many morphemes came in related pairs, for example, the establishment of a misfortune/lack and its liquidation, the pursuit of the hero and his rescue, the introduction of a false hero and his exposure. Propp also noticed that the order of the elements in a story seems to be constant, even though any particular version of the story might lack some of the elements. For instance, the test of the hero always occurs after he leaves home and before he acquires the magical agent. In a particular version of the story, the test might be left out, but it would not be transposed. Like a cook who analyzes a dish to understand how it was prepared, Vladimir Propp has arrived at a recipe for the Russian folktale.

More than that, Propp's analysis makes clear that the formulaic underpinning makes folktales more intricate; it allows storytellers to weave together multiple different story sequences without becoming confused. For instance, a hero might receive more than one magical gift in the course of a story, a variation that would require a repetition of the elements that cluster around the gift pattern; or a second hero could be introduced to go on his own quest, forming a second story sequence that would be embedded within the first. Propp's abstract notation allowed him to chart such complex story structures. For instance, here is his representation of a story that grows out of two acts of villainy, each of which is resolved separately:

A14   I _____ K9

A2   II _____ K1

Here the villain commits abduction (A2) and murder (A14). The first part of the plot resolves the murder by reviving the dead person (K9). The second part of the plot resolves the abduction when the hero completes a search by an act of cleverness (K1). Propp's notation also reveals some of the rules for creating more divergent variants while still keeping the same basic story line. For instance, he noticed that the "struggle/victor" pattern (elements H-I) could be substituted for a "difficult tasks" pattern (M-N). When he finished analyzing all the extant tales, Propp was able to summarize all the variants of the Russian folktale in one inclusive representation. His work suggests that satisfying stories can be generated by substituting and rearranging formulaic units according to rules as precise as a mathematical formula.[8]

THE COMPUTER AS STORYTELLER

Propp's algorithm is much more complex than most electronic games currently on the market but considerably less complex than current attempts to model stories in computer science laboratories.

The story line in most gaming software can be described in terms of two or three morphemes (fight bad guy, solve puzzle, die). MUDs also rely on the repetition of a narrow set of plot actions, often limited to combat, negotiation and ceremonial events. Indeed, the lack of plot progression in MUDs is an advantage, since a limited repertoire of stereotyped activities makes for more easily sustained role-playing. Adventure and puzzle games usually provide only one route through various game levels, which results in a very linear story despite the high degree of participation activity. Games that do offer choice-points leading to variant plot events are usually constructed with only shallow detours off the main spine of the plot. This is because even a story of less than a dozen branch points, with only two choices at each branching, would require hundreds of endings. Any branching story interesting enough to sustain our attention would therefore be too dense and confusing to write, since writers would have to work their way down each branch separately.[9]

Games that do provide narrative variety often do so through a simple substitution system. Just as one "magic helper" can replace another in a Russian fairy tale, so too can one hero replace another in a fighting game, often changing the emotional tone along with the joystick moves. But games do not allow substitution of thematic plot elements (e.g., a heroic labor instead of a struggle with a villain) the way fairy tales do. Games are limited to very rigid plotlines because they do not have an abstract representation of the story structure that would allow them to distinguish between a particular instantiation and a generic morpheme. That is, "level two" of a fighting game always refers to the same configuration, not to a set of rules by which it can be constructed. A morphological approach (a generic "level two") would require more ambitious programming but it would offer much greater plot variation; it would give the writer the power to tell the system how to generate variants without having to make each possible version individually.

Several kinds of abstract schema have been proposed by computer scientists as ways of representing stories, many of them based on a model of story structure grounded in cognitive theory. Most of these systems, however, have an unnervingly reductive quality to the humanist. For instance, Patrick Winston's analogy-making program Macbeth summarizes the plot like this:

> This is a story about Macbeth, Lady Macbeth, Duncan, and Macduff. Macbeth is an evil noble. Lady Macbeth is a greedy, ambitious woman. Duncan is a king. Macduff is a noble. Lady Macbeth persuades Macbeth to want to be king because she is greedy. She is able to influence him because he is married to her and because he is weak. Macbeth murders Duncan with a knife. Macbeth murders Duncan because Macbeth wants to be king and because Macbeth is evil. Lady Macbeth kills herself. Macduff is angry. He kills Macbeth because Macbeth murdered Duncan and because Macduff is loyal to Duncan.[10]

This summary certainly fits Forster's definition of a plot as "a narrative of events, the emphasis falling on causality," but it is a sledgehammer causality that few literary critics or psychologists would accept because of its disturbing flattening of motivation. Of course, Winston is not trying to understand the play as a literary critic or a psychologist or to be moved by it as a member of the audience. He wants to use it as a pattern from which to predict behavior in similar situations, as a way of mimicking human reasoning by analogy in complex situations. For instance, here is a story that Winston's system finds analogous to Macbeth:

> This is a story about Linda and Dick. Linda is a woman and Dick is a man. Dick is married to Linda. Dick is weak because he is drained. He is drained because Linda is domineering.[11]

Stereotypical thinking is both useful and pernicious. It is useful because it is a form of abstraction that helps us to organize information. It is pernicious because it distorts the world and can make it hard to see things individually. I had always felt that Lord's Serbo-Croatian bards were a wonderful cultural treasure until I reread his account after the recent war in the region and was chilled to come upon his matter-of-fact mention of the "willing" abduction of women from the enemy as just another variant of the rescue theme. It is important to remember that any abstract story system ultimately refers to the sorrows and pleasures of human life and that the story of any event depends heavily on who is doing the telling. A storytelling system that further calcifies the distortions of stereotypical thinking would be as destructive as the most bigoted and bloodthirsty bard. We humans already do enough mechanical thinking without enlisting machines to help us.

Furthermore, stories told from an abstract representation of narrative patterns but without a writer's relish for specific material can be incoherent. Here, for instance, is a computer-generated fable based on a representation of a plot as the solving of a problem or the attainment of a goal:

> Joe Bear was hungry. He asked Irving Bird where some honey was. Irving refused to tell him, so Joe offered to bring him a worm if he'd tell him where some honey was. Irving agreed. But Joe didn't know where any worms were, so he asked Irving, who refused to say. So Joe offered to bring him a worm if he'd tell him where a worm was. Irving agreed. But Joe didn't know where any worms were, so he asked Irving, who refused to say. So Joe offered to bring him a worm if he'd tell him where a worm was. . . .[12]

The program goes into a loop because it does not know enough about the world to give Joe Bear any better alternatives. The plot structure is too abstract to limit Joe Bear's actions to sequences that make sense.

Several ambitious proposals have been made to ensure coherence in computer-generated narrative by creating plot controllers capable of making intelligent decisions about narrative syntax on the basis of aesthetic values. Brenda Laurel, who sees the computer as an inherently theatrical environment, has proposed an interactive fiction system presided over by a playwright who would shape the experience into the rising and falling arc of classical drama.[13] Marie-Laure Ryan has proposed a story-generation system, derived from narratology theories, that would shape satisfying tales exhibiting symmetry, suspense, and repetition.[14] The challenge of all such ambitious schemes is in giving the computer enough knowledge of the story elements to decide what constitutes an Aristotelian recognition scene or a suspense-generating event.

One way of avoiding the arduous task of teaching the computer to understand the world well enough to make such aesthetic judgments is to code very specific story elements in terms of their dramatic function. Michael Lebowitz has created a storytelling system along these lines with morphemic segments derived from the staples of daytime soap opera stories, namely, amnesia, murder threats, forced marriages, and adultery. In Lebowitz's Universe system, the automated author is assigned goals, and the system then looks for fragments that will achieve those goals.[15] For instance, one commonly invoked goal is "keeping lovers apart," which could be satisfied by "lover drafted by the army" and "get partner involved with someone else." Like a soap opera author, the program tries to maximize plot fragments so that they serve the purposes of multiple stories. Here is an example of a story sequence generated with this program:

> Liz was married to Tony. Neither loved the other, and, indeed, Liz was in love with Neil. However, unknown to either Tony or Neil, Stephano, Tony's father, who wanted Liz to produce a grandson for him, threatened Liz that if she left Tony he would kill Neil. Liz told Neil that she did not love him, that she was still in love with Tony, and that he should forget about her. Eventually, Neil was convinced and he married Marie. Later, when Liz was finally free from Tony (because Stephano had died), Neil was not free to marry her and their trouble went on.[16]

Why is the story of Liz and Tony so much more engaging and coherent than the story of Joe Bear? Both are formulaic and machine generated, but Universe starts off with story fragments that are much closer to a writerly source and with a much more particularized representation of a plot. But Universe is also a limited model, since it does not provide for a participatory narrative or for a plot that comes to an end.

In fact, very few efforts have yet been made to create a system that accommodates both interactivity and directed plot. Although Brenda Laurel has been urging the development of such systems since the 1980s, they have received very little attention so far, perhaps because they would require closer collaboration between writers and computer scientists than has been possible up to now. The most promising work in this area has been done by the Oz group, at Carnegie Mellon University, led by Joseph Bates. The Oz group is attempting to create a system that a writer could use to tell stories that would include an interactor, a story world with its own objects, computer-based characters who act autonomously, and a story controller that would shape the experience from the perspective of the interactor.

The Oz group has modeled this system as a live-action theater game in which an interactor is placed in a threatening situation in a bus station.[17] Acting students improvised the parts of the computer-based characters, receiving instructions through headsets from an offstage director who watched the action closely and set off events at appropriate times. The climax of the story is the moment in which the interactor is offered a gun and must choose whether to use it to protect a blind man from a thug, or to escape onto a departing bus. To an observer of the experiment (which was captured on videotape), the action seems painfully slow and the climactic moment rather chaotic. But to the interactor the scene was quite gripping; the offer of the gun was a difficult moral choice, a self-defining moment, because it seemed to be happening in real time. The work of the Oz group suggests that plot satisfaction in an interactive environment is very different from plot satisfaction in an audience situation. In order to ensure the appropriate dramatic pacing, we may need to develop story controllers that monitor all the elements of the environment, adjusting the fictional world with the same precision and forethought as a chess master choosing among complex strategies.

The complexity of pattern manipulation made possible by the computer seems to be pushing stories into the realm of higher degrees of abstraction and variation. But in pursuing complexity and abstraction, we run the risk of incoherence. Since the success of any abstract representation of plot will depend on how much control remains in the hands of the human author, we may find that less computational abstraction will produce more satisfying stories. Or we may discover new abstraction models that are closer to the way writers like to make up stories than the models that have arisen so far from the collaboration between cognitive theorists and computer scientists. . . .

NOTES

1. See Campbell, *The Hero with a Thousand Faces.*
2. Tobias, *Twenty Master Plots.*
3. For the most influential, lucid, and persuasive description of the differences between oral and literate intellectual processes and linguistic habits, see Ong, *Orality and Literacy.*
4. Cited from "A Story as You Like It: Interactive Version," at http://fub46.zedat.fu-berlin.de:8080/cantsin/queneau_20.html, a World Wide Web version of "Cent mille milliards de poemes" by Raymond Queneau, with text adapted from Motte, *Oulipo,* pp. 156–58. Queneau's experiment was part of the 1960s movement called Ouvroir de Litterature Potentielle (OULIPO). He published the original in the form of a book of ten sonnets with pages cut into one-line strips for interchangeability of lines. In presenting his system for generating "one hundred thousand billion sonnets," he expressed the belief that "poetry should be made by everyone."
5. Lord, *The Singer of Tales,* p. 123.
6. Ibid., p. 100.
7. Propp, *Morphology of the Folktale.*
8. I have simplified Propp's formulas somewhat. See Propp, *Morphology of Folktales,* pp. 103–5. See Lakoff, "Structural Complexity in Fairy Tales," for an attempt to expand Propp's morphemes into a generative story grammar.
9. Amy Bruckman of MIT's Media Lab has pointed out in an unpublished paper, "The Combinatorics of Storytelling: Mystery Train Interactive" (1990), that even a simple "choose your own adventure" story that provides only two menu choices at each choice-point and keeps its branches to a maximum of five choice-points deep would generate an unmanageable thirty-two possible endings if it did not loop back on itself and merge branches. If the stories were a more satisfying ten choice-points deep, there would be 1,024 possible endings.
10. Winston, *Artificial Intelligence,* p. 417.
11. Ibid., p. 417.
12. Schank, *The Cognitive Computer: On Language, Learning, and Artificial Intelligence,* pp. 84–85. See also Meehan, "Tale-spin."
13. Laurel, *Computers as Theatre,* p. 135–39.
14. Ryan, *Possible Worlds,* pp. 248–57.
15. For the UNIVERSE system, see Michael Lebowitz, "Creating Characters in a Story-Telling Universe" and "Story-Telling as Planning and Learning."
16. See Lebowitz, "Story-Telling as Planning and Learning," p. 484, and the discussion in Ryan, *Possible Worlds,* p. 246; see Ryan generally for a more extensive and technical account of artificial intelligence approaches to (nonparticipatory) storytelling.
17. Kelso, Weyhrauch, and Bates, "Dramatic Presence."

DISCUSSION QUESTIONS

1. Why does Murray suggest that the "multiform plot" available through digital environments is not really a "violent break" with the narrative traditions of the precomputer age?
2. How do you respond to the idea of "master plots," a limited number of story structures that incorporate all the possibilities of narrative? What implications do these master plots have for our thinking about originality and genius in writers?
3. What are "primitives" in an interactive narrative, as described by Murray? Review the exercises in the Writer's Workshop at the end of Chapter 2. How do those prompts function in a parallel manner to these "primitives"? Do the prompts seem to be expressive and generative or mechanical and formulistic?
4. What are "themes" in an interactive narrative, according to Murray? Again, look at the exercises in the Writer's Workshop. Which exercises generate this kind of "narrative unit"?
5. To what extent do you agree with Murray that digital, computerized storytelling returns us to the bardic tradition, in which oral storytellers work within recognized narrative patterns, drawing on conventions of style and plot known by the audience?
6. What dangers does Murray see in "abstract schemas" used by computer programmers to describe human actions and the consequences of human choices? What is left out of these narratives due to the computer's current limitations, both experiential and aesthetic?
7. What does Murray mean by the "moral physics" of a story? How can a computer be programmed to provide moral density as part of the narrative provided to the person interacting with the machine?

WRITING ACTIVITIES

1. Following Baldwin, write an "autobiographical note" that tries to account for your fiction in terms of who you are. What life influences can't help but be expressed in your writing?

2. Keep a diary, as Woolf does, as you work on a piece of fiction from beginning to end. Try to chronicle the first inspiration you have for the story, the decisions you make as you proceed, the ways in which you change your mind, the worries you have for it, the extent to which the finished piece fulfills your hopes for it, and its reception by readers.

3. Write a fictional autobiography of your growth as a writer patterned on Malamud's "Long Work, Short Life." Begin with your childhood, and extend the memoir to the age of sixty.

4. Write a third-person biographical account of a young writer, akin to Bly's story about Jill in "Writing Whole Literature." Show how the character's circumstances and life experiences lead to a certain kind of writing.

5. Write a scene featuring a character performing a morally ugly act; place the character in a wide periphery, or context, so the ugliness of the act is not the only impression generated by the scene.

6. Make a list of stories that you consider "good" and "bad," and then write about why you categorize them that way. Can you discern the "slyly political" reasons for your judgments that Allison refers to in "Believing in Literature"?

7. Write an account of your parents' effect on your development as a writer; you may emphasize positive contributions (like Lamott), negative feedback (as in Bly's story of Jill), or a mix of both.

8. Using the second person, like Dillard, write about the writer's life, offering several analogies exploring and illuminating what it's like to write.

9. Write a dialogue between your conscious and unconscious selves, as suggested in Nelson's "The Master-Slave Relationship." Have these two parts of yourself discuss writing, as well as any related topics that affect how you write. What do you discover about yourself and your writing?

10. Try conceiving an overtly political story, perhaps inspired by recent headlines, a story that makes the current political situation a motivating part of the characters' lives. How will you balance the needs of fiction (characterization, plot, meaning) with the need to make a political statement?

CHAPTER 4

The Teaching and Learning of Fiction Writing

In "Writing Short Stories" (see Chapter 1), Flannery O'Connor discusses the central role of the "habit of art" in the life of a fiction writer, asserting that fiction writing is an activity in which the whole personality takes part. Continuing, she claims that "teaching any kind of writing is largely a matter of helping the student develop the habit of art." More concretely, she adds that the "teacher can help the student by looking at his individual work and trying to help him decide if he has written a complete short story, one in which the action fully illuminates the meaning." Recognizing the complexity of acquiring the habit of art, and the long period of time necessary to achieve such a goal, O'Connor assigns to the teacher of fiction writing an advisory role, not the otherworldly powers of a guru or shaman. In this way she evades to some degree the question that has long been posed about creative writing instruction: Can creative writing be taught at all? O'Connor seems to answer that the principles for the writing of fiction can be stated—perhaps illuminated—by the teacher, but that the work of becoming a fiction writer, of cultivating the essential habit, must be done by the student.

However, the sense that a creative writing teacher, or a creative writing program, should do more than point the way haunts many of the selections in this chapter. In the arts, young people have long apprenticed themselves to experts, trusting that great artists can somehow not only share the knowledge of craft but also bestow a measure of genius on the novice. When the apprenticeship does not result in this alchemical transfer of artistic essence, the whole enterprise of teaching an art like fiction writing may be called into question. The student may feel betrayed, duped, deceived, cruelly misled. If writers are going to set themselves up as teachers of the art, then they have an obligation to deliver on the implied promise, despite warnings to the contrary voiced in class or printed on the syllabus. So, while teachers may have a clear sense of what a class can and cannot do for student writers, these expectations may not match those of the students around the workshop table.

The first section of readings in this chapter explores, primarily, the experiences of students in creative writing courses. Lorrie Moore's "How to Become a Writer," from her collection *Self-Help,* is foremost a short story, but in dramatizing a young writer's struggles and frustrations, Moore shines a sharp satirical spotlight on the seemingly arbitrary variety of teaching methods her main character encounters. Francie, who wants to become a writer, is bombarded by mixed messages about how and what to write, and the comments she receives about her work and aspirations are dismissive and judgmental. Very little in the story represents creative writing instruction as nurturing or as a consistent source of guidance to the apprentice writer. In an interview with Alexander Neubauer, novelist Jane Smiley also questions the value of her experiences as a student; in her own classes, she offers a more structured, analytical approach to learning how to write fiction. She tries to limit the subjective and competitive aspects of the workshop setting, substituting an emphasis on specific elements of craft (similar to those discussed in Chapter 2) and how they function together in the work being discussed. By banning praise and blame, Smiley aims to shift the focus from personalities to the work itself. This attention to the work is prominent, too, in Raymond Carver's "Creative Writing 101," an account of a class Carver took from novelist and teacher John Gardner. Gardner, unknown at the time, treated his students as writers; one way he demonstrated his respect for their work was by paying painstaking attention to their fledgling literary efforts. Carver characterizes Gardner as opinionated and directive in his comments, but at the same time supportive, including his students in a charmed circle of writers. The novices' imitation of the master (they took to carrying their stories around in binders, like Gardner) indicates the power (and perhaps the potential risk) of this kind of teaching. Bonnie Friedman's narrative about her time at the Iowa Writers Workshop, "The Paraffin Density of Wax Wings," follows a young writer in search of a mentor like Gardner, someone to light the way and also validate her talent, her chosen path. What happens as Friedman moves through the large, prestigious Iowa program (quite a contrast to the smaller undergraduate program in northern California described by Carver) is unsettling and complicated. While Friedman comes to appreciate her experience, she has to fight her way through a series of emotional challenges to reach this appreciation, ultimately highlighting both the benefits and limitations of writing school.

The second section, "Reading as a Writer," begins with R. V. Cassill's piece of the same title. Cassill, like many teachers of fiction, directs young writers to study craft, advising that "all your reading ought to be a search for the variety of technical means by which various writers achieve their ends." While he recognizes that the reading habits of the general reader and the literary critic have their uses, he foregrounds that the writer-as-reader must be aware of the author's choices and the unity of the fiction that results from these choices. Richard Ford, in "Reading," offers a narrative showing such an analytical process in action. Ford's relationship with his professor Howard Babb illuminates for Ford a way to read stories, a "path-in signaled by a prominent formal feature," which leads to careful consideration of the feature's effects and its connection to other formal elements. Ford writes that such an approach leads to a more complete understanding of stories, though he ends by paying respect to the "haphazard" element of stories and the pleasure of not being able to understand any story fully. Rita Mae Brown's "An Annotated Reading List" immerses writers in the history of literature. Brown believes that such a course in reading can "reveal you to you," helping writers define themselves as part of a long literary chain of being. Like many other writers and teachers of fiction, she is less interested in "terms of good and bad" than in "terms of what works and what doesn't."

The third section of readings is slightly more theoretical in nature, though the writers consistently translate their theory into practice as they contemplate how best to teach creative writing. British novelist and critic David Lodge, in "Creative Writing: Can It/Should It Be Taught?" carefully considers Henry James' warning that the organic art of fiction cannot be broken into teachable chunks. While recognizing that the processes are in large part mysterious, Lodge does argue that "descriptive vocabulary," technique, and a heightened rhetorical sense of fiction's effects can indeed be taught. Novelist and teacher Madison Smartt Bell, in the introduction to his craft-oriented textbook *Narrative Design,* also addresses the challenge of teaching creativity, particularly the processes surrounding an art that utilizes language rather than more concrete materials like paint or clay. He contrasts craft-driven and inner-process workshops, concluding that there is room for both emphases in the creative writing teacher's range of strategies. While Bell respects the boundaries of the "black box" of creativity and warns against the teacher who would demand total access to the students' inner processes, he argues that students can learn to analyze craft *and* to improvise within the forms of fiction. Joe David Bellamy, likely the most theoretical of the writers included here, argues forcefully for the value of creative writing as a humanistic discipline in "The Theory of Creative Writing I and II." He critiques standard educational practices—heavy on arcane language and overspecialization—and lauds creative writing as an antidote capable of expanding students' moral awareness and capacity for empathy. Finally, fiction writer John Casey, in "Dogma," surveys nine platitudes of creative writing instruction. His meditations on the uses of dogma, and the counterdogma built into almost any assertion about writing, reinvigorate such familiar advice as "Write what you know."

The final section, "Creative Writing in the Academy," begins with Andrew Levy's close reading of Bobbie Ann Mason's career, focusing on the much-anthologized story "Shiloh." Levy understands Mason's form of "dirty realism" as illustrative of a long-standing tension in American literature between regional and class concerns and more academic, potentially elitist approaches to literature. D. G. Myers' historical overview in "The Elephant Machine" of the growth of creative writing programs contextualizes this phenomenon within the development of research universities in the United States. Universities, in Myers' view, wished to expand their influence in the wider culture, and so provided an institutional home for writers and creative writing programs in order to bring the production of literature into their orbit. In "The New Assembly-Line Fiction," John Aldridge attacks what he deems the consequences of this relationship between writers and the academy, claiming that the culture of creative writing programs insulates writers from the challenges of writing for a wider audience, substituting a "complex network" of cronies and peers for the general reader. Further, Aldridge sees the workshop method as inhibiting the writer's individual vision and willingness to take risks, suggesting that writers' social isolation is an integral part of the creative process. Like television and other media, creative writing programs can disrupt the writer's development.

Can fiction writing be taught? If not, how can it be learned? If so, what is the best way to teach it and learn it? What are the rewards and dangers of creative writing classrooms? These are open questions that can be answered only with reference to our own experiences in those classrooms. And, with the number of creative writing classes proliferating on campuses across the country, they are questions that should be pondered by every teacher and student of fiction writing.

LORRIE MOORE

How to Become a Writer

Lorrie Moore (b. 1957) started early, winning Seventeen *magazine's fiction-writing contest in 1976, when she was only nineteen. Her first collection of stories,* Self-Help *(1985), was a finalist in the AWP contest for short fiction. She has published two more volumes of stories,* Like Life *(1990) and* Birds of America *(1998), as well as two novels,* Anagrams *(1986) and* Who Will Run the Frog Hospital? *(1994). She is currently a professor at the University of Wisconsin at Madison.*

First, try to be something, anything, else. A movie star/astronaut. A movie star/missionary. A movie star/kindergarten teacher. President of the World. Fail miserably. It is best if you fail at an early age—say, fourteen. Early, critical disillusionment is necessary so that at fifteen you can write long haiku sequences about thwarted desire. It is a pond, a cherry blossom, a wind brushing against sparrow wing leaving for mountain. Count the syllables. Show it to your mom. She is tough and practical. She has a son in Vietnam and a husband who may be having an affair. She believes in wearing brown because it hides spots. She'll look briefly at your writing, then back up at you with a face blank as a donut. She'll say: "How about emptying the dishwasher?" Look away. Shove the forks in the fork drawer. Accidentally break one of the freebie gas station glasses. This is the required pain and suffering. This is only for starters.

In your high school English class look only at Mr. Killian's face. Decide faces are important. Write a villanelle about pores. Struggle. Write a sonnet. Count the syllables: nine, ten, eleven, thirteen. Decide to experiment with fiction. Here you don't have to count syllables. Write a short story about an elderly man and woman who accidentally shoot each other in the head, the result of an inexplicable malfunction of a shotgun which appears mysteriously in their living room one night. Give it to Mr. Killian as your final project. When you get it back, he has written on it: "Some of your images are quite nice, but you have no sense of plot." When you are home, in the privacy of your own room, faintly scrawl in pencil beneath his black-inked comments: "Plots are for dead people, pore-face."

Take all the babysitting jobs you can get. You are great with kids. They love you. You tell them stories about old people who die idiot deaths. You sing them songs like "Blue Bells of Scotland," which is their favorite. And when they are in their pajamas and have finally stopped pinching each other, when they are fast asleep, you read every sex manual in the house, and wonder how on earth anyone could ever do those things with someone they truly loved. Fall asleep in a chair reading Mr. McMurphy's *Playboy*. When the McMurphys come home, they will tap you on the shoulder, look at the magazine in your lap, and grin. You will want to die. They will ask you if Tracey took her medicine all right. Explain, yes, she did, that you promised her a story if she would take it like a big girl and that seemed to work out just fine. "Oh, marvelous," they will exclaim.

Try to smile proudly.

Apply to college as a child psychology major.

As a child psychology major, you have some electives. You've always liked birds. Sign up for something called "The Ornithological Field Trip." It meets Tuesdays and Thursdays at two. When you arrive at Room 134 on the first day of class, everyone is sitting around a seminar table talking about metaphors. You've heard of these. After a short, excruciating while, raise your hand and say diffidently, "Excuse me, isn't this Birdwatching One-oh-one?" The class stops and turns to look at you. They seem to all have one face—giant and blank as a vandalized clock. Someone with a beard booms out, "No, this is Creative Writing." Say: "Oh—right," as if perhaps you knew all along. Look down at your schedule. Wonder how the hell you ended up here. The computer, apparently, has made an error. You start to get up to leave and then don't. The lines at the registrar this week are huge. Perhaps you should stick with this mistake. Perhaps your creative writing isn't all that bad. Perhaps it is fate. Perhaps this is what your dad meant when he said, "It's the age of computers, Francie, it's the age of computers."

Decide that you like college life. In your dorm you meet many nice people. Some are smarter than you. And some, you notice, are dumber than you. You will continue, unfortunately, to view the world in exactly these terms for the rest of your life.

The assignment this week in creative writing is to narrate a violent happening. Turn in a story about driving with your Uncle Gordon and another one about two old people who are accidentally electrocuted when they go to turn on a badly wired desk lamp. The teacher will hand them back to you with comments: "Much of your writing is smooth and energetic. You have, however, a ludicrous notion of plot." Write another story about a man and a woman who, in the very first paragraph, have their lower torsos accidentally blitzed away by dynamite. In the second paragraph, with the insurance money, they buy a frozen yogurt stand together. There are six more paragraphs. You read the whole thing out loud in class. No one likes it. They say your sense of plot is outrageous and incompetent. After class someone asks you if you are crazy.

Decide that perhaps you should stick to comedies. Start dating someone who is funny, someone who has what in high school you called a "really great sense of humor" and what now your creative writing class calls "self-contempt giving rise to comic form." Write down all of his jokes, but don't tell him you are doing this. Make up anagrams of his old girlfriend's name and name all of your socially handicapped characters with them. Tell him his old girlfriend is in all of your stories and then watch how funny he can be, see what a really great sense of humor he can have.

Your child psychology advisor tells you you are neglecting courses in your major. What you spend the most time on should be what you're majoring in. Say yes, you understand.

In creative writing seminars over the next two years, everyone continues to smoke cigarettes and ask the same things: "But does it work?" "Why should we care about this character?" "Have you earned this cliché?" These seem like important questions.

On days when it is your turn, you look at the class hopefully as they scour your mimeographs for a plot. They look back up at you, drag deeply, and then smile in a sweet sort of way.

You spend too much time slouched and demoralized. Your boyfriend suggests bicycling. Your roommate suggests a new boyfriend. You are said to be self-mutilating and losing weight, but you continue writing. The only happiness you have is writing something new, in the middle of the night, armpits damp, heart pounding, something no one has yet seen. You have only those brief, fragile, untested moments of exhilaration when you know: you are a genius. Understand what you must do. Switch majors. The kids in your nursery project will be disappointed, but you have a calling, an urge, a delusion, an unfortunate habit. You have, as your mother would say, fallen in with a bad crowd.

Why write? Where does writing come from? These are questions to ask yourself. They are like: Where does dust come from? Or: Why is there war? Or: If there's a God, then why is my brother now a cripple?

These are questions that you keep in your wallet, like calling cards. These are questions, your creative writing teacher says, that are good to address in your journals but rarely in your fiction.

The writing professor this fall is stressing the Power of the Imagination. Which means he doesn't want long descriptive stories about your camping trip last July. He wants you to start in a realistic context but then to alter it. Like recombinant DNA. He wants you to let your imagination sail, to let it grow big-bellied in the wind. This is a quote from Shakespeare.

Tell your roommate your great idea, your great exercise of imaginative power: a transformation of Melville to contemporary life. It will be about mono-mania and the fish-eat-fish world of life insurance in Rochester, New York. The first line will be "Call me Fishmeal," and it will feature a menopausal suburban husband named Richard, who because he is so depressed all the time is called "Mopey Dick" by his witty wife Elaine. Say to your roommate: "Mopey Dick, get it?" Your roommate looks at you, her face blank as a large Kleenex. She comes up to you, like a buddy, and puts an arm around your burdened shoulders. "Listen, Francie," she says, slow as speech therapy. "Let's go out and get a big beer."

The seminar doesn't like this one either. You suspect they are beginning to feel sorry for you. They say: "You have to think about what is happening. Where is the story here?"

The next semester the writing professor is obsessed with writing from personal experience. You must write from what you know, from what has happened to you. He wants death, he wants camping trips. Think about what has happened to you. In three years there have been three things: you lost your virginity; your parents got divorced; and your brother came home from a forest ten miles from the Cambodian border with only half a thigh, a permanent smirk nestled into one corner of his mouth.

About the first you write: "It created a new space, which hurt and cried in a voice that wasn't mine, 'I'm not the same anymore, but I'll be okay.'"

About the second you write an elaborate story of an old married couple who stumble upon an unknown land mine in their kitchen and accidentally blow themselves up. You call it: "For Better or for Liverwurst."

About the last you write nothing. There are no words for this. Your typewriter hums. You can find no words.

At undergraduate cocktail parties, people say, "Oh, you write? What do you write about?" Your roommate, who has consumed too much wine, too little cheese, and no crackers at all, blurts: "Oh, my god, she always writes about her dumb boyfriend."

Later on in life you will learn that writers are merely open, helpless texts with no real understanding of what they have written and therefore must half-believe anything and everything that is said of them. You, however, have not yet reached this stage of literary criticism. You stiffen and say, "I do not," the same way you said it when someone in the fourth grade accused you of really liking oboe lessons and your parents really weren't just making you take them.

Insist you are not very interested in any one subject at all, that you are interested in the music of language, that you are interested in—in—syllables, because they are the atoms of poetry, the cells of the mind, the breath of the soul. Begin to feel woozy. Stare into your plastic wine cup.

"Syllables?" you will hear someone ask, voice trailing off, as they glide slowly towards the reassuring white of the dip.

Begin to wonder what you do write about. Or if you have anything to say. Or if there even is such a thing as a thing to say. Limit these thoughts to no more than ten minutes a day; like sit-ups, they can make you thin.

You will read somewhere that all writing has to do with one's genitals. Don't dwell on this. It will make you nervous.

Your mother will come visit you. She will look at the circles under your eyes and hand you a brown book with a brown briefcase on the cover. It is entitled: *How to Become a Business Executive.* She has also brought the *Names for Baby* encyclopedia you asked for; one of your characters, the aging clown-school-teacher, needs a new name. Your mother will shake her head and say: "Francie, Francie, remember when you were going to be a child psychology major?"

Say: "Mom, I like to write."

She'll say: "Sure you like to write. Of course. Sure you like to write."

Write a story about a confused music student and title it: "Schubert Was the One with the Glasses, Right?" It's not a big hit, although your roommate likes the part where the two violinists accidentally blow themselves up in a recital room. "I went out with a violinist once," she says, snapping her gum.

Thank god you are taking other courses. You can find sanctuary in nineteenth-century ontological snags and invertebrate courting rituals. Certain globular mollusks have what is called "Sex by the Arm." The male octopus, for instance, loses the end of one arm when placing it inside the female body during intercourse. Marine biologists call it "Seven Heaven." Be glad you know these things. Be glad you are not just a writer. Apply to law school.

From here on in, many things can happen. But the main one will be this: you decide not to go to law school after all, and, instead, you spend a good, big chunk of your adult life telling people how you decided not to go to law school after all. Somehow you end up writing again. Perhaps you go to graduate school. Perhaps you work odd jobs and take writing courses at night. Perhaps you are working on a novel and writing down all the clever remarks and intimate personal confessions you hear during the day. Perhaps you are losing your pals, your acquaintances, your balance.

You have broken up with your boyfriend. You now go out with men who, instead of whispering "I love you," shout: "Do it to me, baby." This is good for your writing.

Sooner or later you have a finished manuscript more or less. People look at it in a vaguely troubled sort of way and say, "I'll bet becoming a writer was always a fantasy of yours, wasn't it?" Your lips dry to salt. Say that of all the fantasies possible in the world, you can't imagine being a writer even making the top twenty. Tell them you were going to be a child psychology major. "I bet," they always sigh, "you'd be great with kids." Scowl fiercely. Tell them you're a walking blade.

Quit classes. Quit jobs. Cash in old savings bonds. Now you have time like warts on your hands. Slowly copy all of your friends' addresses in a new address book.

Vacuum. Chew cough drops. Keep a folder full of fragments.

An eyelid darkening sideways.
World as conspiracy.
Possible plot? A woman gets on a bus.
Suppose you threw a love affair and nobody came?

At home drink a lot of coffee. At Howard Johnson's order the cole slaw. Consider how it looks like the soggy confetti of a map: where you've been, where you're going—"You Are Here," says the red star on the back of the menu.

Occasionally a date with a face blank as a sheet of paper asks you whether writers often become discouraged. Say that sometimes they do and sometimes they do. Say it's a lot like having polio.

"Interesting," smiles your date, and then he looks down at his arm hairs and starts to smooth them, all, always, in the same direction.

DISCUSSION QUESTIONS

1. Moore's narrator describes several types of creative writing classes in this story. What are the most vivid features of each kind of class? How does Francie respond to each experience? Do any of the classes help Francie become a better writer?

2. Francie is repeatedly told in the story that she has problems with plot. What are the other characters objecting to in Francie's handling of plot in her stories? Do you agree with their judgments? Why or why not?

3. Early in the story the narrator mentions the "required pain and suffering" in the writer's life, and Francie accepts, or at least labels, many of her misfortunes as part of her training as a writer. Why do you think pain and suffering are often associated with the writer's life in literary representations of writers?

4. One motif in the story is Francie's plan to study child psychology; people tell her that she would be great with children. Why do people say this about her? What is the connection between Francie's desire to write and this advice that other characters offer about an alternative career?

5. Francie describes herself as "a walking blade" toward the end of the story. Why does she choose this image? How does this image fit in with her actions and reactions during the rest of the story?

6. Although the story focuses on Francie, Moore chooses to use the second person "you" as a narrative strategy. Why, do you think? What effect does this relatively uncommon strategy have on your reading of the story?

ALEXANDER NEUBAUER

Interview with Jane Smiley

Alexander Neubauer (b. 1959) is a New York writer. This interview with Jane Smiley is from his Conversations on Writing Fiction: Interviews with Thirteen Distinguished Teachers of Fiction Writing *(1994). The biographical note on her preceding the interview covers everything except the novel* Moo *(1995) and her most recent novel about raising horses.*

Born in Los Angeles in 1949, Jane Smiley attended Vassar College and the University of Iowa Writers' Workshop, where she received both an M.F.A. and Ph.D. Between "a competent murder mystery" called *Duplicate Keys,* her third novel, and *The Greenlanders,* her fourth, her writing underwent "a significant aesthetic sea change," she says here. What followed were the critically lauded novellas *The Age of Grief* (1987) and *Ordinary Love* and *Good Will* (1989), succeeded in turn by the novel *A Thousand Acres* (1992), for which she won the Pulitzer Prize for fiction.

As a teacher of creative writing at Iowa State University since 1981, Jane Smiley has devised an original, highly structured method that forswears critical praise of any kind for students' work. In so doing, she ushers writers away from the arena of criticism and into one of analysis. "The key is not thinking of student stories as 'good' and 'bad,'" she says in these pages, "but thinking of them as examples of some mode of analysis that can be used in an educating way." With insight into the process of creativity, her own and her students', she also speaks of the "rituals of evasion" that every writer develops. What emerges here is a serious, innovative blend of analysis, experience, and objective standards, all rendered into practical terms for the developing writer.

Q: You've developed an analytic method of teaching creative writing at Iowa State that excludes praise of any kind. First of all, would you give me a little history—how did it develop?

Well, the graduate side of our program was very minimal until about 1984, when we decided to use some fellowships we had to lure better students. So by fall of 1984 we had a fairly decent group of graduate students, and they were in a class with a colleague of mine here, but almost all of them were men.

Q: By the luck of the draw?

Just by coincidence. And he had had some trouble with that class. They had problems with antagonism and rivalry that worked against any sort of coherent teaching method. I knew I was going to get all or most of the students the next semester and that there had been bad blood, so I thought, "What can I do to minimize the bad blood between the students and take the pressure off of me as a kind of judge and chooser between them?" One of the things that is true here, as well as elsewhere, is the wide difference between the amount of experience and talent of the class members. You'll have some very good students and some beginning students in the same class, and that can create a lot of friction in fiction.

Q: Fiction friction?

A lot of fiction friction, because obviously students are suspicious of what they are getting from one another. So I decided that the best thing to do, for a number of reasons, was come up with a structure that in some sense would be impersonal and would direct their attention away from me and each other and toward the ongoing progress of their work. To begin with, I divided them up into smaller groups of five, although I didn't dictate who would be in each group. Also, I had been thinking for quite a long time about a structure that would allow constant revision. Since we have a sixteen-week semester, including exam week, I decided each student would have to write four stories with four drafts per story. That meant that in each small group we would read everyone's draft for the week, and talk about them.

Q: So you had to put in a good deal more time.

Well, it requires about four and a half hours each week instead of three, since I meet with three groups of five for an hour and a half each. It *is* more time-consuming but it has a good payoff, so I'm not bothered.

Q: Do the students ever meet all together?

No, not after the first group. Once in a while they say, "Oh, gee, we'd like to," but what turns out to have happened is that the smaller groups have learned to speak a certain language among themselves, and they experience the other groups as a kind of intrusion. So even if they want to, it usually doesn't work. What they discover is that they've become quite intimate with their own group and they don't want to give up that intimacy.

Q: What happens during the course of a student's four drafts of each story?

Well, the first draft they turn in they're usually pretty proud of, and they think of it as fairly polished. And with the first story always, no matter how hard I've prepared them and no matter how hard they've tried not to, what they're really seeking is praise. They want for the impossible thing to happen, for me and the class to say, "This is great, you don't have to do any more drafts, just send it off now and it'll get published, I guarantee it." In my experience the first drafts are fairly short, fairly polished, and with some problem in them that seems fairly minimal. Let's say the section that's supposed to be the climax will be confusing. So we'll talk about that and we'll say that the person has to clear up the confusing parts of the climax for next week. But usually that involves all sorts of other things, too, like a more careful defining of the characters, or making the rising action move more slowly and clearly. It ends up requiring a kind of narrative restructuring just to make the climax less confusing.

As soon as they open up this box of the first draft, which is in, what shall we say, a state of *faux* completion, then the whole thing starts to fall apart. And the second draft is often a mess, because they are trying to bring in or explore elements that aren't in balance anymore. They're usually disappointed with the second draft; there's more to it but it's more of a mess, too. The third draft is better but still in a state of "uncontrol." But often by the time we've talked about the third draft we're all saying, "Aha!" and what we're saying "Aha" about is that we as readers feel that we finally understand what the author is getting at, and the author finally understands where *he's* going, too. Usually then they feel a certain amount of self-confidence about going on to the fourth draft, and it's really much better and more complete but often still unfinished. So they say they want to do a fifth draft, and I say, "No, you have to go on to the next story."

Q: Are you trying to get them to stay in the swim of the process of writing longer without having to produce a finished product?

Oh, absolutely. Ultimately, because they have to turn in a draft a week, they have to get in the habit of sticking with it, and the effect is that a lot of rituals have to be broken down. They resent that and resist it, because in my opinion rituals are a way of evading commitment to your work. When the rituals get broken down, they resist, because that means they can't evade it anymore. There's a whole separate subject I've thought a lot about, which is various types of evasion of commitment. This method is pretty good at breaking down those evasions, but it's not foolproof. We can go into that a little bit later.

Q: OK. For now, how about the progression, as you see it, of the four stories you get per person? Four is actually a pretty sizable number per semester.

Yeah, it is. Well, most of the stories, in a sort of bumbling and starting fashion, get better over the semester. At the same time the students go deeper and deeper into despair, because when you're doing four stories in sixteen weeks you kind of have your face pushed right into your characteristic problem. That problem keeps coming up and coming up, and it can lead to despair. But almost always the students solve some of the problems and so the despair they're feeling by the third story dissipates a little, because they see by the fourth story they've made a breakthrough.

Q: And you offer no praise at all?

Right. That was partly incidental because I had all these students who I knew would be seeking praise, since that had been their downfall the previous semester. And with the diversity of talent in the class, inevitably some people would get praise and some people wouldn't, and I wanted to keep them all on the right track and didn't want the ones who were less talented to feel alienated from the class. So I decided that I would try an analytical approach to their work.

Q: You never say, "Gee, I really liked this part of the story."

Never. I never say "like," I never say "don't like," never "good," never "bad." I say instead, "Why do you think so-and-so did this?" One of the things that I've discovered is that they get more interested in their own and each other's work when you start talking about artistic choices and stop talking about "good" and "bad," because they get interested in the system that's at work and they want to analyze that system. At first they're resentful of the fact that they aren't getting any praise, and often the most resentful ones were the most highly praised in the past; they perceive the absence of praise as a criticism. But I try to warn them, I try to tell them early on that they're going to have these feelings—but they're never going to know that I personally like their work or not.

Q: Isn't it difficult not to hint at an opinion? A raised eyebrow?

Not anymore. It was in the old days, but now it's automatic. You see, when you teach writing, you're teaching to students and beginners, and you owe it to them not to praise them. Well, *I* would say you owe it to them not to praise them; others would say you owe it to them not *simply* to praise them. Either way, with praise you are passing up an opportunity to help them see what the goal is, to intellectually see it and to instinctively perceive it.

Q: And you say the students eventually stop looking for that praise?

Right. Because they realize that if I give them praise it's a way of not engaging them with analysis. They come to see praise as a shortcut and they don't want it anymore. They find it unserious. They really do want to be taken seriously. At first they don't realize that's what they want. They think to be taken seriously is to be praised; but eventually they become convinced that to be taken seriously is to be analyzed and delved into. And so if I just say, "Gosh, this is good, I really like it," they'll wait and be upset if I don't go on.

Q: And what do you find comes out of that? It's almost a retooling of the way one thinks about the process of reward and punishment in one's work.

I think a number of things happen. One thing is everybody feels pretty much like an artist. Everybody feels like they're on an equal footing. And I think in some ways, though not all ways of course, they're on an equal footing with *me* because I'm no longer dishing out the rewards, I'm just asking the questions. They certainly feel like they're on an equal footing with one another.

Mostly, though, I think the best thing about it is that their work becomes more and more fluid. They don't have to protect or defend anything. What I always tell them is, "If I tell you that this paragraph or this sentence or this character is good, and then if you decide that the character has to be changed, you're going to be torn between your sense of the character and the praise you've received for it." I want the work to continue to be fluid until the writer says—or publication says—this is finished.

Q: Were there any teachers in your development who you liked very much and learned from?

No.

Q: None?

I had teachers that I liked personally, and I had teachers who liked my work, but part of the reason I developed this method was that I felt I didn't get effective teaching.

Q: So the next question of course is, what do you do in place of praise? How do you critique a story?

Well, the main problem with saying you're going to use an analytical method rather than a critical one is that you have to have a theory to back up the analytical method. Because of that, I've devised my own theory of how fiction works that I bring into the classroom and use as the basis for the analysis. It's fairly simple and easy to understand, but I think it works pretty well for beginning fiction writers. It's not all that sophisticated.

There used to be a book called *Writing Fiction*—there probably still is—by a man who taught at Brown named [R. V.] Cassill. I remember he spoke about five elements of fiction, but I lost the book so I had to come up with my own five. I decided the elements of fiction are: action, character, theme, setting, and language. In most short stories one or another of these elements predominates. And each predominating element has a particular payoff. For example, the payoff for action would be suspense; the payoff for setting would be a sense of the exotic. And if the writer has that as the main element but doesn't give that payoff, then the story fails at the bottommost level.

Q: The expectation must be met between reader and writer.

Right, right. That kind of analysis leads to the theory of the story as an exchange of expectations, or let's say a negotiation about expectations on the part of both the reader and the writer. The student writer's responsibility is not to fulfill the reader's expectations but to understand them, and to use that understanding to manipulate them. And there's a degree to which, if the writer wants to take something away from the reader, he must also give something back.

So for example: Most experimental fiction writers, like William Gass, took away from the reader a lot of things, such as belief in character, belief in suspenseful action. The thing they had to give back to the reader, since they were relying almost completely on theme, was a real sense of learning something, a real sense of enlightenment. If they fail to say something intellectually new or complex, the reader feels that that piece of experimental fiction has failed in some essential way.

Another example would be a writer of comic fiction. Now, comic fiction relies very profoundly on language rather than anything else. That means when the language fails, even if the characters are good and the action is interesting, the reader feels that the promise of this being comic or funny all the way through is broken, so it fails as a piece of comic fiction.

We talk about those things. We talk about plotting, we talk about character transformation, we talk about willing suspension of disbelief. We talk about things that are very basic, but we talk about them as an exchange: How do you get your reader to invest in this piece of fiction, and once the reader has made his investment, how do you not jeopardize it, or, if you're going to jeopardize it, how do you regain it?

Q: And it's these five elements that provide you with the tools of conversation in the class?

Right. It takes them a while to learn the language but pretty soon they learn that, too.

Q: How would you analyze a Raymond Carver story, say, using your five elements? Which of the elements predominates?

Oh, I would say probably a combination of character and theme. Language and setting are important, but if we weren't drawn into a deep sympathy with the characters, the individual stories might fail.

I guess I came up with this method because I'm not a judgmental person. It's not that I consciously don't like it, it's that I don't have a habit of mind of doing it. Having an analytical structure is a protection for the student as well as a way for him to learn about his own work. Where every student eventually arrives is a place where the formal problems of the work are the same as the psychological problems of the student and the philosophical problems of the student's worldview. And that's a good place for students to arrive; it also shows that the formal problems of the work are now deeper.

Let's say you have a student whose fictional characters are wafty and undefined. After you've had that student for a while you realize that *that's* the student, *that* is his or her problem. Every teacher, I think, has an instinctive perception that the problems in a student's work are in some sense beyond the teacher, that they are rooted in the student. But if you give that student an analytical framework and an understanding of the formal elements of fiction, while you may never solve the student's psychological problems, you may give them a way to attack the formal problems and come to an imaginative understanding of them. Do you see what I mean?

Q: I think so—and you yourself as a teacher don't involve yourself with the psychological elements.

No. See, I keep that to myself. If I come to see a student in a certain way and come to see the link between what's going on in his work and his life, I never say anything. I think that's intrusive. But I might become focused on what you could call the formal dilemmas of the work, and then we can talk about them as if they were purely formal dilemmas. Maybe the student will never solve these things in his life, but he may be able to address these formal dilemmas in his fiction.

Q: Tell me, do you use this method in your undergraduate as well as graduate courses?

Well, not so much with the undergraduates, because they aren't as dedicated to writing fiction. What they need more is to develop their imaginations, and so what I do in class is to give them a number of types of assignments that will let them think about different subjects in different ways.

Q: One question people might have is how easy it was for you to learn to teach this way—and how easy, or difficult, it might be for others to learn your method.

Sometimes I think you have to have a knack for getting the students not to focus on you, not to write stories *to* you, not to try to please you. And I don't know if I even have that knack as much as I'd like.

Q: *In some classes for some teachers, of course, being on stage is part of their method.*

Well, the last thing I would want to be is charismatic, a charismatic teacher. I almost think it's better to play away from any imputation of that, to downplay it, to be more self-effacing than you even want to be.

It *is* comfortable for me to do it this way, but after all I took it from Cassill. And so I think people who weren't me could learn to do it this way, too. Of course the method would change as they did it, but I think they could learn to be structure oriented and analytical and uncritical, and they could learn to reward the students, in a sense, for following their own desires.

I mean, in order for the students to get any benefit from following their own desires, they need to understand what a competent story is, what the mainstream, well-written story is. If you didn't believe as a teacher that there were any objective standards, then you couldn't teach the students the way I teach them. You wouldn't be able to raise them above a certain level of competence and then rely on them to bring their own ideas and personalities into the culture.

To me, it's all an exchange, you know. It's an exchange between the student and the teacher, an exchange between the writer and the culture. The culture exists apart from the writer and the writer hopes to bring his or her individuality to bear on the culture, but also to be penetrated by the culture, so that the product is a recognizable cultural product but also unique to that writer. I have to believe simultaneously in the individuality of the writer and the reality of the culture, that they both exist and that there can be an exchange between the two. And to believe that is basically to have a formalist, or structuralist, theory of literature. That's what I have and that's how I do it.

Q: *In one way you sound similar to William Stafford in his poetry workshops. He is also nonjudgmental. But at the same time, I've heard he's passive in class. You're not passive.*

No, I'm not. Because I also want them to have a theoretical basis: I want them to have *my* theoretical basis. They can have another one later, but I want them to have mine in my class. Lots of times students resist on all kinds of grounds. They don't want to do it my way. What I always say to them is, "Before you drop the class, remember, you will always do it your way. I just want you to do it my way for four months, just to see if you can learn something from my way."

Q: *Tell me about the rituals of evasion you mentioned earlier.*

They involve being willing to give up rituals that you've already developed as a writer. Let's say a student says to me, "Well, I write one draft and then I put it away for six months and then come back to it." That's a question of evasion of commitment. When I say commitment to the work, I mean the willingness to take up a set of characters or themes or actions that you really want to explore, to fiddle with it and change it and work on it consistently until you feel like you've explored it as well as you can. I think what a lot of students do, and maybe a lot of writers do, too, is develop rituals which don't actually allow them to spend time with or become engaged with their chosen themes or characters.

Sometimes you'll have students who, no matter how much a story demands big changes, will focus on sentences and fiddle with this one and that one obsessively. Or, I had a student whose evasion was never to take one piece to completion. He would write a first draft and take every little criticism as an occasion for totally blowing out the first draft and going on with something completely different. He'd come back with the story that he'd said was the second draft but it was just not recognizably related to the first draft in any way. That was a kind of evasion, too, because his talent was invention. Since he had no control, he had to be made to gain control, whereas a lot of other students who have no real invention have to be made to invent new themes and new characters, instead of fiddling with one or two sentences or touching up an ending.

Q: Doesn't that place a burden on you to see each writer individually: what they're good at, what methods of evasion they use?

But that's the thing about this revision method. I see sixteen drafts over sixteen weeks, so it becomes pretty clear what each student's repeated evasions are.

The other thing is, I never would go back to the normal workshop method, where I read a story once and then talk about it, because I now don't believe I ever really understand what the student is doing in the first draft. I mean, increasingly I feel it takes me to the third or even fourth draft to really get a handle on what's going on in the story, me and the class both, seeing the suggestions we've made that haven't worked out, earlier analyses of the story we've made that have been wrong.

And we haven't even talked about all these issues from the point of view of the class, as opposed to the point of view of the writer. It's a much more interesting class session because the students have a larger investment in each other's writing. They make suggestions; they say "do this, do that," and a week later they see the results. The students are more committed to one another's work over the course of the semester and that builds a sense of *esprit de corps*—or it can; it doesn't necessarily, but it can. And it becomes an ongoing dialogue about a given story. In a good class—and not every class is good—the other students come to have a real attachment to the writer's characters and the writer's themes and the writer's stories.

This leads to what I think is the biggest drawback to my method, and maybe a reason why sixteen weeks is enough. And that is, often by the end of the class we can't read each other's stories anymore, because we do have an investment in them. Usually at the end I say, "Now it's time for you to show these stories to fresh readers." As hard as we try to be critical for sixteen weeks, pretty soon familiarity begins to overwhelm our critical faculties.

Q: William Gass, who you mentioned earlier, said in a Paris Review *interview, "I resent spending a lot of time on lousy stuff. If somebody is reading a bad paper in a seminar, it is nevertheless on Plato, and it is Plato we can talk about.*

Whereas if somebody is writing about their hunting trip—well—where can one go for salvation or relief?" Does your use of an analytical method, from a personal point of view, ease your burden emotionally as a teacher?

Oh, sure. It used to be a trial. I don't feel that way anymore, even with undergraduate stories. I think it's because the pleasure of analysis is various enough that if you bring an analytical frame of mind to almost anything you can enjoy it. And I do find that since I am no longer looking at the stories as "good" or "bad," there is a kind of alienation I no longer feel.

I have a friend whose basis of teaching writing is really judgmental, and he can barely stand to read their stories. I don't want to criticize him, but I think it's all part and parcel; they resent him for not liking their stories, even if it's all unspoken, and he resents them for writing bad stories. The key is not thinking of them as "good" and "bad" but thinking of them as examples of some mode of analysis that can be used in an educating way.

Now, we can go back and say—or maybe Gass would say—that some stories are so bad to begin with you're grateful for anything by the time you're into the third draft. And in a less negative way maybe I would say that, too. If I were William Gass, I might say that, having been aware of how far from my intellectual standard students had been, I now recognize how suddenly and in some sense surprisingly they were approaching it.

But all that does is say they're educable, and that writing fiction is a learnable skill. I think there are plenty of people in the world who don't feel that way. In some sense, if they're writers, it's somehow self-aggrandizing to feel that way because then they're saying they never learned anything, they just burst full-blown onto the scene as fully developed writers. Well, that may be true if you've written one or two books and don't know where it came from, but if you've written eight or ten or twelve books and can look back and see the progress in your work, then you know that at some point you were *less* competent and now you are *more* competent.

Q: But the question remains whether people recognize being helped along the way, or whether they feel simply self-taught.

Sure, and maybe they *weren't* helped along the way, maybe they did put it together on their own.

Q: As you seemed to have done.

Well, I think I wasn't, let's say, wonderfully analyzed along the way.

Q: You never had that idealized mentor–protégé relationship, where someone took you under their wing and you suddenly blossomed? That wasn't part of your particular development?

No, but I did blossom, and in a semester—but in some sense I don't know why. It still took me a long time after that to write a publishable story. I also think there's a distinct break in my work between *Duplicate Keys,* which is my third novel, and *The Greenlanders,* which is my fourth. What I always imagined people saying in reviews of *The Greenlanders,* but nobody did, was, "Who would ever expect *this* from the person who wrote *Duplicate Keys*?" I mean, *Duplicate Keys* is a competent murder mystery. It's all about New York, and it's fun. But I underwent a significant aesthetic sea change between those two novels and I don't know why. It had nothing to do with teachers or anything like that.

Q: An added dimensional quality?

Well, I think it was about engaging ideas and emotions that were long-standing. I felt very apocalyptic as a child, because I grew up in the fifties with the atom bomb, and when I went to Iceland in 1977 and discovered that people had lived on Greenland for 450 years or more and then disappeared, that really appealed to a part of me that had been afraid of that precise thing. And there was another part of me that was really taken with the tone that was part of Icelandic literature in particular and Scandinavian literature in general. There's a kind of dryness and recognition of the workings of evil and expectation of the worst in some ways, and a very interesting and subtle understatement and irony, which has always appealed to me. So there were a lot of things that came together when I wrote *The Greenlanders*.

Q: Is there an ordered, inevitable world in that literature? I don't know it very well.

I think so. What happened in Greenland was predicted by Norse myth, which predicts the end of the human world. It's the only mythical system that has an unhappy ending. No one comes to redeem the human world. It's predicted that the gods will finally come to a great battle with the forces of evil, but the gods will fall short; the forces of evil will overwhelm the world. Well, the only happy ending is that all the warriors will get to have one last fling before the final darkness.

I have never heard of another mythical system that predicts the end of the world, and in Greenland it happened, the world ended by the degree to which the people overextended themselves by living there. The history of Greenland is about how much margin you have for survival. And in some sense the early history of Scandinavia is about that, too, but then the modern world came along and expanded their margin just in time.

What I'm saying is, I found something that appealed to me on some kind of deep aesthetic level in Icelandic and Scandinavian literature. I came to know I'm very susceptible to it. So, as I look back on my career, I see that I was educable. When I look at my students, I see that they are educable, too: When, over three drafts, they progress from farther from the ideal to nearer the ideal, that's when I put my judgment of their work in abeyance; I don't feel I have a right to judge.

Even the least competent writer is unique. They are, just by definition, themselves. But they should come up with something that is not only unique but also interesting. The problem is, who's interesting when they're nineteen; who's even interesting when they're twenty-five, the age of most graduate writing students? And so I think any educator who disdains his students because they're not interesting or good is not an educator, not really interested in students; he's interested in other aspects of university life. I see teaching in some sense as a *pro bono* thing. You give back what you received.

Q: It's a pleasure, in that sense?

And the pleasure's enhanced all the time. I had a student who didn't have a great sense of grammar, the stories were very trite, typical undergraduate stories. But he finally decided to work through his revisions of a story, and it was very easy to see as the story progressed that he did bring his own original vision to it. It still wasn't a publishable story, but it was enjoyable to us. Once again, it's a lesson to me that you can't count out any, any, *any* student.

Q: A number of teachers have said that the good students will write well without help anyway.

Well, I would agree, but they might not get as far as quickly. If you can give them the right teaching, maybe you can help them not reinvent the wheel. I don't know what you can give the good ones, but the ones who aren't so good, who don't have native talent, those can get published if they have a great deal of drive and something to say.

And then there's this other whole group who will never get published but who will conform to other kinds of educational goals. They'll get a new appreciation and a new interest in writing and reading. So in some sense you're teaching the writers who will come after you, and in another sense you're teaching your readers. Not every student of philosophy is going to be a philosopher, but if you're a philosophy teacher you hope they'll approach their life with a moment's pause once in a while because you've taught them ethics. Well, if you're a teacher of writing you hope they'll approach their writing life with pause before they go buy another Danielle Steel novel. Maybe, just maybe, they'll buy something else because you taught them something.

DISCUSSION QUESTIONS

1. Smiley's workshop method features small groups and constant revision. What are her reasons for emphasizing these elements? Have your workshop experiences been anything like what she describes? If not, do you think small groups and required revisions would be helpful to your development as a writer? Why?

2. Smiley claims that most first drafts exist in a state of "faux," or false, completion. Do you accept this judgment about your own work? About the work of peers that you have read in workshops? How does your sense of whether your story is complete affect your experience in the workshop?

3. One controversial element of Smiley's method is the banning of explicit praise of students' writing; she states that teachers "owe it to them not to praise them." Why does she assert this belief so strongly? Do you agree with her that "to be taken seriously is to be analyzed and delved into"? If you agree in principle, do you still feel that there is a legitimate place for praise in the workshop?

4. Smiley offers an analytical method for discussing stories, focusing attention on the elements of action, character, theme, setting, and language. What does she mean when she says that each element has a particular payoff for the reader? How can this analytical approach to how a story works in terms of these elements help the writer revise?

5. Smiley discusses "rituals of evasion" that writers develop to avoid confronting the work of creating fiction. What are your rituals of evasion? Do you feel that your rituals serve an important purpose? How?

6. Smiley tells her students that they can always return to their accustomed writing strategies after they complete her course, but that she expects them to "try it her way" for at least one semester. Does this seem to be a reasonable request to you, or should creative writing teachers steer clear of their students' methods and focus instead on the work itself?

RAYMOND CARVER

Creative Writing 101

Raymond Carver (1938–1988) burst onto the scene with his collection Will You Please Be Quiet, Please? *(1976), and the American short story was never quite the same. He continued to create a new minimalist style in* What We Talk About When We Talk About Love *(1981), and he also published ten books of poetry. In the collection* Cathedral, *he found a more expansive voice, but a generation of short story writers tried to re-create the stripped-down simplicity and emotional power of the early stories. In essays and interviews, Carver explained the principles of his style, revealing a writer making his craft serve the ends of his meaning.*

A long time ago—it was the summer of 1958—my wife and I and our two baby children moved from Yakima, Washington, to a little town outside of Chico, California. There we found an old house and paid twenty-five dollars a month rent. In order to finance this move, I'd had to borrow a hundred and twenty-five dollars from a druggist I'd delivered prescriptions for, a man named Bill Barton.

This is by way of saying that in those days my wife and I were stone broke. We had to eke out a living, but the plan was that I would take classes at what was then called Chico State College. But for as far back as I can remember, long before we moved to California in search of a different life and our slice of the American pie, I'd wanted to be a writer. I wanted to write, and I wanted to write anything— fiction, of course, but also poetry, plays, scripts, articles for *Sports Afield, True, Argosy,* and *Rogue* (some of the magazines I was then reading), pieces for the local newspaper—anything that involved putting words together to make something coherent and of interest to someone besides myself. But at the time of our move, I felt in my bones I had to get some education in order to go along with being a writer. I put a very high premium on education then—much higher in those days than now, I'm sure, but that's because I'm older and have an education. Understand that nobody in my family had ever gone to college or for that matter had got beyond the mandatory eighth grade in high school. I didn't know *anything,* but I knew I didn't know anything.

So along with this desire to get an education, I had this very strong desire to write; it was a desire so strong that, with the encouragement I was given in college, and the insight acquired, I kept on writing long after "good sense" and the "cold facts"—the "realities" of my life told me, time and again, that I ought to quit, stop the dreaming, quietly go ahead and do something else.

That fall at Chico State I enrolled in classes that most freshman students have to take, but I enrolled as well for something called Creative Writing 101. This course was going to be taught by a new faculty member named John Gardner, who was already surrounded by a bit of mystery and romance. It was said that he'd taught previously at Oberlin College but had left there for some reason that wasn't made clear. One student said Gardner had been fired—students, like everyone else, thrive on rumor and intrigue—and another student said Gardner had simply quit after some kind of flap. Someone else said his teaching load at Oberlin, four or five classes of freshman English each semester, had been too heavy and that he couldn't find time to write. For it was said that Gardner was a real, that is to say a practicing, writer—someone who had written novels and short stories. In any case, he was going to teach CW 101 at Chico State, and I signed up.

I was excited about taking a course from a real writer. I'd never laid eyes on a writer before, and I was in awe. But where were these novels and short stories, I wanted to know. Well, nothing had been published yet. It was said that he couldn't get his work published and that he carried it around with him in boxes. (After I became his student, I was to see those boxes of manuscript. Gardner had become aware of my difficulty in finding a place to work. He knew I had a young family and cramped quarters at home. He offered me the key to his office. I see that gift now as a turning point. It was a gift not made casually, and I took it, I think, as a kind of mandate—for that's what it was. I spent part of every Saturday and Sunday in his office, which is where he kept the boxes of manuscript. The boxes were stacked up on the floor beside the desk. *Nickel Mountain,* greasepencilled on one of the boxes, is the only title I recall. But it was in his office, within sight of his unpublished books, that I undertook my first serious attempts at writing.) . . .

For short story writers in his class, the requirement was one story, ten to fifteen pages in length. For people who wanted to write a novel—I think there must have been one or two of these souls—a chapter of around twenty pages, along with an outline of the rest. The kicker was that this one short story, or the chapter of the novel, might have to be revised ten times in the course of the semester for Gardner to be satisfied with it. It was a basic tenet of his that a writer found what he wanted to say in the ongoing process of seeing what he'd said. And this seeing, or seeing more clearly, came about through revision. He *believed* in revision, endless revision; it was something very close to his heart and something he felt was vital for writers, at whatever stage of their development. And he never seemed to lose patience rereading a student story, even though he might have seen it in five previous incarnations.

I think his idea of a short story in 1958 was still pretty much his idea of a short story in 1982; it was something that had a recognizable beginning, middle, and an end to it. Once in a while he'd go to the blackboard and draw a diagram to illustrate a point he wanted to make about rising or falling emotion in a story —peaks, valleys, plateaus, resolution, *denouement,* things like that. Try as I might, I couldn't muster a great deal of interest or really understand this side of things, the stuff he put on the blackboard. But what I did understand was the way he would comment on a student story that was undergoing class discussion. Gardner might wonder aloud about the author's reasons for writing a story about a crippled person, say, and leaving out the fact of the character's crippledness until the very end of the story. "So you think it's a good idea not to let the reader know this man is crippled until the last sentence?" His tone of voice conveyed his disapproval, and it didn't take more than an instant for everyone in class, including the author of the story, to see that it wasn't a good strategy to use. Any strategy that kept important and necessary information away from the reader in the hope of overcoming him by surprise at the end of the story was cheating.

In class he was always referring to writers whose names I was not familiar with. Or if I knew their names, I'd never read the work. . . . He talked about James Joyce and Flaubert and Isak Dinesen as if they lived just down the road, in Yuba City. He said, "I'm here to tell you who to read as well as teach you how to write." I'd leave class in a daze and make straight for the library to find books by these writers he was talking about.

Hemingway and Faulkner were the reigning authors in those days. But altogether I'd probably read at the most two or three books by these fellows. Anyway, they were so well-known and so much talked about, they couldn't be all that good, could they? I remember Gardner telling me, "Read all the Faulkner you can get your hands on, and then read all of Hemingway to clean the Faulkner out of your system."

He introduced us to the "little" or literary periodicals by bringing a box of these magazines to class one day and passing them around so that we could acquaint ourselves with their names, see what they looked like and what they felt like to hold in the hand. He told us that this was where most of the best fiction in the country and just about all of the poetry was appearing. Fiction, poetry, literary essays, book reviews of recent books, criticism of *living* authors *by* living authors. I felt wild with discovery in those days.

For the seven or eight of us who were in his class, he ordered heavy black binders and told us we should keep our written work in these. He kept his own work in such binders, he said, and of course that settled it for us. We carried our stories in those binders and felt we were special, exclusive, singled out from others. And so we were.

I don't know how Gardner might have been with other students when it came time to have conferences with them about their work. I suspect he gave everybody a good amount of attention. But it was and still is my impression that during that period he took my stories more seriously, read them closer and more carefully, than I had any right to expect. I was completely unprepared for the kind of criticism I received from him. Before our conference he would have marked up my story, crossing out unacceptable sentences, phrases, individual words, even some of the punctuation; and he gave me to understand that these deletions were not negotiable. In other cases he would bracket sentences, phrases, or individual words, and these were items we'd talk about, these cases were negotiable. And he wouldn't hesitate to add something to what I'd written—a word here and there, or else a few words, maybe a sentence that would make clear what I was trying to say. We'd discuss commas in my story as if nothing else in the world mattered more at that moment—and, indeed, it did not. He was always looking to find something to praise. When there was a sentence, a line of dialogue, or a narrative passage that he liked, something that he thought "worked" and moved the story along in some pleasant or unexpected way, he'd write "Nice" in the margin, or else "Good!" And seeing these comments, my heart would lift.

It was close, line-by-line criticism he was giving me, and the reasons behind the criticism, why something ought to be this way instead of that; and it was invaluable to me in my development as a writer. After this kind of detailed talk about the text, we'd talk about the larger concerns of the story, the "problem" it was trying to throw light on, the conflict it was trying to grapple with, and how the story might or might not fit into the grand scheme of story writing. It was his conviction that if the words in the story were blurred because of the author's insensitivity, carelessness, or sentimentality, then the story suffered from a tremendous handicap. But there was something even worse and something that must be avoided at all costs: if the words and the sentiments were dishonest, the author was faking it, writing about things he didn't care about or believe in, then nobody could ever care anything about it.

A writer's values and craft. This is what the man taught and what he stood for, and this is what I've kept by me in the years since that brief but all-important time.

DISCUSSION QUESTIONS

1. Carver writes of his excitement about taking a creative writing class from a "real writer." What is the source of this excitement? What ideas about "real writers" do you bring to class with you?
2. Carver recalls with gratitude Gardner's offer to open his office space to the aspiring young writer. How is this offer a part of Gardner's teaching method?
3. Gardner's emphasis on revision goes beyond Smiley's, as he requires his students to stay with one piece of writing throughout the course. What do you think of this intense attention to one piece of writing, which will be revised as many as ten times? Why would Gardner choose this approach?
4. In another essay, "On Writing," Carver writes of his disdain for "tricks" in fiction. How does this relate to the anecdote in the essay in which Gardner warns students against keeping "important and necessary information away from the reader in the hope of overcoming him with surprise at the end"?
5. Carver describes Gardner's conference method, which included line-by-line criticism and editing, bits of praise, and discussion of the larger concerns of

the work. Have you had this kind of conference about your work? If so, was it useful? If not, which parts of the method are most appealing to you?

BONNIE FRIEDMAN

The Paraffin Density of Wax Wings

Bonnie Friedman (b. 1958) received her M.F.A. from the University of Iowa's Writers' Workshop and has taught at Dartmouth College, Northeastern University, and the University of Iowa. Her popular memoir and guide Writing Past Dark *(1994) has been praised for its beauty, its generosity, and its understanding heart. In it, she says, "Successful writers are not the ones who write the best sentences. They are the ones who keep writing. They are the ones who discover what is most important and strangest and most pleasurable in themselves, and keep believing in the value of their work, despite the difficulties."*

When I went to writing school, I craved rules. I craved a mentor, and the revelation of secrets, and the permission to write scads, and most of all I craved the confirmation that I could write. In other words, I was like practically everyone else.

What a mystique writing programs have! A sense of promise emanates from their doors, wafts up from the embossed paper bearing their letterheads. I felt that being accepted to one, and especially to that bizarrely exotic one nestled in the middle of America, Iowa, was like being chosen for an initiation into mysteries. After all, what could be more mysterious than learning how to write? A friend of mine had gone there. I received a postcard back from her crammed with tiny type. It pictured a man in a straw hat driving a mule-led wagon, and on the back the remark that her writing had undergone a quantum leap in excellence. And this was just October.

In February I visited her and gazed at the bowl of warty gourds on her vast farmhouse table and the typewriter covered with a deep blue silk scarf, like a tarot deck. At 5 A.M. I walked the boarded sidewalks of Oxford (population 660), the town outside Iowa City where my friend lived, inhaling the odor of manure as if it were perfume, too thrilled to sleep, standing beneath a sky that was absolutely the biggest thing I had ever seen, and perhaps the clearest, while a truck that was also of colossal proportions bore down on me, I noticed, at an astonishing pace. It emitted a roguish honk that banged back from the heavens and shimmered away over the fields, and that left me, after the thing itself vanished in a tide of dust, feeling inordinately calm, as if nothing would ever be able to surprise me again. Behind me the town of Oxford looked like the set of a Western: five or six storefronts facing a single street. I walked onto the set and slipped into the door that was ajar.

My friend was frying eggs. A scratchy old Dylan tape played on her cassette player, hard-bitten lyrics with a fiddle reeling wildly in the background. I sat at the table and gazed at my friend's bookcase. It was filled with slender volumes of contemporary poetry. She hardly used to own any poetry, being a believer in libraries. Now she possessed all this. While I helped cook, my eyes kept returning to those slim books, and, because I could hardly understand even their names, they appeared to me as rare and foreign as slivers of gold shaved from distant domes.

Men came over, and a woman or two. We had brunch. We drank. My friend was dating a soft-spoken ginger-haired second-year who was a "TWIF," a Teaching-Writing Fellow, the rank given those few whom Iowa deemed its absolute best. This man had a roommate, Jackson, a poet who had already published. He was the first Southerner I'd ever met. He said "po-eem," and "woe-m'n," and we argued about possessiveness, I maintaining the absurd position that a poet should be able to steal any line from another poet if it resulted in better art. I wondered what his parents said about his work. He said he had stopped showing them his writing years ago. He asked about my bus trip from Chicago. I told about the green windows, the highway set between vast fields, the gargantuan McDonald's, the woman in a pink felt hat who told the driver that she was going to visit her two sisters in Dubuque, and how the driver waited in his seat while the three old women linked arms, stepped off the curb, and crossed the road before him. "Three sisters," he announced. Jackson gazed at me, and I thought, This is what it feels like to be a storyteller. This is it, at last.

I attended a poetry workshop and then a fiction workshop. The poetry workshop was actually at the poet's house. At one point the poet stuck out his arms and said, "Okay. I'm the tree. The birds are here, and here," gesturing to one arm and then to the top of his head as he tried to show us how one of the poems on the worksheet quite literally did not make sense. To my friend, who had written an exquisite poem set in medieval China and reminiscent of Ezra Pound, he said little. He merely wondered why she chose to write poems set in medieval China these days. I was surprised. What did he want? My friend shrugged, but seemed to understand.

The fiction workshop was less focused. People discussed a few of the sentences here and there in the story. No one seemed that interested. The people who did speak spoke in a very slow dry way, their throats raspy, their remarks trailing off as if they had become too depressed to finish. When the break came I walked out a door at the end of the hallway. It gave onto a gravel roof. The sky was brittle blue. Inhaling was like drinking cold water fast. I wished it would numb the aroused way I'd felt ever since I arrived in Iowa. I gulped and gulped, and then skipped the second half of the workshop to get a walk-in haircut.

The haircut cost six dollars. I watched the beautician's hands fly swiftly all over my head and hoped I would end up looking marvelous, but no. I looked like myself with less hair. Ever since I had come to Iowa I was writing on every scrap of paper I could find. I had drunk so much wine I awoke still drunk, although perhaps it was just excitement that made me feel that way. Am I drunk, I wondered, or is it Iowa? It's Iowa, it's Iowa, I thought. And applied to the school right away.

I arrived with a vast manuscript I had worked on for two and a half years. Parts of it were written longhand, parts of it were typed, parts of it still existed only in my head. It had no name. It had no end. I had been writing it the entire time I lived in Boston, in a room off an endless corridor. Doors swung open and closed. The smell of nail polish, burnt coffee, Ban deodorant spray, Chanel drifted in. Everyone had her own schedule. Not even the phone ringing bothered me. When I had first come to Boston I bought a massive gray industrial metal desk and wedged it by the window. This desk looked indestructible. You could stab this desk with scissors and knives, or kick it with a steel-toed boot, and it would make no difference. I sat down and wrote on my novel at this desk every morning. Sometimes I glanced up and the sapling outside was in leaf. Sometimes I glanced up and it was bare. The alarm clock burst into a frantic buzzing at noon, and I set down my pen and stepped into my skirt and heels and departed for the Mutual of New York Life Insurance Company. The building had sealed windows that tinted the world outside a brownish gold, and hidden vents that hummed with the perpetual exhalation of processed air. As I stood filing insurance policies into a green metal cabinet, rubbing one itchy stockinged leg with the toe of my shoe, I wondered what my life meant. Then I thought of that day's pages, the bit of episode I'd dreamed forward.

At Iowa I crammed as much of the manuscript as I could into a spring-back binder, and gave it to my teacher. I thought, Whatever she says about that book I will absolutely believe. I wanted to be absolved of having to believe in my own book by myself any longer. I felt light and hopeful while I waited for her response. Everything I did—chopping broccoli, reading Willa Cather, listening to a story about Bible camp written by a new friend—partook of this same feeling of detached suspense, as if my job right now was to keep my attitude benign.

"Come in," came my teacher's basso voice when I knocked on her door after two weeks. Hers was a blank door, with just her name printed on an index card in a firm, neat hand. She sat facing the cinderblock wall. There was my manuscript, on the desk. She slid it back to me, and told me three things.

"Please turn to page 127," she said.

The word "I" had been circled every time it appeared on the page.

"How many circles are there?" she asked.

I counted fourteen. The page nearly jumped and jostled with circled I's. But I was not sure what to make of this. Every time I'd written "I," I meant "I." Was it wrong to mean "I" so much? Or did the problem have to do with the word itself? Ought I find a synonym—*is* there a synonym?—for "I"? But no, I suspected the problem ran deeper.

The second thing she said to me was to please look at the comments on the back of page 32. These were comments my earlier teacher had written. He was a conscientious instructor for an extension school class that met in a suburban library. "Those are good comments," she said. "I suggest you do exactly what they say." I was surprised. If that teacher was as good as Iowa, why had I come?

The third and last thing she told me was, "Every writer has a book they do not publish. This," she said, "will be yours." She glanced at her watch, and stood.

"Thank you very much. Thank you," I said, stumbling for the door. Five minutes had elapsed.

Once upon a time I was sure I knew exactly what this story meant. She was a bad teacher. She was mean. Even if the manuscript were terrible, certainly there was more she could teach about a piece that was hundreds and hundreds of pages long. Why, two years later another writer on the faculty spoke about the book encouragingly for over an hour, although while she was speaking I realized that the novel was for me by then effectually dead.

Perhaps this first teacher, dismayed, thought, Why try to convey the whole workshop in one meeting? Then too, there was the business of her irritation, for I felt her irritation as soon as I walked in. At the time I took it for granted, but now I wonder, Whatever was it doing with us in that room? Was it the irritation of feeling your ears have been chewed off, of encountering a narrator who just won't go away, of having to sit across from a student with shining eyes and a terribly hopeful manner and a big book that at the moment seems to personify a bloated ego or some voracious personal demand, and having to say the very things she will most hate to hear? And what had all that to do with me?

I wept, and resolved immediately to begin writing short stories. Everyone here wrote short stories. Maybe stories would teach me what I needed to learn. I threw my novel into a corner, where it lay for a long time like a shameful body part that another person could not bear to regard for more than five minutes.

I had learned my first grand lesson of writing school. It had to do with power, and belief.

What we learn most deeply is usually what we do not know we are learning at all. Years later, if we are lucky, we recognize the shape of what we have learned, its true anatomy. Writing school was like that. I always thought I was learning something multiple and complicated, when I was learning something singular and simple. I attended so avidly to particular lessons—when to use the simple past tense, when to suppress the narrator's emotion—that I did not notice the grand lessons that I took in unconsciously.

I wrote stories. Almost everyone I knew wrote stories. The one woman I knew who was writing a novel soon shaped each chapter into a short story. She came over, clattering through the streets of Iowa City in high heels and a pillbox hat, and toting Parliament's and a red plastic pocketbook and flurries of pages scrawled in her wire-bound notebook. She read aloud in a voice withered by smoke and sleeplessness and by pure will. (I once asked her if she would care to swim with me. "Swim?" she asked, looking at me askance. "Honey, these lungs are shot." She was twenty-five.) Nevertheless, she was the best reader I had ever heard. She gave each word perfect, weighted dignity, so that you yearned to hear her read a soup can, to know if even that most banal list could withstand the measured drama of her voice. She was a cross between Joan Didion, Mae West, and Eloise of the Plaza Hotel—fragile and urbane, a child in a scoop-neck dress—and did not weather the Workshop well. Criticisms assailed her like a cloud of gnats.

She scratched and clawed blindly, explaining and defending and firing excuses before the critique was half out of the other student's mouth (this was outside of workshop; in workshop she sat blinking, her crossed leg bobbing like wild), so that you sensed both how utterly she refused to let her work be imperfect, and how despairing she was of ever, ever getting her work right.

She had come to Iowa, she once confided, in possession of a letter from Scribner's. Did she have a novel? the letter asked. If so, please send it. She had published a short story in the magazine *Ploughshares,* a ribald, rowdy story featuring some college students who were friends. The Scribner's letter stemmed from that, but its glow diminished as the semesters wore on, so that, by graduation, although she finished the novel and typed it up in thesis format (*Autumn Song,* I think the elegiac title ended up being), it was with a sense of something disappearing down a well. Her temperament was ill-suited to critiques. Something eroded in her as the months passed so that eventually her play-anemia approached the waxy fatigue of real anemia, and the dark glasses she now wore didn't seem a chic accessory. Her father had not wanted children, she told me on one of the rare afternoons we spent together that second year. He was jealous of the attention they took from his wife. "Is that so?" I said, sensing she'd given me one of the skeleton keys to her life. But it was late afternoon, and I was tired of drinking her coffee. I left before she told me much else.

Yet it was at Iowa that I became a writer. Before I went there, I wrote, but blindly. I had no idea what I put on the page. Words came in a flood. I gushed, and never looked back. I could write a chapter a day. I didn't see what was the big deal. Of course, sometimes I stopped to groom a sentence, brushing it up so it plumped and shone with many attractive words. But I rewrote nothing. Why should I? Hadn't I said what I meant?

This was the problem with the novel. It was like a file cabinet that is all one file. It got going and it just went, over hill and dale, around and around the block, like an electric toy with a tireless battery, never quickening or slowing or ever acknowledging it had seen these sights before. I wrote the same thing over and over because I didn't trust it had communicated. And I thought, The more words the better. People read because they enjoy reading. Wouldn't they enjoy reading more words more?

Writing school worked as a marvelous brake. It slowed me powerfully. It allowed me to see exactly what I was doing. People had, in fact, been advising more slowness for years. In a Spanish course at college, the teacher beckoned after class. "We are all intelligent here," he said. "When you speak, pay attention to your grammar." My face blazed. It was true: when I spoke I cared only about getting my idea across. I was still at the age when one thinks the idea itself—freshly invented—is what is extraordinary, and that it must be told fast before it vanishes. Spanish became just a bothersome obstacle, like a stile to a galloping horse.

Writing school turned out to be all about grammar, the grammar of fiction, the syntax and inflection of rhetorical choices. "Strategy" was talked about a lot here, as if a story consisted of troops on various maneuvers. How did you deploy your forces? How did you manage your subject's inherent strengths, and compensate for its weaknesses? No longer was your story something bodied forth in a sort of rapture; no longer was it something as natural and mysterious to you as your own foot. Now it was revealed to be a series of specific choices: why this phrase here, why that explanation there, was this ending "earned" or was it a bit of fancy eloquence glued on, like a false facade on a house? You couldn't answer. The story itself had to provide all its reasons. What it couldn't justify remained troublesome, dubious, a bit of "indulgence," even—so that you realized there was a morality to telling, and that everything in a story must be in the service of its final shape.

It started to become clear how strong writing got strong. Your eyes counted more than you'd known, and your hands and tongue and the shivery sensitivity of your skin. Your vocabulary counted less. All those years of collecting words, assuming by themselves they'd get you out of any jam! Words had been my abracadabra, and I'd hoarded them in little bound books, prying them from novels and reviews like arrowheads, amulets, charms whose use I would live to discover. Rows of words stacked one below the other and descending through the rococo flourishes of their third and fourth gradations of meaning—all because I knew that one day I would be baffled, stopped before a locked door, and at that moment the "shazam" might occur to me from out of the archives. Words were tricks, and I meant to know lots of them. At Iowa I saw that all those words led me no closer to real writing. They reeked of the library and secondhand life, and of the shiny red apple placed on the teacher's desk, and which holds on its laminated skin a tiny blue window in which one sees oneself looming, looming, unable to get out of one's own way.

Phi Beta Kappa counted for nothing here. Theoretical methodology counted for nothing, too. One of the finest writers was a shaggy man without college who said he slept in a tent pitched in his living room for fear that a turtle would crawl on his head. He spoke his stories into a tape and a secretary he paid typed them, ineptly. Broken glass, a yellow dress, a swing rushing up to the sky carrying a boy who at last leaps, a woman in a doorway bleeding from the mouth—who cared what this writer's philosophy was? Days later you noticed you still had his story in your head. He had what lots of us work to learn: a shucked vividness, as if he'd peeled the world's things and seen their pulp.

Sometimes I felt my earlier education had ruined me. I'd shunned the world to get at books. Now I saw books milked the world; they thrived on it. The world was pressed between their pages, like the leaves my sister saved in the encyclopedia. Two decades later I looked up "Abyssinia" and a leaf fluttered out: mustard-green, crushed thin as foil but brittle, its veins risen to the surface like an old person's. What mad thought possessed a girl to stuff a tree into the World Book, what longed-for hope? Was it for this? This startling autumn? This memento mori from Girl Scouts? At writing school I found books were lined with the world; it was pressed into them, crammed into them until the bindings bulged. Writing set me back in the world the way reading never had.

Although what mattered was not the world, but how you used it. How convincing was this dialogue? Why was this scene prolonged by three relatively plodding sentences? The elderly mother in the story—wasn't it going too far to give her liver spots, a trembling neck, *and* teary eyes? One should be cut: the neck or the eyes, preferably. "Sincerity is technique," a friend quoted Auden, and now I understood: technique was how to achieve sincerity. Did you care deeply, deeply about your subject? That was nothing. What mattered was how your story read.

"What rich material you have!" came to seem the most condescending remark possible. The world was strewn with material. Like dust, it was everywhere. If your material bunched uncomfortably, if you stitched and snipped it with ease, if it crimped like haute couture or draped like the most natural garment on earth—that was its worth. The same material could make melodrama, or strike with hushed truth. The same material could generate scenes so vaporous, so fogged with verbiage, that the reader emerged merely irritated, as if he'd been blindfolded for an hour while someone whispered excitedly in his ear. Or it could set you quite simply in the middle of events, so that when a woman entered you saw her, and when the narrator drank old coffee it was old coffee, sludgy and bitter, in your own mouth. What was sex, even? Written one way, it made you wish to shut the door and daydream; written another, you wanted never to see a naked body again. Even God was only as strong as you wrote Him. Here truly was the promised magic. It was taught here, after all—and it was almost all that *was* taught here. Its name was technique.

One much-envied woman wrote sentences like mute faces. They meant several things at once or else they meant nothing at all. They had a killing grace. Reading them, you never thought of a person writing them; they seemed to have dropped straight from heaven or rolled off an assembly line. This writing was all the rage. Emotion existed in these stories like a distant moon, a pathology, a suicide the narrator had recovered from. They were complicated pieces, with an iron beauty that locked itself into your memory.

As did their author. She sat amid a torrent of red hair, circling around and around with her Bic pen in her notebook while her work was discussed, and chewed Bazooka bubblegum. The candy smell drifted through the room: cherry, grape. One day as I stood in a long line outside the bursar's office I heard this woman shout, "I don't have time for this!" It was an altercation with a dean. She held a slip of green paper in her hand—it needed signatures—and rattled it, incensed. Then she swept past. I thought, Why is her time so important? What does she mean to do with it? My own line inched forward. If my time were more important to me, I wondered, would I write stories like hers? For her soul was in them, apparently, even if it was hidden. She cared passionately about the hours of her life, and so she must care about her pages, even if the blaze in her stories was invisible.

Another man wrote stories that always led to white space. There would be some paragraphs and then a poignant rim of white space gaping like an antiseptic wound, as if speech could only go so far before mute agony intervened. This man ended up working for Hallmark. Occasionally, buying an anniversary card or a birthday card, I wonder about him.

Here, in both writers, was a style dedicated to technique. It was technique as triage, as refuge, as glittering fortress, and yet in its commitment to form this way of writing taught tremendously.

Stories are machines inhabited by a god. School pointed out the cranks and spindles. It showed how to get the most leverage possible by grasping the jack-handle at the farthest point. It taught me to recognize grit in the system, the tiny distracting particles that can draw the whole thing to an abrupt halt—a wobbly point-of-view, a pompous phrase. The method was mostly cautionary; it was easier to see where a story was broken than where it ran smooth.

The god part, though, remained unmentioned. That was the writer's own business. How you wrote, where your ideas came from—everything that preceded class scrutiny of a piece went unacknowledged. This was writing school but we did not talk about writing. We talked about what had got written. We came to find it faintly embarrassing to hear how these words came to be on this page. The writer's vision, the vocabularies we wished to dwell in, the hints of dreams and memories that haunted the edge of our work—verboten, not discussed. We had come here because as children we'd clasped books to ourselves, running down the streets laughing after reading a particularly marvelous sentence in a particularly exciting scene, thinking, This is the best book in the world!—before, gasping, we stopped on a street corner to read on. We had come here because one day, bent over a sheet of yellow, green-lined paper, we smiled, having just then rendezvoused with ourselves like a Doppler effect of two waves surging into a big wave twice their height. How to have this pleasure more? How to turn on the switch in ourselves that made writing possible? How to transform the texture of life—the heat shimmer of a highway in which everything attenuates and billows skyward, every solid thing a form of smoke—into the lucid corridors and conclusions of a short story? How to write despite fear? Questions we did not ask.

On Thursday or Friday afternoon, and sometimes as late as Monday morning, a stack of copies of a stapled, Xeroxed story appeared on the workshop shelf. The Xerox machine was tired, and tended to erode the type, so that the stories we read were printed in wavery, broken letters in a field of dust, as if the words were receding from us. We read with pen in hand. We discussed the overall impact of the story, whether the story "worked"—the way a magic trick may or may not "work"—and all the various moves of the author along the way. Every choice was questioned. Our talk was technical, respectful. Like scientists, we did not ask how the creator functioned, but what he or she had done.

I, for one, managed to do only less and less. I wrote some sentences, studied them, and wrote them over again. Meaning drained from them while I worked. When all the meaning was gone I set my writing aside for the day and took a walk. My brain felt like a wad of chewed gum. I gaped at the simple reality of a tree. The point of all this work was not to banish meaning. Quite the contrary: it was to find the optimal arrangement of words to convey the most meaning possible. I wanted to arrive at words just saturated with meaning, but it was a crooked path that led there. The goal was a sort of perfection, and I could see that the only hope of arriving at this perfection was by way of revision. Revision, I realized, allowed an ordinary intelligence to achieve greatness. Through revision even a sloppy writer could achieve the tailored figure of elegance. And yet, since there was a sort of salvation to be found in revision, it was, ironically, easy to get lost in it, too.

It could, in fact, take on a compulsive energy of its own. The first time I took a bath as a young teenager (we had moved from an apartment where I took only showers), I stepped out of the tub and rubbed a towel against myself. Suddenly I saw little gray nubbly growths all over me—rolls of dirt! They were the size of pinky nails, rolled up like minuscule cigars. The more I rubbed to get rid of the dirt, the more dirt appeared. It seemed to generate from within me, like parthenogenesis. Frightened, I called my mother, who told me, "Honey, that's *skin*."

Rubbing away at a story, every word can look like dirt. You brush eraser dust from the page and stare again at an incident that appears less and less familiar, wound through as it is with blank white, becoming, you hope, more and more perfect, more and more timeless, as if before your eyes condensing into an artifact —and yet somehow leaving you and all you meant behind. Is this what you came for? Is this why you write? As if beauty were death. As if art holds life in contempt. As if when you yourself have been utterly expunged, it will be complete.

A whole season might net just one story, a story carved through so many drafts it dwindled limply, scarcely alive, its heart grafted to its lungs, its arms and legs missing entirely. One regarded such botches amazed. Love had engendered it. Conception had come all in a wild heat. Yet here the thing lay after weeks of surgical concern, barely recognizable. One suspected the worst: nothing is ever finished. Meanwhile, the page itself had gotten bigger and whiter, and more forbidding. Sitting down to write, one regarded it with alarm. It glared like a search-beam. More and more courage was required to face it.

Yet where was this courage to come from? The fiction program was better at rapping knuckles than encouraging the wild leap. If you chose to jump off a rooftop with wax wings or creep along the ground in baby steps crying, "Mother, may I?" no one would stop you. No opinions were offered on this. Discussion was restricted to the technical position of your feet on the ledge, and the paraffin density of the wings, and the exact velocity of the baby steps. If you crashed on the sidewalk, though, a circle of colleagues might appear to analyze the mess. So it was easier to creep; there was less distance to fall.

"Courage" is from the word for heart. School had little to do with heart, and everything to do with technical perfection.

How we learn is what we learn.

While the private act of the writing program may or may not be writing, the defining weekly ritual is public scrutiny. It doesn't matter whether it's your work that's up for discussion or someone else's: what is heard is criticism, what is said is criticism, until, for many, as they sit before their typewriters at home, what occupies their minds is criticism, criticism devouring their latent words.

Eudora Welty says, "I believe if I stopped to wonder what So-and-so would think, or what I'd feel like if this were read by a stranger, I would be paralyzed." And Joan Didion says, "When I first started to write pieces, I would try to write to a reader other than myself. I always failed. I would freeze up."

Yet at the Workshop we were trained to wonder all about So-and-so; we learned to write always to a reader other than ourselves. Once a week for two years we sat across a table with a Xeroxed story between us. It was tempting to write stories like a suit of armor: hollow, but impervious to attack.

And yet many of us became writers at Iowa. It was here that we noticed the nature of words.

It is possible to write for many years and never notice. It is possible to write so much one's pages swarm, and still not detect how an individual word behaves. Writing school changes that. It taps its pencil against each particular word and says, "See this." Focusing on particular words can feel niggling. It can feel pedantic, even willfully obtuse—as if the viewer insisted on standing too close to a pointillist canvas and then complained that all she saw was dots. Where are the promised sunbathers, the river, the boats? Well, if you'll just take a step back, if you'll just squint. *Squint? Step back?* The audience stares, granite-faced. No, the text must convey itself from here. When I read, I read one word at a time.

So, faced with a table of granite readers, you look at your words again. The same scene might be described in another way entirely. You might ax all the adjectives, like chipping barnacles from the sleek prow of a ship. You might shift the whole thing into interior monologue and allow adjectives to bloom like cabbage roses, saturating the telling with the deep color of emotion. If you can change anything, you can change everything. A gulf appears; you have lived on a fault line and never noticed it. Now it has broken open, leaving you over here, and what you wrote over there. Forever after, this is how it shall be.

No longer can you assume, as I did, that the way you feel writing something will be pretty much the way a person will feel reading it. I used to go to a diner under the Number 1 elevated train, and order a grilled corn muffin and jelly, and many cups of coffee, and I wrote in a sort of pounding exaltation. I assumed my readers would experience a similar thrill. The method was to get very, very excited. The story was just the conduit to convey this excitement. The writing was the same as my jumpy fingers, or the train racheting overhead and making my heart vibrate.

Writing school detached the words from the vibration. I saw that the inchoate mood and the particular words—the heart's rattle and the lines of prose—may approach each other more and more closely, but they will never merge. You may fling a million strings of words, and lace them tight, and still there is a gap.

And then, astonished, you see something else: the reader isn't granite. It is words themselves that are stony. A sort of gritty earth-bound gravity inheres in them. It is they who are stubborn, not the reader. The reader *does* squint, *does* step back and approach and turn things every which way trying to discern the depicted shape. The reader wants a good story. It is words themselves that are reluctant to cooperate.

The workshop does have a treasure to bestow. It teaches a new way of seeing. This is a loss of innocence that opens the way to all the pleasures of consciousness. It is often beautiful to revise, to enrich one's story and focus it more clearly. Moments spring to sharp life that before lay blurry. The real purpose of the story may now reveal itself. One increases the chances for a story's success.

Yet learning to write hurt me. I had to give up a sense of natural unity with my writing—of the rightness of my intuitive way. I recall the sensation that a certain story of mine had atomized. All its parts were sprayed out in various directions and hung, unrelated to one another and divorced from me. How far away they looked! Losing trust in the instinctive aptness of one's words is a form of exile. My anger at writing school is in part due to this necessary loss, and to that extent my anger is misplaced.

The formal training needs a counterbalance. Training in caution needs training in danger. So much polish needs rawness. So much restraint needs wildness. So much head needs heart. Before there was light there was "Toehu-vavohu," to use the original Hebrew: there was a mishmash, a topsy-turviness. The earth was "unformed and void," which does not mean that the earth did not exist. It existed, but without shape. It existed unrecognizably, shrouded, wanting.

It is easier to make sense saying what has been said before—we already know how to hear what we've already heard—than saying something new. We need to make nonsense on the way to making sense. We need to allow our work to be unrecognizable, shrouded, wanting, and still know it is real.

The best art risks most deeply. It is intended not for a group of readers but for one. It descends into the subterranean, the shameful, the fraught, the urgent and covert. What could not be said aloud because it defies conversation. What could not be said aloud because it could exist only as this constellation of scenes, this concatenation of details on this page. What passes invisibly over the earth because you have not yet pointed a finger at it.

To supplement the formal workshop we need an informal one, where students are told, Write about what is most frightening to write. Write what makes you feel guiltiest. Write about the most passionate you ever have been. Write images, a whole string of images you do not understand. An ear full of earwax that you scoop with your finger and it turns out to be a contact lens. A house you left where someone lies dead. You have to go back and bury them. Your husband digs a big trench in the backyard. You are worried the landlady will see.

Write about the time you were so sick you heard sirens although there were none, or the time you were so healthy for so many dull sane days you wished you were sick. Write what you are afraid will be sentimental, boring, melodramatic, pornographic, derivative, trite, vulgar, indulgent, sick, and/or stupid. There are a hundred reasons not to write what you most want to. Fuck that. Write it anyway.

We should be told: Write fast, write close to the bone, write for ten hours straight until you're not thinking in words anymore but in colors, in smells, in waves of memory. Write what you care about. Don't write one more word you don't care about. Don't waste any more of your life on what does not matter to you. Write only what matters to you—those scenes, those dialogues. Get messy. Before you get neat, get very, very messy. Write until you are more alive than you have ever been before.

So many of us were good in school, and we wanted to be good in school some more. We needed someone to say, Don't be good in school anymore. Be done with school. Be in school, but be done with school. Writing teaches writing. Your writing will teach you how to write if you work hard enough and have enough faith.

How to learn faith? My friends taught me. I saw how they lived, and it made my own way possible.

Imagine a page of text with a gigantic margin. The brief typeset part is the formal workshop. The margin, swirling with various scenes in croissant shops and bars and bedrooms and apple orchards, is the rest of the life of the place, where I learned much, unexpectedly, uniquely, implicitly. Certain scenes from it belong to me like objects:

Sitting on Gary's second-floor back porch beside the yellow torrents of willow leaves shining in the dusk lamps. We reclined in rusty lawn chairs while he read aloud from a children's book he was writing called, I think, *Families Under the Sea.*

Mary grinding coffee beans in a giant corn grinder riveted to a table which I had to press down on with all my might so it didn't shimmy away. After the coffee was brewed and cut with cream, she read me William Carlos Williams, leaping up when she heard an odd sound. It was goats. They filled the back garden, chewing the tops off the red geraniums. We laughed because it was like some dumb TV show—"Please Don't Eat the Daisies"?—laughed amid those miles of sunlight careening down. Mary said the goats had leaped loose because of William Carlos Williams. Williams was in the air and they had to jump free.

Going to a party at Indira's—there were parties every weekend—where the music was thrillingly loud, and we all knew everyone, and these were all people I admired, all people who loved the same things. It was dark and smelled of cold beer and early spring, and nearly everyone was dancing.

My neighbor Susanna and I being invited to Margie's farm to read sex scenes from our work. When we arrived lentil soup was simmering on the wood stove, and there was buttery corn bread and a green salad with tahini dressing, and red wine. We scarfed up great hunks of bread, and plate after plate of soup, and when evening shrank the room into a little glowing bowl, we read. We bent toward one another around the small wood table, and candlelight flickered on each reader's face, and I knew, listening and reading and then listening again, that I was one of the privileged of the earth.

Olga Broumas visiting Iowa, and after her talk I asked her a question I had wanted to ask someone for years: "How do you endure the long times when you cannot write?" She said in that room full of writers and readers, "Even when I cannot write, I know I am still a writer, just the way I know I am still sexual even if I have not had a lover for many months."

I have thought of her answer many times over the years. It is the sort of thing that I imagine it is possible to hear—or to hear personally, transformatively—only in a place dedicated to writing.

When I went to school mattered. Everyone had read *Will You Please Be Quiet, Please?* and thought understatement could accomplish all that was worth accomplishing. We could all be quiet, please, and we were.

My mistake was to believe this way of writing was *the* way to write. It is the mistake of the diligent student: to grasp for rules, to confuse the values of the moment with the values of all time, to want to please. "There is no hierarchy in learning," Krishnamurti says. "Authority denies learning and a follower will never learn." Or, as Lao-tzu puts it, "When they lose their sense of awe / people turn to religion. / When they no longer trust themselves, / they begin to depend on authority."

Many people are enraged at what they find when they come to writing programs. Why do teachers so often slight their students? Why do they give so little of their time? The teachers are writers, and their first loyalty is usually to their own writing.

Students come expecting to find a true mentor, someone who cares about their own writing with much of the fervor with which they care about it themselves. Some people find this guide, it's true. One friend was told, "Race your horse up a crystal mountain." This image spoke to her in her own language, and has inspired her to try for the heights ever since. Another writer was invited to meet time and again with her teacher, an *Esquire* editor, to go over drafts of her story. In the last class, the editor announced that he was publishing her story in his magazine.

For many, though, the mentor does not appear, at least not from the ranks of the writing faculty.

Jane Gallop, a literary critic, writes, "One morning while I was reading Freud, I realized that what I wanted from analysis was to understand everything enigmatic about me, what my dreams mean, why I was so afraid of fishbones and of diving into water. I realized that when I read Freud (but not Lacan) I got the impression that all this could, someday, be understood . . . I saw myself expressing various forms of psychoanalyst-envy . . . I believed psychoanalysis knew, and that if I were analyzed, or better yet if I became an analyst (my analysis was started under the guise of a training analysis), then I would get 'it.'"

I believed writing school had "it" and that by my going to writing school, "it" would be transferred to me. I thought school would make me a writer, and then thought school had failed me when it did not. But how contradictory this is! For of course at the same time that I craved the transformation from without, I would have been alarmed by any attempt to transform me, since in fact I wanted what most of us want: not to become someone else, but to find endorsement for who we already are; not to be told, "This is how to write," but to be told, "Yes, you are writing."

I read part of this essay to a friend, who told me, "But that is precisely what your first teacher said to you, only you didn't hear."

"Where? Where?" I asked, flipping through the pages.

"Well, when she said, 'Every writer has a book they do not publish. This will be yours.' She said you were a writer. She predicted you would publish books."

I nodded, abashed. For all I knew the message had been many places. Perhaps I heard only what I'd listened for. At night, wanting silence, I hear only the creak of my neighbor's foot over my head, or the poised absence of the creak before the creak occurs. I do not hear the reassuring silence washing all around me, although I wish for it with all my might. Thinking of her apartment, I hardly inhabit my own. Waiting for my words to establish something, assuming I would know exactly how I would feel when they had established that thing (I would feel established, good), I missed the clear signs.

My very first teacher, who I had regarded with such fury because she denied me, in fact gave me what I asked for. She merely assumed it was something I already possessed.

And yet, five minutes is still five minutes. I was right to expect more. That teacher had come to writing late, after her many children were grown. I suppose she felt that the time she had left she must hoard for herself, and that her heart had already been consumed by too many others.

In the first writing class I ever took, at the New School for Social Research, a woman sat in front of me. Her body was crooked—she was a dancer who'd fallen onstage. She wedged a book under one buttock so she could sit up straight. It was always the same book: a paperback with an electric pink cover and a title I did not understand, *If You Meet the Buddha on the Road, Kill Him!* Why kill the Buddha? Why not embrace the Buddha, follow the Buddha, cherish him? I longed for Buddhas, their compassionate eyes and knowing half-smile, the sense that they could see me through and through like gazing to the leafy bottom of a lake. I longed to deliver myself up to a Buddha.

But being brushed off is the lesson. Worshipping another is not useful; desire for approval leads the artist astray. My Buddha pushed me away from her. I had read all her books the summer before, and I thought, If only I can meet the woman who wrote these sentences! If only the writer who conceived these scenes would be unfolded to me! In pushing me away from her, she pushed me toward my own self. I didn't like this. I was too full of questions. I'd come here for answers. I wanted to be different by the time I left. I wanted to make contact with the Buddha in her, but she needed every last bit of her Buddha for herself, and I was forced to discover my own way.

DISCUSSION QUESTIONS

1. Friedman begins by describing the mystique surrounding writing programs. What contributed to this feeling that such a program would offer her a mentor, revelations about writing, and confirmation of her talent? Was she overly idealistic in her expectations?

2. Friedman, like Moore in "How to Become a Writer," uses narrative to illuminate a particular writer's educational experiences. How do Friedman's episodes contrast with Moore's? Are there similarities in Francie's and Bonnie's experiences? What do these narratives communicate about the nature of "writing school"?

3. When Friedman first meets a prospective mentor, the teacher circles all the "I's" on a page of Friedman's novel, refers her to a previous teacher's comments, and pronounces that the novel will not be published. How would you describe this teacher's method?

4. Friedman characterizes writing school as a "marvelous brake," forcing her to slow down and focus on the "grammar of fiction" rather than the sudden flash

of her ideas. What does she mean by this shift in focus? Do you see a similar rush in your own writing, an engagement with inspiration at the expense of craft? Does the kind of brake Friedman describes seem attractive to you?

5. Friedman calls into question the usefulness of traditional academic achievement for writers, discounting "theoretical methodology" and claiming that her "earlier education had ruined her." Do you agree that certain kinds of academic work are detrimental to a fiction writer's development? Why?

6. Like many of the writers in this book, Friedman decides that technique is a kind of magic and comes to value craft consciousness. Have you had a similar experience in your life as a writer? How did you come to know and appreciate the value of technique?

7. Friedman comments that personal motivations and life experiences were not discussed by the students in the workshops. The discussions were "technical" and "respectful," not personal: "School had little to do with heart, and everything to do with technical perfection." Why do you think this was the case?

8. Friedman does explore what the emphasis on technique cost her as she progressed through writing school: her "intuitive way" of working, the "natural unity" of her work. In sum, she mourns her "loss of innocence" and suggests that there is a need for a less formal kind of school that allows students to "play." Can these two kinds of experiences be blended? How?

R. V. CASSILL

Reading as a Writer

R. V. Cassill (b. 1919) is Emeritus Professor at Brown University and has taught at the University of Iowa, Columbia University, and the New School for Social Research in New York City. He is the author of two dozen novels, a half dozen collections of short stories, several collections of poetry, several anthologies of literature, and the important textbook Writing Fiction *(1962). His best-known novel may be* La Vie Passionnée of Rodney Buckthorne: A Tale of the Great American's Last Rally and Curious Death *(1968); other novels include* Clem Anderson *(1961),* The President *(1964),* The Goss Women *(1974),* Labors of Love *(1980), and* After Goliath *(1985).*

If you're awfully impatient to get to work, I can tell you now *exactly* how a story is made. It is made by uttering a declarative statement—"Joe wrote Maureen a dishonest, flattering letter"—and answering the questions naturally provoked by such a declaration: Who is Joe? Who is Maureen? What involvement have they with each other that motivates Joe to write a dishonest letter?

These questions will be answered by further declarations, which in turn require explanations. If you keep on giving explanations, presently you will have a story—of sorts.

This is exactly how all fiction is made. In the beginning there is an utterance. Then there is explanation.

However, like any "exact" formula in the arts, this none-too-serious prescription leaves a great deal to be said. To make it serious one must point out exhaustively how a writer learns *which* questions to ask, how they are best answered, and when enough has been said.

Certainly the writer can acquire technical principles otherwise than by distilling them from the fiction he reads. Yet reading remains essential because most technical concepts are learned more quickly and thoroughly from examples than from abstract definitions.

Consider this. It is generally agreed by modern critics and practitioners of fiction that nothing is more characteristic of the art than concreteness of expression.

Concreteness ought to be your aim in all you write and revise. Very well, you say, but what is this concreteness?

It can be abstractly defined as the rendition of actions, people, places, and things in language that relates how they would be registered by an observer's senses of sight, sound, taste, smell, and touch. Concreteness is about the same as what Henry James called *realization*—the achievement of a sort of evoked reality from mere words.

Such an abstract definition is not without value. But keeping it in mind, read this passage from Flaubert's *Madame Bovary:*

> It was a fine summer morning. Silver gleamed in jewelers' windows, and the sunlight slanting onto the cathedral flashed on the cut surface of the gray stone . . . the square, echoing with cries, smelled of the flowers that edged its pavement— roses, jasmine, carnations, narcissus and tuberoses interspersed with well-watered plants of catnip and chickweed. The fountain gurgled in the center . . . bareheaded flower-women were twisting paper around bunches of violets.
>
> The young man chose one. It was the first time he had bought flowers for a woman; and his chest swelled with pride as he inhaled their fragrance, as though this homage that he intended for another were being paid, instead, to him.

Note, in the first paragraph, how many senses are appealed to in this realization of a summer morning in a French city. The gleam of silver and the sunlight on the cathedral illustrate the visual sensations; the gurgling fountain and the cries of merchants and customers appeal to the sense of hearing; the flowers and the wet plants stir the reader's recollection of actual smells.

Then, in the second paragraph, we see a young man in the midst of this color, sound, and smell. Within the quoted passage this young man is not described, characterized, or even named. Yet he is as real as fiction can make him, because here he serves as a focal point for all the sense impressions set loose by the previous paragraph. We cannot, of course, quite smell, or see, or hear this busy city square. (Unlike the theater or the movies, fiction can't rely on immediate sensual impact.) But we are induced to imagine that the young man is literally assaulted through every sense—and it is the concreteness of the objective world acting on his mind and emotions that gives him his fictional reality.

An experienced writer, criticizing the work of an apprentice, is apt to say repeatedly, "Don't tell us what your character or scene is like. *Show* us." Certainly you can learn how to *show,* to make your story concrete, by studying this example from Flaubert. If you return to it twenty times, it will still have things to teach you. . . .

In urging you to read, I am doing no more than reminding you that a writer has many teachers. Good writers are your real teachers of how to write fiction, and their novels and stories are the means by which they teach. We know that Flaubert taught one other writer in a formal sense of the word. He coached, criticized, and advised Guy de Maupassant for several years before allowing him to publish anything. But it is also true that, in a less formal and direct way, Flaubert has taught most of the good writers of the past century—all those who "read as writers" when they looked into *Madame Bovary.*

"Reading as a writer" differs in a number of ways from other readings of fiction. The ordinary, intelligent nonprofessional expects, quite rightly, that fiction will give him a kind of illusion that something meaningful is happening to characters who have become very interesting in a particular situation. He recognizes traits of character that resemble those he has observed in life. He finds recognizable values at stake in the action of the story. (Will Joe harm Maureen by his dishonest letter? Will Lambert Strethers achieve magnificence or lose his self-respect?) Whether those values are preserved or destroyed conveys some meaning to the reader about the world he shares with the author. This sort of communication between author and reader is fine. It is the primary justification for fiction.

But there is another sort of transaction going on when a critic pauses to analyze a work. The critic generally wants to determine where to place this particular story. What *kind* of fiction is it? Is it realism or parody or fantasy? If it is realism, is it kin to the realism of Conrad, or that of Dreiser? Does the psychological insight of the story conform to the revelations of Freud? Or is it, perhaps, more intuitive—closer to the intuitions of D. H. Lawrence? Is the style derivative or original? Is the form of the story adequate to the meanings the author tried to load onto it? The critic's way of reading fiction is a good way, too, and a very valuable approach for a writer. If he has time and opportunity, a young writer ought to supplement his writing program with classes in the analysis of contemporary fiction.

But what the writer wants to note, beyond anything that concerns even the critic, is how the story, its language, and all its parts have been joined together.

The writer will look at the way the opening sentences and paragraphs are constructed to put certain information immediately before the reader.

> A new person, it was said, had appeared on the esplanade; a lady with a pet dog. Dmitry Dmitrich Gurov, who had spent a fortnight at Yalta and had got used to the place, had also begun to take an interest in new arrivals. (Opening sentences of "The Lady with the Pet Dog.")

There is a watchmaker's precision evident in the form of this opening. The first sentence implies, without a direct statement, that the setting will be one in which rumor has the force of authority, that here people are to some extent free of custom and the rigidity of their family or social position. We will learn from reading farther into the story that Yalta, a resort city, is such a place as is implied. In this atmosphere of transience and rumor, it is common, though a bit odd nevertheless, that ladies should be identified by such superficial trivia as their possession of pet dogs.

The second sentence, which names the principal character, develops our awareness of social fluidity in Yalta by its restrained, wry statement of how quickly one becomes an old-timer in a place where none stay very long.

Thus, from the very beginning Chekhov has begun to develop the peculiarities of the setting in which the love of Gurov and Anna will begin its unworldly flourishing.

Dramatic, concrete, and already ironic, Chekhov's opening draws the reader swiftly into the heart of the experience to be endured by his characters.

Noting the skill of such an opening, the writer who reads it must, *above anything else,* be aware that the story might have opened otherwise. For instance:

> In the year 1883, Dmitry Dmitrich Gurov was vacationing at Yalta. His wife and children had remained at the family home in Moscow. While on vacation it was his daily habit to take sweets at a café on the esplanade. The gossips whom he met there one day told him that a new arrival had attracted the attention of many idle vacationers. Her name was not known. They spoke of her as the lady with the pet dog.

The point I wish to emphasize is not that my alternative opening is inferior to Chekhov's—which it certainly is—but that such another possibility for a beginning exists. *A writer reading must be forever aware that the story exists as it does because the author chose his form from among other possibilities.* From this recognition of author's choice comes the key to understanding what is excellent in the fabrication of Chekhov's story or any other good work.

To the ordinary reader-for-pleasure it ought to seem that the story is told in the language he finds on the printed page because it *has* to be told in just those words. As soon as we know better than that, we are reading as writers.

It is not always easy to understand why the author made the choice he did. For instance, why did Chekhov choose to caricature Gurov's wife as an intellectual shrew instead of picturing her as becoming pathetic as she grows older? That other choice would have served the purposes of the story—but it might have required greater development of her character, thus changing the proportions and center of interest.

We cannot be sure how this other possible choice would have fitted. But mere speculation on it should make us realize that *no choice of character, action, language, names, or anything else is an isolated one.*

Each successive choice made as the writing progresses has to be made with respect for what has already been established. This is a respect for what I will call the overall unity of fiction. Suffice it to say for now that when you read as a writer you will keep asking how did the author harmonize A with B and B with C and C with D—on through a very long series of decisions that finally resulted in the story as we have it. We can't understand all the secrets of unifying a story at once. But the recognition of author's choice stimulates a fruitful curiosity.

For an example of another particular a writer ought to look for in his reading, let us recognize the obvious truth that characters in fiction have to be developed as the story rolls along. No character can be fully revealed the moment he is brought on the scene. They are developed by encountering situations in which they act to reveal themselves and act on other characters to affect the outcome of the story.

So one ought to note what sort of occasions in a story extend and amplify the first impressions given of each of the characters. How large an opportunity for character revelation is provided by the particular few situations that constitute any one story?

For a modest approach to understanding how a limited number of situations can reveal as much about character as they do, let's start with a recognition that they were contrived or chosen by the author exactly because of their capacity to expose significant qualities in his characters. We should ask constantly whether another set of circumstances would have served this purpose better or worse, remembering that in the writing, alternative choices could have been made.

In most stories that cover any span of time greater than several minutes, we are aware that only a part of the action that might have been given in detail has been fully presented. Why did the author omit some bits of dialogue that might, in actuality, have been spoken? How has the author covered the gaps that he chose to leave? Has he left some important realities up to the imagination of the reader? Of course he has, unless he is a real bumbler. But a skilled author will have chosen ways to make sure the reader imagined something consistent with what is given, rather than something irrelevant.

And while the author was contriving so many clever joints and putting in so many bolts, hinges, and braces, what else was he doing? Why, he was taking pains to hide all his carpentry work for the sake of the illusion he wants to give the reader.

Perhaps the last thing you need to find out, reading as a writer, is how an author has managed to disguise his own presence, how he has kept the curtain always between himself and the reader.

A writer must read, then, with close concentration. But, a writer also ought to read widely. What becomes of concentration and close attention to detail when one tries to plunge through a lot of stories, novels, and other reading matter in a short lifetime? Well, obviously there have to be occasions when he reads hastily, avidly, skipping like a stone flung across a pond. There's no need to be afraid this reading is wasted. Thomas Mann's *The Magic Mountain* and James Joyce's *Ulysses* are novels that might reward months or years of concentrated effort. But I suppose it is better (just a *little* better) to have dipped into one or the other during an afternoon's bus ride than never to have opened them at all. . . .

Read poetry. Nowhere are there such possibilities of the language on display as there are in poetry. Not all these possibilities are suitable for fiction, but the fiction writer ought, by all means, to know that they exist. Furthermore, some of the finest and most subtle narrative forms are found in poetry. Read the ballads "Little Musgrove," "The Demon Lover," or "Lord Randall" for a tiny sample. Read William Morris's "The Haystack in the Floods," or "Sir Gawain and the Green Knight," or Robinson Jeffers' "Thurso's Landing" if you want to see how wonderfully stories can be told in verse.

Read drama. It can be useful reading for a fiction writer. Contemporary fiction has borrowed a great deal from the literature of the theater. For economy and deftness in giving information to the reader—for learning how to *show* him instead of telling him what he has to know—we can find worthwhile examples in many plays. Beyond this—it ought to go without saying—means of character delineation have had to be worked out to a high degree of subtlety for the stage.

So read widely. Read good things when you can find them. But don't—if you really mean to master your craft—be afraid of soiling your mind by reading works not exactly of first rank. In my experience, students who purposely confined their college reading to "the best"—meaning Shakespeare, Dante, Cervantes, Dostoevsky, Melville, and Henry James; all great writers, all writers in an idiom no longer common—had more than usual trouble in developing for themselves a supple style that would express their own experience. Sometimes more of one's basic craft can be learned from second-rank work.

It has probably occurred to you that I have outlined a reading program that will take years to complete, a reading program with no outside limit. I'm afraid I have. Certainly I do not mean to suggest that all this reading should be done before you put paper in your typewriter and strike out boldly for yourself. . . .

DISCUSSION QUESTIONS

1. Cassill, analyzing the descriptive passage from Flaubert, writes of the character in the scene "that it is the concreteness of the objective world acting on his mind and emotions that gives him his fictional reality." How is this claim more complex and challenging to the writer than the usual admonition "Show, don't tell"?

2. Do you feel that Cassill's advice that "all your reading ought to be a search for the variety of technical means by which various writers achieve their ends" is too limiting? Why?

3. How does Cassill contrast the reading habits of the general reader, the critic, and the writer? How can each way of reading contribute to the development of the writer?

4. Why does Cassill emphasize that "a writer reading must be forever aware that the story exists as it does because the author chose his form from among other possibilities"? How does this awareness change, specifically, the way a writer reads?

5. Another point of emphasis for Cassill is that "no choice of character, action, language, names, or anything else is an isolated one." How does this awareness of "unity" in fiction affect, specifically, the way a writer reads?

6. Cassill recommends that fiction writers read poetry and drama, too. What other genres would you add? Why does Cassill suggest that "basic craft can be learned from second-rate work"?

RICHARD FORD

Reading

Richard Ford (b. 1944) studied with E. L. Doctorow while earning an M.F.A. from the University of California at Irvine (1970) and first became widely known with the publication of The Sportswriter *(1986).* Independence Day *(1995) won both the Pulitzer Prize and the PEN/Faulkner Award. Among his other works are* A Piece of My Heart *(1976),* Wildlife *(1990), and* Women with Men *(1997). He has also been an important editor of the* Best American Short Story *series (1990) and the* Granta Book of the American Short Story *(1992), generously anthologizing many less-well-known writers.*

For H. S. B.

I learned to read—I mean learned to read carefully—in 1969, when I was twenty-five years old. I was in graduate school then and trying to figure out if I should begin to write short stories. I was married and living in a small apartment. I'd quit law school the year before. I had gone a long way from home—to California—and I did not know very much. I didn't even think I did.

Nineteen sixty-nine was an awful year in the Vietnam War and a bad year in the country. The Tet offensive had been the year before, and everyone saw the whole war as a loss. Among us graduate students there was a related and distinct unease, almost a squeamishness, about what *we* were doing—writing; an unease that manifested itself as a hot and unforgiving demand for relevancy in everything we said and intended and studied and, most important, asked of others. And, especially, we measured our courses that way. They needed, we felt, to be very, *very* relevant; to our lives, but to our dreads also, to our predicaments, our genders, our marriages, our futures, to the war and to the sixties themselves—an era we knew we were living through even as we did it.

And, naturally, nothing quite measured up. I had a course in the *bildungsroman,* read Lessing, Rousseau, Mann, Henry Adams. And it all seemed just too bookish by half; too much to do with history and Freud, both of whose lessons we distrusted and made fun of as reductive. I read all of Hardy's poems after that, all seven hundred or so pages in the big green Macmillan edition, and couldn't bear them either. They seemed oldish, pale and insulated from my interests. What we did like, of course, we didn't need or mean to study: *Man's Fate,* a clear book of truth; both the wonderful Kesey books; *The Crying of Lot 49, At Play in the Field of the Lord, The Ginger Man*—books premised in ironies, a mood more and more attractive when the sincere and practical connections between us and the world could not be convincingly drawn.

Contemporary writing itself had not been in much of a signifying mood. Donald Barthelme's stories were in our minds. Ron Sukenick's. Barry Hannah. William Kotzwinkle. They were all writing wonderfully. And the disjointures and absurdities, the hilarity, the word-virtuosity of those writers—all of whom I still admire—seemed right for our time and us. The world was a whacking wreck, California its damned epicenter. And we were stranded there, absurdly. And absurdity is never completely irrelevant to the facts of any life.

Exactly what we wanted is not clear to me. Though likely it was not one thing, alone. We were young. We were not particularly educated. And, like many beginning writers, for a time we were addicted to the new in everything. We were makers and less so takers-in, and we thought *ourselves* in the relevance business. Barthelme and those other guys were our colleagues, whether they knew it or not. And to be vulnerable to teaching suggested about us and these classics we resisted—tameness. Encapsulability. There wasn't time for Mann. *Irrelevant,* I have come to believe, is a word one often uses to put oneself forward. And what I truly think is we wouldn't have recognized relevance if it had come up and kissed us on the lips.

Part of my school training as a writer, however, provided that I could learn how to teach. It was felt by my teachers—writers themselves—that if we students ever became the real things, we would probably never be able to support ourselves that way and so could teach as a fallback while we busied ourselves toward agents, book contracts, editors, movie and paperback deals, big bucks—whatever else is at the end of that line of hopes. And strange to say, if my classes did not seem spot-on relevant to me, this prospect of teaching somehow did. Teaching *was* a kind of practical preparation for life, after all, and it did not seem hard to do. It had pleasures. It involved the admiration of others—something I wanted. And teaching literature seemed allied to writing it in some way abject studenthood did not. And so I said I would do it, and in fact was very glad to do it.

What exactly this teacher training entailed was going before a class of undergraduates, asking them to read several short stories and novels chosen and discussed among us assistants by an overseeing professor, and then, for three days a week, teaching. Teaching fiction. And what I found my problem to be was that I couldn't imagine the first thing to do, because I didn't, in any way I could convey to another human, know how to read.

Oh, I'd read plenty. I felt I was a *reader,* and I expected to be a writer. I'd been an English major at a big midwestern university and escaped with good grades. I had actually "taught" high school English a year and worked as an assistant editor for a Hearst Corporation magazine, and had, it seemed, experience to make me worth the risk of being put in a classroom full of eighteen-year-olds. Only as I began to prepare I was drawing a blank.

I can still say the things I knew about fiction then—most of it brought along from college. I knew several terms: Characters were the people in fiction. Symbols were the objects in stories to which extra meaning adhered (the raft in Huck Finn, for example, was a symbol). Point of view, I understood, referred not to a character's opinion about something, or the author's, but to what means the story was told by. First, third, omniscient. I knew that beginnings were important parts of stories and, as in "The Lady with the Pet Dog," sometimes they contained the seeds of the entire story (I did not know why that mattered, though). I knew primitive myths sometimes underlay fairly simple-seeming stories. I knew irony was important. I knew, nervously, that the language of a story or novel often meant more or less or even something entirely different from what it seemed to, and that understanding it—the story—meant understanding all the meanings at once. Meaning itself was a term, though I'd never been altogether sure what it meant.

And I knew other things. I knew how to "read like a writer." We talked about such things in our workshops. Certain books had practical lessons to teach. Nuts and bolts: how to get characters efficiently in and out of fictional rooms (Chekhov was good here); how to describe efficiently that it was dark (Chekhov again); how to weed out useless dialogue ("Hi, how are you?" "I'm fine, how are you?" "I'm okay. Thanks." "Good to hear it." "Good-bye." "Good-bye." That sort of stuff). I learned that a good opening ploy in a novel was to have Indians—if there were any—ride over a hill screaming bloody murder. I learned that when in doubt about what to do next, have a man walk through the door holding a gun. I learned that you couldn't get away with killing off your main character in a short story—though I was never told why, and neither, I guess, was Hemingway.

All these hands-on lessons were things I was mulling. Yet they didn't really seem worth teaching to young readers, people for whom making literature was not yet a career selection, nor was reading it even a given in their lives—in fact was possibly as disagreeable as a dentist's visit. Going about teaching literature in this way seemed like teaching someone to build a sleek and fast car without first treating them to how it felt to split the breeze in one. They'd never know exactly what it was all good for.

What seemed worthwhile to teach was what I *felt* about literature when I read it—those matters of relevance set slightly aside. That was why I wanted to write stories, after all. Literature was pretty and good. It had mystery, denseness, authority, connectedness, closure, resolution, perception, variety, magnitude— *value,* in other words, in the way Sartre meant when he wrote, "The work of art is a value because it is an appeal." Literature appealed to me.

But I had no idea how to teach its appealing qualities, how to find and impart the origins of what I felt. I didn't even know when to bring in my terms, or if they were right. I quickly came to feel that being an intermediary between an expectant mind and an excellent book is a conspicuous and chancy role to play. And I imagined myself sitting behind a metal desk staring at them, *Madame Bovary* open before me, passages underlined, silence commanding every molecule of the still air, and having nothing whatsoever to say, while being certain something should be said. Or worse—having only this to say: "What's the point of this book?" And *then* having nothing to say when the right answer came and as a voice inside me screamed, *mystery, connectedness, authority, closure, magnitude, value.*

These first preparations for teaching occurred over the Christmas holidays, in 1968. I went to my tiny graduate-student office and pored over my stories, over and over and over, without advance. "A Guest of the Nation"; "Death in the

Woods"; "The Battler"; "Disorder and Early Sorrow"; "The Wind Blows." I could practically recite them. But I had no idea what to say *about* them. I still can feel the panic of pure inessentialness cold on my neck as literature rose against me like a high wall behind which was a deep jungle. I was to take people through there not just safely but gainfully, only I had no business even setting out.

In an office down the hall from where I was panicking that winter was a man named Howard Babb. I knew him because he was to be the chairman of our English department the next fall, and he was director of the course I was readying to teach. Mr. Babb liked us writers—even more, we felt, than he liked the Ph.D. types whose literary training he saw over. We seemed like true amateurs to him, not even serious enough to be gloomy, and it was in his good character to think of himself, or at least to portray himself, in precisely that way. Later, when I knew him better in the few years before he died, and I was his young colleague, I would overhear him say again and again to some student, about some piece of literature he was instructing, "Now, of course, I don't pretend to know a goddamned thing about any of this business, mind you. I would only in a simpleminded way venture to say this . . ." And then he would go on to say what was truest and best and smartest about a story or a novel. He merely did not claim to be an expert, and possibly he wasn't, though he knew a great deal. Simplest just to say that his mind stayed remarkably open to literature, whereas an expert's sometimes does not.

I will say a word or two about Howard Babb here because he was a singular man—human and inspiring—and because his influence over my life as a writer and as a reader was direct and unqualifiedly good. A day, indeed, doesn't go by now that I do not think of him.

At that time, I knew about him only a very few things, as was once the case between students and their professors—no first names, no dinner invitations or ball games attended together. He was a big Yankee man—in his late forties—with a Maine accent, a bluff, good temper and a deep, murmurous voice with which he would occasionally talk loudly for effect. He had left college to be a sailor, and cursed like a sailor, though he was not undignified. He had tattoos on his arms that you could see when he rolled up his white sleeves. He smoked Tareytons in secret when he was at school, and sometimes drank at faculty parties and talked even louder. He'd been a student of Walter Jackson Bate at Harvard, and later a colleague of John Crowe Ransom and Peter Taylor at Kenyon. He was married and had a son. He walked with a heavy, hod-carrier's purposive gait—bowlegged, arms a little out from his shoulders, as if he was always stalking something. He seemed like a tough guy to me, and I liked him the first moment I saw him.

Toughness aside, though, he loved Jane Austen and George Eliot. He loved Conrad and Richardson and the eighteenth century. He knew a world about narrative and wrote and talked about it smartly, though he never became famous for it. He was, I thought even then, as out of place in southern California as a man with his history and affections for lasting virtues could ever be. And possibly to accommodate those divisive forces—though maybe the line of cause runs exactly opposite—he immersed himself with a fury in literature: reading it, teaching it, and talking about it. And for our purposes—his students—his fierceness, his zeal for teaching, his fervor for literature and its importance to us, comprised his entire attitude toward life, his whole self. No discrepancies. No ironies. No two-mindedness about how he felt, say, when the Irish soldiers kill their poor prisoner in "A Guest of the Nation," and how he might feel were such an awful dilemma ever to be his own. Or our own. Literature had direct access to everyday life. The day, in fact, that he read aloud to me those fearsome final words of O'Connor's, sitting alone in his shadowy office on a winter afternoon almost twenty years ago, I listened without moving. And when he was finished he just stared at the floor, leaning on his knees, the book opened in his big hands, and maybe for five minutes we did not speak a word—not one word—so large were both our feelings for what we'd heard. And what I knew was that anything that happened to *me* afterward, after that seized moment, I would never feel the same about again. Here, I think, was relevance, first encountered, and here was pleasure of a quite rare kind.

But before then, back on that cheerless snowless Christmas, I had yet to encounter it. And what I did, at my wits' very end, was pick up my book of stories and walk down the empty corridor to Mr. Babb's office at the end of the hall. He was there through those holidays, reading alone without overhead light, making his minute margin notes, preparing for his courses while his colleagues were elsewhere—on their sailboats or skiing or attending conventions. I stood in his open doorway until he looked up and saw me. He stared a moment. "Well," he said softly, "what in the hell do you want? Shouldn't you be off farting around back in Mississippi, or wherever it is you're from?" This was friendly.

"No," I said. "I have a problem here."

"Well okay, then." He sighed and closed his book. "Come on in and sit down." And that is what I did.

Not surprisingly, if I could not teach those stories, neither could I say to Mr. Babb how or why I couldn't. This seems axiomatic now—proof of ignorance. But even more awful was that I didn't want to admit I didn't know. Silence has always been the accomplice to my ignorance; and ignorance, unsuitedness, unpreparedness always my coldest, most familiar fears. I have never approached anything difficult and truly new without expecting to fail at it, and quickly; or without generalizing how little I knew and dreading being told.

What I said was this: "I am having trouble knowing *exactly* how to go about teaching this Anderson story."

The Anderson story, as I've said, was "Death in the Woods," one of his great, signature stories, written in the thirties and separate in style and sympathy from the famous "Winesburg" tales from fifteen years earlier and the aftermath of the war. In "Death in the Woods," as in those few other Anderson masterpieces, "I Want to Know Why," "The Egg," "The Man Who Became a Woman," an adult narrator tells a series of events recalled from his childhood, a seemingly simpler time, when the speaker was but a receptor—though a keen one—for whom life's memorable moments became the stuff of later inquiry and recognition. It is a classic story structure, one I have come to know well.

In Anderson, a man remembers a woman he saw once years earlier, in the small town where he was a boy. The woman was poor and poorly treated by her brute husband and her brute son. Yet she fed and provided for them on their poverty farm while the two men went off drunk and carousing. On a certain trip back from town, where she had traded eggs for meat and flour, the woman—named, sadly, Mrs. Grimes—pauses to rest at the foot of a tree, and surprisingly though painlessly freezes to death as snow and then clear night set on. In a spectral and unforgettable scene (one the narrator imagines, since he could not have witnessed it) Mrs. Grimes' dogs begin to run wild circles around her body and eventually drag her out into the night radiance and feed themselves on the provisions she was bringing home—though not, it should be said, on Mrs. Grimes, whose palely beautiful body goes untouched—". . . so white and lovely," the speaker imagines it, ". . . so like marble."

Much is plain in this wonderful story, even to the least lettered reader. When I first read it, in 1969, it seemed longer and complexer than when I read it today. But its large concerns seem the same ones I must've known then, if intuitively: the cruelty inherent in us all; our edgy similarity to the spirit of wild beasts; the uncertain good of advancing civilization; the mystery and allure of sex; adulthood as a poor, compromised state of being; the ways by which we each nurture others; the good to be got from telling. Mystery, closure, connectedness, magnitude—value. Anderson wrote inspired by all these grand disturbances and their literary conceits. I think of him still as one of our great, great writers.

And I meant to teach him. He was on the syllabus, though I could not then have found the words I've just said.

"Tell me, Mr. Ford," Mr. Babb said, still softly, when he'd sat in silence for a while, flipping pages through the story in my anthology, glancing at my underlinings, raising his eyebrows at my notes, sniffing now and then, humming at a line of Anderson's he admired. He knew the story by heart and loved Anderson. I knew that in the way a graduate student must know the tastes of his professors and assume them shamelessly. "Tell me just this," he said again, and looked up at me quizzically, then at the ceiling, as if he'd begun rehearsing some life of his own from years ago, which the story had pleasantly revived. "What, um, what do you think is the most interesting formal feature of this story? I'm, of course, not talking about anything particularly complicated. Just what *you* think about it." He blinked at me as though in the mists of this marvelous story and of his own memory, he couldn't quite make me out now.

And at the instant I write this, I know what was in his mind—though I have never known it before, and would've guessed it was something else; that I would give him the wrong answer, or an incomplete one, and that our talk would commence there. But I understand now that he was certain I had no idea in the world what he could be talking about, and that our tasks would begin from that point—the perfect point of origin. Zero. The place where all learning begins.

"I don't know what you mean by 'formal feature,'" I answered in a good, clear voice. And with that I gave up some large part of my ignorance. I must've sensed I'd learn something valuable if I could only do that. And I was right.

"Well," he said, bemused. "All right." He nodded and sighed, then turned in his swivel chair to a green chalkboard on the wall, stood, and with a chalk wrote this list.

Character

Point of View

Narrative Structure

Imagistic Pattern

Symbol

Diction

Theme

These, of course, were words I'd seen. Most of them had been swirling around my thinking for days without order or directive. Now, here they were again, and I felt relieved.

These expressions, Mr. Babb said, sitting back in his chair but still looking at the list, described the formal features of a piece of fiction. If we could define them, locate them in a particular piece of fiction, and then talk about any one of them in a careful and orderly way, reliant on the words of the story and common sense, asking perfectly simple questions, proceeding to deductions one by one, perhaps talking about other features as they came to mind—eventually we would involve ourselves in a discussion of the most important issues in a story, or in a novel.

In every story he himself read, he said, some one formal feature seemed to stand out as a conspicuous source of interest, and he could investigate the story that way. *The Great Gatsby,* for instance, was *narrated* in a way he thought especially interesting. Point of view was then the issue: Who was Nick Carraway? Why was he telling the story? What peculiar advantage or disadvantage did he have as its teller? Was our understanding of the story affected by the fact that he told it? If so, how? Did he—Nick—judge other characters? How? Was he always telling the truth? What if he wasn't? Why did I think so?

In "Silent Snow, Secret Snow," the lustrous, enigmatic master-story by Conrad Aiken (also on the syllabus), how could one make sense of this unusual snow that seems increasingly to buffer the child whose life is at the story's center? Is it actual snow? Why do we think it is or isn't? Could we reasonably imagine it to represent anything besides itself? Only one thing? What did this have to do with other features of the story? The child's character? The setting? His parents? Here we were investigating an image.

Story to story, each had a path-in signaled by a prominent formal feature, with one feature's effects and our observations about it implicating another—point of view leading naturally to an interest in character, leading onward to some wider sense of how, as the story progressed through its own structural parts (scenes, settings, flashbacks), character and image and narrative strategy intertwined and formed the whole, until by our directed questioning we could say what seemed most complexly at issue in the story. Theme, this was—though no one should hope to identify that matter succinctly or to say it in a phrase. It was last but not foremost. Foremost was one's intimacy with the story.

In the Anderson, Mr. Babb said, one might start with a simple-minded set of questions and observations about who it was who told that story to us. Was it just a straightforward matter of an anonymous voice telling a story in the most unembellished way? *No.* Wasn't the teller a character? *Yes.* Did he tell it as it happened? *No.* Could one, on close examination of the very words chosen in the story, distinguish different concerns—even preoccupations—of the speaker besides just the facts of the old woman's death? *Yes, yes, yes.* And with each answer elicited couldn't we reasonably say, "And how does this materially contribute to my understanding of the story?" Or, in plainer words: "So what if this is true?" "So what if this is not?"

What opened for me in the course of this single conversation was a larger number of small lights, partial recognitions I could only partially appreciate, but that over the years have developed and seemed among the most important I've ever made and, toward reading literature, the most important of all. Mr. Babb, naturally, never told me exactly what to do, and our talk never left the plane of the hypothetical/conditional ("one *might* ask this; isn't it possible to wonder that? surely this is not completely irrelevant . . ."). But he taught. He taught me not only an orderly means to gain entry to and intimacy with a complex piece of narrative, but also that literature could be approached as empirically as life, to which after all it was connected. As in life, our literary understandings, even our failures at understanding, were founded on a series of commonsense responses—not necessarily answers—that were true to the small facts, the big movements, and the awes and dreads and pleasures we all felt as we made our way along. Literature was not only accessible, but relevant to life, inasmuch as the same matters were of issue in both: How do I love whom I love? How can I go on each day with or without those persons? How will this day end? Will I live or will I die?

It will be understood that when I left Mr. Babb's office that late December afternoon, I did so with a much less clear view of reading literature than I have today, even though my view now is still clouded by the ignorance of all I've yet to read and will never read, and by the "complicating" experience of having spent the next eighteen or so years trying to make stories as good as those Anderson ones I loved and that affect me to this moment. Still, I went away feeling confident—pleasurably confident—that the method I'd just seen practiced bore an utterly natural relationship to any piece of fiction I would ever read, examine, or teach. I believed that the stories which had pleased me, awed me, frightened me with their interconnected largeness were actually *constructions of* those formal features Mr. Babb had described. Good stories—whether or not they were made so intentionally by authors—were basically arrangements of knowable images, word patterns, of dramatic structure and symbols. They were *made of* characters and points of view and possessed themes. Moreover, reading any story with this knowledge amounted to the truest experience of knowing it. I'm certain I taught my first students that, and taught others, too; made discovering forms and verifying them an end, not just a pedagogy, a device. It is almost inevitable I would, given my novice's need to order a universe and since fiction can be fitted in so nicely to this symmetry. My mind rested there, I suppose I can say. And many people, I suspect, students and their teachers, too, never get beyond that static, intermediate stage of reading—knowing which point of view is which, sensing what an old symbolizing animal man is, comparing and contrasting poor Jake Barnes and lucky Bill Gorton *as characters;* never get around to asking what all this has to do with life—asking the final question of relevancy: So what?

Thinking back to then, I'm sure Mr. Babb didn't believe in such a pat, synthetic view of literature, but instead that we synthesize these forms in an effort to organize our progress through difficult writing, tracing their shapes like constellations in a wild heaven. The proof was the awe he preserved, the affection, the eagerness with which he returned to the same passages and stories over and over, still curious, pleasantly baffled, willing to be amazed, reverent of all that the books continued to give him. It was I—not smart enough and just beginning—who championed a method before the method's full use and limits could be understood.

And it is—I suppose appropriately—only because of writing stories rather than being an excellent reader that I figured out that this formalism was a faulty account of how stories of any length got made and are best known.

Stories, and novels, too—I came to see from the experience of writing them—are makeshift things. They originate in strong, disorderly impulses; are supplied by random accumulations of life-in-words; and proceed in their creation by mischance, faulty memory, distorted understanding, weariness, deceit of almost every imaginable kind, by luck and by the stresses of increasingly inadequate vocabulary and wanting imagination—with the result often being a straining, barely containable object held in fierce and sometimes insufficient control. And there is nothing wrong with that. It doesn't hurt me to know it. Indeed, my admiration for the books I love is greater for knowing the chaos they overcame. But there is very little I can say, then, about the experience of writing stories that will make the experience of parsing them formally seem a completely apt way to know them. Even the word—formal—seems wrong-spirited to such an amateurish and un-formal business. *Characters,* those "rounded" people in good books whom we say we recognize and know like our cousins, are at heart just assemblages of sentences, ongoing, shifting arrangements of descriptions and purported human impulse and action hooked to a name—all of it changeable by adding and subtracting or forgetting words—yet hardly ever sharply convincing to me as "selves." Point of view, that precise caliper for measuring meaning in Mr. Babb's scheme, is chiefly an invented mind's voice which I can hear and "write through," and whose access to language and idiom seems, at least to start, adequate for some not quite certain telling. Imagery—at best—is a recurrence of sentence patterns and emotional tics and habits I would often rather trade in for more diverse and imaginative resources in language. And symbol. Well, symbol is anything the reader says it is.

And for every writer it's different; different means and expectations, different protocols under which a story accumulates, different temperaments and lingo about how to do it—different work in every way—as should be.

A formal template for studying narrative can guide us orderly into such creations as these, permit a desired intimacy with sentences, aid our confidence and encourage our thinking by abstracting us from parts of the story we can't grasp yet, then in due time leading us to the other parts, so that eventually we see and can try connecting all that's written. But an organizing or explaining system which doesn't illuminate the haphazard in any story's existence can't be a real comprehension. Such schemes are always arbitrary and unstable—wrong (if still useful) in that at their worst they reduce a complex story to some matter of categories, and pose as cure-alls to our natural wonder and awe before great literature —reactions that originate less in ignorance than in the magnitude of the story itself; reactions we shouldn't relinquish but hold on to for dear life—as pleasure.

But pleasure can arise even from this very friction between the story read and the story written. And not a single, simple pleasure, but several, with shadings and history. Even as unsevere and practical-minded as the formal procedure taught me when I learned to read closely is in some sense an imitation of its subject—one with a consoling use, in this case. And imitation has always appealed to us: "The pleasure . . . received is undoubtedly the surprise or feeling of admiration occasioned by the unexpected coincidence between the imitation and its object." That was Hazlitt's idea. And Addison takes it straight to the point: ". . . Our imagination loves to be filled with an object or to grasp at anything that is too big for its capacity"—which is what happens when a method of knowing cannot altogether account for its natural subject in all its complexity.

This friction between my school method and my experience might just as well be renamed pleasure. Each is valuable to me, each quickens interest in the whole truth, and each can accommodate the other. Pleasure, in this scheme, arises when what was unknown, or unknown as pleasure, can be perceived that way; when, in a sense, pleasure is reinvented.

I still feel dread and wonder in the face of literature from time to time—usually in a novel, often so much that I can't parse it with satisfaction. Maybe my spirit for parsing has been worn down. Joyce makes me feel that way. Ford Madox Ford, sometimes. Céline. Gide. Pynchon: awestruck—although I think these writers' aim is to make me feel that. And I simply experience chaos—literary chaos, the story's apparent nearness to its own disorderly beginnings—more agreeably than I once did. I try to accommodate the story read to the one written, which is what Mr. Babb did and would've had me do from the beginning. He probably knew, however, that there's pleasure in first learning and then unlearning, that it is one of literature's other great relevant lessons for life. And I am satisfied that his pleasures have finally become mine, and that I was at least a willing student. For that I could not be more grateful.

DISCUSSION QUESTIONS

1. Ford begins by describing what it was like to read in 1969, as a graduate student. How is your time different from the politically charged era that Ford lived in? Do you feel the same craving for "relevance" in your reading? Why or why not?

2. In retrospect, Ford judges that he and his classmates "wouldn't have recognized relevance if it had come up and kissed us on the lips." What is the older Ford asserting about his younger self?

3. Why does Ford list all the things he knew about fiction when he began teaching? Are these things familiar to you from your previous education? Why are they of no use to him as he prepares to teach?
4. Why does Ford claim that Howard Babb's approach to reading was in some ways better than the literary expert's way? How does Babb help redefine "relevance" for Ford?
5. Why does Ford emphasize that the admission of his own ignorance was a crucial moment in his interaction with Babb?
6. Babb models for Ford a particular way of reading: "Story by story, each had a path-in signaled by a prominent formal feature, with one feature's effects and our observations about it implicating another." Does this method seem familiar to you? How does it orient the reader to the craft of the story?
7. Why does Ford end by contemplating the chaos of literature's "disorderly beginnings," the need to illuminate the "haphazard in any story's existence," and the pleasure of not being able to understand something fully?

RITA MAE BROWN

An Annotated Reading List

Rita Mae Brown (b. 1944) has been infamous since the publication of her best-selling comic novel of lesbian life, Rubyfruit Jungle *(1973). Her many other novels include* Six of One *(1978),* Sudden Death *(1983),* High Hearts *(1986),* Bingo *(1998),* Venus Envy *(1993),* Riding Shotgun *(1996), and* Outfoxed *(2000). Her fiction textbook* Starting from Scratch: A Different Kind of Writers' Manual *(1988) continues to be popular. Her memoir* Rita Will: Memoir of a Literary Rabble-Rouser *(1997) is an account of the importance reading and writing have had in her life.*

This list is prepared for you from a writer's point of view. Delightful though it is to read for story (and you will read for story) you have other concerns. You must study structure, evolving metaphor (if it exists within the work), style, originality, and boldness of theme. Does the dialogue work? Are the characters real or are they stick figures manipulated to serve the story? Is the voice an honest voice or is the author hiding something from you? (Hiding something is not necessarily negative; it may serve the story.) Does the author trust the reader/audience? Has ego gotten in the way of the work itself? Does the work hark back to earlier works by other writers?

There are many more questions than these, but as you can see, your concerns are both emotional and technical. This is what makes our work so subjective.

In the beginning of this list you will be absorbing our language in its primitive state. You begin your reading in the seventh century A.D. As you read, keep in mind that other languages (Greek and Latin for Western culture) have reached their full genius. Look at where we started. The language is stark, not fluid. The concern of the author is usually to inform you of an historical event. *Beowulf* is the first work to reveal the raw visual power of Anglo-Saxon.

These early works—and I've picked out only a few—serve to ground you in your language and in some of the consistent themes of our culture/language. As the centuries progress, so does the language. Chaucer, at the end of the fourteenth century, brought forth the revolution. You and I are indebted to him. He raised up the language. He understood the peculiar affinity of our language/people for comedy/comic relief.

After Chaucer, improvements are rapid. You will be amazed at just how quickly the language evolved. English writers took advantage of each improvement. Nor did they mind stealing from one another or plundering writers from other times and nations.

Writing was, and essentially remains, an aristocratic pursuit. In order to get the time to write you must be an aristocrat or be sponsored by one. Today, sponsorship has been taken over by your publisher. But writing is a time-consuming occupation. Your literary ancestors, recognizing the need for patronage, wrote about kings, queens, dukes, and duchesses. Naturally, a flattering reference to one's own patron is found within the work. Don't be put off by this "class" concern. The common people found their outlet in plays. Since they couldn't read and write, plays were extremely important to them not just as entertainment but as education. So as you move through this list you will see the difference between what was written to be read and what was written to be performed. Keep this uppermost in your mind or you will miss the point the author was trying to make.

Reading these works in chronological order will begin to reveal you to you. You will find that you have predecessors. Even though you may feel isolated historically, you are not. Somewhere in this reading list is a writer or writers with whom you have a natural affinity. When you find them, cherish them. They will teach you a lot.

Another fact that may be revealed to you is your own attention span. If you are under forty-five you have probably always known television. (I did not. We were poor and I didn't see a television until I was about seven.) The misery of television is commercials. On the average, you watch for twelve and a half minutes and then the show cuts to a commercial. Today, our attention span is shorter than that of even one generation ahead of us. If you find yourself getting fidgety or bored, ask yourself if it's the material or if it's you. Granted, some of the selections contained here are boring but you must address them. Still, people under forty-five have been damaged in terms of their attention span. They also need action in the plot. I don't know if people can be weaned away from this need for hype or a fix. I cannot single-handedly change our collective attention spans. All I can do is alert you to something that's happened to you as a result of circumstance. This is a dangerous development for writers, because some subjects can only be approached slowly. I think of them as sleeping cobras. If the public has to have action and false drama (i.e., melodrama), then the more upsetting issues of human life are going to lie dormant because we won't have the patience to understand them.

If that paragraph isn't clear now, it will be as you go through this list. When you come upon the late eighteenth and nineteenth centuries you will see that novels were expected to consume your time. Readers had tolerance for embellishments, the exploration of tangents to the plot, and so on. Of course, they didn't have film and television to distract them. There were no professional sports as we understand them, although there were sports. Reading was a primary form of entertainment and writers rose to the occasion. You do not have that pride of place.

Originally, this list was much more complete. My publisher beseeched me to cut it down to the bone because it would take up too much space and raise the price of the book. I apologize for many of the important works left out. . . .

In some instances I have assumed you have read what is considered a writer's masterpiece. Often I have included a writer's first work so you could see the beginnings of talent. If the writer is important I have included later works too. I have also included some failures and some popular novels. You need the comparison. You can't understand what is good until you know what is mediocre or bad. I find that often the most interesting works from the past are the ones in which the author had an original idea and couldn't fulfill it.

Another thing: Try to cleanse your mind of what your English teachers told you. They were reading with a different purpose from yours. They were also confining themselves to what has been generally accepted as high-quality literature. High quality, depending on where and when you went to school, can mean sterile and sanitized. Beware. You can't afford to think in terms of good and bad right now. You must think in terms of what works and what doesn't. Once you are secure about the mechanics of literature, you can apply yourself to the aesthetics of literature.

After this reading list, which is restricted to writers of English, I wish I could make one from all Western literature, but there just isn't room.

I wish we were gathered among other working writers to read together. Each person brings something unique to a work of literature and I will miss the discussions we aren't having. However, I do hope this helps you and that you'll stick with it over the years.

Reading List

The dates below are dates of publication, or public showing in the case of plays. They do not correspond with the dates of authorship.

665–670

Caedmon, *Caedmon's Hymn,* recorded in the Venerable Bede's *Ecclesiastical History of the English People.*

ca. 700

Anonymous, *Beowulf.*

700–800

Anonymous, *The Rhyming Poem.*

780–830

Cynewulf (attrib.), *Andreas, Christ; Elene; The Fates of the Apostles; Juliana; Riddles 1–59, 30b, 60–95; The Dream of the Rood.* Pick one of Cynewulf's works.

856–915

Anonymous, *Judith.* Begins the written tradition, as the influence of Cynewulf can be clearly seen in this poet's work.

Bede, Venerabilis, *An Ecclesiastical History of the English People.*

973

Anonymous, *The Coronation of Edgar,* in *The Anglo-Saxon Chronicle.* The poet-monk's rhapsodizing on the fact that the apocalypse was only twenty-seven years away is entertaining, and more interesting than the story of Edgar's coronation.

975

Anonymous, *The Death of Edgar,* in *The Anglo-Saxon Chronicle.*

ca. 800–1000

Anonymous, *The Banished Wife's Complaint.*

Anonymous, *A Love Letter.*

Anonymous, *The Ruined City.*

ca. 1300

Anonymous, *Piers Plowman.* First extant copy dates from 1360, but it is mentioned before then.

ca. 1350–1400

John Barbour, *The Actes and Life of the Most Victorious Conqueror, Robert Bruce, King of Scotland.* First extant copy, 1487.

Geoffrey Chaucer, If you haven't read *The Canterbury Tales,* do. It's a delight. If you have, then pick another of Chaucer's work.

ca. 1394–1395

Sir Thomas Clanvowe, *The Cuckoo and the Nightingale.*

ca. 1400

"The Pearl Poet," *Sir Gawaine and the Green Knight.*

1423

James I, King of Scotland, *The Kingis Quair.*

1470

Sir Thomas Malory, *Le Morte d'Arthur.*

1481

Anonymous, *Reynard the Fox.*

1483

John Gower, *Confessio Amantis.*

1528

John Skelton, *A Replication Against Certain Young Scholars.* The language is antiquated but the ideas are current.

1533

John Heywood, *The Play of the Weather.*

1545

John Skelton, *Why Come Ye Not to Court?*

1551

Sir Thomas More, *Utopia* (first edition in English, translated by Ralph Robinson).

1566

Nicholas Udall, *Ralph Roister Doister.* This will give you an idea of how humor was used, and it will also show you how different Shakespeare was from his contemporaries. The play smacks of the schoolroom.

1581

Barnabe Rich, *His Farewell to the Militarie Profession.*

1583

Robert Greene, *Mamillia, A Mirrour o Looking-Glasse for the Ladies of England.*

1590

Robert Greene, *Greenes Never Too Late.*

Christopher Marlowe, *Tamburlaine the Great, Divided into Two Tragical Discourses.*

1591

Thomas Lodge, *A Margarite of America.*

Sir Philip Sidney, *Astrophel and Stella.*

Edmund Spenser, *Complaints, Containing Sundry Small Poems of the World's Vanity.*

1593

William Shakespeare, *Venus and Adonis.*

1594

First production of Shakespeare's *Comedy of Errors.* You should buy a *Complete Works of Shakespeare* and read it in chronological order. There's no way around this, and in addition, once you get the hang of the language you will be swept into its beauty.

Christopher Marlowe, *Edward the Second.*

1596

Michael Drayton, *The Tragical Legend of Robert, Duke of Normandy; The Legend of Matilda; The Legend of Piers Gaveston.*

1598

John Dickenson, *Greene in Conceipt: New Raised from His Grave to the Tragique Historie of the Fair Valerie of London.*

John Marston, *The Metamorphosis of Pigmalions Image, and Certaine Satyres, and The Scourge of Villainy: Three Books of Satyres.*

1600

Ben Jonson, *Every Man Out of His Humour*. See also *Complete Poems,* edited by Ian Donaldson, 1975.

Thomas Nashe, *Summer's Last Will and Testament*.

1601

Ben Jonson, *Every Man in His Humour*.

1603

Thomas Dekker, *The Wonderful Yeare, Wherein Is Shown the Picture of London Lying Sick of the Plague*.

1604

Christopher Marlowe, *The Tragicall History of D. Faustus*.

Thomas Middleton (with Thomas Dekker), *The Honest Whore*.

1606

John Marston, *The Wonder of Women, or The Tragedy of Sophonisba*.

1607

Ben Jonson, *Volpone, or The Fox*.

George Peele, *The Merrie Conceited Jests of George Peele*.

1608

François de Belleforest, *The History of Hamblet*.

Thomas Middleton, *A Mad World, My Masters*.

1609

Edmund Spenser, *The Faerie Queene, Disposed into Twelve Books, Fashioning XII Moral Virtues,* with *Mutability Cantos. The Faerie Queene* was originally published 1590–96, without the *Mutability Cantos*.

1611

John Donne, *An Anatomy of the World*.

1612

Ben Jonson, *The Alchemist*.

1613

Francis Beaumont, *The Knight of the Burning Pestle.*

1620

Thomas Middleton, and William Rowley, *The World Tost at Tennis.*

1633

John Donne, *Poems.*
Christopher Marlowe, *The Famous Tragedy of the Rich Jew of Malta.*

1641

John Day, *The Parliament of Bees, with Their Proper Characters.*

1650

Anne Bradstreet, *The Tenth Muse Lately Sprung Up in America.* Anne Bradstreet strikes a blow for women writers.

1653

Izaak Walton, *The Compleat Angler.* A gentle, enjoyable book even if you don't like fishing.

1656

Margaret Cavendish, Duchess of Newcastle, *Nature's Pictures Drawn by Fancies Pencil to the Life.* The Duchess of Newcastle fancies too much.

1658

Sidney Godolphin, *The Passion of Dido for Aeneas.* "Sidney Godolphin is an almost perfect example of a truly minor poet . . . of the nearly 1,000 lines of his original verse, not one is memorably bad; nor is there a single line that is memorably good"—THOMAS WHEELER. (Couldn't resist.)

1667

John Milton, *Paradise Lost.* I don't like Milton, even as I recognize his exalted gift for poetry. Still, he must be read and he must be mastered.

1669

John Dryden, *Tyrannic Love, or The Royal Martyr.*

1671

Bryce Blair, *The Vision of Theodorus Verax*. This gives you a sense of Milton's contemporaries.

John Milton, *Paradise Regained, to Which Is Added Samson Agonistes*.

1673

John Dryden, *Marriage A-la-Mode*.

William Wycherley, *The Gentleman Dancing-Master*. Wycherley is working out the "new" comedy of manners for English speakers.

1675

William Wycherley, *The Country Wife*.

1677

William Wycherley, *The Plain Dealer*.

1678

John Bunyan, *The Pilgrim's Progress from This World to That Which Is to Come*.

John Dryden, *All for Love, or The World Well Lost*, and *MacFlecknoe*.

1679

Andrew Marvell, *Advice to a Painter*. See also Marvell's *Complete Poems*, edited by Elizabeth Story Donno, 1972.

1680

Thomas D'Urfey, *The Virtuous Wife, or Good Luck at Last*.

1684

Aphra Behn, *The Adventures of the Black Lady*.

1686

Aphra Behn, *The Lover's Watch*.

1688

Richard Blackbourn, *Wit in a Woman*.

1689

Nathaniel Lee, *The Princess of Cleve.*

1692

William Congreve, *Incognita, or Love and Duty Reconciled.* Congreve takes on Wycherley, in a sense. He is good and he's going to get better.

1693

William Congreve, *The Old Bachelor.*

1695

William Congreve, *Love for Love.*

1697

William Congreve, *The Mourning Bride.*

1698

John Crowne, *Calisto.* I threw this in by way of contrast. Crowne is not especially gifted but he's trying.

1699

William King, *Dialogues of the Dead.*

1700

William Congreve, *The Way of the World.* You can't get much better than this. Restoration drama in its exalted state.

1701

Nicholas Rowe, *Tamerlane.* Precedes Arnold Schwarzenegger by 286 years! Rowe would have made him Tamerlane.

1704

Jonathan Swift, *A Tale of a Tub, Written for the Universal Improvement of Mankind, to Which Is Added an Account of a Battle Between the Ancient and Modern Books in St. James's Library.* The first appearance of this satiric genius.

1707

George Farquhar, *The Beaux' Stratagem*. Farquhar lacks Congreve's and Sheridan's natural talent but he works hard; he pays attention to structure although this may be difficult for a modern reader to realize. This is a very fine piece of work.

1708

Ebenezer Cooke, *The Sot-Weed Factor, or A Voyage to Maryland*.

1709

Susanna Centlivre, *The Busie Body, A Comedy*. Susanna makes a stab at it.

1714

Alexander Pope, *The Rape of the Lock*. Divine artifice. Even if an author could achieve this in our time, our public is not sophisticated enough to enjoy it. (I hope I'm wrong.)

1715

Susanna Centlivre, *The Gotham Election*. Never acted, due to censorship. Susanna has not given up, but she's in trouble.

1719

Daniel Defoe, *The Life and Strange Surprising Adventures of Robinson Crusoe, of York, Mariner*. Here's a "newspaperman" turned author.

1726

Jonathan Swift, *Travels into Several Remote Nations of the World, by Captain Lemuel Gulliver*. What can I say that has not already been said? Swift is savage and very secure in his style.

1734

Jonathan Swift, *A Beautiful Young Nymph Going to Bed*.

1737

Elizabeth Boyd, *The Happy Unfortunate; or The Female Page*. An old theme.

1739

Jonathan Swift, *Verses on the Death of Dr. Swift*. Swift's mind is beginning to go.

1740

Samuel Richardson, *Pamela, or Virtue Rewarded*. You can argue about whether or not this is the first true novel. I think the *Satyricon* is the first real novel in Western literature and I know I'll get an argument there. But sticking to English, this has importance and we all need to read it at least once.

1743

John Gay, *The Distress'd Wife*.

1747

Thomas Gray, *Ode on a Distant Prospect of Eton College*. Early Gray.

1749

Henry Fielding, *The History of Tom Jones, a Foundling*.

Samuel Johnson, *The Vanity of Human Wishes: The Tenth Satire of Juvenal Imitated*.

1751

Thomas Gray, *An Elegy Wrote in a Country Church Yard*. Gray in best voice.

1756

Christopher Smart, *On the Goodness of the Supreme Being*. "Confinement in the madhouse allowed Smart to escape some of the restrictions of demand and tradition, and create the distinctive religious verse which is his main achievement"—MARCUS WALSH.

1757

Thomas Gray, *Odes*.

1762

James Macpherson, *Fingal: An Ancient Epic, with Several Other Poems Translated from the Gaelic Language*. Macpherson's claim that these poems are the work of an ancient Gaelic Makar named Ossian is fantasy. They are his own work.

Tobias Smollett, *The Adventures of Sir Launcelot Greaves*.

1766

Oliver Goldsmith, *The Vicar of Wakefield*. Another giant steps on the scene.

1768

Oliver Goldsmith, *The Good Natur'd Man*.
Thomas Gray, *Poems*.
Lady Mary Wortley Montagu, *Poetical Works*.

1769

Tobias Smollett, *The History and Adventures of an Atom*.

1770

Oliver Goldsmith, *The Deserted Village*.
Phyllis Wheatley, *An Elegiac Poem on the Death of the Celebrated Divine Georg Whitfield*.

1773

Oliver Goldsmith, *She Stoops to Conquer, or The Mistakes of a Night*. Sheer, audacious fun!

1775

Richard Brinsley Sheridan, *The Duenna* (music by Thomas Linley). A respectable beginning for another magical writer.

1777

William Combe, *The Diaboliad. A Poem. Dedicated to the Worst Man in His Majesty's Dominions,* Vol. 1. The concept is better than the execution.

1780

Richard Brinsley Sheridan,*The School for Scandal*. How lucky were our forebears that they lived at the same time as Goldsmith and Sheridan. Our theater, today, doesn't even come close.

1781

Richard Brinsley Sheridan, *The Critic, or A Tragedy Rehearsed*.

1785

James Boswell, *The Journal of a Tour to the Hebrides with Samuel Johnson*. Welcome to modern biography, the first bud.

1789

William Blake, *Songs of Innocence*.

1791

James Boswell, *The Life of Samuel Johnson*, 2 Vols. The full bloom.

1796

Joel Barlow, *The Hasty Pudding*.

Samuel Taylor Coleridge, *Poems on Various Subjects*.

Thomas Morton, *The Way to Get Married*. It isn't great literature but it's interesting to note that this subject is still addressed today.

1798

Samuel Taylor Coleridge, and William Wordsworth, *Lyrical Ballads, with a Few Other Poems*.

William Cowper, *Poems: On the Receipt of My Mother's Picture; The Dog and Waterlily*.

1810

Marjorie Fleming. A child poet writing 1810–1811. A literary curiosity worth looking into. Accessible in various collections and referred to sporadically by Victorian writers. Her *Complete Works* is available at most closed-stack research libraries.

Sir Walter Scott, *The Lady of the Lake*. This man eventually became an industry. The story line of each of his novels is strong. The tone is unabashed romanticism.

1813

Jane Austen, *Pride and Prejudice*.

1814

Fanny Burney, *The Wanderer, or Female Difficulties*.

1816

Samuel Taylor Coleridge, *Christabel; Kubla Khan: A Vision; The Poems of Sleep.*

Percy Bysshe Shelley, *Alastor, or The Spirit of Solitude, and Other Poems.* It's interesting to contrast Keats with Shelley. I'll let you make your own judgment.

1817

John Keats, *Poems.*

Sir Walter Scott, *Rob Roy.*

1818

Jane Austen, *Northanger Abbey* and *Persuasion.* See also *Love and Friendship,* edited by G. K. Chesterton, 1922; *The Watsons,* edited by A. B. Walkley, 1923; *Lady Susan,* edited by Q. D. Davis, 1958.

Hannah More, *Stories for the Middle Ranks of Society* and *Tales for the Common People.*

Sir Walter Scott, *The Heart of Midlothian.*

Mary Wollstonecraft Shelley, *Frankenstein, or The Modern Prometheus.*

1819

Sir Walter Scott, *Ivanhoe: A Romance.*

1820

Washington Irving, *The Sketch Book of Geoffrey Crayon, Gent.,* 2 Vols. The first American author to attain international fame. He is much better than we give him credit for being. Literature has fashions and right now Irving is out of fashion.

Percy Bysshe Shelley, *Prometheus Unbound: A Lyrical Drama with Other Poems.*

1821

James Fenimore Cooper, *The Spy.*

Sir Walter Scott, *Kenilworth: A Romance.*

1824

Washington Irving, *Tales of a Traveller.* Irving is getting better.

Walter Savage Landor, *Imaginary Conversations of Literary Men and Statesmen,* 5 Vols. I find this work rewarding to read.

1825

Sarah Kemble Knight, *The Journal of Sarah Kemble Knight*. Sarah learned the secrets of self-advertisement.

1826

James Fenimore Cooper, *The Last of the Mohicans*. His dark vision, almost devoid of women, remains intact. It would have been impossible for a European to write this novel.

1827

Edgar Allan Poe, *Tamerlane and Other Poems*.

1831

James Fenimore Cooper, *The Water Witch*. It's a good idea to read one of his novels that isn't his best. Gives us all hope.

Edgar Allan Poe, *Poems*.

1832

Washington Irving, *The Alhambra*. I think this is an underrated book. It's travel writing of the highest order.

1837

Charles Dickens, *The Posthumous Papers of the Pickwick Club*. Even from the first, Dickens was different.

Nathaniel Hawthorne, *Twice-Told Tales*.

1838

Elizabeth Barrett Browning, *The Seraphim and Other Poems*.

1840

James Fenimore Cooper, *The Pathfinder*. Pure Cooper. Pure homoerotic myth-making, I think!

Edgar Allan Poe, *Tales of the Grotesque and Arabesque*.

1841

James Fenimore Cooper, *The Deerslayer*. Even better than *The Pathfinder*.

1843

Edgar Allan Poe, *The Murders in the Rue Morgue* and *The Man That Was Used Up*. Poe was clever, original and completely misunderstood.

1845

Edgar Allan Poe, *Tales* and *The Raven and Other Poems*.

1847

Anne Brontë, *Agnes Grey*.

Charlotte Brontë, *Jane Eyre: An Autobiography*. See how background and family impose upon literature.

Emily Brontë, *Wuthering Heights*. See also her *Complete Poems,* edited by C. W. Hatfield, 1941.

1848

James Russell Lowell, *A Fable for Critics*. A "civilized" voice for the Northeast.

William Makepeace Thackeray, *Vanity Fair: A Novel Without a Hero*. Not true. The hero was the author.

1849

Robert Browning, *Poems,* 2 Vols.

James Russell Lowell, *Poems,* 2 Vols.

1850

Nathaniel Hawthorne, *The Scarlet Letter.*

Alfred, Lord Tennyson, *In Memoriam*. Tennyson's voice is elegant. If you've been reading your poetry, you will "hear" the difference instantly.

1851

Nathaniel Hawthorne, *The House of the Seven. Gables* and *The Snow Image and Other Twice-Told Tales.*

Herman Melville, *Moby-Dick, Or The Whale*. More homoerotic, desperate literature. There is a doom-ridden quality to Melville and Cooper that astonishes me.

George Meredith, *Poems*. Technically, Meredith is superb, but I still find him boring.

1852

Harriet Beecher Stowe, *Uncle Tom's Cabin, or Life Among the Lowly*. You have to read it to grasp how bad it really is and to wonder at its tremendous political impact.

1853

Walter Savage Landor, *Imaginary Conversations of Greeks and Romans*. More joy.

1854

George Washington Harris, *Sut Lovingood's Yarns and High Times* and *Hard Times*. Serialized, beginning November 4, 1854, in *Spirit of the Times* magazine; first published in 1966–1967, 2 vols., with M. Thomas Inge as editor. Harris gets "cute" but it's a minor school of writing still in vogue today, usually among columnists and magazine writers. The style is updated, obviously, but you will recognize the tone and possibly be nauseated.

Henry David Thoreau, *Walden, or Life in the Woods*. Overrated and over-indulged. One has to read him to try to grasp the phenomenon, particularly as it affected Americans in the late 1960's.

1855

Henry Wadsworth Longfellow, *The Song of Hiawatha*. He's better than you think.

Walt Whitman, *Leaves of Grass*.

1857

Herman Melville, *The Confidence-Man: His Masquerade*. You should read a novel that wasn't a big success. Each of us needs to be reminded that famous, dead writers struggled as much as we struggle.

1858

Oliver Wendell Holmes, *The Autocrat of the Breakfast Table*.

1862

George Meredith, *Modern Love*. Extremely interesting, especially when compared to his other poems.

1865

Lewis Carroll, *Alice's Adventures in Wonderland*.

1866

Christina Rossetti, *The Prince's Progress and Other Poems.*

Algernon Charles Swinburne, *Poems and Ballads.*

1867

Samuel L. Clemens (Mark Twain), *The Celebrated Jumping Frog of Calaveras County and Other Sketches.*

Ouida (pseudonym for Marie Louise de la Rámee), *Under Two Flags.* A wonderful example of a "popular" novel.

1868

Louisa May Alcott, *Little Women,* Vol. 1. True Americana.

Walt Whitman, *Poems.*

1869

Louisa May Alcott, *Little Women,* Vol. 2. More of the same.

Samuel L. Clemens, *The Innocents Abroad.* Conceptually, this was a big jump (forgive the pun) from *The Celebrated Jumping Frog.* . . .

Henry Kendall, *Leaves from Australian Forests.* At last, something about Australia.

1870

Edward Lear, *Nonsense Songs, Stories, Botany, and Alphabets.*

Dante Gabriel Rossetti, *Poems.*

1872

Samuel Butler, *Erewhon, or Over the Range.* There are other Butlers, but this clearly demonstrates his themes.

George Eliot, *Middlemarch: A Study of Provincial Life.* This was a trial to read in eleventh grade but from a technical viewpoint it is a successful novel.

1873

Ambrose Bierce, *Nuggets and Dust Panned Out in California.* If you get "hooked" on him, you'll read everything he wrote.

1874

Thomas Hardy, *Far from the Madding Crowd.*

1875

William Cullen Bryant, *Poems,* 3 Vols.

1876

Samuel L. Clemens, *The Adventures of Tom Sawyer.*
Henry Wheeler Shaw, *Josh Billings, His Works Complete.*

1877

Sidney Lanier, *Poems.*

1878

W. S. Gilbert, *H.M.S. Pinafore* (music by Arthur Sullivan). How did Gilbert learn to be Gilbert? Where is he now that we need him? Don't mistake him for just a lyricist.

1879

W. S. Gilbert, *The Pirates of Penzance* (music by Arthur Sullivan).

Bret Harte, *An Heiress of Red Dog and Other Sketches.*

George Meredith, *The Egoist.* The concern of "Modern Love" is now disguised as a novel which is almost a comedy of manners. I believe it is the same idea from a new angle. Meredith appeals to intellectuals. In my mind, T. S. Eliot picks up where Meredith left off.

1881

Joel Chandler Harris, *Uncle Remus, His Songs and His Sayings.* Still remarkable, although you must steel yourself for the "cute" racism.

Oscar Wilde, *Poems.*

1883

Samuel L. Clemens, *Life on the Mississippi.* He's learned a great deal about writing. It shows.

Robert Louis Stevenson, *Treasure Island.* He's much better than a popular novelist, yet rarely is he regarded as "literary." Make up your own mind.

1885

Samuel L. Clemens, *The Adventures of Huckleberry Finn.*
Walter Pater, *Marius the Epicurean: His Sensations and Ideas.*

1886

Robert Louis Stevenson, *The Strange Case of Dr. Jekyll and Mr. Hyde.* Much, much more than a horror "movie." This work is thematically brilliant.

1888

Edward Bellamy, *Looking Backward: 2000–1887.*
Rudyard Kipling, *Plain Tales from the Hills.* Rivers will flow from this pen.

1890

James Whitcomb Riley, *Rhymes of Childhood.*

1891

Oscar Wilde, *The Picture of Dorian Gray.* Close, in a thematic sense, to *Dr. Jekyll and Mr. Hyde,* yet filled with cynicism. Wilde is always stylized. Stevenson is more "natural."

1892

Sir Arthur Conan Doyle, *The Adventures of Sherlock Holmes.* Elementary.
W. S. Gilbert, *Rosencrantz and Guildenstern.*

1893

Samuel L. Clemens, *The £1,000,000 Bank Note.* Mark Twain off-form is as interesting as other writers on-form.
Oscar Wilde, *Lady Windermere's Fan: A Play About a Good Woman.*

1895

Stephen Crane, *The Black Riders and Other Lines.* You've already read *The Red Badge of Courage.*
Sir Arthur Wing Pinero, *The Second Mrs. Tanqueray.*
H. G. Wells, *The Time Machine: An Invention.* He was never anything like any other writer. A true original, although not "great."

1896

Samuel L. Clemens, *Personal Recollections of Joan of Arc.*

1897

Kate Chopin, *A Night in Acadie.* Kate Chopin did a brisk sale in books and she wrote many. She is very much a product of her time.

Bram Stoker, *Dracula.*

1898

George Bernard Shaw, *Plays Pleasant and Unpleasant,* 2 Vols. He asked for no quarter and he gave none, from youth to old age.

H. G. Wells, *The War of the Worlds.*

Oscar Wilde, *The Ballad of Reading Gaol.* This was a shift, for Wilde.

1900

L. Frank Baum, *The Wonderful Wizard of Oz.* See what happens when a work is adapted for the screen.

Joseph Conrad, *Lord Jim.* Pay attention to how a non-native uses English.

Theodore Dreiser, *Sister Carrie.*

1901

George Washington Cable, *The Cavalier.* Cable was much admired in his day. He filled the shelves of book stores.

Frank Norris, *The Octopus.* This floored people.

1903

Samuel Butler, *The Way of All Flesh.*

George Bernard Shaw, *Man and Superman: A Comedy (and a Philosophy).*

1904

O. Henry (pseudonym of William Sydney Porter), *Cabbages and Kings.* Fantastic command over the short-story form.

1905

Edith Wharton, *The House of Mirth.* This is a sharp, new American voice. In my mind she is the counterpoint to Dreiser.

1906

Upton Sinclair, *The Jungle.* What did he learn from Frank Norris? Do you think there is a connection?

1907

J. M. Synge, *The Playboy of the Western World*.

1908

Kenneth Grahame, *The Wind in the Willows*. Utter happiness/silliness.

1909

Samuel L. Clemens, *Extracts from Captain Stormfield's Visit to Heaven*.

Gertrude Stein, *Three Lives: Stories of The Good Anna, Melanctha, and The Gentle Lena*. She is rough going but her experiments with language helped her generation of writers break from the adjective-heavy style then so popular. If Hemingway had not found Stein, he would not have become Hemingway.

1910

Saki (pseudonym of H. H. Munro), *Reginald in Russia and Other Sketches*.

William Butler Yeats, *The Green Helmet and Other Poems*. He is to poetry as Cezanne is to painting.

1911

Max Beerbohm, *Zuleika Dobson, or An Oxford Love Story*.

Frances Hodgson Burnett, *The Secret Garden*.

Edith Wharton, *Ethan Frome*. Remember reading this in high school? Bet it looks different now.

1912

Zane Grey, *Riders of the Purple Sage*. These cowboy stories were gobbled up by little boys in America and also in Germany.

1913

D. H. Lawrence, *Sons and Lovers*. More interesting than *Lady Chatterley's Lover*.

Vachel Lindsay, *General William Booth Enters into Heaven and Other Poems*.

1914

Edgar Rice Burroughs, *Tarzan of the Apes*. Another one of those boys' books which affected so many people.

Booth Tarkington, *Penrod*. Tarkington, for a time, was a beloved American writer. Read this and see if you can figure out why he is out of favor. Almost forgotten.

1915

Edgar Lee Masters, *Spoon River Anthology* (revised and expanded in 1916). This is a deceptive work.

1916

Samuel L. Clemens, *The Mysterious Stranger.*

George Bernard Shaw, *Pygmalion; Overruled;* and *Androcles and the Lion.*

1917

Clemence Dane, *Regiment of Women.* She was very celebrated in her time.

Siegfried Sassoon, *To Any Dead Officer.* He is not a great or perhaps even good writer by literary standards, but he is effective and his reserve is probably what cost him greatness, for the talent is there. Also, he did not devote himself to the craft.

1918

Gerard Manley Hopkins (d. 1889), *Poems,* edited by Robert Bridges.

Booth Tarkington, *The Magnificent Ambersons.* This book should not be in the literary doldrums.

1919

P. G. Wodehouse, *My Man Jeeves.* The beginning of an industry much more appreciated by the British than by Americans.

1920

Dame Agatha Christie, *The Mysterious Affair at Styles.* Doyle's spiritual "daughter" begins to weave her web.

Wilfred Owen (d. 1918), *Poems,* edited by Siegfried Sassoon. See also *Collected Poems,* edited by C. Day Lewis.

Edith Wharton, *The Age of Innocence.* A devastating book—and it fools you. She has become so sure of herself she doesn't have to show off.

1921

Clemence Dane, *Will Shakespeare: An Invention in Four Acts.* What do you think is going on here? Is this clever or is there something else?

1922

T. S. Eliot, *The Waste Land*. The post–World War I world found a voice.

John Galsworthy, *The Forsyte Saga*.

James Joyce, *Ulysses*. Where would university professors be without *Ulysses*? By this time, this work has become a parody of itself and it is the fawning of university English teachers that has ruined it. What a pity.

Katherine Mansfield, *The Garden Party and Other Stories*.

1923

Edna St. Vincent Millay, *Poems*. A crystal clear, unyielding voice.

1924

Emily Dickinson (d. 1886), *The Complete Poems,* edited by Martha Dickinson Bianchi.

Edna Ferber, *So Big*. Her sense of story is sure. You may or may not find her "dated." She enjoyed stupendous success in her lifetime.

George Bernard Shaw, *Saint Joan*.

1925

Noel Coward, *The Vortex*. Daring at the time. Coward's subject was VD.

Countee Cullen, *Color*.

Hilda Doolittle (H.D.), *Collected Poems*.

Theodore Dreiser, *An American Tragedy*.

F. Scott Fitzgerald, *The Great Gatsby*.

Robinson Jeffers, *Roan Stallion, Tamar, and Other Poems*.

Sinclair Lewis, *Arrowsmith*.

1926

Ernest Hemingway, *The Sun Also Rises*. I never tire of this novel.

Sean O'Casey, *The Plough and the Stars*.

Sir Sacheverell Sitwell, *All Summer in a Day: An Autobiographical Fantasia*. You may hate it or love it. This is what happens when a writer is "superior" to his audience. Very different from his sister, Edith.

1927

Rosamond Lehmann, *Dusty Answer.*

Jean Rhys, *The Left Bank and Other Stories.*

Thornton Wilder, *The Bridge of San Luis Rey.*

Virginia Woolf, *To the Lighthouse.*

1928

J. M. Barrie, *Peter Pan, or The Boy Who Would Not Grow Up.*

Radclyffe Hall, *The Well of Loneliness.* Historically important as regards women. Stylistically absurd.

D. H. Lawrence, *Lady Chatterley's Lover.* Another historically important work of questionable literary value. As time passes the cracks in the plaster widen, and Lawrence fanatics will blow a fuse when they read this assessment.

Virginia Woolf, *Orlando: A Biography.* I believe this is her greatest work. I know I'll get lots of arguments but that's why Woolf is special. She involves you in her work in a personal way.

1929

Djuna Barnes, *A Night Among the Horses.*

Dashiell Hammett, *The Dain Curse.*

Edmund Wilson, *I Thought of Daisy.*

Thomas Wolfe, *Look Homeward Angel: A Story of the Buried Life.*

1930

Dorothy Canfield (later Fisher), *The Deepening Stream.* She was very popular.

Noel Coward, *Private Lives.* Bliss. Pure bliss.

W. Somerset Maugham, *Cakes and Ale.* His is a "distant" style. Very readable. He is tricky but you don't know you are being tricked—or maybe it's just me.

Carl Van Vechten, *Parties: Scenes from Contemporary New York Life.*

1931

Elizabeth Bowen, *Friends and Relations.*

Kay Boyle, *Plagued by the Nightingale.*

Pearl S. Buck, *The Good Earth.* Another writer in eclipse.

Gertrude Stein, *How to Write.* Dare we try after reading this?

1932

Erskine Caldwell, *Tobacco Road*. Certain Southerners were very upset with Caldwell. He didn't flinch.

William Faulkner, *Light in August*. Another Southerner despised, in the beginning, by his own people. He didn't give up either.

Zelda Fitzgerald, *Save Me the Waltz*.

Rosamond Lehmann, *Invitation to the Waltz*.

James Thurber, *The Seal in the Bedroom and Other Predicaments*.

1933

Richard Aldington, *All Men are Enemies: A Romance*. Another popular novelist.

Ivy Compton-Burnett, *More Women Than Men*. She was much praised back then.

Dorothy L. Sayers, *Murder Must Advertise*.

Gertrude Stein, *The Autobiography of Alice B. Toklas*. At last, you can understand what she's writing.

Nathanael West, *Miss Lonelyhearts*.

1934

Robert Graves, *I, Claudius* and *Claudius the God*.

Dashiell Hammett, *The Thin Man*.

Lillian Hellman, *The Children's Hour*.

Zora Neale Hurston, *Jonah's Gourd Vine*.

Frederick Rolfe (pseudonym of Baron Corvo), *The Desire and Pursuit of the Whole*. A curiosity then. A curiosity still.

1935

T. S. Eliot, *Murder in the Cathedral*. If only he hadn't been so intellectual!

Hugh MacDiarmid, *Second Hymn to Lenin and Other Poems*.

John O'Hara, *Butterfield 8*. A smashing success. Most of his books were best sellers. Can you figure out why?

Muriel Rukeyser, *Theory of Flight*.

1936

Djuna Barnes, *Nightwood*. This is considered her strange, isolated masterpiece.

Margaret Mitchell, *Gone with the Wind*. Don't laugh. If you pay attention to this novel you might learn something.

Dorothy Parker, *Collected Poems: Not So Deep as a Well.*

Laura Riding, *Progress of Stories.*

1937

Moss Hart and George S. Kaufman, *You Can't Take It with You.*

1938

Elizabeth Bowen, *The Death of the Heart.*

John Dos Passos, *U.S.A.* Another odd work. Think about his structure. Why did he choose to present material this way?

Marjorie Kinnan Rawlings, *The Yearling.* This deceptively quiet book, as you know, was made into a successful film.

Muriel Rukeyser, *U.S. 1.*

Thornton Wilder, *Our Town.* This has been done to death. Why? Because it is so accessible.

1939

Moss Hart and George S. Kaufman, *The Man Who Came to Dinner.*

Lillian Hellman, *The Little Foxes.* By now, the South was center stage in American literature.

Katherine Anne Porter, *Pale Horse, Pale Rider.*

William Saroyan, *The Time of Your Life.* Can you make the connection between *U.S.A., Our Town,* and this work?

John Steinbeck, *The Grapes of Wrath.*

Dalton Trumbo, *Johnny Got His Gun.*

Nathanael West, *The Day of the Locust.*

1940

Arthur Koestler, *Darkness at Noon.*

Carson McCullers, *The Heart Is a Lonely Hunter.* People back in Columbus, Georgia, wouldn't speak to Carson after reading her books.

Christina Stead, *The Man Who Loved Children.*

James Thurber and Elliott Nugent, *The Male Animal.*

1941

Noel Coward, *Blithe Spirit.*

Eudora Welty, *A Curtain of Green and Other Stories.* People in Jackson, Mississippi, did and still do speak to Ms. Welty. On the surface she is gentle, but her themes are not slight. Her voice, while very Southern, is quite different from the other celebrated Southern authors of this time.

1942

Sir Rabindranath Tagore (d. 1941), *Poems,* edited by Krishna Kripalani.
Thornton Wilder, *The Skin of Our Teeth.*

1943

Edna St. Vincent Millay, *Collected Lyrics.*
Delmore Schwartz, *Genesis: Book One.* Most definitely not a Southern voice.

1944

S. J. Perelman and Ogden Nash (music by Kurt Weill), *One Touch of Venus.*
Sir Osbert Sitwell, *Left Hand! Right Hand!* The Sitwell siblings strike again.

1945

Walter de la Mare, *The Burning Glass and Other Poems.*
Nancy Mitford, *The Pursuit of Love.* I still don't think the English have recovered from the Mitford sisters.
George Orwell (pseudonym for Eric Arthur Blair), *Animal Farm: A Fairy Story.*
Tennessee Williams, *The Glass Menagerie.*
Richard Wright, *Black Boy.*

1946

Christopher Isherwood, *The Berlin Stories.*
Carson McCullers, *The Member of the Wedding.*
Terence Rattigan, *The Winslow Boy.*
Robert Penn Warren, *All the King's Men.*
Frank Yerby, *The Foxes of Harrow.* He was a popular novelist.

1947

Malcolm Lowry, *Under the Volcano.*
Sean O'Faolain, *Teresa.*
S. J. Perelman, *The Best of Perelman.*
Tennessee Williams, *A Streetcar Named Desire.*

1948

Hortense Calisher, *In the Absence of Angels*.

Truman Capote, *Other Voices, Other Rooms*. Like a comet, this beautiful talent reduced himself to dust.

Ezra Pound, *Cantos*. There is nothing easy about Ezra Pound, but you can't afford to ignore his work.

James Thurber, *The Beast in Me and Other Animals*.

Gore Vidal, *The City and the Pillar*. This was a concern, a style, left behind by Vidal.

1949

Truman Capote, *A Tree of Night and Other Stories*.

Christopher Fry, *The Lady's Not for Burning*.

1950

William Inge, *Come Back Little Sheba*.

Carl Sandburg, *Complete Poems*. He styled himself a poet of the people.

Isaac Bashevis Singer, *The Family Moskat*.

Tennessee Williams, *The Roman Spring of Mrs. Stone*.

William Butler Yeats (d. 1939), *Collected Poems*.

1951

Langston Hughes, *Mortgage of a Dream Deferred*.

J. D. Salinger, *The Catcher in the Rye*. Will this stand the test of time? We won't know.

1952

Ralph Ellison, *The Invisible Man*.

Ernest Hemingway, *The Old Man and the Sea*.

Mary McCarthy, *The Groves of Academe*. She doesn't write with a pen. She uses a scalpel! Here is a writer with terrific control—what does that do to the material?

1953

James Baldwin, *Go Tell It on the Mountain*.

Arthur Miller, *The Crucible*.

Ogden Nash, *The Private Dining Room and Other New Verses*.

Mary Renault (pseudonym for Mary Challans), *The Charioteer.* She has a huge cult following. Think about the material. In another writer's hands this novel would have died. As it is, the tone of the book is a problem, at least, for me.

1954

William Golding, *Lord of the Flies.*

Dylan Thomas, *Under Milk Wood: A Play for Voices.* You've probably read this.

1955

Vladimir Nabokov, *Lolita.* Another non-native writer who wrote in English. He is important to study for his use of our language and for his themes. Would an American have selected this? What about an English writer? If they had, imagine how they would have presented the story. Why was/is he so celebrated? Does Cold War politics have anything to do with it?

Sir Terence Rattigan, *Separate Tables* (two plays).

Tennessee Williams, *Cat on a Hot Tin Roof.*

1956

James Baldwin, *Giovanni's Room.*

Brendan Behan, *The Quare Fellow.*

Allen Ginsberg, *Howl and Other Poems.*

Eugene O'Neill, *Long Day's Journey into Night.*

1957

Stanley Kunitz, *Selected Poems, 1928–1958.*

John Osborne, *Look Back in Anger.*

1958

Archibald MacLeish, *J.B.: A Play in Verse.* Much admired at that time.

C. P. Snow, *The Conscience of the Rich.*

Tennessee Williams, *Garden District: Something Unspoken* and *Suddenly Last Summer.*

1959

John Ciardi, *39 Poems.*

Lorraine Hansberry, *A Raisin in the Sun.*

Grace Paley, *The Little Disturbances of Man.*

Muriel Spark, *Memento Mori*. Quite a wicked little book, displaying Spark's distinctive characteristics as a writer.

1960

Harper Lee, *To Kill a Mockingbird*.

Brian Moore, *The Luck of Ginger Coffey*.

Tillie Olsen, *Tell Me a Riddle*.

Harold Pinter, *The Birthday Party and Other Plays*.

Sylvia Plath, *The Colossus and Other Poems*.

Anne Sexton, *To Bedlam and Part Way Back*.

Gary Snyder, *Myths and Texts*.

1961

Muriel Spark, *The Prime of Miss Jean Brodie*. You probably know this one.

1962

Edward Albee, *Who's Afraid of Virginia Woolf?* Caused a sensation when first produced. Would it today?

Doris Lessing, *The Golden Notebook*. She has passionate admirers. Your reaction to her work ought to tell you something about the kind of books you want to write.

1963

Hortense Calisher, *Extreme Magic: A Novella and Other Stories*.

1964

James Dickey, *Two Poems of the Air*.

Denise Levertov, *0 Taste and See: New Poems*.

Robert Lowell, *For the Union Dead*. This harks back to another Lowell.

1965

May Sarton, *Mrs. Stevens Hears the Mermaids Singing*.

1966

Truman Capote, *In Cold Blood: A True Account of a Multiple Murder and Its Consequences*. A twist: nonfiction treated almost like fiction. You're on dangerous ground here. After Capote this "form" took off. The form makes me uneasy. I feel that it is intrinsically dishonest.

Bernard Malamud, *The Fixer*.

1967

Marianne Moore, *The Complete Poems*.

Joyce Carol Oates, *A Garden of Earthly Delights*.

Joe Orton, *Crimes of Passion: The Ruffian on the Stair, and The Erpingham Camp*. Why did this kind of drama come forth in England? Something happened there after World War II.

Tom Stoppard, *Rosencrantz and Guildenstern Are Dead*. Gilbert used Rosencrantz and Guildenstern in 1892. What's the pull of these two Shakespearean characters?

William Styron, *The Confessions of Nat Turner*.

Thornton Wilder, *The Eighth Day*. This is an interesting "failure."

1968

Gore Vidal, *Myra Breckinridge*.

1969

John Berryman, *Dream Songs*.

Kurt Vonnegut, *Slaughterhouse Five, or, The Children's Crusade*.

1970

Maya Angelou, *I Know Why the Caged Bird Sings*. Maya is still singing, thank God.

Enid Bagnold, *Four Plays*.

Denise Levertov, *Relearning the Alphabet*.

1971

Cynthia Ozick, *The Pagan Rabbi and Other Stories*.

1972

Barbara Deming, *Wash Us and Comb Us*. This is a personal book, essays disguised as memoirs. Pay attention to her style.

James Merrill, *Braving the Elements*. A style 180 degrees from Deming—yet, how are these writers similar?

1973

Adrienne Rich, *Diving into the Wreck: Poems 1971–1972*.

Gore Vidal, *Burr*. Gore Vidal uses history as a mirror for the political life in the 1970's. Even if you don't "get" it, the book reads well as a story about Burr. This has Vidal's trademark: superb structure, suspicion/fear of emotion. Also, this is a good example of a book in which something is withheld from you until the end without its being a trick. It relates to the emotional blindness/innocence of the main character.

1975

Seamus Heaney, *Bog Poems*.
Ruth Prawer Jhabvala, *Heat and Dust*.

1976

W. H. Auden, *Collected Poems*.

1980

Margaret Drabble, *The Middle Ground*.

1981

Anthony Burgess, *Earthly Powers*.

Please excuse the lacunae from 1981 until today. I am weary. I've read many recently published novels, but with the exception of *The Color Purple* by Alice Walker, I'm drawing a blank. Of course, right now there is an avalanche of books being published and I know I've missed some fine ones. The closer one gets to one's own time the harder it is to see clearly.

DISCUSSION QUESTIONS

1. Brown begins with a matter-of-fact list of chores and questions for the reading writer. How does her advice reinforce or contrast with Cassill's and Ford's?
2. Why does Brown begin her list with works that present language "in its primitive state"?
3. Brown insists that "reading these works in chronological order will begin to reveal you to you." What does she mean by this? How strong a sense do you have of yourself within a historical tradition? Has your reading of literature helped you define yourself as a writer?
4. Why does Brown distinguish between "terms of good and bad" and "terms of what works and what doesn't"? Why does she disdain the lessons of English teachers that foreground "great literature"?

DAVID LODGE

Creative Writing:
Can It/Should It be Taught?

David Lodge (b. 1935) taught at the University of Birmingham (England) from 1960 to 1987,
when he retired. His novel Changing Places *(1975) won the Yorkshire Post Fiction Prize and*
the Hawthornden Prize, *while* How Far Can You Go? *(1980) won the Whitbread Award*
for Fiction. His other novels include The Picturegoers *(1960),* Out of the Shelter
(1970), Ginger, You're Barmy *(1982),* Paradise News *(1992), and* Therapy *(1995).*
He is also an important critic, with books on Jane Austen, Evelyn Waugh, and Graham Greene,
as well as the collections The Novelist at the Crossroads and Other Essays on Fiction and Criticism *(1971),* Working with Structuralism: Essays and Reviews on
Nineteenth and Twentieth Century Literature *(1981),* After Bakhtin: Essays on
Fiction and Criticism *(1990).* The Practice of Writing: Essays, Lectures, Reviews,
and a Diary *(1996) reflects upon his own forty years as a writer, as well as the experiences of*
other writers.

In April 1995 the Royal Society of Literature held a one-day seminar on the
subject, "Creative Writing: can it be taught?" The idea for the event originally
came from Hilary Mantel, and it was chaired by P. D. James. The audience consisted of a mixture of writers, aspirant writers and teachers of writing. This was
my contribution (slightly expanded here) to the opening panel discussion.

PENNY You told me earlier what I was doing wrong. I understand that, I
think. Now I want to know how to do it right.

LEO (*slowly*) You want me to tell you how to produce literary works of enduring value?

PENNY Please.

LEO *shakes his head.*

PENNY I know it's not a simple matter.

LEO You bet your sweet—bet your life it isn't.

PENNY But you *are* a teacher of creative writing.

LEO I offer criticism. What my students do with it is up to them.

—The Writing Game, Act I Scene 5

How does one become a writer? One thing is certain: nobody ever wrote a book without having read at least one—and more probably hundreds—of approximately the same kind. Most writers, whether they take courses in creative writing or not, are kick-started—that is, they begin by imitating and emulating the literature that gives them the biggest kicks. The pleasure and the enhanced sense of reality that you get from reading gives you the urge to try and produce that effect on others. And it is from reading that you acquire basic knowledge of the structural and rhetorical devices that belong to a particular genre or form of writing. To a large extent this learning process is intuitive and unconscious, like learning the mother tongue.

Three writers who I believe had a formative influence on me when I started to try and write prose fiction were James Joyce, Graham Greene and Evelyn Waugh. No doubt the fact that all three were Catholics, and wrote, in very different ways, about Catholic subjects, was one reason why I was drawn to their work in late adolescence, for I was brought up in that faith myself. I also read them as a student of modern English Literature, with exams to pass and degrees to get. But from my immersion in their work I absorbed many lessons about the techniques of fiction, some of which I did not put into practice until many years later. For example: from Greene, how to use a few, selected details, heightened by metaphor and simile, to evoke character or the sense of place; from Waugh, how to generate comedy by a combination of logic and surprise, of the familiar and the incongruous; from Joyce, how to make a modern story re-enact, echo or parody a mythical or literary precursor-narrative. I learned many other things from these writers as well—above all, I would like to think, a craftsmanlike approach to the business of writing, a willingness to take pains, a commitment to making the work as good as you can possibly make it.

Can such things be taught, systematically, rather than personally discovered and intuitively assimilated? Henry James thought they couldn't, and said so in a famous essay called "The Art of Fiction." This was written in 1884 as a riposte to a lecture with the same title, delivered in that year to the Royal Institution by Walter Besant. Everybody interested in the subject knows James's essay, but not many have read the text which provoked it, for it is quite difficult to obtain. Besant was a prolific and versatile man of letters, typically Victorian in his energy and industry. He boasted of having written 18 novels in 18 years, and also wrote on and translated French literature, and published books and journalism on many other subjects. He was a tireless philanthropist, and a key figure in the professionalization of authorship in the late nineteenth century.

In the same year that he published his "Art of Fiction," Besant founded the Society of Authors, and it is clear in retrospect that the lecture was part of his mission to raise the professional status of writers. He begins by arguing that novelists are not taken seriously as artists because, unlike painters, sculptors and musicians, they receive no national honours and awards, they "hold no annual exhibitions, dinners or conversazione; they put no letters after their name; they have no President or Academy," and they do not attempt to teach their art to aspirant practitioners:

> How can that be an Art . . . which has no lecturers or teachers, no school or college or Academy, no recognized rules, no text-books, and is not taught in any University? Even German universities, which teach everything else, do not have Professors of fiction, and not one single novelist, so far as I know, has ever pretended to teach his mystery.

All these things have come to pass, for good or ill, and Besant can take some of the credit for that. Certainly, if anyone deserves the title "Father of Creative Writing Courses" it is he. To tyros who lightly assume that "anyone can write a novel," he sternly recommends "that from the very beginning their minds should be fully possessed with the knowledge that Fiction is an Art, and, like all other Arts, that it is governed by certain laws, methods and rules, which it is their first business to learn."

Henry James welcomed Besant's insistence that the novel is a work of art, which might be analysed and discussed, counteracting the "comfortable good-humoured feeling" more common in England, that "a novel is a novel as a pudding is a pudding, and that our only business with it could be to swallow it." On the other hand he was sceptical of Besant's claim that "the laws of fiction may be laid down and taught with as much precision as the laws of harmony, perspective, and proportion":

> The painter *is* able to teach the rudiments of his practice and it is possible, from the study of good work (granted the aptitude), both to learn how to paint and how to write. Yet it remains true . . . that the literary artist would be obliged to say to his pupil much more than the other, "Ah well, you must do it as you can!" If there are exact sciences, there are also exact arts, and the grammar of painting is so much more definite that it makes the difference.

The essence of James's argument, eloquently developed later in the essay, is that the novel is an organic form:

> I cannot imagine composition existing in a series of blocks, nor conceive, in any novel worth discussing at all, a passage of dialogue that is not in its intention descriptive, a touch of truth of any sort that does not partake of the nature of incident, or an incident that derives its interest from any other source than the general and only source of the success of a work of art—that of being illustrative. A novel is a living thing, all one and continuous, like any other organism, and in

proportion as it lives will it be found, I think, that in each of the parts there is something of each of the other parts.

Since you cannot isolate and identify the various components of a novel, James seems to be saying, it follows that you cannot teach people how to use them.

Was he right? Well, one hesitates to disagree with Henry James, but I think he overstates his case. Let me invoke another great modern writer, T. S. Eliot. In his essay "The Function of Criticism" Eliot said: "the larger part of the labour of an author in composing his work is critical labour, the labour of sifting, combining, constructing, expunging, correcting, testing: this frightful toil is as much critical as creative." That is precisely what I mean by the willingness to take pains. It can be done intuitively—but it can also be done consciously and analytically. We learn our mother tongue without learning grammar first, but we need the metalanguage of grammar to understand and explain (explain to ourselves as well as to others) how a language works—what are its rules and possibilities, and why some utterances fail in their communicative purpose. I don't say it is *essential* for a writer to have such a metalanguage at his fingertips—just as Molière's M. Jourdain found he had been speaking prose all his life without knowing it, a novelist may use, for example, free indirect style without knowing what it is called or being consciously aware of what its rules and constraints are—but I don't think it does any harm, either, to acquire the metalanguage, and it may help in that essential process of self-criticism which Eliot describes so well. In short, I see no incompatibility between the formalistic critical study of literature and the effort to produce new writing of one's own.

Walter Besant's mistake was to base his proposals not on rhetoric, which can be taught (*that* effect is produced by *this* technique), but on general aesthetic "rules" or "laws" which are either matters of subjective opinion or so vague as to be useless for pedagogic purposes. He sums them up as follows:

> The Art of Fiction requires first of all the power of description, truth and fidelity, observation, selection, clearness of conception and of outline, dramatic grouping, directness of purpose, a profound belief on the part of the story-teller in the reality of his story, and beauty of workmanship.

Well, yes—but whose truth, whose beauty? And what makes one description more powerful than another? On what principles is "selection" based, and what exactly do the terms "outline" and "dramatic" mean in the context of narrative prose? Besant never tells us, and he never illustrates his maxims with quotation—an abstention that becomes almost comically frustrating at times. One would dearly like to know how

> in some well-known scenes which I could quote, there is not a single word to emphasize or explain the attitude, manner and look of the speakers, yet they are as intelligible as if they were written down and described.

In short, Besant's "rules" and "laws" of the art of fiction amount to little more than vague invocations of the conventional literary taste of his time. As Henry

James observed, with his usual suave courtesy, "They are suggestive, they are even inspiring, but they are not exact, though they are doubtless as much so as the case admits of."

Creative writing courses can help the aspirant writer to acquire a descriptive vocabulary for and explicit awareness of such technical matters as (in prose fiction, for instance) point of view, narrative voice, frame-breaking, time-shifting, etc., etc., to entertain a wider range of possibilities in these respects than the writer might have discovered independently, and to appreciate how important are the choices made in these categories to the final effect of a narrative text. These things can be "taught" in a variety of ways: by systematic exposition, by practical criticism of model texts, by set writing exercises, and by workshop or tutorial discussion of the student's own spontaneously generated work.

Those words, "own" and "spontaneously," however, bring us to the problematic heart of the matter. I have suggested that the teaching of creative writing is best seen as a special application of formalist criticism. But it is a peculiar feature of criticism, and especially of literary criticism, that the licence to criticize does not carry with it an obligation to explain how the fault complained of might have been avoided or how it might be repaired. The reviewer of a novel may complain that a certain phrase is a cliché without being obliged to produce a fresher one; may protest that a certain character's actions are implausible without having to suggest more credible behaviour. Indeed, for a critic to propose such emendations would be regarded as out of order. The reason is very simple and very obvious: once you start trying to rewrite somebody else's work, you take it away from them and make it your own. To that extent James was right: creative writing cannot be "taught"—as, say, perspective can be taught to an aspiring artist—by correcting the student's work or showing him how it should be done. Indeed a creative writer who tries to make his students clones of himself is doing them the worst possible service.

I believe anyone's expressive and communicative skills can be improved by practice and criticism. If the teacher is competent, anyone who takes a creative writing course ought to be producing or capable of producing better work at the end of it than at the beginning. And certainly the experience of trying to write under systematic guidance will enhance the student's understanding and appreciation of literature as a reader. For that reason I believe there should be a creative writing component of the set-exercise type in all English education up to and including the tertiary level. But no course can teach you how to produce a text other people will willingly give up their time—and perhaps their money—to read, although it has no utilitarian purpose or value.

This raises another kind of problem as regards courses which are offered to students with serious aspirations to become professional writers. Since you cannot guarantee that any of them will succeed in this ambition, is it ethical to take their money to teach them? Responsibly taught courses do their best to mitigate this problem by careful selection of students. But ultimately success cannot be guaranteed and this should be made clear to everybody involved. In one sense, literature is not differently placed from any of the other arts in this respect. You can be taught to draw and paint competently but you cannot be taught to produce paintings of enduring value. But there is a difference too: you can draw and paint for your own pleasure, but, to be satisfying, writing needs an audience and a permanent existence in print. It needs to be published. And as we know, crossing that threshold is very difficult. There is no such thing as an "amateur" novelist, or a "Sunday novelist"—or if there is, it is not a status that anyone would take much pride or satisfaction in, I think. One common argument in favour of creative writing courses, especially long-term ones, is that they provide a supportive yet critical community in which the budding writer can develop and test his or her talent. Certainly many graduates of such courses have testified that this was their experience. Others find the competitiveness and self-exposure of the situation intimidating and inhibiting. But in either case, the community of the course is a small and artificial one. Sooner or later the students must submit their work to the judgement of readers—publishers, agents, editors, scavengers of the slush-pile—who don't know them personally, and this can be a deeply discouraging experience. The more advanced the course, the more heartbreak is likely to be associated with it.*

"The only obligation to which in advance we may hold a novel, without incurring the accusation of being arbitrary," said Henry James in his essay, "is that it be interesting." It goes without saying that not every successful novel can be interesting to every potential reader. But there are novels which are interesting to nobody except the author and perhaps his or her family and friends, and it is inevitable that a great many, perhaps the majority, of works produced in creative writing classes will fall into this category.

What makes a novel "interesting," however, is as difficult to define as any of Walter Besant's categories; though we all recognize the quality when we encounter it and are aware of its absence when it is missing. It is not subject-matter, as James himself was anxious to affirm: "We must grant the artist his subject, his idea, his *donnée:* our criticism is applied only to what he makes of it." But it is not just a matter of technique either. It is like a chemical, or alchemical, reaction between form and content. So many factors are involved in the production of a literary text: the writer's life-experience, his genetic inheritance, his historical context, his reading, his powers of recall, his capacity for introspection, his fantasy life, his understanding of the springs of narrative, his responsiveness to language —its rhythms, sounds, registers, nuances of meaning, and so on. Even a single sentence in a novel is the complex product of innumerable chains of cause and effect which reach deep into the writer's life and psyche. To distinguish, analyse and retrace them all would be impossible. Even the most sophisticated literary

---

*Walter Besant's advice for dealing with rejection is brutally blunt: "if a novelist fail at first, let him be well assured it is his own fault; and if on his second attempt, he cannot amend, let him for the future be silent." In an appendix to the printed lecture he relented somewhat: "persevere, if you feel that the root of the matter is in you, till your work is accepted; and *never,* NEVER, NEVER pay for publishing a novel."

criticism only scratches the surface of the mysterious process of creativity; and so, by the same token, does even the best course in creative writing.

DISCUSSION QUESTIONS

1. Lodge begins with the perennial question about creative writing mentioned in this chapter's introduction: Can it really be taught? What are your beliefs about this question? Have your beliefs changed as you've taken classes and developed as a writer?
2. Lodge cites the importance of reading to the fiction writer's growth, echoing R. V. Cassill's, Rita Mae Brown's, and Richard Ford's views in the previous section. Make your own list of writers from whom you have "absorbed lessons" in the way Lodge describes. What specific things have you learned from these writers?
3. Lodge gives careful consideration to Henry James' claim that the organic nature of the novel works against the teaching of the art of fiction. What does James mean by this? What analogies other than the one to painting can you develop to support or challenge James' point?
4. Lodge lists several ways that creative writing courses can aid writers: by providing a "descriptive vocabulary," by increasing awareness of "technical matters," and by building an understanding of the effects of the writer's choices on the work's effectiveness. Have your courses provided these things? How?
5. Lodge ends by acknowledging the "mysterious process of creativity" and states further that even the "best course" in creative writing can only begin to illuminate this mystery. If this is so, why do growing numbers of young writers continue to fill creative writing classes across the country?

MADISON SMARTT BELL

Introduction to *Narrative Design*

Madison Bell (b. 1957) has been Writer in Residence at Goucher College since 1984. His many novels include Waiting for the End of the World *(1985),* The Year of Silence *(1987),* Doctor Sleep *(1991),* Save Me, Joe Louis *(1993), and* Ten Indians *(1996).* Soldier's Joy *(1989) won the Lillian Smith Award, and* All Soul's Rising *(1995) was a finalist for the National Book Award. As a teacher as well as a writer of fiction, he has much to say about how fiction should be taught. The selection we've included is the introduction to his textbook* Narrative Design: A Writer's Guide to Structure *(1997).*

To teach creative writing, or to be taught it, is a paradox. "Creativity," whatever it is, must be innate. Our intuition tells us that much. But creativity is now taught constantly, in reasonably formal settings all across the country; this teaching has become a totally common classroom activity. The creativity which is thus professed takes many forms: the plastic arts, dance, theater, and music are commonly taught, as *crafts,* along with the writing of poetry and fiction.

To be the target of creative writing instruction, a student whether novice or advanced, is quite a different experience than to be apprenticed in any other art. You have no paint or clay, no instrument, no concrete material to work with. Nor can you use your body as material to be shaped, as an actor or a dancer would. The substance of creative writing is (relatively) abstract.

On the other hand, creative writing is qualitatively different from other abstract fields of study. You will not encounter universal axioms and theorems, as in mathematics, or a fixed corpus of information to be learned, as in history, or even a generally agreed-upon set of rules for procedure, as in expository writing. More likely, you will find yourself adrift in a cloud of conflicting opinions: your teacher's, your classmates', your own. Out of this perhaps salubrious confusion you are asked to make something—a structure of words—which this audience will *for some reason* find to be aesthetically satisfying.

The lack of fixity, the flux of most creative writing classes, permits at least some kind of freedom—but freedom can be a spooky thing to handle. Precisely because the methods of instruction tend to be in a process of constant metamorphosis, it's important for the student to understand what that process is and where it may lead. Let the student beware, or at least, be aware.

One of the difficulties of creative writing as an academic discipline is that it is so new. The teaching of music and visual art as crafts in some systematic fashion is centuries old; it goes back as far as Renaissance ateliers, even to the medieval guilds. There is no long-standing tradition of guilds or ateliers for fiction writers. The form itself, as we now understand it, is quite new. The novel itself did not completely find its feet until the nineteenth century. As for the modernist short story (still and likely long to remain the fundamental writing workshop text), it is mainly a twentieth-century phenomenon.

Imaginative writing has always been a solitary and indeed a somewhat antisocial activity. Apprenticeship existed, no doubt, but it was an apprenticeship to books and not to living masters of the craft. Fifty years ago, there was no such thing as a creative writing workshop; forty years ago, such workshops were novelties. Now there are hundreds of them all around the United States, both in and out of colleges and universities. The rate of change has been so very rapid that the big surprise would be if there were not a huge welter of confusion surrounding the whole enterprise.

But creative writing education is also judged (hostilely in a great many cases) by the result, that is to say, by the published and often popular work of that interesting *minority* of creative writing students who do go on to become "professional writers" and who are indeed charged with the burden of creating the literature of the future. To say that a book smacks of the creative writing workshop has become a sort of reviewer's cliché, a shorthand expression for the idea that the work in question is trite, hackneyed, stale, spiritlessly mechanical, mediocre, myopically self-involved, and so on and so on.*

This hostile description of work by writers who have served their apprenticeships in creative writing workshops is by no means universally true. However, it is sometimes true, and perhaps turns out to be true a little too often. Therefore, it has to be taken quite seriously.

Several years ago, I spent two semesters teaching at the Iowa Writers' Workshop. It is the oldest "studio" writing program in the country, and by many standards it is still probably the best. The Iowa workshop not only attracts the best applicants to graduate writing programs in the nation, it also *turns away* more than half of them. It was there that the workshop method, now common to about 95 percent of all creative writing programs across the academic landscape, first evolved. The Iowa workshop, in short, is the ur-creative writing program.

It has also been, for a very long time, a bugaboo for critics hostile to the workshop method. In the mid-seventies, the Iowa workshop already had a reputation not only for attracting talented writers and launching successful literary careers, but also for turning out mechanized, soulless, homogenized fiction. There was, supposedly, an official Iowa academy style, as tyrannical in its own way as, for instance, the editorial policy of a magazine such as the *New Yorker* of those days. As a student, I was sufficiently put off by this latter reputation that I did not even consider applying to the Iowa graduate program. Later on, I went there to teach with a certain amount of trepidation.

What I found was not quite what I'd expected. If Iowa-generated fiction did have a distinctive academy style, I'd have looked for it to be handed down from the masters. That was not at all the case. No one teacher or teaching approach was dominant; the very size of the program, and the way it was organized, made it virtually impossible for any one teaching method, or the influence of any one teacher, to gain the kind of ascendancy that was rumored without the walls.

In the fiction half of the Iowa workshop, there were then about fifty graduate students in either their first or their second year, enough to make it far and away the largest program in the country, I believe. These students were divided in roughly equal numbers among the four fiction workshops which ran concurrently each semester. Of the workshop leaders, only two were permanent members of the faculty. The other two were visiting writers like myself, likely to be on the scene for no longer than a semester or two. Furthermore, none of these workshop leaders had any oversight of what the others were doing in their classrooms. No particular approach to the task was endorsed or promoted by anyone. Within the limits of law and propriety, we were free to do whatever we damn well pleased.

---

*For an exhaustive discussion along these lines, see *Talents and Technicians: Literary Chic and the New Assembly-Line Fiction,* by John Aldridge (New York: Scribner's, 1992). The extreme bias against the workshop system suggested by Aldridge's title is more than fulfilled in the body of the book—but although Aldridge's discussion is very one-sided, his description of the disadvantages of creative writing education as it's practiced today is accurate enough to be informative reading for anyone involved in writing workshops either as student or as instructor.

Under these conditions, it was virtually impossible for any one teacher to accumulate much influence over the writing style of even *one* student (although that might have happened, occasionally, if one particular student sought out the workshops of one of the permanent faculty again and again, thus in effect choosing a specialized apprenticeship). And it was completely impossible for any one teacher to dominate the group at large. The students just weren't in the hands of any particular workshop leader for long enough for a singular influence to harden. The students rotated among workshops, and the teachers themselves rotated in and out regularly. There was a lot more variety and diversity in the whole situation than I would have supposed before I arrived there.

However, there *were* enormous, crushing pressures to conform in those Iowa fiction workshops. The pressure came not from any teacher but from the students themselves. It was a largely unconscious exercise in groupthink, and in many aspects it really was quite frightening.

The basic strategy of a fiction workshop is probably well known to anyone who's read this far—or if not, it soon will be. The mold for it was originally cast at Iowa. The student writes a piece of fiction, most likely a short story, in solitude, with some degree (quite large, we hope) of psychological privacy. He brings it in and distributes it to twelve or fourteen classmates and the teacher, who take it home, read it, make their notes, and bring it back the following week for perhaps an hour-long discussion of its merits and defects. The task of the teacher is to guide this discussion, with a hand gloved in either velvet or iron, depending, and to produce a synthesis of the result: a prescription for revision—if revision is required.

What's wrong with this picture? It sounds almost idyllic: a happy community of cooperating artists. But there are snakes in the garden.

I was aware of the first pitfall before I ever came to Iowa. Fiction workshops are inherently almost incapable of recognizing *success*. The fiction workshop is designed to be a fault-finding mechanism; its purpose is to diagnose and prescribe. The inert force of this proposition works on all the members, and the teacher too. Whenever I pick up a student manuscript and read a few pages without defect, I start to get very nervous. Because my *job* is to find those flaws. If I *don't* find flaws, I will have *failed*. It takes a wrenching sort of effort to perform the inner *volte-face* that lets me change from a hostile to an enthusiastic critic and start rooting for the story to succeed. (Though in fact there's nothing more exciting than that moment, and probably it's the main thing that makes me want to teach.)

As for the other students, they are just as influenced by the factors above as the teacher, and on top of that, there's the probability that in confronting a successfully realized piece of fiction, the classmate has to cope with a certain amount of conscious or unconscious envy. (Indeed, envy may sometimes arise for the teacher too, but with a little effort it can be transformed into an enjoyable experience.) Well, once the group is back in the classroom, these forces militate against any *consensus* that a given story has succeeded, is finished, and requires no further work. Take that to its logical extreme and you see that the student as writer has been assigned the task of Sisyphus. There is no way to ever finish anything. . . .

A smart teacher, though, will learn to beat this demon. There are certain signs, in classroom discussion, that a work has in fact succeeded in whatever its intended mission was. When the talk begins to shift from flaws in realizing the story's apparent intention to the idea that the intention itself ought to have been different—i.e., that the writer should have written some different *kind* of story— that's a signal to the teacher that the story may have been successfully completed. It's a good thing for students whose work is under discussion to learn to listen for that signal, too.

And when a teacher identifies a piece of finished work in preparing class, it calls for a different kind of classroom presentation. Instead of performing the customary autopsy, the teacher must present the story as literature. (Well, it *is* literature now. Isn't it?) The teacher has to show how and why the story has succeeded (and thus, how it is exemplary for the others). The fault-finding force of inertia inherent in all workshops means that it will be hard for the teacher to convince all the other students that the work has succeeded, but if he argues skilfully he will probably manage to convince the author, which is the main thing that matters at the end.

At Iowa, I began to recognize some other hazards of the workshop method of which I'd been previously unaware. At Iowa, the students were very diligent about annotating each manuscript and writing an overarching commentary at the end—each student producing a separate version of the instructor's work (and some of them were already teaching undergraduate workshops). When the classroom discussion was finished, these fourteen annotated copies would be handed over to the unfortunate author, along with mine. My heart misgave me every time I watched the student (victim) gather them up, and an inner voice whispered, *Please, when you get home, just burn those things.*

But of course they didn't do that. It would be idiotic if they had. After all, this was the criticism they'd come to receive—they'd paid for it, worked for it, striven for it. I found out through private conversations that many of these students, if not all, would indeed spread out the fifteen different annotated copies and try somehow to incorporate *all* the commentary into a revision of the work.

The results of this kind of revision were often very disheartening. I'd get second drafts that very likely had less obvious flaws than the first, but also a whole lot less interest. These revisions tended to live up to commonly heard, contemptuous descriptions of workshop work, being well-tooled, inoffensive, unexceptional, and rather dull.

Bear in mind that I myself, the teacher, was particularly trying *not* to exert any undue influence at this stage of the game. I let the group have its head and do much as it would. It was all very democratic. Those depressing revisions were the outcome of the individual student trying to please the group mind—trying to please everyone at once—trying to satisfy fifteen different line editors. The inevitable result was to put the work toward the middle. The middle, of course, is where mediocrity flourishes.

Well, I was beginning to understand how a specific "Iowa style" could develop, how any workshop anywhere could develop its own academy style over time, and how there were a lot of things about this process that really weren't so great. There are inherent tendencies in all workshops to enforce conformity, *no matter who is leading them.*

At Iowa the situation was actually exacerbated by the fact that the students were so good. The uniformly high level of talent meant that the students were more deferential to each other's opinions than they might have been in a more average program with a wider spectrum of ability among its writers—allowing the leaders to separate more quickly from the pack. And so the group mind's pressure to conform was magnified.

What was going to happen to all that talent? Fifty students in fiction at the Iowa workshop . . . Admission to the program was so competitive that all of them must have written at least one story that was publishable or the next thing to it simply in order to get in. But I knew it was statistically impossible for all of them to succeed in becoming "professional writers." Most would probably not publish even one book. They all wanted to. Desire was not an issue. But there had to be some trait that separated the ones who would "make it" from the ones who would not.

I remembered writing two-thirds of my own first novel under the scrutiny of a graduate workshop. Every few weeks I'd have my hour of attention. I'd listen to the discussion and the summation, infrequently make a few notes. At the end I would smile and say thank you and go my way. By the time I got home, most likely I'd forgotten most of what had been said. I'd sit down and write the next five chapters. . . .

Now this was a kind and nurturing workshop where the group mind did not withhold its fundamental approval of what I was doing. But still, my classmates liked to editorialize as much as any workshoppers. If I had set out to satisfy everyone in matters of *detail,* I might still be fiddling with the first chapter even today.

I opened my second-semester workshop at Iowa with remarks along these lines: Assume that when your work is being discussed, about 90 percent of what you hear will be useless to you and irrelevant to what you have done. Learn to listen carefully and to discriminate what's useful to you from what's not. Remember the relevant part and ignore the rest. If even *one* person understands what you intended to be understood, then you can say you have succeeded. Past that, the only issue is just how widely accessible you want your work to be. Don't try to please the group. Don't even try to please *me.* The person you have to please is yourself. Your job is to become the best judge of your own work. If you *do* become a professional writer at some point, you'll need that skill more than ever before.

Well, okay, this is pretty weird. It is tantamount to declaring at the outset that everything that you're about to do is pointless. I can't think of any other form of pedagogy that would require such an opening disclaimer. It is a large paradox to swallow, though no larger than the paradox of claiming that creativity can be *taught,* when we all know, intuitively, that it can't be.

I have been opening classes that way ever since. Thereafter, things went on very much as before. It wouldn't have been completely impossible to alter the nature of the process radically, but I felt that the risks and costs would well outweigh the gains. Let the process remain as it was and try to change the attitude of the students—show them where the pitfalls are laid in the forest and teach them to be wary and suspicious.

Workshops on the Iowa model (95 percent of all workshops in academia) are nothing if not craft-driven. Their general mission is to teach a repertory of techniques. Probably these techniques will not be taught in any specific programmatic order, but instead are more likely to be brought up apropos of a particular student's needs for a particular story. Thus a student who is ambitious to write many different *kinds* of stories will acquire a larger bag of technical skills than one who is not.

But the talk is always technical. It is all about the mechanics of plot, of characterization, setting, description, point of view, voice, tone, and so on. The attitude of the group toward the work is surgical. A process of dissection is going on. The text is handled as a machine in need of repair. Or at best, the successful functioning of the machine is analysed and admired.

All this is much as it should be: You cannot really learn anatomy without dissection. But the risk is that the process will lead the student to forget that the story is supposed to be a living organism. Tilted too far in the direction of mechanics, the process will turn out monsters of mere technique.

The procedure for passing on that craft tends to ignore that no stories are *originally* written on craft intelligence alone. There's something else operating at the inception, something which needs to operate all the way through the period of composition, something which is much, much harder to talk about than craft. The overworkshopped student is at risk of losing this indescribable thing. You go home from class with your head crammed with specific techniques. When you pick up your pencil to write, you no longer think, This or that is *happening* in my story, but, I am implementing this or that technique. Even worse, you are no longer alone. Your teacher and classmates have burrowed through your earholes into your skull and are now taking up a whole lot of space in your brain. Without your psychological privacy, it's very hard for you to function. With a tremendous amount of stress and strain, you may achieve an anatomically correct sort of Frankenstein monster, but it's not very likely to get up and walk on its own.

Even worse, this whole paradigm is a recipe for writer's block. Once you have internalized the voices of your whole workshop, you're not just second guessing yourself, you've multiplied it by a factor of fifteen. How to go forward in that situation? In situations where craft-training becomes overwhelmingly dominant, writer's block spreads faster than bad news or viruses.

There is another way. The great defect of craft-driven programs is that they ignore the writer's inner process. Creativity, the inner process of imagination, is not discussed. So far as the craft-driven workshop is concerned, creativity is sealed in a black box; you're supposed to remember that the box is there, but there is a tacit agreement not to open it in public.

Some teachers, though, take the opposite tack. They try to attack inner process head-on. A teacher of this stripe wants to pry or coax open the black box and come up with hands dripping with that mysterious ectoplasmic creativity stuff.

The tactics of such teachers may be either gentle or violent, but the ultimate strategy is the same in either case: to open to the teacher and to the group that private area of primary process where the imagination does its work. They may employ meditation, or soporific music, or various mental and writing exercises intended to bypass the left brain hemisphere and activate the right. By putting inner process in the center of the whole enterprise, these approaches seek to remedy the great defect of craft-driven workshops, which is to be so polite about not discussing inner process that students are at risk of forgetting that it ever existed.

On the more violent end of the spectrum is found a more jolting technique which a hostile observer might define as brainwashing. More neutrally, one might call it hypnosis by confusion. In fact these two are one and the same. The strategy is to assume tremendous authority, elicit enormous trust, and then abuse both, deliberately and to the maximum. Psychological shock tactics. Similar methods are used by hypnotists when they're in a hurry, and by cult leaders everywhere. The purpose is to reach areas of the target personality that are otherwise inaccessible. For the religious, it's the soul; for the Freudian, it might be the id. The cult leader wants to get into this place to awaken the disciple to the glory of God. Your more bloody-minded writing teacher, meanwhile, wants to get into this place to awaken his disciple to the glory of art. He is in one hell of a hurry and he is willing to use dynamite to open the black box.

The inner-process teaching strategy can indeed get interesting results. But to my mind the risks it presents to the individual student writer are too great. One's inner process should in fact remain private. If you admit into it the writing teacher, and/or the writing group, you risk forming a quasi-pathological dependency. What happens if the group dissolves or the teacher withdraws (or withdraws approval)? All inadvertently, they may take the irreplaceable contents of your black box with them.

To put it in metaphysical terms, while you may with good reason choose to offer up your soul to God, or to a lover, it probably is not a smart idea to hand it over to a creative writing instructor. The writing teacher probably didn't want your soul all *that* much in the first place, is unlikely to be equal to the responsibility of caring for it, and will probably be incapable of returning it to you in a useable condition.

Where do we go from here? Consider the two halves of the brain. Research in psychology has assigned specific faculties to one hemisphere or the other with a reasonable degree of certainty. The right brain is generally supposed to be the locus of creativity, among other things. Dancing, music, intuition, imagination, and falling in love are all the provenance of the right hemisphere. The left brain, meanwhile, is in charge of math, logic, chess-playing ability, income tax, and . . . language.

What this means for creative writers is that the two hemispheres must somehow be trained to cooperate in the process of realizing imaginative work in a concrete form. Presumably the two faculties should cooperate on a roughly equal basis, without one gaining great ascendancy over the other. They must work in concert and in harmony.

The left brain is the home of craft consciousness. Here is the warehouse for however many specific technical abilities you are able to acquire. Somewhere in the right brain, meanwhile, the black box full of creativity is stored. Craft-driven workshops have a natural tendency to exercise the left brain at the expense of the right, with craft consciousness becoming so dominant that creativity is squelched. Inner-process approaches, on the other hand, may concentrate so exclusively on releasing creative energy by whatever means available that the necessary craft controls are overwhelmed and anarchy ensues.

Good teachers have always known, intuitively, how to guide students between these two extremes. Wise and discerning students may often find the right path on their own. But the fact remains that both the student writer and the teaching writer really do have to have two heads and considerable facility in shifting their consciousness from one to the other. You cannot do without critical intelligence. Much, most of the time in workshops is spent on developing the critical faculty. It is indispensable for talking about texts, for finding their flaws and also their merits, for both appreciation and troubleshooting. But critical intelligence *originates* nothing.

Critical analysis is a perfectly safe and acceptable group activity. Creative process, on the other hand, is by nature private and solitary. The writer must maintain psychological privacy in order to remain capable of imagining the work. The strange paradox of all imaginative writing is that it is an isolated and secretive project that one undertakes in order to communicate (in most cases, for the desire of your private writer for public recognition is usually quite insatiable) with the greatest possible number of other people.

. . . One must never forget that the inner process is not only where all ideas begin but also where final recognitions are made. Everything of *primary* importance happens inside the black box. Difficult and dangerous as it is to talk about it, it is the most important thing of all.

A few years ago, I began to visit a hypnotist because I had noticed with some consternation that the force of circumstances seemed to be quite rapidly changing my personality from Type B to Type A. Alas, hypnosis was not able to retard this transformation very much. Still, it was not wasted time.

I went into the first session with the false expectations common to most people who never have been hypnotized. I thought I would be swiftly and more or less against my will plunged into a black trance, that while unconscious I would be made to impersonate a chicken, and that afterward I would (mercifully) be unable to remember anything that had transpired.

The actual experience was quite different from that. I was first of all advised that my conscious consent to the whole procedure was crucial—if I withheld it, the hypnosis would fail. All hypnosis is essentially *self*-hypnosis, I was told.

All right, I was good to go with that. He dimmed the lights. There was even one of those Op-Art spirals on the wall, quite similar to those HypnoDiscs you used to be able to order out of the back of comic books, and I regarded this for a couple of minutes. I was told that upon completion of a countdown from ten, my eyes would involuntarily close. They did so. I descended into a state resembling twilight sleep, that condition between deep slumber and waking where, for instance, you may be aware that you are dreaming at the same time that you dream, know that you have a choice whether to awaken completely or dream on. . . .

The hypnotist began to direct my dream by reciting to me a sort of story, a narrative in the present tense, starring myself as the ostensible protagonist. Many hypnotists use these routines as part of the "deepening" stages of hypnotic induction, to intensify the level of hypnotic trance. It went more or less like this.

You are walking on a warm grassy hillside, spangled with yellow sunlight . . . Tall grass is stroking at your ankles, it makes a whisking sound as you walk through it . . . The sun is very warm on your back, you begin to sweat a little, though you are still quite comfortable, feel a warm trickle of sweat down your back . . . The field is full of red and yellow flowers, and all the flowers are swarming with bees, and as you pass you hear the buzzing of the bees, a growing, rising hum . . . You smell the flowers as you pass, sweet dusty aroma of pollen . . .

At the foot of the hill there is a lake, clear blue water and dark at the center . . . You are very warm, you are quite hot, you take off your clothes and go in to swim. The water is cool on your face as you break the surface, cool in the cups of your hands while you are swimming . . . Your strokes are strong but completely relaxed. You are swimming alongside a granite wall, in the shadow of the rock, and near you a shaft of sunlight strikes a lily pad where dragonflies are hovering . . .

At the center of the lake you dive. The water changes color as you go down, dark blue, purple blending into black . . . You hear only water rushing past your ears, then silence, and you are going deeper now . . .

. . . Now you are climbing out onto the flat rocks by the shore. Dip your cupped hand in for a drink of water . . . It is cold and fresh to your taste . . . You let what's left run out between your fingers, back into the lake. You stretch out on the warm flat rock and let the sun's warmth dry you slowly . . . When you close your eyes, your eyelids are stained a deep warm red with the sunlight and the heat, you drift, you dream, you are going deeper now . . .

And so on. I made this one up, but that's the way they go.

While listening to all this (it went on for quite a lot longer), I felt that my awareness was dividing. The sensation was not like being split with an ax, but a slow, gradual, willing process, like the division of a cell. The actor in the induction narrative was not my whole self, but I did occupy his sensibility, so that I could experience, sensorily, everything he felt, as you *feel* the experience of characters in your dreams.

At the same time as a part of me was actually responding to the experience it was suggested I was having, another part was watching the whole business and taking account of what was going on. Some sort of a little left-brain homunculus with a stopwatch, which was by no means my whole self but another partial *I* that saw, among other things, that the whole deal was *working,* that indeed I was entering an altered state. Soon after, the hypnotist, satisfied with the induction's progress, was able to open direct discourse with my autonomic nervous system, while my left-brain consciousness (which had not been put to sleep) was able to watch everything that happened, with wonder and a pleasurable level of fright, as if through the porthole of a diving bell. . . .

Afterward, the whole experience seemed to have important ramifications beyond the therapeutic. The first thing I noticed was how well that induction narrative succeeded in the task that you try and try to get beginning writing students to achieve: that is, to make a convincing address to all five senses. Literarily speaking, the induction narrative didn't do much of anything else (it wasn't supposed to), but it did this one thing extremely well. It created what writer George Garrett calls a *sensuously affective texture,* a sculptural surface that, so far as the mind's experience of it was concerned, was virtually indistinguishable from reality. And the purpose for hypnosis was much the same as it would be for writing: to convince the subject/reader of the visual/auditory/tactile *reality* of what was being described. For the hypnotist it was very important to win this conviction at some location below the level of ordinary workaday left-brain awareness. It occurred to me then that the process of imagining a work to be written (as well, perhaps, as the process of reading it) might also require a similar kind of "deepening."

Because after all, that sense of bifurcation, slow division of the consciousness, was really quite familiar. *All hypnosis is self-hypnosis.* Yes, I had been there before. Often. At my desk, for three or four hours every day.

Then I remembered something the novelist Andrew Lytle had told me about the process of composition. The first step and for him I believe the most important: "You put yourself apart from yourself, and you enter the imaginary world."

You put yourself apart from yourself. If he had set out to describe the initial stages of hypnosis, he couldn't have done a better job. That state of being slightly out of yourself . . . detachment . . . obliviousness, as the people who are trying to get your attention may irritably describe it . . . isn't it familiar?

I remembered a photograph I had once seen of a friend of mine, a writer, caught behind her typewriter and clearly in the midst of deep concentration. She was a beautiful woman, but not in this picture. In a fundamental way she had ceased to be physically present at that moment. She had withdrawn so profoundly into the recesses of her imagination that her features had actually lost their form.

I remembered all the time I had spent in my childhood, daydreaming—out to lunch, as they say. When it got good, I would often talk to myself quite audibly (to the dismay of my classmates). I have since partially broken myself of this habit —I still talk to myself (plenty) but I have quit moving my lips. And as for daydreaming . . . when you get right down to it, daydreaming is my vocation. *You put yourself apart from yourself, and you enter the imaginary world.*

Then I recognized that the process of imagination that underlies creative writing, what happens as or just before you are putting the words down on the page, must inevitably involve a process of autohypnosis. Not that the practitioner would be likely to call it that. You could be doing it without knowing that you were. Most likely you would never have heard of hypnosis, certainly not in such an application. You might call it meditation. You might not call it anything. But you would sure enough be doing it, any time you worked successfully, happily, and well.

Here's the explanation for all those strange little tics and ceremonies you hear about writers having, the ones that interviewers always try to ferret out and put on display, as if they were themselves the magic secret. Sharpening a dozen pencils, caressing some lucky charm such as a rabbit's foot or a netsuke. . . . At an extreme is Graham Greene's going down into the street and waiting to see a certain combination of characters on the license plate of a passing car before he began work for the day (which must have produced considerable delays, I fancy). Here's why so many writers prefer to break off in the middle of some passage, fearing that if they stop work at the end of something it will be too difficult to begin again—as when, upon your next stretching out to sleep, some tendril of your last night's dream may once again appear to you. . . . Here's why you'll frequently start your work by rereading the last few pages of what you've done, futzing around with unimportant corrections, simply as a way of *getting into it* again. . . . All these rituals belong to a process of autohypnotic induction, though you may call it what you will.

Now the implications for students and teachers of writing become quite interesting. You will recognize that if the inner process of imagination involves a process of antohypnosis, then teachers who concentrate on inner process are, knowingly or not, actually functioning as hypnotists. The sorts of exercises beloved of this kind of teacher are all tools of hypnosis, really. Soothe yourself with relaxing music. Lay your head down on your desk and try real hard to *picture* something. Use cutups and arbitrary combinations of images, words, or situations to try to jump-start your right brain.

Hypnotic approaches can work in the classroom—sometimes rather impressively—but the drawbacks should by now be fairly obvious. Even assuming the best will in the world, if you are a teacher who relies, knowingly or not, on hypnotic strategies, you risk drifting over the line from pedagogy into psychotherapy, and since you are unlikely to be qualified as a *therapist,* all sorts of inadvertent abuses are likely to occur. And if the teacher's good will is less than perfect, well . . . what a nasty thought.

It's not that a student's inner process can't be influenced from without. It's that it shouldn't be. Inner process is the student's business and not the teacher's. An ethical teacher may *recommend* devices to stimulate the process of imagination, but that is a different matter from *participating* in them. It's probably true that, for the individual, the practice of art is not entirely distinct from the practice of working out one's private psychological problems, but as a teacher, you don't want to go fooling around in the area where these two overlap. As a student, you really probably don't want anyone else messing around with the *inside* of your head.

As a matter of fact, most students and teachers do understand all these things, consciously or unconsciously, and for this reason inner-process-focused workshops are much in the minority, and have never really caught on in academic contexts. We are left with the Iowa-model workshop: craft-driven. Here the participants leave the black box shut, they don't get their hands all sticky with that creativity goop, there are no projects of group hypnosis by any description, nothing on the order of a Vulcan mind-meld. All they want to do is teach you technique.

So you go home from class with your pumped-up craft consciousness sitting on your shoulder. Your left-brain homunculus has been elevated to a position of absolute power (when it should be operating in concert and harmony with your right-brain homunculus). When you sit down to write, you are stuck in yourself, paralyzed by self-consciousness, unable to separate yourself, unable to relax your mind, unable to pass through the autohypnotic gate into the realm where the narrative you are working with becomes true and alive for you. Whatever you write falls over dead on the page. Anyone with any experience of writer's block will know exactly what that feels like.

The composition of fiction can, at least theoretically, be broken into two stages. First, and most important, comes imagination. Next is rendering. Imagination is no more or less than a highly structured form of daydreaming. Daydreaming is fun, a form of play. Once the people, the places, the events you are imagining become fully present to your senses, then it's time for rendering. The left-brain homunculus must go to work to express your vision in language. But the problem has been made much easier because it is no longer a task of creating a separate reality constructed of words, but only of describing what your inner eye has *seen*. For an experienced writer on a good day, the synapse between imagination and reading fires so rapidly as to be imperceptible; conception and realization are one.

Ultimately, you have to believe. If it is not real for you, you cannot talk about it persuasively. Because the writing of fiction is all about producing an illusion, it's all-important that *you* believe in the illusion absolutely. You will never fool anyone else if you can't fool yourself.

All the rest is craftsmanship.

There is not a whole lot of difference between teaching writers and student writers in the end. As Norman Mailer once put it, the main difference between an experienced and an inexperienced writer is the ability to work on a bad day. That's not inconsiderable, but you wouldn't call it essential either. The worst, most paralyzing periods of my own career have come when I thought I finally knew it all. . . .

DISCUSSION QUESTIONS

1. Bell reprises the paradox of trying to teach creativity, a paradox that underlines the question of whether creative writing can be taught. He adds that creative writing is even more difficult to teach than the arts that involve material objects or use of the body (painting, sculpture, dance). Do you agree with Bell that the "substance of creative writing is (relatively) abstract" in comparison to other arts? Why?

2. Compare Bell's description of teaching in the Iowa Writers' Workshop to Bonnie Friedman's account of being a student in the same program. How do these

narratives, read side by side, illuminate each other? How do Bell's and Friedman's differing roles and expectations affect their experiences?

3. Bell contrasts craft-driven workshops with courses that focus on inner process, or creativity. What are the features of each type of workshop? Do you feel more drawn to one kind of class than the other? Why? Do you agree with Bell that students should not hand over their "souls" to a creative writing teacher who aims to open the "black box" of creativity? Why?

4. Bell ultimately endorses a blending of craft and creativity, of critical analysis and the processes of the imagination. What might the elements of such a blended approach be? Have you had any courses that effectively serve craft and creativity?

JOE DAVID BELLAMY

The Theory of Creative Writing I and II

Joe David Bellamy (b. 1941) is a poet, short story writer, novelist, critic, editor, and textbook author. He has taught at St. Lawrence University since 1972. His poetry collections include Olympic Gold Medalist *(1978) and* The Frozen Sea *(1988). His fiction has won the* Editors' Book Award *(Suzi Sinzinnati, 1989) and the AWP Award (Atomic Love, 1993). As an editor, he has created important anthologies of contemporary writers, including* Superfiction, or the American Story Transformed *(1975),* New Writers for the Eighties *(1981), and* Love Stories/Love Poems *(1982). His most recent book of criticism is* Literary Luxuries: American Writing at the End of the Millennium *(1995).*

CREATIVE WRITING I: KEEPING THE FROG ALIVE

After nearly sixty years of trying it, what are we to make of the peculiar American experiment of permitting creative writers to teach in English departments? If you wanted to know about an automobile, Ezra Pound asked, would you go to a man who had merely read about an automobile, or to a man who had made one and driven it? Most Americans, I feel sure—and most students—would rather talk to the second man. But most English professors in my experience would probably agree with Harvard professor Roman Jacobson, who remarked upon hearing that Vladimir Nabokov might be appointed to the faculty that he had nothing against elephants but he would not appoint one professor of zoology.

It is a sad fact that many of my scholarly colleagues—even some of those who are not theorists—seem to think that creative writing is a frill or a waste of time. In the ongoing battle over college and university airtime, neither traditional English professors nor theorists seem willing to agree wholeheartedly that the teaching of creative writing properly embodies many of their guiding principles, or even supplements them adequately. Observers will have noted a great deal of heated debate about what English departments should or should not be doing and considerable hostility directed toward theory, or toward creative writing in particular.

The critic Gerald Graff maintains, however, that to "attack theory as such is equivalent to attacking thinking," since theory "denotes nothing more than *philosophy,* the sort of reflection on our assumptions and practices without which any person or institution goes brain dead." Very well. If that is the case—since, above all, I hope to discourage further brain death, which seems to be closing in around our necks like so much toxic waste—then I suggest that we badly need a *theory* of creative writing, because it is clear to me that many of these "camps" within English departments truly don't understand one another.

My hypothesis is that this is an ancient and inevitable misunderstanding, but one that we should make every effort to alleviate. The dispute goes back several thousand years: Plato, you may recall, claimed that there was an ancient argument between philosophy and poetry. If it was an ancient argument in Plato's time, then it must be very ancient indeed; and Plato, you may remember, made the strange and unforgivable mistake of siding with the philosophers when he decided to ostracize the poets from his ideal republic, fearing, apparently, that poets represented a dangerous potential for arousing passion, discord, and insurrection. Like good fascists everywhere, Plato apparently wanted a nation of sheep, or perhaps, sheep who enjoy chess.

I will proceed to the matter of defining *the theory of creative writing* momentarily, but first . . . some additional thoughts.

Even before the current debates, there were problems in the English department. One complaint I used to have as an undergraduate was that most of the English professors I knew wanted us to dissect literature as if it were a frog in a lab experiment. My objection to the intense analytical process of what was then called "the new criticism," especially before I learned how to perform it, was that *it killed the frog.* I thought I wanted to find a way to study literature that would keep the frog alive.

What I valued in the study of literature, as a naïve undergraduate, was the energy of art, the emotional power, the effortless release into worlds of the imagination and pure language, and, even then, I think, the potential for what John Hawkes has called "aesthetic bliss." I believed that literature was—far and away —the most important field of study because it was, for me, the most meaningful way of understanding the world and my own life. I was willing to put up with almost any silliness my English professors devised for us because I thought it would lead me to greater levels of understanding.

But then I had had a most unusual introduction to the English department and to what the study of literature might have to offer. Completely by chance, my freshman English instructor at Duke University was a young man named Reynolds Price—a creative writer, we understood, though no one had ever read or heard of anything written by him, since in 1959 he had not yet written very much, although he was, at that time, working on his first novel, *A Long and Happy Life.*

We all referred to him as Mr. Price. In like manner, he referred to me as Mr. Bellamy and to each of his men's-campus charges as Mr. Somebody. Mr. Price was twenty-six years old and had just returned from Oxford University in England, where he had attended as a Rhodes scholar. His accent was an ear-catching mixture of a North Carolina dialect and aristocratic British.

I must say I soon discovered that this Mr. Price was the most interesting teacher, and one of the most interesting persons, I had ever encountered. All my professors were good, and they were all demanding. But this Mr. Price was almost magical. Everything he said was fascinating, and he talked about everything from British politics, which I knew nothing about and cared nothing about, to literature, to the nature of art, to writing. He assigned a series of essays that we were required to bring, in hand, to his office; and there, on the spot, while we stared at the Modigliani nude above his desk, he would read our handiwork and inscribe comments and corrections and discuss the work as if it were of the utmost importance. No one had ever read my work this closely and with such intensity and had such surprising things to say about it. Nearly everything he said came as a revelation to me.

Not everyone has the luck to study with a genius who is also a great teacher. Perhaps I can be forgiven if my prejudices all seem to fall on one side of the arguments that need to be made here. But I think it safe to say, over thirty years later —and absolutely true—that I have never been the same since I accidentally walked into that freshman English class in 1959. Such is the power of art. Such is the persuasive influence of great teaching.

In contrast, I ask you to consider the experience of most students today in our colleges and universities. How many of these students emerge from their undergraduate experiences with a coherent sense of the world, a useful set of values and goals, commitment to *any* discipline, or confidence that they have had a good education? I think most of them survive their college experience feeling somewhat damaged and tired—thankful to have endured it but disillusioned with education and disappointed because they didn't get anything close to what they expected and for which their families paid enough to ransom the king, the queen, and half the court. If they applied themselves, they learned some useful skills perhaps. They learned a certain form of nit-picking analysis and how to manipulate abstractions—what passes these days for "thinking." They learned how to become functional bureaucrats and technocrats and businesspersons and "professionals." They endured; they learned how to be bored for an hour or an hour and a half at a stretch, and still not lose their sanity or good humor—an important job skill in itself—though some, of course, could not learn it well enough. They learned some useful social skills. Far too many learned that one way to endure the meaninglessness and tedium of adulthood is to throw off the veneer of seriousness and *rationality* at regular intervals with cathartic binges of partying, overeating, or drunkenness.

One cause for this sorry state of affairs is that most university-level disciplines address a more and more specialized audience in a more and more abstract form, and they scarcely ever try to address undergraduates at all. As Maynard Mack has written: "We are narrowing, not enlarging our horizons. We are shucking, not assuming our responsibilities. And we communicate with fewer and fewer because it is easier to jabber in a jargon than to explain a complicated matter in the real language of men [and women]."

Creative writing, on the other hand, does attempt to address a general audience, using concrete language and conventions that all can understand. Thus, creative writing—to use an example from one of the arts that might speak for all of them—flies in the face of currently accepted practices and tendencies within the university, though its goal of addressing the broad general audience is discounted by a comfortable majority of scholars as pedestrian or boorish, as evidence of its lack of sophistication or rigor. The difficulties of addressing the general audience are not appreciated by those who have given up the desire to do so or never considered the possibility worthy of their attention. The fact that creative writers can speak in a common tongue, however, gives them a decided advantage when addressing undergraduates, or the world at large, most of whom have no inherent need, wish, or penchant to venture into the airy realms inhabited by most of their scholarly mentors.

In fact, this is true of what creative writers *do* as well as of what they *say* about what they do. As Scott Russell Sanders has noted: "The making of a poem or novel is an act of inclusion, a drawing in of readers to share an experience." Too often, "the making of literary theory is an act of exclusion, shutting out all but the cognoscenti."

The university at large is too given over to purely abstract and so-called rational modes of discourse and behavior. This is one reason that so many universities are boring students nearly to death. The arts and humanities are the natural corrective for this problem; and, in many cases, it is the absence of the arts or of a humanistic orientation in the humanities that has aggravated this difficulty. The influence of the natural and social sciences on the American university and on the arts and humanities, which has been so pervasive in our time, has often been to replace the arts and humanities with questions and procedures, with modes and methodologies, more natural to the sciences. We have seen the wholesale takeover of the curriculum by the abstract thinkers, the empiricists, and the political and social scientists. Often professors in the arts and humanities are behaving as if they were, in fact, scientists or social scientists.

Our primary curricular obsession these days, which we owe chiefly to the social sciences, is the insistence on viewing every subject through the filters of race, class, and gender. Certainly race, class, and gender are important issues—greatly in need of attention—but they are not the only issues. We also need to consider aesthetic, literary, and artistic issues again within universities. Analysis is an important mode for students to understand and use as well, but it is not the only mode worth studying, the only skill worth acquiring.

One difficulty with race, class, and gender—as rallying points or as avenues of inquiry—is that we are all born into these categories with very little opportunity to escape them. Thus, some are destined, it seems, to be victims, and others, victimizers from birth. Too often, rather than encouraging us to be more tolerant of those who were born into a different niche than ourselves, the new education encourages just the opposite—hatred, resentment, and feelings of entrapment. The old humanistic virtues—tolerance, communication, respect for the other— too often seem to be of little interest to those of the oppressed who are bent on defining their victimhood.

There are other ways of seeing and thinking that go beyond politics. Politics should not be at the intellectual center of our university culture because political thinking is endlessly contentious, finite, and adversarial—an excuse for everyone to pursue a purely personal or self-centered agenda, to attempt to climb one more mile up the slippery mountain of status and position. Too often the outcome of political thinking is that people end up yelling, "Me, me, me." I am more attracted to almost any metaphysics that moves further beyond the self and the limitations and cloying egotism of the self—which used to be one of the goals of the so-called liberal arts.

This, for me, is one of the many attractions of the arts. The arts teach empathy, and empathy is a powerful basis for moral action as well as a viable mode for understanding the world. The prophets had it right: life is suffering. I'm convinced that life is suffering for just about everyone, regardless of race, class, or gender—and that suffering *can* be redeeming, though sometimes it is only suffering. The arts open a window to help us understand others' misery, and, in this way, our hostility is blunted and we have a chance of finding peace ourselves. As Bob Dylan used to sing, "If I could stand inside your shoes, I would know what a drag it is to be you."

The natural and social sciences are not "the enemy," of course. We owe them a great deal, and we need to cultivate them and the perceptions they make possible. But these disciplines should *not* constitute the entirety of the curriculum. Some of those in the arts and humanities go about the business of perceiving the world and reflecting upon it in a somewhat different way than their counterparts in the sciences, and this is exactly why we need them.

Another way of thinking about these essential differences—between "philosophy" and "poetry"—may go beyond Plato's historic dichotomy, or offer a contemporary explanation for it. I owe this idea to some reading I have been doing in reader-response theory, an as-yet-unpublished series of interviews with writers and critics concerning their subjective responses as readers entitled "Seeing Their Way Through the Text," by Ellen Esrock. I must say that I was surprised to learn that some readers, some very intelligent people, apparently do not visualize when reading, and some do not participate in any reading experience "kinesthetically," in the ways that I always have automatically. I had always assumed that such experiences were fairly common and similar for all readers of a certain level of intelligence and education.

Esrock set out to discover if "creative" writers and critics share the same perceptions *as* they read. If one reads, for instance, about a "locomotive in a jungle," what perceptions follow? Does everyone tend to visualize an actual engine sitting there, its wheels sinking into the quicksand, moss, and muck, ants exploring its crevices, snakes and giant termites crawling over its surfaces, moisture beading up along its hard surfaces, collecting in its gearbox and drivetrain, rust setting in everywhere, indignant monkeys squawking?

The novelist John Hawkes's description of his experience of reading about the locomotive was very close to what mine would be, what I previously took to be "normal." That is, all the visualizing and sensory experiences that Hawkes describes seem familiar and obvious to me; yet Hawkes must have felt as if he were trying to explain something nearly equivalent to the experience of being "on key" to someone who is tone-deaf, or who is pretending to be for the sake of the interview.

In contrast, when respondents such as philosopher William Gass and critic Geoffrey Hartman attempt to describe their experience of reading literary texts, their subjective responses to the "locomotive in the jungle" for instance, it sounds to me like the subjective description of a type of mental retardation. It is all abstraction to them, just words on a page. (But poems, one is reminded, should be "wordless as the flight of birds," and so should novels!) They don't see and feel the locomotive! Their discussions of the event are so abstract as to be stunningly tedious and mind-numbing. . . . Yet I know, of course, that Hartman, like Gass, is quite a brilliant fellow in his own way.

I conclude that, as humans, we must differ remarkably in some ways that I had previously thought we were mostly the same—in the ways we respond along the concreteness/abstractness spectrum, for instance; and, therefore, we must differ equally remarkably in our abilities to find significance both in literature and in life. Whether through training or inclination, these may be essential brain differences that determine us. If so, it would help to explain why we value different experiences and modes of discourse, why we may have trouble agreeing with one another about the ideal curriculum, and why certain abstract thinkers do not value art. *They've never tried it!* In any case, if these insights are real, we certainly need to account for such differences within education.

I remember the first time I attended a meeting of the Modern Language Association (MLA) as a young man. In the splendid corridors of the convention hotel I took note of the many bright-looking persons milling about, the corduroys and tweeds, and started to feel a sense of community and identity. I thought, "Yes, this is it—I've finally found it—this must be where I belong"—until I discovered what most of these same people were saying to one another when they got down to the business of the meeting. The goal there seemed to be to speak in more and more esoteric languages, often to trivialize, and to exclude, through what seemed to me to be the worst kind of intellectual arrogance.

We learn from the anthropologists that primates are creatures bent on establishing status hierarchies. We cannot really blame them for this, I suppose—since it is so entrenched in their natures. It is my theory that this is what the smartest people at the MLA were doing primarily—not laboring to explain the universe in ever more useful and intellectually challenging ways; laboring, rather, to establish better and better status hierarchies. It was a clever game of "we chosen few." We chosen few with IQs over 150 (or who wish our IQs were over 150) will now address one another in our own newly coined theoretical jargon and thereby distinguish ourselves from the rabble—from all those who are too stupid or ignorant to know what we are talking about—just as the social scientists do so well. Like the social scientists, our goal should be to attempt to make the obvious unreadable or, possibly, unknowable.

But I am not really opposed to these disciplines, to theory, or to abstract thought per se. I am only opposed to these methodologies so greedily, often inadvertently, pushing out all other avenues of thought and inquiry. Now, their triumph is so complete, their hold so great, that it is possible to say, with some poignancy: "Where are the *arts* in the liberal arts? Where are the *arts* in the arts and sciences? Where are the *arts* in the arts and humanities? Where is the *humanity* in the arts and humanities? I understand that it has become fashionable in certain critical circles to consider *humanistic* as a pejorative term for an outdated community of discourse. If so, I refuse to accept such usage and will work to rehabilitate the concept—because I believe that we badly need humanistic thought (and action). We badly need the humanities and the arts and all that they can tell us about the world and our own lives. Without them, we would be quite a different species.

All right. I think it is time to get down to the business of trying to describe my *theory of creative writing*. Since this is "new" and provisional, what I say here is not in the nature of an empirical proof. Let's just say it is, demonstrably, every bit as true as all the other theoretical rubrics we have seen circulating in English departments over the last several decades.

Creative writing can be, especially at the undergraduate level, one of the great undiscovered crossroads areas of the modern liberal arts curriculum, providing access to the study of literature—our treasury of style and language and our best ideas about human life—and an entrée to all sorts of vistas and mysteries, to the scaffoldings and underpinnings of the human imagination in all its forms.

Students are immersed in the process of imagination and synthesis and in the experience of relying on their own emotional, aesthetic, and visionary resources in ways too rarely explored in our curricula. Through participation as "creators," students come to understand, with greater immediacy, the motivations and accomplishments of the great writers of the past (or present), and their appetites are whetted to explore all literature (philosophy, history, theology, autobiography, criticism, even theory) in greater depth.

"A subject becomes liberal," according to Charles Frankel in his defense of the liberal arts, when it considers "ubiquitous and recurrent characteristics of the human scene and human destiny . . . [and] liberate[s] the individual from the parochialisms and the egotisms of time and place and self." According to that description, and others, the subject of creative writing, properly taught, is surely liberal, ameliorative, humanizing, civilizing, and capable of being used for the organization and illumination of ideas across the spectrum of human knowledge.

At the minimum, instruction in creative writing should cause students to become better writers and more discerning readers—and beyond that, more sensitive, knowledgeable, and articulate beings. My ongoing ambition as a teacher is to live up to these possibilities, to understand and articulate the most catholic dimensions of the subject area, to appreciate its mysteries, to seek serendipitous connections to other modes of thought and inquiry; to carry on, at the undergraduate level, in the best liberal arts tradition; to hold forth, at the graduate level, as a mentor, sympathetic critic, and fellow voyager who offers help on the way to professional development.

The "workshop method," sometimes maligned by those who know very little about it, is quite suitable for these purposes, so long as it includes close reading of manuscripts and clear and abundant feedback, allows room for potentially edifying digressions on craft, theory, terminology, and formal concepts, and includes some reading of outside examples as models or landmarks.

George Garrett points out in his essay "The Future of Creative Writing Programs" that the methodology of the writing workshop did not, in fact, originate at Iowa in the thirties but goes back to at least the sixteenth century.

> In the days of standard classical education, education in and about the classics, the composition of original Latin poetry and prose was one of the key elements. This practice continued for as long as the classics were the heart and guts of education. Thoreau, for instance, came out of exactly this kind of system, as did so many of the American nineteenth-century writers. . . . When we talk about the beginning and growth of creative writing in our time, . . . we are really talking about *a renewal, a revival,* the return, in somewhat different form and circumstances, of an old-fashioned, centuries-old form of teaching and learning rhetoric. The aims were different, but the ways and means are surprisingly alike.

Using this method, then, the main distinction I make between beginning undergraduates and more advanced students is that beginners need more guidance and more raw information, and therefore they usually benefit from a more prescriptive and structured approach. They also need, I think, to be impressed with the larger issues more frequently than their more knowledgeable peers, to be shown, for example, that creative writing is far more than mere technical mastery, far more than the effort merely to concoct a more elegant mousetrap, but is at the center of a number of crucial questions often posed by the liberal arts tradition: What is art and what is it good for? Is it good for anything? I argue that it is. What is the status of the imagination as a faculty of perception? Is the imagination educable? I argue that it is both educable and practical. What is human nature? Is it understandable? What is the nature of poetic truth? Even—what is life? And so on.

I try to avoid posing such questions in a purely abstract way, as a philosopher might, but try to make them implicit and concrete, to surround them with metaphor, fable, anecdote, and literary allusion. In my experience, undergraduates are desperate for answers to such questions—their faces show it—and they are desperate to hear the questions because, most of the time, no one has ever posed such questions to them before.

Creative writing is one of the few formal opportunities in American higher education for "self-discovery and self-creation," as Dave Smith has pointed out, and for an exploration of the imaginative faculty, perhaps our most underrated quality as human beings. Undergraduates, in particular, can benefit enormously from their activities in these areas, whether or not they will ever prove to be gifted writers who may wish to consider working toward professional status.

The problem with the idea of teaching creative writing as a form of technical mastery is the fallacy that the art of writing may be taught using the principles of science. But the presumption that writing is the same intricate kind of purely formal or technical achievement as science and that it can only be performed by someone who has had years of study of the rational, analytical, and theoretical sort in order to understand the *principles* of writing is a bad idea. Students may be made to feel that unless they understand all these higher principles, which are at least as difficult as nuclear physics and which only someone like their professor has already mastered, they can't possibly even begin to perform the difficult feat of writing. The opposite problem sometimes occurs as well—when students are made to feel that the realm of art is so mystical and intangible that it is always just out of grasp, and that no standards or rules or conventions are there to guide them. Students may be caused to feel inadequate to the task of writing for several different reasons because a certain type of professor wants to feel indispensable.

I believe that there is useful technical information that can be transferred in the classroom, and that, through a steady diet of good reading and careful teaching, students can begin to get a grasp of the conventions. But more important than acquiring this "knowledge," even from the beginning, is pointing out what the student brings to the classroom, the quality of the imagination he or she already possesses and how that valuable attribute can be expanded. We are not primarily rational creatures. We can exercise rational thought, though it takes some considerable effort, discipline, and training. But we are, much more essentially, imaginative creatures. We use our imaginations without trying or thinking or even being aware that we are using them. We enjoy doing it.

The first issue of the creative writing class might be what sort of discipline and useful training can we bring to this very powerful attribute that students already possess and have quite a lot of unexamined experience exercising. Whatever else happens, they must be given permission to use it, since most of their previous teachers seem to have conspired to shut it off.

What's wrong with teaching only interpretation, analysis, history, and theory in English departments? I have to say: Because of what it leaves out, namely, the energy of art! the vision! the beauty! the suffering! It would be as if, in a music symposium, the "experts" spent all their time arguing about the rules of grammar and syntax of song lyrics and failed altogether to mention melody or rhythm or what the lyrics *mean* or the capacity of the whole beautiful, throbbing ensemble of attributes to make you feel goose bumps on a particular morning in June. My trouble with many of the theorists and abstractionists is that they don't seem to be able to hear the music at all. They are like the man John Cheever describes who "had lost the gift of evoking the perfumes of life: seawater, the smoke of burning hemlock, and the breasts of women. He had damaged, you might say, the ear's innermost chamber." Or perhaps he never had it to lose. But, to put the best face on it, let us simply say that when the room grows still, in the privacy of their minds, these people simply hear different music than I do. These are, perhaps, basic perceptual differences over preferred ways of seeing and essential habits of knowing.

My point is that all would benefit by recognizing that critics and creative writers have certain goals and pedagogical practices in common and much to gain by cooperation with one another—though they do inhabit different discourse communities and therefore have a difficult time communicating. Also, in some major respects, critics and writers are trying to accomplish very different ends and using different modes and styles of knowing to achieve their ends. But these differences are perfectly all right so long as they do not lead to internecine hostility, for, ultimately, writers and critics must sink or swim—together.

CREATIVE WRITING II:
THE USES OF THE IMAGINATION
AND THE REVENGE OF THE PINK TYPEWRITER

Literature, like all the arts, is primarily *about* imagination, empathy, emotion, and aesthetic and poetic truths—not *about* analysis or intellect primarily, though it may, of course, represent a challenge to the intellect. Therefore, if we wish to experience the arts and to know them, why spend all our time engaged in purely analytical and theoretical approaches? Pure reason and abstraction are fine— necessary—in the sciences, but they are often useless in the arts and humanities, as should be evident from the present predicament of those disciplines. The rationalistic mentality is responsible for every sort of mischief, for reducing great art— that which gives us a reason to live—to nihilism, absurdity, and futility.

What the creative writer brings to the classroom is a healthy contrast to the usual sorts of analytical and theoretical practices. Although the writer may engage in practical criticism, when the writer asks students to write a poem or a story, he or she asks them to pay attention to the imaginative, the emotional, and the aesthetic aspects of writing and to explore and use these resources within themselves. The students must approach the work from the point of view of the artist or creator, and that experience is . . . playful, . . . infuriating, . . . exciting, . . . challenging— potentially all the things that art is, at its best. This process, this creative effort, is an attempt to synthesize the world, to see it as a whole, rather than to tear the world apart or to systematize it in order to understand it; and in many ways it is a more demanding activity than the purely cerebral processes of analysis or theorizing.

I believe strongly that the mental processes exercised in creative writing classes need much more attention in our culture—the attempt to integrate instead of, always, to analyze or to make abstract; *not* to take feeling out of our mental processes, but to put it back in. Everyone engaged in teaching in *every* subject area ought to teach imaginative inquiry. Some of our so-called well-educated college students are not so well educated without such experience.

Perhaps it is not surprising that former president Bush, who had such trouble with the "vision thing" and who copped out so completely in his responsibility for defending the National Endowment for the Arts, would neglect to put the arts in any form in his educational recommendations for the future as described in his America 2000 plan. But he did not act alone. He had help!

What the best art has to offer us is vision, and we need it! The worst of popular culture oversimplifies the world and teaches citizens to leap to foolish conclusions about character, motive, loyalties of every sort, and the nature of the world. It creates a world of black-and-white choices where human character is easily, instantaneously readable. Art says not so fast—life is not that simple. Art teaches empathy, a higher and wiser form of knowing.

The longer I think about it, the more I am amazed at the small place given in the curricula of American colleges and universities to the education of the imagination—our most important mental faculty. I believe the imagination is the great underrated domain of human perception, far more natural to us, and therefore far more practical, than analytical and other abstract modes of perception. Yet analytical and abstract modes have so dominated the college curriculum that there is hardly any place left for education of the imagination—except in the arts and, occasionally, in the humanities.

The imagination is like a muscle—it can be strengthened through use. It is educable. Conversely, without use, the imagination can wither and atrophy, or never develop properly. If we do not expose our citizens to an education of the imagination, we may have a high price to pay; for failure of the imagination is certain to have serious consequences—not only an absence of innovative technologies and competitive businesses, but also imperfect and inaccurate perceptions, a lack of ability to understand and cope, and even violent crime. We may be breeding a nation of sheep, citizens unable to discriminate between the truth and the lie, citizens easily swayed by spurious appeals, citizens incapable of imagining the consequences of their actions or alternatives to violence.

At present we have a substantial and growing segment of the population in the United States made up of moral and imaginative idiots. Such citizens go through their lives committing moral outrages. Most normal people play out their violent impulses through fantasies and thus have no need to act them out in the real world. It is, in a sense, through the suppleness of their imaginations that they navigate the choppy waters of life, which, I'm convinced, represent a struggle for nearly everyone.

Jerome L. Singer has written of the link between lack of imagination and aggression in several studies of delinquents and criminals.

> The risks of an undeveloped fantasy life may include delinquency, violence, overeating, and the use of dangerous drugs. . . . Children of equal intelligence but unequal imaginations also differ in their sensitivity to reality. We often assume that children with active fantasy lives have a weaker grasp on hard facts than their pedestrian brothers and sisters. But the truth may be just the opposite. Research indicates that children whose games are poor in make-believe and fantasy are likely to have trouble recalling and integrating the details of events they hear about. . . . A well-developed fantasy life seems to be partly responsible for independence, tranquility, and realism.

We have Freud to blame for the view that the imagination is escapist. Freud recognized that children's play is succeeded by adult fantasy but tended to treat both activities as evasions of reality. (Freud considered science and art evasions as well.) But Erikson, Jung, and other major thinkers since Freud have regarded fantasy much more positively and have been interested in its implications. According to Erikson, play "provides the infantile form of the human propensity to create model situations in which aspects of the past are relived, the present re-presented and renewed, and the future anticipated." Erikson also felt that humans should "vie with each other for the right vision."

Another persuasive commentator on this subject was the noted child therapist Bruno Bettelheim. In *The Uses of Enchantment,* Bettelheim set out to show "how fairy tales represent in imaginative form what the process of healthy human development consists of, and how the tales make such development attractive for the child to engage in." Bettelheim insists that his work made obvious to him the realization that if children were reared "so that life was meaningful to them, they would not need special help." He was confronted, he says,

> with the problem of deducing what experiences in a child's life are most suited to promote this ability to find meaning in his life; to endow life in general with more meaning. . . . [S]econd in importance [after the impact of parents] is our cultural heritage, when transmitted to the child in the right manner. When children are young, it is literature that carries such information best.
>
> In child or adult, the unconscious is a powerful determinant of behavior. When the unconscious is repressed and its content denied entrance into awareness, then eventually the person's conscious mind will be partially overwhelmed by derivations of these unconscious elements, or else he is forced to keep such rigid, compulsive control over them that his personality may become severely crippled. But when unconscious material is to some degree permitted to come to awareness and worked through in imagination, its potential for causing harm—to ourselves and others—is much reduced; some of its forces can then be made to serve positive purposes.
>
> Freud's prescription is that only by struggling courageously against what seem like overwhelming odds can man succeed in wringing meaning out of his existence. . . . This is exactly the message that fairy tales get across to the child in manifold form: that a struggle against severe difficulties in life is unavoidable, is an intrinsic part of human existence—but that if one does not shy away, but steadfastly meets unexpected and often unjust hardships, one masters all obstacles and at the end emerges victorious. . . . Morality is not the issue in these tales, but rather, assurance that one can succeed.

Morality may not be the point of fairy tales, or the primary purpose of grown-up art either, but I would argue that the empathetic awareness fostered by fairy tales and other childhood excursions into the imagination that begin to teach us to see the world from someone else's point of view is a strong incentive to moral behavior.

Art helps create a readiness to experience that strange process where you actually move outside your own body and for a while you feel what it feels like to be someone else. Surely this feeling is a basis for kindness, for forbearance, for communication, for moral response. Without empathetic awareness, we are hopeless, I think, as a species. Art teaches empathy, and many students need experience in this area, some students in particular. If they don't get it somewhere along the way, they've wasted their educations, I think.

I have said that the imagination, which is sometimes thought of as a purely escapist faculty, is, in fact, practical. How can this be? Whether we are reading about characters in a novel or simply trying to understand the people in our own lives, we must use our imaginations minute by minute to get through our lives. We must imagine one another—and ourselves. We do, in fact, use our imaginations to understand one another; and, if we are normal, we do *not* imagine without any basis in fact. We imagine *given* the facts. Most of us know that simply making things up to please ourselves—without regard for the facts—is a strategy that does not work for anyone for very long. If we are intelligent, we adjust our visions of one another each time we receive new information. An important aspect of intelligence is the ability to use your imagination, given the facts, to understand someone else, simply to be better able to predict that person's behavior and to be able to understand your relationship to them. This is, of course, one of the essential concerns and *processes* of fiction and drama, exercising this particular human capacity and pushing it, in the best work, to very high levels of discrimination.

As humans, we are forever engaged by the mystery of human character and behavior, by the potential revealed in a human face. It is said that dogs, who mark their territories by urinating, can detect one part of urine in fifty thousand parts of water. This is why dogs behave as they do, constantly sniffing and making fine distinctions that we know very little about. Humans have, I think, a similar peculiar obsession with face reading, and we go about it with equally stupendous powers of differentiation. All of us look essentially the same, after all: two eyes, a nose, and a mouth in approximately the same locations; yet we are able to detect differences that must be nearly microscopic. We are so adept at this that we can tell one another apart! Further still, we seem to think that we can read character, motive, and intention in the human face. We do not accomplish this through reason or logic but through the imagination. We seem to think we know when virtue may be found there, and it pleases us. We seem to think we can recognize beauty, and we worship it without reason. Most probably, this natural face-reading talent that we have, as in canines, has powerful survival value, especially in such a highly social species as ours and one with such inferior noses. The dogs have their mighty proboscises to get them through their lives, and we have our good eyesight and our luminous imaginations to do the important work.

Another aspect of getting through life moment to moment—which undoubtedly makes use of the imaginative faculty—is in figuring out what you want for yourself, what and who you want to *be,* and then setting out to live your life, to do things in such a way that you will end up at that point, if possible. It seems to me that this process is almost entirely practical and almost entirely imaginative in basis. And one's ability to perform it shrewdly or not has enormous consequences. A French wit of the nineteenth century who was apparently in awe of the writer Victor Hugo is said to have remarked: "Victor Hugo is a madman who believes he is Victor Hugo." One could say the same in our own time, I suppose, of Madonna. Each of us is a creative or not-so-creative imaginer who believes that we are who we say we are. Each of us creates an identity, a self, through imaginative means and our best understanding of the facts of the case, and we can choose to enjoy a relatively generous interpretation or conception of ourselves, as Hugo did, or a relatively more conservative one; and then, as new facts come in, we make adjustments.

Often these adjustments are based on further imaginative constructions. We live constantly on the basis of imaginings that we revise from day to day. We are essentially mind-creatures, and our essential mental activity is to use our imaginations in a purely practical way to live our lives.

Yet another illustration of how literature and the imaginative faculty have a practical benefit is their ability to help us navigate in *time*. One of the original pleasures of the novel as a form was that the novel permitted the reader to imagine the *whole* of a life. We have the unfortunate problem that we never get to *see* our whole lives. We live our lives minute by minute, in a fragmented sort of way. We try to cast ahead and imagine the shape of what will come, as best we can. We try to remember in some detail what life has been, as best we can, and to use that information, if possible. But we never really know what it will be, until we live it; and we never really know entirely what it has been, until we get to the end of it. But when we get to the end of it, it's over. The value of the novel in this regard is that by seeing others' lives, as a whole, we are better able to imagine our own lives, as a whole, and thus better able to compose our own lives, better able to choose how to live them.

Also, of course, literature gives us the incredible opportunity to "live" lives we could never even imagine on our own, trapped as we are within the confines of our own lives. So literature offers the priceless additional benefit, not only of revealing the whole of lives, but also of providing a wide range of totally different lives for us to contemplate, so that we can compare the content of other lives, minute by minute—the aspirations, the mistakes, the victories, the things said and done and the things not said and done—to our own.

In trying to navigate in *time,* we constantly replay the past and we constantly project alternative futures; and these memories and projections are functions of the imagination as well. If there is anything in particular that distinguishes us from what we call the lower creatures, I think it is this capacity to range through time within ourselves, to escape the eternal present of the animal world. Quite possibly, this process is the first step in a new stage of evolution.

In any case, memory is a peculiar thing. We think of memory as having an exact factual relationship to the events we recall, but in many instances it does not. Memory is rather elusive, in fact. Every time you remember the past, a little bit of the place, time, and mood of the present rubs off onto the past. By the time you remember the same experience twenty years later, the memory will have evolved and you may have changed considerably as well, and the original event might seem very different both from the original event itself and from your earliest memories of it. So I would argue that even memory is a product of imagination.

It is probably of some importance to make every effort to remain accurate as we remember our lives, to keep the imagination in line with what actually happened. Otherwise, we take the chance of losing our sense of everything, of losing our sense of ourselves.

One thing that creative writers want, and one luxury that writing allows them to have, is a better, clearer relationship to their pasts—a better sense of memory and a clearer relationship to the present. Writing allows them to slow down the rapid-fire progression of events and examine them, evaluate them, and store them—otherwise, life escapes. Otherwise, the merry-go-round of events overwhelms memory. How *can* one hold it still long enough to get any sense of it? Life is fleeting. How else *can* one preserve it? Writing fiction is one way. Reading fiction is another.

Creative writers, like other artists, are people who are perhaps more frequently overwhelmed by their own feelings and imaginings than ordinary citizens. Writers have the habit of writing their feelings down in order to try to understand them and to try to relieve the pressure of excessive emotion. Some writers are more able than others to translate their efforts to achieve clarity—through groping with bewilderment and anguish—into useful social documents.

Once the writing is finished, however, if the writer has done the job well enough, the experience is trapped right there on the page, permanently and indelibly, for anyone to use. This seems quite obvious, but it is, in fact, quite miraculous. To see the world *through* the mind, through the memory, through the imagination, through the language, of a great writer is potentially a consciousness-expanding experience in the best sense. Potentially, it is as powerful as a brain transplant, without half the difficulty. It changes you. It changes your imagination and your capacity to imagine, so that you may never be the same again. If it works, it makes you smarter, more empathetic, and more eloquent. If you cause it to work often enough, you finally have a chance to experience what we might wish to call, without any irony whatsoever, "a good education."

In 1963 I lived in an old house in Yellow Springs, Ohio, that had been split into apartments. Upstairs from me lived a student-artist who spent most of his time out in our backyard banging on, prying at, and unscrewing a truckload of dilapidated school desks. While I would be sipping my coffee and trying to write a new story, I would stare at him out my kitchen window and wonder what in God's name he was doing out there. What he was doing was this: He made a huge pile of these disassembled desk parts, and then he laboriously reassembled them into absurd sculptural shapes and painted them pink, so that, soon, we had a backyard full of odd pink objects that had never before been seen on the planet. You might say that he was an early sixties deconstructionist, working in an uncharacteristic medium, somewhat ahead of his time.

Another of his creations had been mounted prominently on a wall at the art building on campus. It was a typewriter that he had jumped up and down on several times and then smashed with a sledgehammer and painted that unmistakable pink. The keys were bent around in a truly heartbreaking sort of way. I imagined that he was seeking revenge for too many painful years spent in classrooms that bored him, which I could understand, but I found his pink-typewriter piece especially haunting and upsetting. It seemed to me a potent symbol for the hatred and distrust that some feel toward the written word and the world of literacy and, perhaps, for civilization itself.

I had shared some of this same suspicion, frustration, and anger—who hasn't who's been to school?—but I had not given in to it so completely as my friend with the pink typewriter. My own response to the pressures of undergraduate angst, unfulfilled potential, too many deadlines, and too many papers to write had been to give in in a different way, to perform what was asked of me, to meet the deadlines, to *use* the typewriter and to value what it produced.

Many nonliterary artists, of course, rightfully distrust the verbal as a manifestation of the conscious mind, something they associate with tyranny and stereotypical responses and bad art. Many artists, in their art, are busily trying to escape the strictures of the conscious mind; and this is, perhaps, why they represent such a worry to Plato and to the left-brain-abstraction-and-reason addicts within the university and beyond. But the pink typewriter had in it a level of despair and misunderstanding that troubled me as well.

I suppose you could say that the pink typewriter was a subversive piece of art, and Plato and William Bennett and George Will might wish to banish my former apartment mate—and *me* for living in the same house—for the shocking overtness of his creation, or what they might imagine to be its foolishness. (For all I know the young man who created the art may have gone on to become an insurance salesman, and, unless he received some encouragement, he probably did.) But I, for one, have come to value the example of the pink typewriter because it reminds me in a vivid way—as a writer and a teacher of writing—of what I am up against, of what we are all up against, if we value civilization.

DISCUSSION QUESTIONS

1. Bellamy begins by describing historical tension between literature and creative writing, or literature professors and creative writers. Have you observed such tensions in your educational experience? Does your college or university separate the study of literature from the creation of literature? How? Why?
2. Bellamy refers to Plato's banning of poetry from the ideal republic because of its potential for arousing unruly passions. How might this fear of poetry provide a basis for a college's or university's uneasiness about housing a creative writing program?
3. Bellamy claims that creative writing "flies in the face of currently accepted practices and tendencies within the university," which privilege arcane scholarly language and specialized topics of study. Is this description of the university true to your experience? How have your experiences in creative writing courses differed from those in your other courses?
4. Bellamy discusses different reading styles, contrasting his own imaginative visualizations of objects and actions with the abstract, symbolic reading he ascribes to philosophers and critics. How does your reading fit into this discussion? Is it possible to read differently in different situations? To blend reading styles?

5. What are the features of Bellamy's "theory of creative writing" that make it a liberal art, one of the humanities? How does Bellamy see the workshop supporting these educational and moral aims?
6. Bellamy argues that using the imagination to create art leads to empathy and an expanded capacity for moral behavior. Do you agree that this can be a result of creative writing? Has your own writing affected you in the ways that Bellamy describes?

JOHN CASEY

Dogma

John Casey (b. 1939) is the author of Testimony and Demeanor *(1979);* An American Romance *(1987);* Spartina *(1989), which won the National Book Award for fiction; and, most recently,* The Half-Life of Happiness *(1998). A frequent contributor to* The New Yorker, Sports Illustrated, *and* Harper's, *he taught at the University of Virginia for twenty years.*

The most common thing people ask me about writing is "Where on earth do you get those ideas?" Perhaps there'll be time for that question a little later.

The second most common thing people ask is "Can you teach someone to write?"

I have two answers.

The first is "No" . . . but if someone is talented to begin with, I can save her a lot of time.

The second answer is also "No" . . . I can't teach someone to write, but I can sometimes teach someone to rewrite.

For a long time I taught the way I'd been taught. I'd been in classes taught by Peter Taylor, Kurt Vonnegut, Vance Bourjaily, José Donoso, and what they did—after you turned in a story—was to tell you what they thought you'd done. Basically they'd say "Here is what all those marks on the pages meant to me."

And then I could figure out if that's what I'd wanted to do . . . or if there was now something else I could do that looked better.

This holding the mirror up is a good way to be helpful to a beginning writer. Writing a story or a novel is like finding your way around a strange room in the dark. When you get through the first draft you think the light will go on. But it often doesn't. At first you need a reader you can trust to tell you what you've done . . . and that there is or isn't hope for this particular effort.

I think this process is useful because the majority of good beginning writers are at first less in love with structure or pattern and more in love with the *words* in a foolish but sweet way.

I don't think people should skip this sweet foolishness. There is this to be said for it: you are falling deeply in love with language; you are, at last, learning your own language. If the sweetness outweighs the foolishness, if the genuine outweighs the synthetic, if the verbal inventiveness and precision outweigh the clichés of plot and callow characterization, it's a helpful stage. It may be as good for the future as plowing under a field full of oats.

When Katherine Anne Porter taught at the University of Virginia, her method was to sit the student writer down and read his story to him aloud. That's all there was to it, or so I've heard tell. I've also heard that one student, before his story was half read, broke down and ran.

I'm sympathetic. Long ago a kind editor at a Boston publishing house took an interest in my earliest novel. Over lunch he told me, "You have talent, dear boy." I felt for an instant like one of those saints in Italian paintings on whom a beam of divine light falls. He then said, "Of course, some of this writing is . . . embarrassing." "Oh yeah," I said, "Like what?" (Sometimes you just can't help leading with your chin.)

He opened the manuscript and read aloud.

After a bit I said, "Ahh." Or maybe it was "Arrrgh."

He advised me to plow it all under. I did.

Three years later I salvaged a part of a chapter, turned it inside out, and used it in a story, the first piece I sold. (Moral: plow under, but save a copy just in case.)

But the sophomore, the wise fool, the sweet fool, has to be done away with sooner or later. So what comes next?

From the writer's point of view it seems like more of the same: the inspiration, the rise of hope, the realization, on one's own now, that some part of the piece has failed. You've had your hand held, someone has held up a mirror, but now it's time for sterner stuff. Dogma.

Is dogma helpful? Let us hear some:

- "Write for yourself"—*J. D. Salinger,* or at least one of the Glass boys.
- "Write about what you know"—*Everybody* says that.
- "Above all, I want to make you see"—*Joseph Conrad.*
- "You must tell your story in the fewest words possible"—*Sean O'Faolain.*
- "A short story must have a single mood and every sentence must build towards it"—*Edgar Allan Poe.*
- "Tell the truth"—Everyone again.
- "Stalk the many-headed beast—be a reporter"—*Tom Wolfe.*
- "Conventional narrative bores me; you must experiment"—*Robert Coover.*
- "Culture is local"—*William Carlos Williams.*

There are many other dicta, but these are all at the core. They are also ones I've been told, have told myself, and have told others; frequently they were just what the doctor ordered.

Salinger's "Write for yourself." Yes, there is something wonderful about a writer who has her own voice. And there is something horrible about the sound of an imitated voice. There are writers whose works you can pick up and the particular hum of the prose is immediately recognizable; there is an intimacy your inner ear recognizes even before the rest of your brain approves. This intimacy is not necessarily gentle or nice, but I'm pretty sure that the only way to achieve it is in communion with yourself, a communion that is in some way innocent, however fierce or forgiving.

Of course, the dictum applies to subject matter as well as tone or style. It can be a good prescription for the stylishly voiced but timid. Find the subject that leaves you mute, then tell it.

BUT. If you were to take this dictum as your only course and not a course correction, you could end up on the rocks.

Arthur Koestler, in the second chapter of his autobiography *Arrow in the Blue,* justifies himself and apologizes for autobiography in general. Among his warnings, the chief is against nostalgia.

Twenty years ago I covered a bass-fishing tournament for *True* magazine. The winner of the tournament was a laconic fishing guide from Arkansas. I spent a day with him picking up tips on how to catch fish—the conditions of structure, season, sun, etc. I asked him at least if there were things to watch out for in all this finding the right spot to fish.

"Nostalgia," he said.

I figured out what he meant. I'd spent hours plugging away at a stretch of water where I remembered with great pleasure catching a beauty. But if the fish aren't there now, all you catch is nostalgia. Moonbeams of your peculiar unrelatable memory.

BUT. There's another *but.* Kurt Vonnegut used to say to his class at Iowa, "You've got to be a good date for the reader." The rest of the metaphor of courtship could be inferred. Query: Can you bring flowers and write for yourself? Can you wear perfume and write for yourself? As long as it's still you.

But surely you have some friends to whom you would never ever say just before they set out for a blind date—"Oh, just be yourself."

There is a falsity or pandering one must rid oneself of, but there is often a sincere but boring side too. If I were to go on a blind date, I'm sure that my wife, four daughters, and three sisters would all call out "For God's sake, don't talk about rowing!"

"Be a good date" can let you be a mere entertainer.

"Write for yourself" can let you be a nostalgic bore.

But in the sense that "write for yourself" is "know yourself," "find your own demon, your own angel," it is the first commandment of useful dogma.

"Write about what you know." An example of this as good advice:

I had two students who were writing costume drama. One was writing about Mayan warriors—sacrifice, sex, and slaughter. The other about gentlewomen in Alabama in hoop skirts. Both went on and on. I finally said to each, "Stop."

The woman who'd been going on about hoop skirts, said, "What shall I write about then?"

"Talk to me a bit, tell me what you know."

She said, "I see you're looking at my knee . . ."—This was back in the first round of miniskirts. She went on, "See how it doesn't quite fit? It's going to make me lame unless I have an operation but I have had a phobia of hospitals ever since I was strapped to a gurney when I was little. It was a Labor Day weekend and the room was full of people screaming, I was there for hours, days, I can still hear them whenever I smell that hospital smell . . . whenever I smell that hospital smell I get migraines so bad I can't see, literally, can't see . . ."

I said, "Come back in two weeks with seven pages about your knee."

She wrote a five-page piece called "Patella" that was riveting. It was, in the apt phrase of my first wife, "hysterically calm." It won the $500 prize for the best short story at the University of Virginia.

So I told the man the same thing. Write a five-page story, about something closer to you than Mayan slaughter. He came back with a wonderfully condensed piece about a man sitting at mass (about a quarter of the writing was simply the words of the mass). There was a woman next to him. Her sleeve brushed his sleeve. He concentrated on prayer. Her shoulder brushed his. Was she doing it on purpose? Was she sick? Fainting?

They stood for the Gospel. He wouldn't let himself look at her. He only saw the hem of her raincoat when they sat down. He listened to her breathe. He tried to concentrate on the sermon.

I don't remember how it ended. It was abrupt I think. *Ite, missa est.* Go, the mass is ended. He (the character) was still caught in uncertainty; he'd half resisted the temptation, half succumbed . . . if the temptation was really there. He was freed by the fact that he could never possibly recognize her, never find out what she'd meant. Perhaps there was some regret.

I thought how much more full of conjured sensuality, of tension, of a real psyche and spirit this piece was than all the hundred and fifty pages of exotic Mayan sex and slaughter.

"Write about what you know". . . could there be any *buts*? Two occur to me. Suppose Tolstoy had decided to end *The Death of Ivan Ilych* before Ivan Ilych is dying and has a vision—because Tolstoy didn't really know what dying is. One answer is that Tolstoy imagined it so vividly that he *did* know. Flaubert imagined the death agony of Madame Bovary so intensely that he vomited. Perhaps the best version of this dogma for some people is "Write about what you know, but move into that rich intertidal zone between the dry beach of what you know and the sea of what you don't."

Kipling wrote wonderful stories about the Indian Army. He'd hung out with them when he was a reporter in India. Later, when he'd become famous and was living in England, the Royal Navy made him an honorary officer and asked him to come on training cruises. He got royal tours of the ships—the engine room, the bridge, the officer's ward room, etc. Kipling was an inquisitive man and a quick study. He used his navy material, but the navy stories are lifeless. They are filled with navy lingo and detail, but they don't live. What is the moral of this experience? It may be that if you acquire technical knowledge quickly, without the slower sense of the emotional forces carried by these *things* in a communal life, you will prattle. Even if you are Kipling. Perhaps the qualifying dictum is: he who learns a little soon repeats it. Kipling had some of his best work still ahead of him from "They" (1904) [to] "The Wish House" (1924) and on into the thirties. I love stories about writers with rich autumnal years.

Conrad's "Above all, I want to make you see" is a wonderful motto. Fiction often fails because it isn't visible enough. I see my own early bad writing repeated year after year by otherwise gifted young writers because they want to get right to the metaphysics. But when they or I get to what things look like—not just picturesque landscapes but people's expressions, light on water, the way a worker works—things perk up.

Hemingway had a similar motto something like Conrad's. It's more or less this: write about what people did, what people said, and what the weather was like. Cyril Connolly in his wonderful and odd book *The Unquiet Grave* gives Hemingway his due for having succeeded in awakening the readers' senses.

But the real wonder of fiction is that it not only appeals to the senses—it makes all of your shadow senses receive the world of the story—but also at its very best it gives us a sixth sense: a sense of the invisible forces that make people more than the sum of their five senses. Conrad, though he is the author of the motto, certainly conjured the invisible as well as the visible. As writers, you do finally have to conjure, whether by implication or direct statement, invisible forces as specifically as you have conjured a bullfight, a bank robbery, a kiss. Consider the end of *The Great Gatsby*. The end of *The Sun Also Rises*. All of *Nostromo*.

So perhaps we can amend Conrad and say "First of all, I want to make you see." If you can do that then you can go on, then you have earned the right to the invisible.

"You must tell your story in the fewest words possible." The book in which Sean O'Faolain says this, *The Short Story,* is one of the few useful works on the subject. It is one half anthology, one half commentary.

I can't explain why shortness is a good thing. I can only think of how many gallons of maple sap it takes to make one gallon of maple syrup—forty. Maple sap tastes like water—very good water, but water. Maple syrup is a miracle.

Sean O'Faolain doesn't mean you have to send a telegram. Nor does he mean that you must tell simple stories that begin with the beginning, go through a middle and stop at the end. Supreme examples of rigorous cutting and condensations are Isaac Babel's *Red Cavalry* and Muriel Spark's *The Girls of Slender Means*.

I believed this dictum even before I read it. It was in the babbling gossip of the air. The first story I sold was one I condensed. For ten evenings I more or less copied the handwritten pages of the third and what I thought was the final draft onto new pages, and, at the end of each evening, I would count with satisfaction, "There: four pages into three:" Next time—"There: six pages into four and a half."

Reading aloud helps. You can feel the places where the density isn't what it should be. Reading aloud to prepare a piece for reading aloud in public helps even more. You tend to ask yourself, "Do all those people need to know all of this?"

BUT. Even here there is a *but*. Sean O'Faolain tries to demonstrate how Henry James's long story "The Real Thing" can be cut. He puts brackets around the unnecessary parts. He was brave enough to pick a story by a master. It's a very close call whether he has improved the James story. My students have split about fifty-fifty on this question.

My own further experience is odd. My first published novel, *An American Romance,* was 604 pages in typescript when I sent it to my agent and to my editor. They both said, "Way too long. Make it shorter."

I worked for six or seven months. There were 100 pages on the floor of my workroom when I finished. I did write a few little additions. I typed it up again. It came to 640 pages. What the hell. I sent it in.

My agent and my editor wrote back independently of each other, "Good. It's much shorter."

An Italian fencing master I once knew used to ask his students, "How does the frog catch the fly? Because he is quickest? No! Because he has *tempo!*"

Tempo, timing, pace, rhythm. The shortest distance between two points is a frog's tongue. Thank you, maestro.

"A short story must have a single mood . . ." Poe went on to say that every sentence must contribute to it. He wrote this in a review of Hawthorne's stories, saying that Hawthorne brilliantly fulfilled this requirement of unity and coherence. So do a lot of Poe stories. The dictum is a terrific idea, one I'd guess he came to from his reading and writing lyric poetry. It is a short-story writer's alternative to the suggestions about unity made by Aristotle for tragedy, which show up sometimes as rigid law (one main character, one day, one place). If you haven't already read Aristotle's *Poetics,* it's worth the two or three times you have to read it to sift out the message. The difficulty is in part due to a patched together text, so some scholarly apparatus, available in most modern paperbacks, is helpful. Aristotle's mood is much sweeter than his descendants'. It is something like this: You playwrights have given me such great pleasure, I hope you don't mind if I make a few suggestions about how you can increase my tragic pleasure.

This is a critical mood I wouldn't mind seeing make a comeback.

Both Poe and Aristotle are trying to be helpful in this quest for unity. But what's so hot about unity?

I can't explain unity any more than I did brevity. In *The Biology of Art,* Desmond Morris writes that certain apes and a few monkeys produce paintings that show an instinctual urge toward both symmetry and unity. It is a fascinating book with lots of beautiful pictures, particularly some by chimpanzees (Picasso owned a picture by Congo, the star chimp artist); I also like the delicate spirals turned out by the capuchin monkeys, and some of the work by Sophie, a gorilla who would only paint when she was separated from her mate.

Kurt Vonnegut has a nice sentence about yearning for unity—and brevity too —in *Slaughterhouse Five.* The beings of Tralfamadore, a distant planet, have novels; each is a single dot that fits on your fingertip and zaps you with the essence of the novel.

My own daydream of unity could have been the Parthenon, the Pantheon, or a well-wrought urn, but at the particular right moment I happened to see a cat-boat on her cradle. Her lines defined her perfectly, yet didn't seem to be limits. Every line curved toward another, but didn't end when it met the other. All the lines seemed endless continuations of each other, an endless continuation of the whole. She was a single idea that looked enormous in a neat way, but also as if you could pick her up in the palm of your hand.

Virginia Woolf describes a character in *The Years* having a physical experience of architecture. Considering a building, she (the character) feels weights move inside her until (I may be making up this part) on their own they find the balance the building has. It is possible to read some buildings in that way: standing in the center or sensing their center from outside, you feel their balance so enormously but so wholly that you imagine you could extend your fingertips to every part.

Are there stories or novels like that? One of the pleasures of the days following reading *Pride and Prejudice, Moby Dick, Madame Bovary*—and many others —or stories like Gogol's "Overcoat," its descendant, Frank O'Connor's "Guests of the Nation," Eudora Welty's "Why I Live at the P.O.," Faulkner's "Barn Burning," Flannery O'Connor's "A Good Man Is Hard to Find" is that sensation of feeling the lines moving out and around and back through the whole.

Could there be any *buts* about the unity that Poe or Aristotle, each in his own way, wish for us?

There *are* buildings like the one in Virginia Woolf's *The Years,* like the Pantheon and its descendants by Palladio and Jefferson. Yet there are others like that in which the prince in Lampedusa's *The Leopard* lives. As I remember it, he thinks that it would be boring to live in a house in which you knew all the rooms. I imagine his house as a history of Sicily—each century adding another piece in its own style with lots of accidental spaces caught inside like air bubbles in amber.

There are novels like that: old ones, perhaps *Don Quixote,* and at least one new one, Graham Swift's *Waterland.* And I can think of one wonderful story: Alice Munro's "Oranges and Apples," which starts in a mood or mode of chronicle of provincial life, but turns into something else and something else again: larva, chrysalis, imago. The last instar something so gorgeous you could never have guessed it from the first pages.

Would Aristotle or Poe have helped her? But that doesn't mean that they're not helpful to her or the rest of us on the many occasions of pondering what to do with the jumble of incidents and tones that we're trying to rewrite.

Perhaps these pieces of dogma are like saints for different perplexities: St. Antony of Padua for finding lost things, St. Blaise for curing sore throats, St. Christopher for traveling safely (though I hear he's been displaced, alas).

Everyone says "Tell the truth." But I have in mind Konstantin Stanislavsky.

I used to assign and still suggest Stanislavsky's *An Actor Prepares* to my writing classes. There are two main reasons. Stanislavsky gives a good argument against cliché. If you use a cliché in your preparation for a role, you put a road-block in front of any further imagining. Clichés are vague, large, inert, and there-fore terminal. The other reason is less a warning, more a positive aid. If a character in fiction is lifeless, it often helps to play the part. Do all the preparation Stanislavsky asks an actor to do. Imagine the character's life offstage. What does she eat? How? What does she fear? How does she dress? How does she feel going home? etc., etc. Out of this imagining will come a hundred details, and usually one of them will provide a life-giving drop.

I had an odd experience with the narrator of a long story of mine called "Connaissance des Arts." He was an okay guy, but was neither hot nor cold. Per-haps I was afraid someone would think he was me. So I changed his clothes, put him in a good suit and a custom-made striped shirt with a white collar. I gave him narrow feet and put good shoes on them. I didn't need to mention any of this in the story. He began to act differently. The gulf that he perceived between him and his favorite student at the University of Iowa became more painful for him, at the same time his feelings for her became sharper. I don't know if the story is good, but it became more alive.

An Actor Prepares is a simply written series of lessons at a rhetorical level of *Dick and Jane*'s "See Spot run." It is a work of genius. But . . . I sometimes have misgivings about it. One is that Stanislavsky didn't have a great sense of humor. Chekhov kept writing him, when Stanislavsky was directing Chekhov's plays: "Please, Konstantin, it's meant to be funny." The other misgiving is that Stanislavsky seems to hold that the memory of one fear, for example, can animate the fear of the character to be portrayed. You might, relying only on your own emotions, inflate your jealousy at your junior high prom into Othello's. There is a danger of using emotions as isotopes or platonic ideals. It can work; I have only a misgiving about this, not an objection.

The antidote to this last misgiving about Stanislavsky's method, as valuable a tool as it often is, can be found in the work of another Russian, Vladimir Nabokov, specifically in *Speak, Memory*. Among the many, many things *Speak, Memory* is, it is a manual on the art of memory. Nabokov's memories are not interchangeable, although he could bestow them on certain of his characters as dangerous gifts. They are conjured for themselves, in all their infinite particular-ity. It is infinite particularity that is Nabokov's argument against cliché.

There is a wonderful chapter on his drawing teachers. Without deploying his whole pattern of development, from the facile and sweet to the labored and expressionistic to the precisely observed and rendered (so precise was Nabokov's observation and rendering that he was once employed by Harvard's Peabody Museum to do drawings of butterfly genitalia!), I'll simply characterize that chap-ter as perfect miniature commentary on the dialectic (how he would grind his teeth at that word) of becoming an artist, whether visual or verbal.

So there are at least two saints in this tell-the-truth-niche. Tell the truth, im-plore the intercession of one saint or the other or both, and tell it again. A tenor in an Italian town was called back for a third encore. "Thank you, thank you," he said, "But I can't—." A voice from the crowd called out, "You'll sing it again until you get it right!"

Tom Wolfe's dogma: "Be a reporter." Here's an easy one, but it comes up frequently enough to be worthwhile. Wolfe wrote an essay in *Harper's* magazine in 1989 on how to write a novel. In essence it said, "Go out and be a reporter. The material is out there! Get out of your ivory tower, stick a pencil stub behind your ear and do it the old-fashioned way. You could be Balzac, you could be Zola, you could be me!" There are some writers you'd like to see kicked in the pants in just this way.

I read a very good book (now out of print) several years ago: *Nimrod of the Sea* by William Morris Davis, a story of American whalemen. Every reportorial detail that is in *Moby-Dick* is in there, and then some. In addition to harpooning, a Nantucket sleigh-ride, the tryworks etc, there are icebergs in the Bering Sea, surfing in Hawaii, and a wealth of other lore. But *Nimrod of the Sea* is no *Moby-Dick*.

I like *Nimrod of the Sea*. It should be reprinted. But still, a first-rate way to learn the difference between very good reporting and the art of the novel is to read both books.

"Conventional narrative bores me." Robert Coover then went on to say, "You must experiment."

He was one of the smartest teachers at the University of Iowa when I was there. At that time it looked as if he, along with John Barth, would be the North American answer to Borges. It could still work out that way.

Both Coover and Barth appear in a dozen, no, a score of recent anthologies of short fiction. Their best stories are wonderful. The best of Barth is probably "Lost in the Funhouse." It *is* experimental. It plays with language, with received ideas, with the convention of narrative, with the architecture of the fun house and the architecture of the very fiction we are reading. There is a host of Barth works on which the same descriptive label could be pinned. Some are good, some are sterile. All the smart stuff is there, but it's solving a chess problem.

I think the qualification of the command to experiment is this: variation for variation's sake, experiment for experiment's sake is for the notepad, for the sketchbook. Experiments work in art when they contain the same emotional charge that good fiction always has. Originality is not a sufficient condition for storytelling. When the experiment is attempted as a way to produce a charged state of being, so that less of the charge is lost in transmission, *then* you're trying for the big gold ring.

"Culture is local." William Carlos Williams was a pal of Ezra Pound. Ezra Pound whirled off to England and Italy, learned Latin, Italian, maybe Provençal, and delighted in Chinese poems. His allegiance, his literary allegiance, was European. In the *ABC of Reading,* a rich swath-cutting primer with a great reading list, Pound says intimidatingly that if you want to know poetry and don't know Latin and Provençal, you might still have some fun in English. He's not an antiquarian—he's in favor of writers who've brilliantly upset the applecart—but he harks back and abroad.

William Carlos Williams stayed home. He did do a young man's European tour, but then he set up in New Jersey and practiced medicine, wrote about Paterson, his patients, his home ground.

I like teaching Williams's *The Farmer's Daughters* because in those prose pieces he does find what is wonderful down the street, around the corner. There are famous stories in it—"The Use of Force," "The Girl with the Pimply Face"— but my favorite is "Old Doc Rivers," the life of an old-time country doctor, with a kind of genius and a terrible restlessness. (*The Farmer's Daughters* is also reassuring to students because some of the stories are great successes and some are instructive duds.)

Once again we have two patron saints. Do they cancel each other out? Is it an either/or?

I was wandering around Washington, D.C. one day, wondering why there's so little good fiction written about it. The good American political novels are set elsewhere. *All the King's Men* is set in Louisiana, other good political fiction comes from Boston, or Chicago. (There's a little bit of good stuff about journalism—a subculture that is local in the sense of sealed in and centripetal.) It occurred to me that politicians, like most TV shows, are trying to write themselves as broadly appealing, and, because they aren't truthful, they end up as clichés. But then at my feet I saw another answer. In front of the National Theater there's a plaza on whose paving stones are inscribed quotations about Washington. The one on which I was standing said, "Washington—neither Rome or home."

I wish I'd said that. (When Oscar Wilde wistfully murmured that he wished he'd said a smart wisecrack he'd just heard, Whistler said to him, "You will, Oscar, you will.")

Washington, so far at least, hasn't been a matrix for either the Pounds or the William Carlos Williamses. (One footnote exception comes to mind, a good book of stories—*Lost in the City* by Edward P. Jones—which is set in Washington, but it is about black Washington, a population by and large excluded from the national media nonculture, but with a William Carlos Williams culture of its own.)

As to our two saints—Pound of Rome and Williams of home—there's another way of setting up the difference. It is the distinction between the tale and the modern short story. A tale occurs when someone leaves home, goes over the hills and far away, and comes back to tell the folks what amazing things are out there. A short story occurs when someone stays home and ponders local life until she can produce what is amazing about the things going on in her own culture, in her own words. Both the tale and the short story can be all the things our first eight points and counterpoints of dogma exhort us to write.

After considering these exhortations and their undertows, are we back where we started? Nobody thought that when you are facing the imperfect, half-alive matter you have committed to the page, that you could dial 1-800-OUR-DOGMA. As so often happens in law, the question isn't just what the laws are, but which ones apply to the case. Writing fiction—rewriting fiction—is trial and error, intuition and amended intuition. But in the effort to find your way through your own material, an application of one or another of these suggestions from our inherited lore may provide the right course correction.

DISCUSSION QUESTIONS

1. Casey describes the helpfulness of a teacher "holding the mirror up" to the work of a beginning writer. What does he mean by this? How does this compare to the methods described by Smiley and Carver (in the first section of this chapter) and Bell (in the third)?

2. Why would Katherine Anne Porter's method of simply reading the student's story aloud to the student cause the reaction Casey recounts? Does this reading aloud seem like an effective method of instruction? Why or why not?

3. Casey's exploration of the nine examples of dogma he quotes illuminates the paradoxical nature of such rules for writers, or at least suggests qualifications that must be considered. Which of these bits of dogma are most puzzling or contradictory to you? How can you begin to make sense of them?

4. Casey writes of how fiction gives us a sixth sense, "a sense of the invisible forces that make people more than the sum of their five senses." What does he mean by this? What fiction have you read that gives you this sixth sense?

5. Casey characterizes the examples of dogma as "saints for different perplexities." If you were to wear one or more of these dogmas as a medal around your neck to protect you from writerly harm, which would you choose? Why?

6. Casey pronounces that "originality is not a sufficient condition for storytelling." What does he mean by this? Do you agree?

7. Casey's distinction between the tale and the short story differs from that of John Gardner (see Chapter 1). What are the important contrasts between their definitions? Can these definitions be made to work together?

ANDREW LEVY

Back Home Again: Bobbie Ann Mason's "Shiloh"

Andrew Levy (b. 1962) teaches at Butler University and is the author of many books of poetry including Values Chauffeur You *(1990),* Democracy Assemblages *(1990),* Curve *(1994),* Continuous Discontinuous: Curve 2 *(1997), and* Elephant Surveillance to Thought *(1998). He has anthologized fiction in* Postmodern American Fiction: A Norton Anthology *(1997, co-edited with Paula Geyh and Fred Leebron), published criticism about fiction in* The Culture and Commerce of the American Short Story *(1993), and offered instruction to fiction writers in* Creating Fiction: A Writer's Companion *(1995, co-authored with Fred Leebron).*

For American writers simply to avow that they have the education, or the cultivation, that they very often have, is something that isn't done—they're like politicians who want to adopt a folksy accent.

—SUSAN SONTAG, "The Quote Box,"
Philadelphia Inquirer Magazine, 11 June 1989: 8.

In 1980, Bobbie Ann Mason's first major short story, "Shiloh," appeared in the *New Yorker.*[1] The story was an immediate critical success. It was reprinted in *Best American Short Stories* in 1981, and became arguably the most heavily anthologized short story of the last decade; the collection that followed, *Shiloh and Other Stories* (1982), was nominated for the National Book Critics Circle Award, The American Book Award, and the PEN/Faulkner Award, and won the Ernest Hemingway Award for First Fiction.[2] Mason's distinctive style traits—popular culture references, present tense, blue-collar and rural subject matter—have, with or without her direct influence, become dominant trends in the contemporary American short story. She is considered one of the chief representatives of a school of fiction variously named "dirty realism," "K-Mart realism," or "minimalism": linguistically spare, thematically populist, and consciously antiliterary.[3] This school developed such vogue during the 1980s that Mason's own work went from being perceived as a "refreshing" or "improbable" change from what usually appeared in commercial magazines and literary journals, to being the exemplar of one of the two kinds of fiction found in those venues. "If," in the words of Lila Havens, "Ann Beattie is giving us 'bulletins from the front' "—portrayals of middle- and upper-class angst—Mason is "telling us what it's like back home."[4]

Back home, of course, is a place the American short story has spent a great deal of time. From the 1830s and 1840s, when Eastern magazines and newspapers published anecdotes of frontier life gathered from papers and readers in the South and Southwest, the short story has always been a site of discourse in which a comparatively well-educated, middle-class audience could read about the fictionalized lives of the more marginal participants in the American political project. The major trends in short fiction during the nineteenth century—realism, local color, dialect—all told stories about rural residents, the poor, and ethnic minorities, in magazines distributed to audiences that either had no link with those socially disenfranchised groups, or had left them "back home."[5]

In the twentieth century, these trends continued, in new transformations. . . . Regional, ideological, and ethnic literary movements were spearheaded by the evolution of a system of "little" magazines that, with their shoestring budgets, provided for the distribution of editorial power among economically marginal groups.[6] At the same time, numerous authors and critics argued that the short story, for structural reasons, was the art form best suited for the description of a heterogeneous culture of "submerged population groups"—the American melting pot.[7] This vision of the short story was then realized in published form within the modern anthology, with its all-but-invisible editor and seemingly unranked inclusion of a multitude of individual voices, which appeared like an ideal metaphor for a diverse and democratic culture. Institutionally, historically, and structurally, everything about the short story implied heterogeneity—everything, perhaps, except the audience, which at its apex consisted of perhaps the upper one-fifth of the social pyramid, and which now rarely extends beyond the comparatively small and homogeneous readership represented by the circulation lists of the *New Yorker* and the university presses.[8]

Mason's work is infused by many of these same tensions and ambitions. She writes stories of blue-collar Kentuckians for the decidedly nonblue-collar readers of the *New Yorker,* the *Atlantic Monthly,* and the *Paris Review.* Having earned a Ph.D. in literature and composed (and published) a dissertation on Vladimir Nabokov's difficult *Ada,* she nevertheless has crafted an antiliterary narrative style, and authorial persona to match: Laughing at an interviewer's insistence that she "must know some big words," for instance, Mason responded that "I don't say them out loud."[9] In this context, it is worth wondering precisely how much cultural distance separates the *Atlantic* publishing one of Mason's blue-collar tales in the name of "dirty realism" in 1983, and publishing a story composed entirely in a Newfoundland patois and lauding its "realism" in 1862.[10] Although Mason's writing is often represented as somehow radical, it is difficult to resist the observation that her populism, and the populism of other "dirty realists," is almost entirely consistent with the ideological composition of one hundred and fifty years of American short story telling.

In this event, the nature of Mason's innovation might not be her much-lauded populist edge, which is neither particularly populist nor innovative. Rather,

Mason represents a significant chapter in the history of the short story because of the extent to which she combines many of the century-old narrative strategies of the American short story with a peculiarly postmodern (and postliterate) self-consciousness. Susan Sontag, in the epigraph that prefaced this chapter, observes that one way an American writer copes with life in an anti-intellectual culture is by playing dumb. If America is anti-intellectual because intellectualism constitutes an ostentatious show of superiority that is anathema to democratic culture, however, then the American writer has a second option: He or she can create fiction that undermines the myth structure from which intellectualism (and authorship) has drawn its power. That writer can attempt to "democratize" literature by using models of authorship, narrative, and protagonism that suggest authors and heroes work within a community, rather than rise gloriously and rebelliously above it.

In doing so, of course, the author risks undermining his or her own authority. The short story "Shiloh" illustrates how Mason has developed a narrative strategy that combines radically democratic visions of creative activity with a residual faith in what she calls the "alienated, superior sensibility."[11] It is a highly seductive strategy, one in which the author balances the conflict between the desire to celebrate oneself and to celebrate one's community by consciously and conscientiously playing dumb, as though playing dumb was, in itself, another American art form. It is also a strategy in which the traditional energies of the short story have provided an institutional and intellectual framework within which Mason and other "dirty realists" could operate, and thus add another chapter to the long and thriving history of one class of Americans writing about another.

THE GOOD LIFE

> I didn't understand the conflict between the type of mind I had and the type of mind I was trying to be.
>
> —Bobbie Ann Mason, "Conversation" 133–4.

In published interviews, Mason has been straightforward about the tension inherent in her fiction between home and away-from-home. When asked in 1984 how the people in her hometown—the kind of "everyday people" that populate her stories—have reacted to her success, she responded that "since I hardly know anybody there, I don't really know." She similarly observed that "lower-middle class people"—again, the residents of her stories—"don't have much access to fiction," and would probably "rather be reading *Princess Daisy*" than her work. Despite these limitations, Mason clearly perceives her fiction as having populist ramifications. Her stated ambition is to include in high-culture discourse the kind of characters and models for narrative that would normally be excluded:

> Throughout American literature, the hero was the alienated superior sensibility, the artist, the sensitive young man. I read so much of that in school that by the time I was ready to write, I was sick of reading about that guy, and I thought, "At

least he could be a woman," or maybe someone who was not sensitive and not superior. I think that's how I finally arrived at knowing who I was going to write about . . .

For Mason, the issue is not who reads literature, but what kinds of lives are considered worthy of being literature. She perceives herself as part of a larger populist "cultural shift" where the spread of education and wealth allows the "masses" to get access to the "good life"; and just as the masses get access to the good life, Mason gets them (and herself, the daughter of dairy farmers from western Kentucky) access to the "good" magazines. The result is that, in theory at least, high-culture discourse is transformed and democratized by this infusion of "popular culture," and that "suddenly," in Mason's phrase, "we're discovering that store clerks and cowboys also have valid lives."[12]

Initially, the critical response to Mason's fiction focused on this aspect of her work, on how she seemed to be crossing demographic barriers by presenting her "farmers, store clerks, and truck drivers" in the elegant typescript of the *Atlantic* or Harper and Row publications.[13] The *New York Times* wrote that "the gap to be bridged empathically between her readership and her characters was formidable." The *Chicago Tribune* wrote that "the details of her characters' lives must seem as remote as Timbuktu to the readers of the *New Yorker* or the *Atlantic*." The temptation to consider her fictions valuable simply because they contained factual data about an "exotic culture" was so strong that the *Village Voice* critic reminded his readers that *Shiloh and Other Stories* "was not anthropology." These critical reactions indicate that what made Mason's work exciting in 1982 was not just what she said, but where she said it. She was genuinely perceived as having infused high- and middle-culture sites of publication and readership with a realistic, uncondescending dose of low culture—and, more important, as having somehow bridged an empathetic gap that divided Americans into those separate classes.[14]

These are, of course, high-culture voices who are deciding what constitutes a realistic, uncondescending portrait of low culture. Mason has said that she has heard "rumors" that some residents of her hometown who have read her fiction dislike it because it makes them seem "too much like country people."[15] It is, in fact, almost too easy to deconstruct Mason's populism (and the cheerful response it has received), given that the entire project is virtually invisible to the classes of people it is supposedly empowering. Her literary politics are founded upon the troubling and decidedly unpopulist assumption that "store clerks' lives" are valid only to the extent that they are discussed in the *New Yorker* and taken seriously by an upper-middle-class audience. Similarly, her critics (if not necessarily her readers) do not question the possibility that her work might not be a "realistic" vision of lower-class life at all, but an imaginative reconstruction that appeals to an upper-middle-class audience for many reasons, some of them potentially antagonistic. Given her own tension regarding her Kentucky roots—she has spoken of feeling "threatened" by home, but recently relocated there from Pennsylvania—the possibility that her fiction contains ambivalent impulses toward home is rarely considered.[16]

Just as the praise for Mason fails to account for the possibility that her success might have more to do with the empathy she shares with her readership than with her characters, however, these criticisms ignore the possibility that Mason herself is both conscious of, and fascinated with, these very issues. Thus, although Mason has congratulated herself for "validating" lower-class lives, she more often observes that the "strength of my fiction has been the tension between being from there and not from there."[17] She has similarly suggested the popularity of her fiction can be attributed to the large number of people who, like her, have left behind blue-collar upbringings and joined a rising middle class. For that audience, reading her stories, like writing them, constitutes an act of reconciliation with the home that is left behind:

> My work seems to have struck a chord with a number of readers who have left
> home and maybe who have rejected it, and I think it startles them because they
> thought they were rid of it . . .[18]

For Mason, her work appeals to a broader audience because she brings to a high-culture site of discourse the sort of popular culture references and concerns that she believes have been repressed from high-culture discourse. The "home" that is left behind is not just rural Kentucky, but the "popular culture" that is repudiated (or diluted) by a rising middle class, or an entrenched upper class. As Mason recognizes, however, the repression of that popular culture is rarely complete: The appearance of her K-Mart brand names and rock music references on the pages of the *New Yorker* represents something like the bubbling up of a political subconscious, intruding itself on high-culture lives in a manageable form.

In many ways, Mason's consciousness of class difference is the key to her fiction. She has said that "it's the most extraordinary thing to move out of your class," and the quote resonates across virtually every aspect of her narrative project.[19] Not only does it describe her own rise from the daughter of dairy farmers to respected writer, but it also seems to describe her stories themselves, which appear like representatives of an entrenched underclass in sites of discourse in which that underclass theoretically rarely finds a voice. As she herself suggests, most of her audience is also displaced out of its class of origin, and finds her stories appealing for the reconciliation they offer. And, unsurprisingly, class and cultural displacement are also the major thematic matter of her stories: The *New York Times,* for instance, wrote that "ominous forces of disorientation are loose in Masonland," and observed that Mason's stories invariably deal with the personal and emotional consequences of sweeping social change.[20]

In this context, whether or not Mason is a working-class heroine is not a relevant issue. If the most significant aspect of her fiction is the manner in which it seems to jump across demographic barriers (while dealing thematically with the consequences of social dislocation), then we should value that jump (and her exploration of the consequences) as the central element of her work, not a tangential one. Caught between her sympathy for the underclass and her desire to run away from it, Mason has constructed a body of fiction and a narratology for the rising middle class, a way of telling stories that tries to balance the dictates of a radical populist program with an affection for the individual that rises above populism. "Shiloh" provides the first, and best, example of that narratology.

COUNTRY PEOPLE

The two protagonists of "Shiloh," Leroy and Norma Jean Moffett, are not in control of their lives. Rather, they appear to be moved by larger external forces which they only dimly recognize and certainly do not understand. The most active force in "Shiloh," for instance, appears to be the feminist movement, which makes its way to the Kentucky couple through a television set broadcasting "Donahue."[21] The story presents Norma Jean's evolution toward what Donahue himself might call "self-actualization" (she takes college courses, begins working out, gets a job, and eventually tells Leroy that she wants a divorce), and Leroy's lapses toward a childlike confusion. Her movement toward fulfilling some ideal of individuality, however, is mitigated throughout by her confusion over the reasons for her actions. When Leroy asks Norma Jean if her request for a divorce is a "women's lib thing," for instance, she answers, "don't be funny"; later, she adds "I don't know what I'm saying. Forget it."[22]

Similarly, Leroy, who has come to realize that "he never took time to examine anything," nevertheless "forgets where he hears things anymore," and seems lost in nostalgic fantasies of starting over, exemplified by his desire to build a log cabin as their "new" homestead. Neither he nor Norma Jean seems to recognize the stress that losing their baby several years earlier has had on their marriage, even though Leroy recalls having heard "that for most people losing a child destroys the marriage."[23] Fittingly, Norma Jean's announcement that she wants a divorce takes place in a cemetery, where Leroy seems to sense the link between his failing marriage and death in general, but cannot quite make the more personal connection between his imminent divorce and the loss of their son: "Leroy is trying to comprehend that his marriage is breaking up, but for some reason he is wondering about white slabs in a graveyard."[24]

That final scene is set, appropriately, at a National Historical Site, the Civil War battleground at Shiloh, Tennessee. Leroy, attempting to explain the failure of his marriage, widens his perspective and seeks to locate his and Norma Jean's place within a larger scope of historical change:

> General Grant, drunk and furious, shoved the Southerners back to Corinth, where Mabel and Jet Beasley were married years later, when Mabel was still thin and good looking. The next day, Mabel and Jet visited the battleground, and then Norma Jean was born, and then she married Leroy and had a baby, which they lost, and now Leroy and Norma Jean are here at the same battleground . . .

Leroy's epiphany, however, comes not when he successfully locates his place in history, but when he recognizes his inability to understand the forces of social change that have affected his life, an inability reflected in his rote listing of battleground names and family milestones. In a central line, Mason poetically describes these forces as "the insides of history":

> Leroy knows he is leaving out a lot. He is leaving out the insides of history. And
> the real inner workings of a marriage, like most of history, have escaped him . . .

At this point, Leroy recognizes his desire to build a log cabin as a refusal to adjust to social change, and dedicates himself to "get moving again." This optimistic moment is undermined by the very conclusion, however: Leroy, with one bad leg and one leg asleep, barely capable of "moving" in any sense, nevertheless strides hopefully toward Norma Jean, who is gesturing in what is either a welcoming wave or a muscle exercise designed to increase her own strength. The story ends at that ambiguous moment: It is as if Leroy's recognition that he has not understood the "inner workings" of past events is no guarantee that he will understand them in the future.[25]

The third-person narrator, interestingly, seems to be in a similar position. The story is told in an artfully awkward prose, on a level of vocabulary equivalent to that of Leroy and Norma Jean (Mason has said, probably exaggerating, that she limits herself to a six-hundred-word lexicon).[26] Just as Norma Jean and Leroy seem confused over the reasons for their own behavior, the narrator seems unwilling or unable to locate, and emphasize, the "meaningful moments" within the story. "Shiloh," like most of Mason's stories, has a flat texture, seems unplotted, and ends with an ambiguous and elliptical image ("The sky is unusually pale—the color of the dust ruffle Mabel made for their bed") that provides no sense of closure.[27] Superficially at least, Mason refuses to appear any more in control of the narrative than her characters are in control of their lives.

In doing so, she creates an authorial persona that is bound empathetically to the lives of the people she believes to be trapped inside history. She is unafraid of analyzing herself from the same historicist perspective, even though that perspective often undercuts her own authority by implying that she is not in control of the process of composition:

> I can't analyze it in detail and I'm not sure I can say why I choose to write that
> way, or even if I choose. I think things like that must be determined by larger
> social forces . . .[28]

Much of what Mason says about her own work is informed by this same self-deprecating, and antiliterary, perspective. Responding to a student's complicated interpretation of the dust-ruffle image that closes "Shiloh," for instance, she denies knowledge of the implications the student found, and instead observes that she writes "innocently."[29] Similarly, she has described her decisions about plot and closure in terms that suggest she dislikes making conscious choices about composition, and prefers instead to do anything she can to "get at that subconscious": "When you're writing a story, there comes a moment when it feels right to quit. Sometimes that just happens . . . It comes out of a feeling . . . It's—I'm not used to being analytical about it."[30] In describing her own work process as a sequence of unplanned choices dictated by subconscious or external forces over which she has little control, Mason creates a vision of her own creative activity that is identical to her vision of the lives of her characters, and that is modeled on a distinctly historicist perspective on behavior. Just as she says that her stories are composed "innocently," and conclude at a moment she has neither planned nor analyzed afterward, her characters "don't think of their lives as a story with coherence: They're just in it, they don't know what's going to happen next or why anything's happening."[31]

This is, as Sontag notes, an old game; but Mason practices it with unusually intricate self-consciousness. Unlike her characters, who appear both trapped within history and unable to recognize its influence on their lives, Mason's knowing "innocence" is coordinated with a deliberate effort on her part to control the effect of external conditions on her creative output. Her acceptance of these effects, in turn, places her in a position of both superiority over and sympathy with her characters: sympathy, because she accepts her own helplessness as well as theirs; superiority, because she recognizes and identifies them, and makes them major elements in her empowerment as a writer. In an interview with Lila Havens, for instance, Mason echoes Norma Jean's comments on the feminist movement, but with a telling difference: Where Norma Jean denies that feminism is a factor in her behavior, Mason notes that she "internalized" feminism, and then "moved on"—that is, she consciously accepted an external social movement into her subconscious, so that it would become an element in her "innocent," socially unaware poetic.[32] It is the precise difference enacted in her demographic relationship to her characters: Norma Jean and Leroy Moffett and Mason were all born and raised in lower-middle-class rural Kentucky, but while the Moffetts labor at rising above or repudiating the conditions of their lives, Mason has "moved on," acquired a Ph.D., and gained control of those same conditions (and the Moffetts themselves) as the resources of her fiction.

In a like manner, she denies being explicitly "political," but her thoughts on the purpose of her writing are laced with phrases such as "class struggle," suggesting that she has also, to some extent, internalized Marxism, and then moved on. This internalization of Marxist ideology is perhaps the most crucial aspect of her fiction. Throughout interviews, she has used the term "superior sensibility" (or variants thereof) to describe the model for fiction she believes has been unnecessarily dominant in the past.[33] In its place, Mason substitutes a model for the behavior of characters in fiction in which they move in coordination with communal values, or are moved (hesitatingly or not) by the force of those communal values. Similarly, her model of authorship appears to disdain the notion that the serious writer is a superior sensibility by presenting narrators and implied authors that seem neither more alienated nor more sensitive than their characters: "I don't feel superior to these people," Mason notes of her subjects, "I feel I'm luckier."[34]

THE INSIDES OF HISTORY

As mentioned earlier, "Shiloh" has been one of the most anthologized stories of the 1980s; along with selections from Jayne Anne Phillips, Louise Erdrich, Raymond Carver, Ann Beattie, and a handful of other authors, Mason's story has been consistently selected by textbook and commercial anthology editors as a representative of the best the 1980s short story had to offer.[35] In a significant sense, the popularity of "Shiloh" provides a further illustration of the most radical implications of Mason's narratology, and the kinds of publishing patterns that would be produced by the institutionalization of that narratology. The inference of Mason's poetic is that worthy fiction is not produced by individuals who control the resources of their fiction and the circumstances of its reception, but by individuals who respond "innocently" to a mixture of external and subconscious forces. In the past, it has been a commonplace of literature that special individuals might possess this special innocence—they might, for instance, be the Aeolian Harps through which God chose to communicate to Man. But the peculiar nature of Mason's repudiation of the alien, superior sensibility is that it widens the franchise of "innocence" to people who lack any special spiritual insights or charismatic gifts of artistic ability, as well as to those who have no knowledge of tradition or craft. She widens the franchise of potential artists to those who are truly "innocent," and respond "innocently" to external social forces—which is to say, virtually everybody. This model of creative activity, carried to its institutional fulfillment, would justify a system of publication and canonization where multivocal sites of discourse such as anthologies or magazines dominate, and where conservative assumptions about the consistent quality of an author's oeuvre are replaced by greater accessibility to the processes of publication and canonization.

Mason's own descriptions of the composition of "Shiloh" and her other early stories vividly illustrate the degree of her commitment to this model. Rather than describing the act of writing (about which she is almost consistently unforthcoming), Mason focuses on the correspondence between herself and Roger Angell of the *New Yorker,* who rejected nineteen of her stories before accepting one:

> We developed a correspondence and he really encouraged me a great deal, and I got very excited about what I was doing and worked very hard. Usually what he told me were not bits of advice on revising but just sort of subjective responses about the central reasons he didn't think they could publish the story, and he would offer a general criticism . . . it was fairly general, but usually he would make one or two comments that would hit right at the problem with the story, and it would give me something to think about. . . .[36]

As Mason describes it, "Shiloh" and her personal writing style were the product of a lengthy, impressionistic dialogue between herself and Angell who, as fiction editor of the *New Yorker,* might reasonably be called a living metonymy for the short-story publishing establishment. That her personal style could be perceived as the product of an engagement between herself and an external representative of the publishing community, rather than the product of some isolated, alien poesis, is a possibility that Mason characteristically does not seem to mind.

In fact, "Shiloh" itself, with its reliance on historicizable forces and the present tense, seems to invite the interpretation that it was generated by a moment of interaction between editor, author, genre, and culture, rather than by an isolated author. Mason relentlessly uses brand names, and references to songs that are popular at a given point in time, to historicize her stories to points in history (responding to a question about why she refers to songs and cultural figures by name in *In Country,* for instance, Mason says that *"In Country* was in the summer of '84. There are only a few years in which that story could take place").[37] In effect, this use of popular culture references creates a special language that not only dates the story to a specific moment in time but also makes it less readable as the years pass after its publication. These are all factors that justify "Shiloh"'s presence in current anthologies as a representative of the kind of short stories contemporary culture has to offer to the tradition. These factors also moderate the criticism Mason so often receives for writing *"New Yorker*-type stories"—a contemporary subgenre (to be distinguished from the "New Yorker" stories of previous generations) that she, in fact, did much to help create. As a study of her poetic clearly indicates, composing a story that contained within itself the unconscious traces that define a community was the entire point of her creative efforts, not an awkward after-effect.

These factors also suggest that "Shiloh" will not be so heavily anthologized in the future, unless contemporary culture remains static enough so the special language of popular culture references means as much in 2002 as it did in 1982. To a certain extent, Bobbie Ann Mason is writing a kind of disposable *literature*: serious fiction that addresses specific moments in time, which could be written only in specific moments in time, and that is initially published in sites of discourse (magazines) that are themselves more disposable than the bound volumes within which serious writing is usually enveloped. Friction occurs when this ideology clashes against more conservative assumptions about authorship: When, for instance, Mason herself keeps writing and publishing, she is implying that she can continue deliberately to produce those extraordinary moments when a community interacts with an individual (or an individual interacts with her subconscious) to produce a memorable story, a notion that contains within itself the main elements of the alien, superior sensibility with a uniquely Marxist twist.

Of course, Mason has continued writing and publishing her stories in bound volumes. The irony of Mason's philosophical flexibility concerning external social forces is that it accommodates the kind of self-deprecation that might be expected from a beginning, but not an established, author. That flexibility is part of a narratology for a rising class of people with divided sympathies; but not for an entrenched one. And a survey of the interviews Mason has granted in the seven years since her initial success suggests that as she has grown more confident with her own authorship, she has also repudiated the self-deprecating models of behavior that formed the philosophical underpinning for her rejection of the alien, superior sensibility, and—to some extent—for her preference for the short story.

In an early interview, for instance, she dwells on her relationship with Roger Angell and the *New Yorker,* and speaks in modest terms about her own critical success: "I'm still really quite surprised that my work has made the impression it has."[38] More recently, however, she dwells on the fact that she now composes alone, and shows her work to no one prior to sending it to her publishers. In a similar manner, her stance toward the alien, superior sensibility has altered considerably. In an interview conducted in 1989, Mason describes her evolution as an artist, and describes her repudiation of that sensibility using the same anecdote found in earlier interviews, but with a crucial twist at the conclusion:

I thought, "Well, I'll write a kind of *Huckleberry Finn* novel about *a girl*. I won't write about the sensitive young man, won't write about the artist, the sensitive youth coming of age. I'll write about somebody who is insensitive, and who doesn't wear glasses." And I found out that you couldn't do that! There's no story there . . .[39]

Interestingly, though, there is no conspicuous way to tell from Mason's fiction exactly when she made this discovery; her subject matter and her major themes have remained comparatively unchanged, and it could be easily argued that her most recent novel, *In Country,* is very much a kind of *Huckleberry Finn* about a girl. All Mason seems to have discovered, rather, is the point where her life has finally diverged completely from those of her characters—where her private story cannot be told without a sensitive artist figure performing at the center, and possibly wearing glasses. . . .

NOTES

1. Bobbie Ann Mason, "Shiloh," *New Yorker,* 20 Oct. 1980: 50–57. Mason's "Offerings" was published in the *New Yorker* earlier that year.
2. *Best American Short Stories 1981,* ed. Hortense Calisher and Shannon Ravenel (Boston: Houghton Mifflin, 1981), pp. 171–84. Bobbie Ann Mason, "Residents and Transients: An Interview with Bobbie Ann Mason," *Crazy Horse,* Feb. 1984: 87. Bobbie Ann Mason, *Shiloh and Other Stories* (New York: Harper & Row, 1982).
3. Mason, "Residents," p. 95. See, for instance, Nancy Pate, "The Real Small-Town South," review of *Me and My Baby View the Eclipse,* by Lee Smith, *Philadelphia Inquirer* 12 March 1990: E-2. Kim Herzinger, "Introduction: On the New Fiction," *Mississippi Review* 40/41 (Winter 1985): 8. Joe David Bellamy, "A Downpour of Literary Republicanism," *Mississippi Review* 40/41 (Winter 1985): 31–39.
4. Mason, "Residents," p. 87.
5. For a discussion of the development of the short story of the 1830s, see Eugene Current-Garcia, *The American Short Story Before 1850: A Critical History* (Boston: Twayne, 1985), pp. 91–99.
6. Frederick J. Hoffman, Charles Allen, and Carolyn Ulrich, *The Little Magazine: A History and a Bibliography* (Princeton, NJ: Princeton University Press, 1946), pp. v–vi, 1–6.
7. Frank O'Connor, *The Lonely Voice: A Study of the Short Story* (New York: World, 1963), pp. 20, 40–41.
8. James Hart, *The Popular Book: A History of America's Literary Taste* (New York: Oxford University Press, 1950), p. 286. Theodore Peterson, *Magazines in the Twentieth Century* (Urbana: University of Illinois Press, 1964), and F. L. Mott, *A History of American Magazines, 1865–1905* (1938; Cambridge, MA: Harvard University Press, 1967), both discuss magazine circulation rolls in detail.

   See also Peter S. Prescott, Introduction, *The Norton Book of American Short Stories* (New York: Norton, 1988), p. 14. "I decided to resist the temptation to define to any strict degree what a short story is. To define is to exclude, and there's something in the American character that resists exclusion; for a collection of American stories I needed a vulgar comprehensiveness."
9. Bobbie Ann Mason, "A Conversation with Bobbie Ann Mason," ed. David Y. Todd, *Boulevard* 4-5.3-1 (Spring 1990): 135.

10. F. L. Pattee, *The Development of the American Short Story* (1925; New York: Biblo & Tannen, 1975), p. 170.

11. Mason, "Residents," p. 95. In Bobbie Ann Mason, "An Interview with Bobbie Ann Mason," ed. Enid Shomer, *Black Warrior Review* 12.2 (1986): 98, she refers to the "alienated hero," and the "superior sensibility." In Mason, "Conversation," p. 134, she speaks of the "sensitive young man," in the same context.

12. Mason, "Residents," pp. 89, 90, 95, 96.

13. Suzanne Freeman, "Where the Old South Meets the New," review of *Shiloh and Other Stories,* by Bobbie Ann Mason, *Chicago Tribune Book World,* 31 Oct. 1982: 3.

14. David Quammen, "Plain Folk and Puzzling Changes," review of *Shiloh and Other Stories,* by Bobbie Ann Mason, *New York Times Book Review,* 21 Nov. 1982: 7. Freeman, "Where," p. 8. Geoffrey Stokes, review of *Shiloh and Other Stories,* by Bobbie Ann Mason, *Village Voice Literary Supplement,* 9 Nov. 1982: 7.

15. Mason, "Residents," p. 90.

16. Mason, "Conversation," p. 135.

17. Mason, "Conversation," p. 135.

18. Mason, "Residents," p. 88.

19. Mason, "Residents," p. 102.

20. Quammen, p. 7.

21. Mason, "Shiloh," p. 50.

22. Mason, "Shiloh," p. 57.

23. Mason, "Shiloh," p. 50.

24. Mason, "Shiloh," p. 57.

25. Mason, "Shiloh," p. 57.

26. Mason, Shomer, "Interview," p. 96.

27. Mason, "Shiloh," p. 57.

28. Mason, "Residents," p. 101.

29. Mason, "Residents," p. 97.

30. Mason, "Conversation," pp. 138–39.

31. Mason, "Residents," p. 101.

32. Mason, "Residents," p. 94.

33. Mason, "Residents," p. 95.

34. Mason, "Residents," p. 88.

35. Eugene Current-Garcia and Bert Hitchcock, eds., *American Short Stories* (Glenview, IL: Scott, Foresman/Little, Brown, 1990), for instance, includes Ursula Le Guin, Raymond Carver, Bobbie Ann Mason, Alice Walker, Joy Williams, Tobias Wolff, Tim O'Brien, David Michael Kaplan, Jayne Anne Phillips, Louise Erdrich, and Michael Martone in the "Contemporary Flowering" section. Ann Charters, ed., *The Story and Its Writer* (New York: St. Martin's Press, 1987), includes Ann Beattie, Raymond Carver, Alice Adams, Louise Erdrich, Mark Helprin, Jamaica Kincaid, David Leavitt, Ursula Le Guin, Bobbie Ann Mason, Alice Munro, Cynthia Ozick, Grace Paley, Jayne Anne Phillips, and Alice Walker. Michael Meyer, *Bedford Introduction to Literature* (New York: St. Martin's Press, 1987), uses Carver, Erdrich, Mason, Phillips, and Mark Strand for the "Album of Contemporary Stories." Laurie G. Kirszner and Stephen R. Mandell, eds., *Literature: Reading, Reacting, Writing* (Fort Worth, TX: Holt, Rinehart & Winston, 1991), includes Amy Tan, Anne Tyler, Alice Walker, Alice Munro, Mason, Madison Smartt Bell, Lorrie Moore, Charles Baxter, and Louise Erdrich.

36. Mason, "Residents," p. 98.

37. Mason, "Conversation," p. 141.
38. Mason, "Residents," p. 104.
39. Mason, "Conversation," p. 134.

DISCUSSION QUESTIONS

1. Levy affiliates Mason's work with "fiction variously named 'dirty realism,' 'K-Mart realism,' or 'minimalism': linguistically spare, thematically populist, and consciously antiliterary." Have you heard these terms before? What do they mean to you?
2. Levy describes "back home" as a common setting for American short stories. How does his sense of American fiction's focus on "marginal participants in the American political project" relate to Frank O'Connor's image of "submerged population groups" in Chapter 1?
3. What does Levy mean when he claims that Mason blends traditional narrative strategies "with a peculiarly postmodern (and postliterate) self-consciousness"? How does this relate to Levy's image of writers "playing dumb"?
4. Why does Levy assess Mason's work as dealing with "sweeping social change" in the United States? What are the elements of this change? Do you recognize the class differences and class shifts he refers to in his analysis? How do they function in your life and work?
5. What does Levy mean by describing "Shiloh" as written in "artfully awkward prose"? What writers have you read who utilize this style? Why would a writer choose to write this way?
6 What does Mason mean when she claims she writes "innocently"? Why does Levy state that this is a knowing, self-conscious innocence?

D. G. MYERS

The Elephant Machine

D. G. Myers (b. 1952), a professor of English at Texas A&M University, is the author of The Elephants Teach: Creative Writing Since 1880 *(1996). He has published essays in literary journals such as* Comparative Literature *and* Philosophy and Literature, *and in creative writing journals such as the* AWP Chronicle. *In a recent amazon.com interview, he said, "In* The Elephants Teach, *I quote the Italian Renaissance critic Castelvetro, who says that the theory of poetic inspiration was invented by poets to keep outsiders from inquiring too closely into their methods. That may be the basic commitment of poetry and fiction-writing. Scholarly writing is committed to openness, to full disclosure. And the question is whether it is possible to write well, even beautifully, under such conditions. For a writer, it is an interesting problem."*

Outside of Iowa the first graduate programs in creative writing were set going in the first few years after the defeat of Hitler and Japan. Elliott Coleman founded the writing seminars at Johns Hopkins in 1946; Stanford began its fellowship program in writing in 1947, the same year that Alan Swallow started the program at the University of Denver; Baxter Hathaway set up the program at Cornell in 1948. The purpose was to fashion a separate master's degree for teachers of creative writing, courses in which were becoming a fad on the postwar campus, according to Wallace Stegner. "If candidates are properly screened and trained," said Stegner, who assembled the program at Stanford, "they are competent to teach writing in any college better than it has customarily been taught in most, and more competent to teach it than teachers who have been thoroughly trained in the Ph.D. system."[1]

For two decades the first five programs performed the bulk of the work. Under the poet Paul Engle, who had been appointed its director in 1942, creative writing at Iowa filled up like an auditorium, reaching a peak enrollment of 250 in 1965. Engle, who was said to have been carefully groomed for the job, was the right man to oversee Iowa's expansion: he was an academic entrepreneur who had to cultivate his talents as a press agent and fund raiser, because until the mid-sixties the Iowa Writers' Workshop subsisted on gifts and contributions. The real growth in creative writing programs came after this date, and was symbolized by the turn at Iowa to state funding. By 1970 the number of programs had climbed to forty-four and by 1980 to over a hundred. The history of creative writing since the Second World War has been the 'history of its development into what American industry calls an "elephant machine"—a machine for making other machines. Creative writing programs became a machine for creating more creative writing programs. As early as 1964, Allen Tate warned that "the academically certified Creative Writer goes out to teach Creative Writing, and produces other Creative Writers who are not writers, but who produce still other Creative Writers who are not writers."[2]

The development came in two stages. First there was an age of criticism, a period during which men like Stegner, Coleman, Swallow, Hathaway, and Engle —all of whom were critics in their way, even if none was in the front rank—consolidated the gains of the earlier generation of university critics; and then, once creative writing was set firmly on its feet, it was swept up into a period of expansion within the university as a whole. In both stages creative writing might be described as going through an interval of "professionalization," although I would prefer to say that in the first stage creative writing settled into a *discipline* while only in the second stage did the teachers of this discipline make themselves bodily into a *profession*.

In the first stage creative writing was the perfection of one tendency in the history of criticism. It was an effort to handle a single order of human discourse in a way that would yield a unified body of theory. It was the movement of criticism toward constructive knowledge—knowledge *how* conceived as both the only means of access to and somehow the equivalent of knowledge *that*. This view of the matter led the first generation of full-time teacher-writers (as one of his students said about Tate) to consider "teaching to be an integral and consistent part of the creative work of a professional man of letters." To think of oneself as a professional writer in the years immediately following the Second World War was to perform all the duties of a man or woman of letters, including what Horace had called "the role of whetstone." It was to seek to integrate and make consistent the knowledge and creative practice of literature. Literary professionalization was a way of taking oneself seriously; it was not a campaign for prerogative and authority. In some other professions by contrast—business, education, the military—attempts to standardize professional training predated the existence of any special knowledge in which to train anyone. And in this regard postwar writers in the university were closer to engineers and commercial artists, who have to master a growing body of knowledge or techniques without a comparable degree of control over the conditions of their employment. At the same time writers *were* becoming professionalized in the more usual sense of the term: they were less worried about the opinion of outsiders, including common readers, and more concerned with the judgment of their fellow writers. Even here, though, the insistence upon autonomy might be put in disciplinary rather than professional terms, as when Stegner tries to cheer up a writer who has (he says) "the uncommon touch" and who will find readers (he assures her) "vertically through many years rather than hoizontally in any one publishing season"; or when Saul Bellow differentiates the "great-public novel" from the "art-novel," in which "a reduction in human scope must be compensated or justified by brilliant workmanship—by art." In the first stage of its postwar growth creative writing might be described as an effort to systematize and transmit the knowledge required to enjoy the vertical compensations of art rather than satisfying the horizontal demands of a great public.[3]

In the second stage creative writing became one of the primary engines driving the postwar expansion of the American university. The boom of creative writing coincided with an unprecedented growth in higher education, but it did not merely coincide with it. Creative writing was a means—a justification—for expanding the university's very role in society. During the period from the late forties to the early seventies the university began to reach beyond its traditional function as a site of teaching and research to provide institutional sanctuary for the arts, including literature. Ezra Pound had said in 1950 that

> this much is certain, if America has any desire to be a center of artistic activity she must learn her one lesson from the Ptolemies. Art was lifted in to Alexandria by subsidy, and by no other means will it be established in the United States.

Only a decade later Pound's challenge seemed well on its way to being met. In 1961, Engle observed that "It is conceivable that by the end of the twentieth century the American university will have proved a more understanding and helpful aid to literature than ever the old families of Europe." He could have said "the not so very old families of America," because the university began to assume a role that had previously been left to families like the Guggenheims, Rockefellers, and Fords, who endowed philanthropic foundations, and the MacDowells, Trasks, and the owner of the Bread Loaf Inn, who turned their homes into artists' retreats. . . . Summer conferences like Bread Loaf and summer colonies like Mac-

Dowell and Yaddo were attempts to subsidize and give sanction to the life of art, but at best they were temporary accommodations. After the Second World War the university stepped forward to become the permanent center of artistic activity in America, and this aggrandizement of its historical mission seemed to be abundantly justified by the expansion of its size.[4]

The poet Theodore Weiss shows how the two stages of creative writing's postwar progress are brought together, although in reverse order. In explaining how he had benefitted from a university career, Weiss says that

> it has provided some official status for what I do, a kind of societal approval. The workshop also has obliged me to sharpen and to justify my own attitudes toward writing, to rationalize and articulate them. Thus it has ripened my awareness of what I am—or ought to be attempting to do.

But what exactly is it that Weiss does or attempts to do at his job in the university? Does he write poetry? Teach other people to write poetry? Some combination of the two? This points to a confusion at the heart of postwar creative writing. It is a confusion that materializes every time the question is asked *Can writing be taught?* According to the novelist Walter Van Tilburg Clark, there is only one answer to the question. "[T]he teaching of writing can have but one purpose, the production of writers," he said in 1950. "That must be its central purpose, just as surely as the central purpose of teaching law, engineering or medicine, is to produce lawyers, engineers or physicians." And by writers Clark meant those who are devoted to "'serious poetry and fiction,' as distinguished, presumably, from commercial or formula writing. . . ." To seek anything else from creative writing than to produce serious writers is to fall back upon "secondary values." Indeed, no other account of their "central purpose" would suffice to rationalize and articulate the many graduate programs in writing that were founded after the war.[5]

And yet the purpose of a *program* would appear to be different from a *course*. By the early eighties, for instance, undergraduate enrollment in creative writing courses at Western Michigan University was running above 100 per semester. This was advanced as a good reason for founding a master's program there—the students in these courses were described as the "clients" for such a program—but it is a little difficult to believe that many of these students were being "produced" as writers.[6] When conceived as a mere course instead of a full-scale program, creative writing was defended in terms of its older "secondary value" as constructive knowledge, a way of seeing literature from its makers' point of view.[7] The divergence in aims between the program and the course suggests the real nature of creative writing's professionalization, which did not occur until the late sixties and early seventies. It was not until then that creative writers —graduates of creative writing programs—gained the nearly exclusive right to teach a course whose presence in the curriculum was argued for on different grounds. When it finally occurred, professionalization as such had little to do with literature as such: writers were not professionalized as writers but as writing teachers. If their aims as writers diverged from their aims as teachers, if they were hired and promoted on the basis of criteria that were established by their colleagues and not their "clients," this made them very little different from professors in other walks of university life who also experienced (as Le Baron Briggs had put it many years earlier) a difficulty in adjusting their academic specialties to the needs of general education. This is the true meaning of academic professionalization. Creative writing reached its full growth as a university discipline when the purpose of its graduate programs (to produce serious writers) was uncoupled from the purpose of its undergraduate courses (to examine writing seriously from within).

Despite a steady immigration of critics, poets, and novelists into university teaching positions, the American writer's problem of how to get a living had not been solved for good. By the end of the Second World War, as one historian of authorship has said, five different categories of writers could be made out:

> the independent, free-lance writer stood at the top of his profession; another group of writers supplemented their free-lance earnings with occasional stints of salaried work; a third group relied exclusively on service writing to pay their bills; a fourth group relied on another occupation for their main financial support while occasionally selling a story, novel or poem; finally, a vast pool of amateur writers rarely if ever sold their work.

When the critic and editor Malcolm Cowley addressed the Iowa Writers' Workshop during the 1949–1950 academic year, he warned students that only five or six writers of serious fiction were able to make a go of it, chasing at least one of the students into law school. "Writing novels is not a career, or a profession, or even a trade," agreed Vincent McHugh in a 1950 *Primer of the Novel*. "It is a gambling game. The player's chances are somewhat less favorable than if he were betting on the horses, though the stakes are sometimes larger."[8]

Although the nation's gross domestic product averaged 2 percent growth per worker per year from 1950 to 1973—although it was a period that stood witness to what the historian John Brooks has described as "one of the most dramatic redistributions of income that any nation ever went through in so short a time"— American writers did not immediately share in the prosperity. In the five years from 1953 to 1957, for example, it was found by one investigator that

> the average professional author earns insufficient income to live on from his chosen profession. . . . There are many thousands of men and women who are freelance writers, or are trying to be. Probably no more than a dozen really make a good living at it.

The average income of a full-time freelancer was $3400—this during an era when, while the population rose by 11 percent, the number of Americans who earned less than $5000 a year declined by 23 percent. Meanwhile, writers who supplemented their income with occasional stints of salaried work made nearly five times as much money from their employment as from their writing: annual literary earnings of not quite $1500 compared to almost $7000 a year from working for someone else. While one American in twenty held down a second job, for writers—counting their writing as a "job"—the number was one in three.[9]

One cynic speculated that, as writing declined in profitability, writers turned to teaching instead. It was not quite as simple as that. Long before the rise of the movies and the slow collapse of the pulp fiction market that once made it possible to earn a living at writing stories—long before the Depression and the Second World War—as I [have elsewhere] argued . . . teaching was an option that was available to writers; but unless they were writers like William Vaughn Moody, Alfred Noyes, or Robert Frost—one of those about whom (in Frost's words) "you can hear along other highways," who were "known all over the country for something not too bad"—a teaching post was not likely to be a sinecure. After earning his Ph.D. at Iowa but before going to Stanford, Wallace Stegner taught at several other colleges. "It is possible," he wrote from the University of Utah in 1937,

> to conform to the mores of the pedagogical profession, grind over comma faults and agreement errors and faulty parallelism during working hours, and yet keep close and inviolate a certain artistic integrity which labors to learn the craft of writing. . . . [N]o matter how hard the apprenticeship in pedagogy for the average man, it can be withstood, and it cannot ruin him as an artist. It can perhaps retard him, but it can also pay his board bill while he struggles with his fundamentals—and it is notable that with the first success or two writers consistently abandon the classroom.

Two decades later, though, the attitude toward teaching had begun to change. In a 1958 study of the poet in American society, the Harvard sociologist Robert N. Wilson found that opinion among poets was still divided on the question of what else besides poetry they should do to earn a living. At that time, apparently, teaching was still merely one option among several, including the professions of law and medicine, the business world, manual labor. And yet teaching increasingly struck poets as a "job close to poetry," because it called upon them "to double up on the one outstanding skill they possess—facility with language. . . ." Many poets taught college English, Wilson found, "and despite the traditional horror of mixing pedagogy and creativity they appear to be happy and productive." What was the cause of their happiness and productivity? According to him,

> Teacher-poets report that many university appointments are better suited to the poet's needs today than has been true in the past, since some administrators have come to realize that writers require leisure and are not overloading them with class hours.

It is just as likely that teacher-poets had convinced administrators that grinding over comma faults and agreement errors and faulty parallelism was not what most needed doing.[10]

The improvement of writers' lot—both economically and pedagogically—depended on upholding the distinction between "serious" and "commercial or formula" writers; a distinction, for that matter, which is related by marriage to the one between creative writing and practical composition. These distinctions . . .

date from the earliest years of the century and are central to the development of creative writing as both an institution and a system of ideas. Creative writing is at least partly an effort to solve the problem that has always faced serious writing in America: a lack of economic viability. It does not follow, however, that the distinctions between serious and commercial, creative and practical, are wholly ideological. The economic neglect is merely the end result of a habit of disregard that starts at a much more basic, much less conscious, level. As Howard Nemerov once said, "A primary pleasure in poetry is surely something low enough to be beneath the notice of teacher or critic"—or consumer, he might have added—"the pleasure of saying something over for its own sweet sake and because it sounds just right." And yet the distance between "pleasure" and "seriousness," between saying something because it sounds just right and expecting to receive something for it, is the distance between a logical distinction and an ideological claim. In a 1959 letter of advice to a young writer, Stegner demonstrates how one shades over into the other. "To go on writing" with integrity, he says—in a way that is not calculated to win popular success, "slowly, carefully, with long pauses for thinking and revising"—a writer needs "some sort of subsidy. . . . Of the possible jobs," he goes on, "teaching probably offers most, because its hours are flexible and because it entails a three-month summer vacation." Anyone can write with care but not everyone can expect a subsidy and a three-month vacation. What is going on here is the identification of a certain kind of writing with a certain class of writers. The historian Barbara Tuchman objected to something similar: the narrowing of the word *literature*. In an article published in 1966 she said, "I see no reason why the word should always be confined to writers of fiction and poetry while the rest of us are lumped together under that despicable term 'Non-fiction'—as if we were some sort of remainder." The reason of course is that the hiring of fiction writers and poets to teach in the university had narrowed the scope of "serious writing" and "literature" to what the writers wanted to teach. For the writers themselves this was not experienced as a narrowing at all. On the contrary, they believed passionately in literature, viewing it as the most important of the humanities, even if they confined it to fiction and poetry. "I come of a generation, now largely vanished," Saul Bellow said recently, looking back upon his generation's heyday, "that was passionate about literature, believing it to be an indispensable source of illumination of the present, of reflective power."[11]

The first generation of full-time teacher-writers neither ground over comma faults and agreement errors and faulty parallelism nor produced serious writers; they taught literature. The poet and critic Randall Jarrell was on staff at the University of North Carolina at Greensboro when the school founded its master's program in creative writing, but as Fred Chappell recalls, "Randall made it clear that he had no interest in teaching writing on the graduate level." Not all teacher-writers shared Jarrell's clear lack of interest, but most of them felt the need to teach literature. As the critic Ray B. West reported in 1950,

> Most 'writing' instructors also offer more or less standard 'literature' courses. It is true that they often confine themselves to fields (such as recent criticism and literature, foreign literature, or the study of contemporary forms) not adequately

supplied by the traditional English program, quite often not because this represents their preference, but because these courses fulfill a need which the literary scholar does not feel.

The writers taught literature because it—or at least as they conceived it—continued to be neglected by the scholars. As more and more of them broke into the university after the war, literature came more and more to be identified with them and what they did or attempted to do.[12] . . .

. . . Instead of being studied for the sake of a "secondary value"—its moral effect—literature was studied for the knowledge of how *literary* effects are attained. The shift, as the poet Karl Shapiro urged, was toward vocationalism:

> Let us give up the old pedagogical idea that the effect of poetry on the world is salutary. To believe that men are bettered by poetry is as narrow as to believe that they are worsened by it. Let us think of it another way. Let us think of creation in art as the vocation, and only the vocation of a certain kind of man. Let us then give it the honor of any vocation for knowledge.

At all events, the vocation for literary knowledge remained the first justification for a program in creative writing, and the name for this special knowledge continued to be *criticism,* although it was beginning to be defined in a new way. Three decades later the story writer Donald Barthelme would give the definition most clearly. He agreed that a writing program probably cannot make students into serious writers. "But you can teach the notion of what's dead or alive," said Barthelme, who taught at the University of Houston. "You can teach them how to be critics of their own work." Even in the fifties this idea of vocational criticism was becoming fixed. Ray B. West, who taught at Iowa starting in 1949, doubled back on Foerster's idea of the writing program as a school of criticism. Because "every writer must learn as best he can," West said, "to distinguish exactly what it is in his work which succeeds from that which fails," and because this ability to distinguish success from failure—this critical sense—"operates . . . at all points in the creative process," it follows that "[i]t is in the cultivation of this sense that the writing program can achieve most." If the emphasis was vocational, though, it was not yet fully professionalized. "The problems of recognition and publication will always be secondary," West said, "and they will arise as a result of the writing"—that is, as a consequence of having written—"not as a professional aim in the sense that the student would be encouraged to 'slant' his unfinished writing toward any particular publisher or publication."[13]

Over and over writing teachers said that writing itself cannot be taught, but a discipline of criticism that is associated with it can be. Jean Stafford, for example, suggested there was more to be learned in a writing class than how to write, saying that

> the student who, in class, learns to analyze a story or a novel, to separate its components, and then to see how the author has united them into an infrangible integer may never himself write a publishable piece of fiction, but he will know better

what writing is, and his enjoyment of reading—and therefore, of life—will be greatly enriched. It is more fun to watch a tennis match if you know how to play; but even if you don't know how, if you learn the rules, then you can differentiate among the idiosyncratic styles of individual players and be a judicious spectator.

Not everyone was as blunt as James Whitehead of the University of Arkansas. "I teach reading," he said, "and I teach reading the way writers read." *Reading as a writer*—it became the unexpected bonus of creative writing. Dorothea Brande had coined the term in the mid-thirties in *Becoming a Writer,* but it fell to R. V. Cassill, in *Writing Fiction* (1962), to develop the term into a concept. A novelist and Iowa professor who went on to found the writing program at Brown in 1966, Cassill defined "reading as a writer" as the kind of literary study that distinguishes creative writing from the on-the-job training of journalism on the one hand and from literary scholarship on the other. Good writers are interested in something more than the application of commercial formulas, and so they must study texts in addition to principles. Unlike scholars, though, they are not particularly interested in determining the sources of literary texts. Above all they are interested in how texts are *made*—how the parts are united into an infrangible integer—which means they are committed to the view that a text might have been made otherwise than it is. "A writer reading must be aware," Cassill says, underlining every word, "that the story exists as it does because the author chose his form from among other possibilities." Again, this is clearly a vocational concept of knowledge, embedded in a highly organized discipline of work. But, again, it is not truly a *professionalized* concept, because it does not depend upon a literature or a set of problems accessible only to specialists. "You know," an undergraduate student of creative writing told his professor, James K. Folsom, in the early sixties. "This is the best course in criticism given in Yale College." Pondering what he had meant, Folsom decided that the course

> had given him an insight into the techniques of literary analysis by making him aware of how other writers had succeeded where he himself had failed. It taught him by example rather than by precept that the proper question to ask in the interpretation of literature is not "What does the story mean?" but rather "How does the story work?"

Creative writing remained a discipline of criticism, but the criticism was neither "know-how" nor an absorption in technical detail; perhaps even "vocationalism" is too hidebound. Creative writing was the knowledge of how literary texts are made, how they work; it was a discipline of constructive knowledge.[14]

Howard Nemerov explained how he happened to become a college teacher. He was twenty-six, and though he had got a Harvard education, he held no advanced degree. He was just back from the war in Europe where he had served as a pilot in the Army Air Corps, flying combat missions against German shipping in the North Sea. He was also newly married; he had to start earning a living. "[I]n 1946," he said, by the exemplary generosity of our government in establishing the G.I. Bill and so inducing colleges and universities to find warm bodies to put up against the veterans (twenty of them, and still in combat boots), I became a teacher, or anyhow a kind of dogsbody responsible for The Bible and Shakespeare and The Modern Novel and Modern Poetry (with my first book [*The Image and the Law*] coming out, I was presumed to know something of that) and whatever else needed doing.

The need to find warm bodies to put up against the veterans explains much about the postwar influx of poets and fiction writers into the university. Under the G.I. Bill—officially, the Servicemen's Readjustment Act of 1944—veterans were allotted forty-eight months of free education at the college or university of their choice. Although the administrator of Veterans Affairs predicted that only 700,000 of them would do so, under the provisions of the bill 2,232,000 veterans crowded into American universities and colleges after the war, with more than a million of them enrolled during the single academic year 1947–1948. An army of warm bodies was needed to put up against them—and quickly. Small wonder so many poets and fiction writers began their academic careers about this time. Accounts of its effect upon the curriculum tend to be overstated—creative writing, to name one subject, had already begun to grow prior to the war—but the G.I. Bill left its mark on the university in other ways. "The uncritical acceptance of largeness became a major legacy of the G.I. Bill," says the historian Keith W. Olson. "This legacy, in turn, served as perhaps the most important intellectual foundation for bigness that characterized higher education during the 1960s and 1970s." Another legacy, tied to the first, was the uncritical acceptance of the practice of hiring writers—who, with books coming out, were presumed to know something about it—to teach modern writing. As the postwar university expanded so did the need for writers.[15]

The mass expansion of American higher education received political backing when the President's Commission on Higher Education, consisting of twenty-eight members appointed in July 1946 and chaired by George F. Zook, president of the American Council on Education, linked physical enlargement to an enlargement of the university's public role. "American colleges and universities must envision a much larger role for higher education in the national life," said the Commission's report, *Higher Education for American Democracy:*

> They can no longer consider themselves merely the instrument for producing an intellectual elite. They must become the means by which every citizen, youth and adult, is enabled and encouraged to carry his education, formal and informal, as far as his native capacities permit.

The colleges and universities did their best, although the first thing that was noticeable was their growth in sheer physical size. From 1930 to 1957 college enrollments more than doubled, going from 1,101,000 to 2,637,000. Then between 1960 and 1969 they doubled again, rising to over seven million.[16]

Although the enlargement of the university was seen politically as a democratization of it, within the university this was seen as an occasion for enlarging its domain. The spokesman for mass expansion was the University of California chancellor Clark Kerr, who sang the praises of what he liked to call the "multi-versity," a social and cultural institution that had to be many things to many different people. Playing on the title of Karl Polanyi's famous 1944 account of the emergence of a market economy, Kerr said the university was going through a great transformation. "Knowledge is exploding along with population," he said. "There is also an explosion in the need for certain skills." One field that was "ready to bloom"—whether it was a field of knowledge or skills he did not make clear—was the creative arts, "hitherto the ugly ducklings or Cinderellas of the academic world." Kerr acknowledged that

> in the arts the universities have been more hospitable to the historian and critic than to the creator; he has found his havens elsewhere. Yet it is the creativity of science that has given science its prestige in the university. Perhaps creativity will do the same for the humanities, though there may be less need to create than has recently been true in science and the tests of value are far less precise. A very important role remains for the historian of past ages of creativity and for the critic of the current productions. But the universities need to find ways also to accommodate pure creative effort if they are to have places on the stage as well as in the wings in the great drama of cultural growth now playing on the American stage.[17]

Kerr's logic is interesting, but it is obscured a little by the exuberance of his rhetoric. The argument of his last sentence goes something like this. If the university is to play a central role in American culture (that is the major premise), and if the arts are at the center (American culture, Kerr said, was currently having a "great period of cultural flowering"), the conclusion is that the university must become an arts center. This is an exception to the general rule that the minor premise is the point at which most arguments go astray. What is perhaps most revealing about Kerr's thinking is his assumption that the major premise is unexceptionable. True, he was speaking in his capacity as a representative of the university. And true, the "explosion" in enrollments suggested that the university *was* destined to play a central role in the American future. But on Kerr's argument the creative arts, including literature, are subordinated to the university's need for public prominence. They become a mere *means* by which the university takes its place at center stage in the American drama. It is not so much the growth in population, knowledge, and skills that is at issue; what is important is the expansion of the university's cultural role.

In the nineteenth century the university transformed itself from a college into a research institution. In the second half of the twentieth century it added the function of providing a haven for the arts. Apologists for the second transformation, like Kerr, made the case that the arts were not so different from scientific research. "At their most creative edge," Wallace Stegner said, "science and art both represent original questionings—pure research—and both rely upon a galvanizing and originating intuition." The last phrase was an attempt to supply a rational defense of poetic inspiration, but the attempt was negligible. Far more compelling were lists of prizes and honors won by the writers connected with a university—in a 1961 anthology of Iowa workshop writing Engle listed two Lamont Poetry Awards, a Pulitzer Prize, and two National Book Awards among the faculty and students—suggesting that the real benefit of creative writing was that it could endow a university with prestige. (Engle was careful to dedicate his anthology to the University of Iowa, praising it as "a creating source.") The comparison of artistic creation to scientific research suggests something else too. As in the nineteenth-century university there was a shift away from teaching. If writing is the equivalent of research the old stumper *Can writing be taught?* is off the point. The question, as Stegner observed, assumes that literary talent, being innate, is sufficient to make someone into a writer. But it is not; talent also needs to be developed. "And this means that in the game of literary futures," Stegner said, "luck, economic and social pressures, personal preferences, and character— a word that few use any more—matter quite as much as talent." Among the things that have to be dealt with if a talented writer is to be developed are "the economic circumstances which must allow for practice and growth, the social pressures for success that must be read in dollars. . . ." Thus the university was advanced as a solution to the economic and social problems of writers. For them meanwhile it was—again in Stegner's words—a place to live and write that would remove at least for a while the economic insecurity that came close to unnerving them. Or as Engle said in explaining why so many of them had taken academic posts or enrolled in graduate workshops after the war: "They have found the campus a suitable combination of security with time to work." Over and over it was said that the primary function of a graduate program in creative writing is to give young writers the time to develop themselves. What went unstated was that this pointed to a new cultural role on the part of the university. It was no longer a mere research institution. It was now a writers' colony.[18] . . .

By the late sixties and early seventies, then, creative writing was ready and waiting to be professionalized. And so, in due course, a professional organization— the Associated Writing Programs—was founded. The AWP started at Brown University in 1967, and after rough financial times led to a cutback, it moved in 1971 to Washington College in Maryland. The next year the AWP received $10,000 from the National Endowment for the Arts that enabled it to hire its first full-time staff worker and to set up a placement bureau. In the fall of 1972, fifty writers sought its assistance in finding work; within two years the number had grown to 300. The group staged its first independent annual convention—the earlier meetings had been held in concert with the Modern Language Association—in Denver in January 1975. That year the first edition of the *AWP Catalogue* carried listings for 81 writing programs. By the next year the number of job-hunting writers had climbed to 500. The AWP offices were moved again in 1978, this time to Old Dominion University, and the number of writers using its placement bureau reached 950. The growth of the organization can be charted by its budget, which doubled in just two years from 1972 to 1974 and then doubled again between 1974 and 1978.[19]

In 1979 the AWP issued its Guidelines for Creative Writing Programs and Teachers of Creative Writing. These guidelines were an explicit attempt to set the terms of the relationship between writers and their academic employers. "Academic degrees," for instance, "should not be considered a requirement," the organization said. "If however a terminal degree is required, it is recommended that

the Master of Fine Arts rather than a Ph.D. be considered the appropriate creden-
tial for the teacher of creative writing." The AWP was not setting itself up as an
accrediting agency; it was merely acknowledging reality. The very next year, in
proposing the establishment of a degree program in creative writing, the English
department at Virginia observed that the MFA had become a degree that "is often
a prerequisite for employment by schools and colleges seeking to staff courses in
creative writing." In defending its proposal to the upper administration, the
department said that there were "abundant career opportunities open to those
who have earned the MFA in this field. . . ." The department had found, for
instance, that of the 51 four-year colleges advertising creative writing positions in
the Modern Language Association *Job Information List* for 1979–1980, nineteen
specifically required the MFA. There was a clear "preferential pattern," it con-
cluded, "favoring the MFA over the M.A. in creative writing. . . ." What the preferential pattern may have indicated was that academic creative writers were
seeking and beginning to attain the exclusive right to judge one another's performance. The AWP noted as much in its guidelines. "AWP believes," it said, "that
writing program faculty, who as creative writers are best qualified to make assess-
ments of a candidate's work, should be given the responsibility of making professional decisions about their peers. . . ."[20]

Creative writing was originally an enterprise for bringing the understanding
of literature and the use of it into one system. The plan for doing so was not
always adequate to the task. And too sometimes the nature of the task was not
fully grasped, and those who undertook it nodded long enough to neglect one
portion of it. Even then, however, the coherent view of literature sitting at the bottom of creative writing was not abandoned; it was only neglected. The idea of creative writing was to join the study of literary texts to the act of creating them, and
the culture would have a place for it as long as these things were put asunder.

In 1976, nearly a century after Barrett Wendell taught the first course in
advanced composition at Harvard, the American Philosophical Society reclassi-
fied "creative arts" as being separate from the criticism of them.[21] On one hand
this registered the fact that creative writing had cut the apron strings, establishing
itself as a fully autonomous branch of the curriculum. But on the other hand it
suggested that the original intention behind creative writing had been lost sight
of. "As things stand now," R. V. Cassill said, "even the best of the writing programs are not integrated with other facets of literary studies. 'Creative writing' is
a (usually) suspect *alternative* to 'criticism' or 'scholarship.'" What had begun as
an alternative to the schismatizing of literary study had ended as merely another
schism. The poet and critic Robert Pinsky was even harsher, speaking of "what
can sometimes seem the sharp distinction" between creative writing and formal
literary scholarship—a sharp distinction that had come about to the detriment of
both. On one side there is "an immense elaboration of the techniques of composition" accompanied by "a fatal ignorance of the past"; on the other side an "elaborate sophistication regarding poetic theory" that goes with "a fatal ignorance of
composition." The consequence, he said, is "rhetorical pedantry in the poets; and

arid nihilism in the critics." Technique had been divorced from theory—composition from the past—as each section of the English department sought to perfect its own specialty.[22]

The mystique of professionalism had obscured the reasons why creative writing was ever taught in the first place. For some it had become a means, not of exposing the lie that literature is a "holy mystery" and teaching it instead as something that is unmysteriously *made,* but merely of furthering the enterprise with no clearer idea of what it was all about. "Creative writing is the only real growth area in American literary education," said the novelist William Harrison, who founded the program at the University of Arkansas. "Traditionally, English teachers have taught others to be English teachers. This isn't what we do. We teach writers, not critics." The clientele of creative writing had shrunk as the programs had expanded. Harrison was echoed in Arkansas's self-description: "writers who do take the MFA degree are prepared to teach a wide range of courses at the college and university level. The program is well suited to those who wish to become writers who teach." *Writers who teach*—the phrase was telling, and it marked the end of an era. "Finally," Wallace Stegner said, "we are staffed by writers—not teachers who write, but writers who teach, and whose writing is the principal basis for their tenure and promotion." Finally, creative writing had become a national staff of writers who teach writers who go on to teach, and to hope for tenure and promotion.[23]

NOTES

1. Wallace Stegner, "Writing as Graduate Study," *College English* 11 (1950): 430.
2. Allen Tate, "What Is Creative Writing?" *Wisconsin Studies in Contemporary Literature* 5 (1964): 184. On Engle see Wilbers, *Iowa Writers' Workshop,* pp. 83–108. It was Janet Piper who said that Engle had been carefully groomed for the job of director. See Piper, *Iowa Writers' Workshop in Retrospect,* unpaginated. In the third edition of the *AWP Catalogue of Writing Programs* (1980), 101 institutions are listed as offering advanced degrees in creative writing or an M.A. in English with the option of a creative thesis. I stumbled upon the term "elephant machine" in George Riemer, *How They Murdered the Second "R"* (New York: Norton, 1969), p. 236.
3. Warren Kliewer, "Allen Tate as a Teacher," in *Allen Tate and His Work: Critical Evaluations,* ed. Radcliffe Squires (Minneapolis: University of Minnesota Press, 1972), p. 42; Wallace Stegner, "To a Young Writer," in *One Way to Spell Man* (Garden City: Doubleday, 1982), p. 31; Saul Bellow, *It All Adds Up: From the Dim Past to the Uncertain Future* (New York: Viking, 1994), p. 282. Stegner's essay was originally published in the *Atlantic* in 1959. On the distinction between discipline and profession see Everett C. Hughes, "Is Education a Discipline?" in *The Sociological Eye,* pp. 408–16. On the relationship between knowledge and professionalization see Christopher Jencks and David Riesman, *The Academic Revolution* (Garden City: Doubleday, 1968), pp. 199–207.
4. Ezra Pound, *Patria Mia* (1950), quoted in Robert N. Wilson, *Man Made Plain: The Poet in Contemporary Society* (Cleveland: Howard Allen, 1958), pp.153–54; Paul Engle, "Introduction: The Writer and the Place," in *Midland,* p. xxx.
5. Theodore Weiss, "A Personal View: Poetry, Pedagogy, Per-Versities," in *The American Writer and the University,* ed. Ben Siegel (Newark: University of Delaware Press,

1989), p. 154; Walter Van Tilburg Clark, "The Teaching and Study of Writing," *Western Review* 14 (1950): 170. According to one of his students, Yvor Winters shared Weiss's view of the relationship between poets and the university. "The analogy Winters used to offer was with the English clergy in the 17th century," Donald Justice recalled. "Poets like Herbert and Herrick were members of an institution that gave them and their poetry a kind of credit in society." See "An Interview with Donald Justice," *Sequoia* 28 (Autumn 1984): 28.

6. Proposal: Master of Fine Arts in Creative Writing, Western Michigan University, 1981. I am indebted to Michele McLaughlin-Dondero for a copy of this proposal.

7. For example, Paul Murray Kendall of Ohio University said creative writing would lead to "a heightening of perception leading to deeper realization of the value of experience and a more knowing and sensitive exploration of that experience. . . ." Quoted in Richard Scowcroft, "Courses in Creative Writing," in *The College Teaching of English,* ed. John C. Gerber, National Council of Teachers of English Curriculum Series 4 (New York: Appleton-Century-Crofts, 1965), p. 135. Almost verbatim, Kendell reasserts what Barrett Wendell had given as the aesthetic benefit of a writing course ("the deliberate cultivation of perception"). Somewhat differently, the poet Reed Whittemore hoped creative writing would serve as propaedeutic to the study of poetry. After taking a course or two, students "would all have been indoctrinated in the disciplines and conventions of verse and would not have to question them—at least not for every class and every poem—before going on to see how well or badly the disciplines and conventions had been observed, used, capitalized upon." Reed Whittemore, "Aesthetics in the Sonnet Shop," *American Scholar* 28 (1959): 350.

8. Richard Fine, *James M. Cain and the American Authors' Authority,* p. 58; Ronald A. May, letter to the author, December 4, 1986; Vincent McHugh, *Primer of the Novel* (New York: Random House, 1950), p. 268.

9. U.S. Bureau of Labor Statistics, unpublished tabulations, August 1987, in *Encyclopedia Britannica,* 15th ed., s.v. "Economic Growth and Planning"; John Brooks, *The Great Leap: The Past Twenty-five Years in America* (New York: Harper & Row, 1966), p. 132; William Jackson Lord, *How Authors Make a Living* (1962), quoted in Robert Byrne, *Writing Rackets* (New York: Lyle Stuart, 1969), pp. 135–36.

10. Wallace Stegner, "Can Teachers Be Writers?" *Intermountain Review* 1 (1 Jan. 1937): 3; Wilson, *Man Made Plain,* pp. 151–52.

11. Howard Nemerov, *A Howard Nemerov Reader* (Columbia: University of Missouri Press, 1991), p. 287; Stegner, "To a Young Writer," p. 30; Barbara Tuchman, "The Historian as Artist," in *Practicing History: Selected Essays* (New York: Knopf, 1981), p. 46; Bellow, *It All Adds Up,* p. 279.

12. Fred Chappell, "Welcoming Remarks," *Greensboro Review* 52 (Summer 1992): 83; Ray B. West, "A University Writing Program," *Western Review* 14 (1950): 238. Chappell offered his remarks November 9, 1991, at the Peter Taylor Homecoming on the Greensboro campus. Thanks to Steve Gilliam for this citation.

13. Karl Shapiro, *A Primer for Poets* (Lincoln: University of Nebraska Press, 1953), p. 66; Donald Barthelme quoted in Susan Squire, "The Best Writing Workshop West of Iowa City," *Los Angeles Times Magazine* (9 Aug. 1987); West, "University Writing Program," p. 240.

14. Jean Stafford, "Wordman, Spare That Tree!" *Saturday Review/World* 1 (13 July 1974): 17; James Whitehead interviewed in John Graham, *Craft So Hard to Learn: Conversations with Poets and Novelists About the Teaching of Writing,* ed. George Garrett (New York: Morrow, 1972), p. 68; Dorothea Brande, *Becoming a Writer,* pp. 99–104; R. V. Cassill, *Writing Fiction* (New York: Pocket Books, 1962), p. 9; James

K. Folsom, "Evaluating Creative Writing," in *Writing and Literature in the Secondary School,* ed. Edward J. Gordon (New York: Holt, Rinehart & Winston, 1965), pp. 137–38. On the circumstances surrounding Cassill's leaving Iowa for Brown see Wilbers, *Iowa Writers' Workshop,* pp. 109–16.

15. Nemerov, *Nemerov Reader,* pp. 308–9; Keith W. Olson, "The G.I. Bill and Higher Education: Success and Surprise," *American Quarterly* 25 (1973): 596–610. Whatever the consequence of hiring writers "to put up against the veterans," Olson argues that in general it is wrong to suggest that the G.l. Bill brought about deep and lasting changes in the university curriculum. "Because they received preferential administrative treatment, and because they shared with non-veterans similar attitudes toward college, society and courses of study," Olson says, "veterans demanded no changes in the basic structure or values of higher education. And colleges during the veteran era simply were too busy to study and restructure themselves" (607). Olson wishes to defend veterans against the glib accusation that they received a watered-down university education: "easy" curricula were not needed, he says, because the veterans academically outperformed their younger peers (604–5).

16. President's Commission on Higher Education, *Higher Education for American Democracy* (New York: Harper & Row, 1947), 1: 101; Oscar Handlin and Mary F. Handlin, *The American College and American Culture: Socialization as a Function of Higher Education* (New York: McGraw-Hill, 1970), pp. 72, 84. On the postwar expansion see David Dodds Henry, *Challenges Past, Challenges Present: An Analysis of American Higher Education Since 1930* (San Francisco: Jossey-Bass, 1975).

17. Clark Kerr, *The Uses of the University* (New York: Harper & Row, 1966), pp. 110–13. Originally delivered as the Godkin Lectures at Harvard in 1963.

18. Stegner, "One Way to Spell Man," p. 8; Engle, "Introduction: The Writer and the Place," in *Midland,* pp. xiii, xxx; Wallace Stegner, "What Besides Talent?" *Author and Journalist* 41 (March 1956): 13; Stegner, "To a Young Writer," p. 26.

19. Kathy Walton, "A Brief History of the Associated Writing Programs," typescript on AWP letterhead dated March 1980. I am beholden to D. W. Fenza for a copy of this typescript.

20. Ellen Bryant Voigt and Marvin Bell, "AWP Guidelines for Creative Writing Programs and Teachers of Creative Writing," *AWP Newsletter* 19 (Sept./Oct. 1987): 12–13; Proposal for the Master of Fine Arts in Creative Writing, University of Virginia, pp. 1, 9–10. The AWP Guidelines were originally drafted in September 1979 and signed by a committee the members of which included Max Apple, George Cuomo, George P. Elliott, Daniel Halpern, John Clellon Holmes, David Madden, William Matthews, Philip F. O'Connor, Susan Shreve, David J. Smith, James Whitehead, Dara Wier, Charles Wright, and Al Young.

21. Fritz Machlup, *Knowledge: Its Creation, Distribution, and Economic Significance,* vol. 2: *The Branches of Learning* (Princeton: Princeton University Press, 1982), pp. 101–2.

22. R. V. Cassill, "Teaching Literature as an Art," in *In an Iron Time: Statements and Reiterations* (West Lafayette: Purdue University Studies, 1969), p. 43; Robert Pinsky, "The Interest of Poetry," *PN Review* 17 (1980): 34.

23. *Springdale* (Ark.) *News,* February 27, 1977; The Programs in Creative Writing and Translation, informational brochure (Fayetteville: University of Arkansas, n.d.); Stegner, "The University and the Creative Arts," p. 34.

DISCUSSION QUESTIONS

1. Myers' central metaphor comes from industry: An "elephant machine" is a "machine for making other machines." How does this metaphor apply to the proliferation of creative writing programs after World War II?

2. How does Myers, quoting noted writer and teacher Wallace Stegner, distinguish between "vertical" and "horizontal" success for a writer? How do these contrasting forms of success affect the functioning of creative writing programs?

3. How does Myers see the growth of creative writing programs as "expanding the university's very role in society"? How do creative writing and other arts fit in with the university's traditional purposes?

4. What is the key to creative writing's professionalization, according to Myers? How do graduate programs in creative writing fundamentally differ from individual undergraduate courses in creative writing?

5. How does Myers see creative writers shaping curriculum as they move into university teaching positions? How do writers differ from traditional literary scholars in choosing what works to teach their students?

6. How does Myers lay out the connections among "vocationalism," "criticism," and "technique" in his description of creative writing's evolution as an academic discipline?

7. What in the history Myers describes accounts for such contrary characterizations of creative writing programs as either a "pyramid scheme" defrauding students or a "cultural flowering" supporting the growth of literature?

JOHN ALDRIDGE

The New Assembly-Line Fiction

John Aldridge (b. 1922) is a literary critic who taught at the University of Michigan. His books include After the Lost Generation *(1951),* In Search of Heresy *(1956),* Time to Murder and Create: The Contemporary Novel in Crisis *(1966),* The American Novel and the Way We Live Now *(1983), and, most recently,* Talents and Technicians: Literary Chic and the New Assembly-Line Fiction *(1992), from which this selection is excerpted. As the author of a novel,* The Party at Cranton *(1960), he understands as few critics do the pressures on fiction writers to embrace popular styles and the struggle to remain true to a vision in spite of the pressures.*

. . . The newer writers now beginning to become known for their first work or, in a few fortunate cases, already famous enough to be represented on the *Esquire* map belong to the first literary generation in American history—or, for that matter, in any history—ever to be created almost exclusively through formal academic instruction in creative writing. Unlike some of the most prominent members of the older generation—Pynchon, Mailer, Heller, and Vonnegut, among others—who have neither been formally trained to write nor become full-time teachers of writing, a surprising number of their descendants are the products of the advanced-degree writing programs that began proliferating around the country in the 1960s and that have since had more to do than any other force with shaping the characters of the writers they instruct as well as the literature those writers produce. In fact, the various differences between the typical neophyte writers who are graduates of these programs and their predecessors in all previous generations are dramatic and extremely instructive because they illustrate the remarkable changes that have occurred in the ontogeny of literary apprenticeship in very recent times.

The most significant of these changes is also the most obvious. The process by which a young person traditionally awoke to the discovery that he had somehow become a writer was until now almost always a mysterious, painful, and lonely one. There had occurred at some unknown time in the turbulence of his psychic life an accidental conjunction of experience and temperament that brought the discovery about, most often in a state of relative social isolation and most assuredly not as a result of benevolent collective or institutional effort. American writers, in particular, perhaps because they are not naturally nurtured here, have, at least in modern times, usually been, like Auden's Yeats, hurt, irritated, or provoked into becoming writers by their sense of estrangement from a culture that has been provincially inhospitable, if not downright hostile, to the kind of human beings they found themselves to be or that subscribed to a system of values that they saw either as irrelevant to their deepest concerns or as utterly monstrous.

Very often in childhood they were driven to literature as an unconsciously sought alternative to more damaging emotional disturbance, as a means of escaping their feelings of social isolation, and at the same time of finding in the fictive world of books a confirmation of values more civilized and humane than those in force in the world around them. And eventually they learned to write from reading literature, not from taking courses, by slow degrees forming their literary standards on the work of the best writers and in defiance of the standards of those they ultimately recognized to be the worst.

In view of all this, it is not surprising that over the last hundred or so years American writers have in the main been highly individualistic in their manner in writing and adversarial in their attitudes toward the established culture. As a rule, they have been self-taught and self-motivated, working alone or in only brief proximity to one another and finding little imaginative sustenance in American life except material for books that so often and so poignantly revealed just how little sustenance they had found in American life. Perhaps this is a way of saying that they have been blessed or cursed with that sense of otherness Henry James spoke of as the primary psychic orientation of the natural writer or at least the natural American writer. For their characteristic stance has been that of the alien visitor from outer space or the lone civilized human being set down among savages. Their cultural estrangement, regardless of the many ingratiating guises and disguises it may have assumed, has, in the case of some of them, been such that it has endowed their best work with a kind of subversive clarity of vision in which experience is rendered often through a concentration on realistic detail so obsessive that it seems at times to border on the paranoid.

This development is one of the major reasons why iconoclastic realism became established as the dominant mode of American fiction, and it remained dominant for most of this century, leading to the production of some of the most vital and acerbic novels ever to appear in our literary history. In their profound disaffection with American life many of our writers have given us our most brilliantly realistic portraits of that life. Yet there has also been visible in our fiction a contrary strain that in recent decades has grown much more visible, the tendency of certain of our writers to express their disaffection in ways that push beyond the limits imposed by conventional realism into areas in which realistic details may become transformed into metaphors that embody more fully and precisely than realism the particular character of the writer's disaffection.

An early example of this is John Dos Passos's *USA,* a fictional trilogy usually considered, at least in its central narrative, to be a work of classic realism. Yet it soon becomes obvious that *USA* is not a portrait of any realistically observed America but of a country hallucinated by a malevolent economic conspiracy that has reduced the inhabitants to the condition of slavish automatons in whom all human qualities have been compromised or corrupted. Realism has, in this case, capitulated to political ideology. But behind ideology lies the paranoia of John Dos Passos directing him in the metaphorical portrayal of a culture that is the destroyer of values he believes to be transcendental.

Still earlier and very different examples of this same tendency can be found as far back as the novels of Hawthorne and Melville, which are not, at least in our modern sense of the term, realistic works nor are they works of cultural or political disaffection. Yet some of them give the impression that they are taking place in a sanctified vacuum virtually uncontaminated by the presence of people because the imaginative eye of their authors is so firmly fixed on the cosmos and the heavenly warfare of good with evil. In their case, the disaffection might appear to be with the whole secular world that is there in the novels, one might say, on sufferance and to stand as metaphor of the debasement of the sacred.

Interestingly enough, there are indications that this form of cosmic or mystical vision has resurfaced in a good many of our novelists at the present time. One finds evidence of it in the highly convoluted "systems" novels of Don DeLillo and William Gaddis in which the primary interest lies not in a realistic depiction of the social scene but in the intricate choreography of fictional motifs, the interplay of thematic forces within the narrative ecology, which become in effect an esthetic replacement for, and a considerable improvement upon, the social scene. This vision is present in a much more obvious way in such a work as Mailer's *An American Dream,* where the cityscape of New York is used as a phantasmagoric secular backdrop for the Manichean battle being waged between God and Satan for the moral courage of the protagonist, Stephen Rojack. It is there also in the dark fables of Kurt Vonnegut, which caricature the ills and deceits of our society and so in some degree palliate his and our fears that they will lead us to Armageddon.

These and similar novels are burdened by a heavy weight of abstract speculation—often generated by a realism of detail that one sometimes feels is present simply to serve as its launching platform—about the meaning of sin, guilt, redemption, bureaucratic totalitarianism, political corruption, the tyranny and treachery of sex, the psychopathology of violence and murder—all perhaps in some degree compensations for the failure of the writers to find sufficiently meaningful experience in the quotidian life of the culture and so needing to seek out and confront the extremes of moral and esthetic possibility in some transcendental sphere above and beyond the quotidian.

Alexis de Tocqueville observed with great prescience that in a democracy such as ours "each citizen is habitually engaged in the contemplation of a very puny object: namely, himself. If he ever looks higher, he perceives the immense form of society at large or the still more imposing aspect of mankind. . . . What lies between is a void." As so many of our contemporary novels amply demonstrate, American writers have continued to devote much of their energies to the contemplation of their puny selves. But when not so occupied and they have looked higher, they have tended to fill the void between with portraits of society at large and mankind in general, portraits that often swell to the dimensions of allegory, myth, and the more technical abstractions of metafiction and fabulation.

By contrast, the British, whose literature has traditionally been the kind Tocqueville described as typical of aristocratic societies, have gone on producing work that is generally far less ambitious in scope than ours, more firmly rooted in the social actualities, and much more agreeable and affectionate in its rendition of those actualities. It is, for the most part, a literature that is stoutly secular and pragmatic in its interests and that seems to possess little tolerance for abstract moral speculation. Perhaps because British writers appear not to suffer from our form of cultural estrangement, they can observe their society with a greater equanimity and dispassion and with a livelier because untraumatized fascination with its foibles and idiosyncrasies. Even when they are satirical, as they so often are, their attitude seems to be one of genial delight over the observed pretensions rather than the usual American attitude of horror and disgust.

It would seem that at least in this regard the younger generation of university-trained American writers resemble the British more closely than they do their literary predecessors in this country, for they too seem not to be estranged from their culture, if only for the reason that they belong to a culture of their own, a professional aristocracy or guild made up of young writers like themselves and their instructors. This culture has very little, if any, connection with American society in general. It is extremely doubtful, in fact, whether more than a few people outside the universities are aware of its existence. Yet it provides these writers with some of the same supports traditionally provided writers by a loyal readership or, as happened for a time in the 1920s, by an expatriate community of sympathetic peers. And it actually functions as a substitute for both in the case of those of its members whose work fails to attract the attention of that commercial literary world represented by the celebrity maps of *Esquire*.

The process by which a young writer is selected for membership in this culture is relatively simple, but the rewards of selection can be very considerable. If his qualifying manuscripts—consisting usually of a few short stories or poems—are judged by his mentors to be sufficiently promising to earn him admission to a graduate writing program, his status and security as a writer will be assured for an indefinite time to come. He will be placed in close association with other apprentices in workshop sessions in which his and their work will be closely examined and collectively discussed. If he wins acceptance in the classroom and among his peers and instructors, he will become part of a complex network of in-group patronage through which he will be given access to important career opportunities.

His first novel, collection of short stories, or book of poems—any one of which is the customary written requirement for completion of the MFA degree—may be recommended by his instructors for publication by a small press, perhaps staffed in part by former MFA students, or his manuscript may be entered in one or more of the many literary prize contests that are open to young writers and often are judged by a panel of older writers, some of whom may be friends of his instructors. He will in addition be eligible to join the traveling circuit of young writers who, with their instructors, move from one writers' conference to another during the summers, meeting with and listening to other young writers give public readings from their work. It may happen also that one of his instructors, Mr. A., will at some point call an old conference or reading-circuit friend, Mr. B., who is teaching writing at another university, and arrange for the young writer to give a reading at B.'s university, in exchange for which B. or one of his students will be invited by A. to give a reading at A.'s university.

Before very long, if he has contrived to give readings at the right places and has won favor with the right people, it is quite possible for the young writer to become well known, even slightly famous, on the traveling circuit and to have acquired a supportive audience of his fellow students, his instructors, and their friends without having published much of anything and while remaining entirely unknown to the general reading public. What has happened is that he has become a respectable member of a professional fraternity made up of those who are students and teachers of writing and whose principal means of support consists of one another. Their function is to serve and preserve at all costs the study and teaching of writing, which like any corporate enterprise must be kept going because the survival of its employees depends upon it. Only in a very few exceptional cases are they impelled or sufficiently gifted to resign from the fraternity and make individual reputations in the larger literary world through the creation of a significant body of work. In fact, status within the fraternity serves as a convenient substitute for that kind of achievement and offers its own rewards to the many who would not be capable of it. Among the most tangible of those rewards for the young writer is of course the opportunity to go forth from the university, equipped with his MFA, and be hired by another university to teach even younger young writers how to write.

The writers who belong to this highly politicized fraternity of writing instruction are the academic equivalents of those whose names have become familiar as a result of favorable reviews and publishers' promotion, who may have achieved mention on an *Esquire* map, and yet do not have secure reputations in the literary world. The two groups are comparable in that each has won some status without attaining real position and for reasons of in-group support rather than strong individual accomplishment. Yet the members of the latter group have, for the most part, made some small mark outside the walls of academe and are at least competing with one another to gain recognition and readership for their work.

The academic group of course share this same ambition, but their ambition can so often be too easily tranquilized by the surrogate gratifications offered by their membership in the fraternity, and this can cause them to put off indefinitely the struggle which for any writer is finally the only important struggle—to come to grips with his talent within the stresses and frustrations of the literary marketplace.

The point obviously is that the academic writer is allowed to remain aloof from that struggle for so long as he continues to function within the benevolent precincts of the fraternity and finds an attentive audience, at least for public readings from his work within the fraternity. He need not take the larger risks that writers have traditionally always taken to achieve a hearing for their work because he already has a hearing any time he wants it without taking any risks at all.

In fact, his academic training as a writer will undoubtedly have taught him early on that the taking of risks is decidedly not the gateway to literary success in the fraternity world. In his workshop sessions with his fellow students he will have learned that critical opinion on a particular manuscript is arrived at by consensus, and that critical approval is determined by the number of favorable opinions offered by the class. A piece of writing marked by originality of style or point of view or that does not conform to what is considered fashionable as measured by its resemblance to the work of certain admired mentors such as Raymond Carver or Ann Beattie will undoubtedly be disturbing to many members of the class and so will not be deemed acceptable. Thus, as a result of the democratized process by which critical decisions are reached in the workshop, distinctions are washed out or considered taboo, while a uniformity or homogenization of effects is made to seem a cardinal virtue. One hears more perceptive students complain that after a collective workshop critique, a story or poem will all too often have been denuded of individual character and made to seem anonymous or the product of just anybody or nobody. And it would follow from this that after such an indoctrination a young writer would hardly be disposed to take risks, since his success is measured in the degree of his refusal to take them.

Interestingly enough, this may help to explain the rather astounding absence of critical discussion and debate at the typical public readings that are a regular feature of the program at writers' conferences and the graduate schools of creative writing. So much of the material read on such occasions is so bland, so competently but unexcitingly written, so interchangeable in style and substance that it very seldom stimulates a distinct response from the audience or provides any firm basis for discussion or dispute. Yet, strangely and with an effect that is sometimes eerie, the atmosphere at these readings tends to be downright reverential, as if an awesome spiritual epiphany were taking place, as if the reader on the platform were performing some sacred priestly ritual. And of course that is exactly what he is doing. Through his appearance he is sanctifying the holy function of the writer, and while he is on the platform he is serving as a symbol of the writer in the abstract receiving the adoring attention of the public. He therefore becomes a symbol in turn of all the aspiring writers in the audience and of their own consuming ambition to be the recipients of the same attention. In worshipping him, in other words, they are in effect worshipping themselves and paying homage to the sacramental importance that they attribute to the role of the writer, in preparation for which, after all, they have expended such a large portion of their youth and energy.

This may be a reason why the work being read never seems to be judged on its quality, why there tends to be no discussion of it, and why, in fact, the audience, having heard it read, seems immediately to forget all about it rather in the way they appear to forget the work of the more successful writers whom they profess to admire but also seem never to discuss. For what finally counts in the fraternity system of values is not the quality of the work produced but the continued existence and promotion of writers. Any question raised about quality would surely be considered a form of treason or self-sabotage, since it would threaten to expose one's own grave limitations and might ultimately undermine the system altogether. Hence, it would appear that the members of the fraternity have made an unspoken agreement not to discuss the quality of the work being read by the writer on the platform. That is their insurance against the day when they themselves will be up there reading and will expect to receive unqualified approbation from the audience, not critical judgment.

What is at issue here is a professional fraternity so obsessed with turning out writers that it has lost all regard for the purpose they are supposed to serve and the skill with which they may be expected to serve it. It is rather as if the medical profession were to produce physicians whose ability to treat patients is considered irrelevant when weighed against the fact that the medical profession must be kept going and that the training of physicians is a vital source of revenue and prestige.

But much of the fault is obviously inherent in the premise on which creative writing programs base their function. It might be argued that while universities may be adequate institutions for the study of literature, they are clearly not constituted to train its potential creators, especially given the nature of the training provided. Unlike graduate programs in the visual arts or in music composition, writing programs do not, as a rule, require their students to learn specific techniques, nor do they measure their progress through their growing ability to make use of those techniques in their own work. There is, in short, no formal curricular plan for monitoring the development of writing students as they evolve from apprenticeship through ever more demanding performance requirements until they arrive at a condition at least approaching competence. Writing students are accepted for training on the basis of such signs of creative promise as may be visible in their qualifying manuscripts, and from then on their work is judged on its own terms, that is, on qualities already present in it at the time they entered training. These qualities may be refined after years of practice in the craft of writing, but they are not enriched by instruction in traditional literary techniques or a close study of the work of acknowledged masters in the field—on the theory, perhaps, that such study might sully the originality of the students. As a result, it is entirely possible for a young writer to be graduated from one of these programs in almost total ignorance of the tradition of his craft and, for that matter, with only a superficial knowledge of literature. He will have retained throughout his training the immature approach to writing with which he began. He may have acquired a certain technical proficiency, but he is unlikely to have developed an individual style or a distinctive point of view, since so much of his time has been spent working in an intellectual vacuum, alone wth his manuscripts and unnurtured by any important knowledge beyond the limited experience he had accumulated up to the time he began his studies. He may have learned what he is natively capable of doing as a writer, but not what he *should* be capable of doing now that he has completed his training. For he has not been required to master a series of specific requirements that might have helped him to measure his creative growth and his future creative potential. It is, therefore, not surprising that he would be reluctant to submit his work to critical scrutiny, for his work would be most unlikely to hold up under such scrutiny. Besides, criticism would not only put to the test his abilities as a writer but raise serious questions about the value of the system that supposedly trained him to become one.

But behind the existing deficiencies in the academic training of writers looms the ultimate problem, one so laden with the weight of potential sabotage that one scarcely dares to speak its name. It is that far too many are called to become students of writing and, given the recruiting zeal of the writing programs, far, far too many are chosen. This is not, however, a matter entirely of uncontrolled bureaucratic greed, for in fairness it should be said that many of the applicants for admission to these programs clearly do seem to be promising, at least when judged on the basis of their qualifying manuscripts. Yet too often the promise they show is of the variety most young people show up to the age of about twenty-five, while other qualities far more essential to the continued productivity of writers are not so immediately detectable. There is no way of knowing, for example, that the promising student will possess the kind of obsessive drive to write, or the subject matter to write about, that will keep him functioning for a lifetime. The sad result in too many cases is that writing students will be led by the initial encouragement they receive to spend wasted years trying to become writers when they really do not have the required abilities. What one in fact observes in the majority of writing students is brightness and eagerness, perhaps a certain creative flair, and a religious regard for the holy office of the writer. But rarely do they strike one as having the qualities of mind and spirit that make for excellence. Most of them appear to be nice, well-adjusted, rather conventional, not particularly literary young people who might be equally competent as students of law or dentistry and, therefore, should by all means *be* students of law or dentistry.

It would appear that the writing programs have not yet devised a way to reproduce or incorporate into their curricula the conditions that are best suited to the creation of writers. While it is perfectly true that clonal fabrications of writers proliferate in these programs at an astounding rate, the outlook for their future success remains uncertain. But as some signs already indicate, the future for many of them may hold little more than the production of small, sleek, clonal fabrications of literature.

Part of the problem is that most real writers have already been formed psychologically to become writers long before they are old enough to enter a program. At some time in childhood or early adolescence they will have learned to live with the fact that somehow they are different from others, that there is a detached and perversely watchful ingredient in their natures that causes them to stand just outside those experiences to which their contemporaries so robustly and mindlessly give themselves. Without always being aware of it, writers reenact over and over again, each in his own way, that poignant moment when Mann's Tonio Kröger looks on at the dance and half-despises, half-envies the happy people who are totally and unself-consciously caught up in what they are doing. But the envy in their case as in Kröger's gives way to a superior sense of being the sole custodians of judgment and prophecy, perceiving the scene and foretelling the rest, and knowing that they alone through their artistry will be able to give it a coherence and meaning quite beyond the comprehension of the participants. So the writer becomes a witness and an incurable isolate, doing his work alone and in secret, and being in the end not only fully aware of his otherness but coming to coddle and cultivate it because it forms the perspective necessary to his imaginative re-creation of life.

Behind his knowledge is pride and a feeling that, like the boy in Joyce's "Araby," he is struggling to bear the chalice of his art and otherness safely "through a throng of foes"—those foes being as always the average, the orthodox, the sanctimonious, and the collective. Therefore, a sanctimonious community of writers would be repugnant to him because his entire relation to reality is defined by his productive isolation from community. Perhaps only when he is successful can he view other writers as acceptable fellow workers in the field, but even then the association is strained and laced with suspicion. For he defines himself in relation to them in the way that he defines himself in relation to community —by his difference from them, by the extent to which they do not share his vision of the world and do not intrude upon his imaginative territory but keep within the boundaries of their own.

It is conceivable that at the outset a writing program might give him temporary reassurance that there are others like himself, but again only to strengthen his conviction finally that no one is like himself, no one sees or writes as he does. If, as a result of workshop experiences in which critical judgments are arrived at by consensus and his work is criticized for being original, this conviction is called into question, then his ability to function as he must will gradually be eroded until, if he fails to escape in time, he may well come to share the fate of James's Isabel Archer who, for all her fastidious idealism and determination to lead a superior life, ends in her marriage to Osmond by being "ground in the very mill of the conventional."

Of course by capitulating to that fate he will probably become eligible to join the fraternity of academic writers and may even be invited to give a reading from his work before an audience of his fellows, who will now have no reason not to listen respectfully to his words and applaud him with the greatest enthusiasm when he is finished. . . .

DISCUSSION QUESTIONS

1. Aldridge describes the traditional life path to becoming a writer as "a mysterious, painful, and lonely one." How does he see this difficult process contributing to the vision and work of American writers in earlier times?

2. What does Aldridge mean by "iconoclastic realism" in American fiction? What other forms of fictional vision does Aldridge describe as distinctively American?

3. How does the "professional aristocracy or guild" developed in creative writing programs affect young writers' work, according to Aldridge? How does Aldridge's description of the "complex network" of such programs reinforce Myers' image of "the elephant machine"?

4. Aldridge criticizes the culture of creative writing programs for insulating the writer from the "only important struggle—to come to grips with his talent within the stresses and frustrations of the literary marketplace." To what extent do you agree with Aldridge about this?

5. Aldridge claims that the "democratized process by which critical decisions are reached in the workshop" teaches writers to avoid risk in order to please the collective. How do the workshop methods described by Madison Bell and by Jane Smiley reinforce or challenge this tendency?

6. Aldridge believes that "real writers" are formed in childhood or early adolescence, and that such a writer tends to become "a witness and an incurable isolate." Given this, why does Aldridge believe further that graduate programs are populated by people who are not "real writers"? To what extent do you agree with Aldridge that writers define themselves by their "difference" from others?

WRITING ACTIVITIES

1. Write a scene set in a creative writing workshop. Feel free to caricature the attitudes and behaviors you've observed in past creative writing courses.

2. Write a scene in which an aspiring writer has to explain the desire to write to another character (a skeptical family member, a friend, an academic advisor, a stranger on a bus).

3. Write an analysis of one of your own stories using Smiley's analytical approach. What elements does your story foreground? What's the payoff of foregrounding these elements? How are the elements working together to offer the reader a layered, complex experience of meaning? How can this analysis help you revise the story?

4. Write a scene imitating a writer from whom you've learned something specific about the craft of fiction. Make sure your scene emphasizes the particular element of craft that you admire in the writer's work. (One

possibility for this activity is to add a scene to a story written by the writer you're imitating.)

5. Analyze a story in terms of its choices, using Cassill's questions about character and action in "Reading as a Writer." Note how this kind of analysis heightens your awareness of the craft of the story.

6. Write about a story using the method described by Ford in "Reading." Choose a formal feature to begin the process of asking questions about the story; note how focusing on one feature of the story leads to questions about other elements.

7. Begin writing a scene based on some actual event from your life but then move the scene into what Casey describes as "that rich intertidal zone between the dry beach of what you know and the sea of what you don't."

8. Sketch a story about a character leaving home. Sketch another about the same character staying home and living out life in the same community. How does this fundamental difference between setting out and settling in affect the character in the two stories?

A Modified Smiley
Using an Analytic Approach in the Writing Workshop

by Marvin Diogenes

The traditional workshop method in fiction-writing classes (as outlined in several of the readings in Chapter 4) features class members discussing several student works-in-progress per meeting. Classes generally number between fifteen and twenty-five students, depending on the level, with advanced and graduate courses tending to be smaller. Works-in-progress sometimes are read aloud by the writer, but more often they are distributed beforehand to allow students to prepare comments prior to the workshop. Discussions tend to focus on what readers did and didn't like in the story, with advice about what to keep and what to cut, and suggestions about what to develop further. Instructors may or may not formally lead the discussion by asking questions and amending student comments, but usually they do comment along with the students, often summarizing and highlighting major points. Most instructors also provide written comments with suggestions for revision. After the workshop discussion, students generally revise their work prior to final grading, though many do only minor editing. In almost all traditional workshops, students distribute each piece only once, so having a piece "workshopped" is a momentous event, a public display freighted with tension and anxiety if not fear.

In an interview conducted by Alexander Neubauer (see page 467), novelist and creative writing teacher Jane Smiley outlines her "analytic method" for teaching fiction writing. In designing an alternative to the traditional workshop method (one that she experienced as a student and employed in her early years as a teacher, along with hundreds of other graduates of creative writing programs, including myself), Smiley aims to alter her students' expectations and behavior by directing "their attention away from me and each other and toward the ongoing process of their work." Smiley notes how the traditional workshop foregrounds the competitiveness of students, encouraging them to strive for the professorial stamp of approval in front of their peers; she asserts that this emphasis on polished performance in the workshop impedes students' development as writers and craftspeople.

So, to focus students' attention on craft, Smiley first divides the class into small groups to blunt the competitive dynamic of large group interaction. Then she outlaws the language of praise and blame—"I never say 'like,' I never say 'don't like,' never 'good,' never 'bad'"—and replaces it with talk of "artistic choices" and "the system that's at work" in the story, insisting to the students that "to be taken seriously is to be analyzed and delved into." To structure this analytical approach, Smiley instructs students to talk about five standard elements of fiction: action, character, theme, setting, and language. She couples this formalistic apparatus to a social constructionist view of how fiction makes meaning: "the story as an exchange of expectations, or let's say a negotiation about expectations on the part of both the reader and the writer."

Further, Smiley requires constant revision (four versions of four different pieces in a sixteen-week semester) rather than the single, often perfunctory revision of the traditional workshop, arguing that first drafts exist in "a state of faux completion." These mandated multiple revisions force students to return to the falsely complete first draft and make a "mess," which, in turn, generates the writers' exploration and discovery of their material.

Through this analytical method and regimen of revision, then, students learn to view themselves as crafters of fiction, part of a cultural and artistic tradition, and participants in the contemporary practice of making meaning through writing stories.

In modifying Smiley's method to serve my undergraduate students (she uses the method only with graduate students), I've retained the small groups (from five to seven students per group), the multiple revisions (four versions of two different pieces), and the explicit analysis of craft elements in small-group discussions (to replace subjective responses that do not directly address the inter-relationships of craft, the readers' expectations, and the writer's choices). These substantive reworkings of my classroom practice have allowed me to change my method of responding to students' drafts as well. The traditional workshop method compelled me to communicate everything I could about the one draft I could count on seeing (very few students accepted my invitation to write and discuss with me as many revisions as they desired outside the distribution schedule of the workshop). Although the stories were mostly in embryonic form, or a collection of confidently arranged cliches of plot and character, I had only one chance to influence the students' revisions and thus overloaded students with marginal and summative comments, including evaluation of the draft's handling of craft. With the modified Smiley, since I know I will see the story evolve through several drafts, my early comments aim to mirror or reflect the story (an image used by John Casey in "Dogma"), describing the plot and characters, and providing a narrative of my experience of reading the story. Since the method incorporates the writer's gradual development of action, character, and theme as a natural part of the composing process, I can be less urgent and less directive in my comments. The teacher's evaluations and authoritarian advice do not play a central role in these early exchanges about the story, and though the teacher's authority can not be completely effaced, the method allows the teacher (and by extension the students in the small groups) to respond as a reader rather than as a judge.

Again, this method dramatically alters the roles of both student and instructor, and while my students' responses to the revised workshop have been mostly positive, several issues must be addressed and negotiated with each new group of students. After reading the Smiley interview, most students immediately object to the banning of explicit praise from the teacher, fearing that the spartan analytical method will leave them discouraged and, more importantly, unsure of what's "good" in their work. While most students accept in theory that close analytical attention to their work is indeed a sign of respect from the teacher, most still want some sort of praise to validate their efforts. They predict that a discussion of how their stories function in terms of craft will leave them cold and uninspired. Students also resist the depth of analysis and the specialized terms they are asked to learn and use. They would rather express their opinion unfettered by analysis, in much the same way that the writers of the stories want to express themselves separate from the weight of tradition and the demands of craft. Thus, the allegiance to craft central to Smiley's method, and my modified Smiley, initially seems to students an abandonment of self-expression and an embrace of academic rigidity.

However, as the students grow accustomed to the regimen of revision (and discover that they can still respond to each other as appreciative readers, finding ways to incorporate praise and encouragement into the deliberative discourse of the analytical method), they almost unanimously endorse the modified Smiley, particularly the required revisions.

Credits

JOHN ALDRIDGE, "The New Assembly-Line Fiction." Copyright © 1992 by John W. Aldridge. Reprinted with the permission of Scribner, a Division of Simon & Schuster, from *Talents and Technicians* by John W. Aldridge.

DOROTHY ALLISON, "Believing in Literature" from *Skin Magazine*. Copyright © 1994 by Dorothy Allison. Reprinted by permission of Firebrand Books.

JAMES BALDWIN, "Autobiographical Notes" from *Notes of a Native Son* by James Baldwin. Copyright © 1955, renewed 1983 by James Baldwin. Reprinted by permission of Beacon Press, Boston.

CHARLES BAXTER, "Dysfunctional Narratives, Or 'Mistakes Were Made'" by Charles Baxter. Originally appeared in *Ploughshares*, Fall 1994. Copyright © 1994 by Charles Baxter. Reprinted by permission of the author.

MADISON SMARTT BELL, "Unconscious Mind" from *Narrative Design: A Writer's Guide to Structure* by Madison Smartt Bell. Copyright © 1997 by Madison Smartt Bell. Used by permission of W. W. Norton & Company, Inc.

JOE DAVID BELLAMY, "The Theory of Creative Writing I and II" from *Literary Luxuries: American Writing at the End of the Millennium* by Joe David Bellamy. Copyright © 1995 by Joe David Bellamy. Reprinted by permission of the University of Missouri Press.

WENDELL BERRY, "The Wild Rose" from *Entries* by Wendell Berry. Copyright © 1994 by Wendell Berry. Reprinted by permission of Pantheon Books, a division of Random House, Inc.

CAROL BLY, "Writing Whole Literature" in *The Passionate, Accurate Story: Making Your Heart's Truth into Literature* (Minneapolis: Milkweed Editions, 1998). Copyright © 1998 by Carol Bly. Reprinted with permission from Milkweed Editions, *www.milkweed.org*.

WAYNE C. BOOTH, "Types of Narration" from *The Rhetoric of Fiction* by Wayne C. Booth. Copyright © 1961 by The University of Chicago. Reprinted by permission of The University of Chicago Press and Wayne C. Booth.

ELIZABETH BOWEN, "Notes on Writing a Novel" from *The Mulberry Tree* by Elizabeth Bowen. Copyright © 1986 by Curtis Brown Ltd., London, Literary Executors of the Estate of Elizabeth Bowen.

RITA MAE BROWN, "An Annotated Reading List" from *Starting From Scratch: A Different Kind of Writer's Manual* by Rita Mae Brown. Copyright © 1988 by Speakeasy Productions, Inc. Used by permission of Bantam Books, a division of Random House, Inc.

RAYMOND CARVER, "Creative Writing 101" by Raymond Carver from *On Becoming a Novelist* by John Gardner. Copyright © 1983 by HarperCollins Publishers. Reprinted by permission of International Creative Management, Inc.

JOHN CASEY, "Dogma" from *The Writing Life*. Copyright © 1995 by John Casey. Reprinted by permission of Carlisle & Company, LLC as agent for John Casey.

R. V. CASSILL, "Character" and "Reading as a Writer." Copyright © 1975 by R. V. Cassill. Reprinted with the permission of Simon & Schuster from *Writing Fiction, Second Edition* by R. V. Cassill.

ANNIE DILLARD, "Fiction in Bits" from *Living by Fiction* by Annie Dillard. Copyright © 1982 by Annie Dillard. Reprinted by permission of HarperCollins Publishers, Inc.

Index of Authors and Titles

This index includes the authors and titles of works both contained in the text and discussed in the text.

Subject Index

questions, 497

rationalization, 62, 65
readers
  average, 14
  children as, 417–418
  as critics, 240–241
  distance from, 258
  identification with characters, 40
  intelligent, 14
  unpredictability of, 421–422, 423
  writers as, 497–502, 503–505, 549, 614
reading
  annotated list for, 513–547
  experience of, 571–572
  learning to, 497–502, 503–505, 614
  public, 627–628
Realism
  allegory and, 81–83
  in contemporary fiction, 10
  continuity in, 117
  definition of, 76, 83, 387
  details in, 22–23
  dirty, 594–595
  vs. fabulism, 22
  vs. genre, 20
  history of, 8, 83
  iconoclastic, 624
  image-fiction and, 435
  limitations of, 76
  romanticism and, 109–110
  self-expression in, 22
  summary and, 173
  types of, 82–83
reality
  vs. appearance, 15, 87
  in contemporary fiction, 109
  definition of, 78–79
  of dreams, 78–79
  factual, 393
  in fantasy, 15
  of imagination, 108
  of life, 79
  senses and, 13
realization, 498
realization phrases, 273
reason, 53–54, 87–88
regionalisms, 17–18
relationships, 147, 281–282, 286
relativism, 100–101
relevance, 151–152
religion, 80, 86, 422
Renaissance allegories, 83
reporting, 591
representation, 109–110
resistance, creativity and, 376–377

resolution, 242
responsibility vs. blame, 400
reviewers, 105
revision, 132, 238–280
  of beginnings, 243, 246, 361
  of characters, 242–243, 246, 293
  checklists, 241–243, 245–246
  of descriptions, 246
  of dialogue, 246, 272, 505
  Dillard on, 361, 366
  editors and, 36
  of endings, 243, 246
  exercises for, 291–293
  Kaplan on, 263–280
  Kercheval on, 238–248
  major, 241–245, 277
  minor, 245–248, 277
  perfection and, 247, 277, 365–366, 489
  of setting, 246
  Smiley on, 468–469, 474
  teaching, 468–469, 474, 479–480, 552, 583, 634
  workshops and, 558
rich vs. poor, 54–55
ridicule, 433–434
risks, 492
romanticism, 8–9, 67–84
  definition of, 75–76
  Hawthorne on, 67–74
  James on, 70–74
  latent, 72–73
  Norris on, 75–78
  Plato on, 79–80
  pure, 79–81
  as realism, 109–110
  Scholes on, 78–84
  vs. sentimentalism, 75
  victimization and, 404–405
  worldview of, 77–78
rules, 94–95
Russian literature, 41, 45, 447–449

Scandinavian literature, 476
scenes
  between, 214
  advancing, 150–151
  Bowen on, 145–146
  components of, 167–168
  continuous, 28
  exercises for, 283–285
  relevance of, 151–152
  in short stories, 215–216
  summary and, 156, 170–171, 174–175
  Surmelian on, 165–169
  time lines of, 291
science, 80, 89, 616–617